INSIDE THE
FASHION
BUSINESS

Jeannette A. Jarnow

Edwin Goodman Professor and Professor Emeritus,
Fashion Merchandising
Fashion Institute of Technology

Miriam Guerreiro

Associate Professor, Fashion Merchandising
Fashion Institute of Technology

Beatrice Judelle

Research Consultant

Inside the Fashion Business

TEXT AND READINGS

Fourth Edition

Macmillan Publishing Company

New York

Macmillan Publishing Company
866 Third Avenue, New York, New York 10022

Library of Congress Cataloging-in-Publication Data

Jarnow, Jeannette A.
  Inside the fashion business.

  Includes bibliographies and index.
    1. Fashion merchandising—United States.
2. Clothing trade—United States.   I. Guerreiro, Miriam.
II. Judelle, Beatrice
III. Title.
HD9940.U4J3   1987   338.4′7687′0973   86-16359
ISBN 0-02-360000-4

Printing: 1 2 3 4 5 6 7   Year: 7 8 9 0 1 2 3

ISBN 0-02-360000-4

To the readers of the previous editions whose enthusiastic acceptance of this book encouraged us to undertake this new and revised edition.

Preface

Volatile, exciting, challenging—that is the fashion business. It is a business that changes rapidly, yet the career-oriented student must be knowledgeable on current problems, strategies, and opportunities in order to make a good start on the road to success. Thus, this new edition of *Inside the Fashion Business*.

Our book is dedicated to providing a knowledge of the workings and interrelationships of the many different industries and services that comprise the fashion business. By providing a comprehensive and up-to-date treatment of the complex of enterprises involved in the design, production, and distribution of men's, women's, and children's apparel and accessories, we hope to provide an understanding of the widely varied career opportunities in the fashion field and to help fashion business aspirants achieve faster career advancement.

In addition to the organized factual material in the chapters, the book contains a series of trade articles that discuss the inner workings of the industry.

ORGANIZATION AND CONTENT

Each chapter is an organized presentation of the facts about a specific segment of the business. In each case, the text is followed by carefully chosen readings, which describe the operations of leading companies in their respective fields. These are discussions of how they function under conditions vastly different in many respects from those that prevailed even five or ten years ago. Then, to facilitate further research into the field, each chapter has a bibliography, a list of trade associations, and a list of trade periodicals appropriate to its subject. Each chapter concludes with a series of suggested student learning experiences that require review, interpretation, and application of knowledge. Following the final chapter are three appendixes and a fashion business language guide.

Here is a brief summary of the chapters.

Chapter 1, The Business of Marketing Fashion, presents an overall view of the U.S. fashion industry, its scope, economic importance, and marketing practices.

Chapter 2, Principles of Fashion, discusses the generally accepted definitions of fashion and the principles governing its origin and dynamics, along with the implications for the marketers of fashion. It also discusses the role of designers today.

Chapter 3, The Materials of Fashion, examines the industries that provide the raw materials from which apparel and accessories are made: fibers, fabrics, leathers, furs. Each is discussed in terms of its economic importance, its method of operation, and its tactics for meeting present conditions.

Chapter 4, Women's and Children's Apparel—USA, discusses the design, production, and marketing of women's and children's apparel. It includes the history, development, growth, and practices of this segment of the fashion business, along with the methods used to meet present-day challenges.

Chapter 5, The Menswear Industry, reviews the growth of this industry, its adaptation to the influence of fashion, and its changing methods of operation.

Chapter 6, Fashion Accessories and Intimate Apparel, recognizes the increased fashion importance of these industries by treating them in greater detail than was necessary in earlier editions of this book.

Chapter 7, Foreign Fashion Producers, deals with the importance of foreign fashion producers in the American market, ranging from the inspiration of internationally famous designers to the competition of low-wage countries.

Chapter 8, Imports, discusses the extensive penetration of fashion imports into the United States, the reasons therefore, the procedures involved, and the applicable government import regulations.

Chapter 9, The Retailers of Fashion, explains different types of retailing, the circumstances and periods of their origin, the part that each plays in the business of fashion, and how they are changing.

Chapter 10, Auxiliary Fashion Enterprises, covers the service enterprises that contribute to the effective functioning of the fashion business, such as news media, fashion advisory and information services, advertising and publicity agencies, and resident buying offices, among others. Special emphasis is given to the burgeoning area of fashion information services.

Appendix A is an annotated list of influential designers.

Appendix B, Sources of Current Statistical Information, provides information for those who wish to keep current and update the figures presented in this edition.

Appendix C, Career Opportunities in Fashion, is a roadmap for those seeking a niche in the fashion business. Entry-level opportunities are discussed in terms of personal qualities, skills, and preparation.

The authors feel strongly that readers need statistical yardsticks against which to measure the importance of the various industries, trends, and individual enterprises in the fashion business. This we have sought to provide in the text, within the limits of what was available up to the time of publication.

A fashion business language guide follows the Appendixes.

ACKNOWLEDGMENTS

Each of us wishes to stress that this book, as with its predecessors, reflects the thoughts of many other people. We are grateful to the business leaders who shared their knowledge and experience with us and to the publications and organizations that granted reprint permissions for readings. Also, we thank the faculty members, students, and library staff of the Fashion Institute of Technology for their continuing support and suggestions. Thanks are due also to the patient and willing help of the librarians at the U.S. Department of Commerce office in New York. Finally, we thank the many friends in the academic and fashion worlds who gave advice and counsel. These people helped us shape the previous editions and encouraged and guided us once again in this new work.

Jeannette A. Jarnow
Miriam Guerreiro
Beatrice Judelle

Contents

1

2

WOMEN'S AND CHILDREN'S APPAREL—U.S.A.   127

THE MENSWEAR INDUSTRY   189

FASHION ACCESSORIES AND INTIMATE APPAREL   241

6

Readings   274

FOREIGN FASHION PRODUCERS   289

7

IMPORTS   335

8

Readings   356

THE RETAILERS OF FASHION   373

9

Readings   407

AUXILIARY FASHION ENTERPRISES   431

10

Readings   454

Appendixes:

A
B
C

1

THE BUSINESS OF MARKETING FASHION

Fashion in the United States today is big business. Its component parts—the design, production, and distribution of fashion merchandise—form the basis of a highly complex, multibillion-dollar industry. It is a business that began with small entrepreneurs at the turn of the century and today is a huge, many-faceted business. It employs the greatly diversified skills and talents of millions of people, offers a multitudinous mix of products, absorbs a considerable portion of consumer spending, and plays a vital role in the country's economy. It is, moreover, a business of curious and exciting contrasts. On one hand, there is the rarefied air of Paris couture salons presenting collections of exorbitantly priced made-to-order designer originals; at the other extreme are giant factories that mass produce and distribute endless quantities of low-priced apparel to towns and cities across the country. It is also international in nature, since the United States both imports and exports fashion merchandise.

This chapter presents an overall view of the U.S. fashion industry, its scope, economic importance, and marketing practices. It also introduces the reader to the person who occupies the key position in the entire group of enterprises that constitute this business: the consumer. The readings that follow illustrate marketing strategies in the industry.

Subsequent chapters will discuss in detail the various industries that are concerned with the production and distribution of fashion merchandise: raw materials, apparel and accessories production, foreign sources, retailing, and auxiliary enterprises.

THE BUSINESS OF FASHION: AN OVERVIEW ·

The impact of fashion is all-pervading, but when we speak of the *fashion business*, that term is generally understood to refer to all companies and individuals concerned with the design, production, and distribution of textile and apparel goods. Unlike industries such as tobacco or automotive products manufacturing, the fashion industry is not a clearly defined entity. It is a complex of many different industries, not all of which appear at first glance to have anything of fashion among their products.

Scope of the Fashion Industry

Plainly recognizable as part of the fashion business are industries devoted to the making of inner and outerwear articles of women's apparel; those involved in the production of men's wear; those that make children's apparel; and those that make accessories such as scarfs, jewelry, handbags, shoes, gloves, wallets, and hosiery. Some of these industries serve one sex or the other; some serve both sexes.

When one moves back to an earlier stage of production, to the fibers, fabrics, leathers, furs, metals, and plastics from which the finished products are made, the line between what is and what is not the fashion business becomes harder to draw. Some textile mills that produce dress and coat fabrics also produce bedsheets, carpets, or industrial fabrics. Some chemical companies that produce fibers that are eventually spun and woven to make garments are also producers of explosives, fertilizers, and photographic film. Some producers and processors in fields normally remote from fashion find themselves temporarily with one foot in the fashion business when prevailing styles demand such items as industrial zippers, decorative chains, quilted fabrics, or padding materials, for example. A season or two later, these people may be as far removed from the fashion business as ever but, for the time being, they too are part of it.

The fashion business also includes different types of retailers, such as stores that sell apparel and accessories, and mail-order catalogs from which many consumer purchases are made. It includes businesses that neither produce nor sell merchandise but render advice, assistance, or information to those that do.

In this last category are consumer publications that disseminate news of fashion, ranging from the daily newspaper to magazines devoted primarily to fashion, such as *Vogue*, *Harper's Bazaar*, or *Gentlemen's Quarterly*. Also included in this category are trade periodicals that carry news of fashion and information on production and distribution techniques to retailers, apparel manufacturers, and textile mills. It includes also publicists and advertising

FASHION INDUSTRY FLOWCHART

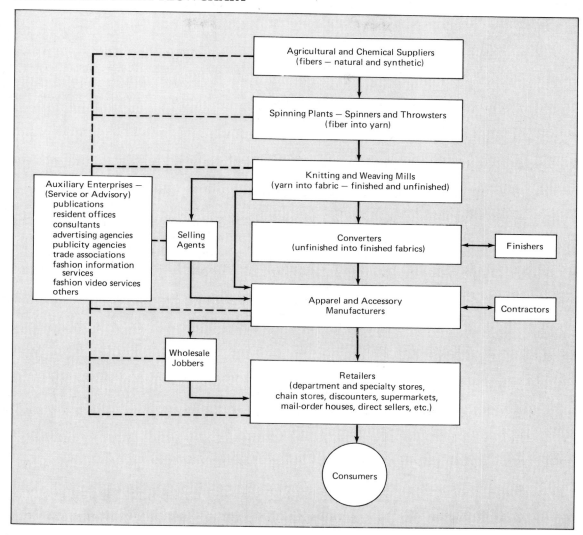

specialists, fashion consultants, and buying offices that represent retail stores in the vast wholesale centers.

All these and more are part of the business—farms and mills and factories, union labor and white-collar workers, tycoons, and creative artists. All play their parts in the business of fashion.

Economic Importance

The business of fashion contributes significantly to the economy of the United States, both through the materials and services it purchases and through the wages and taxes it pays. In assessing the importance of this contribution, it helps to consider such factors as consumer expenditures, the number of people employed, and the amount of wages and salaries paid to them.

In 1985, Americans spent over $155 billion for clothing, shoes, and accessories, an amount that constituted 6 percent of what they spent for all purposes from food to foreign travel. The outlay for fashion goods ran well above that for furniture, or household equipment, or tobacco, for example.[1] A further index of the importance of fashion goods is reflected in department store figures. Typically, the sales of men's, women's, and children's apparel and accessories account for well above half the total volume of such stores.

Still another indication of the industry's importance is the number of jobs it creates—and it creates them in every state of our country. Of the millions of people employed in factory work in the United States, better than one in every ten is employed either in those industries that produce apparel for men, women, and children or in the textile plants that produce the materials from which the garments are made.[2]

Apparel production alone employs more people than the entire printing and publishing field and more than the automobile manufacturing industry. Additional millions are employed in producing such items as fur and leather garments and in staffing the retail organizations that distribute these goods.[3] To this total, add some share of the employment in finance, transportation, advertising, utilities, and other essential services that devote part of their efforts to the fashion industry, and it becomes obvious that the industry has an astounding impact on our economy.

THE CONSUMPTION OF FASHION GOODS . . . .

The role of the ultimate consumer in the fashion business is an important one and, in the final analysis, controlling. This is a fact recognized by all successful fashion professionals. Ordinarily the part that consumers play is a passive one. People do not actually demand new products and designs of which they have little or no knowledge; neither do they demand change. Their individual and collective power is exercised in the selections they make, on the one hand, and in their refusals to buy, on the other. It is by their acceptance or rejection that they influence the goods that will be presented for their favor and even the methods of presentation.

The controlling role of the consumer is not unique to the fashion industry. Every business that serves the public has to guide its operations in the light of consumer demand. The fashion industry, however, moves at a

SELECTED COMPONENTS OF CONSUMER EXPENDITURES (ADD 000,000)

Year	Total	Clothing, Accessories		Shoes and Other Footwear
		Men's Boys'	Women's Children's	
1970	$ 52,396	$15,539	$28,794	$ 8,063
1975	70,021	20,807	38,519	10,695
1980	102,831	30,142	56,909	15,780
1984	139,494	39,219	78,755	21,500
1985	156,500	53,000	80,000	23,500

Source: Focus, Dun and Bradstreet; U.S. Department of Commerce estimates of personal consumption; U.S. Industrial Outlook, 1986.

fast tempo. The rewards of success are great and the cost of failure correspondingly high. As Dr. Nystrom put it:

> Consumer demand is the guide to intelligent production and merchandising. . . . A knowledge of the fundamental facts of what consumers want and why, is clearly of the first importance . . . to those who plan the policies, design the product, determine the price lines, prepare the advertising and sales promotion, sell the goods and make the collections, in fact all who deal with the problems of the consumer.[4]

The Power of Fashion

Few words in any language have as many different implications as the word *fashion*. To the layman, it implies a mysterious force that makes a particular style of dress or behavior acceptable in one year but quite the reverse in another. Economists view fashion as an element of artificial obsolescence that impels people to replace articles that still retain much of their original usefulness even though the new articles may not greatly differ from the old ones. To sociologists, fashion represents an expression of social interaction and of status seeking,[5] psychiatrists find indications of sex impulses in patterns of dress.[6] But whatever fashion may mean to others, it represents billions of dollars in sales to the group of enterprises concerned with the production and distribution of apparel and accessories. As one fashion student said, "Everything that matters, everything that gives their trade its nature and place in the world must be ascribed to fashion."[7]

Fashion, in and of itself, does not create consumer purchasing power, but wherever there is such purchasing power, there is interest in fashion. In times past, when purchasing power was concentrated among the wealthy few, they alone pursued fashion. Today, with widespread ability to spend, the great masses of people follow fashion, and thus fashion determines both the character and direction of consumption. Although such factors as price, durability, convenience of use, and quality of workmanship are also of concern to the consumer, they mean relatively little unless the purchased articles are also clearly identified with the prevailing fashions. Fashion is also an important factor in the replacement market for such utilitarian items as household goods; it is often more important than wear and tear in motivating discard and replacement of furniture, kitchen utensils, and automobiles, for example. Businesses that serve the consumer succeed when they go with the fashion, but are doomed to fail whenever they go against the tide.

Socioeconomic Factors that Affect the Consumption of Fashion

The growth of the fashion business in the United States directly reflects the vast social and economic changes that have taken place in this country's lifetime. As one noted social commentator has expressed it, "Few societies in history have been as fashion conscious as the American, and there have been few in which styles and clothes changed so often. Students of human society know that changing fashions are an index of social change within a society."[8]

Keeping up with the changing social and economic trends is not a one-time or a once-in-a-while research project for fashion professionals. Instead, it is necessarily as much a part of their day-to-day activity as keeping sales and inventory records. The fashion industry is aware of the various social and economic factors that influence the needs and wants of consumers; it is aware also that, as consumers react to these influences, their fashion needs and wants change. The industry is constantly fine-tuning its awareness of these changes and its responses to them.

Every factor that affects the population has significance to the industries that cater to consumers. For example, the age mix of the population, both present and projected into the future, has a definite bearing on the character-istics of current fashions and of those to come. The baby boom that followed World War II gave us the present large population of young adults, a generation that has become a major economic and fashion force in the 1980s. It is among their numbers that we find the strong thrust of women into the work force and especially into executive positions. This trend has not only changed the status of women, but has also affected the way they dress. By the same token, the young men of this age group increasingly participate in home and leisure activities, and accordingly adopt more varied styles of dress. Earlier generations, it is true, had working wives and husbands who partici-pated in home activities, but not in the numbers or with the impact of this group.

In virtually no aspect of life does the United States of the 1980s resemble that of the 1950s. Family life has been turned inside out by the rush of married women, including mothers, into the work force. Households made up of single individuals, once a rarity, are fairly commonplace today; so are single-parent households, in which the unmarried or divorced parent drops the child off at a day care center and spends the major part of the day in the business world, rather than the nursery and the kitchen. These and similar changes in the consumer's way of life have their impact on fashion. Among them: the rise of the "Yuppies," or young upwardly mobile urban professionals, and the fashion spotlight on their preferences in clothes, food, and lifestyle in general.

America is changing. Nowhere is it more evident than in **demographic** shifts largely wrought by the population bulge created by the "baby boom" following World War II combined with a variety of other social and economic considerations. As society fragments and becomes more diverse, a new consumer is emerging with a group of different socioeconomic and geodemographic measurements being developed and applied to better zero in on targeted consumer groups. However, broad demographic trends are vital when viewing future U.S. markets for a wide variety of goods and services. Marketing and media decisions will be heavily influenced by several major demographic shifts perceived to be taking place over the next 20 years.

The statistics of population changes that are presented at the end of this chapter provide an indication of how fashion's customers will change. Obviously, the American consumers of today differ vastly from those of yesteryear—just as those of tomorrow, and their fashions, will inevitably differ from those of today.

THE MARKETING OF FASHION

The fashion industries, like most other consumer goods industries in the United States today, have a productive capacity beyond what the public actually needs. At the same time, most consumers have incomes in excess of what their households require for such absolute necessities as food and shelter. This combination of ample productive capacity and ample discretionary spending power means that consumers have a wide choice as to how they will spend their money. A woman, for example, does not merely choose between one dress or another; she may also choose between a new dress and a new idea in household appliances. Likewise, a man may choose between one jacket or another, or he may choose between a jacket and some new golf clubs.

Producers of fashion have been traditionally backward in many of the marketing techniques that have sparked growth in such other industries as, for example, packaged foods. In recent years, however, there has been a major change in fashion marketing philosophy. Sophisticated research techniques have been applied to the study of consumer wants; emphasis has been put on product development geared to meet these wants; and vast amounts of promotional funds have been spent to establish the identity and enhance the demand for specific brand and designer name products.

These marketing activities take place at all levels of the fashion industry, from the producers of fibers, fabrics, and apparel, to the retailers of fashion merchandise. A basic difference is that producers are concerned with what to manufacture, whereas retailers are concerned with what to select and purchase for resale.

The Marketing Concept

To understand the marketing concept, it is only necessary to understand the difference between marketing and selling. Not too many years ago, most industries concentrated primarily on the efficient production of goods, and then relied on "persuasive salesmanship" to move as much of these goods as possible. Such production and selling focuses on the needs of the seller to produce goods and then convert them into money.

Marketing, on the other hand, focuses on the wants of consumers. It begins with first analyzing the preferences and demands of consumers and then producing goods that will satisfy them. This eye-on-the-consumer approach is known as the **marketing concept,** which simply means that instead of trying to sell whatever is easiest to produce or buy for resale, the makers and dealers first endeavor to find out what the consumer wants to buy and then go about making it available for purchase. Every step—design, production, distribution, promotion—is geared to consumer demand.

Much can be done to stimulate that consumer demand, but to do this effectively one must first recognize that fashion itself is a democratic phenomenon: the sellers nominate and the consumers elect. Customers therefore must be perceived as the motivating force behind the marketing process. Without them, there would be no business.

This concept does not imply that business is benevolent or that consumer satisfaction is given priority over profit in a company. There are always two sides to every business transaction—the firm and the customer—and each must be satisfied before trade occurs. Successful merchants and producers, however, recognize that the surest route to profit is through understanding and catering to customers. This concept has been recognized in such slogans, far removed from the fashion business, as Burger King's "Have It Your Way," and United Air Lines' "You're the Boss." A stunning example of the importance of catering to the consumer presented itself in mid-1985, when Coca Cola changed the flavor of its drink. The nonacceptance of the new flavor by a significant portion of the public brought about a prompt restoration of the Classic Coke, which was then marketed alongside the new. King Customer ruled!

Market Segmentation

Since no business can be all things to all people, it must select one or a few groups of customers as its target. Everything that follows in the marketing process is then geared to the target group, or market segment.

To understand market segmentation, it is first necessary to know what a market is. In general terms, a **market** means a meeting of people for the purpose of buying and selling. Such a meeting is not necessarily physical or personal. Specifically, a market for fashion merchandise refers to people with money (some more, some less) and with an inclination to buy fashion-related goods. Fortunately, the potential consumer fashion market in the United States is so large that there is enough business for a company to operate successfully by satisfying even a small percentage of that market.

A *segment* is any part of a whole market. According to the American Marketing Association, **market segmentation** means dividing the heterogeneous market into smaller customer divisions that have certain relatively homogeneous characteristics the firm can satisfy.[9] The segment will consist of a group of customers (not necessarily physically in one community) who react in a similar way to a given set of market stimuli. The segment may be based on such characteristics in common as income level (high, middle, upper middle, etc.), life-style (suburban, city), fashion preferences (*avant garde* or classic), special interests (jogging, aerobic dancing, disco), sizes (extra large, petite, junior, miss), occupation (career executive, homemaker), and so on. The potential categories are many more than can be illustrated here, and the kinds and types within each category are also more numerous than our necessarily limited examples.

Usually, a market segment includes a combination of two or more of such characteristics as were mentioned here. The individuals who constitute a segment may differ in other respects, but they have a commonality of interest and wants that makes each one a potential customer for the business concern that is courting that particular market. A market segment can even be large and powerful enough that producers and retailers prepare whole new categories of clothing for it. For example, in the 1980s as the baby boomers born in the 1950s and early 1960s entered the work force, they created a market segment for executive career apparel.

If a business, either manufacturing or retailing, is large enough, it may cater to several different market segments at once, creating separate divisions or departments for each. An obvious example is the special shops, both free standing and within department stores, for "big is beautiful" women and for extra-tall, extra-large men.

It must be realized that segments do not always remain static. One of the costliest errors a business can make is to take its market for granted. Economic and social conditions change; competitors develop new market strategies; new products arise and affect consumer purchasing patterns. The only way for a business to expand or even maintain its market position is to keep up with, and even ahead of, such changes. Products, services, and pricing policies must be continuously reevaluated in terms of changing market influences.

The need to target consumer groups is threefold: (1) to identify consumer characteristics most suited to the goals and capabilities of the firm; (2) to provide a basis for formulating and, if necessary, adjusting the firm's policies and products to satisfy these characteristics; and (3) to pinpoint consumer characteristics that affect patterns of buying behavior.

Market segmentation in itself will not ensure success in the fashion business, since it is only one of a combination of many factors in the equation. Not to segment, however, is to choose a sure way to failure. The principle of segmentation is based on the fact that people are different, and that, to make the point again, no one company can be all things to all people. A choice must be made as to which segment of the market a particular business or division or department can most effectively serve.

As a great fashion retailer once put it: "Each store has to edit and present what best fits its own audience. Fashion is not the same for every store. Hot numbers in one store can fall flat in the competitor's."[10]

Channels of Distribution

There are three main links in the production and distribution of fashion products: (1) the **primary markets**, which provide the raw materials of fashion, such as fibers, fabrics, leathers, and furs; (2) the **secondary markets**, which manufacture finished products of apparel and accessories; and ultimately (3) the retail distributors. All three links are interdependent. The primary markets depend on the secondary markets for the sale of their products; the secondary markets depend on the primary markets to provide the materials from which to fabricate finished goods; both markets depend on the retailer to present and sell the merchandise to the ultimate consumer. It is the retailer who is the final link between the consumer and the vast network of the fashion-producing industry. Within that network are enterprises of many different types. A flowchart in this chapter illustrates the main segments and the interrelationships of each. Subsequent chapters will discuss the activities of each in detail.

In some instances, the flow of products to the consumer varies. Instead of selling only to and through retailers, some producers also sell directly to the consumer through factory outlet stores, mail order, or manufacturer-owned retail stores. The existence of a retail division of a manufacturing firm is not news in the menswear industry; such outlets have existed for decades. It is new, however, in women's wear, a field in which it appears to be an emerging trend. These enterprises, in both men's and women's wear, will be discussed in the appropriate chapters, later in this book.

Timing of Product Development and Showings

Each link in the fashion industry chain periodically presents its new styles very early to those in the next level of production, so that producers and sellers may in turn prepare their collections well in advance of the consumer buying periods. For example, the colors, weaves, and fabrics that are expected to receive consumer acceptance are researched and decided on a year to two years before the consumer will see them.

By consensus and custom, each branch of the industry sets its opening dates by balancing many factors against one another: the change of season, the time required to produce goods after trade buyers have placed their orders; and the time required by product developers (whose titles may be fashion director, designer, stylist, retail buyer, or creative director) to assess the pulse of the market. Attempts to change customary dates have been made in some branches of the industry, with no success. Despite the fact that consumers today are more knowledgeable, sophisticated, and more inclined toward seasonless dressing, tradition and custom seem to prevail. Still, everyone in the fashion industry chain seems to produce collections earlier and earlier—possibly motivated by a desire to reach customers with something new a jump ahead of competitors, or possibly to forestall expensive overtime costs when production runs late, or even to avoid the premium charges for super-fast delivery services on last-minute orders and shipments.

The accompanying chart shows the time patterns for the average workings of major links within the fashion industry.

PRODUCT TIMING WITHIN THE FASHION INDUSTRY

Activity	Length of Time before Consumer Buying Season
Development of fiber variants	4 to 5 years (continuous)
Development of fabrics by fiber companies and mills	2 years
Color predictions at fiber level	2 years
Development of new fabric lines by textile producers	1 year
Apparel companies shop fabric lines	6 to 9 months
Development of apparel designs by designers and manufacturers	6 to 9 months
Lines shown to retail buyers	3 to 6 months
Production of garments	2 to 5 months
Retail selling season	Before and at the beginning of the actual wearing season

FEDERAL LEGISLATION AFFECTING THE FASHION BUSINESS ....

Under the American systems of government and economy, businesses enjoy certain rights and freedoms. Although business in America originally operated in a *laissez-faire* economy (i.e., noninterference by government) the emergence and abuses of trusts and monopolies in the late nineteenth century, which minimized competition and made it difficult for small business to survive, created the need for regulation. Two basic categories of federal legislation affect the fashion industry: (1) laws that regulate competition and (2) labeling laws designed to protect consumers.

Federal Laws Regulating Competition

Sherman Anti-Trust Act—1890: This was our first law enacted to restrain unfair competition. It outlawed monopolies and practices that restrained competition.

Clayton Act—1914: This law reinforced the Sherman Act by spelling out some specific restraints pertaining to price fixing, price discrimination, and interlocking directorates.

Federal Trade Commission (FTC) Act—1914: This law created the **FTC** to serve as a "policing" agency to enforce the Sherman and Clayton Acts, to investigate alleged unfair methods of competition, to conduct hearings, and to issue cease and desist orders. This law was amended by the Wheeler-Lea Act of 1938 and gave the FTC authority to prohibit fake advertising and made it an additional offense to injure the general public.

The Robinson-Patman Act—1936: According to this law, which was aimed primarily at giant retailers, large purchasers of goods may not be given so large a discount as to give them monopolistic advantage. This act makes price discrimination between purchasers of like grade or quantity illegal (e.g., it outlawed "phony" advertising allowances).

Celler-Kefauver Act—1950: This law made it illegal to eliminate competition by creating a monopoly through the merger of two or more companies.

Product and Labeling Laws to Protect Consumers

In addition to regulating business to promote competition, the federal government has enacted various product labeling laws intended to protect consumers by requiring that the materials used be listed, that they be safe and accurately identified, that the percentage of natural and synthetic fibers be shown, and that clear instructions to consumers about the care and maintenance of articles be provided. Examples of these labeling laws are as follows:

Wool Products Labeling Act—1939
Fur Products Labeling Act—1951

Flammable Fabrics Act—1953
Textile Fiber Products Identification Act—1966
Fair Packaging and Labeling Act—1966
Care Labeling of Textile Wearing Apparel Act—1972

PENETRATION OF IMPORTS

The rise in American **consumer expenditures** for apparel has not provided a proportionate growth for the U.S. apparel manufacturing industries. Beginning in the 1960s, imported apparel has been increasingly accounting for a rising share of consumer expenditures. For example, domestic production, which was $13 billion in 1960, tripled to a value of $39 billion in 1981—a substantial increase, it would seem. During the same period, however, market consumption of apparel increased four and a half times, from $22 billion at retail to $96 billion. The difference was in imported apparel, which in some merchandise categories equalled and even exceeded domestic production.[11]

PROJECTED DOMESTIC PRODUCTION, IMPORTS, AND CONSUMPTION OF APPAREL
1982–1995

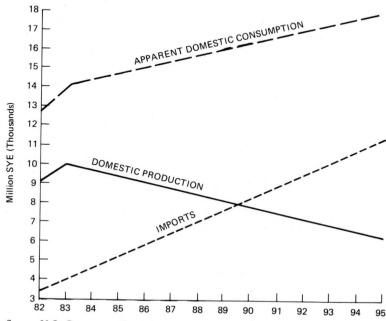

Source: U.S. Commerce Department.

Although the garment industry shares many problems with other import-troubled U.S. industries, its relatively simple technology and smaller capital requirements coupled with its labor-intensive dependence on low-skilled workers make it particularly vulnerable to imports from low-wage foreign countries. The major impact of imported apparel is stiff price competition.

Although it is generally agreed that international trade is in the long-range interests of our country and of the world, the prospect of further dislocations due to increased foreign competition is not pleasant for the industry to comtemplate. The government makes efforts to respond to the needs of the apparel industry by regulating the flow of imports, but it is limited by foreign policy considerations and the possibility of other countries retaliating against what they consider American protectionism.

Since the subject of imports is dealt with in further details throughout this book, it is sufficient to state here that this increasing degree of foreign penetration into the American fashion business has created an economic problem for all segments of the U.S. industry, which has been unable to offset it by corresponding increases in exports.

DEMOGRAPHICS THAT AFFECT THE FASHION INDUSTRY

(a)

**Population growth pyramids 1980–2000,
male versus female**

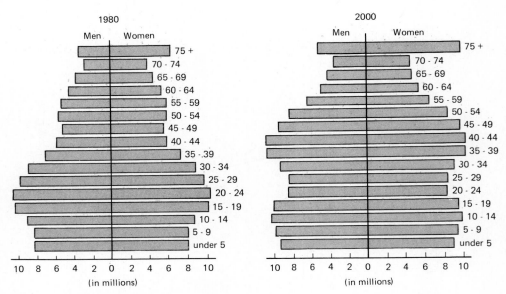

Source: U.S. Census Bureau.

(b)

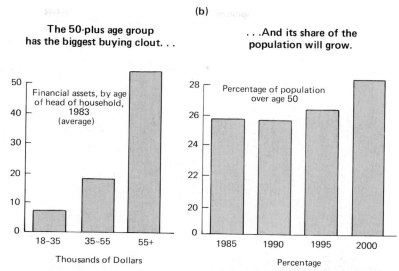

**The 50-plus age group
has the biggest buying clout. . .**

Financial assets, by age
of head of household,
1983
(average)

Thousands of Dollars

**. . .And its share of the
population will grow.**

Percentage of population
over age 50

Percentage

Source: Conference Board Inc., Census Bureau, Federal Reserve Board.

(c)

Regional shifts in population 1980–2000 (percent change).

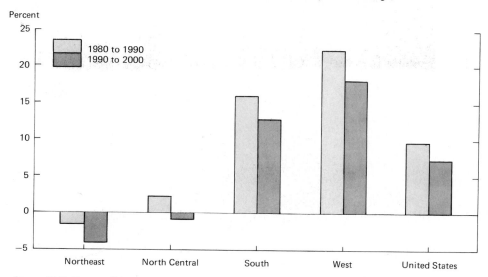

Percent

1980 to 1990
1990 to 2000

Northeast   North Central   South   West   United States

Source: U.S. Census Bureau.

DEMOGRAPHICS THAT AFFECT THE FASHION INDUSTRY *(continued)*

(d)

**Distribution of Families and Income by Income Class: 1980 and 1990
(based on constant 1980 dollars).**

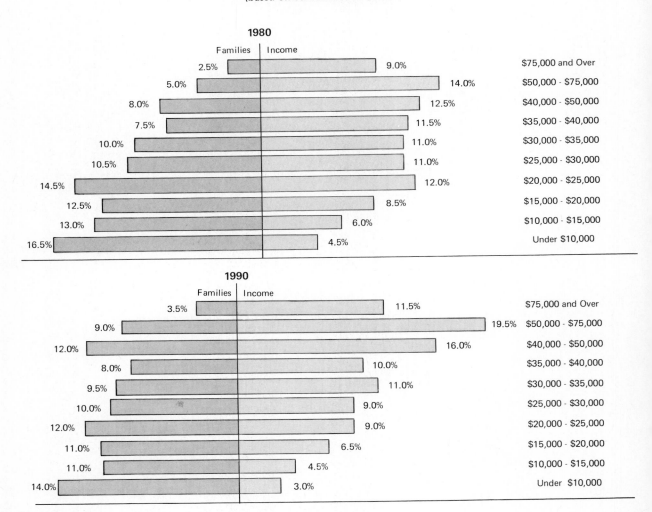

1980

Families	Income	
2.5%	9.0%	$75,000 and Over
5.0%	14.0%	$50,000 - $75,000
8.0%	12.5%	$40,000 - $50,000
7.5%	11.5%	$35,000 - $40,000
10.0%	11.0%	$30,000 - $35,000
10.5%	11.0%	$25,000 - $30,000
14.5%	12.0%	$20,000 - $25,000
12.5%	8.5%	$15,000 - $20,000
13.0%	6.0%	$10,000 - $15,000
16.5%	4.5%	Under $10,000

1990

Families	Income	
3.5%	11.5%	$75,000 and Over
9.0%	19.5%	$50,000 - $75,000
12.0%	16.0%	$40,000 - $50,000
8.0%	10.0%	$35,000 - $40,000
9.5%	11.0%	$30,000 - $35,000
10.0%	9.0%	$25,000 - $30,000
12.0%	9.0%	$20,000 - $25,000
11.0%	6.5%	$15,000 - $20,000
11.0%	4.5%	$10,000 - $15,000
14.0%	3.0%	Under $10,000

Source: U.S. Census Bureau.

(e)

Families by Income Class
(based on 1979 dollars)

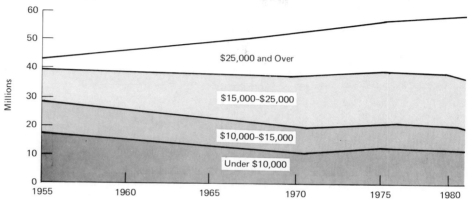

Source: U.S. Census Bureau.

(f)

Labor Force by Sex

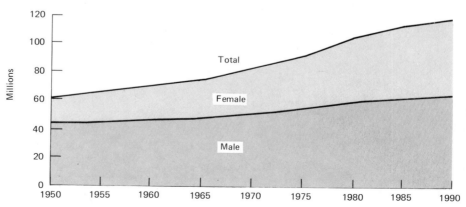

Source: U.S. Census Bureau.

DEMOGRAPHICS THAT AFFECT THE FASHION INDUSTRY *(continued)*

(g)

Women in Working Population by Age.

Year	Number (in thousands)	% of Population Aged 16 and Over	% of Total Working Population Aged 16 and Over
1960	23,268	37.8	32.5
1970	31,580	43.4	37.2
1980	45,611	51.6	42.0
1985	51,700	54.3	44.7

Source: World Almanac, Book of Facts, 1986. New York: Newspaper Enterprise Association, Inc.

(h)

Mothers' Participating in Labor Force (figures in percentage).

Year	Age of Children	
	6–17 Years of Age	Under 6 Years of Age
1965	45.7	25.3
1975	54.8	38.9
1980	64.4	46.6
1985	69.9	53.4

Source: World Almanac, Book of Facts, 1986. New York: Newspaper Enterprise Association, Inc.

(i)

Educational Attainment
Years of School Completed, Persons 25 and Over

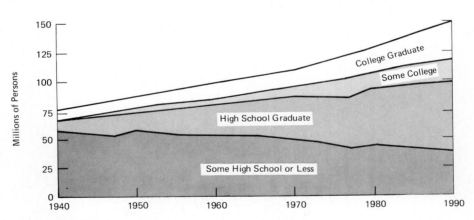

Source: U.S. Census Bureau.

Readings ....

Throughout the fashion industry, everyone's eye is on the consumer, and on how the industry can meet the public's needs quickly and correctly.

Watching Du Pont Watch Du Pont Watching Consumers
The consumer watch in the fashion business begins as far back in the production process as the development of fibers and chemicals. A Du Pont spokesperson explains why and how his company does the job.

The Surviving Companies Will Be Marketing Oriented
This consultant to the apparel industry explains that studying the consumer also means adapting production and distribution methods to meet customer demand and competitive challenges.

Watching Du Pont Watch Du Pont Watching Consumers

For very good reason . . . hopefully not to the exclusion of other endeavors . . . our little commercial world is concerned with the threat of imports. The solution to this problem is the goal of every domestic mill president, apparel maker and federal secretary of something.

Yet there is another, deeper, more complicated, and more interesting revolution or change affecting us today. One that is important for us now and for American apparel and textile business as a whole in the closing years of the twentieth century. It's an issue that will determine how successfully we approach the marketing of our products to the variety of consumers who are now leading the industry. . . . "baby boomers."

This group of 21- to 39-year-olds have reached a higher level of maturity. Like the jeans generation, the hippies, the beatniks, another "cultural" revolution is in the offing. It's nothing new. You've been reading about it for the last few years. And the Du Pont Company has been monitoring it for nigh as many.

Of course when a cultural revolution is under way, it advertises itself; it needs no press meeting or publishers cocktail party. It becomes a mysterious, magnetic force. When I interpret Du Pont's findings about this new "market" as it relates to those 76 value conscious people, I know that something important is happening. It goes beyond the current industry craze for funding political action so I'd better write about it particularly because too many retailers are still merchandising rather than marketing-oriented.

Too many of these retailers are still generalists, seemingly unaware of the need to project a clean-cut image to those who once might have protested the American way. More and more of these retailers I believe will fall harder in the balance of the '80s unless they adopt such a marketing orientation, develop a clear picture of their target consumers and position themselves carefully against this particular age group. They can only do this by understanding what they are now and what is unique about them; deciding what they want to be and what they want to de-emphasize or abandon. Most important, retailers must become experts in communicating with this group—in a language they understand, that this industry is fully prepared to give them what they want!

A few years ago, a trade press article observed that: "for whatever reasons there seems to be a new kind of marketing energy radiating from within Du Pont and although not yet clear enough to characterize completely, a variety of events, actions and activities during recent seasons indicates 'something's up' with big daddy."

Recently, Alan R. Titus, Du Pont's Director of End Use Marketing was quoted: "We will selectively pursue high value market niches with better quality products which provide 'differentiation' and we will define and pick the right market segments and *play our strengths to successfully launch products that are valuable to our ultimate customers.*"

OK: *products that are valuable to our ultimate customers,* Titus said. Which customers? How does one discover what is "valuable" to customers? Particularly the boomers?

Easy. When you have as much at stake as

Source: *New York Connection*, June/July 1985. Reprint permission granted.

Du Pont you spend a bloody fortune to find out how you are marketing your products. One job of "marketing" is to anticipate change. Without a "consumer watch" if you will, a rational fiber manufacturer like Du Pont might just fall into the same tendency to ignore change. It cannot take that chance. There is too much at stake for those who use their fibers—and those at the top who manage Du Pont.

Talking with Steve McCracken, Du Pont women's wear Marketing Manager—and observing big daddy's "Consumer Watch" video (used as a marketing tool for Du Pont products related to new target audiences) is enlightening. McCracken, introspective while warm and himself a boomer, points out that this group, "is demanding more value than ever before in the clothes they buy" based on information gleaned from a number of recent studies of America's largest ever generation.

"A balance of fashion, price and performance is what these savvy, young shoppers mean by 'value,' and what they will demand more and more of in all their apparel purchases," McCracken offers. "Value means getting your money's worth whether it's a consumer buying slacks for $19.99 or another buying a pair for $69.99. Both expect to get the fashion look they want, in a garment that offers quality and comfort, and at a fair price."

McCracken says that fashion still comes first to these young adults. But price and performance follow closely. "As the best educated generation in history," he says, "they pride themselves on getting what they paid for, and don't like to feel they're being ripped off."

The performance element in the value equation is keyed to creating fabric for garments that fit well, wear well and last. Designers admit that when they go out to look at fabrics they test them. They check their wearability and their tensile strength.

"Here's where technology has made its mark on the apparel market," McCracken offers. "Fabrics made of Du Pont fibers such as 'Dacron' polyester or 'Orlon' acrylic can be optimized to their intended end use, making them highly versatile, wearable and easy to care for as well as fashionable."

According to a few of the studies, these young people have learned how to adjust to accelerating change. "After all," said Joseph Plummer, Director of Research for Young & Rubicam, "they've had more psychological and technological change in their lifetime than any of the previous generations in history. They know what their rights are; they know what to expect. But I think the biggest trap is to oversimplify it and view it as one big homogenous group that moves together like lemmings toward the sea."

Other research uncovers more: They want more information. "They have learned and will continue to be exposed to more data about the products being offered to them," McCracken continued. "Right now they are just beginning to focus on what 'value' means to them in the clothing they buy. They will want to know even more about how something is made and what makes it different or better in the same way they've learned about VCRs, running shoes and other tech-based products. To them shopping is work. They know who they are and seek to move beyond the superficialities they find within our culture.

"Society has been catering to them from diaperhood. As the most educated generation, this group also is the most educable. We like the fact that they study and compare before buying. We believe that on comparison, apparel made with man-made fibers offers these discerning shoppers optimum value. We're confident that it's only a matter of time before these consumers respond."

Overview of the "Baby Boomer": A New Breed of Consumer

- Born between 1946 and 1964, baby boomers number about 76 million or about 31 percent of the total American population.
- Baby boomers are the best-educated generation in history, with 86 percent having finished high school, 45 percent at least one year of college, and 24 percent at least four years of college.
- Nearly 38 percent of all baby boomers enjoy a household income of more than $30,000 and, as a total, have more than one-quarter of all the disposable income in the U.S.
- Most baby-boom women work outside the home, and the majority of married couples are two-earner families. By 1995, it is projected that 80 percent of baby-boom women will be employed.
- Baby boomers are engaged in more physical activities than other adults, participating regularly in an average of 4.5 different physical activities, including swimming (46 percent), dancing (39 percent), camping (31 percent), baseball and softball (30 percent), jogging (26 percent), bicycling (29 percent), and calisthenics (23 percent).
- Although more than 58 percent are married and nearly 60 percent of those have children, baby boomers generally marry later, delay parenthood to an older age, and anticipate having fewer children than their parents.
- Compared with their elders, baby boomers are 74 percent more likely to purchase active sportswear; 112 percent more likely to purchase jeans; 154 percent more likely to purchase sporting goods; and 180 percent more likely to attend movies.
- Baby boomers are discerning shoppers, interested in product durability and reliability, quality and value. In apparel purchases, value translates to a combination of fashion, price and performance.

The Surviving Companies Will Be Marketing Oriented
by Peter W. Harding

Projecting the future is both challenging and hazardous. Challenging because the industry is entering an exciting period of technological change and discontinuity that has not been witnessed since the industrial revolution. Hazardous because it is so easy to pick the wrong cues or misinterpret them and come to some false conclusions.

As an example of these hazards, look at the Delphi Consensus Survey conducted in 1977 by KSA on the future of the U.S. knitting industry. Fifty-two leading executives from the knitting industry, its suppliers and customers were asked to make projections on the future of the industry through the year 2000. Their projections were excessively optimistic, and in the cases of warp knits and double knits, they projected increases in production by 1984 whereas both of these sectors had declines.

There were probably two major reasons

Source: Excerpted from *Apparel World*, August 1985. Reprint permission granted.

why these projections were wrong. The first is that the respondents were too close and too involved in the business to take an objective view, and secondly, there was an element of wishful thinking. Many executives, particularly in the double knit sector, had made investments in capacity decisions based on the growth projections which were already turning out to be false.

In thinking about the future it is necessary to guard against this kind of incremental thinking, starting from today and projecting it forward.

In the textile industry, there are two major sets of forces. The first are market forces and the second are broader environmental forces. The market forces fall into two groups, the supplier markets and the product markets. Although changes in the raw material supply, financial and labor markets are important, they do not have the impact on the future of the textile and knitting industries that our product markets, comprising the apparel industry, the retail industry, and the consumer market will have upon us.

The consumer market is the source of all ultimate demand. Significant changes are taking place in the consumer market which have had, and will continue to have, significant impacts on the apparel and textile industries.

First of all, the consumer market is aging. The jeans generation of the 1960s and 1970s has become the "yuppies" of the 1980s. This generation is affluent, often living in two income households either without children or with a small family.

They have money and are value conscious, but to them value does not mean cheap. Time is often more precious than money, and time for shopping competes with the many other activities they want to pursue. They are individualistic, and want clothing that fits their needs functionally for each of their many activities, and also makes them feel good about themselves.

The population is also shifting geographically, and whereas the West showed the greatest growth in the 1960s and 1970s, in the 1980s and 1990s the Southeast and Southwest will be the major growth centers.

This changing consumer market has led to the creation of many new market segments. Individual companies, whether apparel manufacturers or retailers, can focus on these segments and create specialized niche businesses. This segmentation, fragmentation or de-massification of the consumer market is a continuation of a trend that has been going on quietly for many years. Consumers now have different wardrobes for different occasions, and the drive for most of the fashion industry comes not from replenishing the basic inventory, but by making items in the wardrobe obsolete so they have to be replacecd by the current fashion.

In the retail market, traditional retail channels face strong competition in an over-stored world. Different channels have developed their own response to this competition. Department stores, with the highest cost structure in the retailing industry, have continually had to seek increased operating margins.

They are targeting their consumers more precisely and seeking to differentiate their store and its merchandise from the competition. Many have become almost theatrical in creating excitement for the consumer, and the private label programs provide opportunities to build their store's batch sizes, resulting in longer and longer through-put times.

But perhaps the greatest factor in the success or failure of any company is going to be the willingness of management to change from the incremental, narrowly-focused path of the post-war years to a broader vision of competitive opportunities that offer greater chances of profitability and survival.

Endnotes

1. Standard and Poor Industry Surveys: Textile Apparel and Home Furnishings, May 15, 1986.
2. U.S. Industrial Outlook, 1986.
3. *Ibid*.
4. Paul H. Nystrom, *Economics of Consumption*. New York: Ronald Press, 1929, p. 111.
5. See Bernard Barber and Lyle Lobel, "Fashion in Women's Clothes and the American Social System," *Social Forces*, December 1952; and R. K. Merton, *Social Theory and Social Structure*. Glenco, Ill.: The Free Press, 1949, Chapter 1.
6. See Edmund Bergler, *Fashion and the Unconscious*. New York: R. Brunner, 1953, for a provocative work based on his psychoanalysis of many persons connected with the fashion industry.
7. Dwight E. Robinson, "The Economics of Fashion Demand," *Quarterly Journal of Economics*, Vol. 75, August 1962, p. 377.
8. Max Lerner, *American as a Civilization*. New York: Simon and Schuster, 1957, pp. 646–647.
9. American Marketing Association, *Definition of Terms*.
10. "Fashion, the Heartbeat of Retailing," an address by Hector Escobosa at the annual convention of the National Retail Merchants Association, New York, January 7, 1963.
11. U.S. Industrial Outlook, 1986.

Selected Bibliography

Baker, Michael John. *Dictionary of Marketing and Advertising*. New York: Macmillan, 1984.

Calvin, Robert J. *Profitable Sales Management and Marketing for Growing Businesses*. New York: Van Nostrand Reinhold, 1984.

Category, Philip R. *International Marketing*, 5th ed. Homewood, Ill.: Irvin, 1985.

Doroff, Ralph. *Marketing for the Small Manufacturer*. Englewood Cliffs, N.J.: Prentice-Hall, 1983.

Kotler, Philip. *Principles of Marketing*, 3rd ed. Englewood Cliffs, N.J.: Prentice-Hall, 1986.

Langer, Judith. *Consumers in Transition: In-Depth Investigation of Changing Lifestyles*. New York: American Management Association, 1982.

Mitchell, Arnold. *Nine American Life Styles: Who We Are and Where We Are Going*. New York: Macmillan, 1983.

Rogers, Dorothy S. and Linda R. Gamans. *Fashion, A Marketing Approach*. New York: Holt, Rinehart and Winston, 1983.

Trade Associations

Direct Marketing Association, 6 East 43rd Street, New York, N.Y. 10017.

Trade Publications

American Demographics, P.O. Box 6543, Syracuse, N.Y. 13217.
Direct Marketing, 224 7th Avenue, Garden City, N.Y. 11530.
Marketing Communications Magazine, 475 Park Avenue South, New York, N.Y. 10016.
Sales and Marketing Management Magazine, 633 Third Avenue, New York, N.Y. 10022.

CHAPTER REVIEW AND LEARNING ACTIVITIES

Key Words and Concepts

Define, identify, or briefly explain the following:

Channel of distribution	Market segmentation
Consumption expenditures	Obsolescence
Demographics	Primary market
FTC	Robinson Patman Act
Market	Secondary market
Marketing	Sherman Anti-Trust Act
Marketing concept	

Review Questions on Chapter Highlights

1. Name the different types of industries involved in the business of fashion and explain the interrelationships.
2. Explain the importance of the fashion business to the economy of the United States .
3. Give examples of current social and economic factors that are affecting the consumption of fashion.
4. What is the marketing concept? Define market segmentation and give specific examples. Explain its importance.
5. What is the relationship between the marketing concept and market segmentation?
6. Name the three main links in the production and distribution of fashion merchandise and explain their interrelationships.
7. Name the two basic categories of federal legislation that affect the fashion industries and give examples of each.

Applications for Research and Discussion

1. Analyze current demographic trends and discuss their current implications for the business of fashion.
2. Research the business of fashion in your home community and explain its economic importance to the community.
3. Research examples of marketing successes and failures in the fashion business and discuss the reasons for their success or failure.

2

PRINCIPLES OF FASHION

Fashion, which is as old as time and as new as tomorrow, is one of the most powerful forces in our lives. It influences what we wear, the way we talk, the foods we eat, the way we live, how and where we travel, what we look at, and what we listen to. Fashion is what leads us to discard a product that is still useful but is no longer "in." It is also what makes us sometimes wear more clothes than we may actually need, and sometimes less than is needed to protect us from the cold or the sun.

The intensity with which changes in fashion are followed by people everywhere on all levels of society is evidence of its social significance and its impact on human behavior. To be "out of fashion" is indeed to be out of the world.

This chapter discusses the generally accepted definitions of fashion and the principles governing its origin and dynamics. It also suggests some of the many implications of the fashion process for the producers and sellers of fashion goods. The readings that follow the text profile some leading American designers of fashion.

THE LANGUAGE OF FASHION

Many definitions of fashion have been given by wise and witty or learned men and women. For example, to Oscar Wilde, "fashion is a form of ugliness so intolerable that we have to alter it every six months." And according to Ambrose Bierce, "fashion is a despot whom the wise ridicule . . . and obey." Thoreau philosophized that "every generation laughs at the old fashions but follows religiously the new." And Shakespeare wrote that "fashion wears out more apparel than the man."

27

Since an understanding of fashion is obviously of primary importance for fashion practitioners, let us begin by defining the terms that are used by everybody and confused by some. Although the definitions that follow are formulated largely with respect to textiles and apparel—the subject of this book—it must be emphasized that they apply equally to music, painting, architecture, home furnishings, automobiles, telephones, and any other consumer goods or services that one can think of.

A Style: Distinctive Characteristics

The terms **fashion** and **style** are confused by many people who say, "That's the style," when they really mean "That's the fashion." There is a world of difference in the meanings of these two terms. *A style is a type of product that has one or more specific features or characteristics that distinguish it and make it different from other products of the same type.* For example, a crew neck is one style of neckline and a turtle neck is another. All blazer jackets have certain features in common, features that make them different from, say, safari jackets, just as bow ties differ from four-in-hands. Baggy jeans have a common characteristic—fullness—that distinguishes them from other types of jeans. Shirtwaist dresses have a distinctive feature that makes them different from wrap, sheath, or other types of dresses.

Similarly, there are different styles of fabrics, each of which has its own distinctive features, such as denim, gabardine, chiffon, and seersucker, to name but a few. In automobiles, there are such styles as convertibles, station wagons, and vans. Art has such styles as pop art, art deco, and impressionism; houses may be colonial, ranch, Victorian, or other styles. There are styles in penmanship, interior decoration, advertisements. In any one category of product, there is usually an endless variety of styles.

A Design: Variations of a Style

Within a specific style, there can be many variations in trimmings, texture, decoration, or other details. A cardigan sweater, for example, is a distinctive style, but within that style, individual variations could include different types of knits, embroideries, pockets, and neckline, to name but a few. *These individual interpretations or versions of the same style are called* ***designs***. Compared with the number of styles in any given product, the possible variety of designs is limitless. Each design is different from the others in detail; they are all individual interpretations of their respective style.

In the fashion industry, when a style becomes popular, many different designs or versions of that style may be produced. In the trade, each producer assigns a **style number** to each design in the firm's line, which is used to identify it in production, selling, and shipping.

Fashion Means Consumer Acceptance

Among the countless definitions of fashion, the one from Webster's latest unabridged dictionary (the Third International) comes very close to what professionals mean when they use the word: *the prevailing or accepted style in dress or personal decoration established or adopted during a particular time or season.* The most widely recognized fashion authority, the late Dr. Paul H. Nystrom, defined fashion in similar words as "nothing more or less than the prevailing style at any given time."[1] Thus, a fashion is always based on a specific style. A style, however, does not become a fashion until it gains consumer acceptance, and it remains a fashion only as long as it is accepted.

For example, bow ties, tapered jeans, crinoline skirts, and chemise dresses are and will always be styles, but they can only be called fashions if and when they become prevailing styles. It is clearly possible, moreover, for a particular style to come in and go out of fashion repeatedly. Some examples of such "ins and outs" of fashion are peasant blouses, sheath dresses, padded shoulders, and circular skirts, to name but a few.

The element of social acceptance is the very essence of fashion. Acceptance, however, does not mean that a style is necessarily worn by everyone or even by a majority of the public. Acceptance can be and usually is limited to a particular group of people or to a particular location. For example, what New York men and women wear is often unacceptable in other parts of the United States that have markedly different climates or mores. Furthermore, what is popular among a particular age or occupational group may not be accepted by those of different ages or occupations.

Other Key Fashion Terms

There are, of course, many more key words commonly used in the fashion business, and it is necessary to understand their precise meanings to understand fashion itself and follow a discussion of fashion principles.

CLASSICS AND FADS

*A **classic** is a style that continues to be accepted, to a greater or lesser degree, over an extended period of time.* In the fashion world, this means that its acceptance endures for several seasons, or even longer. Typical of classics are blazer jackets, crew-neck shetland sweaters, and men's oxford cloth button-down collared shirts. From time to time, some classics can achieve a peak in popularity and become a mass fashion. That happened to the examples just cited, which in 1983 constituted the "preppy look."

In contrast to classics, there are styles that sweep suddenly into popularity, are adopted with great fervor, and then just as quickly disappear. Their acceptance is generally for a brief period and among a limited following. *These short-lived fashions are called fads*, and they seldom have any lasting impact on future fashions. An example is the Nehru collar, which was adopted by men almost overnight several years ago and died as abruptly as it was born. Often there is a capricious aspect in a fad, as in the case of "pet rocks" and "mood rings," which were briefly and suddenly seen everywhere, and then just as suddenly were gone. Fads go up like rockets and sink without a trace once their brief popularity is over.

LIMITED AND MASS FASHIONS

The term **high fashion** is commonly used to describe a *very new and costly style, whose acceptance is limited to those who want to be first to adopt the very newest fashions and can afford their often astronomical prices.* Some of these styles are limited in appeal primarily because of the high prices they command. Their intricate design and costly workmanship keep some of them out of reach of all but people in top income brackets. Other styles may be limited because they are too sophisticated or extreme to be attuned to the needs of the average man or woman. In either event, high fashion styles are generally introduced, produced, and sold in relatively small quantities, until their newness wears off. If the style has the potential for appealing to a broader audience, it is generally copied and sold at lower prices. The originator and the early purchasers, meanwhile, have gone on to something new.

In contrast with high fashion, which accounts for a relatively small portion of the fashion industry's business, there are **mass fashions** or **volume fashions**. These are *styles that are accepted and worn by a large number of people.* Mass fashions are produced and sold in large quantities at moderate prices and constitute the bread and butter of the fashion industry.

FASHION TREND

Fashions are not static; there is always movement, and that movement has a direction, discernible to careful observers. *The directions in which fashions are moving are called **fashion trends**.* For example, skirt lengths may be moving up from the calf to the knee—perhaps almost imperceptibly from one season to the next, but generally in an upward direction. Short jackets, as another example, may gradually be gaining at the expense of hip-length styles. Men's ties may be getting wider or narrower; women's shoes may be getting clunkier or more elegantly slim; the athletic workout look may be getting more or less popular in other leisure-time clothes; and so on. The change from season to season may be slight, but they generally have a direction. The ability to recognize that direction or trend is vital to fashion practitioners. Since these people must work far ahead of consumers' buying periods, much of their success depends on their ability to read the signs and recognize promptly the incoming and outgoing trends in fashion. The terms "prophetic," **avant garde**, and **forward fashions** are often used to describe styles that are gaining in acceptance.

THE CONSTANT IN FASHION IS CHANGE ....

If there is one absolute constant pertaining to fashion, it is the fact that it is always changing—sometimes rapidly, sometimes slowly, but it is never static or dormant. This element of change is recognized in the definitions of fashion itself cited earlier, by the use of such words as "prevailing" or "a given period of time." To ignore the element of change is like looking at a still photograph in place of a motion picture. The still tells you what is happening here and now; the motion picture shows you what came before and what may lie ahead.

Why Fashions Change

To understand the constant changes in fashion, it is imperative to understand that fashions are always in harmony with their era. As a famous designer expressed it, "Fashion is a social phenomenon which reflects the same continuing change that rides through any given age." Changes in fashion, he emphasized, "correspond with the subtle and often hidden network of forces that operate on society. . . . In this sense, fashion is a symbol."[2]

PSYCHOLOGICAL REASONS

Men and women are complex creatures whose actions are seldom governed by reason alone. Change comes about for psychological reasons. People grow bored with what they have; the eye wearies of the same colors, lines, and textures after a time; what is new and different appears refreshing; and what has been on the scene for a while appears dull and unattractive. Thorstein Veblen, writing at the beginning of the present century, made this clear in his *Theory of the Leisure Class.* As he pointed out: "A fancy bonnet of this year's model unquestionably appeals to our sensibilities today more forcibly than an equally fancy bonnet of the model of last year; although when viewed in the perspective of a quarter of a century, it would, I apprehend, be a matter of the utmost difficulty to award the palm for intrinsic beauty to one rather than to the other."[3]

Changes for such psychological reasons occur also in the fashions for products other than clothing. For example, nothing could be more utilitarian than a broom, a refrigerator, a telephone, a tea kettle, or a hand tool. Yet people about to buy such things will be attracted to, for instance, a broom with a coppertone handle to go with a similarly colored refrigerator that has recently been purchased to replace a quite adequate white model that they discarded. This element of change for the sake of change—artificial obsolescence, in fact—touches nearly all products today. Along with boredom, human curiosity or an innate desire for new sensations leads to change for its own sake.

SOCIOLOGICAL REASONS

Changes in fashion are also caused by rational reasons, such as environmental factors that create new needs. A classic example of a social change that brought about a drastic change in fashions occurred in the early decades of the twentieth century, when women sought, gained, and enjoyed new political and economic freedom. Their altered activities and concepts of themselves encouraged them to discard the constricting garments that had been in fashion for centuries and to adopt shorter skirts, relaxed waistlines, bobbed hair, and other fashions more appropriate to their more active lives. Generations later, as women moved into top executive positions in the business world, the tailored suit, femininely soft blouse, and attaché bags became the "dressing for success" fashion among career women.

Similarly, in the decade following World War II, when the great trek to the suburbs began, those who joined the exodus from the city found themselves needing cars and car coats, garden furniture, and casual clothes for backyard barbecues. The physical fitness movement in the 1970s and 1980s brought about a need for exercise clothing, and as the interest in jogging, hiking, tennis, and aerobic dancing mushroomed, so also did the need for new and different fashions appropriate to each of these active sports.

Changes in Fashions Are Gradual

Although fashions change constantly and new ones appear almost every season, a full-scale changeover is never completed at any one time. In studying the pattern of change in fashions, scholars have observed that changes in fashion are **evolutionary** in nature, rather than revolutionary.

CHANGES IN FASHION ARE GRADUAL

1960	1965	1970	1975	1980	1985

It is only in retrospect that fashion changes seem marked or sudden. Actually, they come about as a result of a series of gradual shifts from one season to the next. For example, when women's skirts began inching up from midcalf in the 1960s, this gradual shortening was not particularly noticeable at first. It was only when skirts moved thigh-high, in the form of minis and micro-minis, that people took notice of the approaching extreme. Similarly, when men begin to abandon ultranarrow ties and suit lapels in favor of more and more width, the changes are not noticed at first. Then, when wide ties and lapels begin to lose their appeal and progressively narrower styles make their appearance, people again mistake their belated recognition of these gradual shifts for a sudden change in fashion.

Even today, when the rate of fashion change has accelerated sharply, the pace of change is really slower than it appears to the unskilled observer who has failed to notice the early evolutionary movements in a new direction.

The evolutionary nature of fashion change is a fundamental principle that is recognized by fashion practitioners; it provides them with a solid, factual foundation for forecasting and identifying incoming fashions. When planning and developing new styling ideas, they always keep the current fashions and evolving directions in mind. Thus, the acceptance of a particular coat or dress fashion during a current season becomes a straw in the wind for experts in search of clues to next season's trends. The degree of its acceptance provides needed clues as to what will or will not be welcomed by the consumer in the next season. Knowing that people do not respond well to sudden changes, the fashion experts build gradually, not abruptly, toward new ideas.

A lone exception to this principle occurred just after World War II. During that cataclysm, fabrics were in decidedly short supply; fashion was at an enforced standstill; women's clothes were built along straight, skimpy lines. By 1947, however, fashion was on the move and making up for lost time. Dior introduced his famous "new look," with long, full skirts and pinched waists. The radical change was accepted overnight. This unique event in fashion history was possible because the years of wartime shortages had precluded the gradual changes that would otherwise have taken place.

Even the slowest, most gradual of evolutionary changes in fashion, however, do change direction eventually. Once an extreme has been reached, shifts begin to occur in a new and different direction—often a complete reversal, like the returning swing of a pendulum. "All fashions end in excess," is a saying attributed to Paul Poiret, an outstanding couturier of the 1920s, and his remark carries as much weight today as it did then.

Examples are readily found in both history and recent times. Eighteenth-century hoopskirts and the crinolines of the nineteenth century ballooned to diameters of eight feet. Later, both exploded into a fragmentation of trains, loops, and bustles that nevertheless provided a far slimmer silhouette. Similarly, when the miniskirts of the 1960s moved up to the micro-minis of the 1970s, hems began inching downward. Whether it be skirt lengths, silhouettes, suit lapels, or general fashion looks, all fashions tend to move steadily toward an extreme, at which point a new direction develops.

FASHION: A "FOLLOW-THE-LEADER" PROCESS ....

In the constant change and movement of fashion, there is a definite orderliness about the pattern of acceptance. Styles become fashions through a "follow-the-leader" process. Understanding the acceptance pattern is a key to understanding fashion movements; it explains how a look or idea begins with a few and spreads to many.

The Fashion Cycle

Every fashion has a life span, known as a **fashion cycle**. This consists of three major stages: a beginning, or rise; a peak or very popular stage; and a declining stage. The acceptance patterns of individual styles and of overall fashion looks both fall into this pattern.

In its first or beginning stage, the fashion is adopted by people who like or can afford to be first with what is new, or who are highly motivated by a desire to dress differently from others. These pacesetters are relatively limited in number. In this first stage, the new fashion is often called a "high fashion," as explained earlier in this chapter.

If and when the new fashion idea spreads and is widely imitated by the greater number of people who tend to follow rather than lead, we arrive at the second stage of peak or mass acceptance. The fashion is then in such demand that it can be mass produced and distributed at prices within reach of many consumers.

Ultimately, each fashion moves into its third or declining stage—usually the result of consumer boredom arising from seeing too much of the same thing. Some consumers will still be wearing it at this stage, but they are no longer willing to purchase it at regular prices. Meantime, other, newer fashions are going through the earlier stages of their cycles.

This pattern of acceptance and decline has been explained thus by sociology professor Neil J. Smelser:

It is important to (style leaders) to be among the first in order to reap the psychological rewards of being in the forefront of fashion, and it is almost as important to flee from a new style when it is assumed by the masses. Further back in the procession, among the followers, the motivation is more purely sociable—persons adapt to styles to avoid being conspicuously traditional, rather than to be conspicuously original.[4]

These stages of public acceptance tend to occur in all products that are subject to changes in fashion—not just in dress. Similar cycles can be traced in home furnishings, architecture, food, and even manners, but the pattern shows up most obviously in what we wear.

Different fashions vary in their life spans, in the degree of acceptance they attain, and in the rate at which they move through their various stages. The length of time a particular fashion may remain in any of its three stages depends on the extent to which it is gaining or losing public acceptance. Some fashions may endure for a year or more; others for a season; and, indeed, some may never get beyond the first stage of acceptance by small groups of people. Therefore, if one were to draw a fashion cycle, it would include the three stages, but its shape would be different for different fashions. The rise and fall may be gradual or sharp; the peak may be narrow or wide. Although no one graph can depict the life story of all fashions accurately, all would have a wavelike appearance.

Academically minded students of fashion have sought to chart the ups and downs of fashions in an effort to determine the length of time a fashion movement takes to run its course. The time intervals, however, elude measurement. The spread of fashion, as of every new idea, is a complicated social phenomenon. The public's needs and interests do not change by clockwork.

The problem of applying the stopwatch technique to an analysis of fashion movements is also complicated by the fact that price differentials, which at one time tended to mark the different stages of style acceptance, have virtually disappeared. Moreover, while some cycles are in their peaks, their successors are already in the growing stage. Many new fashions often reach full growth without ever entirely displacing those that preceded them.

FASHION CYCLES DIFFER

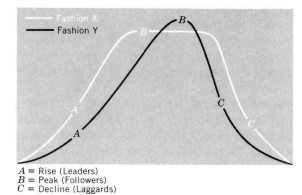

A, rise (leaders); B, peak (followers); C, decline (laggards).

A further complicating factor is that, owing to the evolutionary nature of changes, clearly definable shifts in fashion do not occur at a given time, and it is impossible to pinpoint the exact beginning or end of a specific fashion.

APPLICATION TO MERCHANDISING FASHIONS

An understanding of the fashion cycle is basic to successful merchandising of fashion goods, at wholesale or retail. Because very few concerns, if any, can successfully serve under one roof both the pacesetters and the followers, each firm must have a clear-cut policy on which fashion stages it wishes to deal in.

The main volume of business, in manufacturing and retailing alike, is done in fashions that are widely accepted or well on their way to the top or peak of the fashion cycle. A business that aims to attract a mass customers audience must concentrate on widely popular fashions, or on those that show promise of rising into the mass acceptance stage. These volume fashions constitute the major portion of the business done by the giant firms in the fashion industry. Conversely, those manufacturers and retailers who concentrate on being the first to carry the newest, the most individual, or the most extreme fashions cannot expect to do a large volume of business. Their appeal is to the limited group of customers who adopt such fashions. Their volume contributes only a small part of the total business done in the fashion industries, but a vital one indeed.

MERCHANDISING THE FASHION CYCLE

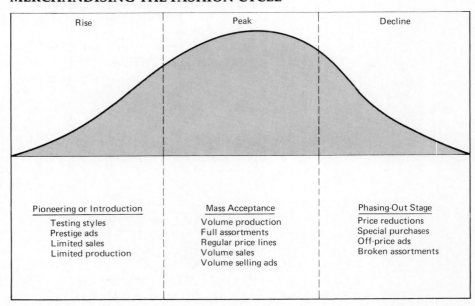

Theories of Fashion Leadership

Social scientists explain the follow-the-leader element in fashion cycles in terms of an individual's desire to achieve status by choosing apparel similar to that chosen by an admired individual or group. This association through choice of fashion is a means of bridging the gap between social classes—that is, becoming in one's mind like "them" by wearing what "they" wear. Imitation and conformity in dress are also explained in terms of insecurity, since it takes more social courage than most of us possess to be conspicuously different from others in the appearance we present to the public. Thus, fashion gives expression to two basic human needs: the need for social status and the need to conform.[5]

Three academically accepted theories categorize the admired groups or individuals from whom fashion leadership flows. These theories are "trickle down," "horizontal, or trickle across," and "bottom up." Each has its own claim to validity with respect to specific fashions and the fashion cycle.

TRICKLE-DOWN THEORY

The **trickle-down theory** maintains that new styles make their first appearance among people at the top of a social pyramid and then gradually move down to progressively lower social levels.

Centuries ago, the persons at the top of the pyramid and therefore the setters of fashion were royalty. Fashions trickled down through the ranks of the nobility and those of the middle classes who had the means. The lower classes, of course, had neither the means nor the temerity to copy, or were even prohibited by law from doing so.

These days, royalty has practically disappeared, and the position at the top of the pyramid is held by individuals at the top of the economic, social, entertainment, and political ladders. Many such people make it their business to dress well, and their activities and appearance are highly publicized. To the large majority of the public, the fashions accepted by the glittering personalities at the top constitute a guide to what to wear, within the limits of their own more restricted budgets and social activities. For most consumers, innovation is risky but imitation is safe. Thus, fashions trickle down from higher to lower echelons, just as they did in the days of royalty.

Simultaneously, those at the top seek to dissociate themselves from those whom they consider socially inferior. They abandon a fashion once it has achieved popularity at less distinguished levels and introduce a new and different idea.

This type of social behavior was recognized and its implications for fashion were propounded by such early economists as Thorstein Veblen, John Roe, and Caroline Foley,[6] and by such sociologists as George Simmel, who spelled it out, step by step, in a paper published in 1904.[7]

TRICKLE-ACROSS THEORY

As the twentieth century progressed, it became clear that fashion was no longer a matter of imitating any single social or economic class, but of choosing one's own role models—and not necessarily from among individuals with glittering genealogy or fabulous wealth. This phenomenon gave rise to another theory of fashion emulation: the **trickle-across theory**, enunciated by Charles W. King in 1963.[8] He observed that fashions spread horizontally within and across homogeneous groups, rather than merely vertically from one social level to another. He believes that each segment of our pluralistic society has its own leader or leaders whom it emulates. For example, a "Big Man" on campus may favor white sweaters and thus set a fashion for them among other students. In the business world, aspirants to the executive office tend to dress as the upper echelons do, be it the gray flannel suit of the 1950s or the attaché cases of the 1980s. Even in so small a group as a suburban bridge club, the dominant member subtly influences the dress of the other members by the fashions she favors.

BOTTOM-UP THEORY

The third and most recent theory espoused by many students of fashion and by fashion practitioners themselves is that the traditional trickle-down movement has reversed itself and many fashions now filter up. This **bottom-up theory**, as advanced by Greenberg and Glynn, maintains that young people are quicker than any other social group to initiate new and different fashions and that fashions filter up, not merely from youth to older age groups, but also from lower to upper economic classes.[9] Typical of fashions initiated by the young and less than affluent are jeans, sneakers, tee shirts, military surplus and safari clothes, black leather pants and jackets. Each of these started in the streets with young people of modest means and streamed upward to well-to-do mothers and fathers. The male espousal of flowing hair and beards similarly was initiated by the young in the 1960s, and that fashion spread to gray-haired, balding men as well. When younger men became reacquainted with razors, their elders soon followed suit.

MARKETING IMPLICATIONS

These three different theories of how fashions spread have major significance for practitioners in the field, since they confirm that there is no single homogeneous fashion public in our pluralistic society. A number of distinctly different groups make up the fashion public, and each has its own leaders and its own perception of fashion. Although we continue to see many new styles introduced at high prices and eventually becoming fashions, this is less often the case than it once was. One successful new style may originate in the studio of a prestigious designer, but another may come into fashion from the stock of an Army-Navy store.

Leadership in fashion these days has less and less to do with price and high-priced merchandise. Therefore, producers and retailers can no longer look only to an elite group of traditional fashion leaders for incoming trends. They must also be aware that some fashions flow upward and others flow across within special groups. Dominant individuals and dominant influences, wherever they reveal themselves within our society, are important influences on fashion. Success depends on identifying and watching these, not just the patrons of elite restaurants, resorts, and entertainments.

HOW FASHIONS ORIGINATE

There is no question but that it is far easier to recognize what is fashionable at a given time and place than to say why or how it became a fashion. When we search for the influences that brought forth such fashions as the hobble skirts and crinolines of the past, or some of the fashions of the present, we are confronted with a complex question indeed. Several things we do know, however. One is that esthetic appeal alone does not produce a fashion. Veblen made this point when he observed that there is no intrinsic difference between the gloss of a patent leather shoe and the shine or a threadbare garment. People, he observed, are ready to find beauty in what is in vogue; therefore the shine on the shoe is beautiful and the garment's shine is repulsive.[10]

Another thing we know is that promotional efforts by designers, producers, or retailers cannot in themselves dictate what customers will accept. If there were such dictators in the past, there certainly are none today. And a third factor that we know is that a fashion does not just happen without a reason. It is a response to many things: attitudes, social changes and movements, major events on the world stage, and new technological developments, for example. Which of these is the most important, no one can say; their relative strengths vary with the times.

The Role of Designers

There are countless styles, each of which has its own distinctive characteristics and most of which have, at one time or another, or more than once, been a fashion. It is a common misconception, however, that all have been "created" by designers and only by them.

It is true, indeed, that many new fashions have been introduced by famous designers. Some examples include the boxy jackets of Chanel's 1920 suits; the bias cut dresses of Vionnet in the 1920s; Dior's "new look" in the 1940s; and the smoking suits of Yves St. Laurent in more recent times.

Often, however, it is a functional garment rather than an individual designer that generates a new fashion. Some examples that have taken the fancy of the public and become fashions in their time are the bomber jackets of aviators, the pea coats of sailors and the trench coats of soldiers, the leg warmers of dancers, and the protective overalls of farmers. Similarly, denim pants. The ultrapractical style created by Levi Strauss in gold-rush days, inspired the jeans that have enjoyed worldwide popularity in the second half of the twentieth century. And let us not forget the many examples of "street fashions" that started among young people and moved out to a wider following. A classic case is the miniskirt: the miniskirt and boots that London working girls adopted in the 1960s attained widespread popularity before being shown in Paris by Courreges.

Designers who acquire a reputation for "creating" fashion are simply those who have been consistently successful in giving tangible expression to the shapes, colors, fabrics, styles, and looks that are wanted and accepted by a substantial number of customers. The fact that a style may be widely heralded as a new fashion does not make it one. Even among the greatest of designers, it is recognized that it is only when customers accept a style, new or old, that the particular style becomes a fashion. Paul Poiret, one of the greatest Paris couturiers, once told an American audience the following:

> I know you think me a king of fashion. It is a reception which cannot but flatter me and of which I cannot complain. All the same, I must undeceive you with regard to the powers of a king of fashion. We are not capricious despots who wake up one fine day, decide on a change in habits, abolish a neckline or puff out a sleeve. We are neither arbiters or dictators. Rather we are to be thought of as the blindly obedient servants of woman, who for her part is always enamored of change and a thirst for novelty. It is our role and our duty to be on the watch for the moment at which she becomes bored with what she is wearing, that we may suggest at the right instant something else which will meet her taste and her needs. It is therefore with a pair of antennae and not a rod of iron that I come before you, and not so much as a master that I speak, but as a slave . . . who must divine your innermost thoughts.[11]

Poiret was at his peak in the early decades of this century, but designers today still see things as he did—although they express themselves in less flowery language. Here is Halston, very much a designer for this part of the century: "I have always felt that all the designer can do is suggest; it is the consumer who accepts or rejects and is the ultimate maker of fashion."[12]

Fashions Reflect Their "Times"

Fashions in clothing have always been more than merely a manner of dressing. A study of the past and a careful observation of the present will make it apparent that fashions are social expressions; they document the taste and values of their era just as painting, sculpture, and other art forms do.

Fashions are a fact of social psychology. They reflect the way people think and live, and are therefore influenced by the same environmental forces that act on any society. Every fashion seems completely appropriate to its era and reflects the spirit of an age as no other symbol of the times does. This is true both for widely accepted fashions and for those that flourish only within small isolated or counterculture groups. To illustrate: Mennonite garb reflects Mennonite ideals; punk dress and hair styles reflect the attitudes of punk rockers.

NEWSWORTHY EVENTS AND PERSONALITIES CREATE FASHION

Fashions are made by outstanding personalities and major events in the worlds of entertainment, politics, art, and sports. To cite but a few examples from the 1970s and 1980s: the popularity of disco dressing resulting from enthusiasm for discotheques and the "Saturday Night Fever" music; the influence of a young and lovely English princess like Princess Diana on women's and children's dress; the Indian-inspired fashions influenced by the widely watched television production of "Jewel in the Crown" and the Indian art exhibits in New York and Washington; the tremendous impact of rock and roll superstars such as Prince, Boy George, Cindy Lauper, and Tina Turner on hair and clothing styles; the popularity of dancers' leg warmers and cut-off tee shirts emerging from the active interest in aerobic dancing.

SOCIAL VALUES AND ATTITUDES CREATE FASHION

There is, of course, no one universal way of life in America today, even among those who constitute the mainstream. Except within fragmented groups, like those mentioned earlier, our values are varied. Some of us are hedonistic; others are antimaterialistic. Some are conservative; some are futurists. Whatever our values and life-styles, our dress reflects that choice, consciously or otherwise. As one commentator points out, clothes nowadays are viewed "sometimes with almost mystical fervor, as the most basic expression of life style, indeed of identity itself."[13] Thus, fashions are a language that communicates self-identity and group identity with instant impact. When youth ideas are dominant, there is a tendency for people of all ages to dress, act, and think like, and to make believe they are young. The expanding use of hair dyes and face lifts by both sexes reflects the desire to appear young, no matter what nature may say to the contrary. The wearing of pants by women for many occasions is not merely a matter of dressing practically; it is also an expression of their freedom from the conventional restraints that they and their mothers had accepted in earlier years. When women, even those who wear trousers for most occasions, prefer to express their femininity, they move into fashions that are frillier, lacier, and sexier. When ostentation is seen as an expression of success, then rich clothes and elaborate home furnishings are "in." At other times, a revulsion against "conspicuous consumption" will express itself in understated clothes and home furnishings. And so it goes.

Fashions also reflect and are created in response to social and economic movements. For example, the career fashions and specialized career shops for women are a response to the rise of women in the ranks of corporate executives. Similarly, the antiestablishment fashions of the 1960s—cut-off jeans, long hair, beards, the "hippie" look—were expressions of the antiestablishment attitude that developed as a reaction to the unpopular Vietnam War of the 1960s. The androgynous fashions in 1983 and 1984, not quite masculine nor quite feminine, but something in between—the women's boxer shorts of Calvin Klein, the angular and ambisexual Japanese fashions, and the men's overcoats that were worn by women—received impetus from the androgynous dress of such entertainment stars as Boy George, Michael Jackson, Prince, and others.

In ways uniquely their own, hair styles have reflected social movements. In the Gay Nineties, women enhanced the luxurious look of their hair with pinned-on puffs, curls, rats, and other devices that have gone the way of tight corseting. In the 1960s, alongside the unkempt locks of the hippies, the blacks let their hair grow long and full, in Afro styles that proclaimed that black was beautiful. In the 1970s, many blacks, looking back with Alex Haley to their roots, returned to corn-row hair styles and then to dreadlocks—two styles almost impossible for Caucasians to copy. In the 1980s, Mohawks and spiky pink and green hairdos were part of punk rock's way of thumbing its collective nose at the establishment.

TECHNOLOGICAL DEVELOPMENTS CREATE FASHION

New technological developments often father new fashions. So simple a thing as a digital clock, for instance, makes it possible to depart from the round-face design that prevailed for centuries. Some apparel fashions seem to have their origins in the development of new fibers and fabrics, new processes for utilizing familiar ones, and other fruits of the chemist's genius—plus a waiting need for the new or a weariness with the old. For example, the synthetic fibers that made wash-and-wear fabrics possible, and thus influenced fashion, might not have had such a rousing welcome if they had come on the scene early in the century, when domestic help was plentiful and when the stiffly starched, beautifully ironed garment was a symbol of a well-run household.

Other examples abound, such as the popularity of skintight bodysuits in the 1980s resulting from the development of stretch fabrics; and the proliferation of graphics on tee-shirts, which were made possible by the advances in heatsetting technology. Plastics in their infinite variety influenced the development of such fashions as raincoats in gay colors, and the leather look of suede-like fabrics that offered the flexibility, easy care and lightweight qualities of cloth.

THE PREDICTION OF FASHION ·····································

Analyzing and predicting which styles will become the fashions for coming seasons has been called an occupational guessing game for the fashion industry, with millions of dollars at stake. Fiber, textile, and leather producers must work from one to two years ahead of the consumers' buying seasons; apparel and accessory designer/manufacturers must prepare their lines from nine months to a year ahead in order to show them to retail buyers three to six months in advance of the consumers' wearing season. Without accurate forecasts and projections of what looks, colors, fabrics, silhouettes, and design details are likely to be acceptable to customers, they would not be able to produce and sell the massive quantities of textiles and apparel that they do.

Such forecasts and predictions of fashion are neither guesswork nor a game, nor a matter of intuition. Rather, prediction is one of the most vital activities in the fashion industries. The successful forecaster recognizes that fashion is neither haphazard nor mysterious, but a tangible force whose progress can be charted, graphed, understood, explained, and projected. Basically, what fashion practitioners do is examine past experiences for clues as to what will happen today, and then analyze and evaluate today's activities for indications of what may happen tomorrow.

Determining Targeted Customers

Whether one is designing, producing or selling, the first step is to have a clear picture of the customer segment that constitutes the firm's targeted customers. A noted economist has said that "the central function of the entrepreneur in a fashion industry is far less the efficient organization of the production of a given commodity and much more the shrewd anticipation of the changing preferences in his numerically restricted clientele—his own small niche in the great neighborhood of women."[14] Just as there can be no universal weather forecast, but only one that is pinned down as to time and area, in our pluralistic society there is city, suburban, and small town; there is young and not-so-young; there is the blue-collar and white-collar background; there is the middle-income and well-to-do; there are followers and leaders; there is the conservative and the avant garde; and so on. What one forecasts for, say, the young juniors in a wealthy suburb of the West may be all wrong for the same age group in a poor neighborhood of an Eastern city.

With a specific targeted customer group in mind, the next step is to collect all the facts one can get. What are they buying this season? What are the activities and occasions for which they need clothes? What are their priorities? Are they innovators or imitators? What people, periodicals, or other influences will affect their choice? And so on. The more answers one has to such questions, the clearer the picture becomes, and the easier it is to forecast. Perhaps the essential element in the prediction of fashion is best pinpointed by one successful merchant's definition of fashion as "a conception of what your customers want."[15]

Analysis of Customers' Fashion Preferences

There is in the fashion industry a constant flow, back and forth, of information about the styles that the customer is buying. The systems that producers and retailers have today for this purpose are extremely rapid and accurate, thanks to the development of the computer. In most retail stores, a record is kept as to the styles, colors, fabrics, and so on, that have been purchased for resale. On this record are also entered the day-to-day sales. Every garment bought by a consumer thus becomes a ballot cast by the customer for the wanted size, color, fabric, silhouette, and style.

From the records, retailers can discern sudden or gradual changes in the preferences of their own customers. These changes become apparent whether the same customers are turning to different fashions, or whether there is a change in the kind of people who make up the store's clientele. In either case, the proprietor or buyer sees that there is less demand for this, and more for that.

These variations in what consumers are buying at that store are reflected in what the store buys from the manufacturers of fashion merchandise. Multiply that store's experience by the hundreds or even thousands of stores that buy from one manufacturer, and you see that producers have a pretty broad spectrum of consumer response as represented in the rate at which their various styles are sold. If they have countrywide distribution, they may see that certain areas are buying certain colors, styles, or fabrics faster or more slowly than others. If they have no reason to believe that this is due to special effort (or lack of effort) on the part of their retail outlets in those areas, they can assume that a regional difference is influencing sales. Typical of such differences are the West Coast's quickness to accept what is new, and especially what is casual and relaxed, or the Middle West's fondness for shades of blue to go with the blue eyes that predominate among the German and Scandinavian groups who have settled there.

From the manufacturer of the finished garment, information about customer preferences, as expressed in customer purchases, flows in several directions. One flow is back to the retail stores, by means of the manufacturer's salespersons, to alert them to trends they may not have noticed for themselves. Another flow is to the fabric producers, in the form of the garment maker's reorders for the most accepted fabrics and colors.

Information about the customer and the balloting that he or she does from day to day at the retail cash register is also collected by other people in

ANALYZING FASHION PURCHASES AT POINT OF SALE

Retail Sales ticket showing manufacturer, style number, classification, season, size, and price. This information is fed into a point-of-sale (POS) register and the data appear on sales and inventory reports.

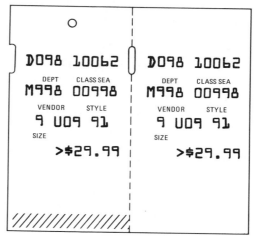

the fashion field. Editors of consumer magazines, for instance, check regularly on trends with manufacturers of raw materials and finished products. They do this to see whether their own previous editorial judgments of fashion trends have been right, and to establish a basis on which to select styles to be featured in future issues. What the customer does or does not buy is watched as closely in the fashion industry as the ticker tape is watched by stockbrokers.

Often the customer is a guinea pig on whom the experts test their judgment. Sometimes he or she is a member of a committee formed by retailers or editors to represent a particular section of the public and to be available for consultation or reaction to new ideas, or just to sound off on any subject. Consumer surveys are also conducted by stores, producers, and publications. More often, the customer serves unknowingly as a test subject. When a new style, color, fabric, or silhouette is introduced, makers and retailers usually proceed on a "sample, test, reorder" system. This means that only small quantities are made up and placed on sale in retail stores. At the first inkling of customer reaction, the retailer reorders the acceptable styles and discontinues whatever other styles may have evoked little customer

FASHIONS REFLECT THE TIMES

1910s		
Events	**Entertainment**	**Looks**
Modern Art	"Birth of a Nation"	The Gibson Girl goes modern
Costumes for plays	"Intolerance"	Looser waists
Ballet and fine art influence fashion	"Peg O' My Heart"	Gossamer fabrics
	"Let Me Call You Sweetheart"	Hobble skirts
	"Alexander's Ragtime Band"	Empire waist silhouettes

1920s		
Events	**Entertainment**	**Looks**
Prohibition	"The Jazz Singer"	Short skirts
The Charleston	"The Sheik"	Flapper chemises
Art Deco	"City Lights"	Bobbed hair
Bootleg liquor	"Tea for Two"	Powdered knees
"Showboat" on Broadway	"Ol' man River"	
"Swanee"	"Swanee"	
The Cotton Club in Harlem	"The Man I Love"	
	"I'm Just Wild About Harry"	

1950s		
Events	**Entertainment**	**Looks**
Television	"Rebel Without a Cause"	The trapeze
The "Beat" generation	"Some Like It Hot"	The chemise
Abstract expressionism	"Gigi"	The shirtdress
Sock hops	"Singing in the Rain"	Pennyloafers
"My Fair Lady" on Broadway	"Psycho"	Bobby sox
	"High Society"	Capri pants
	"Hound Dog"	Ponytails
	"Three Coins in a Fountain"	The sheath
	"I Love Paris"	Saddle shoes
	"Standing on the Corner"	Princess dresses

1960s		
Events	**Entertainment**	**Looks**
Woodstock	"2001: A Space Odyssey"	Ironed hair
Pop art	"The Sound of Music"	Nehru jackets
Psychedelics	"Bonnie and Clyde"	Love beads
The Beatles	"The Graduate"	Teased hair
Flower children	"Z"	Go-Go boots
"Hair" on Broadway	"Let the Sun Shine In"	Miniskirts
	"Strangers in the Night"	Dark eyes, pale lips
	"Moon River"	Pillbox hats
	"I Want to Hold Your Hand"	Prints

1930's

Influences	Fashion	Films / Music
Hollywood glamour influences fashion	Streamlined silhouettes	"Gone with the Wind"
Café society, "Our Town" on Broadway	Body conscious shape	"The Wizard of Oz"
Jazz	Bias cut	"It Happened One Night"
	Shirtwaists	"42nd Street"
	Draping and shirring	"10¢ a Dance"
	Halters and hip wraps	"I Got Rhythm"
	Hats and gloves	"Night and Day"
	Fox trimmed coats	"Putting on the Ritz"

1970s

Influences	Fashion	Films / Music
Roller skating	Granny dresses	"The Godfather"
Disco	Platform shoes	"The Great Gatsby"
A "Chorus Line" on Broadway	Message tee-shirts	"Annie Hall"
	Midis	"Rocky"
	"The Great Gatsby"	"Butch Cassidy and the Sundance Kid"
	"Annie Hall"	"Cabaret"
	Hot pants	"Send in the Clowns"
	Designer jeans	"The Way We Were"
	Punk	"Losing My Mind"
		"Killing Me Softly"

1940s

Influences	Fashion	Films / Music
WW II ends	Short hemlines to long	"Casablanca"
Nylon stockings available	Dior's "New Look"	"Citizen Kane"
"Death of a Salesman" and "Street Car Named Desire" on Broadway	Hepburn pants	"Adam's Rib"
	Sarong drape	"Born Yesterday"
	Peplum jackets	"Notorious"
	Uniform style suits	"The Red Shoes"
	Hats with veils	"So in Love"
	Platform shoes	"If I Loved You"
		"Some Enchanted Evening"
		"Moonlight Serenade"

1980s

Influences	Fashion	Films / Music
MTV	Men's wear	"Ghandi"
New wave music	Sweaters	"Diva"
Tina Turner	The big shirt	"Rambo"
Michael Jackson	Oversized silhouettes	"An Officer and a Gentleman"
Postmodern art and architecture	Stirrup pants	"Born in the U.S.A."
"Cats" on Broadway	Preppy	"Flashdance"
	Cropped tops	"We Are the World"
	Leggings	
	Dusters	

Source: WWD Special Edition, 75 Years in Fashion. November 1985.

47

enthusiasm. The manufacturers, meanwhile, are watching the retail reorders to see which styles they should cut in quantity and which ones should be discontinued.

No one, least of all the customer, may fully understand why one style is chosen in preference to another, but everyone in the fashion industry is observing their selections and thus determining what the current fashions are and evaluating their degree of popularity and their directions.

Recognizing and Evaluating Trends

The logistics of projecting current fashions are relatively simple. Whatever styles have been steadily rising in popularity during the last few months may be expected to continue to rise for a few months more—or at least, not to decline abruptly for some time. For instance, a rising trend for fur-trimmed coats at the end of a fall season is very likely to be followed by a high demand for fur-trimmed coats at the beginning of the next fall season. Likewise, whatever has been steadily declining in popularity up to the present offers little favorable prospects for the future. People in the fashion business seem to develop almost a sixth sense for weighing various factors and judging probable ups and downs of trends. Their apparently instinctive skill arises from years of experience in studying signs that may escape the untrained observer, just as a weather forecaster observes signs the rest of us may not have noticed and becomes adept in his work.

Sources of Information

Fashion practitioners base their predictions not only on their own selling records and preliminary sales tests, but also on facts and observations that are available from other segments within the fashion industry.

The fact-gathering procedure, to continue the analogy to weather forecasting, is similar to preparing a meteorological map, with its isobars, temperature readings, pressure systems, and other indicators of present and future conditions. On the fashion forecaster's mental map of present and future customer preferences, are the factors below—in addition, of course, to a knowledge of the movement of fashions.

With respect to the firm's targeted customer group, the fashion forecaster calls on the following:

• Careful observation of current events that have captured or are likely to capture the imagination of customers and affect the styles they will prefer.

- Awareness of the current life-styles and dress of those men and women most likely to influence what the firm's own customers will ultimately adopt.
- Study of sales trends in various sections of the country, not only for the forecaster's own company, but for competing companies to whatever extent is possible.
- An intimate knowledge of the fashion opinions of their sources of supply.
- Familiarity with professional sources of information, such as fashion reporting services, fashion periodicals, opinions of consultants, analyses offered by resident buying offices, and the like.
- Exchange of information with noncompeting concerns.
- Understanding of and constant awareness of the inevitable and evolutionary nature of changes in fashion.

Thus, a forecaster, whose official title may be designer, fashion director, magazine editor, or department store buyer, may decide that brighter and gayer colors will be more acceptable than they were in the previous year, that oversized tops have run their course for the time being, or that sleek hairdos are coming in.

A fashion forecast, once made, whether in one's own mind or in print, is seldom final and immutable. The unexpected can often happen when some new factor enters the picture. In any forecasting, whether it be weather or fashion, all that can be hoped for is a high percentage of successful projections. Even the best informed and most successful designers, producers, buyers, and fashion reporting services make errors, resulting in merchandise that must be disposed of in some way—usually unprofitably.

Consumers have given proof often enough that they have minds of their own and will reject a so-called fashion before it can even get going, if it does not appeal to them. And if the industry had any doubts about this, it has only to look back a bit. Efforts to induce customers to wear hats when they preferred to go hatless achieved nothing. Similarly, an effort in 1970 to switch customers from miniskirts to the so-called "midi" or midcalf length, met with disastrous results.

The importance of the customer in determining the course of fashion was stated effectively by Bill Blass, the American designer whose leadership has been legendary for decades. He said, after the "midi" fiasco: "I have never felt for one minute that the designers or the press or the industry could force or impose a new fashion on the customer, and that's never been more evident than now. The designer can only propose; the customer decides. This is a time of great individuality in customer buying, so the store merchant must pay more attention than ever to what his or her customers are looking for, and then find the designers who are making clothes that relate to their customers."[16]

AWARD-WINNING AMERICAN DESIGNERS ....

American designers, like practitioners in the American theater, television, and motion pictures, have been selected for awards when their work earns the admiration of their peers. Given annually from 1943 until 1984, the Coty American Fashion Critics Award recognized excellence in design. The awards were made on the basis of ballots cast by a national jury of newspaper and magazine fashion editors. These men and women voted for the designers who, in their opinion, contributed most to fashion during the preceding year. Special awards were given also to designers of accessories, and, beginning in the late 1970s, to designers of menswear. Designers who won three or more awards over the years entered the Coty Hall of Fame, and were no longer eligible for future annual awards. The purpose of this step was to encourage newcomers, since they would not have to compete with the established giant talents of the industry. The first to win Hall of Fame eminence was the late Norman Norell, in 1956. A chart in this chapter lists the names of other Hall of Fame recipients.

In 1984 the Coty Awards were discontinued and a group of leading designers formed the Council of Fashion Designers of America (CFDA) in order to present its own annual fashion awards. Their announced plan was to have committees made up of retailers and fashion journalists choose the nominees and winners. The awards and the winners were then to be announced and possibly presented in a television spectacular. As of the time of this writing, the television plan has not been implemented, but in January 1986, a dinner was held to announce the 1985 award winners.

Another award is the Cutty Sark Award, given under the auspices of the Men's Fashion Association. This award, presented each year in June, has been given since 1979, and is for the most innovative menswear designer of the year.

COTY HALL OF FAME DESIGNERS

Year	Designer	Year	Designer
1956	Norman Norell	1974	Geoffrey Beene: Halston
1958	Claire McCardell	1975	Calvin Klein
1959	James Galanos; Pauline Trigere	1976	Herbert Kasper
1961	Ben Zuckerman	1977	Ralph Lauren
1967	Rudi Gernrich	1979	Mary McFadden
1970	Bill Blass	1982	Louis Dell'Olio, Donna Karan
1971	Anne Klein		(of Anne Klein Co.)
1972	Bonnie Cashin	1983	Norma Kamali
1973	Oscar de la Renta	1984	Perry Ellis

ANNOUNCING AWARDS

*The Council of Fashion Designers
of America
Announces the 1985
Award Winners*

GEOFFREY BEENE
LIZ CLAIBORNE
NORMA KAMALI
DONNA KARAN
"MIAMI VICE"
ROBERT LEE MORRIS
RAY-BAN SUNGLASSES
TANGO ARGENTINO

Special Tribute

RUDI GERNREICH

The CFDA Lifetime Achievement Awards

ALEXANDER LIBERMAN
KATHARINE HEPBURN

*The CFDA Awards Dinner,
January 19, 1986,
is being graciously supported by
The Wool Bureau Inc.*

PURE WOOL

Source: Advertisement in trade papers. RWP: Robert Raymond, Council of Fashion Designers of America.

THE LOOKS FROM 1910 THROUGH THE 1980S

| 1910's | 1920's | 1930's | 1940's |
| 1950's | 1960's | 1970's | 1980's |

Readings

Successful designers are, above all, careful observers of the fashion consumer. As these readings show, those at the top make it very clear that their success owes a great deal to knowing what, how, and when the public wants to buy.

The Making of New York Fashion

New York fashion designers know that fashion does not exist in a vacuum. Thus, they produce fashion for Everywomen—sensible, stylish, businesslike, and straightforward.

Designers on Designing—Norma Kamali

Norma Kamali, interviewed, stresses that customer reaction is so important to the design function that she demands regular reports on the subject from her sales staff.

Bill Blass: Ideas Come at Odd Times, Odd Places

Bill Blass credits his award-crowned success in part to accurate timing. To his mind, the "when" is as important as the "what" in presenting fashions to the public.

Words and Fabrics Spur Ellis Creations

Perry Ellis does not believe in the ivory tower. He credits his varied business experience and his contacts with people, particularly with his talented staff, with contributing importantly to his success.

Donna Karan Takes the Lead

Donna Karan's electrifying success owes much to her clear understanding of the woman she serves: one whose sense of chic is not limited to dress, but extends also to the care she takes to maintain a trim figure—and the confidence that goes with it.

About Ralph Lauren

The life-style of his customers guides Ralph Lauren's designs—designs that have been successful not only in clothes, but also in products as diverse as perfume and home furnishings.

How Calvin Klein Fashions Success

Fashion designer Calvin Klein has helped make the sporty American look internationally popular and has survived the pressures of success and celebrity. An important key, he says, is self-understanding.

Geoffrey Beene and Liz Claiborne Exemplify Divergent Patterns of Success

Design entrepreneurs keep a worldwide view. For Geoffrey Beene, this means exploring foreign market opportunities. For Liz Claiborne, looking abroad means looking for offshore production facilities that help keep her prices in line with what her customer will pay.

The Making of New York Fashion
by Perdrix

Each of the world's great fashion centers has its distinct specialty. Paris glorifies design for design's sake, Milan emphasizes casual luxury, London aims to shock, and Tokyo, to mystify. By contrast, New York produces fashion for Everywoman—straightforward, sensible, businesslike, and increasingly stylish.

Twice a year, members of the international fashion world convene in the crowded showrooms of midtown Manhattan, looking for new ideas and new designers, checking out already-established reputations, and hoping to do a lot of business. Besides these things, they are after a unique commodity—the reality factor.

New York's top designers leave little to chance. They crisscross the country to meet their customers and discover their wants and needs. They are not only creators but master marketers. They know that fashion does not exist in a vacuum. Women want and need clothes that make them look good and do not get in their way. New York's fashion industry responds. No other country's can produce such practical clothes.

Paris merchandises glamour. It is the fashion capital of the Western world, and of a good part of the Eastern world as well. Though Paris clothes can be beautiful both in design and in execution, they take their cue from fashions of the past rather than focusing on what women need now. Milan has established itself as a center for luxurious sportswear, drawing upon its wonderful resources—a wealth of fine designers, fine silks and woolens, and fine tailoring.

As for London and Tokyo, both are retrenching. The wild, irreverent approach of the British designers of the early 1980s is muted. They seem unsure whether to be conventional or outré. And the Japanese insistence on shrouding the body has changed. Colors, sometimes brilliant, are replacing the once-obligatory somber shades. Neither London nor Tokyo pays much attention to women who want to dress simply and elegantly.

New York does. In importance to the world of fashion, it ranks after Paris and Milan. It has specialists in sportswear (such as Ralph Lauren, Calvin Klein, Anne Klein, and Perry Ellis), in dresses (Pauline Trigere and Adele Simpson), and in the shrinking category of coats and suits; but of them all, five stand out: Geoffrey Beene, Bill Blass, Oscar de la Renta, Carolina Herrera, and Donna Karan. Besides talent, all five have an eye for the kind of clothes women actually need. They take for granted the fact that clothes must fit properly: a size eight, for instance, will fit women of different heights as well as of different shapes. The Europeans are just learning this, and the Japanese don't care—often they make just one size, anyway.

Donna Karan sprang to the forefront of American fashion in less than a year. When she started her own business, after more than a decade with Anne Klein, she decided that she would make life easier for working women like herself, providing the perfect jacket, the best-fitting pair of pants, the right sweater, the right jewelry, handbag, shoes, and alligaor belt.

Source: This article first appeared in *Connoisseur Magazine*, February 1986. Reprinted with permission.

Karan went a bit further. She designed a bodysuit, like a leotard, to be worn under skirts and pants so that the top wouldn't ride up. The concept worked. A key to her designs is a skirt the wearer knots and ties herself. As important as its perfect fit is the seductive draped effect. Not every woman, to be sure, wants to drape her own skirt or wear a confining bodysuit. For such women, Karan provides pull-on pants (with elastic waists) and conventional blouses and sweaters that have the same severe, sophisticated look as the rest of the collection.

Though designers everywhere tend to create their clothes on tall, willowy mannequins with broad shoulders and no hips, when clothes go into actual production U.S. designers remake them on bodies more like those of average women. Even so, proper fit is elusive, especially when clothes are cut closer to the body. Though the inventive Geoffrey Beene uses fabrics that cost up to $300 a yard, he knows women resent paying for alterations and has evolved a jacket that will fit anyone. It is a classic solution, and he has used it throughout his spring collection. The jacket has ties that wrap around the waist and button in the back, making it fit as neatly as a second skin. It is effective in wool jersey and silks, worn in company with narrow skirts or long pants, for day or night, and practical as an apron translated into the ethereal realm of fashion.

The sweater is another practical garment that appears in the most elegant collections. Bill Blass achieves effortless sophistication by simply tucking a navy cashmere pullover into white crêpe pants and adding a long navy-and-white striped silk coat. He tosses peach or mauve cardigans over warp-print taffeta pants or skirts, decorates some sweaters with lace, lines others with prints to match the dress or skirt they are worn with. He offers glamorous crêpe evening dresses in hot colors, and tai-lored clothes in houndstooth checks, but the sweater is his leitmotif, showing his appreciation of the utilitarian principle in fashion. Though he is sometimes carried away with his designs, this time everything, including beading, is under control.

Oscar de la Renta is better-known for his extravagant evening dresses, but the sweater is a cornerstone of his collection too. It tends to be rimmed in jewels but can be equipped simply with a white piqué collar and cuffs and worn with a bouffant taffeta skirt. Some sweaters are paired with crystal-beaded short skirts; others are tucked into crêpe pants. De la Renta likes to drape jersey or crêpe dresses close to the body and has a fine hand with chiffon and lace, but his preoccupation with sweater dressing shows that he is at home with down-to-earth designs too.

When Carolina Herrera first appeared on the fashion scene she was not taken very seriously, but she knew instinctively how women want to dress. First her evening dresses clicked, then her day clothes. Her formula was simple: neat suits and jacket dresses by day, slim columns with bare necklines by night to show off a woman's jewels. The day clothes often have contrasting color panels—both pretty and slimming. Glamorous as her clothes are, Herrera has her feet on the ground.

New York designers cannot afford the luxury of untrammeled fantasy, nor can they be persistently outrageous. Their customers want clothes to be flattering but not to interfere with easy movement, and they must fit without alterations more complicated than a hem adjustment. That is their strength. While store buyers and press people from abroad call French clothes too artsy and fussy, designers like Beene have reported orders from stores in Austria, Switzerland, and West Germany. It is a trickle today, with a still-strong dollar and tariff barriers, but observers foresee a time when American clothes will be up there with

American films, pop music, and fast food. The reason is not so much life-style as the designs themselves. The best of them mix practicality with glamour in a way few designers elsewhere even think about.

Some American designers play it safe, and are boring, while others are insecure enough to copy ("adapt") styles by acknowledged leaders. Even in the best collections, echoes of designs by Armani, Valentino, Chanel, and Ungaro can be discerned. Of them all, only Geoffrey Beene seems to be his own man. This is the vestige of a provincialism that lasted through the 1950s, when American designers took all their cues from Paris, and copies and adaptations were the order of the day.

For the handful of New York designers who have carved out their own look, the prospect is encouraging. In the vitality of their customers, they have a great opportunity to explore new ideas and make fashion an active force in contemporary life. While each has his own identity, together they are recognized as representatives of the New York school of fashion—a school grounded on the reality principle. It represents the wave of the future. Behind the baroque mirrored walls of the hotel Pierre's grand ballroom, Geoffrey Beene is so quiet you almost wouldn't notice him. A gentle, soft-spoken southerner, smooth and easy, he watches a woman about eight feet tall slipping into a sleeveless dress with a red bodice and yellow satin skirt. In her high heels she towers above the dressers, who surround her like worker bees attending their queen. Then his attention turns to the sunny model in a black linen suit whose lips are like rosebuds. He adjusts her bracelet, and she joins a line of black-and-white cocktail suits and dresses that look like the dots and dashes of Morse code, an unfinished sentence poised at the runway entrance. . . .

Spring will be dramatic, with black in most collections. Some Texas fashion writers say black has run its gamut, but everyone who attends the show—writers, buyers, photographers, the rich and famous, the feared and dreaded, the models in their own clothes, even the dressers—everyone wears black! No collection is blacker and more dramatic than that of Donna Karan, out on her own for the first time. The showroom is full of whispers: "That wrapped waist, so flattering . . . she's going to be the hit of the season." Backstage, she makes sure everyone is wrapped just right—heads, hips, bosoms, waists, fannies, all wrapped over her little jumpsuit that has replaced the formal blouse.

When Oscar de la Renta arrives backstage at the Parsons School of Design auditorium, the scene begins to move as if it were being directed, models moving to cue, everything so well rehearsed and well versed, with swirls of color dancing about in the rushing to and fro. Just before the finale, while models in evening gowns wait backstage, two of them begin to waltz with each other: a sexy redhead and a dark, mysterious beauty, in gowns of black taffeta and polka-dot chiffon. Afterward, the models gather around Oscar, kissing and applauding him in a great release of joyful celebration, both because of the thrill—this is tops, they won't get much higher than Oscar—and because it is the end. One more down, one fewer to go.

At Carolina Herrera's show, the models manage to look rich and thin. Her sculpted look is set off well on these wafer-thin shapes. Her show is one of the less maniacal—hurried but rarely frenzied, lest a model misplace her shoes. The models look like the Herrera woman until they walk out the door and into the next show; then they seem like the Blass woman. And, of course, they can change to suit Oscar at noon and show up to wow the audience at Karan at three; and each time, these women, long and lanky, can remodel themselves, reiterating the mystery of womankind. The difference between backstage and on-the-runway is determined in the blink of an eye—just about how long it takes a model to fall into character.

Some designers, like Blass and Oscar, have two or three shows the same day. In between shows, backstage is ghostly, with a few models who haven't gone to lunch deep in their thoughts. At Blass, Toko smokes a cigarette as she reapplies makeup to her Oriental eyes. A video crew works with three models in bright silk dresses, reenacting a moment backstage. The dressers sit around little tables set up next to a bountiful buffet. Most of Blass's dressers are older women. Oscar uses students from Parsons. After all the models have left Oscar's last show and Oscar has been swept away by his swell friends, a young student takes an evening dress from the rack, holds it up, and sighs as she surveys the jet-beaded black lace bodice over a blue silk chiffon skirt—for the dress or the elegant man who made it?

The Blass collection is a carnival of colors: stripes, plaids, prints, beaded jackets in lemon yellow and pumpkin orange, and a day suit printed with dominoes, like a jokey wink. If there is one show that's fun, it's Blass's. By the time the third show comes round, a sudden calm falls over everyone, and it turns out to be the most lighthearted. Just before it begins, models and designer watch the video of the previous shows, entranced and happy. So the little pink silk dress rounds the corner of the back hallway that leads to the dressing room at more of a skip than a run.

Blass looks like a movie set. Models lean just so against a chair to prevent wrinkles while they preen and primp and are fussed over. Bill Blass smokes cigarettes while he smooths a model's hair or changes an accessory. A stage manager barks for the girls, but comically, using nicknames, forming them into groups of complementary dresses. The African model Iman smooths her gloves in an elegant gesture, like some dark crane resting on a branch. And there's that scamp Sara Kapp, flirting on the wing with the chefs in the silvery aluminum minikitchen through which models must race from the runway before they sprint down a mirrored hallway and past a screen for a record change. The kitchen is by all odds the best spot in the house for watching the show.

Designers on Designing—Norma Kamali
by Irene Daria

"So," Norma Kamali asks a reporter visiting her workroom, "how many other designers have you seen in their underwear?"

Standing behind a screen, wearing black bra, panties and socks, Kamali is fitting part of her spring sportswear line for Jones Apparel Group, one of her licensees. "I fit the clothes myself so that I know how the clothes feel and look," she says.

Speaking on her method of designing, Kamali says she designs "for myself and other women like me.

"I'm my best reference," Kamali continues. "I design what I want to wear in fabrics

Source: *Women's Wear Daily*, May 5, 1985. Reprint permission granted.

I like. I'm doing it for me, but I think there are a lot of women out there like me. I'm living in 1985, and I'm doing a lot of things that women are doing in 1985, so my personal needs and associations are like everyone else's.

"I look at a dress and ask myself, 'Would I wear this?' and if I can say, 'Yes, I would,' then I'll put it on the line."

The fitting progresses. Kamali and a fitting model are trying on different colored versions of the same samples. A merchandiser and pattern maker look on. Kamali criticizes one of the tops as being too big. Its sleeves are too long. The pattern maker points out that the fleece in the holiday line shrank, and the same possibility exists for this top. The sleeves are left long.

Wearing a skirt, Kamali wriggles in front of the mirror and exclaims, "I hate the stitching." She pulls at the waistband. "It makes a stiff line, and I can feel it." The stitching will be changed. As for a sheer beige dress, Kamali declares, "I wouldn't be caught dead walking down Eighth Avenue in this." The longevity of the dress is dubious.

Kamali spends each morning in this 15,000-square-foot loft on Eighth Avenue, and some part of each of these morning is spent doing fittings. "The fitting process is very long and very tedious," says Kamali, "but for me it's the most important part of designing, because how clothes drape and feel on the body is what is important in the end."

Yet before clothes can be created, they must be conceived. Kamali says she gets her ideas from three sources: her imagination, her staff and from fittings.

On her own imagination, Kamali says, "When you're in this business you think about what you do all the time, and ideas come to you all the time."

As for her staff, she says, "I have a rule in my company where everyone, and I mean everyone, whether they clean the bathroom or

are in high positions of responsibility, must write me a letter once a week and tell me anything they want to tell me—personal feelings or ideas they have for the company.

"Getting that information from them will either reinforce an idea I have or give me ideas about what the customer may need. I mean, they're in the store all day. They talk to the customers." The fittings, she says, "are very creative and very productive because I may fit one piece and from that one piece get ideas for six others."

Once an idea gels, Kamali writes down a description of it. "Even if I only write three words," she says, "I find it's better to write it than to sketch it because a sketch would limit the possibility of where an idea could go. The words are inspiration for what I could still do with it."

To explain this concept, Kamali gives this example: There is a detail that repeats throughout the spring sportswear collection, so that when people put things together there is a connection. That detail is pearlized buttons that are very closely spaced on a fabric tape, and that tape is made out of the same fabric the garment is.

"When I had the idea I wrote 'Pearlized buttons repeated in the decoration and detail.' If I'd taken the time to draw out how I wanted the buttons, I would have been stuck. Instead, I told my merchandiser, 'Listen, I have this idea for buttons. These are the kind I want, and this is the spacing I want.' She's there to facilitate the idea for me. The next day she'll bring me lots of tape and buttons and I'll see how it looks."

Following Kamali's instructions, samples are made. Sample makers for both her designer line and the licensed sportswear line are located in her loft, so work progresses swiftly. Kamali does not sketch until a garment is made. This sketch becomes "a references to the attitude, gesture, feeling and movement of the garment," she says. "I'll sketch it with the personality I want it to have."

"The more things you do, the more they stimulate the other things you do," says Kamali, who was one of the first designers to produce videos featuring her clothes. "I find that when I do videos, I'm inspired for the clothes and that the clothes inspire the videos."

The creative process behind "making videos and making clothes is the same," says Kamali. Both begin with an idea. Kamali's staff then helps her execute the idea. "I say to them, 'I need the following things.' For clothes, it may be buttons. For the video, it may be ghosts.

"Then those things are brought to me, and it's a matter of getting the right people to do the work on it." Work is contracted out to either clothing manufacturers or video cameramen or lighting technicians.

After a clothing line is produced and a video filmed, Kamali edits. "I'm great at editing," she says. "I can rip a piece right out of the line, even though I like it, because it throws the balance of the line off. The same is true with a scene in a video. It could be the most beautiful scene, but if it doesn't work with the balance of the story, it goes."

Kamali says that creating, whether it be a line of apparel or a video or the building housing her store OMO and showroom on West 56th Street, is "the biggest rush."

The one "problem" Kamali says she's had with the creative process is that "I've felt designing is a selfish experience."

"I always questioned what kind of serious contribution we are making here in fashion. I mean, there are people who do things for other people that are profound and wonderful, and I always had a little bit of embarrassment about the quality of what I do. I mean, is this really all that important?"

Kamali came to terms with the meaning of her work when she came to understand that "clothes really do give people a certain kind of joy. It may not be saving someone's life, but it does maybe save a day, or an evening and make them feel a little bit better about themselves."

And her work, Kamali says, brings joy and meaning to her own life. "The advice that's been given to me over the years as my business has grown is to hire assistant designers. I hear this and say, 'What, are you kidding me? My dream all my life has been to do my own designing. Now that I'm doing it and my business is getting bigger, I'm going to not design? I'm going to let other people have all the fun?'

"No way."

Bill Blass: Ideas Come at Odd Times, Odd Places
by Irene Daria

First, of course, there are the ideas, ideas that come "at very odd times in very odd places," says Bill Blass during a recent interview on the creative process of designing.

"I know it sounds perfectly ridiculous, but I often dream about clothes," he continues, as he signs a stack of travelers checks, preparing for his next day's departure to Japan on a

Source: *Women's Wear Daily*, June 3, 1985. Reprint permission granted.

business trip. "And I'm very successful at creating in my mind when I go to the opera or ballet. I do not have a great ear for music, and my mind wanders. Seeing something on stage that has nothing to do with everyday life enhances the creative process. It starts the juices flowing."

Blass pauses to tell an employee, the first of many who will appear in his doorway during the 45 minute conversation, to enter. Throughout the interview, when necessary, he will stop to talk to his staff and then, without skipping a syllable, will pick up where he left off. His method of conversing is indicative of his method of designing.

"My occupation is not a solitary one," he says. "Much of it is done on the run. I find that external interruptions are stimulating. The thing that stimulates me most is when we get going on a collection and while I'm fitting it, I will have 20 phone calls, and then I'll have people walking in and out from production, from selling, from publicity, all asking me questions.

"Some designers lock themselves up," Blass continues. "I don't work that way. It is not possible for me to get the creative juices working by being chained to a chair and saying, 'All right, now this afternoon we have to knock out this or that section of the collection.' If I attempt to sit down and say, 'OK, I have to do five black short dresses by Thursday,' I can't do it. But then I will be someplace and see something there that will trigger inspiration."

Among the places Blass finds most inspiring are museums. "I've been to almost all the great museums in the world," he says. "I never cease to be amazed at what derives there in the sense of inspiration."

Blass expects that the exhibit on India that the Metropolitan Museum has scheduled for this fall will have "some impact" on his upcoming collections. "Perhaps not in the sari or drape costumes, as much as in color."

Once an idea surfaces from his whirlwind of activity, Blass sketches it on a small scrap of paper. His initial drawings are, for the most part, doll-size. "I have sketch pads here and there," Blass says, "and I'm always drawing. I sketch while I'm talking on the telephone, while I'm in the car, while I'm on the plane. I sketch dresses, shoes, hats, anything and everything that might be appealing as a silhouette."

Blass then enlarges the sketches that he thinks are "valid" for a collection. He matches the drawing to the appropriate fabric, and then hands it over to one of his assistants and steps away. "I don't oversee them as they're being worked on," he says. "They're not interesting to me at that stage. They're like children when they're toddling. They're not interesting until they get up and walk. I leave them alone until the first fitting."

Blass says he does not design for "just one" woman but rather "for a composite of many women—small and tall, blond and dark."

He grants that socializing with the women who wear his clothing has been "highly productive."

"Seeing women, seeing how they dress and live, and traveling across the country gives you vital insight into what makes clothing successful," he says.

Blass quantifies the success of his collections according to how well they sell or, as he puts it, on "how many backs it actually got on."

Blass considers this season's collection "a big success." When asked if one collection stands out as being his best, he hesitates and then says, "I can't judge that." He adds that "seven or eight times" he's been presented with awards for designing that "came as a total surprise."

"I would not have considered that collection to be as remarkable as my peers felt it was."

But he does not hesitate when asked what has given him his staying power. "Sticking to it and learning that sometimes you have to wait an awful lot for what you want."

Blass said he developed his capacity for waiting as a child. "As a youngster the thing that I had, the thing that saved me, was patience.

"I knew from the time I was preadolescent what I wanted to do, and I wanted to do it with clothes," he continues. "As a child I was doing rather sophisticated drawings of people in New York penthouses having cocktails." These drawings, he says, represented what, to him, was "the most attractive possible life."

"I couldn't wait until I was old enough to come to New York," he continues, "but I didn't act as if I was dissatisfied with where I was, and that's been partly true of my career. I did not have an early success, but I waited."

Just as Blass filed away his childhood dreams for future fulfillment, he files away any sketches not put into his upcoming collection for possible future use. "I've had sketches that I've held back three, maybe four, maybe five seasons and then brought them out and had a bestseller. Timing is all important. It's a happy combination of the right fabric in the right style at the right time that makes a successful dress."

Blass likens his craft to that of a painter or a writer. "Each time one designs a collection, I suspect it's a little like a painter starting a painting or an author starting a manuscript. Although you want to continue your own style, you want a fresh approach each time.

"The start is the weakest part," Blass continues. "You gain momentum as you get into it. The collection often gets in the last two weeks before you open. I suspect it's a little like a play that is redone and rewritten out-of-town before its New York opening."

Blass has long reached the point where, as he puts it, "people will look at your clothes and say, 'Oh, that's very Bill Blass.'" But he says he works on giving his customer "a fresh approach each season."

The freshness, he says, comes from the fabrics. "Sometimes I choose a fabric that is such a piece of art, such a superb item in itself, that I think, 'What a shame to have to ruin it by making it into a dress.'"

Although he says there are times when fashion design can be called art, he considers his work to be a craft. He cites the work of Balenciaga, Madame Gres and "instances of Yves Saint Laurent," as art. "But I don't consider myself one of them," he says.

"I don't think of this as a deadly serious business," Blass continues. "After all, clothes are meant to be discarded. I take a dim view of people who hold on to their clothes for too long. And I don't like designers who take themselves too seriously, because they are a dreary bore.

"This is a business like any other," he concludes, "and it is also a craft that you perfect, hopefully until your dying day."

Words and Fabrics Spur Ellis Creations
by Irene Daria

Perry Ellis is a designer who does not sketch, drape or sew. He talks.

Unlike most designers, Ellis had no formal design training. Rather than making detailed sketches of his ideas, he gives his staff of 11, all of them graduates of Parsons School of Design, "funny little primitive drawings" illustrating the proportions he has in mind.

These drawings are presented at an initial brainstorming session where Ellis is joined by Patricia Pastor, vice president of design and now a freelancer, and Geoffrey Gertz, assistant designer.

"There are four of us who sit around and talk about what we want to accomplish," says Ellis, referring to the designing of his collection. "It's a group thing."

"It's very important for me to have a group of young people who are wildly talented as part of my day to day being," says the 45-year-old Ellis. "They're very adventuresome with ideas. Sometimes I like their ideas, and sometimes I don't. But they're always pushing me against the wall, which is great because they're moving me on.

"Any designer can only design from his own experiences in life," Ellis continues. "If you design alone, your work tends to be the same. When I started designing the collections were all tan and white with almost no color," continues Ellis, whose wardrobe is heavily weighed with khaki pants and white shirts. "I said I would never do color."

But, he says, "It's important that you move on and try new ideas and not rely on the same things over and over again."

Initial inspiration for the collection always comes from fabrics, says Ellis. "Two or three weeks before one season's show I'm in here looking at fabrics for the next season, really without any idea of what I would like to do for design. From the fabrics I'll get ideas.

"Then we test the fabrics," he continues. "It's important to see not only how fabrics look but how they feel and what they are capable of doing." Once this is done the group sketching process begins.

"I'll give them my ideas, and they'll give me their ideas, and then they'll sketch. We'll meet again, and I'll say, 'That's right,' or 'That's not right.' And if it's not right, they'll resketch, and that's the way it evolves."

Although Ellis has his own office, the rest of the design staff works communally in one large room nearby. The activity in one end of the room often inspires another end, says Ellis. "There's a lot of overlap."

Indeed, showing a visitor fabric swatches for an up-coming Portfolio line, Pastor says, "We stole this from men's." She indicates a bulletin board across the room where swatches for men's wear are hanging.

Later that day, a Chinese lamp for use by the home furnishing licensee was delivered to the design studio. An assistant apparel designer saw the lamp and yelled, "Oh, good! More inspiration!"

Although Ellis is quick to credit his staff for their work, the final design decisions are his. He says he is "totally involved with every product," including those of his 21 licensees. "I don't think there's anything that has my name on it that I haven't approved."

Ellis says he would have liked to study

Source: *Women's Wear Daily*, August 5, 1985. Reprinted by permission.

"formal drawing," but besides this, he says of his own background, "I wouldn't change any of it."

Ellis says he was "lucky to have been born with a mind that keeps presenting me with crazy ideas" and notes he was "always aware of good design and good fabrics." He first chose a career in retailing because "I always loved stores—the mystiques they can create."

He earned a bachelor's degree in business at the College of William and Mary. Then came a six-month stint with the Coast Guard as a member of the White House honor guard during the Kennedy administration. After the service, Ellis attended New York University where he earned a master's degree in retailing.

In 1963 he returned to Virginia and became a sportswear buyer at Miller & Rhoads department store in Richmond. "I was constantly redesigning everything I saw," he recalls, "I would go into the showrooms and the clothes would never be quite right. So, I'd give them a sketch and a cutting ticket and they'd give me the kind of clothes I wanted for the store."

In 1968, Ellis went to work for one of his vendors, John Meyer of Norwich, as a merchandiser. He moved to the Vera sportswear division of Manhattan Industries, Inc., in 1974 as a vice president of merchandising. It was

there that he came out of the back room and began officially designing.

"I'm not sure at what point I stopped merchandising and started designing," says Ellis. "It was an overlapping of positions."

With the success of his Vera collections, Ellis began designing his own line, Portfolio, for Manhattan Industries.

In 1978, at the outset of the fall Portfolio show, Laurence C. Leeds Jr., chairman of Manhattan Industries, announced the firm was setting up a Perry Ellis sportswear division.

That same year, Ellis formed Perry Ellis International, the design studio that holds the rights to his name. Manhattan Industries' Perry Ellis Sportswear is his largest licensee.

Reflecting on the circuitous route he took to design, Ellis says, "Well, you know, being a designer is not just the sketching, draping or fabric. It's also understanding the stores and the customer, the timing and the cost of things. Beyond your creative instincts, all of that is put into a collection too.

"Business experience and knowledge don't necessarily make a better designer, but it's certainly helped me."

Author's Note: Perry Ellis died in June, 1986.

Donna Karan Takes the Lead

When she was growing up on Long Island, the kids at school nicknamed her "Popeye" and "Spaghetti Legs." Except for softball, volleyball and basketball, there wasn't much doing at school that interested her. Her mother was a career woman on SA, and when she came

home from work she was usually too tired to pay much attention to her daughter. In short, no matter where she was, Donna Karan just didn't fit in.

"I was a social misfit, and I wasn't very accepted," she says, recalling two painful

Source: Excerpted from *Women's Wear Daily*, Wednesday, July 10, 1985. Reprint permission granted.

memories from her childhood. In one, a seven-year-old Donna stepped up to bat, pulled back—and smacked her best friend across the nose, breaking it. In another, a "gawky, flat-chested" Donna stuffed her bathing suit top at camp with toilet paper—only to forget and jump into the water.

"I didn't go out, I didn't socialize, so I had to find something that I was good at doing," says the 36-year-old, considerably more confident Karan today.

There was, after all, her passion for clothes and for working in boutiques after school. And one day in Hewlett High, she dreamed up her first collection, using her body to trace the patterns since she didn't know how to make the real thing. As awkward or out of touch as she might have felt then, she hit on the one thing she was good at—designing clothes—and it has stood her in good stead ever since.

Assistant to the late Anne Klein when she was barely out of her teens, Karan today sits at the head of one of the most ballyhooed and eagerly anticipated new lines to come down SA in ages—her new company Donna Karan New York. With a controlled first-year distribution of about 125 stores, the company is projected to do $11 million its first year—and may break even.

"That's not even supposed to happen," says a breathless Karan, reeling in the attention and excitement that has surrounded her since the collection was shown in May.

"I'm still scared, but I don't understand it at all," she says of the line's initial success. During recent personal appearances at Bergdorf Goodman, I. Magnin and Saks Fifth Avenue, in Beverly Hills, the line, sold only from samples, booked some $450,000 in orders.

"I just wanted a few friends to wear it," she says, shrugging back into the self-effacing Karan, a persona that alternates at lightening speed with the confident, brash young woman who tends to talk in the dulcet tones of a carnival barker.

Speaking with her today, there is no evidence of the gawky, quiet teenager who skipped classes to hang out in the art department at school and who longed for her mother's attention. The shy child is gone, replaced by a bubbling, exuberant woman who talks in shrieks of happiness or dismay. Not for her the subtle entrance and exit. At the end of her last Anne Klein collection with former co-designer Louis Dell'Olio, Karan sobbed and bawled on the runway like an out-of-control kid.

Today, she is making clothes for the perfectly poised woman of the Eighties—all muscle-toned chic with slim hips, strong shoulders and buttocks that are packaged neatly in the curve-defining scarf skirts she's made a crucial part of her collection. It's a special look that retailers say is one of the most innovative American collections in years and one that they expect will be something of a challenge to sell due to its high prices and the importance of the bodysuit.

"The clothes are today, the world is ready for them," declares Marilyn Kaplan, senior vice president of Neiman-Marcus in Dallas. "I don't think it's every store's cup of tea, but they've got a very careful strategy of distribution. The potential is excellent for stores like Neiman-Marcus."

Adds Kal Ruttenstein, vice president of fashion direction for Bloomingdale's, "They're modern, sleek clothes based on the bodysuit. You need a good body—not a perfect body—to wear them."

Sonja Caproni, vice president of fashion direction and visual presentation for Magnin's in San Francisco, describes Karan as having "one of the best seasons of any American designer" right now.

With its center of gravity based on the bodysuit—until now a not very intriguing piece of fashion outside of exercise class—Karan has pared down a woman's wardrobe, offering her the ultimate "packable" separates that can be wrapped, tied, switched and swapped using only a few basic essentials. Black is the pivotal color. Despite the practicality of the idea, there is another, completely impractical aspect to the collection—her clothes have some of the highest price tags on SA—with a gold sequined blouse expected to retail for about $1,900. Still, Karan contends there are pieces such as the wool jersey skirt for about $90 retail, that will make the collection accessible to many women. And as she explains it, "Your whole closet isn't and shouldn't be full of expensive clothes. Great pizza is still great pizza."

Karan is a woman with seemingly limitless goals, and she is not shy about voicing them: She wants to open her own boutiques, particularly in Europe, "definitely in the next year"; she'd like to do men's and children's wear, and although it requires a tremendous amount of up front work, she's plenty interested in that hallmark of designer licensing, the fragrance business.

"I have a plan that's all worked out. I've just got to hold back so I don't blow it," she says, her cockiness intact once again.

Fresh from the multimillion dollar success of Anne Klein II, Karan is eager to start her own lower-price line, keeping the Donna Karan collection a select, expensive "laboratory" of fashion where she can test her ideas. This, of course, doesn't even touch on the ancillary businesses she entered when she started her new company backed by Takihyo, the Japanese company that funds Anne Klein—hosiery, bodywear and accessories, from jewelry to belts and hats. With all this frantic activity going on, Karan still has time for a regret or two—for instance, she's sorry she hasn't yet unveiled a loungewear line but promises to do so shortly.

"I worked since I was 14 years old," she says. "I loved clothes and I loved retailing."

That single-mindedness is what has brought her to the numerous highs she has already experienced in her career, but it has also left her with a lot of black holes in her life. Her disinterest in school and her eagerness to work for Anne Klein led her to drop out of Parsons School of Design at age 19. Today, when her 11-year-old daughter, Gaby, comes home with a problem in her lessons, Karan admits she finds it hard to help her.

"Stephan and I are both visual people. I'm not a reader, and it's hard for me to retain written information. It's a one-dimensional kind of life. Sometimes I even feel dumb," she says, revealing a long-harbored desire to go back to school at New York University for a degree in liberal arts.

Married to Weiss for the last two years, Karan says he was her "first love" before she married her ex-husband, Mark. After that marriage dissolved, she went after Weiss with the same determination she uses in attacking her career.

A tomboy while she was growing up, Karan says it is women who fascinate her today.

"Now I think women are more interesting. They're doing so many exciting things, they're confused and they don't have role models. We need tips about other things besides diapers and formula," she says.

Ralph Lauren: Success American Style

Ralph Lauren is America's leading designer in the classic tradition, who has stayed true to his own point of view, despite the seasonal vagaries of fashion. Lauren has always believed that fashion is a function of lifestyle. He believes that clothes should be natural, comfortable and elegant, for the way people live today. His are clothes with a timeless grace, clothes that become more personal and special with age.

For Lauren the starting point is always his overriding concern for quality and attention to detail, but the creative drama comes from his own romantic sense of authenticity and elegance. Always true to his own purely American vision of fashion, his products are nearly as diverse as the country that inspires them. He designs everything from menswear to womenswear, childrenswear, home furnishings, eyewear, scarves, shoes, hosiery, fragrances, handbags, luggage and leathergoods. And the stores that carry his products are located across the United States and around the world.

"I stand for a look that is American," states Lauren. "It is an attitude, a sense of freedom. I believe in clothes that last, that are not dated in a season. They should look better the year after they are bought. The quality holds up. The people who wear my clothes don't think of them as 'fashiony'. They like good clothes and they like to feel comfortable in them." Arising from this philosophy is the perfection of a classic look that offers new excitement each season. That look has put Ralph Lauren in the Coty Hall of Fame for both his menswear and womenswear designs—the only designer to be so acclaimed.

His Menswear: Polo by Ralph Lauren

In 1967, the New York born and bred Lauren started the Polo division of Beau Brummel neckties. Ties at that time were in an Ivy League phase—dark, narrow and undistinguished. But for several years Lauren had been harboring the notion that the time was right for a new look. And so he pioneered the wide tie—a four-inch tie made with opulent materials and fabrications that were unheard of in the tie business. Polo ties soon became the status ties. And Ralph Lauren became the menswear designer to watch, as his ties revolutionized the industry.

But Lauren had more dreams to fulfill. He had chosen the name Polo for his line of ties because that sport represented to him a lifestyle mood of athletic grace and discreet elegance, an image of men who wore well-tailored, classic clothes and wore them with style. With that image in mind, Lauren established Polo as a separate menswear company in 1968, producing a total men's wardrobe. Using only the finest fabrications, Lauren's menswear was distinctive, innovative, but always classic and refined. His suits blended the American Ivy League natural shoulder silhouette with the fitted shape and expensive fabrications of the best European custom-tailored clothing. His shirts were all cotton, richly patterned and expertly made. This same care was and still is applied to every element of Lauren's collection, as it expanded from knitwear to sportswear, outerwear, ac-

Source: Reprinted by permission of Polo by Ralph Lauren.

cessories, and shoes. Today, Polo stands as a bastion of quality and elegance, a menswear institution that maintains a ready identifiable image and a devoted following through its successful blend of creative innovation and classic tradition.

Menswear Licensees

Polo/Ralph Lauren's men's apparel is manufactured and distributed by licensees in Japan, Canada, Hong Kong, Korea, Panama, Mexico, Italy, Germany, Austria, Belgium, the Netherlands, Luxembourg, Switzerland, Spain, England, and France. All are under the Polo by Ralph Lauren label.

Under the Chaps by Ralph Lauren label, Lauren designs a collection of men's clothing, shirts, sportswear and ties for established executives who want an American traditional look at a less expensive price. In 1981, Lauren, the man who established the "preppy look," introduced Polo University Club, a line tailored for the college student and aspiring young businessman developing his first professional wardrobe within the exceptional taste level that Polo has come to represent.

His Womenswear: Ralph Lauren

Ralph Lauren first introduced his clothing for women in 1971, and his impact on women's fashion has been such that the "Ralph Lauren Woman" has become part of the vocabulary of our time. She is active, independent, and mature—the image of a woman who possesses innate elegance, a woman who is understated and feminine. His are clothes for self-assured women, women who would wear tailored clothing much in the manner of Hepburn and Garbo, with their own personal style.

Today, Lauren has established his own medley of signature classics—well-cut hacking jackets, man-tailored skirts, pleated trousers, chic city suits, exquisitely colored hand-knit Fairisle and motif sweaters. His collections offer the most elegant and feminine silhouettes in beautiful fabrics, including delicate, handkerchief linen and lace blouses, tucked shoulder jackets, refined and sophisticated dresses, hand-knit folk art sweaters, elegant sportswear, and evening dresses in rich cashmere.

Ralph Lauren's ready-to-wear lines include Collection, Classics, Roughwear, Active Sport, Swimwear, Bodywear, and as of Spring 1986, the Executive Dressing Collection. Lauren's complete ready-to-wear collection is licensed in Japan, Canada, Hong Kong, Mexico and Europe. Ralph Lauren also licenses a line of patterns to Vogue Patterns.

Awards and Commissions

In addition to his dual Coty Hall of Fame status and three special Coty Citations for contributions to American Fashion, Lauren's other design awards include: The Tommy Award (1971), The Council of Fashion Designers of America Award (1981), The Gentlemen's Quarterly Manstyle Award (1982), The Cutty Sark Career Achievement Award (1983) and the Neckwear Association Special Achievement Award (1985). In 1986, Polo/Ralph Lauren was honored at The Fashion Video Awards for Best Retail Store Concept Video and Best Children's Video. Lauren has also taken time out to accept a few special design projects. He costumed the male stars in "The Great Gatsby" (1973) and Woody Allen and Diane Keaton in "Annie Hall" (1977). In 1978, Lauren also designed a uniform program for Trans World Airlines (TWA).

As part of an ongoing commitment to the

World Wildlife Fund, Lauren has designed a special tie from which all proceeds are contributed to support the World Wildlife Fund. Commenced in 1985 for the World Wildlife Fund's 25th Anniversary, this program is being continued in 1986. The tie is available at Polo/Ralph Lauren stores across the country, including Polo/Ralph Lauren in New York City, as well as a number of other stores in the United States.

Personal Information

With a demanding work schedule, Ralph Lauren at 46 prefers to lead a quiet, personal life with his family—his wife Ricky, and their children. They enjoy jogging around the reservoir near their upper Fifth Avenue apartment and active weekends together at their ranch in Colorado.

How Calvin Klein Fashions Success
by Bob Colacello

He was born in the Bronx 41 years ago and now annually sells a billion dollars' worth of jeans, menswear, womenswear, sportswear and underwear with his name on it in department stores as far away as Brazil and Japan. He won three successive Coty Awards (the Oscars of fashion) by the age of 32, becoming the youngest designer ever to achieve that distinction. He has been married and divorced, suffered through the kidnapping of his daughter, endured rumors of his death from AIDS and somehow emerged from it all intact. He admits that he could not have survived success and its side effects without psychotherapy. He helped to make the sporty American look internationally popular, but he is most famous for his sexy and controversial advertisements, like the TV commercial for his jeans in which Brooke Shields says: "What comes between me and my Calvins? Nothing."

Calvin Klein, tall, tan and fit, sits cross-legged on the industrially carpeted floor of his modestly proportioned, starkly furnished penthouse overlooking Manhattan's Central Park. There is nothing extravagant or fancy

about his surroundings, except perhaps for some very American desert dreamscapes painted by Georgia O'Keeffe. Nor is he dressed like a man who recently bought, for $61 million, the company that manufactures his mega-selling jeans. Typically, the jeans *he* is wearing are not Calvins but Levi's, though his forest-green crew neck sweater and the white cotton T-shirt under it carry his label. White gym socks and black loafers from Brooks Brothers complete his non-outfit. In fact, he looks more like a grad student than America's best-known designer.

"I always think," he says, "that I have been really lucky, because at least I've always known what I wanted to do. I never went through the thing most young people do—going to school and not truly knowing what they want to do until later in life. I mean, I had a major head start—at age 5, I had a pretty good idea of what I wanted to do."

In 1963, when Klein graduated from New York's Fashion Institute of Technology, both he and American fashion still had a long way to go, and the going wasn't always easy.

Source: *Parade Magazine*, August 26, 1984. Excerpted by permission.

"My first job when I came out of school," he tells me, "was working for a person who interpreted French couture designs for American stores. They did what they called 'line-for-line' copies in those days."

After five years of obediently turning out commercial variations on Parisian themes and working on his own simple tailored coat and suit designs at home at night and on weekends, Klein was almost ready to give up on fashion and accept an offer from his best friend, Barry Schwartz, to become a partner in the supermarket Barry had just inherited from his father. As Calvin's father was in the same business, it seemed like a logical and potentially lucrative alliance.

"I didn't know what to do," he says calmly but with an echo of the confusion he must have felt then. "It was so *frustrating* on my job. I was working for an inexpensive, terrible coat house in those days, and I was just miserable. It was one of the few times in life that I went to my parents for advice. I was certain my mother would say, 'Stick to fashion'—she never wanted me to have anything to do with the supermarket business. And I was sure my father would say, 'Take Barry's offer, because who offers you half of something for nothing? And a partnership with your closest friend, what could be better?' *Instead*, my father said, 'I don't know anything about fashion or what you've been studying and doing, but I have a feeling that you haven't given it enough of a chance. An opportunity like Barry's may never come along again, but I think you'll be miserable for the rest of your life if you don't stick it out.'

"I was shocked. My father's a smart man. You know, I always thought I was so independent, that I never needed anyone's advice—but you *do* need advice. This was a serious time in my life, a really big decision, and coming from my father—I don't know, it just meant an awful lot to me. It convinced me. I told Barry, 'No, I don't want half your business.' A year later, *he* was in business with *me*."

Their partnership, which thrives to this day, began with a $10,000 loan from Schwartz to Klein, handed out in dribs and drabs, as needed. "I would run up to his store in Harlem," Klein recalls, "and I'd say I needed money for this sample or that fabric, and he'd take $500 out of the cash register so I could pay the sample tailor in Coney Island, who had his sewing machine in his daughter's bedroom—he was sewing samples for me because I didn't sew. That's how I developed a small group of clothes that, finally, Mildred Custin, then president of Bonwit Teller, discovered."

"She wrote a $50,000 order—it was just incredible for some kid who was in a pair of jeans and a T-shirt. And in those days, my hair was down to my shoulders."

"You know," he goes on earnestly, "I learned one thing—and maybe people can learn from my experience. What I learned is that you just take one step at a time. I've been through so much, both personally and in business. If I had known in 1968 what I would have to go through to get to the place that I'm at right now, I probably wouldn't have attempted it. But instead, I got my order from Bonwit's, and I said, 'OK, what's the next step?' There are a hundred million things you have to do to deliver clothes. You have to sit down with banks, get fabric, establish credit, find a factory to make the clothes, deal with the unions—it's endless. But I learned: One thing at a time, and you can deal with it. Whatever it is, make a decision, right or wrong. Just trust your instincts and decide. If you procrastinate, forget about it."

He pauses, then adds: "And I was terribly determined to be successful. I think you have to be. One thing I always tell students today—I teach at the Fashion Institute of Technology—is not to be discouraged. You have to want it, and if you really want it enough, you can, I honestly believe, achieve anything you want. To this day, I'm still a positive thinker. I think you have to make an enormous commitment to your work. You have to put that in front of a lot of other things."

The fashion press has written that some of Calvin Klein's best clothes—clothes that are both attractive and wearable—represent what an increasingly dominant American fashion is all about. How does Klein feel about being American?

"I have always felt so proud," he states. "What's happened to me could never happen in any other country in the world. I don't believe for one minute that you could experience the kind of success that I have, in a relatively short period of time, in Europe or the Far East or anyplace else. It's just not possible. It's the American dream because it can only happen in this country. I'm a great believer in free enterprise and in freedom of the press—even though there are so many things written about me that aren't true, and it's upsetting. Still, I prefer a free press to one that's controlled by the government."

One last question: Is Calvin Klein—super-success, American-dream-come-true—happy?

"Very happy." He smiles broadly. "I feel good. I'm healthy. I work hard. I don't feel the need to stay out late every night. I've done that, and I think that interesting people, alive and creative people, get bored doing the same thing all the time. Not that I'm through with nightlife, but it's not fulfilling. It fulfilled a moment, that crazy period I experienced, and it's not what I want anymore."

Geoffrey Beene and Liz Claiborne Exemplify Divergent Patterns of Success
by June Weir

In the wide-ranging world of the American fashion industry, where success can take various forms, there is room at the top for more than one. Geoffrey Beene and Liz Claiborne, certainly two examples of the wide extremes between talents, have taken separate roads in reaching the heights.

Beene has found his special niche at the upper limits of creative fashion, where luxurious fabrics and demanding workmanship produce clothing for a selective, dedicated, and limited, audience. Liz Claiborne, on the other hand, is a stylist for women working their way up. She has built her successful business with a more moderate sense of style; she churns out smart tops, bottoms and dresses that have a more moderate range and aim for the mass market. And she has been on target to such a degree that at least one Wall Street analyst has given Liz Claiborne Inc. what might be called a rave review.

Beene first established his name internationally in Milan in 1976. The designer calls it a turning point that showed "my internationalism in the world of fashion." But three years later, the contract in Italy was terminated, he said, because of too much copying of his fabrics and cheapening of his clothes.

"Time has passed," Beene says now. "I feel now is the right time to return to Europe."

Beene already has established himself in Japan, with 13 boutiques. There are also negotiations going on for the opening of boutiques in Southeast Asia, he says. Beene has only good words for the Japanese. "The talent of the Japanese hasn't even been measured," he says. "Their fabrics are something extraordinary. They'll probably be the leaders of synthetics."

Exporting has become a fact of life in fashion, and one that many American designers did not come to recognize until late in life—the last decade. But now, the strength of the dollar has made the exporting of American clothes a difficult and expensive affair—unless those "American" clothes are manufactured outside the United States. "Every other country exports like crazy," says Beene. "Even if they're just starting in fashion, like Japan. I realize how very late we are."

Beene says all this first hit home two years after he started his own business and was in Mexico City to represent American fashion at an international festival in 1965. "Cardin represented France, Valentino was from Italy, as well as Spain's Pertegaz," says Beene. "I saw all these designers had been selling in a world way. I thought: 'Why has America been doing this? Why do we Americans always look to other countries?'"

Besides overseas expansion, Beene's other ambition is to expand his use of synthetic fibers. Though he has usually been a purist who works only with natural fibers, he now says he would like to find enough man-made fibers to produce an entire collection. "Everything," he says, "starts with the fabric."

Beene attributes his designing success to a move from structured shapes to what he calls "soft clothes." Suddenly, he says, "I was doing soft clothes that did not hide the body, but revealed it."

Liz Claiborne, too, knows about change and expansion. "Basically, I think women want change and they want a fresh look each season," she says.

And each season, Liz Claiborne Inc. has the financial figures to prove that her thinking has been on the mark. In about nine years, she has built a multi-million-dollar business based on moderate-priced and stylish clothes. Last year, sales topped the $391 million mark for Liz Claiborne Inc.—which includes Liz Claiborne Missy Sportswear, Liz Claiborne Dresses, Liz Claiborne Petites, Lizkids, plus revenues from licensees.

With all the success, she remains cautious, and she says she has yet to form any major plans to sell her clothes overseas. She says: "We do very little exporting. We have a licensee in Japan. We export to Canada and the United Kingdom. . . . There are ways of expanding in Europe, but at the moment we are not equipped to do it since some of our manufacturing is in the Far East. The quota for each individual country is very complicated."

Her present direction involves the fine-tuning of her manufacturing. Her success may partially be explained by her understanding of her medium, by her use of modern technology, by her extensive research. Her entire organization seemingly is run with computer efficiency. It is a process that means paying careful attention "to our customer," to her changing needs and demands, listening to store workers, studying store displays.

The company has a corps of young people who travel the country and visit stores, where they talk to the sales personnel about their customers, listen to "complaints and requests." "Our 'travelers' go across the country explaining the current clothes," says Liz Claiborne. "They tell what clothes will be coming. They help to merchandise the floor. . . . They take photos of the branches to show us how the shops look. . . . It's very helpful when dealing with the stores. It certainly keeps you up on customer needs.

"Also, we have a marketing department that does nothing but analyze the figures and come up with trends."

With all the research, a prime step for Miss Claiborne is to "try to keep prices affordable and make it possible for a woman to have new things each season. Women want clothes that are easy to wear and comfortable. Our clothes never have a detail that doesn't work. No fake buttons. No fake tabs. . . . I know the average American woman is not as quick as Europeans to pick up fashion trends. She needs a lot of help." That's why 900 store accounts go to Liz Claiborne Sportswear alone.

The price range for Liz Claiborne clothes varies from $26 to $85 for knits, to $80 to $150 for career jackets. Shirts are in the $40 to $50 range, while skirts start at $35.

Unlike the top designers, such as Geoffrey Beene, who work with perhaps a small group of assistants, Liz Claiborne plays a managerial, teaching and supervisory role for her extensive design staff. She is, in effect, now more of a stylist than designer.

Indeed, the aims, workings and markets of Liz Claiborne and Geoffrey Beene are different, but both are essential to the American fashion industry.

Endnotes

1. Paul F. Nystrom, *Economics of Fashion*. New York: Ronald Press, 1928, p. 4.
2. Cecil Beaton, *The Glass of Fashion*. Garden City, N.Y.: Doubleday, 1954, p. 335 and pp. 379–381.
3. Thorstein Veblen, *The Theory of the Leisure Class*, Mentor Edition. New York: New American Library of World Literature, 1963, p. 97.
4. As quoted in Molly Ivins, "The Constant in Fashion Is the Constant Change," *New York Times*, August 15, 1976.
5. Edward Sapir, "Fashion," *Encyclopedia of the Social Sciences*, Vol. VI. New York: Macmillan, 1931, pp. 139–144; and Gabriel Tarde, *The Laws of Imitation*, New York: Henry Holt & Co., 1903, p. 313.
6. Veblen, *The Theory of the Leisure Class*; John Roe, *The Sociological Concept of Capital*. London: Macmillan, 1834, Chapter 13; Caroline R. Foley, *Economic Journal* (London), Vol. 3, 1893, p. 458.
7. George Simmel, "Fashion," *American Journal of Sociology*, Vol. 62, May 1957, pp. 541–558. Reprinted from the *International Quarterly*, Vol. 10, October 1904, pp. 130–155.
8. Charles W. King, "Fashion Adoption: A Rebuttal to the 'Trickle Down' Theory," Reprint Series 119. Reprinted from American Marketing Association Winter Conference, 1963, by Purdue University, Krannert School of Business Administration.

9. Allan Greenberg and Mary Joan Glynn, *A Study of Young People*. New York: Doyle, Dane, Bernbach, Inc., 1966.
10. Veblen, *The Theory of the Leisure Class*, p. 97.
11. Quentin Bell, *On Human Finery*. London: Hogarth Press, 1947, pp. 48–49.
12. RAM Reports to Retailers, January 1977.
13. Charles E. Silberman, "Identity Crisis in the Consumer Markets," *Fortune*, March 1971, p. 95.
14. Dwight E. Robinson, "Economics of Fashion Demand," *Quarterly Journal of Economics*, Vol. 75, August 1961, pp. 395–396.
15. Alfred H. Daniels, "Fashion Merchandising," *Harvard Business Review*, May 1951.
16. RAM Reports to Retailers, January 1977.

Selected Bibliography

Adburgham, Alison. *View of Fashion*. London: Allen and Unwin, 1966.

Alynn, Prudence. *In Fashion: Dress in the Twentieth Century*. New York: Oxford University Press, 1978.

Anspach, Karlyne. *The Why of Fashion*. Ames: Iowa State University Press, 1967.

Batterberry, Michael and Ariane. *Mirror Mirror: A Social History of Fashion*. New York: Holt, Rinehart and Winston, 1977.

Beaton, Cecil W. H. *The Glass of Fashion*. Garden City, N.Y.: Doubleday, 1954.

Bell, Quentin. *On Human Finery*, 2nd ed. London: Hogarth Press, 1976.

Bergler, Edmund. *Fashion and the Unconscious*. New York: R. Brunner, 1953.

Bigelow, Marybelle. *Fashion in History*, 2nd ed. Minneapolis: Burgess, 1979.

Black, J. Anderson and Madge Garland. *A History of Fashion*, rev. ed. New York: William Morrow, 1980.

Boehn, Max von. *Modes and Manners*. Philadelphia: J. B. Lippincott, 1932.

Boucher, Francois. *2,000 Years of Fashion*. New York: Harry N. Abrams, 1967.

Broby-Johansen, R. *Body and Clothes: An Illustrated History of Costume*. New York: Reinhold, 1968.

Calasibetta, Charlotte. *Dictionary of Fashion*. New York: Fairchild Publications, 1976.

Carter, Ernestine. *20th Century Fashion: A Scrapbook—1900 to Today*. London: Eyre Methoen, 1975.

Contini, Mila. *Fashion: From Ancient Egypt to the Present Day*. New York: Odyssey, 1965.

Cunningham, Cecil W. *Why Women Wear Clothes*. New York: Gordon Press, 1979.

D'Assailly, Gisele. *Ages of Elegance: Five Thousand Years of Fashion and Frivolity*. London: Macdonald, 1968.

Everyday Fashions of the Twenties as Pictured in Sears and Other Catalogs. New York: Dover Publications, 1981.

Flugel, John C. *The Psychology of Clothes*. New York: International Universities Press, 1966.

Fourt, Lyman, *Clothing: Comfort and Function*. New York: Marcel Dekker, 1970.

Gold, Annalee. *75 Years of Fashion*. New York: Fairchild Publications, 1975.

Hall, Carolyn. *The Twenties in Vogue*. New York: Harmony Books, 1983.

Harris, Christine and Moira Johnston. *Figleafing Through History: The Dynamics of Dress*. New York: Atheneum, 1971.

Hill, Margot H. and Peter Bucknell. *The Evolution of Fashion*. New York: Reinhold, 1968.

Hollander, Anne. *Seeing Through Clothes*. New York: Viking Press, 1978.

Horn, Marilyn J. and Lois M. Gruel. *The Second Skin: An Interdisciplinary Study of Clothing*, 3rd ed. Boston: Houghton Mifflin, 1981.

Khornak, Lucille. *Fashion, 2001*. New York: Viking Press, 1982.

Kohler, Carl. *A History of Costume*. New York: Dover Publications, 1963.

Kybalova, Ludmila, Olga Herbenova, and Milena Lamarova. *The Pictorial Encyclopedia of Fashion*. London: Hamlyn Publishing Group, 1968.

Lagner, Lawrence. *The Importance of Wearing Clothes*. New York: Hastings House, 1959.

Laver, James. *The Concise History of Costume and Fashion*, rev. ed. New York: Oxford University Press, 1983.

Laver, James. *Dress*. London: J. Murray, 1950.

Laver, James. *Modesty in Dress*. Boston: Houghton Mifflin, 1969.

Laver, James. *Taste and Fashion*. New York: Dodd Mead, 1938.

Laver, James. *Women's Dress in the Jazz Age*. London: H. Hamilton. 1964.

Laver, James and Christina Provert. *Costume and Fashion*, rev. ed. New York: Oxford University Press, 1983.

Lurie, Allison. *The Language of Clothes*. New York: Random House, 1981.

McDowell, Calin. *McDowell's Directory of Twentieth Century Fashion*. Englewood Cliffs, N.J.: Prentice-Hall, 1985.

Milbank, Carolyn R. *Couture: The Great Designers*. New York: Stewart, Tabori and Chang, 1985.

Nystrom, Paul H. *Economics of Fashion*. New York: Ronald Press, 1928.

Parkinson, Norman. *Fifty Years of Style and Fashion*. New York: Vendome Press, 1983.

Pistolese, Rosana and Ruth Horsting. *History of Fashions*. New York: John Wiley & Sons, 1970.

Roach, Mary Ellen and Joanne B. Eicher. *Dress, Adornment and the Social Order*. New York: John Wiley & Sons, 1965.

Rudofsky, Bernard. *The Unfashionable Human Body*. New York: Doubleday, 1971.

Solomon, Michael R. *The Psychology of Fashion*. Boston: D. C. Heath, 1985.

Stegemeyer, Anne. *Who's Who in Fashion*. New York: Fairchild Publications, 1980.

Tozer, Jane. *Fabric of Society: A Century of People and Their Clothes, 1770–1870.* New Jersey, Laura Ashley, 1985.

Wilcox, Ruth Turner. *The Mode in Costume.* New York: Charles Scribner Sons, 1983.

Yarwood, Doreen. *The Encyclopedia of World Costume.* New York: Scribners, 1978.

CHAPTER REVIEW AND LEARNING ACTIVITIES

Key Words and Concepts

Define, identify, or briefly explain the following:

Avant garde	Fashion prediction
Bottom-up theory	Fashion trend
Classic	Forward fashion
Design	High fashion
Evolutionary	Mass fashion
Fad	Style
Fashion	Trickle-across theory
Fashion cycle	Trickle-down theory

Review Questions on Chapter Highlights

1. Give examples of each of the following: a style, fad, classic, design, fashion, fashion trend. Explain the differences and relationships between these terms.
2. "The only thing constant about fashion is change." Explain why fashions change and cite examples.
3. Cite examples of products other than apparel and accessories that are currently being affected by fashion.
4. Do you agree or disagree that there are different fashions for different groups of people? Give examples to prove your answer.
5. Does your current wardrobe represent one or more stages of the fashion cycle? Which state or stages and why?
6. Explain the following statement: "There are three accepted theories that categorize the admired groups from which fashion leadership flows." Give examples.
7. Do designers originate all fashions? Prove or disprove.
8. Explain how fashions reflect their "times" and cite specific current examples.
9. Is there a relationship between market segmentation and the prediction of fashion? Explain.

10. Describe the factors that must be considered by fashion professionals in predicting coming fashions.
11. What awards in the American fashion industry are comparable to the "Oscars." To which current American designers would you give an award and why?

Applications for Research and Discussion

1. Analyze current economic, social and demographic trends that are currently affecting fashion and cite appropriate examples.
2. Select stores in your community that operate on different stages of the fashion cycle and explain the reasons for your conclusions.
3. Research the designers that you consider to be the most influential at this time and discuss their major contributions to current fashion directions.

3

THE MATERIALS
OF FASHION

The expression of every fashion in the form of a garment or accessory owes as much to the fabrics, furs, or leathers that are available as it does to the idea that inspires its birth. As Christian Dior once said, "Many a dress of mine is born of the fabric alone."[1]

To grasp the importance of the producers of the raw materials in the business of fashion, one must recognize that many of the changes are primarily variations in colors, textures, or fabrics rather than changes in style.

This chapter is concerned with the **primary** fashion markets that provide the fibers, fabrics, leathers, and furs that enable designers to give substance to their ideas. The text discusses the most important segments of the primary markets and indicates how each of these influences fashion and is influenced by it. The readings that follow illustrate the operations of leading companies in the field.

FROM FIBER TO FABRIC

The making of fabrics involves a great many processes, uses machines of many different types, and employs the skills and knowledge of a variety of producers and processors.

No matter what the end result, every textile product originates as fiber. Fibers fall into two main categories: (1) **natural fibers**, such as cotton, wool, silk, and flax, which come from plant and animal sources and have been used for thousands of years, and (2) **man-made fibers**, which are basicly chemical products and whose development and utilization are twentieth-century phenomena. Whether fibers are natural or man-made, however, they undergo the same basic fabrication processes in the course of their transformation into textile products: the spinning of fibers into yarns, the weaving or knitting of yarns into fabric, and the finishing of fabric to impart color, texture, pattern, or other characteristics. *Weaving* is the interlacing of 2 sets of yarns, vertical and horizontal. *Knitting* involves machines that make fabric by interlooping of either vertical or horizontal sets of yarns.

Before being made into a fabric, fibers must first be spun into yarns. **Yarn** is produced by twisting together strands of fiber into a continuous thread or filament. This may be as coarse as rug backing or finer than sewing thread. To manufacture cloth, the yarns are knitted or woven together.

Some natural fiber yarns are dyed before being made into fabric. This is particularly true of wool, but sometimes man-made fibers receive similar treatment. In the latter case, the fibers are **solution-dyed** which means that dye is introduced into the chemical "dope" from which the fiber is made. In **yarn dying** the yarn is first spun, put on cones, then dyed on the cone prior to the fabric production process. More commonly, however, yarns are employed in their undyed state to produce **greige goods** which is undyed, unfinished fabric that is later dyed in the piece and subjected to a variety of finishing processes. At every step of the way, from fiber production to finished product, fashion is the primary influence in determining what materials will be used, how they will be treated, and what the end product will be.

FIBER PRODUCERS

Much of the fashion industry's ability to respond promptly and accurately to changes in consumer preferences for apparel and accessories is due to the immense variety of textile products available for use. In turn, the textile industry can more readily present its impressive range of textures, colors, weights, lusters, and other characteristics because the fiber producers are also aware of and responsive to fashion's requirements. That responsiveness, this far back in the production process, was slight in the days when only natural fibers were available, but it has reached enormous proportions now that man-made fibers have opened new doors in the industry.

Suppliers of Natural Fibers

The natural fibers are cotton, wool, silk, and flax. The amounts and qualities available at any given time and place are influenced by environmental conditions, such as climate and terrain suited to the animals and plants that are their source. Suppliers of natural fibers are many, are located all over the world, and tend to be relatively small in size. They generally sell their products in local markets to wholesalers who, in turn, may sell them to other wholesalers in regional markets. In the case of cotton and wool, commodities dealers may buy these fibers from central wholesalers throughout the world and sell them to mills. Thus, it is possible for an American textile producer to create a shirting fabric from Egyptian cotton, or a Japanese knitter to offer a sweater of Australian lambswool.

Before the entrance of man-made fibers, the suppliers of natural fibers were scarcely a part of the fashion industry. Their traditional role was only to produce and sell their raw materials. They were not concerned with the making of these raw materials into yarns for weaving or knitting fabrics, and they had no relationship with the garment makers or ultimate consumers. They certainly were not attuned to fashion. All of this changed with the entrance of man-made fibers into the business of fashion.

The need to compete with man-made fibers forced the cotton and wool growers into reevaluating their marketing procedures. They were impelled to take a more aggressive role and move out to reach the textile producers, the garment makers, and the ultimate consumers. In addition to improving the desirable properties of their fibers, the suppliers of wool, cotton, and other natural fibers each began united efforts to compete more favorably with the man-made fibers. Today natural fiber producers, through their trade associations, act as a source of information about the fabrics processed from their respective fibers and about fashion in general. They also promote their fibers

EXAMPLES OF NATURAL FIBER LOGOS

PURE WOOL

The sewn-in Woolmark label is your assurance of quality-tested fabrics made of the world's best...Pure Wool.

WOOL BLEND

The sewn-in Woolblend Mark label is your assurance of quality-tested fabrics made predominantly of wool.

cotton

True Performance

GIVES YOU THESE FABRIC QUALITIES

COMFORTABLE	Yes
EASY CARE	Yes
BREATHABLE	Yes
WASHABLE	Yes
DURABLE	Yes
PILL FREE	Yes
STATIC FREE	Yes

Source: Reprinted with permission of Wool Bureau Inc. and Cotton Council.

to the trade and to the general public by directing attention to the virtues of their product.

For example, there is an International Wool Secretariat supported by wool growers from all over the world. Their headquarters, which are located in London, are staffed with fashion specialists who advise fabric manufacturers of new developments in weaves, patterns, and colors. This association also publicizes wool in all media and by all means—films, fashion presentations to the trade and to the press, and cooperative advertising programs with makers and sellers of wool garments. There is also a very active cotton association, Cotton Incorporated, which is headquartered in New York City and acts as an information and promotional center for cotton. They prepare and distribute advance information about fashions in cotton and cotton-blended fabrics to designers, manufacturers, the fashion press, and retail stores. They also advertise cotton fashions in consumer and trade publications. In addition, both associations encourage producers and retailers to use their distinctive logos (a cotton boll in the one case, a ball of yarn in the other) in the advertising of fashion garments made of their particular fibers. The promotional activities of their trade associations have drastically changed the part played by natural fiber producers in the world of fashion.

Man-Made Fiber Producers

As defined by the Textile Fiber Products Identification Act, man-made fiber is "any fiber derived by a process of manufacture from any substance which, at any point in the manufacturing process is not a fiber." This is in contrast to the term *natural fiber*, meaning a fiber that exists as such in the natural state.

For hundreds of years, man had toyed with the possibility of duplicating the work of the silkworm by mechanical or chemical means. These small creatures feed on mulberry leaves and are able to produce a thick liquid, which they force out through tiny openings in their heads in the form of silk fiber. Thus, in 1855, a Swiss chemist named Audemars attempted to produce synthetic silk by using the fibrous inner bark of the mulberry tree.

It was not until 1891, however, that the French Count Hilaire de Chardonnet built the first "artificial silk" plant in France. He eventually earned the title of "father of the rayon industry" when, in 1924, artificial silk was renamed *rayon*: "ray" to suggest sheen and "on" to suggest cotton. Rayon was followed by a deluge of man-made fiber experiments and developments in the 1920s and 1930s. The giant breakthrough came with the first public showing of nylon hosiery, introduced by Du Pont, at the 1939 Golden Gate Exposition in San Francisco. Not only did nylon hosiery immediately become one of the most wanted articles of feminine apparel, but nylon itself played a significant role in World War II for such uses as parachutes and uniforms.

With the development of man-made fibers, the importance of natural

U.S. MILL CONSUMPTION OF FIBERS

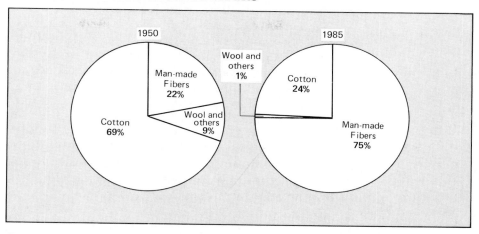

Source: *Man Made Fibers Fact Book*. Washington, DC: Man Made Fiber Producer Association.

fibers declined dramatically, whereas the growth of the man-made fiber industry was phenomenal. These figures illustrate the point: At the end of World War II, man-made fibers accounted for only 15 percent of all fibers used in the textile mills of the United States. By 1965, the man-made fiber industry was providing 42 percent of the nation's fiber needs. By 1985, the man-made fibers accounted for 75 percent of the 11 billion pounds of fiber used annually by American mills. Cotton in that year provided 24 percent of the fiber; wool, silk, and flax combined to provide the remaining 1 percent.[2]

IMPACT OF CHEMICAL FIBER PRODUCERS

The continuing development of an unending procession of new man-made fibers took place and continues to do so in the laboratories of giant chemical companies such as Du Pont, Celanese, Dow Chemical, Monsanto, and Eastman Chemical, for example. The entrance of these chemical producers into the fashion industry has brought about many changes in the fashion business, along with a whole new world of textiles. Since few in the textile industry know how to handle new synthetic fibers, the man-made fiber producers have to teach and guide spinners, weavers, and knitters in the processing and fabrication of new fibers. They also have to create a demand among garment producers for the fabrics made with their fibers and provide them with guidance and encouragement. Finally, they have to educate and create a demand among consumers as well. In short, they not only supply their fibers to yarn makers, but, with their enormous facilities for financing and research, they assume a dominant role in how these fibers are used in yarns, fabrics, and fashion apparel. Unlike the suppliers of natural fibers, the man-made fiber producers made fashion their business from the start.

The entrance of giant chemical companies into the business of fashion has added new dimensions to the fashion industry. The concept of creating whatever kind of fiber is needed or wanted to develop new and different fabrications opened up a whole new world of textiles such as "stretchable," "wash and wear," "durable press," "heat-set pleats," and "wrinkle-resistant," for example, with more to come. The promotional funds provided by man-made fiber producers to help finance the advertising of fabrics and/or garments that feature their fabrics generate more fashion advertising than would otherwise be possible. The financial resources of giant chemical companies are such that they can support continuing research and development of new concepts in technology, merchandising, and fashion, the results of which are made available to fabric and apparel producers.

FLEXIBILITY OF MAN-MADE FIBERS

Two basic types of man-made fibers are used for apparel: cellulosic and noncellulosic. Cellulosics are produced from cellulose, the fibrous substance found in plants, such as softwood trees, and are made with a minimum of chemical steps. They include rayon, triacetate, and acetate. Noncellulosic fibers are made from chemical derivatives of petroleum, coal, natural gas, air, and water. Fiber chemists link the molecules from these sources into long chains called polymers. In this category are nylon, acrylic, and polyester fabrics.

Man-made fibers have been improving the quality of fashion goods by offering a variety of characteristics unavailable in natural fibers. Their production, moreover, is not affected by the vagaries of weather or other natural conditions. They can be manufactured in quantities as large or as small as anticipated demand requires, and they can be endowed with desirable characteristics not necessarily found in natural fibers. For example, triacetate can be used to produce fabrics that are washable, wrinkle resistant, or with pleats that are heat-set for permanency; it can also be used in fabrics with brushed or napped surfaces and textured effects. Acrylic fibers can be employed in pile fabrics that are used in fleecewear, and that simulate furs. Modacrylics, inherently flame resistant, are excellent for use in children's sleepwear, upholstery, blankets, and draperies.

An example of how a fiber can be constantly improved to meet changes in consumer demand is offered by nylon. Today, high-filament nylon is blended with stretch fibers such as spandex to create new swimwear, exercise wear, and dance clothing. Nylon reflective yarn is used in clothes that reflect the headlights of oncoming cars when worn by nighttime joggers and bicycle riders. In the home, nylon has become the leading fiber for carpets; 99 percent of all domestic carpets are made of it.

EMPHASIS ON BRAND NAMES

Under the Textile Fiber Products Identification Act, the Federal Trade Commission establishes generic names for synthetic fibers. A **generic name** is one that designates a general group of fibers with similar chemical composition and properties. Of the more than 20 generic names established, however, relatively few are used for apparel fabrics. Polyester, nylon, and rayon, in that order, are the most widely used for clothing; other fibers used include acrylic, acetate, modacrylic, and triacetate. Within any of the basic broad categories, fiber producers can modify the basic chemical and physical composition to produce a new fiber. Although the same generic names may apply to the newer creations, these *variants*, as they are called, are usually identified by a brand name given them by the manufacturer.

From the first, the producers of man-made fibers have been very aggressive in promoting their **brand names**. A *brand* is a device, sign, trademark, or name that is used to identify and distinguish products as a means of building a market for them. Each company uses its brands to build recognition and acceptance of its product, to differentiate it from other similar products in the customer's mind, and to lessen price competition. To accomplish these ends, producers of man-made fibers advertise their brands in trade and consumer magazines and other public media in their own names, or in conjunction with fabric firms or makers of finished products. Anything from a multipage advertisement in a trade paper to an elaborate fashion presentation on TV may be used. In addition, their cooperative advertising money pays for much of the trade and consumer advertising of textiles and apparel in which their branded fibers are employed and identified. They also arrange or participate in fashion presentations staged by textile firms that identify their fibers, and they distribute free educational booklets to both retail employees and the consumer to acquaint people with the properties and names of their fibers. Some branded fibers are sold under a licensing arrangement that restricts the use of the brand name to products that comply with standards set by the fiber producer. An example of such a brand is Celanese Fortrel. At the other extreme are fibers that are sold as unbranded products, with no specified or implied performance standards or restrictions on their end use.

TEXTILE PRODUCERS

Textiles is a broad term that describes fabrics made from fiber by any of a number of different methods. Thousands of yards and millions of pounds are produced annually in the United States, in infinite variety: wovens and knits, polka dots and stripes, reds and blues, chiffons and seersuckers, and on and on, in every kind and color and texture fashion can demand. In providing the

A QUICK GUIDE TO MAN-MADE FIBERS

Generic Fibers and Major Trade Names*	Applications
Acetate Acetate by Avtex[6] Celanese[8] Loftura[11] Ariloft[11] Chromspun[11] Avron[6] Estron[11]	*Apparel:* Blouses, dresses; foundation garments, lingerie; linings; shirts, slacks, sportswear. *Fabrics:* Brocade, crepe, double knits, faille, knitted jerseys, lace, satin, taffeta, tricot. *Home Furnishings:* Draperies, upholstery. *Other:* Cigarette filters, fiberfill for pillows, quilted products
Acrylic Acrilan[13] Orlon[10] Zefkrome[7] Bi-Loft[13] Pa-Qel[13] Zefran[7] Creslan[2] Remember[13] Fi-lana[13] So-Lara[13]	*Apparel:* Dresses, infant wear, knitted garments, skirts; ski wear; socks; sportswear, sweaters, work clothes. *Fabrics:* Fleece and pile fabrics; face fabrics in bonded fabrics; simulated furs; jerseys. *Home Furnishings:* Blankets, carpets, draperies, upholstery. *Other:* Hand-knitting and craft yarns
Aramid Kevlar[10] Nomex[10]	Hot-gas filtration fabrics; protective clothing; military helmets, protective vests; structural composites for aircraft and boats; sailcloth; tires, ropes and cables; mechanical rubber goods; marine and sporting goods
Modacrylic SEF[13]	*Apparel:* Deep pile coats, trims, linings; simulated fur; wigs and hairpieces. *Fabrics:* Fleece fabrics; industrial fabrics; knit-pile fabric backings; nonwoven fabrics. *Home Furnishings:* Awnings; blankets; carpets; flame-resistant draperies and curtains; scatter rugs. *Other:* Filters; paint rollers; stuffed toys
Nylon A.C.E.[1] Cumuloft[13] Natural Touch[3] Anso[1] Eloquent Luster[1] Natural Luster[1] Antron[10] Eloquent Touch[1] No Shock[13] Blue "C"[13] Enkacrepe[3] Shareen[9] Cadon[13] Enkalon[3] Shimmereen[3] Cantrece[10] Enkalure[3] Softalon[3] Caprolan[1] Enkasheer[3] T.E.N.[3] Captiva[1] Lurelon[3] Ultron[13] Celanese[8] Multisheer[3] Zefran[7] Cordura[10] Zeftron[7] Courtaulds Nylon[9]	*Apparel:* Blouses, dresses, foundation garments; hosiery, lingerie and underwear; raincoats; ski and snow apparel; suits, windbreakers. *Home Furnishings:* Bedspreads, carpets, draperies, curtains, upholstery. *Other:* Air hoses; conveyor and seat belts; parachutes; racket strings, ropes and nets; sleeping bags, tarpaulins, tents; thread, tire cord; geotextiles

Generic Fibers and Major Trade Names*			Applications
Olefin Herculon[12] Herculon Nouvelle[12] Marquesa Lana[5]	Marvess[15] Patlon[5]		*Apparel:* Pantyhose, underwear, knitted sports shirts; men's half hose; men's knitted sportswear; sweaters. *Home Furnishings:* Indoor and outdoor carpets; carpet backing; slipcovers, upholstery. *Other:* Dye nets; filter fabrics; laundry and sandbags; geotextiles
Polyester A.C.E.[1] Avlin[6] Caprolan[1] Crepesoft[3] Dacron[10] Encron[3] Fortrel[8] Golden Glow[3] Golden Touch[3]	Hollofil[10] Kodaire[11] Kodel[11] KodOfill[11] KodOlite[11] KodOsoff[11] Lethasuede[3] Matte Touch[3] Natural Touch[3]	Plyloc[3] Polyextra[3] Shanton[3] Silky Touch[3] Strialine[3] Trevira[4] Ultraglow[3] Ultra Touch[3]	*Apparel:* Blouses, shirts, career apparel, children's wear; dresses; half hose; insulated garments; ties; lingerie and underwear; permanent press garments; slacks; suits. *Home Furnishings:* Carpets, curtains, draperies; sheets and pillow cases. *Other:* Fiberfill for various products; fire hose; power belting; ropes and nets; thread, tire cord, sails, V-belts
Rayon Absorbit[3] Avril[6] Avsorb[6] Beau-Grip[14]	Coloray[9] Courtaulds Rayon[9] Courtaulds HT Rayon[9] Courcel[9] Durvil[6]	Enkaire[3] Enkrome[3] Fibro[9] Rayon by Avtex[6] Zantrel[3]	*Apparel:* Blouses, coats, dresses, jackets; lingerie; linings, millinery, rainwear; slacks, sports shirts, sportswear, suits, ties; work clothes. *Home Furnishings:* Bedspreads, blankets; carpets, curtains, draperies; sheets, slipcovers, tablecloths; upholstery. *Other:* Industrial products; medical/surgical products; nonwoven products; tire cord
Spandex Lycra[10]			*Articles (where stretch is desired):* Athletic apparel; bathing suits; delicate laces; foundation garments; golf jackets; ski pants, slacks; support and surgical hose
Triacetate Arnel[8]			*Apparel (where pleat retention is important):* Dresses. *Fabrics:* Faille, flannel, jersey, sharkskin, taffeta, textured knits, and tricot
Vinyon Vinyon by Avtex[6]			Used in industrial applications as a bonding agent for nonwoven fabrics and products such as tea bags

*Number after the fiber trade name indicates the manufacturer: (1) Allied Corporation; (2) American Cyanamid Company; (3) American Enka Company; (4) American Hoechst Corporation; (5) Amoco Fabrics Company; (6) Avtex Fibers Inc.; (7) Badische Corporation; (8) Celanese Corporation; (9) Courtaulds North America Inc.; (10) E.I. du Pont de Nemours & Company, Inc.; (11) Eastman Chemical Products, Inc.; (12) Hercules Incorporated; (13) Monsanto Fibers & Intermediates Company; (14) North American Rayon Corporation; (15) Phillips Fiber Corporation.
Source: American Textiles Manufacturers.

materials with which to express the designers' ideas, textiles are the very essence of fashion. Without denim, for instance, the fashion for jeans could not have come into being. Nor could there be sweat suits and jogging outfits if the appropriate sweatshirt materials were not available.

Economic Importance

The basic function of the textile segment of the fashion industry is the transformation of fibers—natural or man-made—into yarns and then into finished fabrics. At one end of the industry spectrum are thousands of manufacturing plants that perform one or more of the three major processes involved in the production of fabrics: spinning fibers into yarns, weaving or knitting yarn into fabric, and finishing fabric to impart color, pattern, and other desirable attributes. At the other end of the spectrum are the sales offices that market the finished cloth to apparel and accessories producers, fabric retailers, and the home furnishings industry.

The textile industry plays a vital role in the economy of the United States. It encompasses companies operating more than 3,000 plants and gives employment to over 700,000 people. Its output was valued at the manufacturing level at almost $59 billion in 1985.[3]

Although the bulk of the manufacturing facilities are on the East Coast, some phase of textile activity is carried on in nearly every state of the union with the largest concentration in the South. Marketing, styling, and design

END USE OF FABRICS

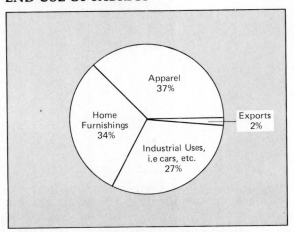

Source: American Textile Manufacturers' Institute, Charlotte, NC.

activities are centered in New York City as the number one location, with Los Angeles second, but selling activities reach into many other major cities.

The textile industry consumes fibers and dyes, machinery and power, services and labor to produce cloth that finds its way into a myriad of end uses—fashion apparel and accessories, to be sure, but also such diverse products as inflatable buildings, tire cord, space suits, sheets, carpets, and diapers. Clothing and accessories take up over one-third of the industry's output, with products for the home ranking second and increasing rapidly.

History and Growth

Although the United States textile industry today is the largest in the world, textile production by factory methods had its beginnings in England. During the eighteenth century, while the United States was becoming aware of itself and struggling for its independence, a series of inventions, each a closely guarded trade secret, had mechanized the spinning of yarn and the weaving of cloth in England and had moved production from the home to the factory in that country. The American colonies were, as England intended, a dependent market for one of the mother country's major products.

Colonial America imported most of its fashion materials: silks from Italy, China, and France; woolens, calico, and cashmere from England; feathers and artificial flowers from France. Prosperous settlers took full advantage of such imports; those who were less prosperous produced their own crude materials with which to clothe themselves. The men raised and sheared sheep, grew flax, tanned leathers, made shoes, and cured furs. Women did the spinning, weaving, dyeing, cutting, and sewing of the family garments.

EIGHTEENTH CENTURY: FROM HAND TO MACHINES

The transition from handcraft to factory production of textiles had its start in the United States when the first cotton **spinning mill** was built in 1790 at Pawtucket, Rhode Island, by Samuel Slater.[4] Slater was a young Englishman who had worked in one of England's leading mills and memorized the machinery his country refused to export. Declaring himself a farmer rather than a mechanic, he was allowed to emigrate to the United States, carrying his knowledge in his head. In 1793, Slater expanded his plant to house all the processes of yarn manufacture under one roof. That same year Eli Whitney introduced his cotton gin, a machine that pulled fibers free of seeds and helped to make a bountiful supply of cotton available to Slater and other early American textile producers.

Slater's spinning mill, now a textile museum, not only was the first successful spinning or yarn-making plant in this country but was also considered to have started the **Industrial Revolution** in America. His contribution to the industrialization of this country was recognized by President Andrew Jackson, who called him the "Father of American Manufacture."[5]

RAPID GROWTH IN THE NINETEENTH CENTURY

The nineteenth century saw a period of great development in textile manufacturing activity. The country was growing rapidly and the continuing improvement of textile machinery and factory methods made it increasingly economical to produce textiles outside the home. Fundamental to this development was the introduction and perfection in 1814 of the power loom by Francis Cabot Lowell, a Boston merchant, importer and amateur scientist, who visited England and memorized the system in factories there.[6] Lowell's factory in Massachusetts was the first in America to handle all operations from raw cotton to finished cloth under one roof. Before Lowell, spinning mills contracted out the weaving of yarn into cloth to individuals or small groups of workers. Spinning was thus a factory industry, and weaving a cottage industry before Lowell.[7] The nineteenth century also saw the rise of a domestic wool industry as a result of the introduction of Merino sheep into America early in that century. By 1847, more Americans worked in textiles than in any other industry.[8]

Additional impetus was given to the industry by the Civil War, which made great demands on American mills for fabrics for soldiers' uniforms, over and above the country's normal requirements. By the end of the war, the textile industry was firmly established and mass production of fabrics, although not yet of top quality goods, was well on its way. As late as 1858, England and France were still our sources for better grade textiles, notably fine broadcloth, and the New York Chamber of Commerce reported "that American wool, when used alone, cannot produce cloth of equal quality and finish as that made of foreign wools."[9]

By the end of the nineteenth century, however, woolens became available in a great variety of patterns and in great quantities, and cotton fabrics were even more abundant and variegated. In the relatively small silk industry, in which imports dominated the market as late as the 1860s, domestic production provided the overwhelming share by the turn of the century.[10]

PUBLICLY OWNED GIANTS IN THE TWENTIETH CENTURY

Spurred on by the booming postwar economy in the late 1940s, and an increasingly affluent consumer market, leading firms in the industry began to expand by means of mergers and acquisitions and to "go public" by offering shares in their companies on the stock exchanges. For some companies, the objective was diversification, as by acquiring carpet and hosiery mills in addition to those that produced garment fabrics. Burlington Industries, for example, originally specialized in weaving rayon fabrics. In 1939, it moved into hosiery production. During World War II, it made nylon parachute cloth. After the war, it continued to expand, acquire new plants, buy up other companies, and diversify. At present, as the world's largest textile producer, it turns out fabrics, hosiery, carpets, household linen, industrial fabrics—and

SALES OF THE LARGEST TEXTILE FIRMS

Company	1985 Sales (add 000)
Burlington Industries	$2,802,134
J. P. Stevens	1,858,190
Springs Mills	1,013,492
West Point Pepperell	1,204,158
Collins and Aikman	1,040,373
United Merchants and Manufacturers	795,360
Fieldcrest Mills	586,092
Guilford Mills	356,521

Source: Fortune Magazine, April 28, 1986.

more. It also produces every conceivable kind of fabric for any use and is vertically integrated. For other companies, the objective of acquisitions was to have an integrated operation.

The drive toward integration and diversification that began in the 1940s continued in the 1950s and 1960s. Between 1955 and 1966, when acquisitions were perhaps at their height, the Federal Trade Commission reported that about 365 textile companies were acquired by other companies.[11] In the 1970s, the Federal Trade Commission moved against excessive mergers and acquisitions, in this and many other industries, to avoid the lessening of competition that could result.

These acquisitions helped to create the huge, publicly owned diversified enterprises that dominate the textile industry today. Largest of these is Burlington Industries, with annual sales of almost $3 billion in 1985.[12]

Geographic Location

Throughout the nineteenth century, the industry was located principally in New England, where it began. Cotton, however, was grown in the warm southern states, and the transportation northward to the mills was slow, inconvenient, and costly. Industry leaders began to turn their eyes southward but, although there were small textile mills in virtually every southern state in the early nineteenth century, they were not especially welcome. Plantation owners found industrialization repugnant, perhaps seeing it as a threat to their way of life and as competition for slave labor.

After the Civil War, however, southern leaders recognized the need for industrialization and offered textile companies special inducements, such as low taxes and utility rates, if they would build plants in the South. The movement of cotton manufacturing plants gained momentum after World War I, and by 1920 more than half the spinning and weaving capacity of cotton textile manufacturing was found in the South.[13] Woolen and worsted plants, attracted by an improved spinning system developed in the South for woolen manufacture, followed suit shortly after World War II. Today, the three southern states of North and South Carolina and Georgia employ over 60 percent of the textile industry's labor force.[14]

Along with the growth of the industry came changes in the selling and distribution of its output. Merchants who had originally started as importers of European fabrics gradually became selling agents for the domestic mills or bought their goods outright for resale. The expansion of domestic output after the Civil War stimulated the establishment of a textile center in downtown Manhattan, on and near Worth Street, that became the heart of the textile trade. The name "Worth Street" became synonymous with the body of textile merchants on whom American mills depended for their orders and often for the financing. After World War II, however, when fashion's impact hit the industry, the textile showrooms began moving uptown, where they are still located, right on the doorstep of the women's apparel industry.

Today, the textile mills are largely situated along a broad arc reaching from New England through the Southeast, but their designing, styling, and sales activities are heavily concentrated in New York City.

Different Types of Textile Producers

In its early history, the U.S. textile industry was highly fragmented. Different companies specialized in different stages of production, each of which required different machines, processes, and skills. Spinning mills bought fibers, which they spun into yarn. Fabric mills purchased such yarns and performed the weaving or knitting into cloth. Much of what the fabric mills produced was greige goods, or unfinished cloth. At this point, finishing plants took over, doing the dyeing, printing, or whatever other treatments were required. In the case of **yarn-dyed fabrics**, commonly woolen cloth, the fabric usually required less finishing than piece dyed fabrics.

Today, the specializations that once characterized the textile industry are disappearing. More and more fabric producers seem to be utilizing a wider range of fibers or combinations of fibers.

VERTICALLY INTEGRATED FIRMS

During and immediately after World War II, problems of scarcity and price made the prewar production and marketing procedures of fragmented operations infeasible. The industry began to integrate itself. In some cases, fabric mills ceased to rely on spinning mills, selling agents, and finishing plants, and acquired or set up their own such operations. Burlington Industries was one such company. In other cases, independent selling agents like J. P. Stevens acquired textile mills and finishing plants. In still others, converting firms like Cohn Hall Marx bought mills to be sure of having fabrics to sell.

Today the textile industry includes companies that engage in all processes of production and distribution—spinning, weaving, knitting, finishing, and selling. This all-encompassing operation is called **vertical integration** and it enables a company to control its goods through as many processes as are potentially profitable. Nevertheless, even in these integrated firms, operations are specialized in their different plants, each of which performs a single function in the production of fabric, and different products are distributed by their different specialized marketing divisions.

SPECIALIZED FIRMS

There are still, however, many more companies that specialize in a single phase of production. Some are large firms that employ hundreds of workers, such as spinners like Dixie Yarns and Wintuk Yarns; weavers like Dan River; giant converting companies such as Concord Fabrics and Loewenstein; and printers such as Cranston. There are also many small firms, some of which limit themselves to narrow product lines, such as velvets and velveteens, or to such dressy fabrics as chiffons, taffetas, and silk failles. Other firms deal only in knits, brocades, metallics, or novelty fabrics. Their limited specialization seems to make them invulnerable to penetration by very large firms.

CONVERTERS

Converting is a specialized textile operation whose function it is to style greige goods and arrange to have it finished. The unfinished goods is contracted out to finishing plants for processing as ordered by the **converter** (i.e., dyeing, printing, waterproofing, etc.). The finished goods is then sold by the converter to apparel and home furnishing manufacturers or to fabric retailers. The converter may be either a division of a vertically integrated textile company or an independent company that owns neither fabric mills nor finishing plants but serves as a middleman between these two stages of production. In that capacity, the converter specifies all aspects of the finished fabric, such as design, color, and other treatments considered necessary to make the goods salable to apparel producers or fabric retailers. Independent converters are usually relatively small operators, but there are big names among them, such as Concord, Loewenstein, and Loomskill.

There are three basic types of converting organizations, each of which performs essentially the same functions. One is the *independently owned converting* company, which has contractual relationships with the mills from which it purchases greige goods, or the finishing plants it uses, or both. A second is the *converter-jobber*, also independently owned, who does not have any contractual arrangements. The third is the *integrated converter*, which is a division of a vertical textile firm. Such a converter works primarily with greige goods from mills of the parent organization and, as a general rule, has the finishing done in its own plants. It may also use outside sources, however, for greige goods or finishing.

BURLINGTON INDUSTRIES: PRODUCTS FOR APPAREL AND HOME*

Products for Apparel	Products for the Home

Domestic Operations

Burlington Blended Fabrics
Cotton/polyeter fabrics for shirting and uniforms and cotton/polyester fabrics, including corduroy, for men's, women's, and children's wear

Burlington Greige Sales
Filament and spun greige fabrics

Burlington Home Sewing Fabrics
Finished apparel fabrics for the home sewing market

Burlington Knitted Fabrics
Yarn dyed and piece dyed spun circular knitted fabrics for men's, women's, and children's wear

Burlington Madison Yarn
Textured nylon and polyester, KDK, and spun synthetic yarns

Burlington Menswear
Worsted and worsted blend woven fabrics for men's and women's wear and uniforms

Burlington Denim
Cotton and cotton/polyester denim fabrics for men's, women's, and children's wear

Burlington Studio Prints
Printed woven and knitted fabrics for men's and women's wear

Klopman Fabrics
Woven fabrics for men's and women's wear and uniforms

JG Furniture Company
Executive office and contract furniture, and auditorium seating

Burlington Carpet Group:

Burlington House Area Rugs
Tufted bath and area rugs for the home

Lees Carpets
Monticello Carpet Mills
Burlington House Carpets
Tufted and woven residential carpeting

Lees Commercial Carpets
Tufted and woven carpeting and tufted carpet modules for the commercial market

Burlington Domestics
Sheets, pillowcases, towels, bedspreads, and comforters

Burlington House Fabrics Group:

Burlington House Converter Fabrics
Drapery fabrics for the custom drapery market

Burlington House Draperies
Ready-made and made-to-measure draperies, custom-made novelty sheers and bedspread ensembles

Burlington House Tickings
Damask and striped mattress tickings for residential, contract, and institutional markets

Burlington House Upholstery Fabrics
Woven fabrics and tufted velvets for the residential and commercial upholstered furniture market

Products for Apparel	Products for the Home

International Operations

Burlington Industries (Ireland) Limited
Tralee, Ireland
Cotton/polyester greige fabrics for leisure wear and uniforms

Burlington Sportswear Fabrics Limited
Longford, Ireland
Denim fabrics for men's and women's sportswear

Klopman Internationa S.p.A.
Frosinone, Italy
Cotton/polyester woven fabrics for leisure-wear and uniforms.

Textiles Morelos S.A. de C.V.
Cuernavaca, Mexico
Woven fabrics for apparel and home furnishings

Burlington Carpet Mills Canada
Bramalea, Ontario, Canada
Tufted carpeting

Nobilis-Lees S.A. de C.V.
Cuernavaca, Mexico
Tufted carpeting

*In addition to the above, Burlington has five additional operating divisions—products for industry, international divisions, and so forth.
Source: 1985 Burlington Industries Annual Report.

Converters fulfill an important function in the textile industry. Since they enter the fabric production process in its end stages, they can work quite close to the time of need and adjust quickly to changes in fashion. Converters (company or independent) keep in contact with clothing producers, seeking indications of colors, patterns, and finishes that are likely to be wanted. For this reason, most of them are located in major apparel markets. The successful converter is a keen student of fashion, observes trends, and anticipates demand.

From Textiles to Apparel

A recent development is that a few large U.S. textile companies have gone into manufacturing basic apparel garments made of their own fabrics. What they are doing is arranging to have garments cut in the United States and sent to offshore assembly plants in the Caribbean area. As of the time of this writing they are selling these garments to their own apparel-producing customers, thus avoiding direct competition with them. This move into apparel production seems almost a sure way to expand the market for their own fabrics. For example, Dan River, West Point-Pepperell, and Springs Industries have tossed their hats into the apparel ring, and it seems more than likely that other large textile companies will follow their lead. It is interesting to note that in 1985 West Point acquired Cluett Peabody, a multiproduct apparel company, in order to expand its lines of consumer products by the acquisition of an apparel company with strong brand name recognition.

FASHION RESEARCH AND DEVELOPMENT

Apparel designers say that "fabric is the designer's creative medium, just as pigment is the painter's. A good designer responds to new fabrics and searches for the quality that will make it—and her designs—come alive."[15] To make possible fabrics that will evoke such response and that will ultimately be acceptable to the consuming public, fiber and textile producers must keep many fashion steps and several years ahead of the design and production of apparel. By the time fashions are featured in stores and magazines, they are old hat to textile designers and stylists, because these are the people who have created these patterns and colors at least a year earlier. And probably two years before the public sees the fashions, the fiber companies and their associations were working with fabric mills on the kinds of cloth to be presented. At that time or even earlier, fiber companies were working on color projections and fiber variants for seasons still further ahead.

Specialized Fashion Staffs

Fiber and textile producers invest a great deal of time and money in fashion research to guide the development of salable fabrics, blends, textures, colors, finishes, and whatever other properties are expected to be wanted. All of the large producers, textile as well as fiber, maintain specialized fashion staffs in menswear and women's wear to research and report on trends in fashion.

Although their individual responsibilities and titles—fashion merchandisers, creative directors, fashion coordinators, stylists, and others—vary from one company to another, the recommendations of these fashion experts guide their company's design and production activities. These fashion specialists tour the world fashion centers looking for fashion inspiration and direction, observe what fashion leaders are wearing, exchange ideas with apparel designers and manufacturers, and fashion editors, and generally use every resource available to anticipate what will be wanted by their customers and eventually by the public. At the same time, many large producers conduct market research in order to analyze consumer attitudes and their ever-changing tastes and preferences as to performance characteristics. Thus armed with their research findings about the performance and fashion features that are likely to be wanted, producers design, develop, and produce fibers and fabrics long before they become available to ultimate consumers.

Early Color Decisions

Fashion decisions in the primary markets begin with color. Fairly typical of the procedures followed in determining the colors to be used are those described by Ed Newman, then vice president and creative director of Dan River, Inc., in this comment:

> When putting together a color line we review the best and worst sellers of the last season, check computer readouts, have informal discussions with manufacturers and check the racks of department and specialty stores. We think of what colors have been missing from the palette for a while and which shades seem "new again." Many colors make the natural progression through the seasons; a wine becomes purple, the purple moves to magenta and the magenta to a pink. No mystery—just logic. The final choice of a color line is logic, research and "gut feeling." With it lies the success or failure of your next season.[16]

The Color Association of the United States, a major force in guiding industry color decisions, has been issuing color projections for textiles and apparel for more than 60 years, and has been forecasting home furnishings and appliance colors for nearly 30 years. It is a nonprofit service organization whose board of directors consists of top industry executives, each from a different industry, and all of whom donate their time. About 700 companies are dues-paying members, ranging from fiber producers to car manufacturers. All receive annually swatch cards that give color forecasts for the coming 18 to 24 months. These forecasts are arrived at by committees of volunteers who evaluate what they call the "color climate." To arrive at that, they consider everything from politics to the economy to cultural events and movements. Among the members of their committees are such distinguished persons as Mary McFadden, the well-known fashion designer, and Jack Lenor Larsen, a famous textile designer.

Intercolor, an association of representatives from the worldwide fashion industry, arranges meetings in Paris twice each year. There, these experts analyze color cycles and the natural evolution of color preferences, to determine specific color palettes for their target season two years in the future. Another color prediction service offered to textile and apparel producers is the International Color Authority (ICA). They, too, meet twice a year to establish their color predictions for fiber, yarn, and fabric producers. Six months later, they send a modified version of their selected colors to member apparel producers.

Textile Design

In addition to the color story, fabric stylists must also be aware of the silhouettes coming into fashion, so that the fabrications they recommend will be appropriate. For example, if the trend is toward a tailored or structured look, firm fabrications are necessary, whereas soft, light fabrics are needed for a layered look.

Once the stylists have their color story set and the fabrications determined, the next step is designing the fabric. Textile designers, unlike apparel designers, are primarily concerned with two-dimensional surfaces, rather than with the three-dimensional human form. A further consideration is the capabitilies of the knitting machines or weaving looms to be used. If a printed design is to be applied to the fabric, the designer must also consider any problem the pattern may present to the garment cutter. The pattern, usually a continuous repetition of a motif, is planned so that it does not entail unnecessary waste or difficulties in the cutting of garments.

Textile designers tend to specialize in either print, woven, or knitted design. Some are full-time employees of fabric mills, converters, or textile design studios. Others work free-lance and sell their sketches to textile companies.

Fashion Presentations

Fiber and fabric producers have developed considerable skill in utilizing their fashion expertise to sell their products. And through the fabrics they make available and the fashions they promote, they exert an important and continuing influence on the fashion industry's chain of production and distribution.

Large producers (both fiber and fabric) are very active in disseminating the fashion information they have collected to all segments of the industry. Most maintain fabric libraries in their showrooms that contain swatches of fabrics currently available or scheduled for production for an upcoming season. In addition, producers and retailers are invited to visit, inspect, and consult special displays of new yarns and fabrics that are set up periodically. These libraries and exhibits are used by apparel makers and their designers, retailers, and fashion reporters as sources of information about future fabric and color trends.

Some conduct seasonal clinics and workshops at which they visually present their fashion projections and illustrate them with garments they have had made up for this purpose and in which their fibers or fabrics are featured. These clinics are open to all segments of industry: producers, retailers, and fashion reporters.

Seasonal Lines and Sales Presentations

Once a fabric line is set and sample yardage is in process, the work of the sales and merchandising staff is put into motion. In the primary markets, two new seasonal lines a year are customary. Fabrics for seasonal apparel lines are shown from six to nine months in advance.

The actual selling of piece goods is broken down into two phases. The first of these, called "preselling," is a presentation by the textile company's merchandising staff to its key accounts—the decision makers. Presentations take the form of color swatches (small fabric samples made on sample machines), cloques (painted samples on paper), color puffs, and sketches set up on story boards for approval. Presentations are made either in the fabric mill's own showroom or in the showrooms of their customers. At this point, all samples shown are **open-line** goods, available for selection. If a customer chooses to have a particular sample "confined," and not available to others, and agrees to purchase an amount of yardage considered adequate by the mill, then no other customers may purchase it. Exceptions are sometimes made, however—for example, for a very prestigious designer label.

The second phase of fabric selling is the sales presentation to all other customers, regardless of size. Appointments are made six to eight weeks in advance of these customers' market weeks (selling periods), and presentations are made to apparel designers, stylists, and even the apparel companies' marketing staffs. Sample yardage is then ordered by the apparel producers for use in making up sample garments. After such garments have been shown to retail store buyers, apparel producers decide how much goods to buy and place their fabric orders. By the time this takes place, the textile creators are well into work on the next season's goods.

Textile Trade Shows

American producers participate in trade shows both in the United States and abroad. Held semiannually, these shows are attended by designers, manufacturers, and retailers who come to look at and perhaps buy the new fabrics. At this writing, the most comprehensive such shows are the **Interstoff Textile Fair** held in Frankfurt, West Germany; the **Première Vision** in Paris, France; the **Ideacomo** in Como, Italy; **Texitalia**, in Milan, Italy; the **New York Fabric Show;** and the **Canton Trade Fair** in Canton, China. Each host country presents the latest lines of textiles developed within its own borders, along with whatever else producers from other countries choose to exhibit. Other

Première Vision

FROM 15
TO 18 MARCH
1986

SUMMER 87

PARC DES EXPOSITIONS DE PARIS NORD
FROM 9.00 a.m. TO 6.30 p.m.
PREMIÈRE VISION INFORMATION
FRENCH FASHION AND TEXTILE CENTER
200 MADISON AVENUE · SUITE 2225
NEW YORK NY 10016
TEL   (212) 2130170 · TELEX   66540

Source: Reprinted with permission: Première Vision.

smaller shows include the Knitting Yarn Fair in New York City, which features new yarns, dyeing, and knitting techniques; and Cotons de France in New York City.

In addition to stimulating sales of fabrics, these shows result in further benefits. First, they make all related industry branches aware of changing fashions. At the same time, they unify and coordinate the thinking of related areas within the industry, so that they change in phase with one another and thereby facilitate the mass production that mass demand requires.

COMPETITION FROM IMPORTS

Despite the ample productivity of our fiber and textile industries, the United States imports a considerable amount of textile fibers, yarns, and fabrics from abroad. End-of-year figures for 1985 confirm the continuing strength and growth of the textile industry's import competition. In 1985 imports increased by 32 percent in quantity and 9 percent in value over the previous year.[17] Figures show that total textile imports just about doubled in the period from 1973 to 1983.[18]

In 1985 imports of textile mill products amounted to almost $4 billion when valued at the foreign sellers' invoice price.[19] After transportation, customs, and insurance costs are added to this figure, these imports would amount to more than the total output of our industry's largest producer. Our purchases abroad include such fibers as wool from the United Kingdom and Belgium, cotton from Egypt, flax from Ireland, and man-made fibers from Japan. The fabrics we import include silks from China and Italy, laces from France, and a variety of other fabrics from the Far East.

Some of our imports are from countries that have traditionally produced superior fibers and fabrics of a particular kind; others are simply a matter of importing from countries whose labor costs and costs of factory operation make it possible for them to sell more cheaply in the American market than domestic producers can.

We do, of course, export some of our own output, but in 1985 the United States had a textile trade deficit of over $2 billion. The downward trend in textile employment over the last decade, from over one million employed in 1973 to 707,000 in 1985, has to a large extent been caused by the drastic inroads made by textile imports.[20]

FEDERAL LEGISLATION AND TEXTILES

Both the Congress of the United States and the Federal Trade Commission have been alert to opportunities for deception in dealings involving fiber, textiles, and, indeed, furs, leathers, and other materials used in the fashion industries. As one of its general and continuing responsibilities, the Federal Trade Commission issues rules against deceptive practices in business of all sorts, since this is a form of unfair competition. Thus, we have both laws (such as the Wool Products Labeling Act of 1939) and FTC regulations with the force of law, promulgated to protect the consumer against misrepresentation. In general, the rules require that such fibers as wool, which can be reprocessed, may not be labeled as virgin wool if in fact they have been reclaimed; they require that furs dyed to simulate other furs should also have the name of the actual animal from which they came; they require textiles to be identified as to the fiber content, with the percentage of each fiber by weight mentioned, unless it represents less than 5 percent of the total; they require treatment to inhibit flammability of fabrics used in children's clothing and some home uses; and they require apparel products to be labeled with information on fiber content, use, and care.

The objective of this section is not to spell out laws and regulations in detail, but to make clear that these laws require that, if the product is not immediately recognizable by the least informed consumer for what it is, there should be an appropriate label to alert him or her to the facts needed for wise buying decisions and safe use and care.

FURS AND LEATHERS

Furs and leathers were used for garments long before textiles were developed, and they are still major raw materials in the fashion industry. Both materials share certain basic qualities: they utilize the skins of animals; the natural habitat of the individual animal determines the part of the world in which the material originates; high degrees of skill are required in selecting, treating, and making garments and accessories of the material; there can be great variations over the years in the availability of a particular animal skin; there has not yet been a way to produce truly equivalent materials in laboratory or mill.

The qualities with which nature has endowed both furs and leathers make them uniquely desirable in today's sophisticated, mechanized age, just as they were in the dawn of history. In the fashion field, dominated by textiles and other machine-made products, each of these two materials occupies a small but important place. Although both materials require skilled handling and slow processing, the fashion industry curbs its appetite for speed when dealing with fur and leather. It has no real choice.

The Fur Industry

The wearing of fur as a status symbol goes back to the ancient Egyptian priests, if not further. Present-day use of fur for prestige and fashion is evidenced most clearly in the parade of sable, chinchilla, mink, and other expensive furs on such occasions as inaugural balls, opera openings, and other gatherings of the socially and financially elite.

NATURE OF THE INDUSTRY

Sales of fur garments in the United States have been rising in recent years. It is estimated that $1.7 billion was spent by consumers on furs in 1985—up by nearly 50 percent from 1981 and more than three times the 1974 total.[21] Not all of these garments were American made; imports have been increasing. An interesting footnote is that men's fur coats, which accounted for practically no sales as late as the mid-1970s, represent about 10 percent of the market today.

The largest proportion of fur garments sold are produced in factories. The balance are made to order for individual customers by retail fur shops. There are many such shops in the United States.

Domestic factory production of fur garments takes place almost entirely in New York City. There, one finds a great concentration of dealers in raw skins, as well as of *dressers,* or firms that prepare the skins for use by the garment producer. In the United States, about 500 plants are devoted to making fur garments. These are mostly small and family owned; only 43 of them have 20 or more employees.[22]

According to the Furriers Joint Council of New York, an organization that represents workers in the manufacturing end of the industry, there are 2500 members of this union in the city, and an estimated 3500 additional nonunionized workers. A high degree of skill is needed in every phase of handling furs—a skill that is often acquired through being "brought up in the business" as a member of a fur family or through long apprenticeship. Most of those now employed in the industry are far from young. According to industry officials, the average age of fur workers is currently 58 years. To encourage the recruitment of younger employees, provision was made for a training program when the union and employers signed their 1983 contract.[23]

MANUFACTURING OF FUR GARMENTS

At every step of the way, from the living animal to the finished fur garment, the industry requires specialized knowledge, plus skills that are acquired through a long learning process. In many phases of the work, hand operations prevail. Mass production methods have little application.

The process begins with a trapper who obtains animals in the wild by methods that do not damage the **pelts**, or with a breeder who raises certain species under controlled conditions on a fur ranch. According to the Fur Information and Fashion Council, about 80 percent of the furs used in the United States are from ranch-bred animals, notably mink and fox. The fur business is necessarily worldwide in scope, with each country offering pelts of animals indigenous to its area. To secure desirable pelts, fur traders attend auctions all over the world: in Russia and Finland; Oslo, Sweden; Montreal, Canada; and Frankfort, Germany.

FUR INDUSTRY FLOWCHART

Auctions are arranged by permanent trade associations (e.g., the Emba Mink Breeders Associates). Some skin dealers sell direct to retailers. Commission merchants often sell direct to manufacturers.

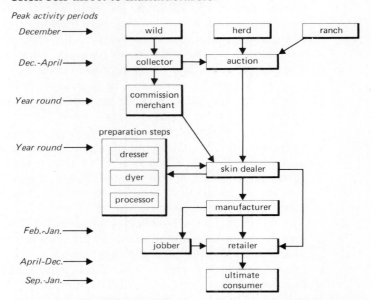

Source: Reprinted with permission of Fairchild Publishing Company.

Once purchased, the raw **skins** are prepared for use by dressers. These companies first immerse skins in a salt-water solution, then scrape off excess fat and flesh from the **hide**. Next, the pelts go into revolving, sawdust-filled drums that remove grease and dirt. Oils are then added to keep the skins soft and pliable. Finally, the fur itself is combed and blown to raise its pile. Only after the furs become part of a finished garment is the last step taken—glazing, to add to the natural luster by drawing the oils to the surface.

To enhance their natural beauty, some furs are subjected to other steps. Beaver or nutria, for instance, may be plucked, to remove the guard hairs and enhance the underfur. On furs like beaver or nutria, shearing may also be used to clip the fur into an even pile.

Colors, too, may be subjected to change. White furs may be bleached to remove stains or discolorations, at least until a few years of exposure to air causes them to yellow. Other furs may be given a dye bath, to change the color entirely. In such cases, a federal law, the Fur Products Labeling Act, requires appropriate labeling. Other beauty treatments are tip dyeing or blended color. The latter is a matter of brushing dye over the fur to even out the color or give additional color depth. All this before the making of a garment begins!

Production of the actual garments involves a number of skills. First comes the selection and matching of bundles of pelts for each individual garment. Then the skins are cut individually by hand, sewn together in garment sections, and wetted, stretched, and nailed by hand, fur side down, to a board and allowed to dry in the desired shape. Only then are the sections sewn together to complete the garment.

For some expensive furs, like sable and mink, the expensive **letting-out** process precedes the garment construction. Again, this is a hand operation that requires great skill. Each skin is cut in half through the dark center stripe. Diagonal cuts are then made down the length of the skin at intervals of $1/8$ to $3/16$ of an inch apart. When the resulting strips are sewn together at a different angle, a longer, narrower skin is formed, presenting the striped effect that is wanted, for example, in mink garments.

MARKETING FUR GARMENTS

There is one major market period when fur garment producers present their wares to retailers—the period from May 15 to June 15, in New York City. Showings are usually held in the manufacturers' showrooms, generally on live models in the larger companies. The majority of fur wholesalers are located on or near Seventh Avenue, between 27th and 30th Streets. In that area, messengers carrying thousands of dollars worth of furs and fur garments stroll through the streets as casually as if they were bringing a bag lunch to the office.

There are approximately 35,000 fur retailers in the United States, of which about 1,000 are specialized fur shops. The overall figure includes small mom-and-pop local retailers, fur boutiques, and large department stores.[24] Because of the huge investment in merchandise required to present an adequate assortment to the consumer, the practice of *consignment selling* is common in the fur trade. This means that the manufacturer ships a supply of garments to the retailer, and is paid for them only when they are sold; unsold garments are returnable at a specified date.

Department stores and large specialty shops almost universally *lease* out their fur departments, thus calling upon the capital and the expertise of the lessee. Under such an arrangement, the lessee supplies stock, hires and trains salespeople, and pays for the advertising. All activities are subject to store policy and approval. The lessee benefits by the drawing power of the store's name and location, and pays a percentage of sales plus rent.

Evans & Co., of Chicago, is the largest such leased fur department operator, with over 800 retail operations all over the United States. Also prominent is Mademoiselle Furs, owned by The Fur Vault, better known through TV ads as "Fred the Furrier." This is a publicly owned company that not only runs leased departments, but operates its own retail stores, owns some of its manufacturing facilities, and maintains a New York showroom in the fur district. Multifaceted operations of this type are expected to become a growing trend.

In addition to the advertising done by retailers, the industry launches advertising and publicity through its trade associations, many of which concentrate on a single type of fur. For example, EMBA (the Eastern Mink Breeding Association); GLAMA (Great Lakes Mink Association); SAGA (Scandinavian mink and fox breeders); the Canadian Majestic Mink Association; and the British-Irish-Dutch conglomerate. Speaking for furs in general and the fur garment manufacturers as a whole, is the American Fur Information and Fashion Council, the industry's trade association.

THE IMPACT OF FASHION

Many factors influence the fashion for furs. When there is a fashion for opulence, furs are "in." When there is a revulsion against ostentation, or against wanton killing of animals for their skins, people swing away from furs. When the fashion world, as it has done in the past, goes overboard for an exotic fur to the point that the animal involved is threatened with extinction, the conservationists and sometimes the government itself will bring pressure to bear against the use or importation of such furs. This happened with leopard, which zoomed into prominence in the 1960s, causing such indiscriminate slaughter that by 1969 the animal was an endangered species. Similarly, revulsion against the use of certain types of seal fur, for which trappers kill very young pups, curtails the market to some extent—but not enough to stop the annual slaughter. These days, a retailer may add a footnote to the store's advertising, stating that no endangered species are among its offerings.

A fashion development since the late 1970s has been the introduction of major American apparel designers into the fur business. Through licensing arrangements with major fur producers, Perry Ellis, Oscar de la Renta, and Bill Blass, among others, now have their names on a variety of high-priced fur garments. Where formerly terms like quality and luxury got major emphasis in the industry, today a new fashion dimension has been added—designer names.

IMPORTS AND EXPORTS

A large part of the retail sales increases in fur garments are accounted for by imports from the Far East, where production costs are lower. Industry sources say that imports now account for almost 20 percent of the U.S. retail sales of fur garments and a much higher percentage in units.[25]

Once a fur garment gets into the channels of trade in the United States, it is not easy to identify its source. The law does require information about the pelts (country of origin, type of processing and dyeing, etc.) but it does not require information about where the garment was made. It could be presented or even labeled "U.S.A." yet have been made in, say, Korea. Industry experts say that the lower the selling price compared with that of similar garments, the greater the likelihood that the coat or jacket was imported. For example, the labor cost of manufacturing a full-length mink coat in the United States is about $1000, whereas the same coat made in Hong Kong would have a labor cost of $300 to $400; in Korea, $125 to $175; in China, less than $100.[26] So far, the finest furs at the top of the price range have no problem with imports. When Russian sables and white lynx garments sell at wholesale for as much as $75,000 to $100,000, they are above price competition. And the pelts used, moreover, are of too high a value to be entrusted to the less-skilled workmanship of cut-price operators at any stage of the game.

International trading in furs, however, is not a one-way street. There is demand abroad for American raw pelts because of their high quality. And in finished garments, the fashion styling as well as the high quality of American goods makes them desirable in foreign countries, especially in the Japanese market.

The Leather Industry

Leather is one of man's oldest clothing materials. Long before they learned to plant cotton and make fabrics, people were skilled in the tanning and use of leather for sandals and crude garments. Leather apparel in this country goes back to the American Indians, who made moccasins and cloaks out of deerskin. Renowned frontiersmen like Daniel Boone and Davy Crockett, and other early settlers wore deerskin and buckskin pants, shirts, shoes and jackets.

NATURE OF THE INDUSTRY

The leather tanning and finishing industry is made up of establishments primarily engaged in tanning, curing, and finishing animal hides and skins to produce leather. Also included are leather converters and dealers who buy hides and skins and have them processed under contract by tanners or finishers. The output of the leather tanning and finishing industry in 1985 was valued at $1.7 billion. In that year, there were some 300 establishments in the industry, of which about 160 were directly involved in tanning and finishing hides and skins. Employed workers totaled 15,800.[27] Since leather is a by-product of the meat packing industry, the industry tends to be cost-efficient. The packing houses derive their primary revenue from the carcass; the skins and hides, which have no food value, are sold to the leather trades.

Processing of the hides and skins is done largely in small plants located mostly in the North Central and Northeastern states. Three major types of companies are involved: (1) converters, who buy the hides and skins from meat packers and contract them out to tanneries for finishing, (2) contract tanners who finish skins but do not market them directly, and (3) regular or complete tanneries that purchase and process skins and hides and sell finished leathers.

Like the fiber and fabric producers, the leather industry promotes and sells its products to manufacturers of apparel and accessories. Yet, unlike fiber and fabric companies, the tanning companies do not make their names known to the consuming public. Advertising for leather garments and accessories may include the name of the fashion designer, the manufacturer, and the type of leather, but never the name of the producer of the leather.

HIDES AND SKINS

These terms, used interchangeably by the layman, have very specific meanings within the leather industry. **Hides** come from animals whose skins weigh over 20 pounds, such as cattle, horses, and buffalo. These hides are so thick they are frequently split into two or more layers, called **splits**. Under Federal Trade Commission regulations, the under pieces must be identified as splits, and cannot be called genuine leather or genuine cowhide. **Kips** is a term applied to skins weighing between 15 and 25 pounds. The term **skins** designates still smaller skins, from such animals as calves, pigs, sheep, and goats.[28]

PROCESSING OF LEATHERS

There are three basic steps in processing leather: pretanning, tanning, and finishing. **Pretanning**, the first, is basically a cleansing process in which the leathers are soaked and rid of all flesh, hair, and dirt. Next is **tanning**, which both preserves the skin and improves its natural physical properties. The varied tanning methods employ such substances as oil, vegetable substances, alum, formaldehyde, zirconium and, most commonly used in the United States, chrome. The techical term "in the blue" refers to hides, skins, or kips that have been chrome-tanned but not yet finished. Final steps after tanning include dyeing and a variety of finishes. Among these is aniline, the most expensive, used only on the finest, smoothest skins to impart a highly polished surface. Other finishes include embossing, which presses a pattern onto the leather, often to simulate expensive alligator or snakeskin; also sueding and napping to raise the surface; or pressing, to give a shiny glazed finish. That last, called glacé leather, is often used for accessories.

LEATHER MARKETING

Because of the length of time required to purchase and process its raw material, the leather industry is among the earliest to research and anticipate fashion trends. Its decisions as to colors, weights, and textures are reached early and presented early. The industry as a whole participates in this process through its strong association, previously known as the Tanners' Council of America, but since 1984 using the name of Leather Industries of America

LEATHER INDUSTRY FLOWCHART

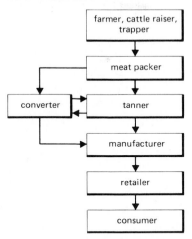

Source: Reprinted with permission.

(LIA). The LIA offers color seminars semiannually and sells swatches of its colors to industry members at nominal cost, some 18 to 24 months in advance of the season concerned. Other functions of the LIA include a Hide Training School for persons engaged in the buying or selling of either hides or leathers; sponsorship of a contest among U.S. design schools to select annually six Student Design Award winners for creative use of leathers in fashions; and publication of an industrywide weekly entitled *Council News* to cover all pertinent information of interest to its members.

As experienced observers of fashion signals and early forecasters of trends, the leather industry is looked to for guidance by other segments of the fashion industry.

At least one to one and a half years before the ultimate consumer sees the finished products in retail stores, there are leather trade shows at which tanners show and sell their latest products to professional buyers. For example, the *Semaine du Cuir* is a long-established major annual show in which tanners from around the world participate, and to which buyers come from all over the world, along with the fashion press. This show is held in Paris, France, usually in September.

The Hong Kong International Leather Fair is a more recently established trade show. It is held in June in Hong Kong and attracts buyers and sellers from many countries, including the United States.

The Tanners' Apparel and Garment (TAG) Show is held in New York City in October of each year and attracts garment manufacturers, suppliers, and retailers, among others. In 1985 there were 21 countries represented, and visitors from 25 of the United States.[29]

IMPORTS AND EXPORTS

The domestic leather industry faces two deterrents to growth. One is the growing use of synthetic substitutes. The other, and greater cloud on its horizon is the competition from imports. Imports of leather materials into the United States rose to approximately $398 million in 1985, from $124.5 million in 1974. The European Economic Community supplied 28 percent, with the United Kingdom, Italy, and West Germany the major suppliers. Developing countries such as Argentina and Brazil represented 57 percent, and South Korea, Canada, Hong Kong, and Korea supplied the balance.[30]

Since it is rapidly losing its share of the domestic market to imported leather finished products, the U.S. industry must increasingly rely on exports to achieve growth or even maintain its present volume of sales. In fact, U.S. exports of leather reached an estimated $307 million in 1985, up from $102 million in 1974.[31] Despite the strength of the U.S. dollar, major countries to which American leathers were exported were Italy, the Netherlands, Belgium, Brazil, and Korea. In addition, Japan imports American leathers primarily for upholstery.

ANNOUNCING THE LEATHER SHOW

Source: Reprinted with permission of T.A.G. Committee of Leather Industries of America.

Readings

The production and marketing of fashion's raw materials begin with someone's shrewd eye on consumers. Before yarn is finished, fabric is woven, or fur is finished, the fashion customer's preferences are carefully studied.

Secrets of a Color Oracle

Color can make or break a product, whether apparel or automobiles. Visualizing the beginnings of color trends is June Roche's job, and she travels the world, looking and analyzing, before developing each season's colors for Milliken.

Look What Celanese Is Doing Now!

Celanese has set itself a task that emphasizes the importance of communication in the fashion business. Their objective: to make the consumer aware of the sometimes forgotten virtues of polyester as a medium for expressing fashion.

Burlington Industries

Changes in customer attitudes and in global competition can lead to restructuring and repositioning within a giant textile company, as these excerpts from Burlington's annual reports shows.

Springs' Drive for a Younger Market

How does a fabric company put youthful appeal into home furnishings? Springs Industries does this by teaming up with Merona, a producer of youthful casual apparel, and tapping their knowledge of that market.

The Fur Vault, Inc.

This company discusses its first year of operations as a public company and the future plans of "Fred the Furrier" to increase their share of the nation's growing fur business.

Secrets of a Color Oracle
by Patti Hagan

Rattan, Hemp, Dill, Turnip, Ginger Root, Bay Leaf, Rosemary, Blue Grass, Barleycorn, Pumice, Malachite, Henna, Olivewood, Smoky Teal. Spring 1985, the current color season as forecast months ago by the fabric house of Milliken.

When June Roche came to work as a textile designer at Milliken 24 years ago, fresh from the New Bedford Institute of Technology, all the men wore white shirts, all the fabrics were wool, and all the colors were numbered. Now, the men at Milliken have taken to wearing color, all the fabrics are polyester, and all the colors are named. June Roche names them, 80 or so, twice a year. As corporate fashion director for Milliken & Company—corporate color forecaster—June Roche calls the colors, three seasons in advance of the natural world, and Milliken turns them out by the millions of polyester yards.

In the fashion world, Roche is regarded as something of a Color Oracle. But she also has devout followers outside of her field, in Detroit, for example, where she takes her "color show" once a year. The business press seems intrigued by the idea of this small, attractive woman preaching to the Detroit auto men, and that they take her color-word seriously. It's not that June Roche is the only color preacher around, but that she has a larger, more diverse congregation than the others.

Milliken's corporate colorist arrives at her advance color schemes by dividing her work year into roughly four seasons: (1) incubating, (2) thinking, (3) creating, (4) communicating. Seasons (1) and (2) keep her on the move ("I don't want to spend a lot of time in one place")

for several months out of the year "peeking ahead" with her camera, mostly in Europe and Japan. She does no peeking in Africa, or Latin America, or much of the Third World. "I'm looking for bigger trends than just the fabrics. I'm looking for what's influencing us. Burma is not influencing us."

Peeking does not include poking into newspapers or magazines, either. "I'm a scanner," Roche says. "I'll look at all the publications on the plane. I read through the *Literary Guild* catalog. I don't have to buy the books. I don't read anything. I get the news on TV. I can see magazine covers on the newsstand. I know what they're all about."

The field observation skills of the naturalist are the same skills necessary to the color oracle; her fall '82 color card, "Audubon Wildlife," included: Mallard, Titmouse, Partridge, Poison Berry, Blue Goose, Redheaded Woodpecker. She is a careful observer of the pop scene—what the kids are wearing, the music they're listening to, the dances they're dancing. She peeks into and photographs the newest, trendiest boutiques in London (Nostalgia of Mud), in Florence (Al Capone), in Tokyo (Comme des Garçons), and museums. What she's after is "the new mood. I want a new story. I want new material. I'm for new ideas, innovation." She trusts to intuition and gut reaction, and then with 4,000 photographs—her field notes—and maybe a hundred pieces of "directional clothing," she returns to New York to let things incubate. This field evidence, what Roche calls "noticing for the industry people, telling them the observations, calling their attention to things," enables

Source: *Across the Board*, May 1984. Excerpted with permission.

her with great confidence to wax color oracular, to decide what colors should appear outside the fashion blind.

Along with the rest of the world, spring is June Roche's "creating" season. "In April I go South and put myself on the line about these colors. I actually create new colors for the fall—better, different, more soft, more light colors." South means Spartanburg, South Carolina, the Milliken color lab. Says Roche, "I go for a few days. Then I bring things back up to New York. I like to look at the colors with the New York eyes." By this month, the fall '86 colors will be frozen.

June Roche's four-month "communicating" season begins in October with the New York opening, just off Broadway at Milliken, of her one-woman, one-hour, multimedia show, known in the trade as "The June Roche Show." (The show goes on the road through February, traveling to Los Angeles, San Francisco, Chicago, Detroit, High Point, North Carolina, and Hilton Head Island, South Carolina, after which it goes on by video, and on.)

She introduces another set of feminine colors, the "Blushing Beauties"—Peaches 'n' creme, Chic Cheek, Baby Blush, Powder Puff—in blouse forms that emphasize "softness, oversize collars, upscale cuffs," and proclaims 1985 "the year of ensemble dressing" and "a transition year," that is, getting away from gray. "The gray thing went along with the economy," she says. "We were in a recession. Everybody's wearing gray now. We created that, and now the whole world's just too gray." And she is not hesitant to remind her audiences from whence they came: that black-and-white, pallid pre-'60s world before the Flower Children liberated color, especially for men. ("The masses now had permission to wear color. The truck driver and not just the preppy.")

There are a number of plums on her current color card, even though "each year we keep waiting for plum to drop dead." (She put three purples on her 1979 card, to general astonishment.) June Roche shows three Marilyn Monroe figures to introduce "hourglass dressing," and says, "Each year, like the purples, we think this is the end of Marilyn." Instead, Marilyn and the purples are beginning to seem immortal. They are carried forward. Color has shades, enabling the color forecaster to make almost imperceptible color changes to complement established favorites. Next year's colors can differ from this year's by a shade and still be "new." The most fashionable colors frequently amount to shades of the past. "All color is relative," says June Roche, who spends her days working the fashion frontier of relativity. Color forecasters are in fact color conservationists, so conservative are colors that have sold well, it's hard to imagine them going very far wrong with the colors they propose.

Some oracles tell parables, but June Roche tells stories: The Color Story for Fall '85, The Gray Story ("now The Gray Story is completely, somberly gray"), The Ivory Story, The Important Brown-Heather Story, the Marilyn Story, The Brand-New Story Coming Up: Softer, Lighter, Cleaner Colors. For fall '76, she told the story of the Shah of Iran's colors (Peacocks, Persian Wines, Bedouin Brown, Sultan's Ruby, Byzantine Blue) a few years before the Ayatollah changed that color story. She foretold the Tut Story (Sphinx, Blue Lotus, Cobra Brown, Scarab, Henna, Sand, Nile Green, Pomegranate, Teal Dynasty) a full year and a half before Tut came to New York's Metropolitan Museum. In 1978, when New York City was still down in the fiscal dumps, her fall '79 color cards told the New York Story (Manhattan Satin, Bronxberry, Queens Green, Staten Ink, Murray Hill Mauve, Stage Deli Mustard, Maxwell's Plum).

One story the June Roche Show omits is The Polyester Story. But Milliken posters hazarding "Bet we can shatter your image of polyester in 30 seconds" need explanation. The polyester image, says June Roche, *was* cheap, tacky, garish. "Those old leisure suits were shiny. All over Europe those were the Americans, in polyester pantsuits, in bright colors." Polyester was "a tough battle, a hard one to turn around." But, she states, by various sleights of dye, "we've changed the whole image of polyester. By using these grayed-off colors, it makes the polyester look softer, more elegant. Polyester does have designer acceptance now." And anyway, she says, "We've become a polyester people. Ninety-five percent of all Americans wear polyester." (June Roche does not herself dress 95 percent polyester. "I wear polyester in the blouse area mostly.")

Milliken is one of the Big Three fabric manufacturers, and Richard Moore, the company's general manager, maintains that "it's pretty hard to have a polyester image problem when 95 percent of the American people are wearing it." And as for the color of that cloth, Moore states, "We take a color-leadership position. We study, research, determine the trends, what's new, and give that information to the market. Our customers look to us for direction," and June Roche not only has the ability to communicate that information colorfully, she has the power.

She says simply, "You get your power by having other people be successful by you. That's why I have this following. Because people experienced good results from what I told them. They give you the power. They give it to me and they come in droves." Roche's communicants, she admits, amount to a fan club. "A lot of people are addicted to the show. I'm preaching it on the stage to 5,000 people who're coloring up products. I'm influencing a lot of people. We're very big so we affect more people. We're for the masses here at Milliken. We're supplying millions of yards of fabric. In

the beginning of the show we didn't invite the belts, the zippers, the threads. But it was hard to stop them." Now her audience regularly includes the buttons, the interfacings, the tanners, the shoes, the millinery, the gloves, the jewelry, the makeup, the linens, the volume apparels, the artificial flowers, the home furnishings, the awnings—and the automobiles.

June Roche's conventional-car fans (no stock) in Detroit number in the 400s, and their allegiance may perhaps explain her recent "discovery" outside the fashion press. She first took her show to Detroit at the invitation of General Motors, eight years ago. It was so popular that it has since become an industry event, attended by the color-and-trim men from General Motors, American Motors, Chrysler, and Ford. What does the show do for Detroit? "It stimulates them," answers Roche. "I whisk 'em around the world in one hour. Every year I dye my hair, fix it differently. I want to exemplify the change."

Chrysler's design chief, Jerry Thorley, finds the Roche Show useful "to verify what we're coming up with—the color direction. We don't react to the trendy stuff. It's of interest, although we don't use it in cars. But you can pick up a definite color direction. We use the Roche Show as another indication of what's happening in the color world." Roche says that each color has its special aura, and Jerry Thorley adds that "all products have a color personality. Some cars don't look as well in one color group as in another. Some forms will read better in one color or another. We are using color now as more of a tool, to give cars more personality. We're relying on color to do a bigger job and to separate economy cars from luxury cars. Certain colors *cost* more. [Reds and blues, for instance.]"

What the business is coming to realize, he says, is that "color is something a lot of the people identify with. And men are becoming more color conscious, whereas women always have been. Women have more sensitivity to color, a greater feeling for color." Biologically this is true, according to Margaret Walch, director of the Color Association of the United States, and June Roche is capitalizing on her biological endowment by following the basic principles of color forecasting: (1) people like change, (2) there's a logical, cyclical color progression, (3) taste will change in an orderly way. Says Walch: "Color forecasting has to do with the human response to color. It's highly subjective, and a good color forecaster will know what to pay attention to." To her mind, "The '80s can be thought to be colored in a pastel way." Sure enough, in 1986 Cadillac is coming out in Light Driftwood, Rose Quartz, and Sun Gold.

"A lot of people used to think color was frivolous or meaningless, especially men. Now, they're beginning to realize that color may be the most important part." She should know. In 24 years at Milliken, June Roche has been over the rainbow and back, repeatedly.

Look What Celanese Is Doing Now!

During reflective moments (publishers have them too) we've often wondered why the general trade press seems reluctant to print certain kinds of stories. ("Studies" is a better word); studies of company (or industry) actions—or techniques of action that bear on certain problems; state of the art problems, etc. Media, serving other industries perhaps because their people are more personally, professionally involved—do much more indeed. "How so and so came to grips with the problem of silicon crunch" . . . "How Cecil B. DeMille conquered the weather in Colorado" . . . "Managing people by the zippo method" . . . "Ten things salesmen do that turn off film buyers" . . . etc. etc. Perhaps you know what we mean. For some reason, in our business we hardly find in media those case studies that teach a lesson or explain a technique—what have you . . .

So how do we find out when and for what reason to applaud? one could ask.

We don't. Our "children," in and fresh out of school also don't get a message and, we go on just the way we've been going . . . and we continue to say, "You know . . . this business isn't fun anymore."

Pity.

But let's look around.

By now everyone knows or should know that Celanese Fibers has announced—and has already embarked on—an extensive marketing and communications effort which, according to John A. Fennie, CFO president, marketing, "is programmed to educate the consumer about polyester in general not just Fortrel® and we hope all polyester producers initiate similar educational programs," Fennie prodded.

In their own way, some fiber makers will tell you they have. We of course have written articles about polyester. Our colleagues across the nation have also written about it and by now most of us are acquainted with the Celanese tag line "Look what polyester is doing now."

So what else is new?

On reflection (I told you we do that a lot) it seems to us Celanese had a lot of guts—if you will—to begin with. After all, to publicly state

Source: *N. Y. Connection*, Vol. 28, August 1983. Reprint permission granted.

the intention "we're out to help change the image of polyester" or "correct a misconception about polyester" seemed, at first blush, to violate all the rules of the game. Sure there are indeed newer polyester fabrics that are in no way even close to the old stuff. They are as different as day is from night; the state of the art has evolved tenfold. But to accent the negative, to use language that almost emphasizes the problem??? Why by gosh you're not supposed to do that, right???

Wrong again . . . because from the way we received the message, "telling it like it is" was and is exactly the Celanese plan. Obviously the decision was a good one. Everybody quickly picked up on it: newspapers, magazines, television, trade papers, etc. Even the staid *New York Times* ran stories about polyester . . . and everybody knows the *Times* doesn't print "developing" news. It prints "already" news.

Indeed, the subject of polyester is extremely topical and becoming more so every day. Celanese was keen enough to move quickly in spite of the "no-nos" and they moved ahead "to help change the image many consumers had about polyester."

We were curious as to what they would do next as were our colleagues. So when we later got the call to learn about how the firm intended to "correct the misconceptions about polyester" we were already primed. They had us and Celanese knew it.

Anyway we got the message: In the light of new fiber, yarn and fabric developments containing polyester—(Fortrel in particular but not only Fortrel) and over and above previous actions that beachheaded the campaign. Celanese was embarking on the second phase of its "look what polyester is doing now" long-range program. I guess you might call it "taking the pitch on the road."

Well, you've probably never heard of Nolan Miller. Certainly you don't consciously think about him on a daily basis and the general trade press is busy pounding out bad news, good news or what have you—so you only see or hear the announcements. You may not see or hear, even know who Gillis MacGillis either. Her name isn't being bandied about West 36th between 7th and 8th Avenues or even other—more main fashion drags around the country. But hang on.

Nolan Miller has been called the "celebrity's couturier." Every week the costume designer on TV's top rated "Dynasty" creates 6–10 ensembles each for Joan Collins, Linda Evans and Pamela Sue Martin. As if that weren't enough he also designs for "Love Boat" and the new "Matt Houston." His designing credits range from Las Vegas shows including "Follies Bergere" to motion pictures. He's designed for Barbara Stanwyck, Joan Crawford, Susan Hayward, Yvette Mimieux, Jaclyn Smith. Natalie Wood, Cheryl Ladd, Farah Fawcett and Jane Wyman to name a few.

Gillis MacGil on the other hand was well on her way to becoming one of the industry's best known models when she founded Mannequin Models 22 years ago. Now her New York agency represents 75 models in the world capital of fashion and beauty. She's often quoted in various publications like *The Wall Street Journal*, *New York Times* and her opinions are highly valued in the fashion and beauty fields. She and Nolan Miller are highly visible, active, always sought after professional figures in our business . . . and they are both national spokespersons for Celanese efforts relative to the subject of polyester and of course Fortrel polyester. (If we had our way we'd photo journalize a week or at least 4 days "on the road" with either of them . . . to show you exactly what life is like on the road. Certainly only the announcement about the effort is merely just an announcement.)

Anyway we were watching one of those daytime television shows. I think it was Bill

Boggs. Miller was the guest. Plenty of fashions and models around. He said, during an interview, "most women don't buy as much on impulse today. It's an investment. Rather than buy expensive silk dresses or blouses they'd be wise to investigate some of the newer polyester fabrics" he mentioned while all the while models were crossing from stage left to stage right or vice versa wearing the new fashions in Fortrel polyester. Remember . . . millions of people are exposed to that and other messages. (Many of them, of course, still retain the "old" image because that's all they still know in spite of the fact all along they've been buying the new stuff.)

Ah the consumer. MacGil knows that her models must look their best at all times. She instructs them to be fashionable and to select apparel which retains its appearance under all modeling requirements. She is aware that polyester fabrics are ideally suited for that.

In her way, and in similar and different public circumstances, MacGil gets the message across of "Look what polyester is doing now." Newspapers pick it up. Editors talk with her, she appears on television shows, and slowly but surely the message begins to penetrate the public sensorium further. People can "see" for themselves the difference between yesterday and today.

Now when you couple all the above and more; newspaper releases, sales promotion procedures, etc., and you add in those new and refreshing double spread Celanese ads that appear in media like *The Times*, *People Magazine*, etc., you begin to realize even further how millions of people begin to "see" polyester consistent with new industry developments. They are prepared to accept "more" of better and the industry, already familiar with the new fabrics to begin with, has every-

thing waiting for them when they enter their favorite store.

It all goes together. One without the other means nothing. Interesting about the Celanese effort is the amount of media pickup around the country. Since the subject of "polyester" continues to be topical, it's all happening faster according to Celanese marketers and communicators. "Not a day goes by," a spokesperson said, "that we don't get a flood of clippings from around the country or receive measurement surveys about changing perceptions."

So it's working. Solid, new, better, different polyester products, and the "education" required to pedestal polyester higher in the hierarchy of consumer values.

But ever and above the new and improved, the acceptance of polyester is being broadened by a vigorous and effective communications program. Interestingly, the program is working not only for Celanese (and Fortrel) but also for other polyester producers, who are working on a group effort, with each campaign reinforcing the other. The efforts are also working for those along the pipeline who buy, sell and promote anything made of polyester.

To us, of course, there's an essential message. If you are out to realign, shift or change the mental billboards stuck in millions of American minds, you'd best find a good way to energize the media. Obviously this is being done.

You know, long ago someone said, "sell the sizzle not the steak." Well in this case someone decided to violate that and other rules and came up smelling like a rose. It isn't easy to tell it like it is in the communications game.

We've been told you're not supposed to.

Burlington Industries

Textiles, one of man's earliest crafts, was the sector that sparked the industrial revolution. Today this old, established business is a hotbed of competition. The marketplace is intensely active, marked by change and diversity, rapidly shifting trends and looks. Thousands of companies, both here and abroad, fight for a piece of the American market, creating the most challenging competitive environment in textile history.

To succeed in this environment a company must have energy, flexibility, a clear sense of what it needs to accomplish and a mastery of the fundamentals. We believe that Burlington has these qualities, as illustrated in the following pages. We have been in the business for over 60 years and we know it inside and out—the marketplace, its problems and potential; the manufacturing process, its capabilities and limitations. Our focus is on our customers, and it is backed up by the most modern and productive manufacturing operation in the world. The customer knows what he wants. We know what we can deliver. Together, we get things done.

Product Performance

To remain competitive, products must be innovative, must perform and must adapt to changing life styles. Responding to consumers' increased emphasis on comfort, Burlington worked closely with Celanese corporation during development of *Comfort Fiber*, used in Burlington's *Quintura* knits. Quintura has a look, feel and comfort comparable to cotton, combined with the durability and easy care features of polyester. For activewear, Quintura provides comfort and ventilation even in a strenuous workout. Quintura knits are also increasingly popular for soft, comfortable loungewear and sleepwear.

Manufacturing Flexibility

A fashion-oriented company must be prepared to change its products rapidly, and its manufacturing systems must be highly flexible. To that end, Burlington has invested heavily in state-of-the-art manufacturing technology. To illustrate manufacturing versatility for this photograph, finished products in a wide variety were returned to their common point of origin, Burlington's highly automated Richmond plant. Plant manager Dale Ormsby displays an array of fabrics ranging from *Silky Wovens* for lingerie and blouses, all the way to traditional blazer fabrics and a new high performance product for lightweight all-weather outerwear.

New Product Development

The nature of fashion is change. Burlington is large, but agile enough to follow the zigs and zags of fashion trends. For example, while continuing as a major supplier of the traditional indigo blue denim that has always been associated with jeans, Burlington has responded to the trend toward looser, flowing silhouettes by developing lighter weight, drapable denim fabrics in an assortment of new colors, patterns and novelty finishes.

Service to Customers

Amid a building boom and renewed interest in architectural excellence, designers of modern

Source: *Burlington Annual Report.*

116

office buildings want furnishings that offer both visual appeal and performance. Burlington's ability to provide the right product for the job has made it the industry leader in contract carpeting.

Partnership with Customers

The competitive marketplace puts a premium on response time and makes it vital for suppliers like Burlington to understand and help meet customers' operational requirements.

Marketing Skill

Capturing the interest of fashion conscious shoppers requires unique products, presented in a striking way. Last fall, in hundreds of stores throughout the country, Burlington Domestics successfully launched its new line of bed and bath ensembles from leading women's wear designer Liz Claiborne. Special displays featured a Burlington-produced videotape in which Ms. Claiborne explains her unique "mix and match" concept.

Technological Innovation

The process of creating new fabric designs traditionally moved slowly from a designer's idea, to sketches, to hand-woven samples, to actual production. Today, Burlington is speeding up the process with computer-aided design systems.

Springs' Drive for a Younger Market

Springs Industries consumer fashion division believes it will offer more than another designer collection at the domestics market next month when it introduces its new licensed Merona Line.

With the introduction of the formerly all-apparel name, the company plans to embark on a major new design, marketing and merchandising program geared to capture younger customers. Until now, Springs' main appeal has been to an older, more affluent consumer, admit company officials.

Besides the casual, youthful patterns that characterize Merona, the bed and bath collection will offer marketing and merchandising features such as a change of designs twice a year, limited production of each line and self-selling packaging with color coding to indicate product sizes. All those features are intended to give the program a fashion orientation that should appeal to a young audience, believe Springs executives.

"We were trying to get more of an apparel, fashion idea with this line," M. L. "Chip" Fontenot, president of the consumer fashion division, said. "We wanted to have the line change frequently to bring in fresh products. Each presentation will be completely different and will replace the previous."

He added that Springs management found that department stores were changing their products as frequently as twice a year and were looking for fresh merchandise. "With the program, we can offer stores a change in merchandise and also reach the consumer we haven't been."

Merona, a successful manufacturer of casual, youthful apparel, decided to enter the

Source: *Home Furnishings Digest*, October 21, 1985.

home furnishings market last year, about the same time that Springs began looking for a new line to reach a younger consumer.

"I guess when you look at our line you see Bill Blass and Jay Yang as having a terrific touch in the master bedroom," Fontenot said. "But there are a broad group of consumers in the 30-to-45-age range out there not looking for the master bedroom look. Merona represented a clean approach in apparel and we thought it could be transferred into home furnishings.

"The logic was not to replace other sales at Springs," he added. "It should represent new sales for Springs in an area where we weren't offering anything."

Thomas P. O'Connor, vice president in charge of retail department stores for Springs, explained that Springs' management was considering numerous other designers to reach the youthful consumer that the company was failing to address, but decided on Merona because of what it offered to Springs. "Most licensing programs have been basically design programs only. In this licensing program we were looking for both design and merchandising."

Since the licensing arrangement was announced last February, Springs and Merona have been working together to develop a multi-faceted program to successfully carry the product from the mill to the consumer. Silberman Davies-Davis, a marketing consulting firm based in New York, has been contracted by Merona to develop and launch the licensing program in conjunction with Springs.

The collection was designed by Merona, along with input from the Springs studio and David Ehrenreich, a free-lance designer who has worked for style leaders Gear and Katja.

The collection will include three sheet patterns with matching bedding accessories, including tab draperies, tailored bedspreads, duvet covers, comforters, quilted and unquilted pillow shams, dust ruffles and decorative pillows. In bath products, towels, bath rugs and shower curtains will be offered.

The sheets, which will be priced to retail at a reachable $9.99 for a twin, will be a type-200, 60 percent combed cotton-40 percent Kodel polyester. All of the designs and matching accessories will be done in the Merona home fashion colors of marine, which is a deep blue, pebble and oyster, and will coordinate with one another so that a duvet cover of one pattern will match the sheets and shams of another. What Merona officials describe as "fun colors," which in November's line are conch and sunshine, will change at each introduction. Every pattern in November's collection will be on an oyster ground. The oyster twill tape that is used on much of Merona's apparel line also will be used throughout its licensed bedding collection. All of the designs also are simple and casual-looking.

One design, Palm Desert, is a bold leaf silhouette emphasizing the colors of aster, conch and pebble. This design represents the clean and simple patterns that have been characteristics of Merona. A second will be Long Beach, a stripe that will contain almost the entire Merona palette of marine, sunshine, and conch. The flat sheet is a multi-colored stripe while the fitted sheet contains just the pebble stripe. Annapolis will consist of two colors, marine and sunshine, printed on the oyster ground.

John Zulch, brand manager of bath products for Springs, explained that the bath products are not identical to the bedding products, although they are compatible. "One of the main reasons we're working with Merona is for their colorations and quality designs," he said, adding that it is unnecessary to completely coordinate the bedding and bath products in order to have a successful collection of goods.

The towels, which are being imported from Portugal and Brazil, are in two basic designs in five colors. The towels will be 100 percent cotton, 27 inches by 50 inches, jacquard loop terry construction. One pattern will consist of a series of woven flowers. Each towel in this design will reverse to white. The second pattern, Block Island, will be a border design towel with the use of two solid colors. The border of each towel in Block Island will be in pebble. The towels are to retail for about $10 each.

The rugs, which will be made by Springs, coordinate with the Block Island towel design. Suggested retail will be about $22. The shower curtains, also to be manufactured by Springs, are vinyl. A retail has not been set.

Although the licensed Merona designs are important to Springs in order to capture that young consumer, the program includes some features that set it apart from others in the marketplace. Lines will be changed at least twice a year to give the program more of a ready-to-wear, fashion appeal and production will be limited in order to cut the high number of markdowns at retail, he explained.

"We often treat this business as a commodity business, not a fashion business," O'Connor said. "We have to give the consumer and retailer a reason to be excited. We should be able to do that with multiple collections. With the limited selection, retailers won't be so tempted to try to quickly turn the product, either."

The packaging and presentation is another way that the Merona program will be distinguished from other licensed designs. Silberman Davies-Davis has developed a number of in-store displays to show the merchandise. But the firm acknowledged that many stores would not have the room to show the merchandise, so it has also developed packaging that could self sell the products. The packaging will be a three-sided vinyl re-useable bag with a three-sided board that will be color-coded to indicate size.

The firm also is offering sales training to both Springs sales people and stores, in order to help them better sell Merona merchandise. The firm also is offering tips about merchandising the Merona products to stores.

"Merona has been a lot more involved in this program than normally happens," said O'Connor. "It is more than a design concept, it is an entire program that we hope will appeal to the younger consumer."

The Fur Vault®, Inc.
Annual Report 1985

To Our Shareholders:

On May 31, 1985, we closed the books on our first year as a public company. We had been public since August 9, 1984—just 295 days.

I doubt that we will face as crucial and eventful a period in our next 295 years.

We made the very critical and difficult decision to abandon two-thirds of our sales volume and profits and pursue the conviction that Fred The Furrier could leave Alexander's without sacrificing either short-term sales growth or profitability. Underlying this decision was the belief that our organization was

Source: The Fur Vault, Annual Report, 1985.

capable of designing, building, staffing, merchandising and successfully operating three complete department stores for furs and fur services in the New York Metropolitan area.

EXPECTATIONS The fundamental premises of our planned expansion and simultaneous public offering were twofold:

The *first* was that the revolutionary social and economic changes brought about by the expanding role of women throughout our society was permanent and increasing. These changes provide an immense opportunity for the sale of fur, related accessories and services. Fur—once the narrow status symbol of the elite—now could be marketed as broadly as automobiles.

The *second* premise related to our organization's ability to respond to this special marketing opportunity. We believed that our lifetime of acquired expertise, our unbroken 35-year record of profitability, our internally-created systems of control, our proven specialized marketing methodology, our capacity to recruit, train, and motivate our excellent staff, and our disciplined inventory and fiscal management controls—would combine to place us in the best possible position to develop this vast potential of business.

REALITIES The 1984–85 fur season continued the growth curve begun 13 years ago. Record sales were achieved, placing the domestic retail industry above the $1.5 billion mark for the first time. The numbers and types of retail outlets for furs continued to expand. The hard statistic that fueled these developments is the burgeoning growth of the largest segment of the female public—women age 25 to 54. Not only are these women the major customers for furs, but they continue to be more upwardly mobile in both job status and income growth. Two out of every three now work, many in previously male dominated occupations such as computer specialists, engineering, and law. Besides the potential growth that this represents in women's discretionary income, these job classifications are conducted more and more in urban environments where higher levels of dress are emphasized. The U.S. Census Bureau projects that this target group of females will continue to expand to more than 40 million by 1990. The opportunity that this growth augers for mutiple sales of merchandise and services is clear as job status levels and income and discretionary funds grow between the age years 25 through 54. Our sales of additional merchandise and services to our existing customer base has grown, as has our average retail sale, by more than 25 percent in 1984–85.

Wholesale Divisions

Our Mademoiselle Furs Division and its subsidiaries continued its profitable operations and expanded in several new directions.

Overseas, it expanded the activities of its Hong Kong buying office, opened in 1983, resulting in closer and more efficient coverage of that increasingly important fur market. We have benefitted from a sustained flow of shopping reports, close monitoring of fur market activities and most significantly, improved quality control by the examination of all purchases for approval prior to shipment. It has resulted in better vendor relations, shortened lead-times on ordering, and reduced risk.

In Montreal the Wholesale Division, in conjunction with the Retail Division, has opened a buying and shipping office. This long-awaited facility will enable both divisions to operate more economically and efficiently in what has become the world's major production market for furs. Our resident staff supervises quality control at the manufacturers and provides an important "window" to this market.

In the United States, we have intensified our market penetration in key areas with the opening of our own permanent sales offices in Los Angeles and Atlanta and have extended our existing representation in Dallas. These efforts will, we believe, result in an expanded customer base and an intensification of our existing customer relationships. It will also enable us to bring new items to market on a continuing basis with less reliance on seasonal trade shows.

Our warehouse in the New Jersey Meadowlands continues to serve our expanding requirements and has proven to be an invaluable asset as we extend our wholesale offerings and open new wholesale sales divisions. With the planned removal of our retail buying and distribution operations from our Seventh Avenue location (discussed below), our Wholesale Division will avail itself of the significant space that is being vacated. We plan to devote the entire area to multiple showrooms as our various wholesale lines expand. This will give us the largest complex of showrooms in the industry located in the heart of the New York fur market at very advantageous rentals.

Two divisions are planned for expansion in these premises in addition to our existing Mademoiselle Division. One, the Andrew Marc Division, has been the shining star of the recent season with its special line of fur-lined high fashion leather sportswear for men and women. The growth and profitability of this Division has been exceptional, having achieved distribution in the finest department and specialty stores. Its success has been widely reported in the trade papers.

A new Division, Ripa Addition, began operations this spring. This Division will also operate in our new showrooms. We initiated an exclusive U.S. arrangement for obtaining high fashion Italian designs by Giancarlo Ripa of Rome, the celebrated world-class designer, believed by many to be superior in good taste and saleability. The Ripa line is manufactured to our specifications and under our exclusive control in Hong Kong. Initial reaction from leading retailers has been promising and corroborates our feeling that Ripa merchandise offers the rare blend of exceptional design and quality at a moderate price.

Retail Divisions

FRED THE FURRIER The Fred The Furrier's Fur Vault Division opened two stores (Paramus, New Jersey, and Westbury, New York) on October 18, 1984. Originally planned for late summer, the openings were delayed by lagging construction. Both stores were prototypes of "The Fur Store of the Future," as heralded in *Fur World* magazine. The term "store" is really a misnomer as these are truly environments featuring a compendium of all that the fur craft encompasses—from the actual craft shops to engaging fur boutiques with separate shops for fur and leather sportswear on up through sable coats, each in their own special settings. Truly an assemblage of fur and fashion that converts a consumer from "whether" to buy to "which" to buy. Adding our comprehensive fittings and alterations services on the premises assures quality control and customer comfort. Several fashion accessory shops feature hats, jewelry, scarves, belts, and scores of unique fashion items enabling a customer to complete her wardrobe for her fur. All of the shops surround a spectacular atrium that provides a domed skylight, flowing fountains, chairs and tables to sit and enjoy wine and cheese or just to ogle. The fountains convert to a 60 foot runway for fashion shows. Since its opening, our stores have been visited and praised by leading retailing executives from Asia, Europe, Canada, and the United States. In their short lives, both stores have already achieved profitability.

Finding the proper location in New York

City was another matter. We believed strongly that a continuing presence in New York City was vital. We were compelled to take the expedient course and open a temporary location in woefully small space (2500 square feet) on West 57th Street. We opened late November 1984 in time for Thanksgiving, and closed on April 30, 1985. We immediately went into business on Fifth Avenue, between 47th and 48th Streets. Early indications are very promising. We have about 6000 square feet and a long-term lease with a unique arrangement that permits us to leave with no penalty should we find a larger space.

This fall we're opening another Fred The Furrier store in the Town Center Mall in Stamford, Connecticut. This new installation completes our plan to cover the New York market with four strategically placed stores in prime locations.

Moving our business from Alexander's to new locations was accomplished with less difficulty than anticipated. We proved that our consumer acceptance and trust was truly "ours" and not theirs. This was the strongest possible affirmation of our original decision to go it on our own.

Now that our stores in the New York market are established, we feel confident that our expansion plans can move forward. Eleven cities have been targeted for Fred The Furrier's Fur Vaults over the next six years. We expect to build one in 1986 and two in 1987. We choose to control the number of new stores in this period because we have established a very high priority for maximizing growth in our existing stores. This is, in our opinion, the easiest and most profitable form of growth. It also enables us to hone and develop our merchandising, personnel, and advertising skills before transferring them to new stores. Funding for this expansion is well within our capacity given our existing cash position and our ability to convert stores to a profitable basis within the first year of operation.

Serving the customer is at the very heart of our business. Probably no subject was more critical to us in this incredible year than was our ability to gain, train, and retain top quality people. In this one year, we added 130 percent to our existing organization. We lost not even one key individual. The caliber of our entire staff is higher than ever, and we salute our personnel and training staff.

Endnotes

1. Christian Dior, *Talking About Fashion*. New York: G. Putnam's Sons, 1953, p. 35.
2. *Man-Made Fibers, A New Guide*. Washington, D.C.: Man Made Fiber Producers Association, Inc., 1986, p. 7.
3. Standard and Poor, *Industry Surveys: Textiles, Apparel and Home Furnishings*, May 15, 1986, and *U.S. Census of Manufactures*.
4. Frederick Lewton, "Samuel Slater and the Oldest Cotton Machinery in America," Smithsonian Report for 1926.
5. *Textiles—an Industry, A Science, An Art*. Charlotte, N.C.: American Textile Manufacturers Institute.

6. *Mankind's Magic Carpet*. Charlotte, N.C.: American Textile Manufacturers Institute.
7. *All About Textiles*. Charlotte, N.C.: American Textile Manufacturers Institute, p. 5.
8. *Ibid.*, p. 1.
9. Herbert Heaton, "Benjamin Gott and the Anglo-American Cloth Trade," *Journal of Economics and Business History*, Vol. 2, November 1929, p. 147.
10. E. B. Alderfer and H. E. Michl, *Economics of American Industry*, 3rd ed. New York: McGraw-Hill, 1957, p. 417.
11. U.S. Department of Labor, *Technology and Manpower in the Textile Industry of the 1970s*, Bulletin No. 1578, p. 10.
12. Burlington Industries, *Annual Report to Stockholders*, 1985.
13. Walter Adams, *Structure of American Industry*, rev. ed. New York: Macmillan, 1957, Chapter 2.
14. Estimates of the U.S. Department of Agriculture, quoted by the American Textile Manufacturers Institute, Charlotte, N.C., 1985.
15. Rosalie Kolodny, *Fashion Design for Moderns*. New York: Fairchild Publications, 1970, p. 79.
16. Ed Newman, "Development of a Fabric Line," *Inside the Fashion Business*, 3rd ed. New York: John Wiley & Sons, 1981, p. 92.
17. Standard and Poor Industry Surveys: Textiles, Apparel and Home Furnishings, May 15, 1986.
18. *Ibid.*
19. *U.S. Industrial Outlook 1986*.
20. *Ibid.*, p. 4.
21. *New York Times*, June 2, 1986.
22. U.S. Department of Commerce, *1982 Census of Manufacturers*.
23. *New York Times*, April 7, 1985.
24. U.S. Department of Commerce, *Census of Retail Trade*.
25. *New York Times*, April 17, 1985.
26. *Ibid.*
27. *U.S. Industrial Outlook 1986*.
28. Tanners' Council of America, *Dictionary of Leather Terminology*, 7th ed., 1983.
29. Tanners' Council of America, *Council News*, June 9, 1986.
30. *U.S. Industrial Outlook 1986*.
31. *Ibid.*

Selected Bibliography

Bagnall, William R. *The Textile Industries of the United States*. New York: A. M. Kelley, 1971.
Clarke, Leslie J. *The Craftsman in Textiles*. New York: Praeger, 1968.
Collier, Ann M. *A Handbook of Textiles*. New York: Pergamon Press, 1970.

Corbman, B. *Textiles: Fiber to Fabric*, 6th ed. New York: McGraw-Hill, 1982.

Ewing, Elizabeth. *Fur in Dress*. England: Batsford, 1981.

Fairchild's Textile and Apparel Financial Dictionary. New York: Fairchild Publications, published annually.

Kaplan, David G. *World of Furs*. New York: Fairchild Publications, 1974.

Pizzuto, Joseph J., Arthur Price, and Allen C. Cohen. *Fabric Science*, 4th ed. New York: Fairchild Publications, 1980.

Pizzuto, Joseph J., Arthur Price, and Allen C. Cohen. *Fabric Science Swatch Kit*. New York: Fairchild Publications, 1984.

Prentice, Arthur C. *A Candid View of the Fur Industry*. Bendley, Ontario: Clay Publishers, 1976.

Sinclair, John L. *The Production, Marketing and Consumption of Cotton*. New York: Praeger, 1968.

The Textile Industry and the Environment. Research Triangle Park, N.C.: AATCC, 1973.

Walton, Frank. *Tomahawks to Textiles: The Fabulous Story of Worth Street*. New York: Appleton-Century-Crofts, 1953.

Ware, Caroline F. *The Early New England Cotton Manufacture*. New York: Johnson Reprint Corporation, 1966.

Wingate, Isabel B. *Fairchild's Dictionary of Textiles*, 6th ed. New York: Fairchild Publications, 1979.

Wingate, Isabel B. *Textile Fabrics and Their Selection*, 8th ed. Englewood Cliffs, N.J.: Prentice-Hall, 1981.

Trade Associations

American Fur Industry, 100 West 31st Street, New York, N.Y. 10001.

American Printed Fabrics Council, Inc., 1040 Avenue of the Americas, New York, N.Y. 10036.

American Textile Manufacturers Institute, Inc. (ATMI), Wachovia Center, 400 South Tryon Street, Charlotte, N.C. 28285.

American Yarn Spinners Association, Inc., P.O. Box 99, Gastonia, N.C. 28052.

The Color Association of the U.S., 24 East 38th Street, New York, N.Y. 10016.

Cotton, Inc., 1370 Avenue of the Americas, New York, N.Y. 10019.

Emba Mink Breeders Association, 151 West 30th Street, New York, N.Y. 10001.

Fur Information and Fashion Council, Inc., 101 East 30th Street, New York, N.Y. 10016.

International Leather Association, 411 Fifth Avenue, New York, N.Y. 10016.

International Silk Association, U.S.A., 299 Madison Avenue, New York, N.Y. 10017.

Knitted Textile Association, 386 Park Avenue South, New York, N.Y. 10010.

Man-Made Fiber Producers Association, Inc., 1150 17th Street, N.W., Washington, D.C. 20036.

Mohair Council of America, 1412 Broadway, New York, N.Y. 10036.
Textile Distributors Association, Inc., 45 West 36th Street, New York, N.Y. 10018.
Textile Fabric Association, Inc., 36 East 31st Street, New York, N.Y. 10013.
Wool Bureau, Inc., 360 Lexington Avenue, New York, N.Y. 10017.

Trade Publications

American Fabrics and Fashions, 24 East 38th Street, New York, N.Y. 10016.
American Fur Industry News Letter, 101 West 30th Street, New York, N.Y. 10001.
America's Textiles, 106 East Stone Avenue, P.O. Box 88, Greenville, S.C. 29602.
Daily News Record, 7 East 12th Street, New York, N.Y. 10003.
Fur Age Weekly, 127 West 30th Street, New York, N.Y. 10001.
Knitting Times, 51 Madison Avenue, New York, N.Y. 10010.
Modern Textiles, 303 Fifth Avenue, New York, N.Y. 10016.
New York Connection, 1 Times Square, New York, N.Y. 10018.
Textile Industries, 1760 Peachtree Road, N.W., Atlanta, Ga. 30357.
Textile Month, 205 East 42nd Street, New York, N.Y. 10017.
Textile Week, 1221 Avenue of the Americas, New York, N.Y. 10020.
Textile World, 1221 Avenue of the Americas, New York, N.Y. 10020.

CHAPTER REVIEW AND LEARNING ACTIVITIES ....

Key Words and Concepts

Define, identify, or briefly explain the following:

Brand name	"Open-line"
Converter	Pelt
Converting	Première Vision
Francis Cabot Lowell	Samuel Slater
Generic name	Skins
Greige goods	Solution-dyed
Hide	Spinning mill
Ideacomo	Splits
Industrial Revolution	Tanning
Interstoff	Texitalia
Kips	Textiles
Letting-out	Vertical integration
Man-made fiber	Yarn
Natural fibers	Yarn-dyed

Review Questions on Chapter Highlights

1. In their correct sequence, name the steps in the production of fabrics.
2. Discuss the various fashion activities of the primary markets.
3. Explain the statement that "unlike the suppliers of natural fibers, the man-made fiber producers made fashion their business from the start."
4. What was Samuel Slater's role in the Industrial Revolution in the United States?
5. Why is Burlington Industries called a vertically integrated textile company? What are the competitive advantages and disadvantages of a vertical operation?
6. Describe the function of a converter and explain the various ways in which different types of converters perform the same function.
7. Give examples of current and past fashions that prove the following statement: "Many of the changes in fashion are primarily variations in colors, textures, or fabrics rather than changes in styles."
8. List and explain the steps in the production of a finished fur garment.
9. What is there about the processing of leather that causes the leather industry to be among the earliest to research and anticipate fashion trends?
10. Select one or more of the readings in this chapter and explain their relationship to the content of this chapter.
11. Discuss and explain the relationships between apparel producers and the primary producers.

Applications for Research and Discussion

1. Analyze and list the fiber content of the clothing in your wardrobe. Tell how important the fiber was in making your decision to purchase and explain why or why not.
2. Select five current advertisements each of which features three names, that of a fiber company, a textile company, or an apparel producer and retailer. Which featured name do you believe is most important to consumers and why? If none, why not?
3. Research the current stock prices of three major publicly owned textile or fiber companies. Based on this information plus any other pertinent information, would you invest in this company if you had the money to do so? Why or why not?

4

WOMEN'S AND CHILDREN'S APPAREL—USA

"And if it be true . . . that the condition of a people is indicated by its clothing, America's place in the scale of civilized lands is a high one. We have provided not alone abundant clothing at a moderate cost for all classes of citizens, but we have given them, at the same time, that style and character in dress that is essential to the self-respect of a free, democratic people."[1]

These words, spoken by a clothing manufacturer, William C. Browning, near the end of the 1800s, aptly capture the essence of today's American ready-to-wear industry. This industry has brought the mass production of fashionable clothing to its highest development and leads the world in the quality, quantity, and variety of its output. Known by many names (the apparel industry, the garment trades, the cutting-up trades, the needle trades) and once even characterized as "the Wild West of United States industrial society,"[2] the clothing-producing industry is a sizable force in our nation's economy.

This section deals with the history, development, location, operations, and economics of the women's branch of the American apparel industry, including that subdivision concerned with children's wear. The readings following the text, which discuss apparel companies, have been selected to give the reader a deeper insight into the unique nature of one of this country's major industries.

ECONOMIC IMPORTANCE

By any of a number of yardsticks, the importance of the women's fashion business is clear. In terms of how consumers spend their money, it is estimated that in 1985 the outlay for women's and children's clothing and accessories, exclusive of shoes, was $80 billion.[3] In terms of the value of its production, the women's fashion industry also ranks high. Using 1985 once more as a yardstick year, factory shipments of apparel for women and children were $28 billion.[4]

VALUE OF SHIPMENTS, WOMEN'S AND CHILDREN'S SELECTED APPAREL (MILLIONS OF DOLLARS)

	1975	1980	1984
Total	$13,268	$20,597	$23,046
Women's Outerwear			
Coats	670	852	753
Suits, ex. pantsuits	242	377	363
Pantsuits	330	163	92
Jackets	239	727	991
Dresses	2,856	3,706	3,424
Blouses and waists	1,286	2,468	2,697
Knit sport shirts	431	710	830
Sweaters	441	480	698
Skirts	405	1,021	1,460
Slacks	1,087	1,705	1,751
Dungarees and jeans	397	878	1,347
Playgarments	125	163	258
Bathing suits	159	307	472
Raincoats	152	223	184
Washable service app.	153	238	288
Other outerwear	680	1,071	1,248
Children's Outerwear			
Coats	84	59	35
Jackets	42	46	57
Dresses	348	504	629
Blouses and waists	99	196	234
Knit sport shirts	215	398	465
Sweaters	44	64	68
Skirts	26	60	42
Slacks & Play garments	475	745	904
Dungarees and jeans	99	209	231
Bathing suits	28	41	57
Raincoats	6	8	2
Other outerwear	154	172	187
Intimate Apparel			
Corsets & brassieres	636	852	933
Undergarments	597	971	1077
Nightwear	762	1182	1274

Source: U.S. Bureau of the Census data benchmarked to the Census of Manufactures.

Another yardstick—employment in the apparel industry as a whole (men's, women's, and children's wear combined) is 1.2 million, or about 5.5 percent of total factory employment.[5] The major divisions of the women's apparel branch, according to the authors' estimates, based on government reports of employment, account for much more than half.

Numbers alone, however, do not tell the full story of the importance of the fashion industry as an employer. Historically, the industry has been a haven for the foreign born and the ghetto resident in search of work; it is a vast source of jobs in all parts of the country for semiskilled labor; and it is notable for hiring and training unskilled workers.

The women's apparel industry, with which we are primarily concerned here, is not only of considerable size itself, but its activities have great influence on many other business areas. Its productive facilities, as will be discussed later in this section, are distributed throughout the United States. It provides an outlet for the talent of gifted, creative individuals and employment for workers who are happiest at routine jobs. In addition, it is an industry that has changed fashion from what was once the privilege of the Four Hundred to something within reach of all but the most deprived women in this country. It is in the United States that the development of mass markets, mass production methods, and mass distribution of fashion merchandise has been most rapid. It is to this country that manufacturers and retailers from other countries turn for the know-how of making and selling fashionable ready-to-wear merchandise.

HISTORY AND GROWTH OF WOMEN'S INDUSTRY ....

Until the midnineteenth century, ready-made clothing was virtually nonexistent, and fashionable clothing was something that relatively few people in the United States wore or could afford. The wants of these few were supplied by custom-made imports, usually from England or France, or by the hand labor of a small number of custom tailors and dressmakers in this country. The dressmakers worked at home, or in the homes of their customers, or in small craft shops. The fabrics they used for their wealthy clients were generally imported from Europe.

Ready-to-Wear in the Nineteenth Century

From colonial times to the end of the 1800s, the majority of American women wore clothes made at home by the women of the house; every home in modest circumstances was its own clothing factory. Aiding these home sewing operations were the instructions for constructing garments printed in such early American women's magazines as *Godey's Lady's Book* and *Graham's Magazine*. And in 1860, Ebenezer Butterick developed paper patterns that provided the home sewer with help with styles and sizes. Home dressmaking continued to prevail.

WOMEN'S READY-TO-WEAR IN 1860

In contrast to custom-made apparel, which is constructed to the exact measurements of the garment's wearer, the term **ready-to-wear** applies to apparel made in standardized sizes and usually produced in factories.

As discussed in the chapter on menswear, the first ready-to-wear clothing in the United States was produced for men. Not until the U.S. Census of 1860 was the commercial manufacture of women's ready-to-wear deemed

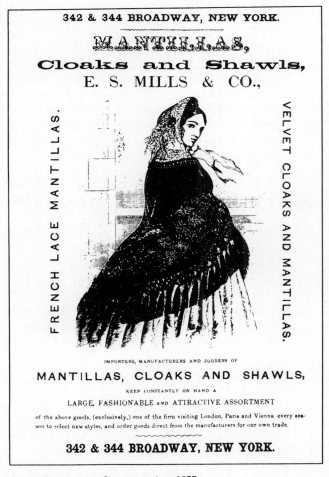

Source: From a city directory, circa 1855.

worthy of enumeration. In that year, mention was made of 96 manufacturers producing such articles as hoopskirts, cloaks, and mantillas. What was available was of poor quality and completely lacking in good design. Although once started, the industry grew rapidly, home dressmaking continued until into the early twentieth century, and it was not until well into the 1900s that the term *store clothes*, applied to early ready-to-wear, was used in other than a derogatory manner.

The women's ready-to-wear business in the United States is indeed young, and its early beginnings were anything but fashion inspired. In not much more than a century, the industry that once served only the lowest income levels of society has worked its way up to acceptance by the very richest of women.

FROM HAND TO MACHINE PRODUCTION

The major event that opened the way to ready-to-wear production was the development of the sewing machine by **Elias Howe** in 1845. Howe's machine was further perfected by **Isaac Singer**, whose improvements made it suitable for use in factories. Singer also promoted it aggressively, thus bringing it to public attention. These machines, first operated by footpower with a treadle, and later by electricity, revolutionized production by making volume output possible in machine-equipped factories.

IMMIGRANTS: A SOURCE OF MANPOWER

A plentiful supply of labor is essential to growth of any industry. This is especially true of an industry like apparel production, that was, and still is, heavily dependent on hand-guided operations such as cutting and machine sewing. Workers to perform those tasks become available in vast numbers, beginning in the 1880s, in the person of immigrants from Central and Eastern Europe. Many of the newcomers were Jews, fleeing Czarist persecutions, and bringing tailoring skills with them; others, without a trade and with no knowledge of the language, were ready and willing to master the sewing machine and work at it to survive in their new country. Hundreds of thousands of immigrants came each year, and the stream never slackened until restrictions were placed on immigration in 1920. This influx of immigrant labor, both skilled and unskilled, made possible an accelerated pace of industry growth.

Developments in the Twentieth Century

During the first two decades of the twentieth century, a number of developments combined to give additional impetus to the industry. In the 1920s, the industry came of age and the output of apparel passed the billion-dollar mark, representing one-twelfth of the country's total output of manufactured goods.[6]

IMPROVEMENTS IN TECHNOLOGY AND RETAIL DISTRIBUTION

Continuing improvements in textile technology in both Europe and America made available a wide variety of fabrics. Improvements in machines for sewing, cutting, and pressing made garment production faster, easier, and cheaper.

Along with the improvements in textile and apparel production technology, there were advances in mass distribution. Retailers began to learn the ready-to-wear business. Dry goods merchants learned to sell apparel; department and specialty stores that prided themselves on their custom-made operations began to establish ready-to-wear departments. Continuing innovation in retail salesmanship and advertising stimulated the demand for the industry's products and contributed to the further expansion of women's apparel manufacturing.

INCREASING NEED FOR READY-TO-WEAR

As manufacturing improved, ready-made clothing overcame the stigma of inferiority and cheapness that had originally been attached to it. It became an acceptable answer to a growing need for reasonably priced and respectably made apparel.

An important reason for this need was the changing role of women. Prior to 1900, there were relatively few women who looked beyond the confines of home and family. Many of those who did work held miserably paying domestic or farm jobs. To be well dressed was the privilege primarily of the wives and daughters of well-to-do men.

At the turn of the century, a whole new breed of busier and more affluent women began to emerge: women in colleges, women in sports, women in politics, and women in factories, offices, and retail stores. World War I further gave many women their first view of an occupation outside the confines of their homes, and stimulated the need for ready-made clothing. Their expanding interests and activities made ready-to-wear for themselves and their families a great convenience, and thus accelerated its acceptance among nearly all classes and incomes.

RECOGNITION OF AMERICAN DESIGNERS IN THE 1940S

In the early years of the twentieth century, the American apparel industry had demonstrated an awareness of fashion but had not yet reached the point of sponsoring or participating in its development. Instead, producers and retailers looked to Paris couture designers for inspiration. Twice a year, heads of apparel-producing firms went to view the Paris collections and bought samples for copying or adapting into mass-produced garments. At the same time, buyers from leading retail stores also bought lavishly from the Paris collections and arranged for manufacturers to copy or adapt the garments chosen. American fashion publications also concentrated their publicity almost solely on what was being shown. The phrase "Paris inspired" was the key to fashions and their promotion.

Inevitably, however, American design talent had been attracted to the industry. By the 1930s, many capable and creative designers were at work in the trade, but so great was the enthusiasm for Paris that their names were rarely mentioned in the press or by the stores. In the war-ridden years of the 1940s, with Paris blacked out by the German occupation, Dorothy Shaver, then president of Lord & Taylor, and an outstanding fashion merchant, smashed the tradition of idolizing Paris designers. Her store, for the first time in retail history, advertised clothes designed by Americans and featured their names: Elizabeth Hawes, Clare Potter, Vera Maxwell, Tom Brigance, and Claire McCardell, considered by many to have been the first true sportswear designer. The rule that only French-inspired clothes could be smart had been broken.

RISE OF PUBLICLY OWNED GIANT FIRMS IN THE 1960S

Until the 1950s, the women's apparel industry consisted almost entirely of relatively small, privately owned, single-product businesses, each concentrating its efforts on its own specialized product. Large or publicly owned firms were virtually nonexistent. In the late 1950s and throughout the 1960s, however, the situation changed and huge, publicly owned, multiproduct corporations made their appearance in the apparel field, usually by means of mergers with and acquisitions of existing companies. Many influences contributed to this phenomenon. Among them was the increase in consumer apparel spending resulting from an expanding economy. Another factor was the need to become large enough to be able to deal successfully with ever-larger textile suppliers, on the one hand, and enormously large retail distributors, on the other.

The rise of publicly owned giants in the apparel field during the 1960s is reflected in the fact that, in 1959, only 22 such publicly owned firms existed in the women's apparel field but, by the close of the 1960s, some 100 multiproduct apparel companies were listed on the stock exchanges and inviting public investment as a source of capital for further expansion.

GOING PRIVATE IN THE 1980S: LEVERAGED BUYOUTS

In the mid-1980s, the trend toward going public began to reverse itself and some large manufacturing firms began to "go private" again through **leveraged buyouts**. In a typical leveraged buyout, a group of investors, aided by an investment firm specializing in the field, buys out a company's public shareholders by leveraging or borrowing against the company's own assets. The investors put up between 1 and 10 percent of the total price in the usual case. The rest of the purchase price, up to 95 percent in some cases, is financed by layers of long-term loans from banks and insurance companies. The company's assets and cash flow are then used to pay back the loans, with or without the sale of bonds. The company's management has reclaimed their autonomy, albeit with a load of debt and interest payments, but without the need to submit their operating decisions to the review of outside stockholders. Some examples of leveraged buyouts were those of Levi Strauss, Leslie Fay, Puritan, and Cone Mills, among others.

THE ILGWU: GROWTH OF THE UNION

No history of the apparel industry would be complete without mention of the International Ladies' Garment Workers' Union (**ILGWU**), and its contribution to the industry's development. In the early days of the women's apparel industry, working conditions, as in many other industries of the period, were generally extremely bad. Men and women worked 12 hours and more a day, seven days a week, in damp, disease-breeding places, referred to in disgust as **sweatshops**. The hourly wage was five cents. Some workers provided their own machines, paid for thread and needles, for the water they drank, and sometimes even for the "privilege" of working in the factories. Work was also taken home to dark, unsanitary tenements that often doubled as sweatshops, and in which children worked long hours side by side with their parents. It was in this environment in 1900 that the ILGWU, then representing fewer than 2000 workers, was founded after two decades of desperate struggle.

ILGWU LOGO

Source: Reprinted with permission of International Ladies Garment Workers Union (ILGWU).

But the union did not achieve strength until after several major strikes and the monumental disaster of the **Triangle Waist Fire** of 1911. This tragic event took place in a factory where 146 persons lost their lives because of locked exit doors, inadequate fire escapes, and one fire escape that actually ended in midair. The shock of this holocaust was the turning point in the sweatshop era, because it awoke the public conscience to labor conditions in the garment industry.

Since the 1920s, industrywide strikes and lockouts have been all but nonexistent. Today, labor–management relations are characterized by cooperation in research, education, and industry development, and the women's apparel industry–union pattern is held up as a model for others to follow.

FROM DESIGN CONCEPT TO RETAILER

There are three major processes in making and marketing apparel: design, production, and sales. The designing department creates new styles; the production division produces them in the various sizes and fabrics required to fill retail store orders; the sales division, acting as liaison between manufacturer and retailer, markets the line. All are interdependent. The top executive (or team of top executives) at the head of the company sets policies, coordinates these functions, and makes all final decisions as to their activities. Throughout the women's apparel industry, this is the basic pattern of operations.

Seasonal Lines

In the women's apparel industry, producers periodically prepare and present (or "open") new lines to be shown to retail store buyers. A **line** is a collection or group of styles designed for a specific season. In the women's apparel industry, four to six new lines or collections are customary: spring, summer, transitional (or Fall I), fall (Fall II), and resort or possibly holiday. Addition-

MARKET DATES FOR SEASONAL OPENINGS

Season	Dates
Summer	Early January
Fall I	Early March
Fall	Early April
Resort/Early Spring	Early August
Spring/Early Summer	October–November

Source: New York Fashion Council.

ally, many firms add new styles to their lines for a given season as that season progresses, and they may also withdraw some styles that do not sell well.

The exact opening dates and number of new lines vary from one segment to another in the industry, but, as a general rule, summer lines are presented in early January, Fall I in March, Fall II in early April, Resort/Early Spring in August, and Spring/Early Summer in October/November.

The Design Function

First of the many steps in the production of apparel is the designing process for an upcoming season. This work may be done by one person or a staff. It may also be performed by one of the owners in a small firm, or by free-lance designers who operate out of their own studios.

RESPONSIBILITIES OF DESIGNERS

The designer, whoever he, she, or they may be, is expected to develop a group of new designs at least two or three months in advance of a seasonal marketing period—which, in turn, is usually six months in advance of the consumer buying period. In many instances, because fashion is basically an evolutionary process, each seasonal collection may include "new" designs that are simply updated versions of the current or past season's best sellers. Also included may be copied or revised versions of some other company's best sellers.

The designer's responsibilities go beyond ideas alone, and there are many practical obstacles to overcome. In addition to creating styles that will fit into the firm's price range and type of merchandise, the designer is responsible for the selection of fabrics, and must give consideration also to the availability and cost of materials, the availability of production techniques, costs of labor, and the particular image that the company wishes to present. Great designers are those who can apply their creative talents and skills to overcome business limitations and produce saleable merchandise.

PREPARATION OF A LINE

Among the fashion innovators, designs originate on the drawing board or in the muslin; among the less-original manufacturers, a style will often start life in the form of someone else's merchandise that has been sketched or purchased for copying.

Once a design has crystallized, the next step if to execute an actual garment. This is generally done by a *sample hand*, an expert seamstress working closely with the designer, or an assistant designer. Revisions are made as needed until a satisfactory sample emerges.

Next, a company executive or team of executives check the garment for costs, production feasibility, sourcing for production, fabric requirements and availability, and profit possibility. At this point, the principals of the firm

FROM DESIGN CONCEPT TO RETAILER

1. Initial Phase
   a. Fabric selections
   b. Fabric sources
2. Seasonal Theme
   a. Seasons determine weight and color (i.e., fall—velvets, wools, dark colors; spring—linens, cottons, light colors)
3. Ordering and Receipt of Fabrics
   a. Review of fabrics per season
   b. Contact and ordering of fabrics
   c. Discussion of color, texture, and silhouette
4. Design Phase
   a. Coordination of color, weights, textures
   b. Draping
   c. Construction
5. Sales Department Market Input—Comparative Analysis
   a. Past season comparison
   b. Number of styles, units sold per style
   c. Price points
   d. Review of void in marketplace (i.e., advice of key buyers)—a need for short cocktail dresses, a need for evening gowns priced to retail for $1200 to $1800; a need for luncheon to evening silk dresses year-round
   e. Weight fabrication relates to regional sales (i.e., market strength in sunbelt—a need for lighter fabrics)
6. Introduction of Collection to Buyers and Press
   a. Public relations firm involvement
   b. List computation and review
   c. Production
   d. Presentation
7. Buyers' Week
   a. Appointments
   b. Actual selling in showroom
   c. Trunk shows/personal appearances (i.e., dealing with fashion coordinator of stores, scheduling of travel, models for formal shows, publicity prior to show, press kits)
   d. Review of merchandising and projections (i.e., pricing, adding and/or editing of collection, after show merchandising)
8. Production
   a. Obtaining firm orders
   b. Logging
   c. Making duplicate samples
   d. Fittings, patterns—designer approval
   e. Marking, grading
   f. Cutting tickets, production list cutting
   g. Production duplicates—designer approval
9. Shipping to Retailers
10. Additions to Line

make the final decision as to which of the styles will or will not be included in the line. Some styles may require minor changes—as, for example, adding or omitting buttons, pockets, or pleats. Other styles may be discarded entirely.

If a design is to become part of a line, it is given a style number, and a highly skilled *patternmaker* makes a master production pattern for it—in one size only (whatever size the firm uses for its samples). From this pattern, one garment is made to see if correction is needed in the pattern, and to work out the final "costing." A change in the pattern, or the stitching, or the details of a garment, it should be understood, may affect the cost of production. Conversely, the need to reduce costs may require some change in the pattern, such as eliminating some of the width of a skirt, omitting pocket detail, or added seaming detail.

When the pattern is right, duplicate samples are made by operators known as *duplicate hands*, usually slightly less skilled than the original sample hands. The duplicate samples are for company salespersons to show in the company's main showroom, in any regional sales offices that it may have, on the road, and at any trade shows in which it participates. In some firms, however, especially those in the higher-priced lines, the master production pattern may not be made until after enough orders are booked to justify the production of the style.

Steps in Production

Some producers may decide at once which numbers they will put into the line. Those less sure of themselves generally await retail buyer reaction before putting any numbers into production. Those styles and designs that do not achieve acceptance must be eliminated to avoid costly markdowns or "close-outs" later in the season. From an initial collection of, say, 100 styles, some will be discarded after they have been shown. Of the remainder, it may be only a relatively small percentage that will warrant continued production after initial orders have been obtained, produced, and delivered. The number of orders received or realistically anticipated that is considered sufficient for a **cutting ticket** (production requisition) varies with each firm's needs and price levels. For example, producers whose dresses retail at medium to higher prices say that they require orders of from 100 to 500 pieces of a number before cutting. On the other hand, one producer whose coats employ carefully hand-cut leather in their designs and whose retail prices are very high indeed has told the authors that he will put a number into production even with orders for as few as 10 pieces. For manufacturers who are producing for mass distribution, the number of pieces considered a minimum for a production order may be counted in the thousands. Each producer has to work out his own minimum, in terms of how many pieces he can expect to sell to his customers, and how much he must realize in profit on the sales of a given number to offset the costs of putting it into production, in addition to all his other costs.

After it has been decided to produce a style in quantity, the master pattern for it is **graded**. This means that the pattern's various parts are "sloped" up and down to create separate patterns for each size that is to be cut. The process, which involves adding or subtracting fractions of an inch for each size, can be done by skilled patternmakers and graders with constant checking to ensure proper fit. Or it can be done mechanically by computers.

Next, after grading, comes the **marker**. This is a long paper guide that shows all of the various pieces and sizes of the pattern as they should be laid out in order to cut the cloth economically and with bias and straight where each is needed. For the actual **cutting,** layers of fabric are rolled out on long tables. The marker is placed on top. Guided by the marker, the cutters use

BEHIND THE PRICE TAG OF A $50.00 SKIRT.
Poly/cotton Skirt: Wholesale Price, $24.00, Retail Price, $50.00.

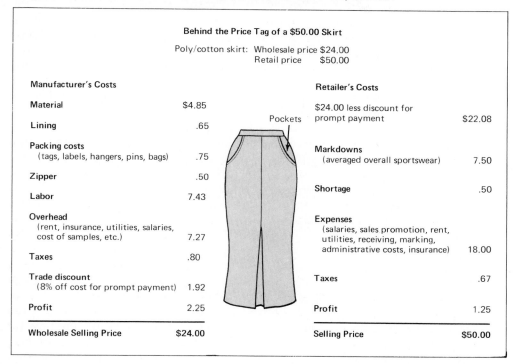

Behind the Price Tag of a $50.00 Skirt

Poly/cotton skirt: Wholesale price $24.00
Retail price $50.00

Manufacturer's Costs			Retailer's Costs	
Material	$4.85		$24.00 less discount for prompt payment	$22.08
Lining	.65			
Packing costs (tags, labels, hangers, pins, bags)	.75		Markdowns (averaged overall sportswear)	7.50
Zipper	.50			
Labor	7.43		Shortage	.50
Overhead (rent, insurance, utilities, salaries, cost of samples, etc.)	7.27		Expenses (salaries, sales promotion, rent, utilities, receiving, marking, administrative costs, insurance)	18.00
Taxes	.80			
Trade discount (8% off cost for prompt payment)	1.92		Taxes	.67
Profit	2.25		Profit	1.25
Wholesale Selling Price	**$24.00**		**Selling Price**	**$50.00**

Pockets

electrically powered knives that cut through a very substantial depth with speed and accuracy. The number of garments cut at one time varies with the thickness of the fabric, the cutter's skill, the price of the garment, the number of orders, and so forth. As many as 6000 garments of a style can be cut on a long table in one operation. The newest use of technology in apparel production is the use of laser beam fabric-cutting systems that cut the fabric quicker and more accurately than an electrically driven knife.

The cut parts of the garments are then collected, identified, and "bundled," to be passed along for the sewing operation. This may be done in the firm's own plant if it is an "inside" shop; more commonly, the bundles go by truck to a contractor's plant for the sewing. In some instances, contractors do the cutting, working from the marker and continuing from that point.

In some plants, a single operator does all of the machine sewing on a garment. This is the tailor system, still followed for garments that require highly skilled workers. More often, team or piece work prevails, and each operator does just one part. Where different machines or different adjustments of one machine are needed for the various elements of the garment, the team system makes for speed. Any hand sewing that is required comes under the heading of trimming, and is done by operators other than those who put together the main body of the garment.

Garments are then inspected, pressed, and readied for return from the contractor (if one is involved) to the original establishment, where they are finally inspected and distributed to the stores that bought them.

The period between design and delivery of a dress or similar fashion garment is a long one that the ultimate consumer knows little about. Yet the important decisions on what type of merchandise customers will find in the stocks of their favorite stores are made during this period.

The women's apparel industry in the United States is distinguished by the relative rapidity with which it produces and distributes its goods. In a business that must keep up with changing fashion, it is vital to surmount time and distance factors by speed and flexibility in production. No matter how early the industry starts preparing its lines, and no matter how early the retailers place their initial orders, the business of production, once started, becomes a race with the clock.

Marketing Procedures

Over the years, the women's apparel industry has established a pattern of selling directly to retailers, supplementing the efforts of producers' salespeople with advertising and publicity. This practice of direct selling, from producer to retailer, is related to the need for speed in the marketing time for ever-changing fashions. Since timing in fashion is of utmost importance, there is no real place for wholesale middlemen in the marketing of fashion goods. Such middlemen would have to buy, warehouse, and sell—distribution procedures too time-consuming to be practical except for staple items such as basic hosiery and undergarments, and any other articles in which fashion change is fairly slow.

INTRODUCTION OF LINES

The methods of introducing new lines to buyers vary. Some firms show their new collections accessorized, dramatized, and professionally modeled in elaborate fashion shows. These shows may be staged in ballrooms, chic restaurants, discos, and other "in" locations. Other companies simply have their lines ready in their showrooms, where the garments are on racks, to be taken down and shown to individual retail buyers for inspection and possible purchase. Some firms stage press previews of their new collections, to which they invite fashion editors in order to get publicity to the consuming public. Others show their lines only to publications in which they are eager to have a "credit"—an editorial mention of one of their numbers. The method and timing of presenting new lines varies from firm to firm, and from one branch of the industry to another.

The initial presentation of a line, however, is only the beginning of a manufacturer's selling effort, since relatively few retail store buyers will be present at the opening. For the benefit of late-comers, the line will continue to be shown at the company's headquarters, although without the initial fanfare and probably without live models. For the benefit of retail store buyers who may not have seen the line while in the market, or who may not have come at all, the firm may send it out with traveling sales representatives, or exhibit it at regional showrooms and trade shows, or it may do all of these.

RELIANCE ON A SALES FORCE

By and large, women's apparel producers rely on their own salespeople to bring the products to the attention of retail store buyers. Most firms maintain selling staffs in their showrooms to wait on visiting retail store buyers and to build a following among retailers who are potential customers. Many firms also employ road salespeople who travel with sample lines to show their merchandise to retailers within their assigned territories. These men and women may also set up temporary display in any regional trade shows that take place in their territories. In addition, many of the larger firms supplement their headquarters showrooms with regional showrooms.

For those manufacturers who do not have their own sales staffs or regional sales offices, there are independent selling representatives that maintain permanent showrooms and represent several noncompeting lines in given areas.

The industry usually pays its salespeople on a commission basis, except for those who staff the showroom in the headquarters office.

NATIONAL ADVERTISING OF BRAND AND DESIGNER NAMES

Before World War II, the names of American designers and garment manufacturers were not generally well known to consumers; apparel was purchased by a combination of approval of a garment's appearance and confidence in the retail seller. The source of a garment or accessory was considered the retailer's trade secret; the store's label was of paramount importance.

The rise of giant apparel firms in the 1960s gave impetus to the development of brand names and their promotion by means of national advertising and marketing campaigns. This promotion was aided by the cooperative advertising funds made available by large producers of man-made fibers, such as DuPont, Celanese, and Monsanto, for example.

The "name game" became increasingly important in the late 1970s, when designers of higher priced merchandise went into business for themselves, either alone or with partners, and established the manufacturing companies that today bear their names. Among the best known and most successful are Calvin Klein, Bill Blass, Geoffrey Beene, Oscar de la Renta, Ralph Lauren, Norma Kamali, and Liz Claiborne, whose firm is the largest of the designer-named apparel producing companies.

Prior to the 1970s, designers, employed by producers, were rarely featured by name. From an apparel producer's point of view, unless there is some assurance of a permanent relationship, there is little advantage in building up the name of a designer who, quite possibly, may be working in another firm next year.

The amount of brand and designer name national advertising done by the apparel industry today is very impressive in comparison with the almost nonexistent industry advertising prior to the 1960s, but it is still quite small alongside what is spent by other major industries such as food, drugs, auto, and electronics.

ADVERTISING AND PROMOTION

In addition to personal selling, fashion manufacturers make widespread use of trade publications as advertising media to bring their names and products to the attention of retailers. The small and specialized circulation of these publications brings their advertising rates far below those of consumer publications, and thus an apparel producer does not have to be large to make good use of them. Among those widely used are *Women's Wear Daily*, *California Apparel News*, and *Body Fashions/Intimate Apparel*, for example. All of these are supported by the advertising of small and large producers.

Also used in the apparel business is **cooperative advertising**, an arrangement under which the manufacturer and retailer share the cost of newspaper advertising that is run in the store's name to promote the manufacturer's name or brand to the consumer. In such an arrangement, the retailer enjoys more advertising space than he pays for out of his own pocket; the manufacturer enjoys advertising that is run in conjunction with the name of a locally known and respected retail store, and that is usually backed up by the store with a substantial stock of that maker's goods. The retailer, moreover, as a large and consistent purchaser of space in his local papers, pays a much lower rate for this space than the manufacturer could obtain for his occasional insertions. "Co-op" money buys the producer more space for less cost.

Other promotional techniques include providing retailers with selling aids: customer mailing pieces, or newspaper advertising mats and photographs for use in store advertisements, for example.

Many of the larger firms also employ publicity agents. It is through their efforts that many of the fashion articles that appear on the women's pages of newspapers have their origin. Press releases, often accompanied by fashion photographs of high quality, are sent directly to newspaper editors or, in some cases, to local stores for forwarding to the editors.

DESIGNER TRUNK SHOWS

Another marketing technique used by many well-known designers is the **trunk show**. A trunk show is a showing by a manufacturing company of its complete line to consumers assembled in a major retail store. A key company salesperson is in attendance, and often the designer makes a personal appearance. There are also live models to exhibit the garments. Such shows are backed by heavy local advertising and publicity. The consumer has the opportunity not only to see the manufacturer's complete line, but also to order through the store any styles, sizes, and colors not available in the store's stocks, since it is usually impossible for any store to stock an entire line. Designers get a firsthand view of consumer reaction; retailers observe consumer response to style numbers they did not select as well as to those already chosen for resale; producers and retailers gain sales from the impact of the promotion. Most designers say there is nothing like a trunk show for stimulating interest in and sales of their merchandise.

Manufacturer-Owned Retail Stores

Seeking to increase their volume of sales, women's apparel manufacturers have begun to engage in retailing by opening stores of their own. Usually, this represents a small portion of the company's total sales, and there appears to be no intention on the part of such producers to abandon manufacturing and devote themselves primarily to retailing. Manufacturer-owned retail stores have long been an established channel of distribution in the menswear industry, as is discussed in the chapter on menswear. In the women's apparel field, however, the establishment of such stores is a revolutionary new development.

This new type of company store should be distinguished from the factory outlets that have been around for decades. The older type of store was usually sparsely furnished, in an out-of-the-way location and stocked with an incomplete inventory of seconds, irregulars, and excess merchandise—the inevitable by-products of mass production. Company stores of the new type, on the other hand, are located in prime shopping areas, carry a large and complete stock of the firm's products at regular prices, have an attractive environment, and offer many customer services. Among the large and well-known branded American companies that began in 1984 to operate their own chains of retail stores are Esprit, with stores in San Francisco and Los Angeles, and the promise of more to come; Merona's in San Francisco and Los Angeles; Ralph Lauren, on New York City's Madison Avenue; the Coca-Cola stores of Murjani (who produces and markets sportswear under a licensing agreement with Coca-Cola); and the Mickey & Co. stores, owned by J. G. Hook. The Hook firm also operates some 25 factory outlets and is licensed by Disney Productions to manufacture an adult line of Mickey and Friends sportswear. The list goes on.

Company-owned retail stores are not new in Europe but the trend toward company-owned retail stores in America is still new, and it remains to be seen how far and how long it will go. There are advantages to the manufacturer: increased sales, and especially the opportunity to observe consumer reaction to new concepts and new styles before putting them into mass production.

FASHION TELEVISION VIDEOS: FTV

The video bandwagon began rolling in the apparel industry in 1984 and has been gathering momentum rapidly. An increasing number of manufacturers are having fashion showing videos produced for point-of-sale use in retail stores. According to the sales promotion director of Liz Claiborne, Inc., "These videos are being produced because we've gotten a lot of requests from the stores to have videos to play in their dress and sportswear departments."[7]

In addition to their use at the point of sale, it is believed that they can be plugged into an increasing number of outlets, particularly domestic and foreign television syndication. Among the firms now using videos as a marketing tool are Norma Kamali, Willi Wear, Liz Claiborne, Ralph Lauren, and Calvin Klein, to name but a few. Of interest as possible indications of future use: WilliWear's videos are being plugged in at nightclubs. Also, the Japanese have asked for fashion videos that they can play on their Sony MTV station in Yokohama and in video coffee bars.

NATURE OF THE INDUSTRY

Apparel producers vary widely as to size, product, and type of operation. Small companies coexist with giant firms. Specialists rub shoulders with firms that, through their various divisions, can dress a woman from the skin out and for every conceivable occasion. Self-contained operations and plants that perform no more than a single step of the production process, publicly owned giant companies and small privately owned firms, fashion creators and flagrant copiers—all are found in the industry.

Different Types of Producers

Apparel manufacturers do not always handle the entire production of a garment in their own factories; they may contract out some of the work. The U.S. Census of Manufacturers, therefore, divides the industry's firms into three classifications according to the comprehensiveness of their production activities: manufacturers, apparel jobbers, and contractors. Common usage, however, employs different criteria and terminology.

MANUFACTURERS

Classified as **manufacturers** by the census are those firms that buy fabric and do the designing, patternmaking, grading, cutting, sewing, and assembling of garments in factories that they own. In the industry, factories that are wholly owned by a manufacturing company are known as **inside shops**, whether or not all steps in production are performed on the same premises. A major advantage of such integrated operation is that there is complete control over the production quality of the product. A disadvantage is that the necessary factory facilities and machinery require large capital investments.

APPAREL JOBBERS

What the census and also the ILGWU define as an **apparel jobber** is a firm that generally handles all processes but the sewing, and sometimes the cutting, and that contracts out these production processes to independently owned outside contracting facilities. The majority of women's apparel firms, both small and large, high priced and low priced, contract out their sewing and often their cutting, as well as any other highly specialized production processes such as embroidery, quilting, and pleating, which require special machinery. One advantage of using outside facilities in this way is that minimal capital investment is required. A disadvantage is that there is less quality control.

The term *manufacturer*, however, as it is generally used within the industry, refers to any firm that buys fabric, designs garments, maintains a showroom, sells to retailers, and ships and bills merchandise. Regardless of whether the firm is an "inside" shop or a jobber, the industry calls such firms manufacturers.

THE CONTRACTING SYSTEM: OUTSIDE SHOPS

There are independently owned factories that own their machinery and employ operators to sew and often cut goods from the designs, materials and specifications of the apparel jobbers that hire them. Both the census and the industry refer to such factories as **contractors**.

EXAMPLES OF THE CONTRACTING SYSTEM

Contractors Wanted	Contract Work Wanted
Seeking low-priced sleep and loungewear maker who can cut, sew, ship. Call Bob 213 554-2725.	15 years exp in garment business. High quality, low price on evening wear. Call 505 277-0405.
Knitwear mfr. looking for contractor, women's and children's knitwear. Steady production and high volume. Contact: Box B35115, WWD.	NY contractor experienced in all types of knitwear, sportwear. Call 212 555-6677.
Seeking sewing contractors for full and half slips. Call 215 333-8585.	Shirt & blouse factory, very high quality, seeks top-quality mfr. Can handle small lots. Contact: WRC Bldg., 432 W. Spruce, Phila., PA 19111.
Cotton/linen line contractors sought. Small lots. Call 212 444-5656.	

Source: Daily advertisements in Women's Wear Daily.

The contracting system evolved early in the history of the industry. Prior to 1880, the manufacture of women's apparel was generally accomplished, in all its steps, under one roof. However, as ready-made clothing began to be produced in volume, it became common practice to perform in one place only such key operations as designing, patternmaking, grading, cutting, inspection, selling, and shipping. Most of the sewing tasks were contracted out to individual women who worked in their homes. This was a "cottage industry" procedure in which women added to the family income by doing piece-work sewing at home. Eventually, this production shifted to privately owned factories that devoted themselves entirely to such work. This system of employing outside production facilities, the contracting process, continues to play an important role. The burden of seasonal idleness and production peaks can be shifted to entrepreneur contractors, along with the investment in sewing machines and the dealings with labor.

Contractors are used by both small and large firms, and an individual company may use as many as 40 different sewing shops at the height of the producing season. Even firms with their own "inside" production facilities also hire independent contractors for extra capacity in busy periods; still others subsidize contracting shops. This system of using outside production facilities also enables manufacturers to diversify their product mix to meet changing consumer demands. For example, sportswear producers may one season need jackets in their lines and the following season need sweaters. The contracting system makes it possible for them to adjust and change their lines without making large dollar investments in new equipment.

Today the women's clothing industry is a maze of inside and **outside shops**, of contracting and subcontracting and contracting beyond that. This system makes it possible for newcomers with salable ideas but limited capital to swing into large-scale production almost overnight, through the simple device of hiring the contractor's plant, labor, and production know-how. Contractors, incidentally, need not be located in the major market centers. Nowadays, they are located not only in every section of the country, but also abroad.

Size of Apparel Companies

In matters of size, as in almost every other characteristic, the apparel industry presents enormous variety. There are huge companies that devote themselves entirely to the women's wear business; there are other enormous companies that have one or more divisions in this field; and there are the small fry. Despite the emergence of giant firms, the trend toward consolidation, the presence of conglomerates, and all the other indications of bigness, the women's apparel industry remains a stronghold of small business—more so perhaps than any other major industry.

MULTIPRODUCT GIANT COMPANIES

As the industry has grown in size, ownership of its firms has become increasingly concentrated through mergers and acquisitions. For example, just 100 companies now account for fully half of the total apparel volume; 42 companies now ship more than $100 million each a year, and 5 companies have annual sales volume figures in excess of $1 billion each.[8]

Large apparel companies, however, are actually multiproduct aggregates of small and medium-sized business divisions, each of which concentrates on a range of products targeted to a narrow consumer market segment and operates quite autonomously.

Today, three basic types of multidivisional companies are involved in the women's apparel industry. All of them have grown either by internal growth or by acquiring subsidiary divisions, or both. One type is primarily specialized in producing ready-to-wear, and in this category are Jonathan Logan, Russ Togs, and Levi Strauss—the last-named being a menswear producer that has moved into the women's field. A second category, exemplified by Warnaco and Vanity Fair Corp., produce undergarments and accessories, in addition to a wide variety of clothing. The final group comprises **conglomerates** whose business activities involve companies operating in widely diversified fields. For example, Consolidated Foods has acquired Hanes Hosiery, Aris Gloves, and Robert Bruce, to name but a few; Beatrice Foods owned Playtex and Halston Enterprises; Gulf & Western had acquired Kayser-Roth, which itself is a consolidation of many once separately owned companies in the apparel field. Some companies that are acquired by such conglomerates

WARNACO: A MULTIPRODUCT COMPANY

Divisions	Product
Warner	Intimate apparel
Olga	Foundations and sleepwear
Hathaway	Women's and men's shirts
Puritan	Men's sweaters and knit shirts
Rosanna	Women's sweaters and knitwear
White Stag	Women's active wear
Chaps by Lauren	Menswear
Dior Accessories*	Women's accessories
Dior Shirts*	Men's shirts
Pringle of Scotland*	Sweaters
Albert Nipon Men's	Menswear
Speedo*	Activewear
Spalding*	Activewear

*Licensed arrangements.

are later resold—sometimes to other conglomerates, sometimes to new owners who will operate them as independent companies. The lineup, like that of a professional football or baseball team, changes constantly.

DOMINANCE OF SMALL SPECIALIZED FIRMS

Today, small, reputable specialized producers continue to set the fashion pace for the industry. What the future will bring remains to be seen, but knowledgeable observers feel that there will always be a place in the apparel industry for the small firm. As one top executive of a major fashion house explained it, the industry "is not capital intensive. You can develop a line on a shoestring . . . the payoff for ingenuity comes up five times a year. As long as there is a free enterprise system, there will be room on Seventh Avenue for the small manufacturer."[9]

The very existence of contractors makes it possible for an enterprising and creative person with a flair for fashion and selling ability to set up business and hope to prosper. Except for the purchase of fabric, little else is needed in the way of capital outlay, since the cutting and sewing can thus be farmed out. The key to success is in producing styles that will find acceptance. In that respect, the small firm is viable and has an equal chance with the larger ones. The small entrepreneur also has the further advantage of being able to move quickly to exploit sudden fashion shifts. On the other hand, a single poor season can wipe out a small, undercapitalized firm—and often does.

Some of the country's major designers give splendid proof of how a small firm can flourish. The companies such as those owned by Bill Blass, Galanos, Geoffrey Beene, and Oscar de la Renta, for example, are relatively small; their individual sales volume figures exclusive of licensing royalties are below $100 million. Although their target customers are women who spend a great deal on a single garment, their combined spending for fashion is a drop in the bucket compared with the volume done by apparel companies that cater to the great mass of American consumers. Dollar volume, alone, however, does not measure the importance of the designers and their firms. The publicity they generate in the news media, plus the impact of the fashion news embodied in their garments and their licensed names constitute a major element in keeping the general public aware of fashion and the American fashion industry.

No matter how much the future holds for further merging and giantism in the apparel industry, one can be sure that there will always be a pool of small manufacturers who are innovative and flexible, and have a clear view of what their small, special target customer group wants. As an element in the apparel industry, the small producer will survive. Those who fall by the wayside are sure to be replaced by newcomers.

Specialization by Products and Prices

Traditionally, there has always been a high degree of product and price-line specialization among industry firms. A typical producer would limit himself to a particular category of garment, such as sportswear separates, evening wear, bridal dresses, coats, or suits within a narrow range of prices, and also in particular size ranges, such as juniors, children's, misses, women's, petites, and the like. Some of the producers concentrated, and some still do, on producing goods to the specifications of mass retail merchandisers, virtually to the exclusion of other potential retail store customers.

Today, however, as many industry companies have expanded by diversifying their product mix and their price-lining structure, specialization seems to be waning. Some firms have created separate divisions to handle each new category they wish to produce. For example, Liz Claiborne, Inc., originally specialized in misses' sportswear separates, but today they have divisions for children's wear, menswear, accessories and dresses.

Other firms moved into new fields by acquiring companies already active in the area in which they wished to function. For instance, under the corporate umbrella of VF Corporation, one will find the following separate divisions: Lee jeans, Vanity Fair knit tops, Bassett-Walker, Inc., and Troutman Industries.

In such a setup, all divisions draw on the parent firm for financing and guidance, but each one has its own name, its own clearly defined product area, its own designing staff, its own contracting firms, its own selling force, and even its own advertising.

PRODUCT SPECIALIZATION

The following are typical products in the women's apparel industry in which companies or divisions of multiproduct companies specialize:

1. Outerwear—coats, suits, rainwear
2. Dresses
3. Sportswear and separates—active wear, pants, tops, sweaters, jackets
4. After-five and evening clothes
5. Bridal and bridesmaid attire
6. Uniforms and aprons—career (other than office) apparel, daytime dresses
7. Maternity
8. Swimwear and beachwear
9. Intimate apparel—foundations, lingerie, robes
10. Blouses
11. Sweaters

SIZE SPECIALIZATIONS

The size ranges in which companies most commonly specialize are the following:

1. Women's—half sizes such as 14½ to 26½, and large sizes 38 to 52
2. Misses—usually 4 to 14 or 16, but may be as small as 2 or as large as 18
3. Juniors—5 to 15
4. Petites—2 to 14 and 3 to 11
5. Children's—special breakdowns of sizes according to age and physical development (discussed in the section on children's clothes in this chapter)

WHOLESALE PRICE SPECIALIZATION

Within the wide spectrum of wholesale prices for garments, there are *price ranges* in which individual manufacturers specialize. Elements in the whole-sale price of a garment are (1) the quality of workmanship, (2) the cost of labor, and (3) the quality and amount of fabric and trimmings. The women's apparel industry generally divides itself into the following four price ranges (or groups of individual prices per garment):

1. *Designer* (highest priced merchandise). This includes the lines of name designers, such as Calvin Klein, Donna Karan, Bill Blass, Oscar de la Renta, and Galanos—whose prices are the highest of all.
2. *Better* (medium to high prices). This includes the lower or secondary lines of designers—Anne Klein II, Calvin Klein's Classifications, and Perry Ellis's Portfolio. It also includes such lines as Liz Claiborne, Evan Picone, Jones New York, and Norma Kamali.
3. *Moderate* (or lower than "better" but higher than "budget"). This includes such lines as White Stag, Russ Togs, Jantzen, Levi Strauss.
4. *Budget* (the lowest prices in which one would find advertised brand names). This includes firms such as Ship 'n' Shore, Judy Bond blouses, and Wrangler jeans.

Prevalence of Style Piracy

Apparel designs cannot be copyrighted; therefore, copying the work of creative designers is standard operating procedure for many firms, both large and small. Design and styling are such important competitive weapons in the fashion industry that **style piracy**, against which U.S. laws provide no protection, is considered a way of life in the garment business. In the language of the industry, however, a design is never "stolen"; it is "knocked off." It is copied, adapted, translated, or even pirated, but the "**knock-off**" is never considered as having been "stolen." This is not hypocrisy but simply the garment trade's way of acknowledging that copying dominates the industry; it is done openly and without apology. The late Norman Norell, who produced garments in very high price lines, indeed, and who was considered in his day the dean of American designers, expressed his philosophy about style piracy: "I don't mind if the knock-off houses give me a season with my dress. What I mind is if they bring out their copies faster than I can get my own dresses to the stores."[10]

Aside from the absence of copyright protection for apparel designs, there are several reasons for this copying practice. Plunging into a fast-selling style, regardless of whose design it was originally, is one way to make a modest investment work to the limit. Another reason style piracy is rife is the highly specialized nature of the firms themselves. If, for example, a dress intended to retail at $150 has features that would make it a fast seller at a lower price, the originator of the style is in no position to produce or market inexpensive versions. His entire purchasing, production, and distribution are geared to customers who are willing to pay for the particular grade of material, workmanship, and details in which he has specialized. In addition, apparel firms' labor costs are established by the union, based on the companies' normal wholesale price lines, and they cannot be reduced. On the other hand, a maker specializing in garments to retail at $50 has much lower labor costs, enjoys access to sources for much less expensive fabrics, knows how to cut corners in production, and has established distribution among retailers catering to the price-conscious consumer. And if a style can be copied down to a still lower level, or can be marketed at some intermediate levels, makers specializing in those levels are likely to step in.

Occasionally, the copying process is reversed, and a style that originates in the lower-priced lines will have features that make it desirable for higher-priced manufacturers to adapt. Normally, however, the procedure is for a style that originally retailed for hundreds of dollars to be "knocked off" at successively lower prices, if it shows signs of popular acceptance by customers.

Financing by Factoring

Many garment manufacturers rely heavily on outside sources for operating capital. These sources are called *factors*. The manufacturer engages a factor to become its credit and collection department. Orders are submitted to the **factoring** company for approval and shipped as designated. The invoices are assigned to the factor, who supplies immediate cash, usually equal to 90 percent of receivables' net value. (The 10 percent reserve of outstanding receivables is usually held to cover returns, allowances, etc.) The factor then proceeds to collect payment from the manufacturer's customers and takes the credit risk. For their services as a credit and collection department and guarantor of credit risks, factors receive a fee known as a factoring commission.

Fashion Designers: Owners or Employees

The authority, position, and name recognition of the designer vary greatly from one firm in the industry to another. In the majority of apparel firms, the designer is simply a hired talent, perhaps only one of several, responsible for developing lines that will be presented under the manufacturer's firm name or brand name. As was pointed out earlier in this chapter, a manufacturer may hesitate to build up the name of a designer who could be working elsewhere next season. Therefore, the vast majority of the industry's designers are nameless as far as the public is concerned. Also in the industry are many small firms that do not even employ designers but rely on free-lance design services or on a patternmaker with a good sense of fashion.

Nevertheless, the number of American designers whose names are well known to the public has increased. This is because they have become owners, partly or completely, of their own producing companies, operating in their own names, and featuring their names on labels, in advertising, and in the fashion press. Among the best known and most successful are the companies of Calvin Klein, Ralph Lauren, Bill Blass, Oscar de la Renta, James Galanos, Norma Kamali, and Liz Claiborne. A recent addition to their ranks is Donna Karan, formerly a designer for Anne Klein. And a conspicuous exception to the prevailing anonymity of designers who before he died was employed by others is Perry Ellis, who was employed by and featured by Manhattan Industries.

Typical of the way a designer wins recognition by operating his or her own company is the story of Liz Claiborne. During the many years she worked for Jonathan Logan, she was unknown to the consuming public. In 1976, she formed her own company, under her own name, and since then has become well known among manufacturers, retailers, the apparel-buying public—and even among investment strategists who take a lively interest in trading shares in her company. Her firm, moreover, is the only designer-owned company with a sales volume of over $500 million a year.

Designer-name firms, as was pointed out earlier in this chapter, generate relatively small sales volume, because their products are aimed and priced for a limited, affluent group of customers. Their importance, however, goes far beyond the dollars in their respective tills, because of the impact of their ideas on the fashion business and the fashion consumer. They are like the icing on the cake—a small but important part of the whole, and a part without which the cake would have little appeal.

Proliferation of Industry Licensing Agreements

The 1970s witnessed the burgeoning of the "name game"—the licensing by prominent American apparel designers of their names for use by manufacturers of accessories and of lower priced clothing. **Licensing** is a legal arrangement covering a specific period of time, during which a manufacturer of goods in a particular category is given exclusive rights to produce and market a line bearing the name of the **licensor**. For this privilege, the **licensee** pays a **royalty fee**—that is, a percentage of the wholesale sales of the goods concerned. Usually a guaranteed minimum payment is specified.

The licensor, however, is not required to confine his or her name to any single product category. For instance, a licensing arrangement with a jewelry manufacturer does not preclude similar arrangements with manufacturers of jeans, sunglasses, shoes, bed linens, scarfs, hosiery, fur coats, perfume, swimwear, or any other product that can profitably become part of the name game. Apparel and accessories, nevertheless, are a major field for such exploitation. It is estimated that in 1985 licensed apparel and accessories represented 38 percent of all licensed name products sold at retail, out of a total of $40 billion a year, an amount still on the rise.[11]

Licensing arrangements are not new to the European couture; some of the most famous among them have long had income of this sort from American manufacturers and stores. Among American designers, however,

Licensing:
Total Sales, $45 Billion

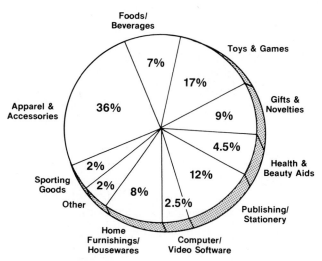

SALES OF LICENSED MERCHANDISE
BY PRODUCT CATEGORY

1985

Source: The Licensing Letter.

this is a relatively new development, but one that has grown enormously. Even as early as the end of the 1970s, some designers were believed to be receiving royalty fees that equaled the total sales volume of their own apparel enterprises.

The proliferation of licensing by both American and European designers has arrived at the point that their names now appear on apparel priced well below the levels at which they operated when they became famous. Examples include the Perry Ellis America line manufactured and marketed by Manhattan Ind.; the Halston name marketed by J. C. Penney; Kenzo's licensing arrangement with The Limited—and many others.

Apparel producers do not necessarily limit themselves to licensing one designer's name alone. They may run several at the same time. For example, Oxford Industries makes lines under licenses with Oleg Cassini and Ralph Lauren, while at the same time manufacturing a variety of other branded lines of their own, such as McGregor and Merona. Another example is Levi Strauss, which markets an Andrew Fezza line along with its own Levi's brand.

The practice of licensing in the apparel industry is not limited to designer names. There are firms that license their names to makers of other products. As an example, Jordache produces and promotes its own line of jeans, but licenses its name for 42 different products among U.S. manufacturers alone. These range from women's panties and slips produced by a lingerie company to sunglasses made and marketed by an optical company.

Also getting into the licensing act are legions of celebrities, including cartoon characters as well as movie and television idols and sports figures. One of the forerunners in the women's market is J. G. Hook, which licensed Mickey Mouse from Disney Productions and formed a division called Mickey and Friends, which generated $211 million in wholesale sales in 1984, its first year of operation.[12] Not far behind is the licensing of different Looney Tunes characters to a variety of apparel manufacturers, among them a producer of misses' sleepwear and loungewear, and a swimwear manufacturer. The popular TV show "Dynasty" has generated a Krystal perfume and Dynasty accessories and apparel. Even a company like Coca-Cola has climbed on the licensing bandwagon; it has licensed Murjani International to produce a line of Coca-Cola leisure apparel, and the producer is now opening retail stores that feature it, as mentioned earlier.

The major value of a licensing arrangement to the apparel and accessories producer is that the merchandise carries a highly recognizable and presold name. To consumers, the name often symbolizes achievement, status, and quality. To the licensor, of course, it means gaining additional income and enhanced name recognition without having to invest in production and marketing costs.

Among the most active American designer licensors are Bill Blass, Calvin

Klein, Anne Klein, Oscar de la Renta, Ralph Lauren, and Geoffrey Beene. As an example of how huge this aspect of designer licensing has grown, consider that Bill Blass alone has 38 U.S. licensees, plus another 50 overseas. The volume of Blass licensed products grew from about $100 million in retail value in 1980 to some $200 million in 1985, for such merchandise as women's apparel, including furs, gloves, and sportswear; sheets and towels; and the Mark VII Lincoln Continental. Calvin Klein's licensing royalties are estimated at $50 million.[13]

It must be remembered, however, that the licensing value of a name is directly dependent on the continuing success and prestige of the licensor. Almost any designer entrepreneur can have an occasional unsuccessful collection. A series of unsuccessful collections can put almost any such firm out of business, and also put an end to licensing, since the licensee has no reason to renew an arrangement with a designer whose name has lost its glamour. No licensing agreement is forever!

LOCATION OF FASHION MARKET CENTERS

Although some phase of apparel production (i.e., contracting and subcontracting) can be found in many states of the Union, the design and marketing activities of domestic apparel companies are concentrated in relatively few major cities throughout the United States. It is in these cities that one finds an enclave of apparel companies that produce and sell merchandise at wholesale level to retail buyers. Known as **market centers** in the trade, these centers are the very heartbeat of the industry since they are the marketing link between apparel manufacturers and retail distributors.

New York, the Leading Market Center

The oldest, largest, and best-known wholesale fashion center in the country is located in the heart of New York City. While other sections of the country have been whittling away at its base, insofar as women's and children's ready-to-wear is concerned, it is still unquestionably the fashion capital of the world.

It is not entirely an accident that New York occupies this dominant position. When Elias Howe first perfected his sewing machine, factory production of garments was not limited to any one city or area. But then came the great wave of immigration, as mentioned earlier in this chapter. New York was a major port of entry for newcomers, eager to find work in the city where they landed. Their assimilation into the garment industry there was often immediate, with some manufacturers and contractors actually meeting incoming vessels to recruit whole families for work in their factories. This pool of labor, growing out of the steady stream of immigrants, was the circumstance that enabled New York to leave its rivals behind in the production of apparel.

New York had the further advantage of being close to both the cotton mills of the South and the woolen mills of New England. It was also the nation's largest city and the center of fashionable society. Once New York had gained dominance, it became a magnet, attracting such auxiliary businesses as embroidery, pleating, trimmings, as well as textile showrooms, consumer and fashion periodicals, trade associations, and the like. With these advantages, the city became the hub of the women's garment industry.

Today, New York still remains and will probably continue to remain the dominant center of the U.S. fashion industry. It is only in that city that one can find the showrooms of an estimated more than 5000 apparel firms, the showrooms of all major fiber and fabric producers, the headquarters of consumer and fashion magazines, and the offices of major trade associations. Add to that the countless opportunities for fashion practitioners to engage in New York's other important activity—"shop talk" with suppliers, friends, competitors, editors, and other sources of fashion information—and it becomes clear why the city retains its position as the hub of the fashion industry. Almost all of the leading American fashion designers work in New York-based firms because, as one major designer explained it: "Everything is here . . . you have to commute to see what kinds of clothes are needed for commuting and working. You have to live through the seasons to design clothes for the seasons. New York is just like fashions: dirty and clean, casual and uptight, alive and changing."[14]

Current estimates are that the area in and around New York employs more garment workers than any other center of the industry and that the production of women's and children's wear constitutes the largest industry in New York City and New York State.

SEVENTH AVENUE

So much of New York City's garment and accessories business is concentrated within a distance of one block east or west of **Seventh Avenue**, from West 41st Street south into the low West 30s, that the term *Seventh Avenue* has become synonymous with the women's fashion industry. The street itself was renamed Fashion Avenue in 1972. Within this area, there are literally thousands of showrooms presenting every known type and price line of women's ready-to-wear and accessories. These showrooms include not only those of New York firms, but also those of many producers whose headquarters are in other parts of the country and even in other parts of the world. There are other apparel centers elsewhere in the country where women's garments are produced and sold, but to those in the fashion business, no other center has the color, tension, activity, or merchandise variety of Seventh Avenue.

Individual buildings within the garment center tend to be specialized,

THE GARMENT CENTER IN NEW YORK CITY

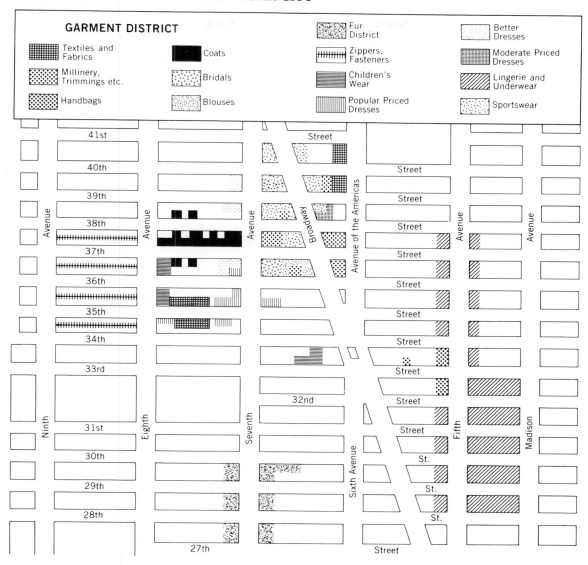

each housing producers of more or less the same categories of merchandise and wholesale price ranges. For example, 1410 Broadway (the next street east of Seventh Avenue) is the market for moderate-priced sportswear, sweaters, and budget apparel; 1407 and 1411 Broadway house the showrooms of more than 2000 sportswear companies; 1400 Broadway is the main building for medium-priced misses and junior dress firms; 1375 houses many bridal and evening dress firms; and 1350 contains many producers of lower-priced apparel, of the type sold by the dozens, sometimes called "daytime" dresses.

The upper end of Seventh Avenue has a range of coat and suit firms and higher-priced designer-name companies, with the overflow spilling into West 39th Street. Coat and suit firms are in 500 and 512 Seventh Avenue. Designer-name companies like Bill Blass, Trigère, Ralph Lauren, Geoffrey Beene, and their peers are in 530 and 550 Seventh Avenue. At the lower end of Seventh Avenue are makers of lower-priced apparel whose names are generally unknown to the public. Children's wear showrooms are mostly on the south and west fringes of the area, with many of them concentrated in a specialized children's wear building at 120 West 34th Street.

The garment center's tenants, however, have been pushing out its boundaries. Recently, two buildings on West 35th Street have attracted many young designer firms.

DECENTRALIZATION OF PRODUCTION

At one time, practically every New York-based firm had its design, show-room, production, and shipping facilities in the garment district, and even all in the same building. Increasingly in recent years, apparel firms locate their cutting and, to a larger extent, their sewing operations in areas outside the city, and even outside the country, whether these production facilities are owned by the companies or simply contracted for. This trend is noticeable not only in New York, but in other large cities as well. The high cost of rent, the unavailability of space that can be adapted to newer methods and equipment, the rising cost of taxes and labor, the almost unbelievable traffic congestion on city streets—all these have encouraged the establishment of factories in small towns in New York State and the surrounding states, in the Southeast, and in foreign countries—Hong Kong, Taiwan, and Korea, for instance. No matter where the goods are produced, however, the finished garments are sent back to the parent firm for selling and distribution. Seventh Avenue remains the nerve center of the design, marketing, and management operations, regard-less of how far afield the production facilities may be.

Secondary Fashion Market Centers

There are other focal market centers outside New York City, but no one of them begins to compare with it in terms of the number of companies based there or the variety, quantity, and dollar sales. Each of these other centers tends to be fairly specialized as to the types and price ranges it produces. Many of the manufacturers in these **secondary design centers** have sales representation in New York City.

LOS ANGELES

Los Angeles, a not very close second to New York, has emerged as an important design and manufacturing center, known for its "California look." Once limited mostly to swimsuits and active sportswear, it now turns out a wide range of moderate-priced garments, including blue jeans, "trendy" junior-sized garments, and boutique items. In 1984, the California garment industry employed some 190,000 people, two-thirds of them in Los Angeles. Statewide production reached $6 billion at wholesale. More significant, however, is the growth rate: the California industry grew by 12 percent in 1985, compared with a 4 percent growth rate for the industry as a whole.[15]

Los Angeles manufacturers have some advantages over New York: cheaper and abundant space, and a large pool of Mexican workers. Unfavorable factors include a shortage of the experienced patternmakers and small specialized fabric and findings firms that are plentiful in New York. California manufacturers, however, have developed their own "look" and are noted for their creative innovations in sportswear styling and colorations.

DALLAS

Once a design and production center primarily for polyester knit garments intended for large-volume apparel chains, Dallas is a wholesale market in transition. As one of their leading manufacturers explains it: "It is still a market that caters to middle America, only middle America has changed. And we've all noticed. None of the merchandise we now produce is faddish, because the middle American customer we're trying to reach isn't faddish."[16] Thus, most of the manufacturers headquartered in Dallas have made the shift from lower-priced polyester dresses to an evenly divided mix of moderate-price dresses and sportswear in a greater variety of fabrications, to meet the changing demands of a large segment of mainstream consumers. Although still a drop in the nationwide bucket, an overview of seven of the city's top-volume producers reveals that their sales collectively accounted for $300 million in annual revenues in 1985.[17] Jerell, Inc., is the largest Dallas company.

MIAMI

Of the more than 1000 apparel manufacturing companies in Florida, the largest segment by far is made up of children's wear companies located in Miami.[18] However, there are also an increasing number of swimwear, sportswear, and activewear manufacturers who are running small but successful businesses in Florida. The state government's fiscal policies are particularly attractive to manufacturers. The corporate income tax of 5 percent is among the lowest of any state in the United States, and there are no taxes on inventory. In addition, Florida attempts to stimulate employment by extending tax credits to manufacturers who create jobs in blighted areas.

Children's wear manufacturers were among the first to establish themselves in Florida—as early as 1940. In the 1960s, some 30 children's wear firms founded the Florida Children's Wear Manufacturers Guild that now sponsors one of the most successful trade shows in the country. The show, held once a year, attracts well over 1000 retail store buyers from major department and specialty stores countrywide.

An interesting point—the Miami manufacturers credit Cuban immigrants, fleeing from the Castro regime, for the growth of their industry. As one head of a children's wear firm expressed it, "The Cuban immigration of the Sixties was the catalyst that allowed us to grow. Once we got the Cuban labor working for us, we could take orders from major stores and know that we could deliver the merchandise."[19] Today, many Cubans have graduated from positions as machine operators to become principals in their own companies—a modern parallel to the European immigrant tide that helped New York City's apparel industry grow in an earlier day!

CHICAGO

Chicago has changed. At one time it had a reputation for conservatively styled and well-made dresses for misses and women, at higher than moderate prices. But here is how an article describes the Chicago market in 1985: "Gone are the days when traditional and polyester were the fashion watchwords here. Gone are the days when moderate-price volume manufacturers and their multi-million dollar business along the crowded banks of the Chicago River were the ONLY game in town. Today, only a handful of these manufacturers, like R. & M. Kaufman, Benderblick, and Henry Lee Co. remain. Today Chicago is fashion. From the fresh young talent not long out of design school, like Richard Dayhoff, Kate Jones, and Peggy Martin, to the long established designers rapidly gaining national notoriety like Maria Rodriguez, Mark Hester and Gina Rossi, Chicago is making a new fashion statement."[20]

OTHER MARKET CENTERS

Some other secondary centers, even further distant from New York in terms of both the value of output and the variety of merchandise, are Boston, whose manufacturers have developed a reputation primarily for well-made, moderate-priced classic sportswear and rainwear; and Philadelphia, for moderately priced classic sportswear and children's wear.

Apparel Marts: Regional Selling Centers

An industry development that began in the late 1970s is the marketing importance of **apparel marts**, or large regional selling centers. Located in major cities throughout the United States, their purpose is twofold: (1) to reach out for and sell to small fashion retailers in the surrounding areas and

(2) to serve as a wholesale selling facility for apparel producers, wherever the headquarters of the companies may be.

In addition to the lines of local producers, these marts house regional showrooms of hundreds of apparel firms from other parts of the country and even those of some foreign fashion producers. The showrooms bring the current and incoming seasons' lines of these companies within easy reach of the area's small retailers, most of whom do not have the time or money to go to New York more than once or twice a year, if that often. Buyers for nearby large retail organizations also find the marts a convenience, as it is often more practical to fill some of their special or urgent needs from a nearby source of supply.

Showrooms are leased both on a year-round basis or for temporary use during major seasonal buying periods. The temporary showrooms are particularly convenient during regional market weeks. Such weeks are scheduled periodically as a means of introducing the new lines of hundreds of out-of-town producers to the retailers of the area at the start of a buying season. Separate market weeks are usually held for different categories of merchandise and range in number from two to five a year. Merchandise categories include accessories, sportswear, intimate apparel, infants' and children's wear, and dresses, among others. A typical calendar of market weeks in major marts is included in this chapter.

The past two decades have seen Los Angeles, Dallas, Atlanta, and Chicago emerge as important regional selling marts, challenging what was once New York's exclusive domain. To attract buyers to market weeks, these marts stage many special events, such as fashion shows, merchandising seminars, and entertainment galas.

THE DALLAS APPAREL MART

Source: Reprinted with permission of the Dallas Market Center Co.

THE DALLAS APPAREL MART

Considered to be the largest of its kind, the Dallas Apparel Mart covers four city blocks on a 20-acre site—in addition to a recently opened menswear facility of 400,000 square feet. The mart houses over 2000 exhibitors of women's, men's, and children's apparel and accessories and shoes along eight miles of corridors. Among its occupants are many prominent designer-name companies. The showrooms are grouped by merchandise category, and annually book orders approaching $2 billion. Its showrooms include 1000 that are permanently occupied, and another 5000 that are taken by exhibitors on a temporary basis. To maintain a flow of customers for these exhibitors, the mart spends many millions on promotion.[21]

Although large Texas retailers such as Neiman Marcus and Sanger Harris may shop this mart, the typical and best customers of any mart are not the buyers from major stores, but a host of small independently owned specialty store retailers from the surrounding areas. Dallas draws these customers primarily from Arkansas, Louisiana, Oklahoma, and Texas as well as others from western and southern states. It is interesting to note that many New York firms "test" their new lines there just before presenting them in their New York showrooms.

THE CALIFORNIA APPAREL MART

Located in Los Angeles, the California Apparel Center contains some 1200 permanent showrooms, plus 300 or so that are available for temporary rentals. This mart is not only a regional selling facility for New York manufacturers, but it is also the showcase for West Coast producers whose merchandise is not exhibited in other marts or even shown in New York. Retail buyers are drawn from the Southwest, the whole of California, Washington, Oregon, and New York.

Various incentives are offered to retail buyers to attract them to the mart: rebates on airfare or gasoline, free meals, and other inducements. Attendance is also promoted by means of a newsletter, a calendar of special events, and market directories. As a service to exhibitors, the mart also publishes a buyer registration list, which manufacturers can use as a mailing list.

THE ATLANTA APPAREL MART

The newest of these apparel selling centers is the Atlanta Apparel Mart, which opened in 1979 and contains some 1200 permanent showrooms, plus several hundred temporary ones. The facility has 1.2 million square feet, on seven floors, each of which is assigned to a specific type of apparel. At each major market period, fashion designers from all over the country are brought in to show their lines to the visiting retail buyers. Such designers have included Oleg Cassini, Bill Atkinson, and Bill Tice. There are also seminar programs, run by industry professionals and outside management consult-

1986 MARKET WEEKS

Below is the revised schedule of 1986 market weeks for women's and children's wear in the various regional markets and New York. An asterisk (*) denotes a combined women's and children's market has been scheduled. In cities where more than one market is being held, the sponsoring organization for each is listed. Dates are subject to revision. Readers are advised to check with the mart prior to a scheduled show.

	Summer	Fall I	Fall II	Resort	Spring
ATLANTA (Atlanta Apparel Mart)	Jan. 31-Feb. 5	April 11-16	June 13-18	Aug. 22-27	Oct. 31-Nov. 5
BIRMINGHAM, Ala. (Civic Center)	Jan. 19-21	March 23-25	June 1-3	Aug. 10-12	Oct. 26-28
BOSTON (Bayside Expo Center)	Jan. 12-15	April 6-9	June 1-4	Aug. 24-27	Oct. 26-29
CHARLOTTE (Carolina Trade Mart)	Jan. 25-29	April 5-9	May 31-June 4	Aug. 16-20	Oct. 25-29
CHICAGO* (Chicago Market Apparel Center)	Jan. 18-22	March 22-26	May 31-June 4	Aug. 16-20	Nov. 1-5
DALLAS* (Dallas Apparel Mart)	Jan. 24-29	April 4-9	May 30-June 4	Aug. 15-20	Oct. 24-29
DENVER* (Denver Merchandise Mart)	Jan. 17-20	April 4-7	June 6-9	Aug. 8-11	Oct. 31-Nov. 3
KANSAS CITY* (Kansas City Market Center)	Jan. 10-14	April 11-16	May 30-June 3	Aug. 1-5	Oct. 17-22
LOS ANGELES (California Mart-Pacific Coast Travelers)	Jan. 17-21	April 11-15	June 6-10	Aug. 22-26	Oct. 31-Nov. 4
children's market (California Mart)	Jan. 19-22	April 13-16		Aug. 24-27	Nov. 2-5
MIAMI (Miami International Merchandise Mart)	Jan. 11-14	April 19-22	June 7-10	Aug. 9-12	Oct. 18-21
(Infant & Children's Wear Exhibitors Inc.,Southern Mart)			May 4-6	Aug. 31-Sept. 2	Nov. 16-18
(Southern Apparel Exhibitors, Inc.)	Jan. 11-14	April 19-22	June 7-10	Aug. 9-12	Oct. 19-21
MINNEAPOLIS* ** (Hyatt Merchandise Mart)	Jan. 19-22	March 9-12	April 6-10	Aug. 3-6	Oct. 26-30
PITTSBURGH (Pittsburgh Expo Mart, Monroeville)	Jan. 19-21	April 13-15	June 8-10	Sept. 7-9	Nov. 2-4
children's market		March 16-18	April 20-22	Aug. 10-12	Nov. 16-19
PORTLAND, Ore.* (The Galleria)	Jan. 19-21		April 13-15	Aug. 3-5	Nov. 2-4
NEW YORK	Jan. 27-31	March 3-7	April 28-May 9	Aug. 4-8	Oct. 27-Nov. 7
SAN FRANCISCO (San Francisco Concourse)	Jan. 11-14	April 5-8	May 31-June 3	Aug. 23-26	Nov. 15-18
(San Francisco Fashion Exhibitors, Hyatt-Regency)	Jan. 11-13	April 5-7	May 31-June 2	Aug. 23-25	Nov. 15-17
(San Francisco Children's Wear Association)	Jan. 12-15	March 16-19	May 4-7	Aug. 24-27	Nov. 16-19
SEATTLE (Seattle Trade Center)	Jan. 25-28	March 22-25	May 17-20	Aug. 16-19	Nov. 8-11

** A show for bridal and other merchandise will also be held in Minneapolis, June 8-11

ants, in addition to fashion shows and entertainment specials. Besides using direct mail pieces and brochures, and advertising in trade publications, the Atlanta mart sends leasing agents to New York to make direct contact with potential showroom occupants.

The primary draw for the Atlanta Mart is among the southeastern states, but attendees come from as many as 30 states to shop there. As in all the other marts, Atlanta's principal customers are small retailers.

THE CHICAGO APPAREL CENTER

The Chicago center, owned by the Kennedy family, is a 25-story building, opened in 1977. It has 11 floors of showrooms, plus a hotel, and a 140,000-

square-foot exhibition hall. There is also a 3000-square-foot exhibit, set up as a model retail store, to offer ideas for store plans, fixturing, color effects, and the like.

Some 3000 resources are represented on a year-round basis. These span all price levels and cover a wide spectrum of manufacturing firms from all over the country. Included are children's wear, furs, accessories, men's, and women's apparel. Among the year-round tenants are such designer firms as Oscar de la Renta, Geoffrey Beene, Yves St. Laurent, and others of similar stature. As in other marts, there are several hundred additional showrooms available for temporary rentals.

Among the Chicago Mart's promotional events, is a center-sponsored "Chicago Is" fashion showing of 29 Chicago-based, designer-named manufacturers' lines.

GENERAL MERCHANDISE MARTS

In addition to the specialized apparel marts described above, there are general merchandise marts in other cities. Such marts include but do not specialize in apparel showrooms. Like the specialized marts, these more general ones serve as regional selling centers and house both permanent and temporary showrooms for local, national, and international producers. And, like the apparel centers, the general merchandise marts hold regularly scheduled market weeks, which are attended mostly by small retailers in their regions. Some examples are the Miami Merchandise Mart, the Carolina Trade Mart in Charlotte, North Carolina, the San Francisco Mart, the Kansas City Trade Center, and the Radisson Center in Minnepolis.

Future of New York

Although more of the buying and selling action has moved to regional apparel marts. New York is still firmly entrenched as the key marketplace of the United States because it offers buyers their choice of over 175,000 lines of goods, an amount that no other area can ever begin to match. It still remains to be seen whether or not the proliferation of regional selling offices will affect the frequency with which buyers for major stores throughout the country shop the New York market.

In any event, the marts have proved not only a boon to the smaller stores in the areas surrounding them, but also a source of sales to firms who lease showrooms in them. As an executive of Halston Originals once explained it: "There's no way we can show our clothes as well in Dallas as we can in New York, but they buy. Last year we sold half a million dollars worth that we wouldn't have otherwise sold."[22]

There is talk of possibly building an apparel mart on 42nd Street in New York City. Whether or not New York should have a mart of its own is a question that is causing controversy on Seventh Avenue. Some manufacturers believe such a mart would help New York business. A greater number, however, feel it would be a bad move to further concentrate showrooms in an already highly congested area. They believe, moreover, that such a building is not needed because the New York garment center is, in effect, just such an apparel market. Another argument against the idea is that, whereas other cities house only showrooms, New York firms still use their headquarters facilities as design rooms, sample rooms, for shipping, some cutting—as well as for showrooms.

As the executive director of the Federation of Apparel Manufacturers has put it: "The huge variety of apparel in the New York market, over 176,000 lines, is more than what is available in all the apparel markets around the world combined, from Hong Kong to Atlanta and more."[23] Nevertheless, more and more New York-based manufacturers continue to show their merchandise not only at home base, but also in facilities closer to its eventual destination.

CHILDREN'S WEAR

In the not-too-distant past, when children were expected to be seen but not heard, they were dressed in miniature versions of adult apparel. Parents chose their clothes. Today, largely as a result of their exposure to television, children have become customers in their own right and have definite opinions about the toys they want, the foods they eat, and the clothes they wear. This "liberation" of children has had a direct effect on the styling of children's wear.

Nature of the Industry

The development of the children's wear segment of the industry and its methods of operation, as far as the preparation of seasonal lines and the production methods used, follow the same pattern as the women's sector. However, the children's industry has a relatively small volume of output, many fewer companies, is less competitive, less aggressive in its marketing practices, and more emphasis is put on ages of their customers.

There are close to 1000 establishments that produce children's wear. The total value of output is over $3 billion.[24] With the notable exception of a few giant firms such as Carter and Healthtex, the majority of companies are small. Most manufacturers produce three collections per year—spring/summer, fall, and holiday.

A relatively recent development in the 1970s was the entrance into some phase of children's manufacturing by large-scale multiproduct adult apparel companies such as Russ Togs, Liz Claiborne, Jordache, Levi Strauss, and Esprit. As discussed previously, these large producers set up separate divisions for each of their product categories, and children's wear is no exception. The design, production, and marketing of children's products has its own division in these firms. Most children's wear companies are located in New York, but there is a substantial contingent in the Miami fashion industry.

Industry Specializations

As in the women's wear industry, manufacturers tend to specialize by price range, sizes, and types of merchandise. In terms of price levels, most companies fall into low, moderate, or higher priced categories. In regard to type, the most common specializations are by age/size groups rather than by merchandise categories. Children, it should be understood, have different body proportions at different stages of growth, and their garments must be designed accordingly. For example, two girls of the same height and weight may require garments from different ranges, because one still has toddler proportions and the other has small-girl proportions.

Thus, the size ranges are related to the age or stage of growth. The following sizes are the same for girls and boys:

Infants: 3 to 24 months
Toddlers: T2 to T4

From children's size 4, the sizes for the two sexes diverge. Children's sizes for girls go from 4 to 6x, then go on to girls' 7 to 14, and preteen, 6 to 14. Boys wear is sized 4 to 7 and 8 to 12, and their garments are made in the children's wear industry. When they pass this age and size, however, the boys move into the menswear industry, wearing boys' sizes 14 to 20, and going on to young men's and students' wear.

In a large retail store, each age/size grouping is often in a section of its own, usually within the infants' and children's department, and usually under one buyer unless the store is quite large. Clothes for boys who have outgrown the children's size ranges are generally bought, displayed, and sold with or near menswear.

Marketing Activities

Marketing practices are similar in many respects to those of the women's wear industry. For example, seasonal lines are presented in showrooms, at company headquarters, and sometimes also at regional marts. The merchandise, however, is not usually dramatized and accessorized as is done in the women's industry. Advertising and sales promotion are relatively minor, with the exception of the few very large firms, like Healthtex and Carter, who have made their names well known through national advertising. Most producers in this industry leave consumer advertising to the retail stores.

CHILDREN'S WEAR ANNUAL
MARKET SHOW

140 DAYS TILL SEPT. 10-14, 1986

23rd ANNUAL MARKET SHOW
FLORIDA CHILDREN'S WEAR MANUFACTURERS' GUILD

Featuring the latest in
Sportswear / Swimwear / Playwear / Dresses / Accessories

ONLY IN MIAMI CAN YOU SEE IT ALL!

DORAL COUNTRY CLUB

Co-sponsored by

EASTMAN CHEMICAL **Kodel**
PRODUCTS, INC. polyester
KODEL is an Eastman Kodak Company reg. TM
FOR INFORMATION WRITE OR CALL:
F. C. W. M. G. Suite 203
3050 Biscayne Blvd. Miami, Fl 33137
305/573-0831 & 305/573-0832

Dress Them in Florida Made Fashions!

EASTERN Airlines, the Official Airline for the
Florida Children's Wear Manufacturers' Guild.
Call for lowest available fare or 35 percent off daycoach fare.
800-282-0244 in Florida and 800-468-7022 Nationally
Refer to easy access No. EZ9P46.

Source: Reprinted with permission of the Florida Children's Wear Manufacturing Guild.

The industry has its own specialized publications: *Earnshaw's, Girls and Boyswear Review, Kids Fashions*, plus a weekly section in *Women's Wear Daily*. All of these focus on trade and product news and carry advertising to the retail trade.

There are three trade shows a year, held in New York, at each of which more than 350 lines are usually exhibited. This is the National Kids Fashion Show, which is in addition to the annual Miami trade show mentioned previously.

As in the women's industry, the licensing name game is very much in evidence and is increasing in importance. Today, many children's wear manufacturers have licensing agreements with both European and American designers. European luminaries like Dior, Yves St. Laurent, Givenchy, and Cardin have licensed their names to producers of higher-priced children's wear, as have Ralph Lauren and other American designers. Also important is character licensing—a trend so rampant in the industry that very few tee shirts, sweatshirts, sleepwear, and similar items are without the licensed name of a Strawberry Shortcake, Mickey Mouse, Hello Kitty, Snoopy, Cabbage Patch Kids, Miss Piggy, Star Wars . . . *ad infinitum*!

COMPETITION FROM IMPORTS ....

Until the 1960s, almost all ready-to-wear purchased by American consumers was produced in the United States by our domestic industry. Imports of apparel products were not of significant size, in either quantity or value, and much of what was brought in from abroad was of poor quality, intended for the extreme low end of the market. Beginning in the mid-1950s, and continuing at a rapidly accelerating pace through the 1960s and 1970s and into the 1980s, apparel imports have been gaining at a rate appalling to the American industry.

These figures tell the story: In 1960, we imported $304 million in clothing for men, women, and children. By 1970, the figure had climbed to $1.3 billion. In 1979 it had reached $5.1 billion. In 1985, imports of such merchandise had grown to a staggering $15.7 billion.[25]

Impressive as the dollar figures are, attention should be paid also to the percentage relationship between domestic production and apparel imports. This is known as the import penetration, a way to measure foreign against domestic goods. In 1961, it averaged 3.9 percent for all women's and children's garments, and varied by category from a low of 0.2 percent to a high of 25.8 percent. By 1978, the import penetration had reached 31.1 percent for the industry as a whole, ranging from 2.5 percent to 119.1 percent for individual categories. In short, for some categories, our imports exceeded our domestic production by almost one-fifth. Since then, the overall figure for imports has grown to an amount equal to 50.6 percent of U.S. production, ranging from 8 to 174 percent for individual categories. The highest, the 174 percent figure, is for items like sweaters and cotton jackets.[26]

What these figures mean is that, overall, for every 1000 garments produced in this country, an additional 506 are imported. That is massive competition indeed, and it is causing the industry to call on the government to exert such pressure as it can to stem the tide.

The subject of imports will be discussed in detail in the later chapter on foreign fashion producers. At this point, it is sufficient simply to realize the enormity of the problem.

Readings

Success in the women's and children's apparel field means knowing one's customer, of course. But it also means knowing when, where, and how to expand, and keeping an eye on markets and marketing.

Style, Image—and Data Processing

The young, confident, business-oriented woman of the 1980s is Esprit's target customer. In the years since it started, Esprit has become a $350 million operation spanning more than 20 countries.

Liz the Wiz

Intelligent involvement in the retail merchandising of her line is an element in the success formula of Liz Claiborne, who combines knowledge of the business with knowledge of the customer.

Acquisitions, Distribution Policies Spur VF Growth

When a company grows at a rate far exceeding that of the industry as a whole, it must be doing something right. This article examines the strategies of VF Corp., parent of Vanity Fair, H. D. Lee, Bassett-Walker, Modern Globe, and Troutman Industries.

Making It on the West Coast

Manufacturing firms and apparel marts combine to make California second only to New York as a center for woman's fashion producers in the United States. Some say the area accounts for 35 percent of the country's wholesale apparel business.

Murjani and Coke: Hoping for Another Classic

Having made a fabulous success with the Gloria Vanderbilt name on jeans, the company is licensing a brand name that is new to the fashion field, but known the world over: Coca-Cola.

Style, Image—and Data Processing
by Mike Ferguson

"We don't sell apparel. We sell a way of life."

San Francisco-based Esprit enjoys quoting that slogan, which to an outsider seems to apply as much to the company as to its product line. In the 15 years since it was started, Esprit has become a $350 million operation.

Esprit now has operations in more than 20 countries on five continents, and employs more than 1,000 people in the San Francisco area alone. The company also operates a score of showrooms across the U.S.A.

MAXIMUM QUOTAS. Because retailers continue to clamor for the firm's products, Esprit has imposed maximum quotas on its sales reps in an effort to hold down excess demand.

"It costs us some good sales people, but it was a necessary step," said Guy Chamberlain, manager of technical services. "Customers were getting mad at us because we didn't always have enough merchandise to fill their orders."

RETAIL OUTLETS. By early 1985 new Esprit retail outlets will be open for business in Los Angeles and New Orleans, and one is slated for New York later in the year—a large step for a company that has been exclusively a wholesaler and mail-order merchandiser. Management looks upon this move as just another step along what for most of the last decade has been a very smooth yellow brick road.

But the path hasn't always been without hurdles. A 1976 fire gutted the company's venerable headquarters building near downtown San Francisco, leaving only its brick walls standing. From the ashes rose a spectacular new interior of natural beams, greenery and skylights, its block square expanse broken by hexagonal, free-standing offices of glass.

After the fire the company needed only three days to get back in business. Its backup computer tapes had survived the 500 degree heat inside a sturdy safe, and shipments went out virtually on schedule.

Redirection

As the 1970s ended, the company was still relatively small ($100 million annually) by today's standards. What has happened in the last four years to triple Esprit's gross?

"We completely redefined our company," Chamberlain explained. "We changed almost everything including our name."

Until then, the firm had done business as Esprit de Corp., a play on a familiar phrase that had started as a joke. Management came to see the name—and quite a bit else about the company—as decidedly cumbersome.

CREATING DEMAND. "We became tired of supplying demand," president Doug Tompkins said later. "We decided we needed to create demand instead."

Within months after changing its name to Esprit, the company had wholly redirected its image. Along with new graphics and a new photography concept, the firm consolidated its product line from eight labels (including the

Source: Reprinted with permission from the January 1985 issue of *Bobbin Magazine*, a publication of Bobbin International Inc. (*Author's note:* Esprit discontinued its direct mail operation in fall 1985.)

well-known Sweet Baby Jane, Plain Jane and Rose Hips) to four (Esprit, Esprit Sport, Esprit Kids and Esprit de Corp. Shoes).

In short order Esprit had come into keen focus—to itself, the retailer and the customer. Its apparel was designed for the young, confident, fitness-oriented woman of the 80s. Business boomed.

DIRECT MAIL. In 1981, design director Susie Tompkins had just distributed another wholesale catalog when an entirely new merchandising idea occurred to her. Why not revise the catalog for mail order, she proposed, and send it direct to customers? Soon Esprit was in the direct mail business. By 1984 it was mailing 10 million catalogs a year, and this new side of the business was grossing nearly $20 million.

Of course growth like this required space and people. In 1983 mail order took over a large building across Minnesota Street from Esprit headquarters; the remainder of the floor space was dedicated to marketing and distribution. A year later mail order had commandeered the entire structure.

"That's what always happens around here," Chamberlain conceded. "We keep growing out of our facilities."

"For years we maintained a greenhouse on the premises that supplied the potted plants so important to our interior appearance. We finally closed it and turned the space into a conference area. We also converted a wood shop, where we made all our own office furniture, and a gymnasium into new office space."

Today Esprit owns a handful of buildings and property covering three acres in the immediate vicinity of its headquarters. In addition, it leases four warehouses, one as big as an airplane hangar and absolutely full of merchandise, according to Chamberlain.

A block square park includes one of the state's few grass-surface lawn tennis courts.

But space remains at such a premium that the factory outlet store has been moved several streets away, and parking is always a problem.

Computers

"None of this could have happened without computers," Chamberlain said. "I've concluded that data processing is as important a part of Esprit as its styles and image."

Chamberlain is hardly exaggerating. If the old IBM System's response after the 1976 fire was not sufficient evidence of the importance of computers, consider the job now done by two 4381 central processors and some 240 terminals and personal computers.

"Since 1979 we're tripled our gross and started a whole new mail-order business," he said. "A company that used to sell pants and blouses now offers belts, shoes, gloves, bags and caps as well. We've even added a whole new line of merchandise for children."

FULL-TIME JOB. Just keeping track of production would seem to be a full-time job. Cloth purchased in Italy or Mexico may become finished goods in India or Hong Kong. Time frames are so critical that the company sometimes charters jet freighters to deliver the merchandise from Asia to its San Francisco warehouses.

GAMBLER'S BUSINESS. In an interview several years ago, an Esprit manager, Henry Gruchacz, referred to the apparel industry as "a gambler's business." Chamberlain wholeheartedly agrees.

"And it's much more complicated today than it was when I came here in 1979," he stressed. "In those days, with fewer seasonal lines per year and longer lead times, we could actually take most of the orders *before* we started production. We knew what the demand would be.

"Today we have four distinct seasons and several lines per season. We're forced to guess—to start production before we know about demand. The computer is the only possible way to keep things straight at all, to make intelligent decisions about what needs to be done and when."

Data Processing

Five years ago the processor offered 500,000 bytes of information on line. The current system provides 80 times that amount to the firm's wide array of terminals. According to MIS director Ken Daly, Esprit presently has 125 IBM 3279 color terminals, 50 IBM personal computers operating as stand-alone units, and other 40 IBM PCs being used as terminals.

"We've also ordered 25 more terminals to add to that, which will give us a total of 240 terminals or PCs for use in our data processing network."

The personal computers are especially noteworthy. They can serve as full-fledged color terminals for one application and as stand-alone processors for the next job. They can receive stored facts from the central computers, then go off-line to process that information—a procedure known as "downloading."

The desktop-sized PC also can serve as an order-entry device in the field. Sales reps enter their orders during the day, then either send the diskettes physically to headquarters or dispatch by high-speed telephone link-up.

"We can issue our cuts by computer, with an IBM Series 1 overseas talking to a personal computer here," Chamberlain said. "It really helps shorten the production cycle."

INSTANT INFORMATION. As the order information is gathered, it becomes instantly available throughout the terminal network. Production and marketing people can find out

specifics: how many units have been ordered today versus yesterday; what specific styles; in what parts of the country (or world) a particular item sells well or poorly; how sales for certain lines compare with the previous year.

"Timeliness is so important," Chamberlain said. "With the computer, if we know how each item is selling and how many were cut, we can make late adjustments—extend or curtail manufacture of a certain garment or switch production from one to another within the same purchase order."

From these facts come the allocation of finished goods, including generating the picking ticket, the packing slip and the invoice. Based on merchandise available and customer preference, the system helps decide whether to ship a partial order or to pack and hold.

CUSTOMER SERVICE HOTLINE. Order entry and distribution information also support the company's customer service department hotline, where inquiries about deliveries, order changes and invoice problems are answered in a matter of seconds by employees using video terminals.

Esprit's wholesale customer base includes thousands of small boutiques, so credit authorization is an important application. By tapping into Dun and Bradstreet and other data bases, the computer helps keep credit problems to a minimum.

A separate application, maintained on a personal computer, tracks manufactured goods from shipment time until arrival and customers clearance. If the shipment does not arrive by the expected data, Esprit is immediately aware of the discrepancy.

Positioned for the Future

The final decade and a half of the 20th century will offer the most remarkable, innovative—and competitive—years the sewn products industry has ever seen. Esprit expects to thrive, not just survive, with its well-defined concepts of market identification, packaging and presentation. Esprit foresees grossing $800 million annually in sales by 1990—and its past projections have been notoriously conservative.

"We've spent the money and put in the time to get ourselves properly positioned for the future," Chamberlain said. "From an all-around company standpoint, we're confident that we'll be able to handle that kind of growth."

Liz the Wiz
by Rayna Skolnik

The First Commandment at Liz Claiborne, Inc., is "Satisfy Thy Consumer." The Second: "Support Thy Retailer." Zealous adherence to those two guidelines is paying off for the women's apparel marketer. Consumers have shown their gratitude by pushing sales for the nine-year-old company to $391 million in 1984, and the projection for 1985 is $520 million. Retailers are also enthusiastic. "It's my most important account because of its size and success," says Jack Schultz, executive vice president and general merchandise manager for the Dallas-based Sanger Harris department stores. Mark Shulman, senior vice president and general merchandise manager for I. Magnin, a group of specialty stores based in San Francisco, says, "I feel it is probably the best-run apparel company on Seventh Avenue today." (New York City's Seventh Avenue is considered the center of the garment industry.)

Like many other companies today, Liz Claiborne is targeting the working woman. The company was formed at a time—1976—when that market was beginning to explode. Liz Claiborne executive vice president, marketing, Jerome A. Chazen describes the company's customer as the "executive and professional career woman who is a little more updated in her taste level, as opposed to a very traditional customer who might wear structured suits and blouses with ties." A major reason the clothing is so appropriate for that customer is company president Elisabeth Claiborne Ortenberg, 56, who was a designer for a division of women's apparel marketer Jonathan Logan for 16 years.

Claiborne (as she is know professionally) says the company aims to "provide all [the consumer's] needs except for formal evening wear, coats, nightwear, and bathing suits. We can take her from the office to dinner to a casual setting to a very casual weekend." Although Claiborne does not actually design the clothing, she is the guiding spirit behind it.

"The result is clothing that meets the needs of the New York customer and the middle-American customer too," says Warren Hirsh, whose many years in the apparel industry included a stint as president of Murjani International, marketer of Gloria Vanderbilt jeans. Claiborne has given women fashion that is "up-to-date but not avant-garde," says Sanger Harris's Schultz. "It's not the cutting edge of fashion, but it's where fashion really sells."

Claiborne clothes, Chazen says, are classified in the "better" price range, which he places a couple of levels below "designer."

Source: *Sales and Marketing Management*, September 9, 1985. Reprinted with permission.

Skirts and slacks in Claiborne's "Spectator" clothing segment retail for $60–$100; jackets, $75–$150; and blouses, $40–$75. In the "Casual" line, skirts, slacks, and blouses are $40–$60. Sweaters in both categories are about $40–$80, and dresses are $90–$170. "What Claiborne does best is thoroughly understand the customer, her lifestyle, and the price she's willing to pay," says Carol Greer, senior vice president and general merchandise manager, ready-to-wear and shoes, for Rich's department store in Atlanta.

It sounds like an unbeatable combination, but Claiborne isn't taking any chances. The company works extensively with retailers to be sure that the clothing is merchandised effectively. Here again, the background of one of the company's principals is a factor. Chazen, 58, one of the founders of the company, spent many years in retailing and understands the needs of that side of the business.

The initial contact with retailers is at the Claiborne showroom, where all sales are made. There are as many as 65 salespeople in the showroom, but there is no road sales force calling on store buyers. That approach is a big plus for the company, Chazen says, because "we were able to establish relationships at a higher level almost immediately. On the road," he says, "a salesman is lucky if he sees the buyer. He almost never sees anyone above the buyer level because those people are busy. But when retailers come to New York," he continues, "top management often comes to see the market. So there's a much greater opportunity to meet these people." Chazen says that every major store president in the country visits his company several times a year. Store buyers still place the orders, however.

There are also cost benefits to making sales in the showroom, says Warren Hirsh, who in his early days was himself a road salesman. (He is now president of Greenwich Office, a growing chain of office equipment stores.) Operating without a road sales force is "the changing scene in the apparel industry," he says. "Because of the cost of travel, it is almost prohibitive" to have a road force. "So more companies have stronger showrooms and are eliminating the road force. But Claiborne never even started with one."

Frequent store visits are made, however, by a cadre of "travellers" who work with retail salespeople. "One of the biggest problems stores face today," Chazen says, is the "lack of trained people on the floor." The problem is especially acute, he says, in branch stores. "Buyers never even visit some of their branches, so people out there operate with blinders on. Stores pay the price in lost sales and in turning off the customer who is looking for help."

Claiborne's travellers—Chazen declines to say how many there are—try to combat those problems by running seminars and clinics for store personnel. They explain the company, its goals, and its fashion point of view. "The most important thing they get across," Chazen says, "is that we care about them and the consumer and we expect them to care in turn."

The people who come into the stores "keep us on our toes," says I. Magnin's Shulman. He says they shop and even take pictures. Then they'll send him a very detailed report on "how we're doing." They might, for example, say that it looked as though a store was short on Spectator wear. Shulman hastens to add, however, that such criticism is "meant to be constructive," and he considers it a plus.

Another way Claiborne aids retailers is with "Claiboards," booklets that list the names and style numbers, by style groups, of every item in the line. Claiboards are, says Chazen, "a road map of the way we put the line together." Initially those booklets also included pictures of all the items, but the booklets somehow fell into competitors' hands. So after about a year they were retricted to internal use only. Now retailers get the Claiboards Receiving Guide, which contains essentially the same information, but without photographs. Sanger Harris's Schultz says the Receiving Guides are "extraordinarily useful in helping us put the goods together." Chazen admits that some stores don't like the guides as much as they liked the earlier Claiboards.

There are, for example, the Liz Claiborne shops that management is helping stores set up on their selling floors so that items of clothing that are meant to be worn together can be displayed together. Liz Claiborne clothing is sold in 5,900 stores, 2,000 of which are department stores and account for 70% of the business. Management began setting up the self-contained shops about three years ago to get more "real estate in the stores," Chazen says, and because they are a "time-saver for the consumer."

Meanwhile, Claiborne management carefully monitors the results of its efforts. Systematic Updated Retail Feedback (SURF) reports come in weekly from 16 stores that represent a cross section of store sizes and geographical locations. Computer programs take the SURF data and "play with it in dozens of different ways to get a feeling for how the consumer is reacting to the merchandise we're shipping," Chazen says. "Most apparel manufacturers tend to identify the best-selling items in the line with how they're purchased by the retailer. We've discovered that there's often no relationship between what the retailer thinks and what the consumer buys." He adds, "I like to think that we use the cash register as the primary tool for market research."

As the company has grown, it has segmented its product line and diversified into new areas. The original category, sportswear, has been broken down into Spectator, Casual, and Lizwear. A "petite" division was created to offer clothing for women 5'4" and under. Then came dresses, and then girls' wear, under the label Lizkids. This month the company begins shipping its first line of men's clothing. It will bear only the Claiborne label, without the Liz, to avoid turning off any man who might not want to wear garments that carry a woman's name. The men's sweaters, shirts, and slacks "are outfits," Chazen says. "We insist that the stores buy and present them as a collection."

Dresses have sold exceptionally well. The line was budgeted to do $10 million in sales in 1982, its first year, and it did. The game plan was to grow to $13 or $14 million in 1983, $17 or $18 million in 1984, and then level off at $25 million a year or two after that. But the rules of the game were changed when sales hit $23 million in 1983 and $55 million in 1984. For 1985, Chazen says, "we anticipate sales in the neighborhood of $90 million." As the Seventh Avenue wags would say, that's a pretty good neighborhood to be in.

Diversification has also extended to licensing agreements for items including handbags, belts, shoes, and even bed linens. This fall, the company will begin contributing to the cost of the advertising it requires its licensees to run. Previously, advertising had been limited to coop, which will continue.

The company has just entered into a joint venture with Avon for a line of fragrances and cosmetics that is expected to debut early next year. Avon, Chazen says, "has fabulous research, development, and manufacturing facilities." Beyond that, it has "expertise in 26 foreign countries. If there are foreign sales in our future, Avon will make a good practical partner for us."

The continued diversification is both good and bad. Industry analyst Jay Meltzer of Goldman Sachs & Co. says that if the company is to continue to grow, "they'll have to diversify." At the same time, there are risks because management is "no longer just doing what it does best and knows well," he says.

With so many new projects under way, it is clear that Liz Claiborne "doesn't rest on its laurels," says Brenda Gall of Merrill Lynch, Pierce, Fenner & Smith. "They're open to anything that seems right for them." What's right for the company is presumably whatever will help Chazen reach his stated goal: "We want the consumer to be Liz-programmed forever."

Acquisitions, Distribution Policies Spur VF Growth
by Herbert Blueweiss

Apparel growth is estimated at two to three per cent a year in the U.S., real growth. But most companies feel their growth should be 5 to 10 per cent a year. For a company to advance two to three times more than consumer purchasing, it must be taking share of market from somebody else . . . or else improve internal efficiencies to achieve income comparable to an 8 or 10 per cent sales increase.

Those are the numbers that inspire marketing and merchandising strategies for VF Corp. . . . outlined and discussed during a conversation with Lawrence Pugh, chairman, and Robert Gregory, president. VF, a $1.167 billion corporation, parent company of Vanity Fair, H.D. Lee and the recently acquired Bassett-Walker, Modern Globe and Troutman Industries.

The acquisitions, they explain, were made on the basis of three criteria . . . "the companies produced basic and basic fashion merchandise, not what we consider fashion merchandise. They are low cost producers. And

they make products that we can assist them in marketing for future growth, based on Lee experience.

"We might also add that the assets of these companies can be used to complement other divisions . . . Modern Globe making fabrics for Vanity Fair . . . Troutman making bottoms for Lee. There's a synergy between the three acquisitions and the other divisions."

This fulfills one aspect of the growth strategy for VF . . . and that is to expand through the acquisition route. The other is to grow by taking market share from someone else, which means, for VF, looking at other forms of distribution.

The big question is what distribution policies to pursue to ensure the future, and both Pugh and Gregory make it very clear that "department stores are important to us. They represent about 20 per cent of Lee Co.'s $900 million volume and around 65 to 70 per cent of Vanity Fair."

But department stores have been battling

Source: *Daily News Record*, May 7, 1985. Reprinted with permission.

off-price and low-price stores, and this has set up all sorts of conflicts of interest for apparel companies vis-a-vis retailers.

Pugh elaborates "in deciding how we are to be positioned . . . we saw that department stores, going back about two years ago, were disappointed in jeans sell-through and in the impact they were making in jeans . . . and they began decreasing space for jeans.

"Yet we knew consumers wanted to buy jeans. So we made a decision to put them into Sears and Penney . . . and 1984 was a very good year in jeans for them because they had the product we knew consumers wanted to buy.

"Not just our brand. The consumer wanted jeans, and department stores had far less space devoted to jeans. What they had was mainly private label . . . and there was no choice available for consumers."

All manufacturers must deal with the realities of the retail world. And what they find are low cost concept stores growing and growing and taking share from someplace, as more and more consumers shop there . . . at Wal-Mart, Target, Mervyn's Family Dollar Stores, and so on.

At the same time department stores have continued their own expansion. Gregory provides some pertinent background to this development, pointing out "we supply basic and basic fashion needs. That's our product mix . . . and the value added is X-amount. But department stores with their expense structure need X-amount plus . . . so they have to shift into fashion goods which have a higher mark up. There is a constant pull internally, regardless of what consumer is saying, to move onto fashion merchandise . . . and there is constant stress on 'what's new?'

"It becomes most difficult to establish a product statement . . . and confuse the consumer.

"Furthermore, department stores may attempt to compete with mass marketing retailers in jeans . . . or basic like the white dress shirts, socks, underwear, lingeries . . . where the mark up is 30 or 35 per cent, and is profitable because of the tightly controlled cost structure. The department stores can't compete at 50 or 55 per cent and they can't live at 30 per cent . . . so they go to 40 per cent.

"The consequences are that the department stores don't get their mark up, and they don't get the same turnover as the mass marketing stores. Sooner or later they just get out of the product . . . or minimize it in favor of the higher mark up fashion merchandise."

Gregory takes note of requests made by department stores to make up the difference in mark up desired and mark up obtained, and adds "they take it out on the manufacturer, and then also expand private label programs."

Continuing to deal with the relative merits of different retail groups, both Pugh and Gregory explain "some aggressive discounters may not be the best merchants around, but mass marketing stores really make their money on a cost efficient distribution system.

"Department stores, on the other hand, have not concentrated on that type of efficiency. They take a different view of the world, preferring to consider themselves merchants, in the fashion business.

"The mass marketers are in the process of more efficiently distributing what the consumer wants . . . using highly advanced computerization and high-technology warehousing.

"If department stores could lower expenses at the bottom, they could then go over to 40 or 50 per cent mark up, and volume would go up X-amount."

There are department stores, say the VF executives, like Dillard's and Belk's, that spend time on being efficient rather than just on being merchants . . . and are in tune with what the consumer wants, and know their profile.

The VF strategy is to constantly and realis-tically examine the market, and put the proper pieces in place to continue the corporation on its growth pattern.

In 1986 VF acquired Blue Bell (Wrangler Jeans), putting it in direct competition with Levi Strauss as the largest jeans producer in the world.

Making It on the West Coast
by Mandy Behbehani and Steve Ginsberg

It started in 1853 in San Francisco when Levi Strauss fashioned heavyweight brown canvas into a pair of jeans. By the early 1900s apparel makers in Los Angeles started making knits and swimwear. Today California has mushroomed into the nation's second largest apparel center offering diversified products ranging from polyester doubleknits to 100 percent silk dresses. California boasts the world's largest apparel company, Levi Strauss & Co., and has several of America's fastest growing apparel manufacturers—Esprit, Ton Sur Ton, Jag, and Carole Little for Saint-Tropez West.

California's post-World War II population boom brought out many East Coast apparel entrepreneurs who recognized Sunbelt retailers' growing needs for lightweight goods that Seventh Avenue couldn't meet. Today there are approximately 3,500 apparel manufacturers in the state and with 170,000 employees rank as the the 10th largest industry in California. While accurate figures on the industry's overall wholesale volume are not available industry estimates put the total somewhere in the $6 billion range. Levi and Esprit de Corp. are the giants and together account for $3,600,000,000.

Other pioneers—along with Levi's—include Catalina, Cole, Graff California-wear, Elizabeth Stewart and Koret, now part of Levi's. Each play major roles today. Catalina was founded in 1909 as a knitwear house and gradually made the transition into swimwear and in the fifties into sportswear separates. Cole was a trend-setting swimwear house in the twenties, and Graff California-wear was probably the first pure sportswear house, opened in 1933. Lee Graff, president recalls, "when we started sportswear was unheard of, not even New York had a sportswear industry."

It was difficult starting in the post-Depression era and it was a slow climb until World War II. After the war the sportswear business exploded.

Bernie Brown has been working with Koret for 40 years and his uncle Joe founded the company in 1938. "In the early days we had California colors. California was only doing the lighter shades and we would put a California label on the casual wear. When my uncle got out here there were no sewing machines, but they really wanted to live here."

While misses' moderate-price sportswear

Source: "75 Years in Fashion, 1910–1985," *Women's Wear Daily* (Special Issue). Reprint permission granted.

and swimwear were the foundations for the market and remain pillars there has been significant growth recently in the junior, contemporary and career markets. Esprit de Corp. has become an international juniors juggernaut with worldwide sales hitting $900 million. Susie Tompkins, an owner and design director of Esprit said, "California is definitely a leader, and people listen to California now. And when you're listened to, you're more apt to speak up. I think people look to California as being optimistic, innovative, young, fresh and honest, and that's what the lifestyle is about these days."

Along with Esprit, the surging California junior companies include Santa Cruz, Organically Grown, Guess, Ton Sur Ton, Domino of California, Gunne Sax, Judy Knapp and Byer California. These companies have all spurted in the last five years and have picked up the volume slack after Bronson of California, the state's biggest junior house in the seventies, shut its doors unexpectedly in 1979.

Bronson's closing sent shock waves through the industry which are partially felt today. Leonard Rabinowitz, chairman of Carole Little for Saint-Tropez West, observes, "Bronson's closing hurt the industry because retailers depended on that company. The flaky 'only in California' image was reinforced. The retailers saw that lifestyle distractions could cause a company to close."

Rabinowitz in building Carole Little into a $43 million career dressing company has had to establish a strong New York presence, which many other California companies also are doing. "When we started there was Bronson, Lou Bella, Alex Colman and Phillippe handbags. They were big important resources in the market and they drew the buyers out. Today we can't do the volume we want without a major New York presence. We think of ourselves as a New York resource that ships out of Los Angeles."

The advantages of operating apparel companies in California, however, are many. The Pacific Rim nations are closer to California and many firms are producing goods in Hong Kong and Taiwan. Landed costs are less here. Los Angeles has been a magnet for Oriental and Hispanic immigrants and provided a large, quality labor pool. Los Angeles has always been a non-union town, and without major heating costs, manufacturers can keep overhead down. There has been adequate financing for start-up companies with Union and Mitsui Manufacturers Banks serving as important catalysts.

Although there are many more companies in the Los Angeles area, San Francisco has a high concentration of large volume companies. Of California's top 10 volume producers five are located in the Bay Area and include Levi Strauss ($2,700,000,000), Esprit ($900 million), Santa Cruz ($100 million), Gunne Sax, Ltd./Jessica McClintock ($75 million) and Fritzi of California ($72 million). Byer California is also a major volume San Francisco resource but owner Alan Byer declines to give any figures on his firm. Byer does say, "Twenty five years ago 90 percent of the industry was located in New York and probably 10 percent in California. The numbers today more likely look like 65 percent in New York and 35 percent on the West Coast. San Francisco is a very good market for the size of the industry. I don't believe anyone has the success ratio we have here."

The big houses in Los Angeles include Catalina ($115 million), Tomboy/Domino ($110 million) and Ton Sur Ton ($100 million). Jag did $55 million last year and is expected to finish 1985 around $100 million. These companies want to be recognized as international resources and constantly fight the stereotyped image of being provincial, casual wear California resources. Steve Gordon, chairman of Tomboy/Domino said, "I really fight the connotation of being a California resource. We happen to be here because that's where the pools of talent are and this is where we live."

Despite having successful fashion forward companies, the California market has yet to spawn a celebrity status designer of the SA ilk. The state does have three resident designers, Galanos, Bob Mackie and David Hayes who have done well but don't come close to the widespread consumer recognition of SA's top designers.

Press hype is partially blamed for the failure of California to produce a national fashion celebrity. Sid Morse, a partner in the California Mart observes, "There has been lack of press coverage and that has hurt the market tremendously. The New York fashion press has taken

a parochial attitude toward California designers who want to be called national commensurate with Calvin Klein."

Morse and his Mart have played an important role in consolidating the myriad companies in Los Angeles and making it easier for buyers. Since 1964 the mart has grown steadily and now has 2,000 showrooms and is the only 52-week-a-year showplace in the U.S. apparel industry.

San Francisco is not as well organized. The mart in downtown San Francisco has a few local manufacturers exhibiting and recently changed its name to "The Pacific Center." The women's apparel associations don't show at the mart forsaking it for the Concourse building and the Hyatt Regency Hotel.

Murjani and Coke: Hoping for Another Classic

"If we did it once, we can do it again."

This is Mohan Murjani's business mantra. What the 38-year-old chairman of Murjani International did was turn a name, Gloria Vanderbilt, previously unknown as a label in the apparel industry, into a brand that last year, Murjani claims, reached a total wholesale volume of $500 million for all Gloria Vanderbilt products.

Now, armed with a $12 million advertising and marketing budget, he is aiming to do the same, and more, with his firm's line of Coca-Cola sportswear. The line has already begun checking out of Speigel's fall winter catalog and is scheduled to hit most retail floors next month.

"Coca-Cola is a far greater business op-

portunity than Gloria Vanderbilt ever was or could be," said Murjani during an interview. Dressed in his requisite suit and tie, Murjani, normally self-contained, was very animated while discussing his plans for Coca-Cola sportswear in his corner office here at 1411 Broadway.

Seated facing a framed portrait of a Hindu saint he calls "Ma," and from which he says he draws daily inspiration, Murjani said, "Coca-Cola is already the number one brand name in the world.

"We didn't have to build it from scratch, the way we did Gloria.

"Consumer loyalty to Coke is even larger than the Coke people dreamed," Murjani said, referring to Coca-Cola's announcement this

Source: *Women's Wear Daily*, July 12, 1985. Reprint permission granted.

week that, in response to consumer pressure, it will reissue the old formula Coke soft drink as "Coca-Cola Classic" to coexist with the controversial newsmaking "New Coke."

Murjani may also divide its sportswear line into Coca-Cola Classic, consisting of base items with a long shelf life such as jeans and rugby shirts, and New Coke, composed of more fashion-forward merchandise, at the suggestion of Tommy Hilfiger, who designs the Coke sportswear along with Carol Anton. Anton was hired away from Esprit to design Coca-Cola clothes.

Building the Gloria Vanderbilt name into a licensor's dream was simply a matter of "taking marketing and making it work for you," Murjani said. He plans to do the same with Coke, capitalizing, he said, on the "fun" image Coke has built for itself over the years.

Murjani's $5 million advertising program for the Coca-Cola clothes has begun. A teaser campaign was launched in New York City bus shelters in June. Ads reading, "It's small" or "It's medium" or "It's large" and "It's coming soon to a body near you" were hung in the shelters. This month the ads will be changed to read, "It's Coca-Cola clothes and it's coming soon to a body near you." In August a national ad campaign with copy reading, "It's Coca-Cola clothes, now playing on a body near you," will be launched in national consumer magazines.

A television campaign will be launched in August. The advertising has been prepared by McCann Erickson, Coca-Cola's advertising agency for the past quarter of a century.

Besides the $5 million ad campaign, another $7 million has been allocated to marketing the clothes. This money is being put toward a Coca-Cola clothing store, scheduled to open here on Columbus Avenue and 73rd Street in September.

"We're looking at our stores as a marketing tool as opposed to a business," said Murjani. In addition to drawing attention to Coca-Cola apparel, Murjani said, the store will serve as a prototype for in-store boutiques retailers can set up in their stores for the line.

The new store, tentatively called Cocateria, is under construction. It will be set up like a fast-food operation. Customers will pick up trays, slide them down a counter and order clothes from salespeople dressed in red-and-white striped uniforms. Pictures of the clothes will hang on the wall behind the counter, the way photos of Big Macs and fries are displayed in McDonald's.

Not all stores are following this prototype, however. Macy's New York will open a Coca-Cola clothes shop resembling a diner in its arcade next month, said a store spokesperson.

Carson Pirie Scott & Co., Chicago, will open an 1,800-square-foot shop modeled after a Coca-Cola bottling plant in its flagship. Smaller versions of the bottling plant shop will be opened in Carson's branch stores, said James Meyers, vice president of advertising at the store. All the shops are scheduled to open Aug. 11.

Rich's, Atlanta, based in the same city as Coca-Cola, is opening a 4,000-square-foot "Coca-Cola section" in its flagship on Aug. 1, said Murjani. They will serve Coca-Cola beverages and will have a Coca-Cola shop similar to the free-standing prototype within this section, Murjani said.

In the freestanding Coca-Cola store, all of the selling will take place in the store's basement and will not be visible from the street. Only a bridge spanning the sales floor and five large video screens will be visible from outside.

The entrance to the 1,000-square-foot three-level-floor-through will be on 73rd Street.

Once the customers enter the store, they will be handed a "menu" listing the store's inventory and its prices. They must cross the bridge to get to the staircase leading to the basement. On their way across, they will pass two terminals connected to two of the video screens. Via these terminals they will be able to call up information on the Coke apparel— namely a large still projection of an item listed on the menu—its size, color ranges and the price.

The other three screens will continuously play kaleidoscopic videos that have no story line. They feature about a hundred segments of 1½ to three-minutes in length, which can be run in any order, so that what the consumer will see on the screen will be constantly changing. Floating around, appearing and disappearing on the screens will be dancers, geometric shapes, and, of course, Coca-Cola clothes.

Murjani believes these videos alone will cause people to "be crowded around the windows watching and lined up around the block waiting to get in to see what's going on inside."

Besides marketing its Coca-Cola clothes to the consumer, Murjani has also begun a large-scale corporate public relations campaign, marketing itself to the press, the financial community and to potential licensees and licensors.

In January it retained Mitchell-Manning as its public relations firm and through that firm has produced a video and an elaborate, heavy-stock print material, detailing Murjani's past, present and planned future.

Murjani International was founded in 1942 as a trading organization by Mohan Murjani's father. The firm set up its first manufacturing plant in Hong Kong in 1952. It continued to add factories, and when the quota system was set up in Hong Kong in 1958 Murjani was allocated approximately 10 million units of quota.

Mohan Murjani, one of four children, was born in 1947 in Hyderabad Sind, which was then in India and today is in Pakistan. He attended Babson College in Wellesley, Mass., graduating in 1967 with a business degree.

That same year, he joined his father in Hong Kong. "I arrived, and my father told me I was now the managing director of the company, which is the same as being president, and that was the end of my social life. Right there, I had to plow in and learn everything about the company."

As Murjani got to know the family business, he learned that he "hated being in the client-servicing business," he noted. "Although I was the head of a huge manufacturing organization, I found I was always at the hands of the importers. They can threaten you with pulling their business from you, and you have to do whatever they want.

"I wanted to control my own business," Murjani said. And so, he came to America and started the Gloria Vanderbilt jeans business in 1976. This past January, in a desire to "move beyond Gloria," Murjani divested itself of marketing responsibilities for Gloria Vanderbilt apparel by licensing that name for all categories of jeans and sportswear to the Jones Apparel Group.

Besides Coca-Cola clothes, Murjani markets Tommy Hilfiger men's wear, for which it is opening a freestanding store this month next door to the Coca-teria, Lois jeans and Pierre Balmain. It is trying to divest itself of its Roger Baugh men's wear, which Murjani called "too haute couture for us." It still has the license to the Elizabeth de Senneville name but is distributing that line only in Europe. The de Senneville line "just didn't work" in the U.S., said Murjani, citing prices that were too high.

Besides being a marketer and licensor, Murjani said he also wants his company to continue its growth as "a major production resource for U.S.-based manufacturers and retailers." Murjani owns 10 factories in Hong Kong and Macau that manufacture woven goods and employ 3,000.

Murjani also has a Far Eastern sourcing organization that will open a department in New York this September. "Our sourcing organization is the key to our being able to service almost unlimited volume levels," Murjani said. "It makes the Far East our oyster."

One-third of Murjani's needed manufacturing is done by its own facilities. The rest is contracted out. Jones Apparel Group and T.Y.C.E.S.A. are its major manufacturing clients, Murjani said.

The firm will continue to develop or acquire other designer or brand names to join those it already markets. "Major conglomerates that specialize in fields other than apparel are looking to divest themselves of their apparel divisions," Murjani said. "I would go out and buy almost any company, and the money is freely available."

Murjani has already taken the first step toward licensing the Coca-Cola brand in apparel related categories. It will soon announce that it has licensed Coca-Cola name to Swatch for watches which will wholesale for $15, said Murjani.

Murjani admitted that certain major retailers were less than receptive to Coca-Cola clothes. Indeed, the fact that "retailers' initial investments were much more conservative than we expected," rubbing against Murjani's goal of "major business immediately with Coca-Cola rather than a slow buildup," was what led Murjani to plan its freestanding store.

"We couldn't expect retailers to assume the same entrepreneurial risk that we can," said Murjani, a veteran to the scorn of retailers.

"They laughed at Gloria, too," he said. "Initially Bloomingdale's ordered only 60 pairs of Gloria Vanderbilt jeans, and that was only after great arm twisting.

"They were conservative with Coca-Cola clothes, but we'll be able to supply their reorders," he said.

Endnotes

1. Claudia B. Kidwell and Margaret C. Christman, *Suiting Everyone: The Democratization of Clothing in America*, published for the National Museum of History and Technology by the Smithsonian Institution Press, Washington, D.C., 1974, p. 15.
2. S. Freedgood, "$100 Million in Rags," *Fortune*, May 1962, p. 151.
3. U.S. Department of Commerce, annual studies of personal consumption expenditures.
4. U.S. Department of Commerce, *U.S. Industrial Outlook 1986*, pp. 48-5, 48-6; and Research Department, ILGWU, New York.
5. *Ibid.*
6. U.S. Department of Commerce, *Long Term Economic Growth 1860–1965*, October 1966, p. 84.

7. "Manufacturers Plugging into Videos," *Women's Wear Daily*, April 15, 1985.

8. Kurt Salmon Associates, presentation at Fashion Institute of Technology, New York, April 8, 1986.

9. Jacqueline McCord, "Restyling the Fashion Business," *Modern Bride*, December 1976.

10. "He's a Fashion Purist with the Golden Touch," *Business Week*, September 12, 1964, p. 64.

11. The Licensing Letter, Scottsdale, Arizona, May, 1986.

12. "Cartoons and Celebrities Showings Muscle," *Women's Wear Daily*, February 20, 1985, p. 28.

13. "Selling Their Good Names," *New York Newsday*, May 18, 1986.

14. "The City That Dresses a Nation," *New York Sunday News*, February 15, 1976. Speaker is Donna Karan, then a designer for Anne Klein, Inc.

15. *Los Angeles Herald-Examiner*, May 16, 1986.

16. "Dallas, The Business of Fashion," *Women's Wear Daily*, October 15, 1985, p. 6.

17. *Ibid.*

18. U.S. Department of Commerce, *Survey of Current Business 1986*.

19. "More Than Just Kid Stuff," *Women's Wear Daily*, April 16, 1983.

20. "Chicago Is," *Women's Wear Daily*, March 13, 1985.

21. "Dallas Mart: Marketing the Concept," *Women's Wear Daily*, May 26, 1985; and "Opportunity Calls Beyond Seventh Avenue," *Advertising Age*, May 1985.

22. "Trammel Crow's Fashions," *Forbes Magazine*, October 16, 1979, p. 46.

23. "Marts and Markets," *Stores Magazine*, New York, April 1983, p. 46.

24. Dun & Bradstreet, *Focus*, 1985 edition; ILGWU, and *U.S. Industrial Outlook, 1986*.

25. U.S. Department of Commerce, *U.S. Industrial Outlook 1980*, for 1979 figures; 1960 and 1970 figures from *Statistical Abstract of the United States*, 1971 edition, p. 778; *U.S. Industrial Outlook, 1986*.

26. Industry Surveys, *Textiles, Apparel and Home Furnishings*, Standard & Poor, May, 1986.

Selected Bibliography

American Apparel Manufacturers Association. *Focus—Economic Profile of the Apparel Industry*. Washington, D.C.: AAMA, 1985.

The Chinatown Garment Industry Study. New York: Local 23-25 International Ladies' Garment Workers' Union, 1983.

Daves, Jessica. *Ready-Made Miracle: The American Story of Fashion for the Millions*. New York: Putnam, 1967.

Dubinsky, David. *David Dubinsky: A Life with Labor*. New York: Simon & Schuster, 1977.

Fairchild's Market Directory of Women's and Children's Apparel. New York: Fairchild Publications, 1985 (revised periodically).

Frank, Bertrand R. *Progressive Apparel Production.* New York: Fairchild Publications, 1970.

Hall, Max. *Made in New York.* Cambridge, Mass.: Harvard University Press, 1959.

Hamburger, Estelle. *Fashion Business: It's All Yours.* San Francisco: Canfield Press, 1976.

Kidwell, Claudia B. and Margaret C. Christman. *Suiting Everyone: The Democratization of Clothing in America.* Washington, D.C.: Smithsonian Institution Press, 1974.

Lee, Sarah Tomerlin. *American Fashion.* New York: Quadrangle Press, 1978.

McCardell, Claire. *What Shall I Wear?* New York: Simon & Schuster, 1956.

Pope, Jesse E., ed. *Clothing Industry in New York.* New York: Bert Franklin Publishing, 1970.

Stein, Leon. *The Triangle Fire.* Philadelphia: J. B. Lippincott, 1962.

Vecchio, Walter and Robert Riley. *The Fashion Makers, A Photographic Record.* New York: Crown Publishers, 1968.

Walz, Barbara and Bernadine Morris. *The Fashion Makers: An Inside Look at America's Leading Designers.* New York: Random House, 1978.

Weitz, John. *The Value of Nothing.* New York: Stein and Day, 1970.

Trade Associations

Affiliated Dress Manufacturers, 1440 Broadway, New York, N.Y.

American Apparel Manufacturers Association, 1611 North Kent Street, Suite 800, Arlington, Va. 22209.

American Coat and Suit Manufacturers Association, 450 Seventh Avenue, New York, N.Y. 10123.

Bureau of Wholesale Sales Representatives, 1819 Peachtree Road, N.E., Suite 515, Atlanta, Ga. 30309.

California Fashion Creators, 110 East 9th Street, Los Angeles, Calif. 90015.

Childrenswear Manufacturers Association, 112 West 34th Street, New York, N.Y. 10120.

Costume Designers Guild, 11286 Westminster, Los Angeles, Calif. 90066.

Council of Fashion Designers of America, 1633 Broadway, New York, N.Y. 10019.

Federation of Apparel Manufacturers, 450 Seventh Avenue, New York, N.Y. 10001.

Infants' and Children's Wear Salesmen's Guild, 45 West 34th Street, Room 1102, New York, N.Y. 10001.

Infant and Juvenile Manufacturers Association, 100 East 42nd Street, New York, N.Y. 10017.

Infants', Children's, and Girls' Sportswear and Coat Association, 450 Seventh Avenue, New York, N.Y. 10123.

Ladies Apparel Contractors Association, 450 Seventh Avenue, New York, N.Y. 10001.

National Association of Blouse Manufacturers, 450 Seventh Avenue, New York, N.Y. 10001.

National Association of Uniform Manufacturers and Distributors, 1156 Avenue of the Americas, New York, N.Y. 10036.

National Association of Women's and Children's Apparel Salesmen, Inc., 401 Seventh Avenue, New York, N.Y. 10001.

National Dress Manufacturers Association, 570 Seventh Avenue, New York, N.Y. 10018.

National Knitwear Manufacturers Association, 350 Fifth Avenue, New York, N.Y. 10018.

National Knitwear and Sportswear Association, 51 Madison Avenue, New York, N.Y. 10010.

United Infants' and Children's Wear Association, 520 Eighth Avenue, New York, N.Y. 10018.

Trade Publications

Apparel News South, Atlanta, Ga. 30328.
Apparel South, 6285 Barfield Road, Atlanta, Ga. 30328.
Apparel World, 386 Park Avenue South, New York, N.Y. 10010.
The Bobbin, 1110 Shop Road, Columbia, S.C. 29202.
Boutique Fashions, 210 Boylston Street, Chestnut Hill, Mass. 01267.
California Apparel News, 110 West 40th Street, New York, N.Y. 10008.
Discount Merchandiser, 641 Lexington Avenue, New York, N.Y. 10022.
Earnshaw's, 393 Seventh Avenue, New York, N.Y. 10001.
Infants and Toddlers' Wear, 370 Lexington Avenue, New York, N.Y. 10010.
Kid's Fashions, 71 West 35th Street, New York, N.Y. 10001.
Teens and Boys Magazine, 210 Boylston Street, Chestnut Hill, Mass. 01267.
Women's Wear Daily, 7 East 12th Street, New York, N.Y. 10003.

CHAPTER REVIEW AND LEARNING ACTIVITIES

Key Words and Concepts

Define, identify, or briefly explain the following:

Apparel jobber   Conglomerate
Apparel marts   Contractor

5

THE MENSWEAR INDUSTRY

Until the 1950s, the average man's wardrobe consisted of one or more dark suits with vests, white shirts, subdued colored ties, highly polished shoes, an overcoat, and a hat. Whatever changes in fashion did take place usually expressed themselves in little more than variations in the width of lapels, the style and flap of a jacket pocket, and the location of a vent in the suit jacket. The industry that produced men's garments did not consider itself to be in the fast-changing business of fashion.

Change came dramatically after World War II. Surfeited with khaki drabness, many of the younger men yearned for color, even in undershirts. Suburban living, the shorter work week, and the trend toward family-oriented leisure activities set up a demand for sports and leisure wear and resulted in a much freer style of dress even during business hours. By the 1960s, the presence of a large and highly visible generation of young adults sparked a demand for greater variety, faster change, and new opportunities for expression of individuality. Through the 1970s and on into the 1980s, the winds of fashion change continued to blow up a storm in the men's field.

Today men's interest in fashion has become increasingly pronounced and the industry that serves them has responded accordingly. Obviously then, no book about the fashion business would be complete without a discussion of the menswear industry—the subject of this chapter and the readings that follow it.

ECONOMIC IMPORTANCE

The menswear industry's importance as a segment of the U.S. fashion business is demonstrated by such figures as these: more than 3000 separate companies are engaged in the production of men's and boys' clothing and furnishings. They employ over 300,000 people, more than half of whom are engaged directly in production activities. Factory output is estimated at above $16 billion, wholesale value, for 1985.[1]

Another measure of the importance of the industry is that there is scarcely an area of the United States in which it does not have production facilities. Some segments of the industry, such as tailored clothing, require highly skilled workers. Others, such as shirts and work clothing (including the ever-present jeans) can provide employment even for people with minimal skills, as long as they can guide a seam through a sewing machine.

Still another indication of the industry's importance: consumers spent $50 billion at retail in 1985 for men's and boys' clothing and accessories, exclusive of shoes. Not all of this originated in the domestic industry, of course, nor did all of the domestic industry's output necessarily go to consumers in this country.[2]

HISTORY AND DEVELOPMENT

The U.S. ready-to-wear apparel industry started with clothing for men; it was born in the early 1800s, almost half a century before women's ready-to-wear had its beginnings. Until that time, all men's apparel in this country was either custom tailored, for those who could afford this service, or was made at home for those less affluent.

Early Beginnings in the Nineteenth Century

Like so many other segments of the fashion industry, menswear manufacturing began with the efforts of some enterprising individuals who saw a need and proceeded to fill it. In this case, the need was to supply clothes for men who either had no access to the then-customary source of supply—the housewife's nimble fingers—or could not afford custom-made clothing.

DEVELOPMENT OF MEN'S READY-TO-WEAR

In such port cities as New Bedford, New York, Boston, Philadelphia, and Baltimore, a few venturesome tailoring shops conceived the idea of producing and selling cheap ready-to-wear trousers, jackets, and shirts for sailors who needed to replenish their wardrobes inexpensively and immediately during their brief stops in port. These clothes were poorly made in low-quality fabrics. The cutting was done in the dealers' shops and the garments were then sent out to local women for hand sewing.

This early ready-made clothing was referred to as "**slops**," a term from which the word "sloppy" developed, with the same connotation then as now. It was remarked that these garments "could be readily recognized about as far as the wearer could be seen. Hence, there was a sort of shame in the purchase and wear of such clothing, and it was considered almost disreputable to wear it; it was at once a reflection upon a man's taste and a supposed indication of his poverty."[3] Nevertheless, the market for ready-made clothing soon expanded to serve bachelors who had no one at home to sew for them and plantation owners who needed cheap clothing for their slaves.

FROM TAILORS TO MANUFACTURERS

Since no firms then existed that produced clothing for others to sell, these early shops functioned as both retailers and manufacturers. Some of the proprietors were custom tailors who produced ready-made garments from cheaper grades of cloth in addition to carrying on their primary business of made-to-measure clothing. Others cut the cloth on store premises and contracted to have the sewing done outside by people who worked at home.

As industrialization developed in the early nineteenth century, cities grew and a new mass market began to emerge among middle-class or white-collar city dwellers. To attract these customers, some of the more resourceful

**1849 ADVERTISEMENT FOR READY-MADE
MEN'S CLOTHING**

LABORING MEN, MECHANICS,
TEAMSTERS, &C.

WIL FIND BY FAR THE LARGEST ASSORTMENT OF
BAIZE JACKETS, OVERALLS, PANTALOONS,
GUERNSEY AND FLANNEL SHIRTS, &c.,
that have ever been collected in any Clothing Warehouse in Boston, at
SIMMONS' OAK HALL,

shop owners offered higher-priced and better-made garments. The quality of "store clothes" improved and their acceptance increased. By 1830, the market for "store bought" apparel had expanded so greatly that there were firms specializing in the manufacture of garments for others to sell at retail. The first steps in the establishment of the men's clothing industry as we know it today had been taken. By 1835, some manufacturers in New York City, then the nation's leading center for ready-made men's clothing, reportedly employed from 300 to 500 workers.[4] Boston, Philadelphia, Newark, and Baltimore also progressed rapidly as manufacturing centers, as did Rochester and Cincinnati, toward the middle of the century. Impetus was gained when the sewing machine was developed in the middle of the 1800s.

Among the early producers of men's ready-mades was one of today's most famous and prestigious retailers of men's apparel—Brooks Brothers. Founded in 1818 as a custom-tailoring shop, the company got its start in ready-to-wear during the early period of industrialization. By 1857, it employed 78 tailors who worked on the premises and more than 1500 outside workers.[5]

WORK CLOTHES FOR LABORERS

A development that contributed in a special way to the growth of the menswear industry was the Gold Rush of 1848, which drew thousands of men to the West to pan or dig for gold. Anticipating that these prospectors would need tents to shelter them, a man named Levi Strauss went to California with a supply of heavy fabrics from which to make tents. Among these fabrics was one from France, then called *de Nime*, later Americanized to denim. Seeing a need for work clothes, he used his fabrics not for tents but to make work pants that featured large back pockets to hold mining tools. When he added metal rivets to the pockets to hold them securely, the success of his pants was ensured. The menswear industry grew in a way typical of American frontier life—with work clothes for laborers. Aside from Levi Strauss's contribution, the industry grew generally as a result of the westward migration. The men who pushed the frontier westward, not just in California, but in the prairies and the Mountain States, became a promising market for ready-made clothing. Plants to produce such clothing developed in Chicago and St. Louis to meet the demand.

STANDARDIZATION OF SIZES

The manufacture of ready-to-wear is based on **standardized sizes** in sufficient variety so that almost any figure can be accommodated by one of them. In the early years of the industry, each manufacturer worked out his own set of sizes and made garments to his own specifications, hoping to fit as many people as possible. The fit of these early garments was far from perfect.

One of the biggest boosts to the men's ready-to-wear clothing industry came from the government orders for soldiers' uniforms during the Civil War.

Because hand sewing could not keep pace with the Army's needs, factories had to be built and equipped with the then new sewing machines. Also, in order to facilitate the production of its uniforms, the Army surveyed the height and chest measurements of over a million recruits, and thus provided the first mass of statistical data on the form and build of American men. After the war, the results of the Army study were made available to producers of men's civilian clothing. This put the sizing of men's ready-to-wear on a scientific basis and, by making improved fit possible, hastened the change from homemade and custom-made to factory-made garments.

Twentieth-Century Developments

By the time the menswear business entered the twentieth century, it was no longer an industry of small entrepreneurs; it had its share of large enterprises. As the present century progressed, there came such developments as unionization, public ownership, and, in time, a return to private ownership on the part of some of those who had earlier gone public.

"THE AMALGAMATED"—ACTWUA

Like the women's garment industry, the men's clothing industry presented a dismal labor picture at the beginning of this century, with sweatshops prevalent. Producers contracted to have the sewing of garments done outside their plants, either by individuals who did the work in their tenement homes or by contractors who gathered sewing hands together in equally uncomfortable and unsanitary lofts.

In 1910, a strike that started at the Hart, Schaffner & Marx plant in Chicago spread and eventually drew 35,000 workers from their jobs. Settlement of the dispute brought improved working conditions, reduced working hours to 54 hours a week, and set up machinery for adjusting grievances. A few years later, in 1914, the craft union that formerly represented the men's clothing workers yielded its place to the Amalgamated Clothing Workers of America, an industry union, and one that has established a record of labor peace and pioneering effort.

"The Amalgamated" worked for arbitration and industrywide bargaining; it sought stable labor relations with management as a means of keeping its people employed. It has encouraged scientific techniques in industry management, and it has provided extensive and innovative social welfare services to its members. The union points with pride to its relationship with that same Hart, Schaffner & Marx, at whose Chicago factory a strike triggered the events that led to Amalgamated's birth. For more than 50 years, that plant, now the world's largest in the men's clothing field, did not have a strike.

In the 1970s, the Amalgamated merged with the Textile Workers of America and the United Shoe Workers of America to form the Amalgamated

Clothing and Textile Workers Union of American (**ACTWUA**). Virtually all factories in the United States that produce men's tailored clothing (suits, tailored sports coats, formal wear, top coats, etc.) are unionized today. This is not true, however, of other segments of the men's apparel industry, such as sportswear. In that respect, the Amalgamated does not have control over its industry. In part, this situation arises because production of men's apparel is widespread throughout the United States; and in part, it is due to the varying patterns of production in the different segments of the industry.

PUBLIC OWNERSHIP IN THE 1960S

Until the 1960s, publicly owned firms were the exception rather than the rule in menswear. Just as was the case in women's apparel at that time, most concerns were individually owned enterprises, or partnerships, or closely held corporations. During the 1960s, many firms in the men's field went public, for much the same reasons as prevailed in the women's field. In some instances, it was a way for a proprietor with no family successor to ease his way into retirement; in others, it was a need for expansion capital. The lure of expansion capital is a strong one. Without it, firms can expand only to the extent that they plow back the profits of their operations year after year. Drawing on the public's invested capital is a faster way.

PRIVATE OWNERSHIP IN THE 1980S

Like the women's industry, in the ultracompetitive atmosphere of the 1980s, some major men's apparel producers began to see public ownership as more of a liability than an asset. Publicly owned companies have a responsibility to shareholders, and this includes public disclosure of new marketing plans and strategies to the extent that swift, silent changes of course are difficult to execute. Some firms, therefore, decided to go private—that is, to buy back their corporation's stock. In addition to Levi Strauss, Blue Bell and Palm Beach also took this step. By returning a company to the private sector, a firm is freer in decision making; it is no longer in the spotlight turned on public companies by investment experts; it is protected from the possibility of hostile takeovers.

NATURE OF THE INDUSTRY ....

The menswear industry, which also includes garments for boys and youths, resembles the women's wear industry in some ways and differs from it in others. Their points of resemblance include the following: (1) manufacturers usually specialize in clearly definable categories of garments; (2) producers in the various industry branches present seasonal lines; and (3) designer names are featured. Still another point of resemblance is the growing importance of collections that feature complete, coordinated groups of merchandise, all of which are produced, sold, and ultimately displayed in retail stores under a single brand or designer name.

Points of difference from the women's field are numerous: (1) the larger firms account for a greater share of the men's industry's total output; (2) manufacturers' brand names have been long established and are better known, more important to the consumer, and more influential in marketing than they are in the women's field; (3) the contracting system, so much a part of the women's field, is less common. On that last point, the growing importance of sportswear is increasing the use of the contracting system.

Finally, in the menswear field, many firms have expanded into women's wear, by either creating or acquiring women's divisions.

Industry Divisions

The menswear industry differs greatly from women's wear in that the distinctions between its traditional product divisions and the types of firms that they encompass are not as clearly defined. For example, a women's coat firm is not likely to produce separate slacks and jackets. In the men's field, however, a tailored clothing manufacturer will generally produce slacks, suits, and sports jackets as well as top coats. Another example: in the menswear divisional structure, firms making nightshirts and pajamas fall under the same classification as shirt producers instead of under the underwear division as in the women's industry. And to further the confusion, men's jeans are still being classified under work clothing instead of under the separate trousers division. Be that as it may, the major divisions, as classified by the government and industry alike and for which statistics are available, are as follows:[6]

1. *Tailored Clothing*. This division includes firms that are primarily engaged in manufacturing men's, youths', and boys' *tailored* suits, jackets, slacks, and overcoats. Also included in this classification are firms primarily engaged in manufacturing uniforms.

   In the lexicon of the men's apparel industry, the term **tailored clothing** refers to structured or semistructured suits, overcoats, sport jackets, and separate slacks, the production of which involves a number of hand tailoring operations. This division at one time so dominated the industry that, to the consumer, the term "men's clothing" was synonymous with tailored clothing.

2. *Shirts (Except Work Shirts) and Nightwear*. This division includes establishments primarily engaged in manufacturing shirts (including dress shirts, tee-shirts, and sport shirts) and nightwear for men and boys.

3. *Work Clothing*. Comprises firms primarily engaged in the manufacturing of

THE MENSWEAR INDUSTRY: AN ECONOMIC PROFILE

SIC[a]	Men's and Boys'	Wholesale Value of Shipments (add 000,000)	Total Employment in Thousands
2311	Tailored Clothing	$3,165	62.0
2321	Shirts and Nightwear	3,355	78.8
2327	Separate Trousers	2,532	50.3
2328	Work Clothes (including jeans)	5,101	60.6
2329	Clothing n.e.c.[b]	1,700	44.6
2323	Neckwear	355	6.7

[a]Standard Industrial Classification (SIC) numbers are assigned to various segments of the industry by the Bureau of the Census, for convenience in collecting and reporting statistics.
[b]N.e.c. means "not elsewhere classified;" this includes heavy outerwear and sweaters.
Source: U.S. Industrial Outlook, 1986.

jeans, work shirts, work jackets, and overalls. Many garments produced in this division, which originally were used as functional work clothes, are now commonly considered to be sportswear.

4. *Separate Trousers.* This division includes firms whose major business is the production of separate pants only, including both dress and casual slacks.
5. *Men's Clothing Not Elsewhere Classified.* Firms classified under this division include producers of swimsuits, skiwear, hunting and field jackets, suede and leather sports jackets, mackinaws, and rainwear.
6. *Boys' Wear.* The men's industry also includes clothing for older boys and youths. (Boys up to age five are considered part of the children's field.) Size ranges are 7 to 14 and 12 to 20. Men's apparel is adapted to their needs, with special emphasis on sportswear—jeans, tee-shirts, jogging suits, shirts, and jackets.

Dominance of Large Firms

There are more large firms in menswear than in women's apparel. The men's industry has firms that do half a billion dollars or more in sales a year, and these big companies do a greater share of their industry's total business than the big women's firms do in their field. Nevertheless, although there are several menswear firms whose individual annual sales figures exceed $2 billion, these are no match in size for such companies in other fields as Procter & Gamble, with its $8.1 billion a year, or Philip Morris, with its $9.6 billion a year.

MAJOR MENSWEAR PRODUCERS: SELECTED EXAMPLES

Company	1985 Sales (add 000,000)	Principal Menswear Product
Levi Strauss, San Francisco	$2,584	Jeans, sportswear
Interco, St. Louis	2,508	Outerwear, sportswear
Hartmarx, Chicago	1,111	Tailored clothing
Cluett Peabody, New York	866.4	Arrow shirts
Oxford Industries, Atlanta	514.5	Shirts, sportswear
Palm Beach Industries, Cincinnati	419.9	Tailored clothing
Philips–Van Heusen, New York	550.4	Shirts, sportswear

Source: Fortune 500, *Fortune,* April 28, 1986 issue, © 1986 Time Inc. All rights reserved.

A table in this chapter lists some of the major menswear firms, along with their respective sales volume figures and an indication of the menswear that they produce.

Many menswear firms have grown large by opening up new divisions, or acquiring other companies, or both. One example is Levi Strauss, which started in the menswear business and expanded into women's and children's jeans and other sportswear separates. Other large menswear producers have also entered the women's apparel field in the course of expansion. Thus, Cluett Peabody, initially simply the producer of Arrow Shirts, and still the country's largest producer of men's shirts, has expanded through acquisitions and new divisions into sports shirts, underwear, jackets, sweaters, slacks, hosiery, and women's wear. Among their acquisitions were the boys' wear firm of Donmoor and the men's tailored clothing company, J. Schoeneman. Another multiproduct company that has grown out of menswear is Manhattan Industries, once manufacturers solely of Manhattan Shirts for men. Divisions of that company now include Vera Industries, Perry Ellis, Henry Grethel, and John Henry.

Geographic Locations: Decentralized

Unlike the women's industry, menswear firms are not heavily concentrated in New York City but are widely distributed throughout the United States. The industry's largest, Levi Strauss, is headquartered in San Francisco. **Hartmarx**, a major producer of tailored clothing, is headquartered in Chicago. Philadelphia is headquarters for Greif & Company, After Six, and Pincus Bros. Maxwell. In the Pacific Northwest are White Stag and Pendleton. Haggar and Farrah are in Texas. Oxford Industries is one of the many companies in the South. Production facilities, as well as headquarters offices, are so widely scattered that the industry is truly national and there is scarcely a state that is not involved in menswear. All the firms mentioned, however, have showrooms in New York City, as do many, many others.

IMPORTANCE OF NEW YORK

New York City is the hub of the industry's marketing efforts and houses the sales office of virtually every important producer in the United States. In just a single building, 1290 Avenue of the Americas, several hundred menswear firms have their offices. As the industry has grown, its showrooms have spilled over into surrounding office buildings on 51st, 52nd, and 53rd Streets, from Fifth Avenue to Seventh Avenue. Further downtown, in the Empire State Building at 34th Street and Fifth Avenue, there are sales offices for a major share of the men's furnishings companies. Meantime, the area round 23rd Street and Fifth Avenue, that was once the heart of the industry, has been abandoned to retail and housing uses.

What draws merchants to New York City is the presence of showrooms, showrooms, and more showrooms. The typical retailer has little need or desire to visit production facilities.

CENTERS OF PRODUCTION

The production of menswear, as has been mentioned, takes place all over the United States. Certain areas, however, are more important than others for specific types of apparel. Tailored clothing is produced primarily in the Northeast, with New York, Pennsylvania, and Massachusetts being the major areas. Together with Georgia, these states produce over 50 percent of all tailored clothing.[7]

As to other categories: 48 percent of men's and boys' shirts and nightwear are produced in North Carolina, Alabama, Georgia, and Tennessee; 70 percent of separate trousers are produced in Georgia, Texas, Alabama, and Mississippi; 55 percent of work clothing is produced in Texas, Tennessee, Georgia, and Mississippi; and 70 percent of all men's and boys' neckwear is produced in New York, North Carolina, California, and Louisiana.[8]

DESIGN AND PRODUCTION PROCEDURES ································

The procedures in design and production of men's tailored clothing and in the design and production of men's sportswear differ greatly. In tailored clothing, changes are simple and subtle; in sportswear, changes tend to be more rapid, more drastic, and more trendy. Throughout the entire menswear field, however, men remain slower and less willing than women to accept radical fashion changes in their wardrobes. What has been changing, however, is men's attitudes toward their bodies, with emphasis on health.

Exercise became a fact of life in the 1980s. Fitness, says designer Bill Blass, "is a major preoccupation of people in our time."[9]

This new body awareness manifests itself in menswear in a number of ways. There is, of course, the demand for jogging suits, tennis and running shorts, and workout outfits. So strong is the interest in athletics and athletic clothes that the warmup suit has become known as the leisure suit of the 1980s. At the same time, men's tailored clothing has changed to reflect the interest in fit bodies. Shoulders are wider, waists are narrower, and the drop has lengthened. The **drop** is the difference between the chest measurement and the waist measurement. Traditionally, this was six inches, but nowadays manufacturers are changing their specifications to seven or even eight inches.

Tailored Clothing

The tailored clothing segment of the menswear industry presents a completely different picture from what prevails in other branches, and certainly a picture utterly unlike that which prevails in the women's fashion industry. Production is slow and painstaking; highly skilled operators are required; handwork is still a factor; sizing is complex; emphasis is on selection of fabrics rather than styles alone; and styles change slowly and gradually. With all these elements to consider, it is not surprising that this segment of the industry operates on the basis of only two seasons a year.

SEASONAL LINES

The tailored clothing industry, with its long and complex production methods, traditionally presents its lines to retailers only twice a year. Fall/Winter lines are shown to the trade in December and January; Spring/Summer lines are shown in July and August. This long-established calendar prevails today and continues to do so because the apparel concerned remains largely classic in style. If fashion changes were swifter and more marked in this field, necessitating more frequent introduction of new styles, the calendar would change—and the industry's methods of operation would undoubtedly have to change along with it.

DEVELOPMENT OF A LINE

The development of a tailored clothing line starts with a decision as to the bodies, or basic styles, that will be featured for the coming season. Each major suit and coat manufacturer employs at least one master tailor/designer whose job is to make the subtle changes in last year's bodies that may be needed to produce this year's new shape. Changes may include adding or subtracting length in the jacket and lapels; bringing the garment closer to or further from the body; making the shoulders fuller or less so; choosing between flap and patch pockets; deciding on whether there will be side vents, back vent, or no vent; and so on.

Once the newly modified bodies are ready, the designer, the piece goods buyer, and the principals of the company set to work to choose the fabric assortment. These assortments are quite extensive, as retailers expect to see a broad range when they come in to make their selections for a major season. Finally, sample garments are made up in a few of the fabrics, so that the bodies can be shown in plaids, stripes, and solids. This is the line that is shown to the retailer, along with a swatch book of additional fabrics that are available.

PRODUCTION OF TAILORED CLOTHING

The process of producing men's tailored clothing is long, complex, and quite different from the procedures followed in women's apparel or in other divisions of menswear. Many hand operations are involved in the construction of structured garments; the sizing system is more complicated; and it is fabric rather than shape or silhouette that differentiates one tailored style from another. The manufacturer commits himself in advance to 100 fabrics or more. These he presents to his retail customers, and the retail buyer selects those he wants and the basic bodies in which he wants them made up. To that extent, the retailer designs his own exclusive line. The producer, moreover, may offer PGR—Piece Goods Reservation—a system whereby the manufacturer sets aside fabric for a specific retailer during or immediately after showing the line. The manufacturer does not begin production until sufficient orders have been accumulated for a fabric to justify a cutting ticket. A quality maker will put a fabric into production, if it has been ordered in one or several different models and runs of sizes, as long as he has at least a minimum number of garments to cut. Each producer sets his own figure, of course.

Even after the cutting has been done, production goes slowly. The hand operations involved in tailored clothing are time-consuming; as much as an hour or more may be needed for the pressing operation alone. Quality control is maintained throughout the construction of tailored clothing—a factor that explains why producers in this division of the industry are *inside* shops, using their own production facilities rather than those of outside contractors. This is in sharp contrast with the men's sportswear field, where style and design features are emphasized rather than exact fit and meticulous workmanship.

COMPLEX SIZING.   The dual sizing system that prevails in tailored clothing is a further factor in making production procedures slow and cumbersome. Men's suits are cut in different chest measurements, each one of which is combined with different figure types. This is in sharp contrast with the situation that prevails in the women's apparel industry, in which each producer tends to concentrate on a single figure type, such as misses, junior, or half-size and cuts possibly five or six sizes for that figure type. A tailored suit producer, however, has to cope with all these sizes for any one number in his line:

TAILORED CLOTHING FOR DIFFERENT BODY TYPES

A FITTING TALE FROM SAINT LAURIE
Or, how we make the New York Suit for three distinctly different bodies.

Once upon a time, business suits came in one basic style: baggy. That was fine with the businessmen who bought them. Then something happened. Some of those businessmen started spending their free time pumping iron, swimming in masters meets, and running marathons. And before they knew it, the same old suits had a new look: baggier.

At Saint Laurie, we noticed these developments. And we decided to do something about it. We took three of the basic elements of tailoring – the construction of the shoulder, the width of the back, and the difference between the chest and waist measurements built into the jacket (which tailors call the "drop"); and we combined them in three distinct ways, to create New York Suits with three very different fits:

The Trevor, a comfortable, traditionally cut suit with a soft shoulder and a 6" drop.

The Chairman, a sleeker and more trimly cut suit with a 7" drop and a gentleman's shoulder, which is slightly padded and squared.

The Crew, as well-shaped as the athletes for whom it was designed, with an 8" to 10" drop.

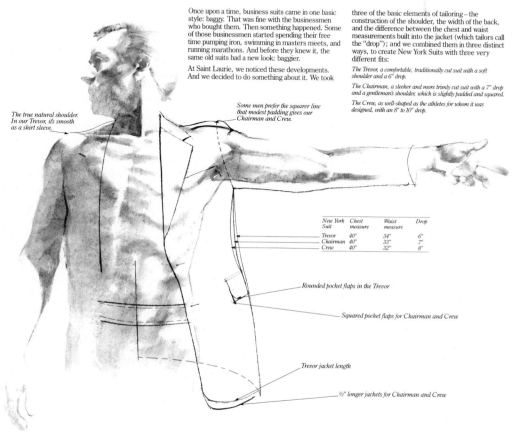

The true natural shoulder. In our Trevor, it's smooth as a shirt sleeve.

Some men prefer the squarer line that modest padding gives our Chairman and Crew.

New York Suit	Chest measure	Waist measure	Drop
Trevor	40"	34"	6"
Chairman	40"	33"	7"
Crew	40"	32"	8"

Rounded pocket flaps in the Trevor

Squared pocket flaps for Chairman and Crew

Trevor jacket length

½" longer jackets for Chairman and Crew

Each of these fits has its own distinctive style. And so that our New York Suits will look as good as they fit, we enhance that style with a fourth element of tailoring – the details. We add a half-inch to the length of the Chairman and Crew jackets and elongate their vents. We square or round the corners of the pocket flaps. And we adjust the angle of the notch in the lapel to make a harmonious design.

And unlike the purveyors of tailored clothing that offer you different fits by bringing you suits from different manufacturers – with different standards of tailoring – Saint Laurie makes the New York Suit just one way. The best way we know how.

We start with a selection of fabrics as varied as New Yorkers themselves; we have Tasmanians and tweeds, midweights, gabardines and flannels collected from mills all over the world. We hand-shape each of our garments, and hand-stitch them where it matters. So that you can find a suit of comparable quality and style every time you walk into our building.

Best of all, because we make all our New York Suits where we sell them, right here at 20th and Broadway, we can price them at $235 to $350 – 30 to 50 percent less than comparable garments anywhere. So at Saint Laurie, you're always assured of finding a suit that fits your budget as well as it does your body.

Send $2.00 for our catalogue.

SAINT LAURIE LTD.

MANUFACTURER OF CLASSIC BUSINESS SUITS SINCE 1913
897 Broadway at 20th St., Dept. T2, New York, NY 10003 (212) 473-0100 Mon. to Sat. 9 to 6; Thurs. until 7:30. Sun. 12 to 5.

Source: Reprinted with permission of Saint Laurie, Inc. and McCaffery and Ratner, advertisers for Saint Laurie.

- *Shorts.* 36, 37, 38, up to 42 chest measurement.
- *Regular.* 36, 38, 39, 40, up to 46 chest measurement.
- *Long.* 38, 39, 40, 41, up to 48 chest measurement.
- *Extra Long.* 40, 42, 44, up to 48 chest measurement.
- *Portly.* 39, 40, 41, up to 50 chest measurement.

Even in the case of separate slacks, the sizing is not simple. Many in the tailored category are sized by waist alone, it is true, depending on the retailer or the customer to measure off the inseam length and hem the garment. But there are also many men's pants that are sold finished at the hem, and these are sized in waists from 26 to 42 for the most part, and in inseam lengths of 29 to 36 inches.

This enormous variety of sizes is important to the retail seller, since many menswear stores continue to alter men's suits to fit individual customers and to absorb the cost of such alterations. This, too, is changing, as the mix of stores selling men's tailored clothing changes to include discounters and others who charge for alterations. Also, stores that have traditionally provided free alterations now charge for some types of alteration in order to keep expenses down. Even Brooks Brothers now charges for some alterations.

The custom of doing free alterations goes back to the made-to-order beginnings of menswear, when accurate fit was expected by the consumer. (In contrast, women, who are supposed by tradition to be competent seamstresses, have always had to pay for any needed alterations.) To minimize alterations, menswear retailers have sought to carry stocks that permit almost any size or figure type to be fitted with a minimum of adjustments. Although it is unlikely that any one style will be carried in all sizes, the average number of sizes bought in one garment ranges from 15 to 25, depending on the type and size of the store and the importance placed on the model and fabric in relation to the total inventory.

HARTMARX MARKETS TAILORED SUITS BY BRANDS

Men's Suits, by Retail Price and Style (The chart below highlights the main focus of each brand)

Retail Price	Contemporary	Designer/Personality	Traditional	Forward Fashion
$525+	Hickey-Freeman – Walter Morton			
$450-$500	Jaeger	Christian Dior Grand Luxe		Walter Holmes – Society Brand
$325-$450	Hart Schaffner & Marx		Graham & Gunn	
$255-$375		Christian Dior Monsieur Pierre Cardin	Austin Reed of Regent Street	Henry Grethel
$215-$275		Nino Cerruti	Racquet	
$170-$245	Jaymar Allyn St. George	Johnny Carson		
$120-$180	Kuppenheimer			

Source: 1985 Annual Report.

HAND TAILORING

The production of men's tailored clothing traditionally has involved many hours of hand tailoring. In the past, tailored clothing was given *grades* from 1 to 6+, based on the number of hand operations that went into the production. In recent years, the practice of identifying suits by grades has disappeared, due to technological developments. Today, many hand-tailoring processes have been eliminated because there is machinery that simulates hand stitching of lapels, turning of pockets, or finishing of buttonholes. Such procedures speed up production and reduce costs. However, top-quality men's suits still involve a great deal of hand tailoring.

CUSTOM TAILORS AND TAILORS-TO-THE-TRADE

Because men's apparel requires a more precise fit than women's clothes, custom tailoring remained important in the men's field longer than custom dressmaking did in women's wear. Most of the men's tailors who did custom work in this country in the early years of this century had been trained in Europe under the apprentice system; they could design a suit, sponge the fabric to preshrink it, cut the garment, run up the seams, sew on buttons, make buttonholes by hand, and supply the fine stitching on lapels. Until the 1920s, a man could enjoy the excellent fit of a made-to-order suit at prices and in qualities that compared very favorably with ready-made clothing.

The supply of custom tailors, however, began to dwindle in the 1920s and 1930s. Immigration had been restricted and, as the older European-trained tailors died or retired, very few new ones crossed the Atlantic to take their places. Work in the factories of this country did not produce craftsmen capable of making complete garments. Efficient methods of operation required some men to specialize in cutting, others in sewing, and still others in the hand finishing.

Today, a number of custom tailor shops still exist in the United States, principally in large cities and at the upper end of the price scale. An outstanding example is Dunhill Tailors of New York City, with a sales volume of over a million dollars a year, and featuring suits that sell for $1500 or more each. To quote Leon Block, one of Dunhill's principals: "Custom is bigger than ever; eight years ago, we planned to phase it out but we couldn't because so many clients wanted it."[10] The store's customer list has included such names as Cary Grant, Paul Newman, Walter Hoving, and New York's former governor, Hugh Carey.

In addition to the retail custom tailors who produce a complete garment on their own premises, there are also *tailors-to-the-trade* or *made-to-measure firms*. These are factories that specialize in cutting individual garments according to the exact measurements of customers who place their orders through retail stores serviced by these firms. The customer selects style and fabric from fashion books and swatches that he consults in the retail store; the retailer relays his selection and his measurements to the factory; and in due course the garment is made up. Although there are still some tailors-to-the-trade, their output is only a small portion of the industry's total and is no longer reported separately in census figures. Much of the made-to-order business nowadays is handled by large producers of ready-made apparel who have set up separate division for this special made-to-measure business.

Sportswear Design and Production

The demand for casual clothing and leisure dress among men has made the sportswear segment of the men's clothing industry increasingly important. The products in this field do not involve the careful shaping and hand operations of tailored clothing, as the garments take their shape from the wearers. Manufacturers can produce sportswear garments quickly and easily enough to respond rapidly to changes in customer demand and to provide the wide variety of merchandise required in a fashion business.

SEASONAL LINES

In men's sportswear, the increasing desire of consumers for fashion newness has resulted in a quickening pace of style change. Instead of the two seasons that prevail in tailored wear, sportswear has three season: Fall, presented in December for delivery beginning in July; Holiday/Resort/Early Spring, presented in July for delivery beginning in November; and Spring, shown in August/September and delivered beginning in January. There has been an effort by sportswear producers to add a fourth season, but retailers have resisted this, in the belief that men are not yet ready to accept such frequent fashion changes.

DEVELOPMENT OF A LINE

The preparation of a sportswear line differs a great deal from the development of a tailored clothing line. In sportswear, as in women's wear, the producer has already preselected the fabrics for the various numbers in his line, and the emphasis is on offering a selection of styles rather than a choice of fabric.

In preparing a line of coordinated sportswear, or of men's separates (such as trousers, shirts, or sweaters), there are both similarities and differences from one company to another. Where a designer's name is involved, the designer usually oversees the sketching, selection of fabrics, making of samples, and selection of colors. A company that specializes in separates, such as Haggar, uses house designers who prepare a line of pants by adding or removing front pleats, narrowing or widening pant legs, or making whatever other modifications are needed to achieve the new season's look. Fabric selection is usually handled by the designer, working with the company's principals and the sales manager, each of whom contributes his or her special expertise to the final selection. Pricing is usually done by the same group, but with the production manager replacing the designer on the team for this task.

PRODUCTION

Since no hand tailoring is involved in the production of sportswear, the sewing and often also the cutting is likely to be farmed out to independent contractors, much as is done in the women's apparel industry. However, in addition to using outside shops, many large producers such as Haggar and Levi Strauss also handle some of the production in their own plants.

With fashion changes, the scope of a line expands or contracts. There may be more or fewer sweaters, fewer tee shirts, more or less active wear, and so on. In such cases, it is necessary merely to find new contractors for the expanded categories and to drop those no longer needed for fading areas of demand. And, as in the women's industry, both foreign and domestic contractors are used.

SIMPLIFIED SIZING

The sizing in some sportswear categories is fairly simple; in others, it is becoming so. Men's sweaters are usually sized Small, Medium, and Large. Sports pants are sold by waist measurement in inches. Some trousers carry both waist and length sizes, in inches, such as 29/30, 29/31, and so on. In these designations, the first figure is the waist measurement, and the second is the inseam or length from trouser rise to hem. More expensive trousers often come without hems, so that the leg length can be adjusted for the individual customer.

Sports shirts are produced in only four sizes: small, medium, large, and extra large. Sleeve lengths are standard for each size. Makers of men's dress shirts have been following the lead of the sports shirt makers in simplifying their sizes, but with limited success. Manufacturers in this field had been accustomed to making their entire lines with neck sizes ranging from 14 (inches) to 17½ or even larger. For each neck size, they produced sleeve lengths ranging from 31 to 37 inches, at 1-inch intervals. Such a wide range of sizes represented a slow production process for the manufacturer and a formidable inventory problem for both retailer and manufacturer.

To permit quicker response to fashion change and to aid operation on lower inventories, shirt producers have sought to pay less attention to fit and increased attention to fashion. They simply produce a very large percentage of their styles with average rather than exact sleeve lengths. This system of producing only average sleeve lengths (ALS) has not been too well received by customers. Today, major men's shirt retailers carry both types—fashion shirts in average sleeve lengths only and classic dress shirts in the customary collar and sleeve length sizing.

IMPORTANCE OF THE COLLECTION CONCEPT

In the past, male shoppers tended to build their wardrobes around tailored clothing and regarded such items as sweaters or sports trousers as merely extra purchases. Today, they may very well make all their purchases in sportswear departments, where they can achieve a look that is properly put together, even if the fabrics in the various garments are different. This has become possible because of the collection concept.

Originally in the realm of licensing designers such as John Weitz, Giorgio Armani, and Allan Flusser, the collection concept has grown to the point that it encompasses almost all menswear, whether designer sponsored or manufacturers' brands, and at all price levels. A menswear retailer nowadays buys and presents a collection from a company that produces jackets, trousers, shirts, sweaters, and even ties and belts, thus ensuring that the customer will be offered varied items, all of which can be worn together and are color coordinated.

For example, Perry Ellis, under a licensing arrangement with Manhattan Industries, designed their lines of clothing, shirts, sweaters, and active wear, so that all can be presented together in a color- and theme-coordinated package. The same is true of Ron Chereskin for Cluett Peabody and Daniel Hechter for Bidermann Industries, among others. Giorgio Armani does three collections, each geared to a separate target market by price and life-style: Armani Couture, the highest priced and most elegant; Armani Boutique, moderate to high priced, geared to the man on his way up the corporate and fiscal ladder; and Mani, the most fashion-forward line in department store price ranges.

MARKETING OF MENSWEAR

The way to achieve growth is to win business away from competing companies. Thus there is greater emphasis on marketing, instead of on production alone, and this in turn has speeded up the industry's use of contractors to facilitate quick response to the changes in demand. As the apparel industry develops and emphasizes marketing strategies rather than production capabilities alone, the field of menswear becomes an ever more important area of potential growth. Today's menswear customer, at every age and economic level, is more interested and involved than ever before in the building of a wardrobe and in the process of selection. Fashion shopping is no longer for women only; it has truly become an activity for both sexes.

Manufacturers' Brands

Brand names in the men's field are older and better established, and have been longer promoted than those in the women's field. Men have been conditioned for generations to purchase apparel in terms of grade, quality, fit, and durability rather than style alone. Thus, until a dozen or more years ago, consumers gravitated to brand names that were associated in their minds with quality: Arrow and Manhattan shirts, Hickey–Freeman and Society brand suits, for example, and such store labels (private brands) as those of retailers like Brooks Brothers, major department stores, outstanding menswear shops, chains, and mail-order companies.

Some of the brand names still prominent in menswear date back to the beginning of this century or earlier. Hart, Schaffner & Marx, now known as Hartmarx, began promoting their name through national advertising in 1890. In 1901, Joseph & Feiss (now owned by Phillips–Van Heusen) embarked on a national campaign to sell their "Clothescraft Clothes," retailing at $10 and upward, by telling their retail customers that "the wearer will be brought to you by judicious advertising. We pay for it."[11] This, of course, was an early and simple form of cooperative advertising.

With some few exceptions, manufacturers have left much of their consumer advertising to retailers, frequently through the medium of cooperative advertising, in which ads are run by the stores and the expense is shared by the manufacturer. More recently, fiber and fabric sources have provided encouragement and funds for national advertising, along the lines followed in the women's industry.

Importance of Designer Labels

Although national brands contributed to market growth for many apparel companies, an increasing number have capitalized on the expanding consumer demand for designer-name clothing. This trend has been evident particularly since the late 1970s. Some of the designers whose names were well established in the women's wear industry took the logical step of moving their design talents over into the menswear area. Calvin Klein, Bill Blass, Cardin, Christian Dior, and Yves St. Laurent were among the early ones to make the transition through licensing their names to menswear manufacturers. Others, such as Perry Ellis, Oleg Cassini, and Giorgio Armani, came into prominence in menswear in the 1980s, many by signing licensing agreements with a number of different companies for a variety of product lines. For example, Pierre Cardin licensed his name to Hartmarx for tailored clothing, slacks, and outerwear, to Palm Beach Industries for shirts and sweaters, to Sheridane for neckwear, and to Roytex for active wear.

The chart in this chapter gives a reasonably complete list of designer licensing agreements—as of the time of publication. Like everything else in the fashion industry, these arrangements change with great frequency.

Liz Claiborne is the most recent to enter the menswear area, with the introduction of the Claiborne men's division late in 1985. This is not a licensing arrangement, however. Claiborne is an example of a designer who does their own manufacturing rather than license their name.

The benefits that accrue to entreprenurial designers from selling the use

LICENSING DESIGNERS AND LICENSEES: A WHO'S WHO FOR MEN'S WEAR

Designer	Clothing	Dress/Sport Shirts	Knit Shirts/Sweaters	Neckwear	Slacks/Jeans	Activewear
Adolfo	Leon of Paris	Aetna	Foremost	Sheridane	Cy Beer	M.C. Apparel
Aigner		P-VH		Schoenfeld		
Amies	Daewoo	Berkley		Hudson		
Armani	GFT	(All classifications, except as noted)	(All classifications, except as noted)			
Barnes 2	Oxford	(All classifications, except as noted)	(All classifications, except as noted)			
Beene	Phillips–Van Heusen	P-VH	P-VH	Randa	Mannor	
Blacker		Mareh	Mareh	J.S. Blank		
Blass	PB-M	Damon	Damon	J.S. Blank	BTK	Laguna
Cacharel		P-VH	P-VH	Rooster	P-VH	
Cardin	Hartmarx	Palm Beach	Palm Beach	Sheridane	Hartmarx	Roytex
Cassini	Greif	Burma Bibas	Oxford	Burma Bibas	Oxford	
Cesarani	Paulman Intl.	Spencer Co. Yangtzekiang	Spencer			
Cerruti	Hartmarx	(All classifications, except as noted)	(All classifications, except as noted)			Robt. Bruce
Chereskin	Cluett				Seminole	
de la Renta	Oxford	(All classifications, except as noted)	(All classifications, except as noted)			
Dimitri	Ratner	Pacific Shirt	Cezar	Wembley	Ratner	
Dior	Hartmarx	Warnaco	Warnaco	Cavaliero		
Ellis	Manhattan			Warnaco		
Flusser	Greif					State O' Maine

	Chequers / Hartmarx	Wm. Stuart Manhattan (All classifications, except as noted)	Wm. Stuart (All classifications, except as noted)	Carter & Holmes (All classifications, except as noted)	Chequers / Bell-Mart
Givenchy	Hartmarx	P-VH	(All classifications, except as noted)		
Grethel					
Halston	Schoeneman				
Hechter	Bidermann			Superba	
Colours/Julian	Greif	Cluett	(All classifications, except as noted)		
Klein	Bidermann		(All classifications, except jeans)		
Lanvin	Greif	Damon		Damon	
Laroche	Weintraub	Vee Elle		Dunleigh-Tuxton	
Lauren/Chaps	Greif	Warnaco		Warnaco	
Nipon	Hartmarx	Warnaco			
Ruffini		Cluett			
Saint Laurent	Bidermann		(All classifications, except as noted)		David Peyser
St. George	Hartmarx	P-VH		Manhattan	Campus
Stock	Oxford	Oxford		Wembley	Campus
Truedsson	Sears/Oxford		(All classifications, except as noted)	Remington	
Valentino	GFT		(All classifications, except as noted)		
Von Furstenberg	Weintraub	Vee Elle			Glen Oaks
Weitz	Palm Beach	Excello/Shelburne		Randa	U.S. Apparel
Wright	Penney/Oxford	Bernette	(All classifications, except as noted)	Schoenfeld	Bernette

Source: Daily New Record. Reprinted with permission.

of their names to menswear apparel producers are many. A major consideration is increased income with little increase in risk. For example, Alexander Julian, having established his reputation with his small, higher-priced collections, increased his earnings substantially by licensing his name under the "Colours by Alexander Julian" label to Cluett Peabody, the manufacturers of Arrow Shirts, among other products. Another such licensing arrangement is that of Gian Franco Ruffini and Cluett Peabody. Warnaco has its Ralph Lauren Chaps collection under license, and Phillips–Van Heusen has Cacherel.

Retail Channels of Distribution

In the past, the largest percentage of the retail menswear business was done in the strictly masculine confines of the men's specialty stores. As men became more interested in presenting an appearance that reflected both the current fashions and their own personalities, and as they sought alternatives to the conventional business suit, they began to shop in other types of stores. And to enjoy shopping! At the same time, that bastion of men's privacy, the menswear store, began to solicit female customers. Examples include Brooks Brothers, Hastings, Paul Stuart, and Barney's. That last-named New York retailer has recently completed a women's annex, six stories tall.

A parallel development has occurred in the traditionally feminine environs of the department store and women's specialty shops. Neiman Marcus now devotes a large part of the main floor of its flagship Dallas store to

CHANNELS OF DISTRIBUTION FOR MENSWEAR

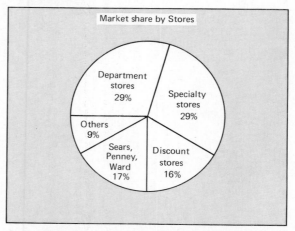

Source: Chain Store Age, General Merchandise Trends, July 1985. Reprinted by permission of Lebhar-Friedman Inc.

menswear. At Bloomingdale's in New York, menswear gets nearly half the main floor, plus another half a floor in the area that was once a low-priced basement sales area. B. Altman, in New York, devotes a third of its main floor to male attire. The same is true of Garfinkel's in Washington, D.C., and the Macy stores in New York and San Francisco. Bonwit Teller, in 1985, reopened a menswear area after closing it two years previously. Says Neiman Marcus vice-president James F. Guerra: "We devote increasing floor space to menswear because it is one of the best performers in the store in terms of sales and margins."[12] At the same time, those specialty chains whose units are primarily located in malls are appealing to young men who shop with young women for the fun of it. Both sexes watch MTV and both react to the same fashion images. Nevertheless, there are still many small men's specialty shops, strictly male, which are an important outlet for men's clothing.

Men's shops, large or small, remain important for several reasons. For one, many men still hesitate to enter the predominantly feminine confines of the department store, or feel so uncomfortable there that even special entrances and special elevators do not entirely break down their reluctance. Another reason is that men's specialty shops are usually arranged in such a way that furnishings and clothing are placed near one another, and a single salesman can escort the customer throughout the entire store and assist him in all his purchases. Such procedures save time for the customer and make suggestion selling of second, third, fourth, or umpteenth items infinitely easier. Still another reason is the convenience of location; men's shops can be found everywhere and anywhere—in business districts, residential areas, and shopping centers.

The menswear business pie, then, is being divided more evenly than ever among department stores, specialty stores, mass marketers, and discount stores, as can be seen in the chart in this chapter.

Manufacturer-Owned Retail Stores: Dual Distribution

Firmly entrenched in the menswear field, is the *dual-distribution system*, whereby some large menswear manufacturers own and operate retail stores through which they sell their products—the same products that they also sell to other independent retailers for resale. Manufacturer-owned stores include in their assortments merchandise produced by other apparel makers—men's furnishings, for example, and women's wear. A prominent example is Hartmarx, whose 257 stores include such chains as Wallach's, Silverwood, and Hastings.[13] Phillips–Van Heusen, the giant shirt company also owns many stores, including Harris and Frank, and Kennedy's. In 1985, the company opened nine additional stores called Titus MacDuff. As these examples indicate, manufacturer-owned stores are usually given names that do not identify them to the public as belonging to the producer concerned.

RETAIL STORES OWNED BY HARTMARX

North Group	West Group	South Group
Baskin	Silverwood's	Jas. K. Wilson
Wallach's	Klopfenstein's	Frank Bros.
Walkers	Arthur Frank	Leopold Price & Rolle
Field Bros.	Hanny's	Merritt Schaeffer & Brown
Roots	Ray Beers	Porter-Stevens
Peer Gordon	Jack Henry	Wolf Bros.
F. R. Tripler	Hastings	Zachry and Divisions
Capper & Capper	Littler's	Schulman's
		J. O. Jones
		Heyward Mahon
		Levy-Wolf

Source: Annual Report.

Marketing Activities by Trade Associations

An important point of difference between the menswear and women's apparel fields lies in the role of trade associations. In menswear, several trade associations are actively concerned with the marketing of the merchandise, acting more or less as go-betweens for producers and retailers. In the women's field, trade associations generally work only at single levels of distribution—that is, retail organizations work only with their retail members, and industry associations only with producers, as far as marketing is concerned.

CLOTHING MANUFACTURERS' ASSOCIATION

The oldest trade association in the menswear field is the **CMA**. This was formed originally by producers of tailored clothing to represent manufacturers in negotiations with the union—the "Amalgamated." Although it still performs this function, the CMA's activities have been greatly expanded. The association coordinates and publicizes the two New York market weeks each year: the January/February showings for fall/winter and the August/September showings for spring/summer. Twice a year, in January and July, the association publishes, in cooperation with *Newsweek Magazine*, a trade periodical for international distribution. Appearing in three languages, English, French, and German, it undertakes to inform retailers about major fashion trends in tailored clothing. Another association function is to compile and distribute periodically to its members statistical and technical reports on developments in tailored clothing. And, of course, like most major trade associations, it is the lobbying voice of its industry.

NAMSB

A second trade association that is very active in marketing menswear is the National Association of Men's Sportswear Buyers (**NAMSB**). This organization was founded and is financially supported by store buyers of menswear as well as owners of men's stores. It was founded in 1953 to give status and identity to a then new category of menswear—sportswear. In its early years, it helped give direction to the styling of men's and boys' sportswear by recommending themes and colors the retailers considered most likely to succeed.

The NAMSB stages three Show Weeks a year: in January at the Sheraton Center and New York Hilton hotels, and in June and October at the New York Javits Center. At each of these shows, exhibit booths are set up on several floors for the use of manufacturers in showing their lines. Although the association was founded by sportswear buyers and originally concentrated on that single category, its function has expanded to include all types of men's and boys' apparel and furnishings, including accessories and shoes. At each show week, more than 1200 exhibitors buy space. The opportunity to view so many lines draws over 25,000 countrywide retailers from establishments of every size and type. NAMSB estimates that more than half of these are store owners and reports that all who come to the shows come to buy. Since show weeks attract more menswear buying power than any menswear trade event, they have become a key marketing tool not only for domestic producers and retailers, but also for importers, foreign producers, and groups of overseas suppliers exhibiting under sponsorship of their governments.

MEN'S FASHION ASSOCIATION OF AMERICA

The (**MFA**) Men's Fashion Association of America is the public relations arm of the industry. It is funded by members drawn from fiber, mill, apparel manufacturing, and retail organizations, and its purpose is to make male fashions newsworthy and to provide information on the subject to the press. Press previews are held three times a year in an area near New York City in June, and in a major southwestern city such as Dallas in January or February. A Press Preview Week is held in September or October, usually on the West Coast. Each preview entails three-day seminars, supplemented by elaborate press kits, to acquaint the media with upcoming trends in menswear fashions. In addition, material is supplied to the press from time to time as the seasons progress. Activity is not limited to the print media; scripts and slides are also provided to television programs. Further encouragement to the media is the award each year of a "Lulu" for outstanding male fashion journalism in various newspaper, television, and radio categories.

THE MAGIC TRADE SHOW

Growing in importance is the Men's Apparel Guild of California; this show was once an association and trade show for West Coast producers only, but since 1979 has been a national men's apparel show with emphasis on sportswear. Its "**MAGIC**" designation is, of course, an acronym for its name. Factors in its development are the energetic promotion of the "California Look" by producers, and the attraction of sportswear lines for retailers eager to capitalize on increasing demand from consumers for such apparel. The show's ability to draw retailers from a widening area has enabled it to move from a regional to a national organization. Held in the Los Angeles Convention Center, it is today considered as important as the NAMSB.

MENSWEAR TRADE SHOWINGS

In addition to the menswear group **trade shows** described above, menswear manufacturers also have the opportunity to show their wares at fashion trade shows held in various fashion centers around the world. In the United States, the **Designers' Collective**, a trade association, presents major season shows in New York City, with emphasis on fashion newness and innovation. Participants are a constantly growing group of menswear designers, both established and newcomers.

Other trade shows are staged by European menswear trade associations. Among them are the European Menswear Show (SEHM) in Paris, Pitti Como in Florence, the English Menswear Designers Collections in London, the Scandinavian Menswear Fair in Copenhagen, and the International Men's Fashion Week in Cologne. These are seasonal showings that are presented twice a year for the major seasons—Fall/Winter and Spring/Summer.

COMPETITION FROM IMPORTS

Competition from imports has affected the menswear industry as it has other segments of the fashion business. In 1985 imports in the four major categories alone exceeded $4 billion, at wholesale, as the following figures show:[14]

Shirts and nightwear	$2,627,000,000
Suits and coats	979,000,000
Work clothing	857,000,000
Separate trousers	62,000,000
	$4,525,000,000

The ratio of imports to domestic production, however, is not as great as in other branches of the fashion industry. Foreign competition has not caused as many disruptions in menswear as it has in the women's branch of the fashion industry.

Source: Reprinted by permission of Men's Apparel Guild of California. Artwork by Bob Wynne.

FASHION EXPLOSION IN MEN'S ACCESSORIES ....

Great as the impact of fashion has been on men's clothing, the American male still wears essentially the same articles of dress that his father and grandfather did before him; coat, pants, shirts, ties. Color, pattern, line, and other elements may have changed, but not the basic costume. Where men have really broken loose from regimentation, however, is in accessories. Not only do they have their hair styled instead of simply cut, and not only do they use perfumes (whose very presence in the home would have scandalized the earlier generations), but they also have let themselves go in wearing medallions and gold chains; in wearing decorative identity bracelets on their wrists; in carrying shoulder and tote bags if they choose to, or in wearing western-look hats and boots if they like the idea. Not since the days of Beau Brummel have men so much indulged in fun things to wear and in uninhibited colors.

Perhaps the most important development in the total men's market is that fashion has become more important in men's lives than it ever has been before.

Readings

There are many ways to reach out for the fashion-conscious male or to make the indifferent male more fashion-conscious. The readings here go into the subject from various angles—including the impact of women on the industry.

Barneys: A New Attitude

Once exclusively a men's store, Barneys has been reaching out for women since 1976, and has been so successful that it has needed a new building for them. The women's facility is close to the men's, to make it easier for couples to shop together.

Haberdasher to the Ruling Class

Brooks Brothers has supplied men's clothing to the rich and powerful since 1818. Now the staid old company is finding itself in the vanguard of fashion.

How Women Keep Changing What Men Wear

Women not only help men choose their clothes, but today they are doing the designing, too. In surprising numbers, women designers are putting color and vitality into menswear.

The Men's Fashion Association of America, Inc.

Informing the public of what is new in men's fashions is a responsibility undertaken by the MFA. Press kits, previews, forecasts, and awards are among the tools described in this outline of its activities.

Hartmarx

Hartmarx for nearly 100 years has been America's leading diversified manufacturer and retailer of men's and women's apparel. Their annual report gives you an inside look into their various divisions and how they operate.

Barneys: A New Attitude
by Pete Born

When Barneys New York opens its new 70,000-square-foot women's store in late January, a project that could represent a $25 million investment, it will be a specialty store with a difference.

Barneys, one of the country's largest men's stores, hopes to make its new store stand out by applying characteristics of the men's wear business to women's apparel: more thorough service, made-to-order clothes and better constructed private label apparel. The company's hope is that this will emerge as a different kind of women's store.

The company also is touting it as the first women's specialty store of this size to open in New York in half a century. The outlet is being constructed out of eight existing buildings on 17th Street behind Barneys' 100,000-square-foot store on Seventh Avenue in Manhattan's Chelsea section.

The project reportedly costs $25 million, according to industry estimates. The new store is expected to generate a volume in the mid-$20 million range during its first full year, sources say.

The store represents an expansion of a beachhead established in 1976, when Barneys first went into the women's business. In 1981, a 6,000-square-foot women's duplex was opened on the top two floors of the main store. This business had grown to $5 million, or about 8 percent of the more than $60 million expected for the fiscal year ending next month, according to sources.

The new venture is being shaped by Gene and Robert L. Pressman, the sons of the family that owns the store. Gene, 34, is executive vice president of merchandising and marketing with additional responsibility for advertising and display. His brother, Robert, 31, is executive vice president of finance and operations. Their father, Fred, is president; their mother, Phyllis, is in charge of the Chelsea Passage gifts, antiques and home furnishings operation.

Gene Pressman, who tends to describe the new store in such words as "revolutionary," pointed out, "Because we are building this anew, we have the opportunity to be the modern women's store in New York City."

Some of the more unusual features of the store's design include a distinct and independently defined contemporary shop with its own entrance and merchandising mix, a circular staircase and atrium spiraling through six floors to a roof punctured by a skylight.

The store was designed to provide liberal amounts of natural light.

The Pressmans decided to stay in Chelsea instead of going uptown and to build the new unit next to the main store because they wanted the advantage of pairing men's and women's stores, according to Robert Pressman. Couples who do not have the time to spend traveling around the city can shop the two stores and fill their individual needs. Many women's stores have a men's floor simply as a "men's afterthought" and conversely, men's stores pay lip service to female shoppers with a "women's afterthought," he added. But Barneys' men's and women's units are meant

Source: *Women's Wear Daily*, June 13, 1985. Reprint permission granted.

to be separate and full-fledged stores. "This will allow couples to shop together," Pressman said.

Since many members of the target audience of 25 to 35-year-olds are professionals, the store has to accommodate their work schedules. The store will be open until 9 p.m. Monday through Friday and until 8 p.m. on Saturday. It will remain open on some Sundays.

To dispel any notion that the women's store is simply an addition to Barneys, there is only one entrance from the men's store to the women's unit. "We wanted to give women their own store," said Gene Pressman.

Robert Pressman said the family decided to renovate the collection of townhouses and old buildings, rather than to replace them with a new structure, because the idea was to project the turn-of-the-century ambience of the surrounding community, which has been undergoing dramatic improvement during the last two years as professional firms relocate their offices there and townhouses are remodeled.

The eight buildings comprising the women's store start with a building connecting to the back of the main store followed by six adjoining townhouses and ending with a co-op apartment building, the bottom two floors of which have been acquired by Barneys. That space, which was divided into four levels, forms the contemporary store which has an entrance of its own on 17th Street and a skylight in the rear.

The first two townhouses, closest to the main store, will be fully merchandised on all six floors. This is the section with the atrium and spiral staircase under the skylight.

Barneys added a mansard roof, complete with slate tile and copper trim, atop these two townhouses. In the other four townhouses, Barneys will only use the ground floor to continue the main floor, plus the basement. The four upper floors consist of apartments.

Each floor in the six-story twinned brownstones contains 5,000 to 6,000 square feet, and the main floor runs for 200 linear feet through the complex. It contains 30,000 square feet of selling space.

The contemporary store on the eastern end of the complex contains 6,000 square feet.

Referring to the main floor with its long run, Gene Pressman said, "Where most stores go up vertically, we decided to go horizontally." He added that the horizontal nature of the main floor, combined with the smaller scale of the floors in the twin six-story brownstones and four levels of the contemporary store, represents an attempt to convey a feeling of "spaciousness and intimacy."

The basement, forming a lower level, was dug 5 feet deeper so the main floor could have a 12-foot vaulted ceiling. Directly under the vault in the ceiling is an opening in the main floor, giving shoppers a view of the lower level, which will house a restaurant and a beauty salon, Roger Thompson at Barneys New York.

Gene Pressman said the interior is being decorated with generous amounts of wood and Art Deco and turn-of-the-century furniture, giving it "almost a townhouse feeling." Describing the decor as "modern classic," he noted, "One of the dangers is that certain stores have designs that are too trendy. The store is dated before the first year's rent is paid. We want something lasting."

He added that even in the construction of designer boutiques, management will try to avoid chopping up the space. "We won't have too many walls," he continued. "We'll use glass or do it in ways with fixtures so the space always flows."

While Barneys already had entered the women's business with the main store duplex, that creation of the new store entails taking on new categories such as intimate apparel, cosmetics and apparel for professional women. In addition, there will be a large expansion of eveningwear, shoes, accessories, the Chelsea Passage gifts and housewares and the designer business.

The duplex carries Giorgio Armani, Gianfranco Ferre, Missoni, Chloe, Jean-Paul Gaultier, Claude Montana, Kenzo, Zandra Rhodes, Azzedine Alaia, Issey Miyake and Ralph Lauren.

The top three floors of the twinned brownstones will have designer merchandise, along with a small, better-price shoe salon on six and a 1,000-square-foot lingerie area on five. The fourth floor will be devoted to avant-garde designers. Gene Pressman says he would like 50 percent of the designer mix to be made up of new resources. "This will give us an opportunity to develop new talent, something we are committed to," he noted.

Floors three and two will house apparel for professional women, 70 percent of it private label. For the women's store in total, the Pressmans would like to build the overall private label business to 50 percent of sales.

Price points of the Barneys New York private label will run from upper-moderate to just below designer.

In doing private label for professional women, Barneys plans to take some of the updated classics from men's wear, such as the "great cashmere blazers and great cashmere sweaters" and design softer versions for women. Referring to the professional women's shops that have sprouted up across the country, Gene Pressman noted, "I find them boring."

The third floor will house a personal shopping service, part of which will be a "Made to Measure" service for women such as the one that is offered in the men's store. Men can pick out fabrics and shapes of bodies and collars for suits that will be made to order by the supplier. That service soon will be expanded to include shirts. This will be applied to the women's store.

Gene Pressman said the price is not much greater than that of regular ready-to-wear, but noted that it can take up to two months for an order to be filled.

In general, the Pressmans intend to invest in more and better-trained sales personnel than usually found in a women's store. "Women are not used to this kind of service," Gene Pressman said, adding that men's wear salesmen are trained to be more helpful because "men hate to shop." Salespeople are trained to stay with customers as they shop the entire store.

In addition to the shoe salon on the sixth floor of the twinned brownstones, there will be a shoe area on the main floor and a third one in the contemporary store. The three will total 2,000 square feet.

Counting the main-floor shoe area, fashion accessories will occupy 8,000 square feet on the main floor, about 40 percent of the total. The floor also will house a 2,000-square-foot cosmetics department.

In addition, Chelsea Passage will take up 3,200 square feet of the floor, a space more than four times larger than the 700 square feet it now occupies in the main store.

"The contemporary store in itself is revolutionary," said Gene Pressman, noting that it has its own entrance, own shoe department, own cosmetics area and its own section of the 2,600-square-foot beauty salon, "We will have a total environment for the contemporary woman," he said. "Department stores do not have enough space to set up a separate environment."

Haberdasher to the Ruling Class
by Maria Karagianis

"Preppy" is not a Brooks Brothers word. In fact, it is a word that makes Brooks Brothers executives wince. The men in the handsome company offices at the chain's main store in New York, overlooking Madison Avenue and 44th Street, wear narrow collars and narrow ties and white cotton boxer shorts, yet they shudder at the word "preppy." For preppy, at this moment in history, is a trend, and Brooks Brothers sees itself as the antithesis of trendiness.

The oldest, most profitable chain of men's stores in America, Brooks Brothers is haberdasher to democracy's ruling classes, the apotheosis of conservative fashion, the *ne plus ultra* of restrained tastefulness. It is a place where buying that first navy blue blazer is, for certain classes of Americans, a rite of passage into manhood—like circumcision, or fasting before an antelope hunt. It's more than a chain of stores paneled in mahogany and mirrors, more than racks of blue and gray pin-striped suits, more than faithful employees and tony customers. Brooks Brothers is a state of mind.

Brooks Brothers is one of the few companies in America that has taken itself seriously enough for enough years to have its own archives. Daguerreotypes, photographs, and other memorabilia tracing its one-hundred-sixty-three-year history are housed on the eighth floor of the Madison Avenue store. For anyone curious enough to pursue the matter, copies of a small blue and gold history of the company, printed in 1943, are available free. Page one features a silhouette of the founding father, Henry Sands Brooks, about whom some Brooks Brothers employees speak so familiarly that it seems as if the old man died just last week, instead of last century.

The son of a Connecticut Yankee doctor, Brooks was in the provisioning business before deciding to open a store that specialized in men's ready-to-wear garments. It was an innovative idea, since most gentlemen's clothing at the time was custom-made. On April 7, 1818, Brooks opened a store near Wall Street, at the corner of Catharine and Cherry streets, in New York. James Monroe was President; the steam engine had not yet been invented; and the total population of Manhattan was one hundred twenty-five thousand.

According to the official history, Brooks possessed "first, a determination to make and deal only in merchandise of the best quality, to sell it at a fair profit only, and to deal only with people who sought and were capable of appreciating such merchandise; and, second, a forward-looking pioneering spirit."

After Henry Brooks died in 1833, the business expanded and flourished under the leadership of his five sons—Henry, Jr., Daniel, John, Elisha, and Edward. In 1850, they changed the name of the establishment from Henry Brooks & Company to Brooks Brothers. And the rest, as they say, is history.

Abraham Lincoln was assassinated in a Brooks Brothers suit. It was black, and in the quilted jacket lining was an embroidered eagle holding in its beak a pennant inscribed: "One Country, One Destiny."

During the Civil War, Generals Grant, Sheridan, Hooker, and Sherman were cus-

Source: *Boston Globe Magazine*, April 4, 1982. Reprinted courtesy of the *Boston Globe*.

tomers. When Grant became President, he was still partial to Brooks Brothers suits. So were subsequent Presidents—both Roosevelts, Franklin and Theodore, Woodrow Wilson, Herbert Hoover, and John Kennedy. Gerald Ford wore a Brooks Brothers morning coat and ascot to meet Japan's Emperor Hirohito, and Richard Nixon wore Brooks Brothers suits both before and after his fall.

Brooks Brothers salespeople in New York were reluctant to reveal whether President Ronald Reagan is a customer, but they confirmed that Treasury Secretary Donald Regan is a Brooks man. So are former Vice-President Walter Mondale, former ambassador Averell Harriman, and former Secretary of State Cyrus Vance.

Passels of Astors, Rockefellers, and Du Ponts and five generations of Morgans have been Brooks Brothers customer. So is Andy Warhol. So were John O'Hara, F. Scott Fitzgerald, and most of the latter's tragic heroes. Although Mary McCarthy didn't shop there herself, she wrote a short story called "The Man in the Brooks Brothers Shirt." Sloan Wilson's classic 1950s novel, *The Man in the Gray Flannel Suit*, also might have been written with that certain store in mind.

Rudolph Valentino wore Brooks Brothers suits. Robert Redford and Paul Newman, Fred Astaire, Cary Grant, Frank Sinatra, Art Carney, Ed Sullivan, and Tony Randall wear them. Jack Dempsey shopped at Brooks Brothers, and the Duchess of Windsor used to buy the Duke his dressing gowns at the Madison Avenue store.

Closer to home, Kathryn White bought her husband, Boston's Mayor Kevin White, a pair of black patent-leather dress shoes at Brooks Brothers two Christmases ago. James Michael Curley used to shop at the Boston store, as did former senator Leverett Saltonstall and Edwin Land, who invented the Polaroid camera. Other recent customers include Faye Dunaway, Carly Simon, Ed McMahon, and Princess Lilliane of Belgium.

And guess what Charles Lindbergh was wearing the day he flew across the Atlantic and was welcomed to New York by the biggest ticker-tape parade in history.

Brooks Brothers' Boston store is on Newbury Street, at the corner of Berkeley, a block from the Public Garden. On a street of elegant shops, Brooks Brothers' building is stately and subdued, three stories tall, with awnings imprinted with the company's golden fleece symbol. In the display windows are headless forms dressed in Brooks Brothers suits.

On Friday at noon, a taxi pulls up to the front entrance and double-parks. The driver gets out and strides through the front door, carrying fifteen boxes of pizza. Moving past salespeople behind counters filled with Shetland sweaters and oxford cloth shirts, he arrives at the wood-paneled elevator and pushes the "up" button. When the elevator door opens, a few customers dressed in herringbone overcoats get out; the taxi driver gets in, pizza boxes stacked to his chin, and pushes 3.

The top floor of Brooks Brothers in Boston, like all floors of all the Brooks Brothers stores, is paneled in mahogany and mirrors and thickly carpeted. It is sedate, dignified, and quiet. There is an almost religious hush. The driver with the pizzas marches across the floor, past a scattering of salesclerks and customers, past racks of tweed, herringbone, pinstripe, chino, and gray flannel. Disappearing around the corner at the raincoat rack, he passes through a narrow archway into another room.

Suddenly it is as if he has stumbled into steerage class aboard a luxury liner. More than thirty men and women are operating sewing and pressing machines in a large, noisy room decorated with crucifixes, holy pictures, and begonia plants. Most are speaking Italian above the din of the machines.

These are the pressers, stitchers, and tailors—a few of the several thousand employees responsible for Brooks Brothers' reputation for fine workmanship and quality. The workers in Boston are mostly Italian-born, craftsmen from Sicily, Calabria, Avellino, and Abruzzi, with skills and an attitude of pride in workmanship less often possessed by workers in this country.

"That girl rips, and that girl marks the pants," Margaret Lifrieri, one of the seamstresses, says proudly, pointing to two middle-aged women hunched over a long wooden table. They look up and smile. "She does all the ripping, and she does the alterations, and she checks the tickets," Lifrieri continues. "She marks with chalk, and she does all the hand work. And if it's not right, we rip it up and do it again."

The pizzas have traveled, someone explains, across the Back Bay, from "Angelina's daughter's sister-in-law's pizza shop on Boylston Street," as they do nearly every Friday. Emilio Sateriale, an 89-year-old presser who has been working at Brooks Brothers for the past sixty-two years, contributes some wine he has made in his cellar in Watertown. On holidays, there is also champagne or vermouth, and a larger assortment of food—zeppole (fried dough), Italian rum cakes, pizzelles (cookies), prosciutto, and pies.

"We celebrate the holidays. We celebrate the birthdays. We celebrate the retirements," Lifrieri says. "We are," she concludes, pausing for a moment to find exactly the right word, "like a family."

Many of the tailors and seamstresses in this room have worked at Brooks Brothers for twenty, thirty, or forty years, or even longer. It is a trend repeated at Brooks Brothers stores

across America. Buddy Holman of the Boston store, for instance, started selling Brooks Brothers suits in 1936 at age 17 and has been there ever since, except for a brief stint as a soldier during World War II. William Slevin has spent forty-one years behind the shirt counter at the Madison Avenue store. This unusual loyalty and continuity results in the specialized service that Brooks Brothers customers often cite as the reason they shop there.

Clerks at Brooks Brothers may wait on three generations of the same family. Some can recall in detail a day thirty years ago when they outfitted a little boy—now a head of state or captain of industry—led in by the hand by his father or grandfather, with camp clothes or a new prep school blazer.

In the jargon of Brooks Brothers, these customers are the CUs (short for "see yous"). They are the ones who come in and ask to "see you," a particular sales clerk, by name. Sales clerks return the devotion by keeping track of their customers' names and sizes, their quirks, their likes and dislikes, in black leatherbound books. Slevin, for example, is proud to show his own tattered book, which lists the shirt sizes of Eleanor Roosevelt's five sons and Clark Gable's sweater size.

In stores across the United States and in Japan, Brooks Brothers sells an image of upper-middle-class respectability, both to those who have arrived and to those who would like to. Its clothes convey stability, status, power, taste, breeding. Like blue-chip stocks, they are a sound investment, since styles change rarely and cloth and workmanship are of high quality. These are clothes to conform in, clothes that are safe, always correct, clothes that eliminate anxiety for the wearer. They suggest the right schools, the right clubs, and an income sufficient to live well without ostentation or vulgarity.

This image of WASP respectability is within reach even if your father was an immigrant or if you went to a state university or if you're Japanese or Jewish or Polish. It is an image available to business and professional men, and increasingly to women, from St. Louis to Cincinnati to Scarsdale.

Even during the tumultuous 1960s and early 1970s, when a revolution in men's fashion resulted in aberrations ranging from wide, wild-patterned ties to Nehru jackets and bell-bottom trousers, Brooks Brothers' best-selling single item remained the oxford cloth, button-down-collared shirt. The chain has never carried jeans. There are occasional bows to changing fashion, as in the four-inch necktie that surfaced briefly in the early 1970s, but that, according to Ed Young, manager of Brooks Brothers in Boston, "was the outer limit." "Ties at Brooks Brothers otherwise," he notes, "have always stayed between two and seven-eighths and three and a half inches."

In the 1980s, Brooks Brothers is finding itself again in fashion's vanguard. John T. Molloy, whom *Time* magazine dubbed "America's first wardrobe engineer," polled fifteen thousand executives over a period of fifteen years on the relationship between wardrobe and success.

"Many critics may charge that my approach to successful dress is snobbish, conservative, bland and conformist," Molloy writes in the introduction to his book *Dress for Success*. "They may further charge that I am encouraging the executive herd instinct," he continues. "To these charges, I must plead guilty, for my research documents that, in matters of clothing, conservative, class-conscious conformity is absolutely essential to the individual success of the American business and professional man." Wardrobe or image consultants like Molloy, who may charge up to two hundred dollars an hour, counsel clients to dress so as to offend the fewest possible people—which means conservatively.

Brooks Brothers is also right in step in the current era of conservative politics and conservative economics, when college students are cramming to get into business school, wearing ties to class, and going to proms and when a new generation of career women is obsessed with climbing to the top. What could be more comforting, more correct in the executive suite and on the way there, than a Brooks Brothers suit?

If the truth be told, Brooks Brothers clothing is rather dull and predictable. Take, for example, Brooks Brothers' classic natural-shoulder sack suit, made in a four-button model around the turn of the century and a three-button after 1918. It is characterized by unpadded, "natural" shoulders, narrow lapels with a button-hole on the left, soft front construction, a center back vent, and straight-leg trousers—twenty inches at the thigh, eighteen inches at the cuff. Like other Brooks Brothers clothing, it is deliberately conformist, reliable, conservative.

Except for those madras patchwork pants, or the screaming pink or screeching yellow ones that some men wear on summer nights at the club, the Brooks Brothers pallette is mousy: charcoal gray, brown, and navy for suits; white, blue, yellow, and an occasional pale pink for shirts. Most of their garments are modest—no tight-fitting slacks or bikini underwear. Shirts and suits are cut full and wide as the mainsail on Daddy's sloop.

"The typical Brooks Brothers customer is a person who recognizes the need to dress well, but who does not have a great deal of time or interest in the latest designer," says Frank Reilly, the company's 53-year-old president. "We like to think that nobody could come to Brooks Brothers and leave in poor taste."

Reilly has an office several floors above Madison Avenue, with a fireplace in the corner, a blue Oriental rug on the floor, leather couches, and a tall palm. On a typical day, he is wearing a Brooks Brothers suit (gray pinstripe); a Brooks Brothers tie (red and blue stripe); a Brooks Brothers shirt (blue oxford cloth with a button-down collar); and Brooks Brothers shoes (black, with tassels). Behind his desk is a Brooks Brothers briefcase embossed with tiny lambs hanging by golden ribbons, the official Brooks Brothers trademark. The same symbol graces Brooks Brothers' storefronts, awnings, elevators, letterheads, bills, wrapping paper, boxes, advertising, and merchandise.

In spite of Brooks Brothers' overwhelming traditionalism, store executives insist that change has been constant—"evolutionary rather than revolutionary." Successfully anticipating the future, they claim, has been the key to Brooks Brothers' longevity and continued good health.

Michael VerMeulen, writing in *TWA Ambassador* magazine in March 1980, cited as Brooks Brothers firsts the silk foulard necktie, introduced to America in the 1890s, the button-down collar in 1900, argyle support hose, the bed jacket for men, cashmere polo shirts, Brooksflannel (a lightweight sport-shirt flannel woven to be worn indoors), madras, Harris tweed, and the Shetland sweater. Perhaps the most dubious innovation, however, occurred in 1953, when Brooks Brothers became the first manufacturer to use a Dacron/cotton blend in shirts, a move that launched the age of polyester. And, more recently, Brooks Brothers has brought its traditional clothing to entirely new groups of customers.

The Japanese pronounce it "Burukks Burazaz." Tokyo was chosen as the site for the first overseas branch of Brooks Brothers in 1979 because it is, according to Reilly, "a city which is enchanted by status, fashion, and foreign names." Behind its gleaming granite facade on Aoyamo-Dori, a chic shopping street in Tokyo, its interiors are carpeted in blue with mirrored walnut pillars and stocked with racks of pinstriped suits and oxford cloth shirts. The Japanese Brooks Brothers "is a little piece of America in Japan," Mike Mansfield, the former American ambassador to Japan, said three years ago on the occasion of the store's opening.

Sales the first year were estimated at $2.7 million. Since then four more Japanese Brooks Brothers have opened, and there are plans for another three. "I'm a very big man in Japan," Reilly says with a laugh. "The Japanese are very respectful of tradition and much more conservative than we are," he continues, "so the Brooks Brothers look really appeals to them. Also, they're very impressed with quality labels and designers."

In this era of multinational business and mass communications, Reilly explains, a bank president in New York doesn't dress much differently from a bank president in Des Moines, New Delhi, or Caracas. That means new vistas for the conservative look. Reilly describes himself as interested in "continued, orderly expansion" and says he is scouting for possible new locations in Europe, Asia, and South America.

Brooks Brothers also reaches other parts of the world through its mail-order catalog. "We send Brooks Brothers clothes all over the world, even to Russia," says the New York store's shipping manager, John Rosado. Around Christmastime, he continues, "we ship three to four thousand parcels a day, everywhere from Bahrain to Moscow."

The most important new market for Brooks Brothers, however, has been female, rather than foreign. Starting in 1949, the year the pink oxford cloth shirt ignited a fashion rage and skyrocketed onto the cover of *Vogue*, Brooks Brothers has been selling men's clothes to women. From the 1950s on, suburban matrons and coeds would slip surreptitiously into Brooks Brothers' men's or boys' department to buy a sweater or blazer. But it was not until the mid-1970s that executives intitiated a Brooks Brothers line of women's clothing.

Realizing what a huge untapped market awaited them in the new legions of business and professional women who wanted, like their male counterparts, clothes that were well-made, correct, and conservative, Brooks Brothers began redesigning its stores to include separate women's departments. Women's clothing is now the company's fastest-growing division. Sales in the new departments, which made up about 1 percent of total volume five years ago, are now up 12 percent, says vice-president Stanley Jaffe. Brooks Brothers executives envision a day when women's clothes will contribute 25 to 30 percent of total sales volume.

The clothes for women at Brooks Brothers look like the clothes for men. There are blazers, conservative suits, button-down shirts, even a version of the silk-foulard tie, which looks like a floppy bow tie. "I recently sold one woman two hundred fifty dollars' worth just in ties," confides a saleswoman in the Boston store. "This is a very classic, conservative, well-designed look," she adds. "There's no way you could shop at Bloomingdale's and leave looking like this."

In addition to fashion news, Brooks Brothers has been making business news recently—a noteworthy fact in itself, since the company is virtually phobic about publicity. Last fall an American retailing conglomerate, Allied Stores Corporation, paid $230 million to acquire a second American retailing conglomerate, mainly because it wanted to get hold of Brooks Brothers. Allied Stores, owner of the Bonwit Teller chain, Jordan Marsh in Boston and Miami, the Stern's stores in New Jersey, and the Gertz stores on Long Island, among others, was so impressed with Brooks Brothers' sales that it acquired the entire holdings of Garfinckel, Brooks Brothers, Miller & Rhoads, Incorporated, of Washington, D.C.

Garfinckel (which also owns nine department stores in Washington, D.C., thirty-two Ann Taylor stores, eight Harzfeld stores in the Southwest, one hundred twenty-five Catherine's large-size apparel stores, and twelve Size-mart discount stores) acquired Brooks Brothers back in 1946, after the last member of the Brooks family, a great-great-great-grandson of Henry Brooks, died. Since then, Brooks Brothers' annual sales have risen from $5.6 million to $160 million. There are now twenty-eight branches in the United States and five in Japan, with plans for further expansion here and abroad.

After that first merger, some customers and employees feared the worst—that Brooks Brothers' traditionalism and attention to quality and detail would suffer under the thumb of a large corporation. Those fears were not realized, however, and employees and customers seem certain that the recent merger with Allied Stores will cause few problems.

"You can't fool with success" is the way one Brooks Brothers executive puts it. "We'll do what we've always done, because for one hundred sixty-three years, it has worked."

How Women Keep Changing What Men Wear

by Marvin Scott

Their names are Davis, Claiborne, Barnes, Canonero, Marcasiano, Knox and Akins. Not exactly household names, but they have more influence over what millions of men wear daily than do wives and girlfriends.

They are the women designers who are to the men's clothing business what Blass, de la Renta and Ellis are to womenswear. Part of a new breed of designers, these women are making innovative advances in a predominantly male domain and pulling a few threads out of the $45 billion annual menswear industry while they design everything from business suits to sportswear, from ties to shoes. While industry leaders feel that the competition is healthy, some of the old-line male designers are voicing concern.

The biggest threat is being posed by Liz Claiborne, whose company launched a menswear division this fall. Demand for her collection from stores nationwide was overwhelming. "The timing is right," says Claiborne. "Men are now more open-minded and are reaching out for a little more fashion."

Between 50 percent and 65 percent of all men's apparel sold in this country is selected by women, according to the Men's Fashion Association. But for the man who shops for himself, Claiborne is taking no chances. The name Liz will not appear on any of her menswear labels. "We don't want men to hesitate," says Jay Margolis, president of the company's menswear division. "Besides, we thought just plain 'Claiborne' on the label has a nice masculine ring to it."

Liz Claiborne, whose womenswear business has grown from $2 million to almost $400 million in annual sales in nine years, says she's venturing into menswear "because there was a void in the market, an absence of a solid men's collection at moderate prices."

But John Weitz, who introduced the designer concept to menswear in 1962, maintains, "Women aren't there because they are desperately anxious to dress men. They're there because the opportunity presented itself, and they recognize the potential for higher profits."

Claiborne doesn't see anything wrong with that but notes. "We think we know our business and can translate it to menswear." She insists her sportswear designs for men are not merely mannish variations on styles in her women's lines. "It's a complete sportswear collection with an identity all its own," says Claiborne. "We're introducing colors and concepts, especially the concept of really putting clothes together for men—not dyed-to-match but separate pieces that work well together."

Jhane Barnes' goal was to put a little color into a man's wardrobe. "All men seemed to look alike," she reflects. "Everything they wore was so conservative and drab." Fresh out of design school, she introduced to menswear a kaleidoscope of colors. "I wanted to radically change the way men dressed," she recounts. "At the outset, I changed everything—the fabric, style, detail. It scared men away."

Back at the sketch pad, she restructured her concepts, which have earned her accept-

Source: *Parade Magazine*, November 17, 1985. Reprint permission granted.

ability by consumers and every major menswear industry award. "I focus on incorporating colors and textures that are of a more subtle and personal nature," notes Barnes. "Men seem to prefer having the color and weave of their suits discovered after they sit next to you, not when they enter the room." A jacket, pointed out from a distance, appeared to be charcoal gray. Close examination, however, revealed that the fabric contained striations of pearly gray, slate, pink and purple.

One of the unusual characteristics of Barnes' creations is that they lack some traditional details. Insisting that they serve no function, she rejects superfluous buttons on jacket sleeves; flaps on pockets, which she says add weight to the wearer; dirt-catching cuffs on trousers; and vents on jackets, which make men look "ducky," declares the designer.

While Barnes says she learns much from her customers, her best barometer is her husband: "He's conservative. If he'll wear 50 percent of my line, then I know it's a success." Her success also is reflected in the way her business has grown from her first order for 1000 pairs of trousers, which she produced with a $5000 loan, to a $15 million-a-year enterprise.

Milena Canonero used to be an enterprising costume designer. After winning Oscars for *Barry Lyndon* and *Chariots of Fire*, Canonero was asked if she could translate her casual, elegant styles from the movies into a line of clothes for men. In collaboration with designer Norman Hilton, her collection is marketed nationally under the name Standards. The hallmark of her designs is simplicity. She focuses on slight changes in detail, such as squared shoulders, and often works directly with the mills to develop the exact texture and color of a fabric.

Canonero advises men not to dress to impress others at a business meeting because frequently they end up wearing the same thing. "Let your individuality come through," she says. "Don't be afraid to wear a lovely tweed or linen suit. Wear whatever enhances your own appearance."

Mary Jane Marcasiano agrees, "If you don't believe in a look for yourself," she advises, "don't wear it."

In 1983, Marcasiano began incorporating some of the ideas from her womenswear collection into a casual line of men's apparel after several men asked her to make some of her women's sweaters in larger sizes. She did, and the result was a runaway seller with men.

"I combine a fashion color with a classic color," she explains. Some interesting combinations in her current line of sweaters: black and olive, black and violet, brown and blue, and brown and turquoise. To a pale gray suit she has added a green pinstripe.

Women have a great sense of color, texture and flair, notes Norman Karr, executive director of the Men's Fashion Association, adding that women designers are on "the edge of a change that is taking place in the menswear business." Menswear designer Alexander Julian observes that while men bring a more practical side to womenswear, women can bring a free spirit to menswear. "Their challenge," he says, "is to do something creative and constructive within the narrow framework of what is acceptable to men."

Vicky Davis, Marsha Akins and Nancy Knox are three designers who have offered men something new in hats, ties and shoes.

Akins is credited with the revival of the men's hat industry. Her man-tailored hats for women caught the eye of many men, who bought the hats for themselves. Akins then changed the shape slightly and came out with a line of hats for men under the label Makins Hats. "The concept for both lines," she says, "is the same: soft, flexible hats that people feel good in." Akins offers 150 colors, including 30 different shades of earthtone. When it comes to men and hats, "it's a lot like kids and vegetables," Akins maintains. "They eventually like them, but the first is the toughest."

Akins, who made her first hats in the kitchen of her walk-up apartment, is still surprised that she's built a million-dollar business. The most important rule, she says, is that a man must feel good in his hat and consider it the finishing touch to his wardrobe—almost an extension of his self-confidence.

What Akins has done for a man's head, Nancy Knox has done for his feet. It was a white leather shoe that catapulted Knox to fame in the early '70s. "Up to that time," she reflects, "most men wore either a wing tip or a saddle shoe—nothing else. White shoes just weren't accepted." But she created an easy-fitting slip-on in one simple pattern. She eventually did the same shoe in 22 different colors, including a small number of lilac suedes to go with white or pink linen trousers. The color was an instant success. Knox recounts the skepticism of her male counterparts: "Everyone laughed—until we ran out of leather."

Knox contends that anyone can make a shoe look good—what's important is to make it fit properly. She maintains that what distinguishes her shoes from the others is the shape of the last, which provides a comfortable fit, and her emphasis on function.

Knox came into the design business out of adversity. Because polio left her with a slight limp and an inability to wear high heels, she wore men's shoes, which she considered unattractive and unfashionable. Now she wears the shoes of her own design—low-heeled creations in pure soft leather that offer as much style as they do comfort.

Vicky Davis gambled with a $27 investment and has tied a $1.5 million-a-year knot around men's neckwear.

Unable to find suitable ties for her husband in local stores, Davis—who was a suburban Michigan housewife—decided to make them herself. Her husband received so many compliments that she made more and began selling them. PTA members assisted with the sewing. Davis sought out unusual fabrics—textures and blends not commonly used in ties, including some fabrics usually reserved for women's apparel. Eventually, she distinguished herself in the industry as the "skinny tie lady" because of the success of her 1½-inch tie. Her initial success, however, came from the opposite extreme—the 5-inch. She was one of the first to introduce cotton, linens, rayons and a variety of blends to ties. Some of her favorite colors are passionate purple, royal blue, bright red, salmon and taupe, and grays with hints of ivory and pink.

Davis contends that men are more insecure about their ties than anything else in their wardrobe. That's why so many men ask women to select their ties. And she feels that a tie really expresses a man's personality. "The man who wears a traditional rep stripe, for example, lacks creativity," she says. "He follows the pack and is seeking the acceptance of his peers. Men should be daring in their choice of ties."

With her array of styles, Davis declares, "I've got men so darn confused. But," she proclaims with a sparkle in her eye, "at least I'm giving them freedom of choice."

After decades of being the silent names behind menswear labels, women designers finally have come out of anonymity and into the closet—a man's closet.

The Men's Fashion Association of America, Inc.

The Men's Fashion Association, the non-profit public relations arm of the male apparel/textile industries, operates on an annual budget of approximately $800,000 which is funded by member companies in the fiber, mill, apparel manufacturing, retail specialty store, chain store and supplier areas, based on their annual volume of sales in the U.S.

MFA has been operating since 1955 when it was created by the industry in response to four urgent problems:

1. The American public was not aware of the new fashions for men and boys.
2. The media generally treated male fashions with neglect or ridicule.
3. An educational program stressing the relationship between good appearance and success in business and social situations, did not exist.
4. Consumer discretionary spending had dropped to the lowest level since the 1930s for male apparel and steps to arrest and reverse the downtrend were urgently needed.

The solution was to proceed with a campaign to make male fashions newsworthy . . . to provide print and electronic media with a continuing flow of photos and story materials . . . and, in the public interest, to develop "Dress Right" materials for distribution to business executives, high school and college seniors and others seeking to improve their image.

MFA therefore structured its program this way:

Press Kits. Aiming for saturation, every seven to nine weeks, MFA distributes press kits to newspapers throughout the U.S. Exclusive photos are provided to newspapers in the same circulation areas. The Fall and Spring kits featuring photos produced for members at cost by MFA staff, covering the top 750 daily newspapers in the nation, are the strongest editorial statement made for the industry. Holiday Gift and Father's Day Gift Guides as well as Back-To-School and Active Sportswear sections are offered to 1,600 daily newspapers and 2,400 weeklies, again in an effort to saturate the media. MFA prepares cover trend stories for all kits. Additionally, MFA produces color slide fashion kits in the spring and fall for distribution to 300 television stations.

Press Previews. To develop a closer contact with the press, three-day seminars were organized—in February to highlight spring fashion news and in June to kick off news coverage of Fall and Back-To-School trends. Attracting an average audience of 150 to 200 reporters from across the nation, MFA conducts generic fashion overviews, sets up interview facilities for newspaper, TV and radio editors with industry leaders and celebrities, schedules fashion shows, panel discussions and other presentations focusing on the newest trends, surveys lifestyles, economic developments, etc. A complete press room, including telex and telecopier equipment, is available along with photographers, cameramen, etc. At the

Source: Press release.

230

Spring Press Preview each year, the "Lulu" Awards for outstanding male fashion journalism are presented to editors in different newspaper, TV and radio categories.

Syndicated Columnists, Wire Services and Special Supplements. MFA works closely with these outlets on a regular basis to obtain coverage of special interest stories, fast-breaking developments and trends, etc.

Network and Syndicated TV Shows. MFA each year places topical and timely fashion reports on such major television programs as those hosted by Mike Douglas, Merv Griffin and Dinah Shore as well as The Today Show, covering varied themes such as formalwear for proms, the western "boom" in fashion, etc.

Public Relations Consulting Services for Retailers. To assist men's wear retailers in doing a more effective public relations job at the community level, MFA maintains an extensive, annually updated library of speeches, fashion show scripts and promotional ideas, institutional filmstrips, "Dress Right" materials for sales executive and school presentations, etc.

Seasonal Forecasts for Retailers. To supply retailers with seasonal fashion updates to show to sales personnel and consumer audiences, MFA produces kits with 80 coordinated color slides and dual scripts.

American Image Awards. To focus attention each year on men of style and achievement, free of the "best dressed" identification, MFA in 1976 initiated the American Image Awards. Each year outstanding men are nominated for awards in the Arts, Business and Industry, Communications, Contemporary, Motion Pictures, Public Affairs, Sports and Television. Ballots are mailed to fashion editors, retailers, apparel industry executives, etc. In addition, a Hall of Fame selection is made annually to a man whose style and achievement are indelibly established, such as Douglas Fairbanks, Jr. (1976), Benny Goodman (1977), Henry Fonda (1978) and Willie Stargell of the Pittsburgh Pirates (1979). The Awards, designed and executed by Cartier and called the "Adam," are presented at a gala banquet in October by outstanding women in U.S. life. The ceremonies are videotaped and syndicated throughout the U.S. by Merv Griffin Productions to reach viewers in the 125 major U.S. markets. In honor of the winners, the Male Apparel Industry each year selects a charity for contributions of apparel and dollars to help needy citizens achieve a better self-image.

Cutty Sark Male Fashion Design Awards. In 1980, in a program to highlight male fashion designers on a platform of their own, MFA joined with the producers of Cutty Sark to inaugurate an awards competition that will create additional publicity for male fashions and scholarships for future designers.

Press clippings and surveys indicate that the programs of the Men's Fashion Association have succeeded in sharply increasing both the number of press outlets regularly reporting male fashion developments and the frequency of such coverage, with the return on industry dollars invested better than 10 to one in terms of the space and airtime gained, via the MFA exposure.

Hartmarx

The Company

Hartmarx for nearly 100 years has been America's leading diversified manufacturer and retailer of men's and women's quality apparel. We provide high quality, excellent value, up-to-date fashion and outstanding service to both customers for our manufactured products and shoppers in our 453 retail stores.

Our business includes: Men's and women's apparel manufacturing, specialty retailing, low markup retailing and international activities. Hartmarx employs 25,000 people.

Men's Apparel Manufacturing. Hart Schaffner & Marx, Hickey-Freeman, Intercontinental Branded Apparel, Jaymar-Ruby, Gleneagles and Hartmarx Uniform/Career Apparel Group. These companies manufacture suits, sport coats, slacks, outercoats, rainwear, sportswear, career apparel for men and women and military uniforms, under a variety of brands, designer and personality labels.

Women's Apparel Manufacturing. Country Miss is a manufacturer of women's moderate to better quality sportswear, dresses and suits. It also operates 56 outlet stores. Austin Reed for Women manufactures and sells high quality women's wear for the business and professional woman.

Specialty Retailing. Hartmarx Specialty Stores, Inc. operates 257 high-quality apparel specialty stores catering to business and professional men and women across the country under such names as Wallachs, Baskin, Hastings, Jas. K. Wilson, Silverwoods and F. R. Tripler.

Low-Markup Retailing. Kuppenheimer is a low-markup, popular-priced, "direct to consumer" manufacturer of men's suits, sport coats, and slacks sold through its 127 retail stores coast-to-coast.

International. Hartmarx has a 49 percent interest in Roberts, a quality Mexico City manufacturer of men's clothing with 25 stores throughout Mexico. The company also licenses its apparel brands and retail names in 13 foreign countries and has a 14 percent voting interest in Austin Reed of Regent Street in Great Britain.

Men's Apparel Marketing

The Hartmarx Men's Apparel Group achieved record sales and earnings for 1984 through greater demand for its established brands and excellent customer acceptance of newly introduced products. Sales were approximately $500 million in 1984, an increase of 12 percent from 1983, including shipments of about $85 million to our men's specialty stores.

Led by the Hart Schaffner & Marx label, a world standard and one of the best performing brands in the U.S., the Hart Schaffner & Marx Clothes Division reported substantial unit and sales increases and earned record profits. "The Right Suit" national advertising campaign, created through extensive market research, has been right on target in reaching executives, and this advertising will be increased in 1985.

The division more than tripled sales of the successful Jack Nicklaus blazer by promoting the Golden Bear label at a lower price point

Source: Annual Report, 1985.

which retailers enthusiastically supported. A blazer/slack package combining a selection of coats and compatible trousers encourages shoppers to choose a complete casual ensemble.

Christian Dior Monsieur, styled by one of the world's most renowned design houses, continues to perform well as it brings an important fashion direction to American clothing. Austin Reed of Regent Street enjoys success with major specialty retailers who feature this prestigious British-influenced line of high-quality tailored clothing. The Walter Holmes label joined with Society Brand in 1984 to introduce an elegant new fashion look. The new Henry Grethel line, focusing on a younger, more contemporary customer, was introduced during the year and has been enthusiastically endorsed by the nation's leading specialty and department stores.

Gleneagles produces weatherwear featuring several brand names including Hart Schaffner & Marx and will become part of that division in 1985. This consolidation will result in a greater market impact and reduction of overhead, which should get Gleneagles back to a profitable basis.

Hickey-Freeman had excellent growth in 1984 with a 15 percent sales increase. The brand benefited from new merchandising and increased advertising aimed at affluent businessmen. Jaeger men's clothing with the fashionable British look was introduced in 1984 as another product of Hickey-Freeman. The Jaeger brand will be featured throughout the U.S. in selected Jaeger stores as well as additional specialty and department stores. The international contemporary look of the Albert Nipon men's collection is being introduced for 1985.

Jaymar-Ruby also increased sales 15 percent in 1984 and earned record profits. In order to maximize the many opportunities for growth, Jaymar restructured its business during the year into three major divisions—tailored clothing and slacks, sportswear and retail. Its Sansabelt Shops, started experimentally two years ago, and a highly successful retail concept, expanded from 5 to 13 during 1984. Pierre Cardin dress slacks and Racquet slacks are proving to be rewarding additions, and the division is expanding its sportswear lines with Jaymar Sport and Austin Reed Sportswear. The Sansabelt Suit leads Jaymar's tailored clothing operations, and the concept is so successful that it launched a new line of Sansabelt blazer suits and tailored slacks.

Intercontinental Branded Apparel, formerly M. Wile, significantly enhanced its merchandising and improved its distribution for Pierre Cardin and Nino Cerruti suits and sport coats in 1984. Intercontinental also added units by selling the famous Johnny Carson apparel through Sears. Racquet natural shoulder suits for younger shoppers proved to be a real "natural" with sales continuing an impressive upswing. Intercontinental's strategy will be to emphasize the strength of its well-recognized names, including the moderately-priced Allyn St. George tailored clothing.

Uniform/Career Apparel Group combines Fashionaire and Thorngate Uniforms, and achieved record earnings in 1984 with sales of over $25 million in career apparel. This group serves the major airlines and fast-food companies, and produces military uniforms. The sales gain of over 20 percent reflects employers becoming more conscious of the need for employees to present a crisp, businesslike appearance when serving the public.

The Men's Apparel Group emphasizes two key strategies: Increase market share through building on its extraordinary strength and diversity of branded products unequaled in the apparel industry and continue its efforts to provide optimum quality at optimum prices through technological enhancements. It has engaged Kurt Salmon & Associates, a leading consulting firm with apparel expertise, to assess our manufacturing. We are determined to be outstanding in state-of-the-art technology.

Each of the companies—Hart Schaffner & Marx, Hickey-Freeman, Intercontinental Branded Apparel, Jaymar-Ruby and the Uniform/Career Apparel Group—are operating under the direction of relatively new chief executive officers, all experienced executives with Hartmarx. We have high expectations for this vigorous new management as they lead the most qualified teams in our industry.

Women's Apparel Marketing

During the past several years, Hartmarx has been expanding its presence as a manufacturer and retailer of women's suitings, sportswear and casual wear, bringing to business and professional women the excellence in clothing long enjoyed by male patrons of Hartmarx labels and stores. A corporate goal is to increase participation in women's apparel markets, and we have achieved considerable progress in positioning ourselves as a leader in women's apparel manufacturing and retailing.

Country Miss is a manufacturer and retailer of women's moderate to better sportswear, dresses and suits that we acquired in January 1981. Its lines—Country Suburbans and Weathervane sportswear, Country Miss dresses and Handmacher suits—are carried in many fine department stores and women's specialty stores nationally. In addition, about 20 percent of the production of Country Miss is sold through its own 56 outlets under the Old Mill name.

Through its unique combination of owned manufacturing and retail stores, competitive sourcing, distribution efficiencies and experienced management, Country Miss has one of the highest returns on investment in the women's apparel industry. We are encouraged by prospects for continued growth as Country Miss, approaching $100 million in annual sales, has attractive styling and pricing.

Complementing Country Miss in the manufacturing of women's apparel, Austin Reed for Women under the Men's Apparel Group is a fine quality line of executive women's suitings and related separates and accessories. It has received excellent acceptance among business and professional women, and is a logical counterpart to our suits for businessmen. In addition, Gleneagles is introducing rainwear for women.

We are seeking ways to expand our participation in women's apparel manufacturing through our existing business and compatible acquisitions.

In developing a successful retail strategy for women's apparel, corporate women's clothing departments have been installed in nearly all of our men's specialty retail stores, and this program was substantially completed in 1984. Our specialty stores have concentrated their focus on business shoppers, with carefully edited lines of apparel. Appealing to professional and business women through our specialty stores will be a strategy of continuing importance during the coming years.

Exceedingly favorable women's demographics in age, income and employment make our emphasis on the manufacturing and marketing of women's apparel an important part of our overall business mix. Throughout the eighties, we expect to be an increasing presence in providing women the quality apparel that their professional status deserves, as we take advantage of our long experience in manufacturing, our comprehensive network of specialty stores and our unequaled reputation as *the* company for executive dress.

Specialty Retailing

Hartmarx Specialty Stores, Inc., our full-service retailing group of 257 stores operating coast to coast, reported record sales for 1984. The men's stores increased nine percent to about $400 million while the women's stores— 26 Chas. A. Stevens in Illinois and 3 deJong's in Indiana—were even at $75 million. Operating profits improved in the men's stores, but much of the improvement was offset by margin pressures from price cutting and heavy promotional expense in the women's stores as well as other business-building productivity improvement programs to aid future profitability. Our long-term strategy based on emphasizing high quality, personal service, wide selection and excellent value continues to draw upscale business shoppers.

Supporting our decision to focus on the business customer, we are providing merchandise selected for business and casual wear by the businessman and have established corporate women's departments in nearly all of our specialty stores, bringing to businesswomen the apparel and image appropriate to their professional status. The businesswoman is an increasingly important customer for Hartmarx in our specialty stores and she is responding very favorably to our well-edited selections, service and ambience.

The specialty stores are also a superb showcase for our manufactured products. Over $85 million of the 1984 purchases by the men's stores was supplied by our manufacturing divisions giving them important planning and manufacturing advantages. Hartmarx Specialty Stores are stressing superior service in a "We Will . . . We Promise" customer service campaign, launched in fiscal 1984. It has been implemented in every retail store and reinforced by national television advertisements featuring the distinguished Peter (Mission Impossible) Graves. Our retail employees are responding enthusiastically to our customer service initiative, and it has become an integral part of the campaign to build our sales and reputation.

During 1984, our store remodeling and Model Store Program continued as several million dollars was invested to improve the appearance and ambience of the specialty stores. We are committed to meeting the expectations of our target customers, who are accustomed to professional attention in a pleasant shopping environment, with attractive displays depicting their lifestyles. Comprehensive management and sales training are increasingly important in the achievement of sales growth and improved productivity.

Major efforts are underway in order to reach our return on investment goals in specialty retailing. The heavy expenditures over the last two years in management information systems have brought us to the point where we can now undertake the centralization of accounting, credit, distribution and merchandising, thus eliminating substantial duplication of effort throughout our previously decentralized specialty store group. The reduction in expense that will result from this program over the next two years is expected to be substantial and the resulting efficiency and better control will add to improved performance.

We are highly encouraged about prospects for Hartmarx Specialty Stores which we believe offer the shopping experience preferred by the growing numbers of discerning, affluent customers.

Low-Markup Retailing

In only its second year as part of Hartmarx, Kuppenheimer's sales doubled from two years ago to $115 million in 1984. The direct-to-consumer manufacturer of men's tailored clothing had 41 outlets when we acquired it in December 1982, and has expanded to 127 stores. This aggressive growth accomplished most of a three-year plan in only two years. However, the expansion program and enlarging the staff, coupled with more competition temporarily slowed Kuppenheimer's earnings and return on net assets, and 1985 will be dedicated to improving profitability as there is now time for a more measured and less expensive approach to store expansion. Existing stores will build their sales base, and no more than 15 to 20 new outlets will be opened in 1985 while less profitable locations in selected areas may be closed. A new marketing program will also be implemented to further differentiate Kuppenheimer from conventional outlet and discount stores and to take advantage of the opportunity it has to be America's leading value clothier for men.

Featuring suits from $120 to $160, sport coats from $70 to $140, and slacks from $25 to $40, Kuppenheimer, which manufactures the apparel it sells in its own stores, complements our higher-end manufacturing and retailing operations. Its garments are directed toward the largest segment of the U.S. clothing market, which is suits under $200, and its retail outlets appeal to the price-conscious customer who is looking for unusual value in apparel designed and tailored for his needs.

Unlike discounters, Kuppenheimer does not rely on over-runs, left-overs or old-season merchandise. It styles the right piece goods and manufactures its own selection of current merchandise to be sold at low markups. Everyday low prices are possible through efficiencies in manufacturing made possible because of production planned only for its own stores, its highly efficient direct-distribution system and by lower cost retail locations, ambience and service.

At the close of 1984, David McMahon, formerly a key executive with Hartmarx Specialty Stores, was named president and chief executive officer of Kuppenheimer. Along with Kuppenheimer founder Sam Forman, who became chairman, it now has an outstanding management team in manufacturing and retailing. New systems management tools will enable Kuppenheimer to streamline its inventories for more precise matching with sales.

Kuppenheimer remains a major growth vehicle for Hartmarx because of its remarkably efficient method of distribution, combined with its quality clothing catering to the mass-middle market of American men to whom value is important.

In low-markup women's apparel retailing, Country Miss has expanded from 19 locations when acquired four years ago to 56 outlets. These Old Mill stores are stocked largely with merchandise from Country Miss factories and serve as outlets for about 20 percent of the production. They are carefully located to minimize any conflict with the sale of Country Miss products through its independent retailers, and the additional distribution improves its overall operating efficiency. The investment in these no-frill outlets, operated with fast-turning inventory and virtually no receivables, is comparatively low so the return on investment and profit margins are excellent.

International

Licensing operations for 1984 achieved record revenues and income, expanded to 27 international licensing programs in 13 countries, and extended our reputation in manufacturing, merchandising, marketing, retailing, technology and trademarks worldwide.

During 1984, we renewed several agreements in Japan that will enhance our exposure in the attractive Asian markets. With our Golden Bear associates, we renewed our arrangement with Asahi for the Jack Nicklaus label in an 11-year agreement involving 10 sublicensees. We expanded a manufacturing arrangement for Society Brand into a 10-year manufacturing and retailing program for that label with Marubeni and Taka-Q and renewed the licensing of our Hastings retail name with Sanko Iryo in Osaka. We also renewed our agreement with Marubeni for licensing of Trumpeter, the international label for high quality men's tailored suits, by our Hart Schaffner & Marx Clothes Division. Renewals in other countries demonstrate our global activities: Society Brand in Taiwan and Korea, Jaymar slacks in Thailand and Pierre Cardin men's suits in Columbia.

Hartmarx launched several new international programs in 1984. A new program with Cambridge Clothing Company of New Zealand for the licensing of Trumpeter is already proving to have a major influence in its market, and new programs for Jaymar were commenced in Canada and Mexico. A new program in Mexico was inaugurated for licensing of Nino Cerruti men's suits.

We are especially pleased with a new program in Japan for Hickey-Freeman. This prestigious suit, retailing for $700 or more in Japan, was warmly received with excellent sales during fall 1984, and is enjoying a favorable reception in a nation noted for attention to quality. The future includes a new program for Jaymar in Finland that will cover the entire Scandinavian market, sublicensing of Pierre Cardin in Columbia and a Jack Nicklaus program in Korea, pending approval by the Korean government. Our retail licensing programs under the Baskin, Hastings, Silverwoods and Field Brothers names continue to grow in importance.

Hartmarx owns a 14 percent voting interest in the Austin Reed of Regent Street Group in England, a successful apparel manufacturer and retailer operating over 50 stores, and this relationship is helpful in the licensing, merchandising and advertising of Austin Reed of Regent Street in the U.S. We also own a 49 percent interest in Robert's of Mexico, that country's foremost manufacturer-retailer of men's quality clothing. Despite Mexico's difficult economic circumstances, Robert's has expanded and just opened its 25th store in the affluent Polanco section of Mexico City. Earnings on our 49 percent equity withstood devaluations this year as Robert's increased sales and earnings in pesos by about 70 percent.

In addition to expanding international licensing activities, more emphasis will be placed on the development of domestic licensing potential during 1985.

Endnotes

1. U.S. Department of Commerce, *U.S. Industrial Outlook 1986*; and Standard and Poor's *Industry Surveys; Textiles and Apparel*, May 1986.
2. *Ibid.*
3. Kidwell and Christman, *Suiting Everyone*. Washington, D.C.: Smithsonian Institution Press, 1974.
4. Cobrin, *The Men's Clothing Industry, Colonial Through Modern Times*. New York: Fairchild Publications, 1971.
5. Kidwell and Christman, p. 53.
6. U.S. Department of Commerce, *Standard Industrial Classification Manual*.
7. U.S. Department of Commerce, *Census of Manufactures*.
8. *Ibid.*

9. "The Impact of Fitness on the Cut of Clothes," *New York Times, Men's Fashions of the Times*, September 8, 1985.
10. "At $1500, His Clothes Make the Man," *New York Times*, July 9, 1982.
11. Cobrin, *Men's Clothing Industry*, p. 317.
12. "A License to Make Money," *Forbes*, December 3, 1984.
13. Hartmarx, 1985 Annual Stockholders Report.
14. *U.S. Industrial Outlook, 1986*.

Selected Bibliography

Bennet-England, Rodney. *Dress Optional; the Revolution in Menswear*. Chester Springs, Pa.: Dufour, 1968.

Boyer, Bruce. *Elegance: A Guide to Quality in Menswear*. New York: W. W. Norton, 1984.

Carlson, Peter and William Wilson. *Manstyle: The GQ Guide to Fashion, Fitness and Grooming*. New York: Clarkson N. Potter, 1977.

Cobrin, Harry. *Men's Clothing Industry: Colonial Through Modern Times*. New York: Fairchild Publications, 1971.

Cray, Edward. *Levis*. New York: Houghton Mifflin, 1979.

Dolce, Donald W. *The Consumer's Guide to Menswear*. New York: Dodd, 1983.

Editors of Menswear Magazine. *75 Years of Men's Wear Fashion 1890–1965*. New York: Fairchild Publications, 1965.

Feldman, Egal. *FIT for Men*. Washington, D.C.: Public Affairs Press, 1960.

Flusser, Alan. *Making the Man; the Insider's Guide to Buying and Wearing of Men's Clothes*. New York: Simon & Schuster, 1981.

Laver, James. *Dandies*. London: Weidenfeld and Nicholson, Ltd., 1968.

Molloy, John T. *Dress for Success*. New York: P. H. Wyden, 1975.

Shapiro, H. T. *Man, Culture and Society*. London: Oxford University Press, 1956.

Tolman, Ruth. *Selling Men's Fashion*. New York: Fairchild Publications, 1982.

Wagenvoord, James. *The Man's Book: A Complete Manual of Style*. New York: Avon, 1978.

Wilson, William and Editors of Esquire Magazine. *Man at His Best*. Reading, Mass.: Addison-Wesley, 1985.

Winnick, Charles. *The New People: Desexualization in American Life*. New York: Pegasus, 1968.

Trade Associations

Boys and Young Men's Apparel Manufacturers Association, 350 Fifth Avenue, New York, N.Y. 10018.

Clothing Manufacturers Association, 1290 Avenue of the Americas, New York, N.Y. 10004.

Designers Collective, Inc., 3 East 54th Street, New York, N.Y. 10022.

Men's Apparel Guild in California, 124 West Olympia Boulevard, Los Angeles, Calif. 90015.

Men's Fashion Association of America, 240 Madison Avenue, New York, N.Y. 10016.

National Association of Men's Sportswear Buyers, 535 Fifth Avenue, New York, N.Y. 10017.

Young Menswear Association, 1328 Broadway, New York, N.Y. 10001.

Trade Publications

Business Newsletter of Menswear Retailers of America, 2011 Eye Street, NW, Suite 600, Washington, D.C. 20006.

California Men's Stylist, 945 South Wall Street, Los Angeles, Calif. 90015.

Custom Tailors and Designers Association of America, Inc., 565 Fifth Avenue, New York, N.Y. 10017.

Daily News Record, 7 East 12th Street, New York, N.Y. 10003.

Made-to-Measure Magazine, 300 West Adams Street, Chicago, Ill. 60606.

Masculines, 225 East 36th Street, New York, N.Y. 10016.

Men's and Boys Scene, Seymour Middlemark Organization, Inc., Lincoln Building, Suite 631, 40 East 42nd Street, New York, N.Y. 10165.

Men's Apparel News, 110 West 40th Street, New York, N.Y. 10008.

Menswear Magazine, 7 East 12th Street, New York, N.Y. 10003.

CHAPTER REVIEW AND LEARNING ACTIVITIES ....

Key Words and Concepts

Define, identify, or briefly explain the following:

ACTWUA	The "MAGIC" show
CMA	MFA
Designers' Collective	NAMSB
"Drop"	"Slops"
Dual distribution	Standardized sizes
Hartmarx	Tailored clothing
Levi Strauss	Trade show

Review Questions on Chapter Highlights

1. Why were the shops that produced men's ready-to-wear in the early nineteenth century known as "slop shops"?
2. Name two developments of the nineteenth century that contributed to the growth of the menswear industry and explain their effect.

3. Why do companies that were formerly publicly owned "go private"?

4. How does the menswear industry differ from the women's apparel industry? In what ways are they similar?

5. Which product division of the menswear industry has the largest volume of sales? Why do you think this is so?

6. How do the procedures of the men's tailored clothing segment of the industry differ from those of the other segments of the menswear industry?

7. How do the sizes of men's tailored clothing differ from those of men's sportswear? Why?

8. What is the meaning of the "collection concept" in men's clothing? Why has it developed?

9. Why do male customers continue to be attracted to specialized menswear retailers?

10. What trade associations play an important role in the marketing of menswear? What is their importance?

11. Select any one reading in this chapter and explain how it illustrates a section in this chapter.

Applications for Research and Discussion

1. Research a given number of menswear stores or departments to determine their target customers. How does their merchandise and merchandising techniques reflect their customers' taste?

2. Give two examples of "designer-name" tailored suits and two examples of manufacturers brand name suits that retail for approximately the same price. To what type of customers do you think each would appeal and why?

3. Research the historical periods in which men's fashions were as colorful and elaborate as women's. Illustrate with examples. Is fashion today as important to men as to women? Why?

6

FASHION ACCESSORIES AND INTIMATE APPAREL

Like a pebble dropped in a lake, every fashion change in apparel creates a ripple of change in the industries that produce fashion accessories and intimate apparel. The total look that the wearer seeks to achieve demands such change. For example, a blazer jacket may invite the use of a tucked-in scarf; a long skirt may require a long slip; short skirts may focus enough attention on the leg to suggest eye-catching patterns in hosiery; shoes may change shape and heel height to become good companions to current clothes; belts may be wide and colorful when waistlines are important, and vanish when dresses hang straight. Jewelry, too, must conform, playing to the high or low neckline, the short or long sleeve, or whatever are the important features of the garment. Even precious heirlooms may be consigned to the vault for a time if the prevailing "look" is wrong for the treasured pieces. Accessories conform to and accentuate apparel fashions to be viable; they cannot afford to lag or clash with the dress or coat or other garment that is the star of the show.

Accessories, intimate apparel, and the industries that produce them are an integral part of the fashion business. This chapter discusses the economic importance and methods of operation of each of these industries. The readings that follow are concerned with different aspects of this segment of the fashion business.

THE ACCESSORIES INDUSTRIES

When designers show their collections on models, and when retail stores put important fashion garments on display, they "accessorize" each dress, or suit, or other featured garment to emphasize the total look that is being

241

Source: Reprinted with permission of FAE, Conference Management Corporation

presented. Consumers also use **accessories** both to accentuate the important fashion points of their appearance and to give individuality to mass-produced clothes. Jewelry in the newest trend, a color-coordinated scarf, a very special handbag, newly textured hosiery—these and similar touches help each woman feel that the outfit she wears is uniquely her own.

Every fashion in the accessory category changes its look as clothing fashions change. Shoes may go from unadorned flats to elegantly pointed high-heeled styles; scarfs and jewelry may vary in length, color, and materials; hosiery may go from neutral to colorful or from plain to textured—all in terms of what best suits the current apparel fashions. Success in accessories production and sales is a matter of moving quickly and surely in step with apparel fashions. Conversely, no amount of promotion and invention can create acceptance for a particular accessory when it simply does not fit into the current fashion picture.

Many accessories have experienced dramatic ups and downs as fashions changed. Belts, for example, went into eclipse for many years when chemise dresses hung from the shoulder, ignoring the natural curves of the body. Millinery, too, has had its problems, reaping only a thin harvest from its industry promotional efforts at times when women preferred to go hatless. Accessories as a whole have had lean years at times when there was little room for them in the fashion picture. Within the past ten years, however, accessories have become a strong area of growth in the fashion industry and have been given ever-expanding areas of prime floor space in retail stores.

The Business of Accessories

The design, production, and marketing of fashion accessories is not a single business, but several. Each category of accessories is produced in its own industry, and these individual industries are as diverse as the merchandise itself. Some, like shoes and hosiery, are large and dominated by big producers. Others, like gloves, handbags, jewelry, scarfs, and millinery, are the domain of small firms. Some of the industries are highly mechanized; others still use hand operations not much changed from those used 50 or even 100 years ago. Some have plants in or near New York City; others are hundreds of miles from that center and merely have showrooms there.

The accessories industries as a whole, however, do have several elements in common:

1. All are extremely responsive to fashion and very quick to interpret incoming trends. Their success depends on how well they reflect the look of the apparel with which they will be worn.
2. All present a minimum of two new seasonal lines a year.
3. All domestic accessory manufacturers, as is the case with other segments of the fashion industry, are confronted with increasing competition from imports.

4. Almost all major accessory producers have entered into licensing agreements with leading apparel designers to produce and market styles bearing the designer's name.

Economic Importance

According to *Women's Wear Daily*, in its premiere issue of "*A*" (accessories), dated May 1985, accessories represent about $9.5 billion in retail sales nationwide. This figure covers jewelry, handbags, small leather goods, scarfs, hosiery, hats, gloves, but does not include shoes.

Another indication of the importance of accessories is their importance in terms of volume achieved and space allotted to this business by department and specialty stores. Macy's, New York, does 6 to 7 percent of total store sales in this category, or from $77 million to $90 million annually. When the company's New York flagship store was remodeled in 1983, accessories departments gained 10 percent in linear footage. Bloomingdale's, New York, was doing less than 10 percent of its total volume in accessories but expects to expand this to 12 percent by 1990. Its accessories sales are estimated at the $90 million level in 1985. Both these stores, of course, are general merchandise stores. In the specialty shop field, Bergdorf Goodman, New York, is estimated to get almost 10 percent of its total volume from accessories, a figure that should be increasing following a 50 percent expansion of selling space for this merchandise on the main floor.[1]

SHOES

If we had no other indication of the importance of the shoe industry, consider the leather industry's estimate that each of us walks the equivalent of twice around the world in the course of a lifetime. No wonder foot protection has always been of prime importance to mankind and shoes take a prominent place in our legends, proverbs, and fairy tales! We are cautioned not to criticize a man until we have walked a mile in his shoes; we grow up on tales of seven-league boots, glass slippers, and red dancing shoes; we tie shoes to the cars of newly married couples as symbols of good luck. Aching feet remind us of the importance of being comfortably shod; a glance into a full-length mirror highlights the importance of shoes appropriate to one's outfit.

The first American shoemaker was Thomas Beard, who landed in the Massachusetts colony on the second voyage of the Mayflower and opened his shop to produce made-to-order shoes. Others followed, some of whom became "visiting shoemakers." These men lived with a household until all members had been shod. Leather for the purpose was usually supplied by the farmer or householder and was obtained from the cured skins of animals killed for meat. During the eighteenth century, shoemakers began producing "sale shoes," made without waiting for specific orders and brought to market to be offered for sale. Thus, ready-made shoes were introduced. These, however, were made only in three widths and five lengths. The well-to-do, therefore, almost universally had their shoes custom made as late as 1880.[2]

The oldest and still active retail shoe organization in the United States is Thomas F. Pierce & Son, of Providence, Rhode Island, established in 1767.

Nature of the Industry

The largest dollar volume of business in the accessories group is done by the shoe industry. This is an industry dominated by large firms. It is not unusual to find among them companies with many divisions, each of which produces and distributes footwear under its own brand name. For example, Joyce is a

THE SHOE INDUSTRY IS DOMINATED BY LARGE FIRMS
Sales and Earnings[a]

1984 Sales			Sales ($000)		Net Income ($000)		
Rank	Company	FYE	$	'83	$	'84	'83
1	Edison Bros	12/84	$1,054,700		$32,900	2	2
2	Nike, Inc.	05/84	919,806	2	40,690	1	1
3	Morse Shoe	12/84	526,546	3	9,092	6	3
4	Wolverine	12/84	378,589	4	2,365	11	8
5	Stride Rite	11/84	289,489	5	5,420	7	4
6	Converse	12/84	265,598	6	14,467	3	6
7	Shoe-Town	12/84	131,929	7	11,513	4	5
8	R.G. Barry	12/84	120,200	10	144	17	17
9	Weyenberg	12/84	108,422	9	4,305	8	10
10	Suave Shoe	09/84	96,430	8	−256	18	14
11	Craddock-Terry	09/84	83,395	11	−1,775	21	12
12	Amfesco	06/84	81,920	13	10,584	5	7
13	Tony Lama	07/84	78,944	12	2,835	9	9
14	Hyde Athletic	12/84	47,313	14	2,681	10	11
15	B B Walker	10/84	42,397	15	174	16	22
16	Sporto Corp.	01/84	37,382	16	1,513	14	16
17	Shaer Shoe	10/84	27,954	18	2,364	12	15
18	Daniel Green	12/84	25,571	17	2,087	13	13
19	Mc Rae Ind	07/84	15,559	20	−599	19	19
20	Penobscot Shoe	10/84	12,623	19	363	15	18
21	Wellco Ent	06/84	12,306	22	−2,618	22	21
22	Simco	07/84	9,239	21	−685	20	20

[a]This table reports on data from 22 companies that derive 50 percent or more of their total sales from footwear manufacturing or retailing.
Source: KSA's 1984 financial performance profile of the footwear industry.

division of the U.S. Shoe Company, which also produces Pappagalo and Red Cross shoes. Thom McCann is a division of Melville Shoe Corp., which also produces footwear under several other labels. The Brown Group manufactures Buster Brown shoes for children, Naturalizer and Airstep for women, and Roblee and Regal shoes for men. Some producers are divisions of conglomerates—for example, Bostonian Shoes is one of the immensely varied divisions of Gulf and Western.

Production facilities are mainly in New England, but Missouri, Tennessee, and Pennsylvania are also important in shoe production. As with most segments of the fashion industry, the major marketing center for shoes is New York City, and most producers maintain permanent showrooms there. For decades, the 34th Street area was the center of activity for American footwear manufacturers. Headquarters were in the Marbridge Building, at 34th Street and Sixth Avenue, and in the Empire State Building, on the corner of Fifth Avenue. Since the mid-1970s, however, many companies have moved uptown to the 50s, close to the hotels where out-of-town retail buyers stay

NEW SHOE LOCATIONS IN NEW YORK CITY

Shoe manufacturers and importers are moving into buildings at (1) 1414 Avenue of the Americas, (2) 4 West 58th Street, (3) 12 West 57th Street, (4) 1370 Avenue of the Americas, and (5) 717 Fifth Avenue.

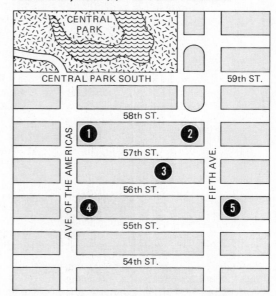

when they come to attend the industry's semiannual trade showings. Most of those who have remained in the 34th Street area are producers of children's and men's shoes. Companies like Ferragamo, Golo, and Joan and David prefer the more fashionable 50s.

DEVELOPMENT OF ATHLETIC SHOES

Not too many years ago, athletically inclined people bought a single pair of sneakers in which to run, jump, bike, or scramble up the side of a hill. Today, all is specialized. There are biking shoes that are stiff enough to direct all the rider's energy into the pedal, cross-country running shoes with spiked soles for traction, high-laced shoes for skateboards, and on and on to a variety of special-purpose sports shoes.

The phenomenal interest of the American consumer in physical fitness has created an entirely new segment within the formerly traditional shoe industry. This segment has its share of giants, such as Converse, with approximately $300 million in sales; Nike, whose sales of almost $1 billion include $60 million in running shoes alone; Wolverine Worldwide, with sales of more than $400 million which includes Brooks and Kaepa running shoes among its divisions. Athletic shoes have also attracted traditional shoe manufacturers, such as Stride Rite Corp., whose Allsport division includes Pumas, and whose total company volume has topped $300 million.[3]

The wearing of athletic shoes has also become acceptable with business clothes. The custom began in New York City during a 1980 transit strike, and gradually was picked up as a fashion for commuters in other parts of the country as a mark of the business or professional person's interest in health and body comfort.

Projections indicate that by 1993 the consumption of athletic footwear and sneakers will reach a total value of $2 billion, comprising more than 300 million pairs each year—that is, more than one for each man, woman, and child in the United States.[4] A further indication of the importance of this category is the increasing presence of retailers who specialize in athletic shoes to the exclusion of all other types of footwear, but offer their customers large assortments of such brands as Adidas, Treetorn, Reebok, Keds, Converse, Puma, and others.

Economic Importance

The **nonrubber footwear** industry includes production of all footwear that is deemed to contain more than 50 percent nonrubber in the upper part of the shoe. Thus, athletic shoes with more than 50 percent of the shoe itself made of suede, leather, vinyl, or any other fabric are considered part of the nonrubber footwear industry. On the other hand, shoes such as jellies, or shoes that are produced by a vulcanizing process, or those that have more than 50 percent rubber in the uppers, are classified as part of the rubber shoe industry. With the enormous growth of athletic shoes, these distinctions are increasingly difficult to perceive. However, a tariff advantage is currently granted to imported rubber footwear, and many canvas-topped athletic shoes contain just enough rubber to qualify for this category.[5]

The domestic shoe industry in 1985 produced 256,600,000 pairs of non-rubber shoes and 64,500,000 pairs of rubber shoes, for a total production of about 320 million pairs—men's, women's, and children's. The production value of nonrubber footwear was over $4 billion in 1985.[6] The industry employed more than 116,000 persons, of whom about 60 percent worked in Maine, Missouri, Pennsylvania, Massachusetts, New Hampshire, New York, Wisconsin, and Illinois. This represents a drop from 1974, when the shoe industry employed over 172,000 persons. Meanwhile, domestic consumption passed the billion mark in 1985, with per capita consumption reaching 4.4 pairs.[7] Retail dollar volume was over $23 billion, the largest percentage of which was in imported shoes.[8]

Shoe Construction

Shoes consist of a number of different parts, all of which must be joined together with precision to make for a comfortable fit. These parts include the shoe **uppers** (the visible outside material) and linings cut to fit inside the uppers. These two elements are joined and draped over a **last**—the form that gives the finished shoe its size and shape. Also included are the toe box, which protects both the wearer's toes and the shape and contour of the shoe, and the **vamp**, which is the front of the shoe from toe to instep.

The lasting of a shoe is one of the most important processes in making shoes, since it gives the finished shoe proper fit, removes wrinkles, and ensures comfort and good appearance. Each size is made on a different last, and it is not unusual for a shoe manufacturer to have thousands of pairs of lasts in a factory. Originally, lasts were constructed of wood, but today newer lasts are made of lightweight plastic or aluminum.

At the bottom of the shoe is the outsole, the surface that hits the ground with each step. Above this is the insole, the lining on which the foot rests. Between these two layers is sandwiched a shank—a metal, leather, or plastic strip that protects and forms the arch of the foot within the shoe itself. Some shoes also contain additional padding within the two sole layers for further cushioning and comfort.

The method by which the sole of a shoe is attached to the upper varies within the industry. Each method is referred to as a "construction," to identify the process used: stitching, cementing, vulcanizing, injection molding, nailing, or stapling. About 60 percent of shoes made today use the cement process, applying adhesives to attach the sole to the upper with a permanent bond. This construction is found primarily in men's and women's casual and lighter-weight dress shoes. The most expensive shoes are usually of hand sewn construction and are referred to as "bench made."

Heel heights of shoes vary, of course; the industry builds them and refers to them in terms of eighths of an inch. Flats measure up to $7/8$ inch, low heels are $8/8$ to $14/8$ inch. Medium heels are $15/8$ to $19/8$ inch; high heels are $20/8$ inch and up. Heels are made of many materials, including leather, wood, plastic, and rubber.

A most important distinction in shoe construction is whether the various parts are made of leather or synthetic material. Leather is highly valued, because it molds to the wearer's foot, is supple and resilient, and breathes to allow moisture to evaporate. Thus, leather is generally used in footwear of the finest quality. Shoes are generally labeled to identify the areas in which natural and synthetic materials are incorporated.

Marketing

The shoe industry is extremely fashion and marketing oriented, and each season presents a wide variety of new colors, shapes, and designs, geared to apparel trends. Perhaps this is why many women seem to be intensely susceptible to the lure of new shoes and to buy them as often as or even more often than they buy the other major components of their wardrobes. The industry does not rely on fashion alone to sell its products, however. Major emphasis is also placed on manufacturers' brand names in selling and in trade and consumer advertising.

SEASONAL SHOWINGS

New lines are brought out twice a year. Because shoe production is a slow process, manufacturers develop and show their seasonal lines in advance of ready-to-wear. Fall/Winter lines are shown in January/February and Spring/Summer lines in August. In addition to presenting their lines in their own showrooms, manufacturers participate in semiannual cooperative trade shows, such as the National Shoe Fairs held in New York. These shows attract thousands of shoe store owners and buyers from all over the country, not only to see the new merchandise but also to attend merchandising clinics and discuss new fashion trends with the fashion directors of the participating manufacturers. A regular feature of the New York shows is fashion presentations, at which retailers see how the new shoes coordinate with apparel fashions. All this is done six months before so much as a pair of the new shoes is likely to turn up in a retail store. In addition, there are other less elaborate regional showings and clinics throughout the country.

LEASED SHOE DEPARTMENTS

Because of the expertise needed to fit and sell shoes, and also because of the tremendous inventory needed to stock a shoe department, department and specialty stores have traditionally leased out some or all of their selling space to experts in the field. Many of these are manufacturers of well-known national brands, such as the U.S. Shoe Company, which uses leased departments to stock and sell its Red Cross and Pappagallo lines, and the Brown Shoe Company, whose leased departments feature its Buster Brown, Regal, and Naturalizer shoes. Other lessees are simply shoe merchants, who operate their departments as they would operate free-standing stores, with as many or few brands as they deem appropriate.

Many of the leased shoe departments, manufacturer-owned or otherwise, also stock related accessories, such as handbags, hosiery, and small leather goods, which they purchase for resale from producers in these various industries.

MANUFACTURER-OWNED RETAIL CHAINS

In contrast with prevailing practices in other accessory industries, there are manufacturer-owned chains of retail stores that specialize in an individual maker's own brand. Some of the brands thus distributed are sold only through such manufacturer-owned outlets. Others are sold both in the owned chains and in independent retail stores. The latter method of marketing, which is an example of dual distribution, is also found in the menswear and women's wear industries.

Among the well-known manufacturer chains are the Thom McCann stores, owned by the Melville Corporation, which produces this and other shoe brands. The Brown Group is another organization that operates retail chains that sell its brands. Like other retail shoe stores, the manufacturer-owned chains stock related accessories, which are usually purchased from other sources for resale.

Extensive Competition from Imports

In 1985, foreign producers supplied more than 77 percent of the total U.S. shoe consumption—a constantly increasing share that has caused domestic production to drop to a 50-year low.[9] Thus, the footwear industries suffer from import competition just as the fashion industries in general do. (A full discussion of imports will be covered in a later chapter.)

The fashion appeal of Italian and other European styling is important; so is their expertise. Important competition is also presented by the price appeal of low-wage labor countries. A further complication faced by shoe producers is that foreign countries are quick to buy up hides and leather in the United States, where our meat-eating habits make us an important provider of these commodities. Then these foreign producers manufacture shoes and other leather goods in their own countries, at lower cost than is possible here, and compete on a favorable price basis with domestic producers.

THE BELEAGUERED U.S. SHOE INDUSTRY

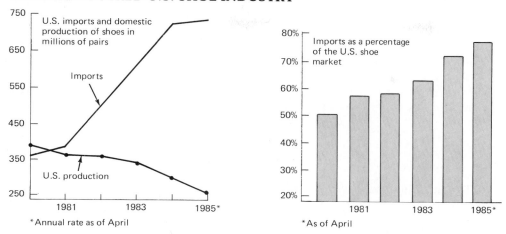

*Annual rate as of April

*As of April

Source: Footwear Industries of America Inc., Arlington, VA. Reprinted with permission.

Total imports of nonrubber footwear were about $5 billion in 1985. Taiwan is the largest exporter of footwear to the United States, accounting for over 42 percent; Korea is second, with 17 percent; Brazil is third, with 15 percent; Italy is fourth, with 10 percent; followed by Spain with 5 percent and Hong Kong with 4 percent.[10] Included in these figures are shoes imported and resold by domestic manufacturers, as well as those purchased directly by retailers. Some U.S. manufacturers, moreover, employ off-shore production. There are those who own their own facilities in Italy, Spain, or South America; others contract out their work to foreign producers. An example of this latter type is the extremely fashion-oriented firm of Joan and David, which has its shoes produced by the Martini factories, among the oldest and finest in Italy.

An example of the inroads made by imported shoes was the fashion craze in 1983–84 of the "jelly bean" or "**jellies**," which are plastic shoes made from polyvinyl chloride or nylon. These shoes, the staple footwear of the poor in undeveloped countries for years, were first imported in cut-out open sandals, styles that overcame their nonbreathing drawback. In 1981, they came into the United States as nonbranded, inexpensive footwear. In 1983, they were colored, restyled, boxed, and tissued, and became a huge retail success. Grendene, a Brazilian factory, produces 200,000 pairs a day, which they ship all over the world. Jellies are also produced and worn in countries such as Mexico, Greece, and China.

Thus, the footwear industry's problems with foreign competition parallel those of other labor-intensive industries in this country. For shoes, however, there are no import quotas. Because of this, and because of the strong American dollar, competition from imports is a serious problem to the domestic shoe industry.

Grim as the picture may be, an occasional manufacturer in this country is able, by ingenuity and enterprise, not only to meet foreign competition, but also to sell domestic shoes abroad. There are not yet enough of these rare birds to make a summer, however, and in the meantime the industry presses for government action to hold back at least part of the import flood.

HOSIERY

The introduction of nylon stockings in 1938 set the stage for vast changes in hosiery, in the industry that produces it, and in its importance as a fashion accessory. Before nylon, stockings were made primarily of silk and also of wool, rayon, and cotton. Yarns were knitted into pieces of flat fabric, each shaped so that when it was folded in half and seamed down the back, a stocking in the form of a leg resulted. Colors were limited and fabric surfaces were plain.

Early nylon stockings were made much as silks and rayons had been. Except during the World War II years, when civilian use of nylon was ruled out to make way for military needs, nylon has made steady progress in hosiery, to the point that it has virtually crowded out other fibers for dress wear. With continuing technological progress, nylon stockings became sheerer, took on more colors, were produced in sandal-foot and other styles, and developed patterns and textures undreamed of in earlier years. In the 1960s, the development and popularity of pantyhose substantially added to the growth and fashion importance of hosiery.

Nature of the Industry

The business of hosiery is one of chemistry, filaments, knitting machines, technology, big production, big promotion, and big competition. It is also the second largest industry in the accessories field, after footwear. And like the shoe industry, it is dominated by large firms. Among the largest are Hanes, Round the Clock, Bonnie Doon, Hot Sox, Kayser Roth, and some that are divisions of giant textile companies such as Burlington and Cannon.

Most of the plants are in the Southeast, notably North Carolina, a state that accounts for more than half the industry's output. Nevertheless, the marketing center for the industry is New York City. There the larger firms have their showrooms and smaller companies also have sales representation. It is there that retail buyers go during market weeks, not only to select merchandise but also to learn about national advertising programs that producers plan to run and to assess the opportunities for tying in at the local level.

Economic Importance

The wholesale value of the hosiery industry's output was estimated at $2.8 billion in 1984.[11] This volume of business represents the output of the 283 companies in the United States in 1984, of which 89 produced women's hosiery and 198 produced hosiery for men, boys, girls, and infants and children. Consumption was estimated at 16 pairs per capita in 1984, compared with 12.8 in 1975.[12] The industry employed 69,700 workers in 1984, compared with 60,900 in 1975—a healthy 13 percent growth in the last decade. Over 90 percent of these workers are employed in North Carolina, Tennessee, South Carolina, and Mississippi.[13]

Hosiery Construction

Hosiery is knitted, either full-fashioned or seamless, and in the greige. Full-fashioned stockings are knitted flat to the desired shape, length, and size; sewn into the shape of the leg; next heat-set or boarded; and then packaged. Seamless hosiery is knitted on a circular machine, at high speed, and then dyed. The same procedure is used for pantyhose, some of which are knitted as stockings and then attached to separate panties. Full-fashioned hosiery

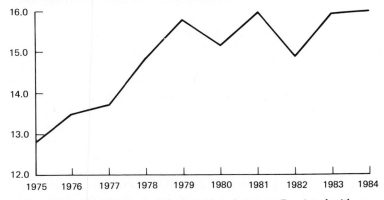

HOSIERY: PER CAPITA CONSUMPTION

Source: National Association of Hosiery Manufacturers. Reprinted with permission.

had the advantage of a better fit than seamless until the introduction of stretch yarns in the 1960s. With them, the fit of seamless hosiery and pantyhose was greatly improved. Stretch yarns also made possible stretch hosiery, support hose, control tops, and comfortably fitted knee-high stockings.

Automation in hosiery production is constantly increasing, to the point that computerized machines can turn out hosiery that features graphics, patterns, and textures and employs many novelty yarns. Such machines were introduced by the Japanese NEGATAS and the British E.T.C.

Marketing of Hosiery

As hosiery moved from almost entirely functional purposes toward becoming an important fashion accessory, the marketing strategies of the industry changed along with its product. Manufacturers' brands acquired new influence; producers' advertising took on greater importance to the retailer; fashion became the watchword of the industry.

NATIONALLY ADVERTISED BRANDS

Manufacturers' brand names in the hosiery field are older and better established, and have been longer promoted than those in other accessories areas. But whereas women had been conditioned to purchase a brand for its fit and durability, they are now bombarded with advertising that stresses the fashion points of the brands. Major producers advertise consistently in national magazines, on television, and through cooperative advertising with retail stores, in newspapers.

Retailers have capitalized on women's devotion to brand names by not only featuring national brands but also creating their own. This approach gives them greater price flexibility, removes them from direct competition with other stores in the national brand arena, and creates a certain exclusivity for their stores. Usually, the same manufacturer will produce both the store's private brand and its own national brand that is also carried in the same department. For example, Macy's has its Clubhouse and Altman's has its Balta, but both stores carry an impressive array of nationally advertised brands side by side with their own. And in that array, the maker of the house brand is sure to be represented. Its source of supply, however, remains the store's secret. The same situation prevails in discount houses, chain drug stores, supermarkets, and others, except that these latter outlets seldom carry as many brands as department stores and major women's specialty shops.

IMPACT OF FASHION AND DESIGNER NAMES

As hosiery has moved into the fashion spotlight, both retailers and manufacturers have been treating legwear much as ready-to-wear is treated. For example, the industry has changed from two to three market weeks a year:

March for the presentation of fall lines; August for the opening of holiday and early spring lines; and November for spring lines. This change in the marketing calendar is a natural outgrowth of the increased number of fashion items attuned to the seasonal apparel fashions. More and more emphasis is put on decorative legwear in a wide variety of textures, colors, and patterns. To coordinate with active sportswear, the industry offers leg warmers in colors coordinated with the clothes themselves. And in response to women's body-building and other exercise activities, the industry produces bodywear in attractive colors, to be sold in hosiery departments.

Inevitably, as the total look became important in fashion, leading apparel designers, both European and American, moved into designer-name hosiery—for the most part under licensing arrangements with producers of national brands. For example, Round-the-Clock has legwear bearing the name of Givenchy; Bonnie Doon has Geoffrey Beene socks; Kayser-Roth produces a Calvin Klein line; Hot Sox has a Ralph Lauren collection. And more!

PACKAGE MARKETING

Hosiery, like so many other products, has been affected by packaging and self-service techniques. For decades, it was sold over department and specialty store counters by saleswomen who slipped their beautifully kept hands into the stockings to show how they would look on the leg. Then came packaging, notably L'Eggs, by Hanes. These were pantyhose, folded into egg-shaped containers, for sale from self-service fixtures conspicuously placed

HOSIERY MARKET SHARE BY TYPES OF RETAILERS

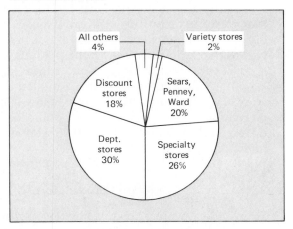

Source: *Chain Store Age* research. Reprinted with permission.

near checkout counters in supermarkets and drugstores. With the marketing success of L'Eggs, other producers soon followed the Hanes lead. Kayser-Roth developed the No-Nonsense brand for similar distribution. Presently, the consumer can find a packaged hosiery rack in almost any self-selection store she patronizes. Even famous designer names are now in the packaging picture: Maro, the largest privately owned hosiery company, now a mere 75 years old, has introduced a Bill Blass line of clam-shell-packaged pantyhose for distribution through mass outlets.[14]

The success of these untraditional channels of distribution has led hosiery producers to seek out more innovative packaging and marketing techniques. Department and specialty stores, too, have had to look to their laurels; their share of the market is now quite small. To compete with the price appeal of discounters, supermarkets, and others, they are using a two-pronged attack. One effort is to push their own brands to meet price competition; the other is to emphasize decorative legwear as a major accessory of fashion.

A chart in this chapter shows the market share of the various types of retailers.

Competition from Imports

Pantyhose, hosiery, and basic socks constitute one area of domestic production that has resisted the inroads of import competition. This is true because the industries involved are capital intensive. Cheap labor, the competitive edge that many foreign merchandise sources enjoy, has little impact in this field. Competition does come, however, from industrialized countries such as Japan, England, and France. These produce goods of high quality, have great technical expertise, and use sophisticated dyeing techniques. Despite attempts by the domestic industry to keep imports to a minimum, some manufacturers say they will bring goods in from offshore because of the quality of foreign yarns, the quality of finishing, and the greater sophistication of dyeing techniques. In the field of casual socks, for example, Hot Sox uses 60 percent of the import quota from Japan.[15]

As to the figures, in 1985 6.2 million dozen pairs of hosiery of all types were imported into the United States. Of these 1.6 million dozen were pantyhose—a category in which domestic production is at the 300 million dozen mark. Total imports for 1985 were nearly double the 1975 figure of 3.5 million dozen pairs.[16]

HANDBAGS AND SMALL LEATHER GOODS ....

From earliest history, people have needed receptacles of some kind in which to carry with them various personal possessions and necessities. Quite possibly, a pouch made of skin or leather and suspended from a belt or girdle was used by primitive peoples who had not yet ventured into clothes, much less clothing with pockets. Handbags as we know them are a creation of the twentieth century; before that, women had only a belt from which to suspend housekeeping keys, and slit pockets in their voluminous skirts to accommodate whatever a lady wanted to carry with her. As women's activities grew more varied in the twentieth century, and as their garments became slimmer and sleeker, handbags became necessary and developed into accessories that would complement and coordinate with the apparel. Today, most women have a wardrobe of handbags in a variety of materials (leather, fabric, and plastic, for example), and in a diversity of sizes and shapes, such as clutch, envelope, satchel, box, duffle, tote, pouch—and the woman executive's briefcaselike carryall.

Nature of the Industry

For the most part, the handbag industry consists of relatively small specialists, the majority of whom are headquartered in New York—primarily in the 30s, between Broadway and Fifth Avenue. They present their lines in two major showings a year: in May for Fall and in November for Spring and Summer. Supplementary collections, smaller than the main seasonal ones, are shown for holiday/transitional in August, for early Fall in March, and for Summer in January.

The industry has been dramatically affected by a great influx of foreign-produced handbags. Because of this factor, some producers have replaced

1986 HANDBAG MARKET WEEKS

N·H·A **SPRING HANDBAG AND ACCESSORIES MARKET** opens November 4th…	**SUMMER** JANUARY 6 **TRANSITIONAL** MARCH 10 **FALL** MAY 12 **HOLIDAY/TRANSITIONAL** AUGUST 11 **SPRING** NOVEMBER 3

Source: Reprinted with permission of the National Fashion Accessories Association.

lost volume by expanding their lines, adding small leather goods, luggage items, or even coordinated belts.

The majority of buyers for retail handbag departments also buy other accessory items, such as gloves, belts, and/or small leather goods. Such buyers demand and usually get coordination in both color and silhouette among the various markets they shop, and they also seek to purchase accessories that will relate well to the upcoming season's ready-to-wear. The handbag industry, through the Handbag Association, establishes market dates that dovetail with apparel openings. It also uses its openings as an opportunity to disseminate both industry and fashion information to the retail store buyers.

Economic Importance

Manufacturers in the handbag industry produce women's handbags and purses of all materials with the exception of precious metals. In 1985, the value of product shipments was reported at $526.9 million, up almost 5 percent from the previous year. This increase is explained chiefly in terms of increased consumer demand and also in terms of the rising costs of labor and materials, resulting in higher unit prices. In 1985, the handbag industry employed over 13,000 workers, in 369 factories, located primarily in New York and New England.[17]

Handbag Construction

Years ago, leather was the principal material from which bags were made. This meant a large amount of hand-guided work and demanded considerable resourcefulness in cutting, since the operator had to work with a natural product, irregular in shape and sometimes with scars to be worked around. Today, many bags are made of plastic or fabric with a uniformity in width and quality that vastly simplifies the cutter's task.

Today's handbags range from classic constructed types to unconstructed, unframed bags of leather, canvas, or other materials. The number and difficulty of the operations required varies with the styling. All, however, begin with a design from which a muslin sample is made. From the muslin, a paper or metal pattern is made, and this is used to cut the handbag materials. The actual cutting is done either by hand or with metal dies, depending on the complexity of the design and the quantities to be produced. Each handbag shape, such as the clutch, envelope, tote, and satchel, for example, requires different types of construction and parts. If the design requires a frame, then all of the inside and outside parts must be fitted into the frame; after that, closures and straps are added.

Competition from Imports

Imports of handbags into the United States in 1985 exceeded $600 million, a 4 percent increase over imports in 1984. Most of the imports are in low- to medium-priced handbags from the Far East. The largest overseas suppliers are Taiwan, accounting for more than one-third of imported handbags; China accounted for 28 percent; South Korea, one-fifth; and Hong Kong, just over 18 percent. Italy, France, and Spain, which export higher-priced, high fashion

EXAMPLE OF DESIGNER LICENSING

ANNE KLEIN HANDBAGS & BELTS*

**The Collections of
ANNE KLEIN & CALDERON BELTS and HANDBAGS
are now being shown at our New York Showroom
and thru our Sales Representatives.
Appointments are suggested.**

 **BELTS & BAGS, INC.**
389 FIFTH AVENUE ■ NYC 10016 ■ (212) 684-0253

NORTHEAST: Gabriel Pecci
DALLAS: Harry Weiss • 1434 Apparel Mart
FLORIDA: Jeff Frankel • Miami Merchandise Mart
ATLANTA: Stan Grey • 6-N-302 Merchandise Mart
CHARLOTTE: Stan Grey • A301/K301 Carolina Mart
WEST COAST: Edith Sheppard Assoc. • A1073 Calif Mart • Los Angeles
CHICAGO: Bernard Nahm & Associates • 580 Apparel Center
KANSAS CITY: Rose Wasser • Apparel Center

*Excluding Metal Belts

Source: Reprinted with permission by Anne Klein for Calderon.

goods, represent only a small percentage of total imports in this field.[18] According to some major domestic handbag manufacturers, "The only way we can compete is to be more creative," and "by using designer labels."[19] Faced with such intense foreign competition, many domestic handbag manufacturers have themselves become importers. Some design handbags in this country but have them produced abroad.

In fact, one of the few remaining domestic handbag producers has been quoted as saying, "Eighty-eight to 90 percent of our industry has been penetrated by imports. Three years ago, it was only about 60 percent."[20] According to the National Handbag Association, most large retailers buy directly from the factories abroad, primarily in the Far East.

Small Leather Goods

Fashion and the changing activities of both men and women have had strong impacts on the industry that produces **small leather goods**, such as wallets, credit card cases, billfolds, key cases, jewelry and eyeglass cases, cigarette cases, and similar items for both sexes. Among the largest are Prince and Princess Gardner, Swank, and Buxton.

In today's world of fashion, many women choose to match such items with the handbags they carry. This is especially true of designer-licensed lines, which coordinate the various items by fabric and color. And among women climbing the success ladder in the business world, special needs are developing for which the small leather goods industry is providing some answers: calculator wallets, credit card cases, pocket appointment calendars, work-and-date organizers, notebooks, and all sorts of handbag and briefcase accessories that project both fashion and businesslike efficiency.

This industry's domestic production in 1985 was reported to have a factory value of $421 million. It employs approximately 8,600 workers, in 469 plants. About 60 percent of the workers are employed in New York, Massachusetts, Wisconsin, and New Jersey. Imports have shown very strong growth, with a 48 percent increase from 1983 to 1985—from $156.2 million to $228 million.[21] Major fashion trends, however, are established by the United States and Italy; other countries that sell their goods here tend to follow their leads.

GLOVES ....

One can trace the wearing of gloves before and through recorded history. In ancient times, they were worn as protection and adornment—as they are today. Objects in pyramids dating back to Egypt's twenty-first dynasty include gloves. In ancient Rome, ladies protected their hands with gloves. In medieval times, kings and church dignitaries wore richly ornamented gloves, symbolic of their status. A knight wore gloves, or gauntlets, reinforced with armor. When he threw one down before another knight, that constituted a challenge to battle.

Gloves today have many purposes, many of them functional. Foundry workers use insulated gloves to protect their hands from heat; Eskimos need mittens to keep out the cold; racing drivers wear gloves that give them better wheel grip; skiers use waterproof kinds to protect them from frostbite. In fashion, gloves play a role that changes in importance, taking a share of the spotlight when dress becomes elegant and fading out when the look is at a casual extreme.

Nature of the Industry

The glove industry suffered a severe blow during the 1960s and 1970s, when fashion took on an ultracasual look and gloves became almost obsolete as fashion accessories. The hard times this situation imposed on the glove industry dealt it a blow from which it has not yet fully recovered.

Many of today's gloves, especially those made of fabric, are produced by divisions of multiproduct companies that also manufacture small leather goods and handbags, such as Etienne Aigner, or by firms like Kayser-Roth that produce intimate apparel and hosiery. There are still, however, some specialists who are glovers exclusively. Among these are Aris Glove, producers of a line of fine leather gloves and also the Isotoner glove. Another is the Foreign Intrigue Glove Company, which has a licensing arrangement with Perry Ellis to design a line of fashion gloves, to be produced in addition to their regular line. Hansen Gloves is another well-known specialist. A relative newcomer to the glove business is LaCrasia, producer of a line of trendy gloves that are unquestionably more fashionable than functional. Companies like these, which are glovers first and foremost, flourish or suffer according to whether fashion smiles on or ignores the glove as an accessory to the total look.

The plants that produce leather gloves are located principally in the Northeast. Many are in the city of Gloversville, New York—where, not surprisingly, the National Glove Manufacturers Association makes its headquarters. That association, unlike many in the fashion field, concerns itself primarily with federal regulations affecting its industry, rather than with product and industry publicity. Gloversville was the site of the first glove production facility in the United States, as far back as 1760, and it is where, by 1900, some 80 percent of American gloves originated.[22] Production of fabric gloves, on the other hand, is more widely distributed throughout the country, with 65 percent of the factories being located in North Carolina, Mississippi, Alabama, and Tennessee.[23]

Economic Importance

Some 6800 production workers are employed in the glove industry, and they produce $208 million worth of gloves at factory value. Of this amount, in 1985 leather gloves accounted for $122.5 million. The balance consists of work glove production. In general, the glove business today is more a business of warm hands and work gloves than one of fashion. A return to a more elegant life-style may change all that, however, at some time in the future.

Imported gloves have been and still are a serious threat to the glove industry, increasing in value to an estimated $105.8 million, up almost 23 percent from 1984. Leading foreign suppliers included China, the Phillipines and Mexico. China alone accounted for almost one-third of the total U.S. glove imports.[24]

Glove Construction

Of all accessories, gloves are probably the most labor intensive to manufacture. Although made on an assembly line, they require the most skill on the part of production workers and involve many steps, since a glove must fit when the hand is closed in a fist and yet not be baggy when the hand is open.

Gloves are made up of numerous small pieces, such as the trank or hand and finger piece, both front and back; the thumb part, which may be made in any of several ways; the fourchettes, or pieces that shape the fingers between front and back; and quirks, tiny triangular pieces sewn at the back of the fingers to provide flexibility and give additional fit. Only the very inexpensive gloves use few pieces; they consist merely of a front and back sewn together—a procedure that earns them the name of "sandwich gloves" in the trade.

Because there are so many pieces in the usual glove, and because they are so small, a great deal of handwork is involved in cutting. This may be done on a table, using a ruler to measure each part, or with the use of a die. The former method is known as table cutting, the latter as clicker cutting. Actual sewing is done on several types of machines and uses lock stitch, chain stitch, and overstitching, depending on quality and style. Since gloves are curved, high-speed production equipment cannot be used.

Glove Marketing

The major marketing center for gloves is New York City, where most glove producers maintain permanent showrooms of their own or use the facilities of sales representatives. These showrooms are usually located in the East 30s, where many of the other accessories industries are also located. Seasonal lines are shown twice a year at the same time as the handbag showings. Compared with the promotional outlays and activities of other fashion accessories manufacturers and retailers, the money devoted to promoting gloves is relatively insignificant.

Some of the more aggressive producers, however, have followed the example of the hosiery industry and are packaging "one size fits all" stretch gloves that can be displayed and sold in self-service fixtures. Others are increasing their volume by packaging their gloves with matching hats or scarfs, or both—a combination with strong consumer appeal during cold winter months.

MILLINERY

Until the middle of the present century, it was unthinkable for a well-dressed woman to be seen on the streets or to enter a store or office without a hat. Every department or woman's specialty store devoted a great deal of prime space to millinery departments, which featured both ready-made and custom-made hats and were usually located adjacent to apparel departments. In the 1950s, there was an enormous exodus from the city to the suburbs and, with it, an emerging fashion for casual living and casual clothes. The outdoor barbecues of the 1950s called for a very different style of dress from the garden tea party of an earlier suburban generation. Country casual dress spread to the city, and the habit of wearing hats went into a decline. The millinery industry, after many years of prosperity when women had whole wardrobes of hats, went into a decline, too—one from which it has not yet recovered.

Nature of the Industry

The millinery industry today is small, because of the diminished demand for its wares. It is made up, as it always has been, of small firms, numbering about 105, all of which are specialists in this one field.[25] The industry has been untouched by the drive to bigness and diversification that has affected other areas of the fashion business. Smallness, however, is no handicap in this industry, as there is little opportunity to mechanize, automate, or develop huge runs of individual styles. The ability to move quickly on a new idea, the strong point of small operations, is an important asset in the millinery field.

The importance of the total look in fashion today may spark renewed interest in millinery. Designers dutifully put appropriate headwear on their models as they parade the runways; retailers show millinery with other outer apparel; some customers even buy hats. But one sees few, indeed, on the streets and in other public places. That tide may turn, as tides often do in fashion. Meanwhile, even the most prestigious of fashion retailers gives minimum space to millinery departments, except for cold-weather hat-and-scarf bars and similar fad or functional sales corners. The day of the huge millinery department, in which expert salespeople helped women choose the right hats for their outfits, or the right hat to enhance their morale for an important date—that has not yet returned. Until it does, the millinery industry will remain small.

Economic Importance

The wholesale value of output in 1985 for millinery alone was $120 million, which represents a healthy increase over the $58 million production in the late 1970s. Hats and caps, which include men's, women's, and children's value of output was $433 million.[27] Approximately 4500 workers are employed in the millinery industry, primarily located in New York City. A small number of these employees are located in St. Louis, Dallas, and Los Angeles. This is seasonal employment, and the figures represent employment at the peak production period. The 105 companies operating today, however, represent a decline from the more than 400 companies operating in the 1960s when hats were worn by a majority of the women.[28]

Construction of Millinery

Basically, the millinery industry's output falls into two categories: hats and caps, and millinery. The former category can be made by machine or by hand. Millinery-type hats are made by sewing velvet, satin, or other fabric and trimmings over buckram frames, or by shaping and trimming felt or straw bodies. Millinery made by these latter methods involves a great deal of handwork, and the processes lend themselves readily to custom work for consumers or for sale through retail shops. The industry is headquartered mostly on a single street in New York City: West 37th Street, between Fifth and Sixth Avenues.

At one time, the industry had its share of well-known designers. Adolfo and Halston, for example, began their fashion careers as milliners. These days, however, the glamorous names bypass the millinery industry and concentrate in the apparel field, where opportunities and rewards are much greater.

Marketing of Millinery

An unusual factor in the millinery industry is the millinery syndicate of Consolidated Millinery, which operates 200 leased departments. Such a firm leases space for millinery departments in retail stores across the country and provides these stores with a continuing supply of new styles. In order to obtain such styles, the buyers for these firms are constantly in the wholesale markets, not only to seek out actual merchandise but also to find and develop talented new producers and stylists. Help, advice, and sometimes even operating capital will be made available by the syndicate to potentially creative resources.

Unlike other fashion accessories, millinery does not function on two lines a year. Seasonality has its influence, of course, but the life of a hat as an accessory is usually short, and, as a rule, the faster a firm gets into and out of a good selling style number, the better the operation is. In millinery, the important element is an unending procession of new styles or new versions of currently accepted styles. At one time, when millinery was in its heyday, retailers sought to have completely new assortments every three or four weeks, and the term *millinery turnover* was used in retail circles to describe extremely fast-moving merchandise.

The great unknown for millinery today is the customer. It still remains to be seen whether promotion, publicity, and fashion creativity can reverse the trend toward hatlessness and convince her that smart millinery is essential to the total fashion look.

JEWELRY

The wearing of jewelry is believed to antedate the wearing of clothes; in fact, among primitive peoples today, even if one sees little that could be called clothing, there is usually a ring or two or ten on the body, the neck, the ears, or the nose. In modern times, jewelry has become a sign of worth and status—and a very important fashion accessory, indeed. No fashion costume is complete without it, whether it be the understated string of cultured pearls worn with a woman executive's office clothing, or the outrageous four-inch earrings hanging from the earlobes of the latest MTV star.

The jewelry industry divides itself into two distinct parts: fine jewelry, made of precious metals and gem stones, and costume jewelry. In recent years, a third category has entered the picture: bridge jewelry, which spans the gap between the other two.

Precious or Fine Jewelry

The metals used in **fine jewelry** are gold, silver, and platinum, worked alone or in combination with gemstones. The 2193 firms operating in this field in the United States produce in excess of $3 billion worth a year of merchandise and employ over 35,000 people. Sixty-eight percent of the factories are located in New York, Rhode Island, California, and Massachusetts.[29]

Gold, the metal of first choice for fine jewelry, is too soft to be used by itself and it is therefore usually combined with base metals. The gold content is expressed in terms of carats, or karats. Solid gold is **24 karats**, or 24K. The most commonly used alloys are rated 18K, 14K, or 12K, and are arrived at by mixing gold with copper (to produce reddish yellow metal), silver (to produce greenish yellow), or palladium or nickel (to produce white gold). Any alloy of less than 10K may not be called karat gold. In the United States, 14K is favored; in European jewelry, 18K is customary.

Platinum, a silvery metal, is rare, heavier, and more expensive than gold, and is a favorite for diamond settings. It, too, is generally alloyed, primarily to reduce its price, with palladium, iridium, rhodium, or ruthenium—all white and hard metals.

Silver, the least expensive of the precious metals, is usually combined with copper. The term **sterling** may be used where there are at least 925 parts of silver per thousand.

GEMSTONES

Precious stones include diamonds, emeralds, sapphires, rubies, and real pearls. With the exception of pearls, stones are measured in carats, one carat being the equivalent of 100 points. Pearls are measured in millimeters of length.

Semiprecious stones include amethysts, garnets, opals, lapis, jades, topaz, and aquamarines, among others. Today, fine jewelry uses more of these than ever, because of the high prices of precious stones.

In addition to natural gemstones, wide use is now made of synthetic gemstones. Laboratories can produce synthetic corundum to look like garnets and amethysts, and synthetic spinel to look like emeralds, diamonds, and aquamarines, among others.

An important element in the value of a piece of fine jewelry is the workmanship that goes into it. It is a hand-made product, with a jeweler creating each setting for each stone at the workbench, one piece at a time. The creativity and skill of the workman are major factors in the cost of the finished piece.

Bridge Jewelry

With the price of fine jewelry climbing and the demand for jewelry increasing, a new area of jewelry has developed to fill the need. This is **bridge jewelry**, which involves silver, gold-plated metals, or 14K gold, and which uses less expensive stones, such as onyx, ivory, coral, or freshwater pearls. Much of the fashion leadership comes from designers such as Celia or Karen Sibiri, Elsa Perretti, and M. J. Savitt, who, among others, create hand-made and signed pieces. Also important here are items such as gold chains; gold combined with the less expensive semiprecious stones; and jewelry that sets many small diamonds in a group to create the look of larger stones. Retail prices range from about $100 to $2000 for these products.

Costume Jewelry

Costume jewelry is mass produced to fill the fashion demand of customers who seek relatively inexpensive jewelry to complete the fashion look of their outfits. The materials used may be plastic, wood, brass, tin, glass, lucite, or any other substance that can be manipulated to achieve the desired effect. Retail prices range widely, from items sold in variety stores to those bearing the names of such companies as Kenneth J. Lane and Miriam Haskell. The total output of the industry is over $1 billion at factory value. There are 785 companies in the field, mostly located in Rhode Island, and many of them are quite small. The industry employs 21,000 people in its plants, but only 186 of the plants are large enough to employ 20 or more workers.[30] Like other accessories producers, the manufacturers of costume jewelry have show-rooms in New York and present two lines a year, timed for the convenience of buyers who expect to coordinate their purchases with what their stores will offer in other fashion departments.

Among the leading names in the costume jewelry field are Monet, said to have a wholesale volume of about $100 million a year; Victoria Creation, with more than $60 million; Trifari, with about $45 million; and Pakula, with about $35 million.[31] A great many bangles and beads, indeed.

Unlike other accessories industries, the costume jewelry industry does not appear to be harassed by import competition. Pearls usually come from abroad, but the assembling takes place in this country. The threat from low-wage countries is felt, it is true, but as one producer points out, the industry offsets that particular differential by offering the retailer such benefits as advertising, adjustment of stock, and dependable deliveries. It also imports some of its components but designs and produces the finished articles in this country.

OTHER ACCESSORIES . . . .

Other accessories include sunglasses, scarves, belts, handkerchiefs, umbrel-las, and wigs. Sunglasses came into fashion prominence in the 1960s, when the then First Lady, Jackie Kennedy, wore "shades" constantly. They have remained important in fashion, not only for daytime, functional outdoor wear, but also as accessories for evening. Wigs, falls, and hairpieces, too, have been important accessories at various times, and to some extent their burgeoning popularity has coincided with the decline of millinery. Under-standably! Skimpy, faded, or neglected hair once hid under hats; nowadays, it hides under a wig or hairpiece. For many women, especially those whose careers leave them little time for the beauty parlor, close-cropped hair under a fashionably styled wig is a convenient fashion move.

Belts gain prominence when waistlines are in fashion. Scarves and stoles fill in low necklines, provide a bit of warmth, add a touch of color, or can be worn to accent broad-shouldered or slender looks, according to how they are draped and according to current fashion requirements. Handkerchiefs, whose utilitarian functions have been taken over by tissues, peep in and out of the fashion picture, tucked into breast pockets or sleeves if and when they enhance whatever the "in" look may be. Umbrellas, too, have their fashion ins and outs, sometimes carried with a swagger like a man's cane, sometimes brightly colored to liven up drab days and drab rainwear, or whatever the case may be. Utility sells many umbrellas; fashion, when it touches this field, sells more.

ACCESSORIES DESIGNERS ....

"Name" designers in the accessories field are almost exclusively those who have made their mark in the apparel field and who license their names to manufacturers of accessories. The designs themselves may or may not originate with the famous individual whose name is attached to them; they may have come from a design studio run by that luminary, or they may have been created by anonymous employees of the producer and then approved by the licensor.

Very few designers become famous through their work in accessories alone. For the most part, manufacturers have design staffs or use free lances; in neither case do they feature the names of these designers. Among the distinguished exceptions are Vera, who began many years ago in scarfs; Elsa Peretti, the house designer of jewelry for Tiffany's, and Kenneth Jay Lane, also in the jewelry field.

Apparel designers moved strongly into licensed accessories in the 1970s, when the total "look" became important in fashion and consumers began putting together outfits in which the accessories were quite as essential as the apparel if one was to achieve the desired casual or elegant smartness. This trend has brought almost every famous American and European apparel design name into the accessories area. It has brought glamour and a useful promotional tool to the field.

It is interesting to note that Liz Claiborne, Inc., who had licensed their name to Kayser-Roth for a line of accessories in 1986, discontinued this arrangement and opened a new division, Liz Claiborne Accessories. Their decision to do this was explained by Jerome Chazen, co-chairman of Liz Claiborne, Inc., as follows: "Since there has always been a synergistic relationship between apparel and accessories, we have decided to make that relationship closer."[32] Whether or not other apparel companies will follow this lead remains to be seen.

DIOR ALSO LICENSES JEWELRY MANUFACTURERS

Christian Dior only uses the licensee's name in advertising that appears in trade publication.

Source: Reprinted with permission of Christian Dior/Grossé Jewelers.

INTIMATE APPAREL ....

The segment of the fashion industry that produces loungewear, nightwear, women's and children's undergarments, and body shapers for women is known as the **intimate apparel industry**. The history of its products is also a history of society's changing perceptions of modesty and feminine beauty. In the nineteenth century and on into the early decades of the twentieth, manufacturers in the United States produced, and women wore, an astonishing variety of devices to shape, distort, and even deform the figure to achieve what was considered fashionable for women. It is a matter for amazement that women of the generations that first fought for suffrage and first entered the business world conducted their activities in garments so constricting that people in the trade referred to them in later years as "iron maidens."

Since undergarments in general come into close contact with the body, they have always had sexual connotations. Even though their appearance to the outside observer is secondary, these garments, other than the actual corsets, have generally been characterized by soft fabrics, a great deal of detailing, and many trimmings. The Gibson Girl might have worn a corset of tough fabric reinforced with whalebone, but she wore a dainty camisole and lacy petticoats with it.

Recent years have seen renewed consumer interest in intimate apparel. The industry had hit a low point in the 1960s when young women burnt their bras as a form of protest and declaration of freedom. This was also the era of tight jeans, worn with little or no undergarments. Nowadays, intimate apparel is well on the road back up again, thanks to the return of interest in dresses, and the concomitant return of slips and petticoats. Today's concern with fitness, moreover, has created a need for jogging bras among women who exercise strenuously, and has revived interest in bras and girdles and support panties among those who want to look even more trim and fit than they may actually be.

Industry Segments

The industry's products fall into three major categories:

1. **foundations**, which include girdles, brassieres, garter belts, and the shapewear that nowadays replaces corsets;
2. **lingerie**, which includes petticoats, slips, panties, camisoles, and sleepwear such as nightgowns and pajamas;
3. **loungewear**, which consists of robes, negligees, bed jackets, and housecoats. The lines between lingerie and loungewear are not always clear-cut, however, and some in the industry categorize their products as daywear (lingerie and housecoats) and nightwear (sleepwear and negligees, etc.).

Many of the producers in the intimate apparel field have products in all three branches of the industry. Nevertheless, there are separate trade associations for each of the different branches within the industry, namely, the Associated Corset and Brassiere Manufacturers; Intimate Apparel Council of the American Apparel Manufacturers Association; Lingerie Manufacturer Association. Each of these has its headquarters in New York City.

Economic Importance

The intimate apparel industry is big business in the United States, with a total output in 1984 of over $3.9 billion, a figure that includes both women's and children's garments. Of this total, the largest segment is produced by the nightwear industry, which includes pajamas, sleepwear, and robes. Nightwear and lingerie employs over 67,000 workers and encompasses 604 companies, of which 422 employ 20 or more employees. Fifty percent of the employees work in North Carolina, Pennsylvania, Alabama, and New York. Foundation garment factories employ 13,800 workers in 151 companies, among which 97 have 20 or more employees. Leading production states are New York, California, Pennsylvania, and Georgia. Loungewear is the smallest area with 135 companies, 83 of whom employ 20 or more persons. The leading production states are New York, North Carolina, South Carolina, and California.[33]

Marketing

New York City is the major market center for all segments of the intimate apparel industry, and the showings are timed to mesh with those of ready-to-wear. The buyer of intimate apparel is usually a specialist, not involved with the merchandising of outerwear. Nevertheless, the close relationship between undergarments and outerwear fashions, and between outerwear fashions and the various categories of at-home wear, make it essential for the intimate apparel buyer to be guided by what the other sections of the fashion customery are presenting.

The intimate apparel industry, which functioned on two markets a year in the days when its major concern was corsetry, now has five seasonal showings: Early Spring in August, Spring in November, Summer in January, Early Fall in March, Fall and Holiday in May. Market weeks are also held in important regional centers: the Dallas Mart, the Atlanta Mart, the Chicago Apparel Center, and the California Apparel Mart in Los Angeles.

IMPACT OF FASHION

Even in this industry's purely functional garments, the impact of fashion is felt. For example, the length and fullness of outerwear skirts necessarily

MARKET WEEKS IN
INTIMATE APPAREL

COMING N.Y. MARKETS
1985

August 12-16
EARLY SPRING

November 11-15
SPRING

1986

January 6-10
MOTHER'S DAY / SUMMER

March 10-14
TRANSITIONAL / EARLY FALL

May 12-16
FALL AND HOLIDAY

August 11-15
EARLY SPRING

Nov. 10-14
SPRING

determines the length and shape of the slips to be worn under them; figure-revealing silhouettes enhance the demand for body-shaping undergarments while relaxed lines diminish their importance; emphasis on the waistline brings waist-cinchers back into production, generally briefly. Changes in women's life-styles and interests, too, affect the industry's output. A notable example is the development of special bras for jogging and aerobic dancing, in response to the interest in fitness. In loungewear and nightwear, in which looks are more important than function, the relation to fashion is clear indeed. The customer, consciously or otherwise, tends to seek out the same general effects, the same overall looks, that she has been seeing in apparel displays and on smartly dressed women in her area.

IMPORTANCE OF BRAND AND DESIGNER NAMES

The brand names of producers in this industry have traditionally been so important that store buyers tend to budget their purchases by resource or vendor rather than by merchandise category. This practice goes back to the days when foundation garments had to be carefully fitted to individual customers. Leading manufacturers, in those days, took a major share of responsibility for planning retail stocks and training salespeople in stores that carried their lines.

Among the best-known names in foundations are Warner, the oldest in the field, Formfit-Rogers, Lily of France, Maidenform, Bali, and Playtex. In the lingerie area, well-known brands include Vanity Fair, Barbizon, Vassarette, and Saybury robes, among others.

As would be expected in a field where brand names are important, producers advertise widely along three fronts: directly to the consumer in print and television, through cooperative advertising with retail stores, and to retail stores through trade publications. Some companies also provide stores with display fixtures, on which their brand names appear, for use in featuring the particular brand in windows and interiors.

The importance of designer names in marketing fashion merchandise is mirrored in the many licensing arrangements that exist between intimate apparel producers and leading designers of outerwear. Bill Blass, for example, designs robes and loungewear for the Evelyn Pearson Company; Monika Telly does a signature sleepwear and loungewear collection for Vassarette; Fernando Sanchez designs a collection of sleepwear and loungewear for Vanity Fair in addition to his own collection; Oscar de la Renta is licensed by Swirl to design sleepwear and loungewear. Even the French designer, Givenchy, has licensed his name to Boutique Industries.

According to the designers themselves, their objective is to apply to their intimate apparel collections the interpretation of fashion that they present in their ready-to-wear collections. Thus, the season's changes in silhouette and fabrication, as they see them, are reflected in intimate apparel as well as in streetwear.

Competition from Imports

Import competition has affected the intimate apparel industry, as it has every other segment of the fashion industry, but not yet to as great an extreme as in some other categories. Imports generally play their greatest role where production is labor-intensive, as in intricately sewn and embroidered loungewear and sleepwear, because of the quality of handwork and the advantageous pricing. In some of the more basic styles of loungewear and sleepwear, retailers have goods produced overseas for presentation under their private labels. Direct import of European-made bras occurs among some of the prestigious fashion stores such as Saks-Fifth and Bergdorf's, which feature French bras from Prima and Lejaby and Italian bras from LaPerla. The major offshore bra production center, however, is the Phillipines, where such companies as Lovable, Bali, and Warner's are major importers.[34] In 1984, imported bras reached a total of 12,331 million dozens—more than half of U.S. consumption.[35] In second place after the Phillipines was Costa Rica. For robes and dressing gowns, Hong Kong and China were the major import sources in that year.[36]

Readings ....

In the extremely diverse field of accessories and intimate apparel, any number of approaches can be used successfully. These readings outline strategies that have worked for a variety of firms and products.

Candie's Bars

Teenagers are a great market, if you can reach them effectively. The elements of Candie's Shoe Bars that are geared toward reaching teens include constant observation and exploitation of the changing pattern of this age group's rapidly changing interests.

Accessories Designers Keep on Going On

Accessory design calls for fast footwork as the fashion spotlight singles out and later abandons individual items. Staying in business involves a large dose of courage and determination, and these designer/ entrepreneurs tell us what kept them going.

Cutting Edge: Hot Sox Spreads Its Empire.

What machines can produce, man can market—and visa-versa. The story of Hot Sox is a lesson in seeking new machines to give substance to an idea, and then developing more new ideas to utilize the capabilities of these machines to the fullest.

Pakula: Chicago's Trendsetter

A moderate-priced costume jewelry company, headquartered in Chicago, explains its operation servicing fashion conscious budget customers in both mass market and specialty store retailers.

Creating Brand Identity in Foundations

When everybody does the same thing, nobody prospers. This reading tells the strategies used by several firms in the intimate apparel industry to lift their brand names above competition and price promotion.

Candie's Bars
by Dorothy Kellett

Mall bunnies are teenage girls, who when they are not at home or in school, socialize in the shopping malls. Last year, they reached into their pockets and forked over $200 million of their allowances in Candie's Bars.

Candie's Bars are the concept stores for Candies, a brand name for the shoes, ready-to-wear, socks, accessories, cosmetics, umbrellas and lingerie sweetmeats dished out by El Greco, a Port Washington, N.Y. shoe company with New York City showrooms on an entire floor of the prestigious Trump Tower on Fifth Avenue.

Charles Cole, chairman and chief executive officer, and his son, Neil, 27, president, have aggressively targeted their Candie's brand exclusively to teenagers, a lucrative market overlooked by most retailers, who "only know the buzz words baby boom and career woman," according to Neil Cole. A recent addition has been diminutive Candie's for little girls who want to dress like their teenage sisters.

With saturation advertising—$8–10 million dollars this year, compared to $5 million in 1983—El Greco's interpretation of the hype, excitement and fantasy of the teen life style has made Candie's a brand recognized by 74% of the teenagers in America, according to a recent Gallup poll.

It is one of the few companies offering a full line under one brand name. El Greco imports Candie's, Crayons and Cities, its shoe brands, from 100 factories in Taiwan, Korea, Brazil and Italy. There are 21 licensees making all of the other merchandise. Among them are Regal, Circo, IFI Industries and Amerex. Five new licensees have been added each season. Belts, swimwear and outerwear will be introduced in Spring '85.

The firm has 26 company-owned Candie's Bars stores, 22 of them converted from R. G. Barry Corp.'s Mushrooms stores; 15 owner-operated stores and there are 14 concepts in major department stores.

"El Greco will be a $1 billion dollar business in three to four years," predicts Neil Cole.

His projection is based on plans to expand the owner-operated stores to between 300 to 500 units by 1989 and to build the company's other teen shoe line, Crayons, which are priced 33% lower than the $10–$35 tag for Candie's. Crayons will be sold in mass merchandising stores.

"It will protect the Candie's line from ever seeping down," Neil Cole says. J. C. Penney, Montgomery Ward and Sears have already signed on the dotted line.

Targeted to the same customer who shops in malls, the Crayons concept will be introduced with a $3 million advertising campaign scheduled for Spring '85.

"Someday Crayons will be a bigger name than Candie's," Neil Cole claims. "We are going to be the next U.S. Shoe Company."

This all started with a simple little shoe from Italy.

In 1978, Charles Cole, who had been manufacturing shoes in the U.S. since 1962, began importing what was to become the shoe of the year, the Candie's slide. It was an inexpensive and simply made plastic, high heel, molded unit bottom with a piece of leather stapled over the vamp. But it was sexy. Five million women bought the slide that year.

Cole closed his U.S. factories and began importing shoes. By 1981, he had licensed ready-to-wear; and hit the media with the jingle he still uses:

> *"I take my own direction*
> *I know the way to go*
> *I want your sweet affection*
> *But I'll make it on my own . . .*
> *And I've got Candie's, Candie's, Candie's*
> *I've got Candie's."*

The message was loud and clear, Candie's was no longer just a shoe.

The jingle and visuals of teen girls identified with their life style—independent, sassy and, as the ads say, "on the fast track."

Neil Cole distinguishes her further. "She's not that fashionable; she likes the basics and still wears jeans, a polo shirt and sneakers. Only a small part of that market is trendy. Ninety-five percent of our business is done in the Midwest."

Candie's ready-to-wear is basic T-shirt and sweatshirt-designed tops and dresses; jeans and cotton knit bottoms. Dresses are priced from $30–60 retail, lingerie $3–18, accessories $5–20, handbags $10–30 in the summer, $20–45 for fall goods. This fall, the company will have leather and back-to-school clothing. "We've decided to work 12 months of the year," Neil Cole says, explaining that 75% of the company's business has been in lightweight clothing. "This year, we'll do 50% of our business in the fall.

"Color is the key to Candie's. The shoes are made in 12–14 colors each; it makes the product jump out. But the typical Candie's customer will end up buying white, black or brown."

Another one of El Greco's strengths has been timing. The teenage market is constantly changing. El Greco conducts its own market studies, and uses *Seventeen* magazine studies.

Neil Cole says he likes to sit in shopping malls in Dayton or Omaha, for instance, to watch his customer in action. "Any study we do (on her habits) is obsolete in a year."

But it is El Greco's persistence in understanding and changing quickly with its market's whims that has kept the company valid to an endearing, but fickle customer while it continued to build its customer base.

The potential for the market has barely been tapped, the Coles claim. In order to capitalize on Candie's growth, the company is concentrating on its program to put owner-operated Candie's Bars in every major mall in the country, including those with major department stores that have Candie's concepts. "This strengthens the market," Cole says.

"We believe we can roll out on a national basis faster with owner-operated stores than we can internally," says Ed Kertz, vice president, store development. "And an owner, who is in the store every day, with his own money invested, pays better attention to his business than any national chain can."

Neil Cole adds that expansion of the concept stores serves another purpose. "With our large factory base, expanded stores will guarantee distribution over the marketplace during the next 10 years."

The Candie's Bars are 1,000–1,800 square feet and cost approximately $80,000–90,000 to open, without inventory. Cost depends on location and whether the store is a conversion or new. Sales per square foot are $400–500. In El Greco-owned stores, the product mix is 70% shoes, 30% other merchandise. Owner-operated stores will split the mix 50–50.

El Greco's team of six specialists with retail and design backgrounds provide store planning, real estate, financial, advertising and promotion advice which includes representatives to help open the stores.

The present store prototype is shiny and electric. The ceiling and walls are silver, with blue and pink naked neon lights. The blare of music and Candie's commercials playing on in-store videos attract teens like actors to Broadway. The ideal Candie's customers are hired as clerks, along with ideal teen boys.

Promotion of a recent opening of a Candie's Bar in Gainesville, Fla. featured a mime, clown, breakdancers, "anything that causes a lot of commotion. The mall was ready to throw us out," according to Kertz.

"If we can find a better way to make our stores more exciting, we'll do it. The mood in the country is still self-indulgence, but if it were to go to soft and romantic, we'll reflect that," he adds.

Four color, double spreads in *Glamour, Cosmopolitan, Mademoiselle, Seventeen* and the *New York Times Magazine* are a montage of a Candie's girl life and fantasy. One page depicts her in motion wearing Candie's action clothes, jogging shoes, plastic sandals or sport flats.

Next she's seen in Candie's jeans and a sweater putting on her Candie's lipstick in the reflection of a shiny red and silver semi-truck. Finally, she is in a fantasy situation, standing by a red convertible in a dark, abandoned factory yard. She's wearing a Candie's knit dress and slides. Steam pours from unseen pipes, the cement pavement is wet. "She's a young woman on her own, here," Neil Cole explains, "away from home, it could be a dream. She's sexy and she's ready to take off."

And when she does, El Greco will be right behind her. The company's 120,000 square feet of warehouse space in Port Washington probably symbolizes El Greco's mobility better than anything. From there, 100,000 pairs of shoes are shipped daily. They flow from the trucks onto conveyor belts where computers read customer orders, label the cartons for shipping and send them back onto the trucks to be shipped out. Streamlined, up-to-date, constantly moving the product, that is El Greco.

Accessories Designers Keep on Going On

Part I

by Hancel Deaton

Eight years ago, apparel designer Bonnie Boynton changed the direction of her career and plunged into the world of accessory design. This year, her company, Bonnie Boynton Enterprises, will generate an estimated $4 million in sales of accessories, sportswear and dresses. Accessories account for 35 to 40 percent or $1,500,000 of that total. For 1986, Boynton projects a modest increase in accessories sales of 5 to 10 percent.

Boynton had a solid background as a ready-to-wear designer with such Dallas-based chain and road line manufacturers as Mr. Fine and Nardis, which are both now out of busi-

Source: *Women's Wear Daily*, August 1985. Reprinted with permission.

ness, and Sunny Isle. In 1977, while still working as a designer at Nardis, she decided to try something on her own.

Boynton designed six different flower-shaped suede lapel pins "when lapel pins were a hot item," she says. Armed with a small suitcase chock-full of her pins, she doggedly pursued representation at the Dallas Apparel Mart. "I walked into an accessory showroom and refused to leave until the representative agreed to take my line," she recalls, laughing. "I started with just a tiny cart to display my pins in the window." During her first market in October 1977, Boynton sold $5,000 worth of lapel pins at $3.75 to $5.75 each wholesale.

Two years later, at the height of the metal trend in belts, the vivacious, determined designer left Nardis to launch her own company. Initially, Boynton worked mainly in brass, but she soon progressed into combining different metals such as brass, silver and copper for a one-of-a-kind look. "I was always experimenting and trying something new," she says, "but I'd definitely give credit to brass for formulating our image with the consumer as a better-price accessory manufacturer."

In 1982, five years after her venture into accessory design, Boynton foresaw an end to the belt boom and expanded her business to include rtw. Last year, she diversified her line of distinctively crafted belts and began to manufacture innovative fine jewelry. "Manufacturing accessories is so much easier than producing a line of ready-to-wear," Boynton says, "because there are fewer steps involved—nothing has to fit." But she also recognizes the limitations of producing a line of accessories exclusively. "It's easier to have unlimited growth in ready-to-wear," she says.

Boynton's belt designs have evolved from a free-form crafted look using mainly hammered brass to an architecturally influenced, polished style using a variety of metals and incorporating unusual woods and geodes as the focal points. All of her belts have leather or snakeskin straps available in an array of colors. Wholesale price points range from $29 for a small trimetal combination buckle on a leather strap to $76 for a metal with ivory buckle on a snakeskin strap.

Although her company has enjoyed steady growth, Boynton says there have been frustrating times. In the early days of her company, when Boynton broke new ground with the hammered metal look, other designers swiftly followed suit. "When that happens," she says, "there's really nothing you can do except try to be first on the market with the product."

Only recently has Boynton overcome a major obstacle in forming her company by developing a good, strong sales force. "Certainly you have to be able to design and produce a good product," says the savvy designer, "but most importantly, you have to be able to sell it."

Boynton has always made a point of working each Dallas market. She shows her lines of accessories and rtw in her 900-square-foot showroom in the Group III designer area of the Dallas Apparel Mart. "I think every designer should have to sell her line," Boynton says. "It makes you a better designer because you're talking directly with the retailers and learning exactly what they want."

The 37-year-old designer attributes her success to persistence and drive. "I think it's very easy to start a company and equally difficult to keep it going," she says. "There's always the pressure of having to come through with a special new look each season. It's impossible to conceive of what's involved in starting your own company until you've already done it."

Part II

by Helena Pohlandt-McCormick

"In the beginning, sheer determination kept me going," says Daphne de la Grandiere, former model and actress, about the first turbulent years of her career as a jewelry designer and owner of Daphne.

"I worked for two years from 9 to 10 every single day, every single night, every weekend. It was insane, I had no capital, and I made everything myself," says the French native, who began designing and manufacturing her own line of fashion jewelry in 1976.

De la Grandiere came to New York after three years of traveling the world as a member of Europe's first free-form 20th Century group—the Living Theatre.

"When I turned 30," she says in her perfect English laced with the trace of a French accent, "I told myself I am going to turn into some old freak. I thought it was time to be serious."

Her traveling years "along the hippie trail to Nepal and Morocco" provided her with exotic ethnic materials, inspired her first designs and insured the success of her first collections. Because she had worked for Dior in Paris, first as a cabine model, later as the house's attache de presse, she was no total stranger to the world of fashion and design.

But nothing had quite prepared her for the intricacies of conducting her own business.

"My biggest problem was my total inexperience," she acknowledges. "I was not being professional, I did not know the professional jargon and I was naive enough to believe people were really nice. For two years I was really ripped off."

It also took some time for her to gain credibility and the reputation for a consistently good line of jewelry with the retailers who bought her collection. "They test you forever," she said, and all the while "you are trying to get to know the way the stores function and the intricacies of merchandising."

Beyond the business aspects of establishing herself as a designer, the single most harrowing problem for this member of a noble French family that got its crest and title in 1050 A.D., was not knowing the American customer.

De la Grandiere speaks of a time when she designed an extremely avant-garde collection of rubber jewelry. "It got enormous amounts of good publicity," she says, "but not one piece sold outside of New York City."

"American women are not trendy, they are not ready to wear something bizarre. It has to be pretty and understandable," she says.

Accordingly, de la Grandiere has had to tone down her designs, and her line now follows American trends very closely. The present line consists of simulated pearl and gold jewelry, rhinestone, baroque pins and earrings, the antique gold look, crystal and gold coins.

It took de la Grandiere four years "not to feel as lost," but by 1981 she had moved the Daphne showroom from 38th Street to its present "established" position on Fifth Avenue. She has expanded her staff from an initial two helpers to 18, including her partner and manager, Herbert Bookstein, and her assistant designer, Paola Attala, and she has doubled her business over the last year, reaching a volume in the $5 million range, according to Bookstein.

More recently, de la Grandiere has experienced new difficulties with her expansion into the French jewelry market.

The Daphne showroom, established in Paris in 1978, is inactive at present, she says, because "it has proven to be a liability.

"The reality is, you have to be big enough to have an organization of people to collect the money and to follow up closely; otherwise you sink all your profits into the foreign showroom."

Beyond that, de la Grandiere's only regret is that she cannot devote more of her time to the more outrageous and exclusive designs she favors.

"Ideally I'd like to be doing 10 fabulous pieces a year, but I'm doing chain work," she regrets. "I tend to have gigantic lines, and as soon as one is finished, we start another. There is never a breather, and the amount of stuff is staggering."

Cutting Edge: Hot Sox Spreads Its Empire
by Karla W. Bausman

"If you think of your company as merely a sock company in 1985, you're missing the point entirely," Gary Wolkowitz says emphatically.

As president and chief designer of Hot Sox, one of the industry's most successful, and certainly trendiest, legwear companies, he is handsomely sitting atop a flourishing $12 million empire. Business includes not only the firm's Hot Sox label but licenses for Ralph Lauren women's legwear and the Polo collection of hosiery for men and most recently Benetton, the Italian sportswear manufacturer.

Kicking around his roomy offices and showroom overlooking Seventh Avenue, Wolkowitz is putting the finishing touches on the coveted Benetton private label agreement under which Hot Sox will domestically produce and distribute a collection of socks in the U.S. and Canada under the store's label.

Hot Sox will sell the collection exclusively to 200 of Benetton's 250 U.S. stores starting in June. The group will retail from $4 to $8 and include casual sport socks and knee-high styles. All will coordinate with the store's stocks of brightly colored and richly patterned goods. The collection will also be shown in Benetton's first catalogue, due in the U.S. by mid-July, according to Wolkowitz.

From Wales, where cashmere cable knee socks and tights for his Ralph Lauren collection are hand-tied by village women, and Japan and Mexico, where high-power computers reel out brightly colored socks, to West Germany for lace goods and here for basic socks, Hot Sox's empire literally stretches to the four corners of the earth.

No one could be more content than Wolkowitz, whose company started as a spark of an idea 15 years ago while on a languorous Cape Cod vacation with some friends, all of whom now are business partners.

The firm's success, Wolkowitz maintains, comes from charting new fashion ground in legwear along with each emerging fashion trend. "Legwear is pure ready-to-wear. That's

Source: *Women's Wear Daily*, May 5, 1985. Reprint permission granted.

how socks and pantyhose have to be designed now," says the man who last year introduced Under Sox, a pair of cotton crews with an elasticized cuff resembling a man's underwear brief. Years before that there was the Toe Sock, a multicolor sock with individual toes knit into it. It was a junior department item that found a broad appeal, catapulting the company into stardom, he easily recalls.

These novelty items are Hot Sox hall-marks. They have consistently won the firm its praise and its growing orders from retailers around the country, says Wolkowitz, who travels to the Orient three times a year to work with 20 mills there. Nearly 60 percent of the Hot Sox collection is manufactured in Japan and the firm controls a large part of the export quota for Japanese-manufactured hosiery goods, he adds.

Wolkowitz first went to Japan five years ago, after being invited to test some state-of-the-art computerized machinery that, up until then, had not been used to manufacture fashion hosiery.

"We worked with those machines and pushed them to do things that even the Japanese who designed them never thought possible. The design potential was astounding and unlimited. It allowed us to create new goods that would have been impossible to do on the antiquated circular knit machinery in this country," he says.

The result was hosiery so uncommon that only Hot Sox had it. Wolkowitz unveiled transparent monofilament socks with intricate multicolor patterns, socks the industry later christened "jellies." New, too, were flat-knit socks with clean, crisp designs knit into them, sometimes in up to five different colors.

This fall, Hot Sox introduced its largest collection of hosiery to date, some 160 styles in all, excluding Ralph Lauren's group. Many of them are the newest generation of "jellies" and encompass designs as intricate as cabbage roses on pantyhose and bold argyle motifs on knee socks.

Aiming for broad market segmentation, prices range from just a few dollars to over $20 for imported lace pantyhose. The majority of the line retails for under $7.

"Buying Hot Sox is like trading baseball cards. For $12 to $16 you can buy three or four pairs of socks and have a lot of fun," Wolkowitz says. As he talks he pulls some favorite items from a showroom display—dealing them out as if he had a fresh stack of playing cards.

Pakula: Chicago's Trendsetter
by Dana Shappro

Pakula, Inc., manufacturer and distributor of costume jewelry here, has quadrupled its sales from $8,500,000 in 1980 to well over $35 million this year, according to industry sources. Company executives predict business will increase at least 15 percent in 1986.

One reason for Pakula's accelerated growth has been a broad customer base that includes both the discount chain store market and the specialty and department store market, said Harry Walker, president and chief administrative officer in charge of finance.

Source: *Women's Wear Daily/A*, January 1986. Reprint permission granted.

"We think we are different because we penetrate the mass merchandise market as well as the specialty shop market," said Dick Calk, vice president for marketing and sales. "Most jewelry companies who serve the mass merchandiser only service that trade. But by servicing both, we can do more internal research. If a look sells in the specialty shops, we know it will go to the mass merchandiser next, because the trends start in the specialty shops."

Among Pakula's mass merchandise accounts are K mart Corp., Troy, Mich., J. C. Penney & Co., New York, and Montgomery Ward & Co., Chicago.

Recently the company added a 52,000-square-foot manufacturing and distributing plant in Cranston, R.I., at an expenditure of more than $2 million. Until this year, the bulk of the manufacturing and distributing was done in the 15,000-square-foot Chicago corporate office and out of a 16,000-square-foot facility in Providence. Now all manufacturing and distributing is done from the Cranston plant. But Pakula, Inc., still claims Chicago as its home base, because its corporate office, accounting, finance, marketing, sales and human resource departments remain here.

Another reason the company chooses to keep its base in Chicago, is that three generations of Chicago families have controlled Pakula. Founded in 1932 by Harry Pakula, the company moved into the Axelrad family when Harry's daughter Marilyn married Milton Axelrad. Today, Axelrad is chairman, and his son James Axelrad is vice chairman and chief executive officer.

"We manufacture a good portion of our line, but also acquire merchandise from 80 different vendors in the Providence area," Walker said. "We had to move to Providence because that's where the jewelry industry is now. But we still do everything else here in Chicago."

When Milton Axelrad took over the company in 1965, Pakula, which was only a regional wholesaler here in Chicago, underwent major changes. Axelrad knew if the company was to become national it had to open a New York showroom and aggressively expand into other regional markets.

Today, Pakula is represented in seven regional markets—Chicago, New York, Minneapolis, Dallas, Seattle, Denver and Charlotte. Its first computer was installed in 1965, and Pakula was incorporated as a manufacturing company in 1970.

The company has three in-house design people who design under the Genevieve for Pakula label, and two contractors who send Pakula their designs on an optional basis. There are six people on the buying staff.

The Genevieve for Pakula collection contains some 2,500 items, and prices range from $3 to $150 retail. The line is divided into four color groupings as well as material groups, with a strong emphasis this year on metals such as silver, gold and brass.

Carson, Pirie, Scott & Co., Chicago has been carrying the Pakula line in its junior department for four seasons, and Pakula makes up 50 percent of Carson's junior jewelry business.

"Pakula is an opening price point-type of jewelry and they go after volume because they are lower-priced," said Norma Foster, divisional merchandise manager. "We've carried Pakula for four seasons and every season we've had it, our volume has grown by 20 to 30 percent. We definitely plan to continue our commitment."

Pakula is considered one of the primary resources at J. C. Penney, which has carried the line for more than eight years.

"We have several primary resources, and Pakula would be one of them," said Mariiyn Delph, regional merchandise midwest for J. C. Penney's. "Our commitment with Pakula this year is even with last year. For us, they are a well-priced moderate jewelry line, and our lowest-priced resource, although they do run the gamut and have more expensive looks."

A divisional merchandise manager at a Northeast budget department store said Pakula makes up 80 percent of its jewelry business.

"We are a budget store carrying Pakula for four years," the Northeast retailer said. "We deal in volume, and our price points range from $4 to $10 retail. Pakula offers us volume and fashion at a price point. Service is very important to us, and their service is exceptional. They do all the fixturing for us. And the company is right on target with the marketplace."

Both Walker and Calk said Pakula sets trends rather than follows them, and agreed it's difficult to know when to get off a trend.

"Sometimes there's danger in being a leader—you get off a trend too early," Calk said. "But we'd rather be off it a month too soon than on it a month too long."

Creating Brand Identity in Foundations
by Joyce Wilson

The foundations industry, which in recent years has been characterized by a high level of off-price sales, rebates and buy-two-get-one-free promotions, now is moving in different directions as manufacturers seek ways to create brand identity and increase market share in retail departments that they feel have become a confusing sea of chrome racks and reduced-price signs.

Manufacturers are striving to heighten brand recognition by staking out subcategories such as large sizes and light-support and sports bras, by introducing new lines that do not have price promotions built in, and by developing enticing shop environments to house their complete lines. The more comfortable boutique-like areas, they assert, also present an opportunity for department stores to separate themselves visually from discount stores and other competition.

One company in the forefront of developing the shop concept is Wacoal America, which expects to have roughly 100 in-store boutiques around the country by the end of this month.

Its in-store boutique concept, which was first presented to stores in November 1984, is an extension of the parent company's successful retailing concept in Japan. The shops began surfacing around the country last spring.

Comparing the approach with that of the beauty industry, Dave Gustafson, vice president of marketing of Wacoal America, noted, "It's no surprise that when you walk into any store, cosmetics are the most exciting things in the store. They sell tons of goods at all price points. It's fun."

"The wave of the future in intimate apparel is the emphasis on how it is marketed at the point the product meets the consumer. There are three integral points: product, environment and service to the consumer," Gustafson said. The service Wacoal can offer through a merchandising staff that routinely visits stores, as well as the fact that Wacoal sells at

Source: *Women's Wear Daily/I*, October 1985. Reprinted with permission.

full price with no special price promotions, will separate the company from its competition as much as its boutique environment on the selling floors, he added.

"I think Wacoal kind of opened some people's eyes to the fact this concept can work," said Jack Cassidy, president of Lily of France Marketing, which is owned by Bestform Foundations. In the May market, Lily suggested its own display environment for its Christian Dior Intimates line.

Cassidy noted that stores must identify their most important brands and stretch the environments for those lines, while setting up less important lines on the periphery of the departments.

At Maidenform, Alan Lesk, senior vice president for sales and merchandising, noted, "There needs to be greater definition between the department stores and all the competition that surrounds them from discount stores, chains and off-pricers.

"Everybody is doing the same thing. Everyone is trying to get a share of somebody's pie. Department stores have to create a sense of individuality in the intimate apparel area, and that means treating the most important brands in an unusually selective manner."

Maidenform, he said, has developed a concept that it is calling the Sphere of Influence, which will put together all the Maidenform updated and fashion collections within a department.

The sphere of influence, which will be unveiled during the November market, includes a showcase tree fixture, with trees of merchandise around it and a chrome display of graphics. It will be rolled out to about 300 store branches for spring.

The Bali Co., part of the personal furnishings group of Consolidated Foods, also introduced a shop concept called Island of Bali during the May market, as a second stage to its Bali boutique concept initiated in 1979. The company, however, has returned to the Bali boutique name since it is more familiar to retailers, said Gayle Brill Mittler, director of marketing.

The new Bali boutique program, which pulls together all Bali products, allows stores to display not only packaged merchandise but also merchandise on hangers. "By emphasizing our brand name and our logo, we expect to not only increase our business for the basic Bali line, but also the Ce Soir, A-OK lines, the Something Else bottoms and the Wonder-Shape girdles," Mittler said.

Beyond displays, however, manufacturers are striving to find niches for themselves in the market with new lines and new subcategories of merchandise.

Maidenform is focusing on key merchandise categories including "fashion-minded basics" at opening price points under the Wise Buys umbrella and is formulating a new upscale line called Lumiere by Maidenform, which will include foundations and daywear aimed at 60 stores and their key branches.

At Warner's, a division of Warnaco, a key direction in developing its business has been the identification of various subcategories, said Brian Tart, president, citing the Just Your Fit back-sized bras, Custom Curves underwire bras, Beautiful Answers full-figure bras and Collector's Items woven daywear.

At Vassarette, a division of Munsingwear, Dorothy Pollack, vice president in charge of merchandising, noted the firm is striving to fill emerging market opportunities. Large-size styles, smaller-proportioned items for the petite woman, the activewear classification and the contemporary market are among the new areas the company is targeting for growth.

Vassarette, in addition, has enlarged its retail merchandising staff, said Pollack, noting that it is "absolutely essential" considering the level of customer service in many stores.

Endnotes

1. All estimates are from *Women's Wear Daily/A,* May 1986.
2. Harold R. Quimby, "The Story of Footwear," *Shoe and Leather Reporter,* Vol. 216, No. 13, December 30, 1936.
3. "Sneakers Gain as a Symbol of Commuting," *Wall Street Journal,* October 17, 1984.
4. *Footwear News,* July 30, 1984.
5. Janet Treber, chief statistician, Footwear Industries of America, in conversation with the author and U.S. Industrial Outlook, 1986.
6. *Ibid.*
7. U.S. Industrial Outlook 1986, p. 9, and *Current Industrial Reports, Shoes,* U.S. Department of Commerce.
8. *Ibid.*
9. *Ibid.*
10. *Ibid.*
11. National Association of Hosiery Manufacturers, Charlotte, N.C., *1985 Hosiery Statistics.*
12. *Ibid.*
13. *Ibid.*
14. *Body Fashions/Intimate Apparel Magazine,* April 1985, Section 2.
15. "Cutting Edge: Hot Sox Spreads Its Empire," *Women's Wear Daily,* May 3, 1985.
16. National Association of Hosiery Manufacturers, *Imports, Ten Years Review,* 1986.
17. *U.S. Industrial Outlook, 1986.*
18. *Ibid.*
19. *Women's Wear Daily,* May 1986.
20. *Ibid.*
21. *U.S. Industrial Outlook 1986;* and *Census of Manufactures.*
22. Leslie Ruth Pelz, *Fashion Accessories,* 2nd ed. Indianapolis: Bobbs-Merrill Educational Publishing, 1980.
23. *Census of Manufactures.*
24. *U.S. Industrial Outlook, 1986.*
25. Burt Champion, publicity director, Millinery Institute of America, in interview with the author, October 1, 1985.
26. *Ibid.*
27. *Ibid.*
28. *Ibid.*
29. *Census of Manufactures;* and *Current Industrial Reports.*
30. *Census of Manufactures;* and *Current Industrial Reports.*
31. "Jewelry: Fashion from the Mainstream," *Women's Wear Daily/A,* May 1986.
32. "Claiborne Buys Its Accessories Line," *Women's Wear Daily,* December 23, 1985.

33. *Census of Manufactures;* and *Current Industrial Reports.*
34. Brian Tart, "The Import Price," *Women's Wear Daily,* June 17, 1985.
35. *Census of Manufactures;* and *Current Industrial Reports.*
36. *Ibid.*

Selected Bibliography

Boehn, Max von. *Ornaments: Lace, Fans, Gloves, Walking Sticks, Parasols, Jewelry and Trinkets,* reprint of the 1929 edition. New York: Ayer Company, 1970.
Gray, Mitchell. *The Lingerie Book.* New York: St. Martin's Press, 1982.
Northampton English Museum. *A History of Shoe Fashions.* England; 1975.
Untracht, Oppi. *Jewelry Concepts and Technology.* Garden City, N.Y. Doubleday, 1982.

Trade Associations

American Footwear Industry Association, 1611 North Kent Street, Arlington, Va. 22209.

Associated Corset and Brassiere Manufacturers, 535 Fifth Avenue, New York, N.Y. 10017.

Association of Umbrella Manufacturers and Suppliers, 11 West 32nd Street, New York, N.Y. 10001.

Belt Association, 225 West 34th Street, New York, N.Y. 10122.

Footwear Council, 51 East 42nd Street, New York, N.Y. 10017.

Intimate Apparel Council for the American Apparel Manufacturing Association, 1611 North Kent Street, Suite 800, Arlington, Va. 22209.

Jewelry Industry Council, 608 Fifth Avenue, New York, N.Y. 10020.

Lingerie Manufacturers Association, 41 East 42nd Street, New York, N.Y. 10017.

Manufacturing Jewelers and Silversmiths of America, Inc., The Biltmore Plaza, Providence, R.I. 02903.

Millinery Institute of America, 37 West 39th Street, New York, N.Y. 10018.

National Association of Fashion Accessory Designers, 2721 Clayton Street, Denver, Co. 80205.

National Association of Glove Manufacturers, 30 South Main Street, Gloversville, N.Y. 12078.

National Association of Hosiery Manufacturers, 516 Charlottetown Mall, Charlotte, N.C. 28204.

National Fashion Accessories Association, 350 Fifth Avenue, New York, N.Y. 10001.

National Shoe Retailers Association, 200 Madison Avenue, New York, N.Y. 10016.

Trade Publications

Accent (Jewelry), Sugartown News, Devon, Pa. 19333.
Accessories, 22 South Smith Street, Norwalk, Conn. 06855.
Fashion Accessories Magazine, 244 Madison Avenue, New York, N.Y. 10016.
Footwear Focus, 200 Madison Avenue, New York, N.Y. 10016.
Footwear News, 7 East 12th Street, New York, N.Y. 10003.
Glove News, 30 South Main Street, Gloversville, N.Y. 12078.
Hosiery & Underwear, 757 Third Avenue, New York, N.Y. 10017.
Intimate Apparel, 757 Third Avenue, New York, N.Y. 10017.
Intimate Fashion News, 309 Fifth Avenue, New York, N.Y. 10016.
Jewelers Circular—Keystone, 825 Seventh Avenue, New York, N.Y. 10019.
Leather and Shoes, 47 West 34th Street, New York, N.Y. 10001.
Modern Jeweler, 133 East 58th Street, New York, N.Y. 10022.
National Jeweler, 1515 Broadway, New York, N.Y. 10036.
National Shoe Retailer Association Newsletter, 200 Madison Avenue, New York, N.Y. 10006.
Wigs, Hats and Accessories, 22 East 42nd Street, New York, N.Y. 10007.

CHAPTER REVIEW AND LEARNING ACTIVITIES

Key Words and Concepts

Define, identify, or briefly explain the following:

Accessories
Bridge jewelry
Costume jewelry
Fine jewelry
Foundations
Intimate apparel
"Jellies"
Last

Lingerie
Loungewear
Nonrubber footwear
Small leather goods
Sterling silver
24 karat
Uppers
Vamp

Review Questions on Chapter Highlights

1. How do fashions in accessories relate to apparel fashions? Give examples.
2. What four factors do all of the accessory industries have in common?
3. What is the difference between rubber and nonrubber athletic footwear? Why is this distinction made?
4. In sequential order, list and explain the steps in the construction of shoes.

5. Why have shoe departments traditionally been leased? What is the current status of leased shoe departments?

6. Why are imports less "threatening" to the hosiery industry than they are to other segments of accessories?

7. How has the handbag industry responded to the deluge of handbag imports?

8. List the various parts and different types of gloves.

9. Give the three major categories of jewelry and explain the differences between each.

10. Discuss the statement that "it still remains to be seen whether promotion and fashion creativity can reverse the trend to hatlessness." Will this industry be revitalized?

11. Name the three major divisions of the intimate apparel industry and give one well-known brand name in each.

Applications for Research and Discussion

1. Research the accessory departments in stores for merchandise identified by designer names. Can you find the same "names" in more than one accessory category? Do you believe that these are licensed names or not? Why?

2. Compare the same category of accessories (i.e., hosiery, costume jewelry, shoes, etc.) in two different large stores. Report on department location, stock assortments, price ranges, brand names, displays, and so on. Which department do you think is better and why?

3. Name and give examples of the most important accessory fashions today. How does each relate to current apparel fashions?

7

FOREIGN FASHION PRODUCERS

A development of major importance in the American fashion business has been the penetration of fashion **imports** into the domestic markets. Producers of fashion merchandise have proliferated in almost every country of the world and are competing for an ever-increasing share of the U.S. consumer dollars. The race is not limited to countries with creative design talent and high-quality products; those with only sewing skills to offer have acquired the know-how to work their way into the world fashion market. In this they have had the encouragement and support of their respective governments. Eager to promote their foreign trade, their governments have developed export incentive programs as well as help in staging international trade shows to attract buyers from around the world. Today, importing from foreign sources of supply is a multibillion-dollar activity of the U.S. textile-apparel-retailing complex.

This chapter deals with the nature, locations, and fashion operations of the foreign fashion producers that supply us with goods. The readings that follow the text focus on the operations of leading foreign exporting companies.

DIFFERENT TYPES OF FOREIGN PRODUCERS

Foreign fashion producers fall into three basic categories, each of which will be discussed in this chapter. First is the **haute couture,** the highly creative designer-name houses that produce very costly garments made-to-order for individual customers. Next, there are the European ready-to-wear fashion centers, known for talented designers, fine quality products, innovative styling, and, in some instances, specialized areas of expertise. Finally, there are the low-wage countries that can mass-produce at costs far below those that prevail in the domestic industry.

PARIS HAUTE COUTURE ....

The fashion leadership of Europe, notably that of Paris, originally derived from a small group of fashion producers known as the haute couture. As used in the fashion business, this term refers to a firm whose designer (in French, **couturier** or feminine **couturière**) periodically creates and presents for sale a collection of original designs that are then duplicated for individual customers on a *made-to-order* basis. The founder of the haute couture is generally acknowledged to be Charles Frederick Worth, a brilliant young English designer with a flair for business, who was appointed dressmaker to the Empress Eugenie. He established his house (and the Paris couture) in the mid-1860s, at about the same time that Elias Howe, in the United States, was busy perfecting his sewing machine.

European haute couture garments are completely different from those of the American firms that produce the high-priced ready-to-wear that is often called "couture ready-to-wear." That description is, of course, a contradiction in terms, since couture implies clothes made to measure for individual customers, and ready-to-wear means garments produced in standard sizes without regard to the individual measurements of the persons who will eventually purchase them. Haute couture garments, moreover, are made of the finest and most luxurious fabrics, use superb needlework and a great deal of handwork, and command astronomical prices. Nothing produced in the United States bears the slightest resemblance to European couture.

Chambre Syndicale de la Couture Parisienne

Shortly after Worth opened his business, a trade association was formed to determine qualifications for a couture house and to deal with their common problems and interests. This was the **Chambre Syndicale de la Couture Parisienne,** founded in 1868. Membership was, and still is, limited to couturiers who meet specified qualifications and agree to abide by a set of rules governing dates of showings, copying, shipping dates, and so on.

To qualify as an haute couture house today, an establishment must do the following:

• Present a formal written request for membership in the Chambre Syndicale.
• Establish workrooms in Paris.

- Present a collection twice a year, in January and July, on dates established and coordinated by the Chambre Syndicale.
- Create a collection of 75 or more original garments designed by the firm's head designer (i.e., without recourse to designs bought from outsiders) and present them on live models.
- Employ a minimum of three models on a year-round basis.
- Employ a minimum of 20 workers in the firm's couture production workrooms.
- Produce only custom-made garments for individuals in its own workrooms (as opposed to the standardized sizes of ready-to-wear garments).

French origin is not a qualification for membership. Many of the most famous Paris couture designers were not French by birth. For example, Balenciaga was a Spaniard, Dessès was a Greek, Mainboucher was born in Chicago, and Molyneux was an Englishman, as was the founder of the French couture, Charles Frederick Worth.

CHAMBRE SYNDICALE DU PRÊT-À-PORTER

Originally, the Chambre Syndicale limited its membership strictly to haute couture houses. As ready-to-wear operations by couture houses burgeoned in France, the Chambre Syndicale expanded its membership to include some designer-named ready-to-wear companies. Today, there is a subgroup called the *Chambre Syndicale du Prêt-à-Porter* (i.e., ready-to-wear) *des Couturiers et des Créateurs de Mode*. To date, 18 designers have been designated *créateurs*, rather than couturiers. Among them are Claude Montana, Dorothée Bis, Chloe, Emanuelle Khan, Kenzo, Sonya Rikiel, Thierry Mugler, and Jean-Paul Gautier. According to Jacques Mouclier, executive vice-president of the Chambre, the number of *créateur* members is expected to grow to 25 by 1990.[1]

ACTIVITIES OF THE CHAMBRE SYNDICALE

The Chambre Syndicale provides many services for both ready-to-wear and couture members. It represents its members in their relations with the French government, arbitrates disputes, regulates uniform wage arrangements and working hours, coordinates the opening dates and times of the collections, issues admission cards for the openings to the press, and registers and copyrights the new designs of its members. Unlike the United States, France considers the copying of a registered design punishable by law.

Designer-Name Couture Houses

The operations of typical couture firms are fairly uniform. Each establishment is known as the *house*, because it operates in a residential building rather than in a commercial neighborhood. The head of the house is generally the chief

HAUTE COUTURE DESIGNERS

Cristobal Balenciaga
de Eisequirre

Captain
Edward Henry Molyneux

Gabrielle Chanel

Paul Poiret

Christian Dior

Mme Vionnet

Elsa Schiaparelli

designer (the couturier or couturière), who more often than not is the owner or co-owner. The house usually carries the name of its designer, and its reputation is essentially a one-man or one woman affair. Occasionally, however, as in the case of Chanel and Dior, the well-known name is retained after the death of the founder, but a new hired designer takes over. For example, Marc Bohan designs for the house of Dior and Karl Lagerfeld for Chanel.

There are usually fewer than 25 dressmaking establishments at any given time that are designated as haute couture, and of these, not all achieve worldwide fashion reputations. Among famous couturiers of the past are Paul Poiret, Vionnet, Schiaparelli, Balenciaga, Dior, Chanel, Molyneux, and, of course, Worth. Of those who show collections currently, the best known of all is probably Yves St. Laurent. Among others are Pierre Cardin, Hubert Givenchy, Emmanuel Ungaro, Marc Bohan, and Guy Laroche, to name but a few. Among the Paris couturiers, many have made fashion history, each for some innovative contribution.

Semiannual Collections and Showings

Twice a year, the couturiers prepare major collections of sample garments. They work with the most luxurious and expensive materials, some of which cost more than $200 a yard, and trimmings of equivalent quality. Each sample is made to the exact measurements of the model who will show it. In addition, accessories are created for each garment shown—shoes, hats, gloves, perhaps a fur, and generous amounts of jewelry. The cost of preparing such a collection is extreme, as high as $500,000. Showings are held in January for Spring/Summer and in July for Fall/Winter.

The heavy costs of preparing the collections, plus the rising costs of labor and materials, have sky-rocketed the prices of custom-made couture garments. They now range from $4000 for a simple dress, $12,000 for a suit, to as high as $50,000 for an embroidered or beaded evening dress.[2] And a crystal and pearl ornamented dress ordered from Givenchy for an Arab princess is reputed to have cost $150,000.[3]

Until 1980 different types of customers, who came from all over the world to attend the openings, included the following:

- Wealthy private customers, to choose styles to be made to their order for their own wardrobes.
- Trade or commercial buyers (i.e., textile producers, designers, apparel manufacturers, retailers), to buy one or several models for the express purpose of having them copied exactly or adapted into ready-to-wear styles to be produced in their respective countries, or both.
- Pattern companies, to buy models or paper patterns to copy as commercial patterns for home sewers.
- Representatives of the press, to whom couture openings were and still are a source of fashion news.

Private customers and the press were admitted without charge, but most houses charged trade buyers a **caution fee** (French for deposit or surety). This right-to-see fee ranged in amount from as low as $500 in some houses to as high as $3000. In others, the caution took the form of a minimum required purchase, generally one or two models. The caution was then deducted from the amount of whatever purchases were made; if no purchase was made, or if purchases did not equal the caution figure, there was no refund.

Trade buyers were traditionally charged more for a garment than a private customer would be asked to pay. The explanation for the higher price was that retailers and producers were actually buying copying rights as well as the garment, whereas the private customer was simply buying for her own use.

The Economics of Couture Today

Today the astronomical prices of couture garments have become prohibitive to all but private clients. Trade buyers no longer attend the openings or buy couture clothing. Even the private clientele, extremely wealthy women from all over the world, whose business accounted for a sizable majority of couture sales at its peak, has eroded from 15,000 in the 1950s to 3000, according to estimates by Jacques Mouclier, executive director of the Chambre.[4]

Figures on the sales of haute couture garments are not publicly reported, nor are authoritative statistics available. In 1985, on the basis of estimates cited in a variety of trade articles and statements from the Chambre Syndicale de la Couture et du Prêt à Porter des Createurs, the authors would place this figure at $40 million as a maximum. This amount, which was a slight increase over 1984, involves only the sales of the custom-made apparel produced by the 22 couturiers who belonged to the Chambre at that time.[5]

OTHER SOURCES OF INCOME

Although the semiannual openings of haute couture houses continue to make worldwide fashion news, the sales of couture garments alone have always cost rather than made money for the houses. To survive, therefore, couture houses have expanded into other, more lucrative ventures, making capital of their names to give luster to more profitable activities, including the following:

- *House Boutiques*. Most couture houses have established boutiques in or adjacent to their haute couture premises. These boutiques feature very high-priced, high-quality accessories such as handbags, lingerie, jewelry, and scarves, all manufactured exclusively for the house by outside producers. Often the accessories thus offered are identical with those worn or carried by the models when the haute couture collections are shown. The merchandise that is carried in the boutiques is designed by the couturier or a member of his staff and bears the designer's prestigious label.

- *Prêt-à-Porter.* Beginning in the 1960s, the decline in couture sales, combined with growing competition from an increasing number of talented ready-to-wear designers, both French and from other Europeans, led haute couture houses strongly into the **prêt-à-porter** (ready-to-wear) field. Although the ready-to-wear lines of the couture houses are designed by the couturiers, production arrangements vary greatly among the different houses, as do the locations of the manufacturing plants. For example, Ungaro's ready-to-wear is manufactured by an independently owned Italian company that also makes Valentino's ready-to-wear. Givenchy's ready-to-wear is produced under licensing agreements by ready-to-wear manufacturing companies in France. The house of Yves St. Laurent has a separate ready-to-wear division, St. Laurent Rive Gauche, whose merchandise is produced in France by a manufacturing company in which it has a financial interest. In all cases, however, the sales volume of their prêt-à-porter lines is far greater than their couture sales and yields a far greater profit.

- *Franchised Boutiques.* Retail boutiques bearing the name of a couturier and featuring his ready-to-wear merchandise made their appearance in the late 1960s and spread worldwide, opening a far-flung consumer market for couturier-designed ready-made clothing. Some of these "name" boutiques are owned and operated by the couture house itself; others are run by independently owned retail stores under a franchising arrangement. Under such an agreement, an independent retail distributor—that is, a franchisee—is given permission by a franchising parent company to sell the producer's product in a store that bears the name of the parent company. Especially noteworthy today are the franchising operations of Yves St. Laurent. He launched his first Rive Gauche ready-to-wear boutique in Paris in 1966 and it met with such enormous success that he now has a worldwide chain of franchised Rive Gauche boutiques that carry only St. Laurent's ready-to-wear. Some of these boutiques are free-standing stores; others are specialized shops within large stores that carry other merchandise as well. Among the couture designers who followed his lead into **franchised boutiques** are Dior, Valentino, and Givenchy, with his Nouvelle Boutiques.

- *Worldwide Licensing Agreements.* In addition to their ready-to-wear operations, major couture houses also license the use of their names on an enormous variety of products—lingerie, shoes, perfumes, stockings, bed linens, luggage, children's clothing, lower-priced women's and men's ready-to-wear, and anything else that is fair game for a well-known designer's name. As in all such licensing agreements, the designer sells different manufacturing companies the right to produce and market specific products bearing his or her name. Although the licensed products are supposedly designed, screened, or edited by the couturier whose name appears on them, it does not always work out that way. However, what does work in all cases is the lucrative royalty percentage of wholesale sales that the licensed manufacturer pays to the designer.

From Haute Couture to "Big Business"

Today, the Paris haute couture has become an industry unto itself, the focal point of which is still its prestigious, although least profitable, haute couture clothing. In the absence of publicly reported figures, the authors present accounts, reproduced from *Women's Wear Daily* of July 23, 24, and 25, 1985. As these clearly indicate, couture operations have indeed become big business, with their fingers very much in the worldwide fashion pie:

- *Dior's Business.* Dior's couture sales for 1984 totaled 39 million French francs (about $4 million), up 57 percent from 1983. The house expects couture sales of over 50 million French francs in 1985. Dior totaled 5,200,000,000 French francs ($550 million) in wholesale volume for 1984 (not including perfumes and cosmetics made by Moet Hennessy). The label encompasses 200 licensees for 84 products distributed in 100 countries. With clients such as Princess Caroline, Betsy Bloomingdale, Lynn Wyatt, Claude Pompidou, Ann Getty, Nastassia Kinski, and Danielle Mitterand, the couture collection sells at prices from 49,000 to 200,000 francs ($5000 to $21,000) for evening dresses.

- *Saint Laurent's Business.* Couture sales at YSL totaled approximately $5,200,000 in 1984, an increase of 11.2 percent from 1983. The house sells an average of 850 to 1000 pieces a season to customers including Rosemary Marcie-Riviere, Annette Reed, Marie-Hélène de Rothschild, Queen Noor of Jordan, Nancy Kissinger, Lynn Wyatt, Anne Bass, Helen Rochas, Paloma Picasso, and Catherine Deneuve. Prices range from $2500 for a blouse to $50,000 for a beaded evening dress. YSL has 40 licensees worldwide, and they did $1 billion in retail sales in 1984, $400 million of which was in perfume.

- *Cardin's Business.* The Cardin empire ranges over 640 licenses for 150 products sold in 92 countries on 6 continents, including China and Bulgaria. Wholesale licensed volume is said to exceed $1 billion. Cardin's couture clients include Claude Pompidou, Estee Lauder, Charlotte Rampling, Queen Noor of Jordan, Joan Collins, Olimpia de Rothschild, Nadine de Rothschild, the Duchess of Bedford, and the Princess of Yugoslavia. The spring/summer 1985 couture collection sold 587 pieces priced at $5,000 to $45,000.

- *Laroche's Business.* Some 180 pieces of the spring couture were sold for approximately $800,000. Couture prices range from $4444 to $20,000. The company, one of the most successful in Paris, has 240 licensees in 20 countries. Wholesale volume in 1984 was $40 million. Top couture clients were Sandy Yturbe, Veronique Peck, Betsy Bloomingdale, Bootsie Gailbraith, Carole Rochas, and Claude Pompidou.

- *Ungaro's Business.* Accumulated worldwide retail sales of $150 million, $80 million of which was sold in Japan, 1984 couture sales totaled $3,500,000, with clients including Marie-Hélène Rothschild, Mica Ertegun, Jackie Onassis, Isabelle d'Ornano, and Ann Getty. The house sold 440 couture pieces in the winter 1984 season, 210 of which were dresses, and 481 pieces in the summer 1985 collection, 320 of which were dresses.

Despite frequent predictions of its imminent demise, Paris haute couture seems destined to remain active in the foreseeable future. Although Yves St. Laurent, for example, claims that his couture garments, each of which sells for many thousands of dollars, are a "gift" to his clients, his business managers do not view his haute couture operation per se as a philanthropic venture. As Jean Szware, general director Yves St. Laurent, explained it: "As long as the losses align reasonably with the value gained in publicity and image, the couture is worth maintaining. But it is possible, in view of rising costs and declining sales, that a moment could arrive when this is no longer the case."[6] Since Yves St. Laurent is still continuing haute couture clothing, it seems evident that "the moment" has not yet arrived.

At the very least, however, it seems apparent that haute couture garments have a new business function: to publicize the name of the house in order to provide a well-known, prestigious label for use in the house's other, more lucrative business activities. As Pierre Berge, president of Yves St. Laurent has said, "No, we don't make a profit on the couture, but it's not a problem. It's our advertising budget."[7]

Italian Couture

While other European countries such as Spain, England, and Italy have at one time had haute couture houses, none has ever approached Paris in importance. Today, the only important couture outside Paris is that of Italy. The Italian couture was organized after World War II along lines similar to those of the Paris couture, but on a much smaller scale. Unlike the French, however, the Italian houses are not congregated in a single city but are located in three: Rome, Florence, and Milan. The Italian counterpart of the Chambre Syndicale de la Couture Parisienne is the *Camera Nazionale dell'Alta Moda Italiana.* Its membership of some 20 haute couture houses includes such famous names as Valentino, Andre Laug, Mila Schoen, Fabiani, Galitzine, and Tiziani. Like the Paris couture, the Italian houses present their collections semiannually, in January for Spring/Summer and in July for Fall/Winter, one week prior to the Paris showings.

The experience of the Italian couture parallels that of the Paris houses: couture prices too high for all but a dwindling clientele of the ultrarich; no more trade buyers; and a largely unprofitable couture operation that is subsidized by income from ready-to-wear divisions, franchised boutiques, and licensing fees from perfumes, accessories, and other goods to which a designer's name adds prestige.

EUROPEAN READY-TO-WEAR FASHION CENTERS ....

While some ready-to-wear was being produced in European countries before World War II, the eyes of the fashion world were focused on its hub, the Paris couture. After that war, as the industrial world developed and expanded, so did important ready-to-wear fashion centers in European countries. They did not, however, achieve their present level of maturity, creativity, prestige, and recognition until the 1960s, due to the dominance of the couture. Even though Paris is still considered one of the major fashion centers in the world, there are now other countries that have gained recognition as fashion leaders and influentials. Italy and England are prominent among them.

French Ready-to-Wear Industry

Ready-to-war, originally a minor sideline of a few couture houses, has blossomed into a large, full-fledged industry in France. Contributing to its development were such ready-to-wear producing firms as Sonia Rykiel, Daniel Hechter, Dorothée Bis, Cacherel, and Emmanuelle Khanh. Such designers began to attract the attention of foreign buyers and the press by developing styles and looks of their own, which were quite different and lower in price than the couture garments. Many of these companies had their beginnings as owner-operated retail boutiques. Many other designer-named ready-to-wear firms have since joined their ranks. Among them are Karl Lagerfeld, Angelo Tarlazzi, Kenzo, Thierry Mugler, Jean-Paul Gautier, and Azzedine Alaia. As was mentioned earlier, many of these ready-to-wear designers have been designated as *créateurs* by the Chambre Syndicale and have been admitted as members.

SIZE OF INDUSTRY

The ready-to-wear operations of the Paris couture and of the 18 designer-named firms that are members of the Chambre represent only a small part of the industry, in both number of firms and value of output. The *Fédération Française de Prêt à Porter Féminin,* a trade association that represents ready-to-wear producers other than those who belong to the Chambre Syndicale, reports a membership of some 1100 companies, with sales totaling $2,600,000,000 in contrast with the $40 million in sales of the ready-made-

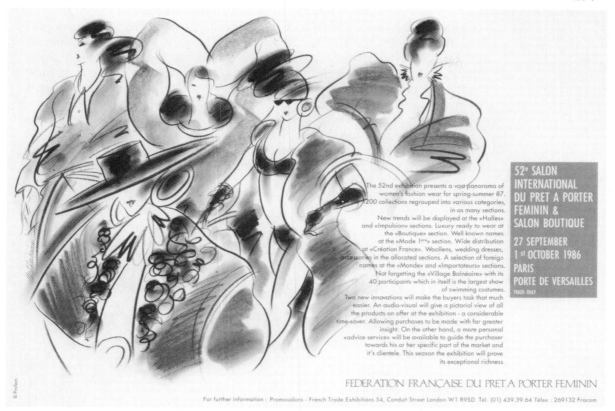

The 52nd exhibition presents a vast panorama of women's fashion wear for spring-summer 87. 1200 collections regrouped into various categories, in as many sections. New trends will be displayed at the «Halles» and «Impulsions» sections. Luxury ready to wear at the «Boutique» section. Well known names at the «Mode 1ère» section. Wide distribution at «Création France». Woollens, wedding dresses, accessories in the allocated sections. A selection of foreign names at the «Monde» and «Importateurs» sections. Not forgetting the «Village Balnéaire» with its 40 participants which in itself is the largest show of swimming costumes. Two new innovations will make the buyers task that much easier. An audio-visual will give a pictorial view of all the products on offer at the exhibition - a considerable time-saver. Allowing purchases to be made with far greater insight. On the other hand, a more personal «advice service» will be available to guide the purchaser towards his or her specific part of the market and it's clientele. This season the exhibition will prove its exceptional richness.

52ᵉ SALON INTERNATIONAL DU PRET A PORTER FEMININ & SALON BOUTIQUE

27 SEPTEMBER 1ˢᵗ OCTOBER 1986 PARIS PORTE DE VERSAILLES
TRADE ONLY

FEDERATION FRANÇAISE DU PRET A PORTER FEMININ

For further information : Promosalons - French Trade Exhibitions 54, Conduit Street London W1 R9SD. Tél. (01) 439.39.64 Télex : 269132 Fracom

Source: Reprinted with permission of the Federation Française du Pret a Porter Feminin.

producing members of the Chambre. The women's industry alone employs some 62,000 people, in addition to those employed by French menswear manufacturers. Exports to the United States in 1985 amounted to $86,000,000.[8]

Innovative fashions and mass production have combined to build a ready-to-wear industry that is a very important resource to the American fashion business. Although our dollar purchases of French ready-to-wear amount to only a small percentage of our total imports, our adaptations and copies of their styles and ideas have enormous impact.

SEMIANNUAL COLLECTIONS AND TRADE SHOWINGS

Unlike the American industry, French ready-to-wear producers prepare and present only two seasonal collections a year, as do all other foreign fashion manufacturers. The Fall/Winter collections are shown in March and April, and the Spring/Summer in October.

In its efforts to court foreign buyers, the French ready-to-wear industry stages week-long semiannual **trade shows** in Paris—actually, two shows each held in a different place at a different time. The mass-producing companies stage the *Salon du Prêt-à-Porter Féminin,* in the *Porte de Versailles,* an exhibition building larger than the New York Coliseum. Some 1300 apparel firms, most but not all of them French, exhibit their lines there. The second show presents the ready-to-wear collections of the couturiers and créateurs, and is sponsored by the Chambre Syndicale. It is located in a central Paris area known as *Les Halles*—one that has developed as a cultural center. In addition to the French designer-named collections, some 20 or so top fashion designers from other countries also present collections at this show.

Both shows are attended by thousands of fashion professionals (buyers, "lookers," and fashion reporters) from all over the world. The French menswear industry also stages its own semiannual seasonal trade shows in the

October dates scheduled for Paris designer rtw shows

PARIS — The schedule of the designer ready-to-wear shows to be held here next month is as follows:

	Wednesday, Oct. 16
3 p.m.	Hiroko Koshino
5:30 p.m.	Junko Shimada
6:30 p.m.	Chantal Thomass
	Thursday, Oct. 17
9:30 a.m.	Dan Beranger
10:30 a.m.	Comme des Garcons
11:30 a.m.	Junko Koshino
2:30 p.m.	Yohji Yamamoto
3:30 p.m.	Michel Klein
4:30 p.m.	Thierry Mugler
6 p.m.	Jean Remy Daumas
7 p.m.	Jean Charles de Castelbajac
	Friday, Oct. 18
9:15 a.m.	Chloe
10:15 a.m.	Bernard Perris
11:15 a.m.	Jean Louis Scherrer
12:30 p.m.	Popy Moreni
2:30 p.m.	Anne-Marie Beretta
3:30 p.m.	Kansai Yamamoto
7 p.m.	Jean-Paul Gaultier
	Saturday, Oct. 19
9:30 a.m.	Karl Lagerfeld
10:30 a.m.	Elisabeth de Senneville
Noon	Claude Montana
2 p.m.	Marie Beltrami
2:30 p.m.	Martine Sitbon
3:30 p.m.	Emmanuelle Khanh
5 p.m.	Issey Miyake
6 p.m.	Dorothee Bis

7 p.m.	Vivienne Westwood
	Sunday, Oct. 20
9:45 a.m.	Angelo Tarlazzi
11 a.m.	Enrico Coveri
Noon	Nino Cerruti
2:30 p.m.	Francesco Smalto
3:30 p.m.	Lanvin
4:30 p.m.	Dik Brandsma
6 p.m.	Sonia Rykiel
	Monday, Oct. 21
9 a.m.	Hubert de Givenchy
10:30 a.m.	Chanel
Noon	Daniel Hechter
2 p.m.	Nina Ricci
3 p.m.	Christian Dior
4:30 p.m.	Madame Gres
5:30 p.m.	Valentino
6:30 p.m.	Torrente
	Tuesday, Oct. 22
10:30 a.m.	Guy Laroche
11:30 a.m.	Emanuel Ungaro
12:30 p.m.	Marithe et Francois Girbaud
2:30 p.m.	Hermes
3:30 p.m.	Tan Giudicelli
5 p.m.	Jacqueline de Ribes
6:30 p.m.	Dietmar Sterling
	Wednesday, Oct. 23
9 a.m.	Hanae Mori
11 a.m.	Yves Saint Laurent
6 p.m.	Kenzo

Porte de Versailles. Held in February and September, these are run in conjunction with makers of knitwear and children's clothes.

The Fédération Française du Prêt à Porter also organizes French participation in international trade shows held in New York, Dusseldorf, Milan, Tokyo, Munich, and Stockholm. It also maintains a permanent office in New York City. This is the French Fashion and Textile Center, whose major purpose is to promote French ready-to-wear in the United States. It represents all branches of the industry except couture and couture ready-to-wear. Additionally, most of the leading couture houses and many of the larger designer-name ready-to-wear companies have established their own offices in New York, along with sales representation at regional apparel marts.

Summing up, it is obvious that the French are not waiting for fashion buyers to come knocking at their doors. They participate in international trade shows, they franchise designer-name ready-to-wear boutiques worldwide, they have global licensing arrangements, and they maintain individual and group sales offices in the United States. It seems apparent that, to the French, creative designers are important players in the fashion game, but the name of the fashion game in France is "MARKETING."

Italy

Today, the most serious challenger to the fashion leadership of Paris is Italy, which has been attracting foreign fashion buyers since the 1950s. Italy's strengths and competitive advantages derive from the superior quality and design of its fabrics, its workmanship, and the innovative, sophisticated styling of its knitwear, sportswear, and accessories—notably leather shoes and handbags. It has also developed a reputation for its interesting and avant-garde styling of men's apparel and accessories.

The Italian ready-to-wear industry developed simultaneously with its couture industry and did not depend on Italian couturiers for fashion leadership and design talent. As a result, it started exporting earlier. Today the well-being of the industry relies heavily on its foreign sales efforts, in which it receives encouragement and support from the Italian government.

SEMIANNUAL COLLECTIONS AND TRADE SHOWS

When Italy first emerged as a major fashion center, foreign trade buyers went to Florence, where the semiannual collections and showings of ready-to-wear were presented in the luxurious and elegant setting of the Pitti Palace. In the mid-1970s, however, ready-to-wear firms in the north of Italy decided to present their own showings in Milan. The initial handful of firms, among them Basile, Callaghan, Missoni, and Caumont, has grown into an avalanche and, today, Milan has become the major staging ground for Italian ready-to-wear presentations. In fact, many of the Florence ready-to-wear firms have defected to the north and show in both Milan and Florence. Their semiannual

Italian Rtw

MILAN
MILANO
MILAN

MILAN — On Via Della Spiga and other fashion thoroughfares, the main topic of debate has been the calendar of the Milan collections.

Here, the schedule to date:

Sunday, Oct. 6
10:30 a.m. — Rocco Barocco
11:30 a.m. — Sportmax

2:30 p.m. — Krizia
4:30 p.m. — Missoni
6:00 p.m. — Ferre
9:00 p.m. — Cadette
10:00 p.m. — Cinzia Ruggeri

Monday, Oct. 7
9:15 a.m. — Miguel Cruz
10:45 a.m. — Versace
Noon — Correggiari
12:30 p.m. — Fendi
2:45 p.m. — Mario Valentino
4:00 p.m. — Byblos
5:15 p.m. — Mila Schon

5:30 p.m. — Ginocchietti
6:30 p.m. — Timmi
8:00 p.m. — Erreuno

Tuesday, Oct. 8
10:00 a.m. — Laura Biagiotti
11:15 a.m. — Complice
12:30 p.m. — Soprani
2:45 p.m. — Moschino
4:00 p.m. — San Lorenzo
5:15 p.m. — Touche
9:00 p.m. — Armani

Wednesday, Oct. 9
9:15 a.m. — Andre Laug

10:00 a.m. — Genny
11:15 a.m. — Ferragamo
12:30 p.m. — Basile
2:45 p.m. — Gianmarco Venturi
4:00 p.m. — Callaghan
5:15 p.m. — Enrica Massei
9:00 p.m. — Armani

Oct. 1 to 2 — Regina Shrecker
Oct. 4-November — Helyett
Oct. 6 to 10 — Gherardini
Oct. 6 to 10 — Lancetti
Oct. 6 to 11 — Claudio La Viola

showings take place just prior to the prêt-à-porter openings in Paris—that is, late March for Fall/Winter and late September or early October for Spring/Summer. The week-long Milan shows include not only those staged by the country's top ready-to-wear designers, but also *Modit*, an exhibition at which 220 other foreign apparel manufacturers are invited to show.

Also, like their French counterparts, the Italian industry participates in trade showings in many other countries—among them, the semiannual New York Pret showings held in early fall and spring. There are many other trade presentations, too, such as the *Uomo Modo*, the semiannual show of Italian menswear manufacturers; an Italian shoe fair staged annually in March in Bologna; the famous textile show, *Ideacomo*, held in May at Lake Como; and the *Mipel* accessories show, held in Milan each January and June. These are but a few of the many trade exhibits staged in Italy.

LEADING READY-TO-WEAR DESIGNERS

Along with those mentioned above, some of the best-known ready-to-wear designer companies in Italy are Krizia, Missoni, Gianfranco Ferre, Gianni Versace, Soprani, and Biagotti. All of these have achieved worldwide reputations for their trendsetting fashions. Consider also the names of Gucci and Ferragamo, who are internationally known for leather products; Fendi, renowned for innovative fur fashions; and Giorgio Armani, who has developed a reputation for interesting and innovative styling of men's apparel. Add these names to those mentioned earlier in this section and it becomes clear that the fashion story, Italian style, represents serious competition to Paris as the prime source of fashion leadership.

ITALY'S FASHION INDUSTRY

After tourism, the fashion industry is Italy's largest national industry. There are more than twice as many apparel and accessory firms in Italy as there are in France, reportedly over 8000. Close to 40 percent of their annual output is exported, with their largest customers being West Germany (number one) and France (second). The United States is Italy's third largest customer.[9]

It is interesting to note that, because Italian workmanship and fabrics are, on the whole, better and cheaper than they are in France, many French designers are steady customers of Italy. Besides the silks from Como, and woolens from Biella, large numbers of sweaters, leather garments and accessories that come from Italy are sold under French labels.

Like their French counterparts, many Italian companies have established retail boutiques, featuring their ready-to-wear in other countries. Some of these "name" boutiques, such as those of Missoni, Armani, and Soprani, are owned and operated by the company itself. Others are owned and operated by franchised retailers. Particularly notable is the worldwide chain of franchised stores of Benetton, whose operations are described in a reading in this section. And also like their French counterparts, many of the Italian designers are involved in worldwide licensing arrangements.

London

The British have long been famous for their tweeds and their men's custom tailoring, but it was not until after World War II that reverberations from their ready-to-wear industry were heard around the fashion world. Their couture effort, which was keyed to the conservative tastes of royalty and the peerage, did not succeed, and is nonexistent today.

FASHION LEADERSHIP IN THE 1960S

The British ready-to-wear industry, unlike the couture, did flourish and made a major impact on both men's and women's fashions in the 1960s. The name "Carnaby Street" became synonymous with colorful, uninhibited, avant-garde clothes for both sexes. The London streets in that area were filled with boutiques carrying unconventional, trendy fashions by new young designers. Their miniskirted dresses, reflecting the free, young spirit of the decade, sent feminine hemlines soaring to incredible highs all over the world. Especially notable was the work of Mary Quant, a young English designer who understood what many other designers around the world were quite late in recognizing: that the young were setting fashions on their own, and that, instead of the young following their elders, the mature folk were following the young.

CLASSICS IN THE 1970S

In the 1970s, the mood of the "swinging sixties" changed, as did the ready-to-wear offerings of that period. English fashion houses focused on their traditional and classic high-quality woolen fabrics in men's tailored clothing, the excellent workmanship of their rainwear (notably Aquascutum and Burberry), and the fine cotton products of Liberty of London and Laura Ashley.

REVITALIZATION IN THE 1980S

Led by Jean Muir, Zandra Rhodes, and Ossie Clark, the British fashion industry was revitalized in the 1980s. All kinds of young, highly individualized, and even outrageous fashion statements began coming out of England. Today, the new and exciting exists side by side with the traditional, conservative, and classic clothing for which England has always been known. There could not be anything more radically different from the romantic cotton prints of Laura Ashley than the industrial cottons and futuristic silks of Katherine Hammett, the bold prints of Betty Jackson, or the unconventional, inventive styles of such other trendsetting firms as Wendy Dagworthy, Rifat Ozbek, Body Map, Jasper Cowran, and Vivienne Westwood, for example. These and other new designer talents are leading the British fashion parade today. That U.S. buyers are taking them seriously is evidenced by the experience of Macy's, New York, where London fashions now account for almost 50 percent of the store's contemporary department.[10]

Even the retail boutiques in London are as inventive as the designers and the styles seen on the streets. For example, there is a shop called the Warehouse, where one can buy white clothes and dye them on the spot, with the dye and washing machines provided for the customer on the premises. In a shop called Spring, clothes are sold Chinese-take-out style.

SIZE OF THE INDUSTRY

There is no question about it: English fashions have captured the hearts of both the young and rebellious and their fashion-conscious elders. What is equally important is that they have also captured the dollars of American buyers. Attendance is on the increase at their semiannual trade showings, in late March and October. Sponsored by the Fashion Council of Great Britain, the event fills the Olympia Fashion Center to overflowing with foreign buyers. Overall wholesale figures for the British industry are above $1 billion, and the export figures have been rapidly escalating. Among Britain's foreign customers, the United States has moved from fourth to second place, with purchases of over $250 million.[11] Whether London will continue to maintain its renewed vitality as the Mecca of the young contemporary market still remains to be seen.

International Shows in West Germany

Germany's expertise lies in its knitwear technology. Its knitting machines are among the best in the world, yet the country's impact on the fashion world arises from a different source. What West Germany is famous for is the international textile and apparel fashion fairs that it stages. They are among the most impressive events of their kind in the world.

For example, in Frankfurt, each May and November, there is the huge international textile trade show, *Interstoff*, at which thousands of fabric producers from many different countries exhibit their wares. Apparel producers from every part of the world attend.

In **Dusseldorf,** each April and October, there is an international women's apparel show, **IGEDO,** which is reported to draw some 2000 producers from 27 countries, to exhibit their merchandise to a worldwide audience of over 30,000.

Cologne, each February and August, offers a week-long *International Men's Fashion Week* that attracts some 30,000 buyers to see the lines of an estimated 1000 exhibitors from 37 countries.

In addition to these, there is an annual *International Footwear Fair*, held in Dusseldorf every March; a semiannual international children's fair in Cologne; semiannual swimwear and underwear shows in Dusseldorf, which are the only trade fairs of their type in the world. And there are still others. Among them, to name but one, is the *Overseas Export Fair*, held in Berlin every September.[12]

Germany's fashion industry and exports may be relatively small, but their international trade fairs are a major source for new fabric and fashion ideas.

In recent years, however, a few West German apparel manufacturers have begun to make their fashion products increasingly felt in the U.S. market. Two German apparel firms, Escada and Mondi, are leading the emerging German fashion parade, but a number of smaller West German designer firms are beginning to follow their lead. A reading in this chapter discusses this development.

Secondary European Centers

Many other countries, in addition to those discussed above, produce ready-to-wear and textiles that attract fashion-hungry producers and retailers from the United States and other parts of the world. Each of these countries is so eager for export trade that its government has encouraged organizations of manufacturers and has offered cooperation and subsidies to help earn recognition for the creative talents of its designers and to promote its apparel and textile industries. With the support of their governments, these countries have developed fashion trade fairs within their own borders and have participated in international trade fairs throughout the world. They are found at such shows as the New York Pret show, the Italian Modit show, and those staged in West Germany. In addition, they have established promotional trade offices in both the United States and other major market centers.

Fashion buyers in the United States are not likely to overlook creative talent, wherever it appears on the face of the globe. For example, they shop in the following places:

- Scandinavia, for jacquard wool sweaters in native patterns, suede coats, sportswear, raincoats, and woolen apparel.
- Ireland, for hand-knitted sweaters, and coats and suits of hand-loomed tweeds.
- Scotland, for cashmeres.
- Austria, for knitwear.
- Israel, for swimwear, leather jackets and coats, and knitwear.
- Spain for leather wear.

In the Western hemisphere, U.S. buyers shop Canada, whose fashion industry of some 2000 firms offers sturdy raincoats, furs, and weather-worthy outerwear for men, women, and children. In shoes, the label "Made in Brazil" is now very common. So is the "Made in Argentina" label on costly alligator bags that are sold all over the world.

Each nation vies with the others for a share of the world's fashion dollars. None of them, however, has achieved the fashion importance of Paris, Italy, or London and it seems unlikely that they will ever do so.

THE ORIENT ....

As the European ready-to-wear markets developed and expanded, U.S. retailers increasingly explored their capabilities and recognized their creative spark. In some cases, they also saw price advantages and exploited them by buying and promoting European products. In the late 1970s however, retail buyers realized that although Europe offered great style ingenuity and often more favorable prices than the domestic market, the prime foreign source for markedly lower priced production, particular sportswear, was to be found in the low-wage countries of the Orient. Countries initially used for this purpose were Hong Kong and Japan, where ready-to-wear could be produced at a fraction of domestic market prices.

Today, foreign buying trips to overseas markets follow a circuitous route: first to European fashion centers to place orders that are relatively nominal in quantity; then to the Orient to place orders in depth.

Japan

In the not-too-distant past, a label reading "Made in Japan" was usually associated with cheap and poorly made products that were carried in low-priced stores in the United States. Today, however, the Japanese industry has been transformed. This is partly the result of the enlightened postwar aid of the United States, and partly the fruit of the Japanese determination to become a major industrial democracy. In the process, that country has become an important fashion center for medium- and high-priced goods, thanks to the presence of many bright, talented designers and to the quality of workmanship in Japanese factories. That country's fashion industry today is indeed a modern miracle.

An excellent description of the Japanese industry is to be found in these excerpts from an advertisement in *Women's Wear Daily* of January 8, 1980. It was placed by the Tokyo Industrial Association of Women's and Children's Wear.

> Dotted with glistening skyscrapers and a gathering place for people from all over, Tokyo is proud of its ability to absorb foreign culture, and especially of being a stage for world fashion trends. . . . Japanese fashion makers have taken their knowledge of world fashion and added to it the traditional Japanese aesthetic sense of beauty, for a higher level of creativity. They believe that the entire fashion world will appreciate the true value of a uniquely Japanese fashion sense. . . . The fashion industry in Japan is at the top of [Japan's] list of growth industries and it is almost certain that fashion will become the superstar among Japanese growth industries in the 1980's. The Sixties were a period when Japanese trade was internationalized, and in the seventies internationalism became a reality in the Japanese world of finance. Now in the 1980's, Japan will push its fashion industry toward internationalization. As Japan's foremost city, Tokyo is striving to raise itself to a par with the world's great fashion centers— New York, Paris, Milan, London.

That they have already raised their par was evident in 1983, when Japanese designers such as Hanae Mori, Kenzo Takada, Kansai Yamamoto, and Issey Miyake first showed their lines at the Paris Prêt-à-Porter showings. They became a design sensation overnight, and Tokyo was hailed by buyers and the press as the fashion frontier of the 1980s.

NEW WAVE OF JAPANESE DESIGNERS

The initial enthusiasm over the Japanese designs grew out of their highly innovative, unconventional, androgynous, oversized, and almost barbaric look—called by some the "bag lady" look. Although the excitement has subsided, no one denies that the new wave of Japanese design continues to be one of the most interesting and influential forces in fashion.

Today there are many designer-name firms in Japan that have become famous for their ingenious concepts. Among them are Rei Kawakubo of Comme Les Garçons, Yohi Yamamoto, and Matsuhiro Matsuzo—in addition to those previously mentioned. Western designers have adapted features of their untraditional designs as well as their unusual color combinations and fabric concepts.

Matsuda has opened his own boutique in New York, and stores such as Henri Bendel and Bloomingdale's set up Comme Les Garçons shops in their stores. Many other leading specialty stores throughout the country also buy and feature Japanese designers. However, as Selma Weiser, owner of Charivari in New York, explains it: "The department stores basically are not able to sell this kind of merchandise; the Japanese are not meant to be mass merchandised; it's a specialty business."[13] Yohi Yamamoto, who is Charivari's lead designer, does as much as $1 million or more in their stores alone, according to estimates by industry sources. The owner of Ultimo of Chicago, who buys from and features Matsuda, Miyaki's Plantation, and Comme Les Garçons, says: "It's definitely a small market, but it's our market. It's for someone who likes interesting cuts and fabrics."[14]

Today, the Japanese are reevaluating their place in the world of fashion. Although they are still focusing on new ways of constructing clothes, their recent designs are less startling and outrageous than those that first burst on the fashion scene.

JAPANESE MARKETING EXPERTISE

The senior vice-president and general merchandise manager of sportswear and junior wear of Saks-Fifth Avenue, a major purchaser of Japanese apparel, appraised it as not being "an incredibly aggressively growing business but . . . an important one."[15] The Japanese would undoubtedly disagree with her assessment of a "not growing business."

Today, Japan is applying to its textile and apparel industries the same marketing efforts and skills that have enabled it to corner the world market in automobiles and consumer electronics. One indication is that in 1985 the country's fashion industry compressed its semiannual trade shows into a two-week period, instead of the former practice of spacing shows over as many as nine weeks. Those long-drawn-out showings dates had made it virtually impossible for foreign buyers to shop the Japanese market thoroughly; the condensed dates are a move toward accommodating buyers.

A further indication of a frontal attack on the world market is seen in the action of Renown, the largest apparel manufacturer in Japan, and one with licensing agreements with many prominent designers. That company now has an office in New York's garment center. In addition, Japanese designers continue to participate in international trade shows. All of these steps, of course, make their clothes more accessible to foreign buyers than if these customers had to come to Japan to see them.

Major Low-Wage Production Centers

As in the case of Japan, apparel made in other Far East countries at one time was of such poor quality and inferior styling that it was relegated to the lowest end of the market. And again, as in the case of Japan, this situation no longer holds. Producers in Asia, although still a source for low-priced merchandise, have also acquired the skills and the modern machinery to produce moderate to high-quality apparel, thus closing much of the technological gap between them and American producers.

LOW COST OF LABOR-INTENSIVE PRODUCTION

In the production of apparel, much of the exporting success of countries such as Hong Kong, Taiwan, South Korea, China, Sri Lanka, Singapore, and India derives from the fact that apparel production remains one of the most labor-intensive and least automated major industries, even in the United States. Labor costs are thus an important element in the manufacturing costs of garments.

As of 1985, the average pay for domestic apparel workers was $4.50 an hour—as compared with $1.08 per hour in Hong Kong, 57 cents in Taiwan and Korea and $5.00 per week in Sri Lanka.[16]

An additional factor is that in each of these countries, the government, like governments in Europe, offers subsidies and tax incentives to producers of textiles and apparel for export. Such incentives have no counterpart in this country. Thus, even with import duties of 16 to 32 percent, and with the cost of shipping goods halfway around the world, the landed cost of these goods is less than production costs in an American factory.

HONG KONG

Hong Kong is the world's largest apparel exporter and the production of apparel is its largest industry. Its more than 10,000 garment firms employ close to 300,000 workers—over 30 percent of its manufacturing labor force. Its apparel exports to its biggest customer, the United States, amount to close to $2 billion.[17] Its five most popular exports have been tee-shirts, trousers (including jeans), blouses, sweaters, and knitted shirts.

A decade ago, the "Made in Hong Kong" label generally meant a cheap, poor-quality item made in a side street sweatshop. But quota restraints that limit their exports to this country have had their effect. So, too, has the competition from other emerging low-wage apparel producing countries. To get maximum foreign currency return on its exports, Hong Kong had little choice but to improve the quality of its workmanship and produce garments of higher quality—and higher price.

Hong Kong's production facilities are being used today for contracting work—cutting and sewing. Leading designers from all over the world use that country for top-price designer-name jeans, garments of silk, linen, and ramie, high-priced sweaters, and sportswear items. Among those whose garments they produce are Calvin Klein and Oscar de la Renta from the United States; Givenchy, Pierre Cardin, and Dior from Paris; Giorgio Armani from Italy; and Yamamoto from Japan, to name but a few. Hong Kong is also used by mass-producing firms such as Esprit and Liz Claiborne, both of whom contract almost all of their production out to producers in that country. In addition, almost every important retail store in the United States that offers private label fashion merchandise has some manufactured to its specifications there.

Close to a decade of producing designer-name garments for such discerning customers has given Hong Kong manufacturers a great deal of experience in the production of high-quality garments. Today, Hong Kong is also nurturing a fledgling designer crop of its own, who are establishing their own businesses. While the colony has not yet produced an Yves St. Laurent or Calvin Klein, fashions by such Hong Kong-based designers as Eddi Lau, Patricia Chong, Jennie Lewis, Diane Freis, and Hanna Pang are featured in leading retail stores such as Saks-Fifth Avenue, Neiman Marcus, and Harrods of London.

Hong Kong's Trade Development Council is promoting the colony's designers in American and European trade shows, including those in Dusseldorf and Paris. They have also arranged for some of their designers to make personal appearances at Harrods in London and at the National Retail Merchants Association convention in New York. Further, they support and stage local fashion fairs.

The colony's best designers still have far to go, however, before they become household names. Having their garments on the racks of some of the world's most respected stores is just the beginning. And there is also a local problem to be overcome. Hong Kong's wealthy women, of whom there are many, do not patronize local producers. They often prefer expensive garments bearing the labels of foreign designers. They do not realize that the clothes were manufactured just down the street!

Hong Kong's future in fashion is still developing; what shape it will take remains to be seen.

THE HONG KONG
CASUAL
APPAREL
SHOW '86

THE HONG KONG EXHIBITION CENTRE
JANUARY 19-22 1986

Make a date now to visit this prestigious fashion event which will highlight *over 80* of Hong Kong's leading manufacturers and exporters of men's and women's casual wear.

The show will also feature both open booth displays and individual house and group shows covering all aspects of *Casual Knitwear; Suits and Coordinates; Active Sportswear; Separates and Designer Collections* suitable for the 1986 Fall and Winter seasons.

For more details about this exciting trade show, simply fill in the coupon below.

HKDTC Hong Kong Trade Development Council
Promoting Hong Kong business worldwide.

Yes, please send me further information about
The Hong Kong Casual Apparel Show '86

Name

Position

Company

Address

Telephone

548 Fifth Avenue, 6/F, New York, NY 10036, USA.
Telephone: (212) 730-0777. Cable: HONGTRADS
NEW YORK. Telex: 710 581 6302 HKTDC NYK.
Facsimile: 1-212-398-0530

Source: Reprinted with permission by Hong Kong Trade Development Council.

TAIWAN AND SOUTH KOREA

Collectively Hong Kong, Taiwan, and South Korea, which are known as "Asia's Bermuda Triangle," are the three biggest exporters of apparel to the United States.

Taiwan, today a low-wage contracting country, was an agricultural area called Formosa until Chiang Kai-shek escaped from China, declared Taiwan to be Nationalist China, became its first president in 1949 and remained its ruler virtually until his death. Within a decade after his installation, he had transformed Taiwan into an industrial nation.

That country's apparel industry, aided by U.S. and Japanese financing, is made up of relatively small producers who for the most part do not have the efficiency, quality, and diversity of Hong Kong's factories. Its main production capabilities are in men's outerwear, shirts and trousers, and in women's low- to moderate-priced sportswear separates and sweaters. As in the case of Hong Kong, quota restrictions on their exports to the United States have encouraged them to upgrade the quality of their work and to attempt to develop a more fashion-oriented and higher-priced product. Under the aegis of the Taiwan Textile Federation, programs have been established to train young fashion designers and technicians who have the potential to help the industry to achieve these goals.

Many industry experts feel that South Korea has the potential to challenge Hong Kong because their factory production is much more efficient than Taiwan's, almost rivaling that of Japan. Their fabrics are generally of excellent quality and their suitings, in particular, are considered to be the equal of anything in Asia. Their main exporting products consist of knitted tops, men's suits and shirts, and women's sportswear.

Although most of their production is still of a contracting nature, Korea, like Hong Kong and Taiwan, is attempting to develop young Korean designers, who hopefully will add a new dimension to their growing industry.

PEOPLE'S REPUBLIC OF CHINA

In 1970, for the first time there was an experimental Canton Trade Fair, attended mostly by Japanese buyers. In the year following, Americans were invited but fewer than a hundred showed up. In 1972, the United Nations seated the delegation from the People's Republic of China. Bloomingdale's, New York, hailed the event by opening a shop called China Passage—the first of its kind in the United States, and so well received that the featured Chinese worker's jacket of quilted blue cotton sold out completely. In that same year, many American retailing executives attended the Canton fair and bought Chinese robes, quilted jackets, men's silk shirts and pajamas, plus jade jewelry, straw baskets, porcelains, and other Chinese craft products. Among the stores represented were Bonwit Teller, Saks-Fifth Avenue, and Macy's, of New York, Neiman-Marcus of Texas, and I. Magnin of California.

By 1975, China had come into fashion. "Slim side-fastened dresses, long slit tunics over pants, flower embroidered and pattern-quilted jackets, intense Chinese colors, and bright satin slippers on high black lacquer platforms—and Saks-Fifth Avenue accelerated deliveries of their large fall orders for Chinese-inspired American fashions."[18] In 1980, Bloomingdale's launched a promotion featuring $10 million worth of Chinese imports.

All of this retail interest notwithstanding, China, as of 1985, accounted for $160 million, or less than 10 percent of the U.S. total imports of textiles and apparel[19] but it is considered to be still a sleeping giant with the potential to become, in the not too distant future, a major force in today's world of fashion. American retailers are being invited in increasing numbers to attend China's semiannual trade fairs, and more and more are accepting their invitations.

EMERGENCE OF OTHER PRODUCTION CENTERS

In the Orient, a void in very low-priced apparel was created when Japan, Hong Kong, Taiwan, and South Korea moved into higher-priced quality goods. Other emerging nations in Asia are now learning to fill that void—in some instances aided by investments from the four Asiatic countries that have vacated that very field. To protect their investments, these same four countries have been helping the newcomers with production technology and expertise.

Among the countries that have developed as low-cost apparel producers and are gaining recognition in that field are the following:

- *Singapore:* for underwear, raincoats, and men's and women's shirts.
- *India:* for cottons, linens, and those coarse gauze fabrics that are particularly popular for dresses and oversized blouses.
- *Sri Lanka:* for sportswear items.
- *Thailand:* for underwear and brightly colored patterned silks and cottons in dresses, skirts, and blouses.
- *The Philippines:* for children's wear, denim products, and embroidered items.

All of these and more are just at the beginning of the industrialization process.

FASHION: A GLOBAL BUSINESS TODAY ....

Today, in addition to shopping European countries for new and incoming fashion ideas and for high-quality products, knowledgeable American producers and retailers travel the length and breadth of the Orient, from Osaka to Kuala Lampur, and from Manila to Calcutta, with a dozen stops in between, seeking low-wage contracting factories for apparel and accessories.

One top fashion executive summed it all up when she was asked about the foreign fashion producers her company shops and buys from: "Where there is a sewing machine, we'll go."[20] The fashion business has indeed become global in all its aspects—design, production, and distribution. In the process, it has made the whole world into a neighborhood garment center. Boundaries, borders, hemispheres—these present no obstacle if there is an idea or a facility that the fashion world can use.

Readings

Foreign fashion producers are making their presence increasingly felt in the United States. These readings discuss some leading fashion firms in France, Italy, Japan, and West Germany.

Fashion Empire: Haute Couture Means High Finance at House of Yves Saint Laurent
This renowned design house reaps big money from their ready-to-wear and their 160 franchised boutiques around the world.

Marc-ing 25 Years at Dior
Marc Bohan says he "makes clothes for real women—not for myself, not for mannequins and not for fashion magazines. I gladly leave the abstract creations to others."

Japan's "New Wave" Breaks on U.S. Shores
Japanese design is one of the most interesting forces in fashion today and Rei Kawakubo is undoubtedly Japan's most influential designer.

The Benetton Group
There are Benetton shops in 53 countries around the world—but Benetton is not a retailer. It is a complex of manufacturing companies based in Italy that produces apparel for men, women, and children.

German Fashion: Making It a Business
According to Ellen Salzman, corporate fashion director of Saks-Fifth Avenue, the fashion industry in Germany is coming into its own.

Fashion Empire: Haute Couture Means High Finance at House of Yves Saint Laurent

by Joan Kron

In 1967, Atlanta banker J. Mack Robinson sold his 80% interest in Yves Saint Laurent S.A. to Charles of the Ritz for $1 million. It is a deal that he prefers not to dwell upon.

"My biggest mistake was ever selling him," Mr. Robinson says of the couturier and his fashion house. "Yves makes more in a month now that I made on the entire transaction."

Mr. Robinson's misery has company. Charles of the Ritz, which was acquired by Squibb Corp. in 1971, didn't find Yves Saint Laurent a dazzling investment either. In 1973, Squibb Chairman Richard Furlaud allowed Mr. Saint Laurent and his partner and business manager, Pierre Berge to buy the company over time at its book value. The sale allowed Ritz to retain the designer's perfumes, from which Mr. Saint Laurent now receives royalties, and amounted to "probably not more than 2 million," says Richard Salomon, chairman and chief executive officer of Ritz at the time and now retired from the company.

Adds Mr. Salomon: "I don't think anyone could prophesy how successful they would become."

It is that lack of prescience that has rebounded to the considerable good fortune of Yves Saint Laurent, 48 years old last month, and 54-year-old Pierre Berge (pronounced bare-SHAY). Today, Mr. Saint Laurent owns 60% and Mr. Berge 40% of what has become a giant fashion empire. Last year, the Saint Laurent name generated about $2 billion in sales. Yves Saint Laurent S.A., the French company, with 332 employees, had a gross income of about $27 million, including $17 million from licensing and $4.5 million from sales of *haute couture*, the made-to-measure outfits that the designer executes each year for some 300 private clients; $6 million of that total was profit. Gross income from North American operations amounted to $8 million in 1983, and Brazilian gross income was $1.5 million.

"We put clothes in the funnel, and the money comes out," says Didier Grumbach, president of Saint Laurent Rive Gauche, U.S., and head of licensing in North America.

Shop in Paris

The funnel includes the house of Saint Laurent at 5 Avenue Marceau here, through which the designer sells his haute couture. But far more important to the company's financial success are the 160 Yves Saint Laurent Rive Gauche shops around the world, which, along with Rive Gauche boutiques in selected department stores, sell Mr. Saint Laurent's ready-to-wear designs. Before 1968, when the first Rive Gauche women's shop opened on New York's Madison Avenue, the name of Yves Saint Laurent was largely unsung beyond major urban centers. But by becoming the first French couturier to offer a complete assortment of his own ready-to-wear clothes and accessories

Source: *Wall Street Journal*, September 10, 1984. Reprint permission granted.

through an outlet that sold only his own creations, Mr. Saint Laurent quickly achieved
widespread fame—and fortune.

Much of that success, observers say, was
due to astute timing. "Saint Laurent has a
wonderful sense for knowing what people
want at the moment," says Sonja Caproni, vice
president of fashion merchandising at the I.
Magnin department-store chain. For example,
the decision to start the Rive Gauche chain
followed a period, in the 1960s, when stores
took designer labels out of clothes: "In the
1970s," Ms. Caproni says, "they wanted them
in."

And they wanted them on everything
from, if not soup to nuts, at least handbags to
umbrellas. Thus, through licensing arrangements with a wide variety of manufacturers,
did the Saint Laurent name and "YSL" logo
begin appearing on various apparel items, accessories and housewares. At the same time,
because of such factors as speed of communications and rapid and cheap transport, women
around the world were beginning to follow the
same style—a trend that dovetailed with Mr.
Saint Laurent's talents: "He's a very international designer," Ms. Caproni says. She adds:
"He understands what women want—con-
stants and change."

Other designers also understand, and
many have also opened their own boutiques
and licensed their names. But Diana Vreeland,
special consultant to the Metropolitan Museum Costume Institute in New York, explains
Mr. Saint Laurent's particular success this
way: "He does the best clothes on earth for the
life of the woman today, and he's been doing it
for 26 years." Indeed, in 1983, the institute
staged a retrospective exhibit of Mr. Saint
Laurent's work, the first time a major museum
has so honored a living designer.

That isn't to say that he hasn't had his
failures. For example, his "1940 collection,"
introduced in 1971, was variously panned by

fashion reporters as "Yves Saint Debacle" and
"completely hideous." (Counters Mr. Berge:
"The [New York] Times loved it. . . . Yves
never made a flop.") In recent years, however,
for the most part, Saint Laurent mannequins
have paraded to wild applause. John Fairchild,
publisher of Women's Wear Daily, called this
year's fall-winter couture collection, shown
here last July, Saint laurent's "best show ever."

The press views the Saint Laurent collections four times a year—in January and July to
review couture and in March and October to
look over the ready-to-wear lines. Their assess-
ments, if occasionally wounding, are considered crucial by the designer. "I will never be
immune to criticism," Mr. Saint Laurent says,
"but criticism teaches and there is always a
basic truth."

Much of the attention goes to haute couture, which is only natural. For if the ready-to-
wear and the licensing are prime sources of the
company's riches, couture is the gold that
backs the Saint Laurent name. "Without it
there would be nothing else," Mr. Berge says.

For their couture outfits, Saint Laurent
clients pay anywhere from $6,000 to $50,000
each. What they get for their money, the company says, is originality and perfection. "Yves
Saint Laurent does the most comfortable
shoulders in the world," says Christophe
Girard, head of the company's licensing division.

But whether it be a $50,000 original ball
gown or a $450 Rive Gauche blouse, it all
begins with inspiration. Diana Vreeland says
of Mr. Saint Laurent: "Everything talks to
him—the streets, the desert."

His listening posts are around the world.
The designer and Mr. Berge share sumptuous
residences in Paris and New York and maintain vacation houses in Deauville, France, and
Marrakech, Morocco. It is to either of the latter
two locales that Mr. Saint Laurent usually re-
treats to sketch a collection. If the destination

is Deauville, he is frequently piloted by Mr. Berge in the latter's private helicopter. Before returning to Paris, usually after two weeks' time, he will often have made some 500 sketches.

His workday here begins at 10:30 A.M. Invariably wearing a white doctor's smock, he goes over his sketches with his six top assistants and picks out the best to form a collection. (A couture collection usually consists of more than 100 outfits, but this year's fall-winter collection had 185, one of the largest anyone has ever shown.)

The designer usually works at a trestle table in the second-floor studio of the Avenue Marceau headquarters; his assistants cluster around another table. The light-filled room is also crammed with books of fabric samples, piles of handbags, jewels and other trimmings. "Mr. Saint Laurent does not go shopping," Mr. Girard explains. Instead, fabric-designers, furriers and jewelers "bring the finest things from all over the world to him."

They don't show their wares in his studio. "This room is like a chapel," Mr. Girard says as he hesitantly escorts a guest into the hallowed place. "No one enters this room—not even we executives."

One flight up from the studio are the major workrooms. Here, all the stitches except the main seams are done by hand. In all, from sketches to stitches, it takes about two months to prepare for each show. "Yves Saint Laurent designs everything for the woman himself," Mr. Berge says, with the exception of hats and jewelry; those items, Mr. Berge says, are designed under Mr. Saint Laurent's direction by Loulou de la Falaise Klossowski, who is known as Mr. Saint Laurent's only assistant *createur*.

Men's styling, however, is left entirely to design assistants, as are the various items that are made by others but licensed to bear the name of Yves Saint Laurent. The company currently has 200 license agreements with 120 licensees, for such products as belts, shoes, handbags, watches and table linens.

Mr. Berge says he manages the Saint Laurent name with care. "A name is like a cigarette," he says. "The more you smoke it, the less cigarette is left. It ends up in the ashtray. I refused to put the name on tires once. That was the most ridiculous request we ever had. And I think it's a bit ridiculous to put the name on chocolates like Pierre Cardin did." (Mr. Cardin, who has 504 licensees, no longer puts his name on chocolates.)

Unlike some other couture houses, that of Yves Saint Laurent cares for its name by supervising the design of licensed products. Twice a year each licensee must make a pilgrimage to the 40-person licensing office headed by Christophe Girard, the first time to pick up designs and patterns and the second time to show their renditions of the designs before putting them on sale. The licensees pay 5% to 10% of their wholesale earnings as a royalty to Saint Laurent.

Designers of the company's licensed products keep regional preferences in mind. For example, Mr. Saint Laurent favors using crosses for jewelry, but they don't sell well in the U.S. Similarly, YSL logos sell better in Japan than elsewhere.

The company's French-made Rive Gauche ready-to-wear line is also manufactured by a licensee, but Yves Saint Laurent S.A. holds a partial interest in the operation. The line is sold through the Rive Gauche shops and department-store boutiques. There are 28 Rive Gauche shops in the U.S., 24 for women and four for men. The owners pay nothing for the franchises, which the company awards to only those applicants it thinks will be successful. And although Mr. Grumbach estimates that the earliest a Rive Gauche shop can break even is in its second year, rewards can come to those who hang on. Ernest Marx, who owns three Rive Gauche women's shops in the Washington, D.C., area, says, "We've had an increase in sales every year for 12 years through depression and recession."

Sue Hartigan is just beginning to break even with the two-year-old Rive Gauche boutique in the Oak Brook Center Mall outside Chicago. She buys $200,000 worth of clothes twice a year. Although Paris headquarters helps her make her selctions, she says, "you have no one but yourself to blame if you choose the wrong styles or colors." Mrs. Hartigan's only complaint is that she and her husband, Jim, a Cadillac dealer, have never met Mr. Berge or Mr. Saint Laurent. "We see the president and CEO of General Motors at least once a year," Mr. Hartigan says.

The free-standing Rive Gauche shops are for the most part welcomed by even those department stores that themselves have Rive Gauche boutiques. "The increased awareness can build business," says I. Magnin's Ms. Caproni. Marvin Traub, chairman of Bloomingdale's, says that as long as the shops' "distribution is limited, it's no problem" for his store.

Such business matters as distribution are overseen by Mr. Berge, who handles the business side of the company. "Yves has never seen one financial figure," Mr. Berge says. "We never tell him, 'Do less embroidery, it's too expensive.' We never say one word. He's the boss." Thus, on the designer's fruitwood and ormolu desk sits not a calculator but a dish of dressmaker's pins.

But Mr. Saint Laurent himself disputes the widely held notion that Mr. Berge is the sole reason for his business success. "I am a good businessman, too," he says. The two partners, he says, always agree on what they should do. He adds, "But Mr. Berge did not make Saint Laurent. Even without Berge, I'd have been Saint Laurent, that's for sure." His manicured right hand, holding the ever-present Rich and

Light cigarette, quivers with indignation. "Since I was nine," he says, "I knew I would be Saint Laurent."

Yves Mathieu Saint Laurent was born Aug. 1, 1936, in Oran, Algeria, then under French control. He first saw Paris at the age of 16, when he accompanied his mother on a shopping trip that included a stop at the couture house of Jean Patou. Inspired, he began doing fashion sketches and in 1953 won first prize in a competition sponsored by the International Wool Secretariat.

In 1955, he moved to Paris to attend couture school and because of his precocious sketches was hired by the house of Christian Dior, Mr. Dior died in 1957, and Mr. Saint Laurent, at the age of 21, was crowned as his successor. His 1958 loose fitting, flare-skirted "Trapeze" collection was wildly successful. Then came 1960's "Beat" collection of knits and leather jackets, which was considered too avant-garde by his employers. Later that year, having been drafted into the army but quickly mustered out because of a nervous collapse, he returned to Dior only to find that he had been replaced by another designer, Marc Bohan. (Mr. Berge says that Mr. Bohan, who is still chief designer for the house of Dior, and Mr. Saint Laurent "do not know each other. They have probably seen each other a few times, but have never raised a glass together.")

Casting about for something to do, Mr. Saint Laurent received encouragement to go out on his own from Mr. Berge, who had been a friend of Christian Dior and was then an art dealer. In 1961, Mr. Berge recalls, "I said, 'Yves, it's your time. We can do it together. We will find the money. Just take a pencil and design.'"

Mr. Saint Laurent agreed. At the same time, J. Mack Robinson was looking for good investments for an insurance company he owned in Switzerland and heard from his Zurich lawyers about Mr. Saint Laurent's need for backing. After meeting with Messrs. Berge and Saint Laurent in Paris. Mr. Robinson says, "I didn't think it was a suitable investment for the insurance company, but I liked the opportunity and invested in it personally." Messers. St. Laurent and Berge retained a 20% interest.

Almost a quarter of a century later, Mr. Saint Laurent is a very rich man, although how rich isn't known. In 1982, Women's Wear Daily estimated that his annual personal income was close to $4 million and that Mr. Berge earned "somewhat less." ("Much too high," Mr. Berge says of the estimate but declines to give correct figures.)

Whatever his income, his life is far from flamboyant. Mr. Saint Laurent "loves to stay home," Mr. Berge says, adding: "It's difficult for him to have fun. Never goes to the theater or movies, doesn't watch TV—never—reads not a lot, always the same book, Proust's 'Remembrance of Things Past.' "

His reclusive life has led to rumors: that he has drug problems; that his physical health is in decline, as evidenced by a walking stick and frequent weight fluctuations; that he has assorted nervous disorders. Mr. Berge counters that his partner has had "nervous breakdowns, yes, but he's never had a problem with drugs," that he uses a walking stick because "in his mind it's very chic" and that his weight gains and losses are caused by a thyroid condition.

Says Mr. Saint Laurent: "I am like an engine—sometimes the engine works and sometimes it breaks down, but I always manage to start again. I consider it my duty—to myself and to everyone who works with me."

Certainly, Messrs. Saint Laurent and Berge take a paternalistic attitude toward employees and the fashion house is one of the few nonunion couture operations in Paris. "My people refuse to unionize," Mr. Berge says. "We have never had a dispute over salary or vacation. We pay a little bit more, but it's not the money that keeps them, it's attitude. We give them respect, consideration." For example, all 10-year employees got paid trips to New York for the 1983 Metropolitan Museum exhibit of Mr. Saint Laurent's past glories.

As for the present, the company recently introduced a ready-to-wear women's clothing line called Variation, which is priced lower than Rive Gauche apparel. The introduction of the new line, which, like Rive Gauche, is a licensed operation in which Yves Saint Laurent S.A. has partial ownership, was partly based on a growing resistance by consumers to the high prices of designer ready-to-wear clothing.

This month brings the launch of a new perfume, Paris d'Yves Saint Laurent, backed by more than $5 million in advertising and promotion. And in the immediate future is next month's showing of spring-summer ready-to-wear clothing.

Looking farther into the future, Mr. Berge sees a potential problem. "I have often wondered what would happen to the house of Saint Laurent if something happened to Yves," he says. "But I'm a pragmatist. I don't answer questions before it's time. I don't know if it's possible to continue without the real designer. If I knew where to find a good designer, I would help him."

Marc-ing 25 Years at Dior
by Patrick McCarthy

A couple of weeks ago, Marc Bohan discovered in an old *Life* magazine photos of one of his first collections for Christian Dior. Rather than being embarrassed by what he saw, or feeling a tinge of nostalgia for a simpler time, Bohan says he was struck most "by how much it looked like what I do today. I could see that I haven't changed all that much."

Few fashion designers would admit to such constancy. But Bohan, who this week officially celebrates his 25th anniversary with Dior, was rather pleased with the discovery. Though given to occasional fits of temper and despondency, he is, by and large, a man on an even keel who doesn't much care for "all the fashion hoopla" and who believes in a "timeless notion of beauty."

"I've never liked gimmicks, perhaps because I don't know how to do them," observes Bohan, as lean now as he was in the 20-year-old *Life*.

"I make clothes for real women—not for myself, not for mannequins and not for fashion magazines. I gladly leave the abstract creations to others."

This unsensational philosophy seems to have paid off for Bohan, the epitome of a good French WASPy designer, and he boasts a roster of loyal clients ranging from Princess Caroline to Betsy Bloomingdale. Moreover, for the last 22 years, double the length of time Christian Dior actually ran the house bearing his name, Bohan and Jacques Rouet, Dior's chairman and chief executive, have presided over the mushrooming of a remarkable fashion empire. From a turnover of $300,000 in 1947, the year Dior and Marcel Boussac established the house, the company's annual wholesale volume now totals $437 million with 160 licensees in 80 countries.

"The name Christian Dior means something to everybody," brags Bohan, who, in addition to the two ready-to-wear and two couture collections he designs each year, also sets the "image and tone" of most of the products carrying the Dior label. "I don't worry that it isn't called the House of Bohan, I've never really cared about that. The professionals in this business know who works here."

Nonetheless, Bohan seems to have developed a classic "love-hate" relationship with the House of Dior, especially since the demise of Boussac, his original patron, and over the past few years there have been repeated rumors that he would leave the company. Now, however, he insists nothing could be further from his mind: "Of course, I've had my ups and downs, but I'm staying, I'm happy here. I will continue to do the couture and I will continue to do the ready-to-wear."

The latter hasn't been as successful, especially in the U.S., as Dior executives had hoped, but Bohan claims "There is a merchandising problem, not a design problem." He is optimistic that "things will work themselves out" now that Dior has been weaned away from the controversial Willot brothers (who took over five years ago when Boussac went bankrupt) and is under the benign control of a government holding company and a consortium of banks. "I have a good job," he adds. "I love to interfere, and that's what I'm paid to

Source: *Women's Wear Daily*, January 24, 1983. Reprinted with permission.

do, and I also like to play politics. Fashion, especially in a house this size, has a lot to do with politics."

Bohan must be a good player, if his vast experience is any guide. He began his career as a sketcher. "I wasn't one of those fashion prodigies who spent my infancy dressing dolls in taffeta," he recalls proudly. "I just liked to draw." In 1945, the 19-year-old Bohan, with the eager complicity of his mother, who was a milliner, got a job with Robert Piquet, then a very fashionable couturier. Hubert de Givenchy was an assistant at the same house.

"I think I liked working with Piquet much more than Hubert," says Bohan. "He was more in my style. He taught me the single most important thing about any dress—bar none—was that it please people. Good design has all to do with proportion and balance and nothing to do with complicated sleeves. A woman shouldn't have to fuss or worry about creases or trying to see the partner next to her at dinner. A woman should feel as relaxed in an evening dress as she does in a skirt and blouse."

Piquet sent Bohan to a fashion school and then made him his principal assistant, which meant doing everything from holding the pins to creating a few dresses for the leisurely twice-a-year couture collections. After three years, Bohan went into the army. Then, after spending two years at Molyneux, he opened his own house in 1953. It lasted one season.

"It was a disastrous period for me," recalls Bohan. "The partners I had pretended to have money, but when it was time to pay the bills I discovered it was all a bluff. The magazines and private customers liked the collection, and so did I, but a couture house, like any other business, requires capital. I risked everything and lost."

Soon after closing his house—"an experience I don't want to repeat"—Bohan became the designer at Jean Patou. In 1958 he went to work for Christian Dior as the stylist in the company's London house. It was just after Dior's death, and Bohan's task was to reinterpret for the British market the designs of Yves Saint Laurent, who had succeeded the creator of the "new look." In 1961, after YSL had been dismissed, Bohan was offered his job as artistic director. Against all the odds, Bohan's first collection was a smash, and the crowd cheered him on the balcony at the Avenue Montaigne almost as loudly as they had cheered Saint Laurent a few seasons before.

Though paid handsomely, somewhere around $300,000 a year, Bohan is not nearly as rich as couturiers like Saint Laurent, Givenchy or Pierre Cardin. This, he insists, doesn't bother him. "I have enough money to live the way I want. This rush to riches—the chateaux and the yachts—doesn't interest me very much. I'd rather spend my time listening to Wagner than counting the profits."

Indeed, Bohan spends a lot of time listening to music, one of his favorite pastimes. His notion of an ideal vacation is to drive his black BMW alone to Beyrouth and attend a week's worth of operas and concerts, something he did last summer. In Paris, he goes to recitals two or three times a week, and, if pushed he'll confess that the most treasured possession in his comfortable rue des Saints Peres apartment is his stereo, which sticks out like a modern sore thumb amind the impeccable 18th and 19th century decor and furnishings.

A widower with a grown daughter who is an antiques dealer in England, Bohan spends most weekends at his graceful country retreat near Fontainebleu, where he likes to cook and where he is taking riding lessons. He stays in shape by swimming every day and by going easy on the Paris social life. "I'd rather be with a few friends at home or at the Brasserie Lipp than at some fancy dinner," he insists.

Bohan is one of the best-dressed men in Paris. His personal style, which he doesn't like to talk about, is a mixture of the fastidious and the unexpected. His suits, which are custom-tailored at Dior, are almost always in soft, conservative shades that blend in with his year-round tan. Ties and shirts are slightly eccentric, but always perfectly matched. The idiosyncratic touches come through in shoes, especially in summer, when Bohan sports white bucks or bowed black patent leather evening pumps, and in coats and sweaters.

At work, the 56-year-old Bohan switches into the customary white smock. His day begins at around 9:30 a.m. and ends around 7:30 or 8. In addition to overseeing the collections, he designs costumes for the theater and movies. He also spends a lot of time with his favorite customers, like Lynn Wyatt, Irith Lan-deau and, of course, Caroline. Princess Grace wore nothing but Dior and the Grimaldi connection has earned Dior a gold mine of publicity. But Bohan seems to be genuinely attached to the family, especially to Caroline, whom he speaks of like an uncle.

Bohan is a devoted admirer of Coco Chanel (he even says he would love to do the Chanel collection anonymously), and it's just not in the man's pure Gallic blood, as it wasn't in hers, to totally upset the fashion applecart. "It's boring to do the same thing every time, it's even antifashion," notes Bohan. "But there has to be some continuity. The object should always be beauty—always. And beauty is never achieved in a season."

Japan's "New Wave" Breaks on U.S. Shores
by Susan Roy

Some have labeled it the "bag lady" look, while others are saying it could revolutionize the way we dress. But whatever the point of view, no one is denying that the new wave of Japanese design continues to be one of the most interesting and influential forces in fashion.

The Japanese are on the cutting edge of fashion. And many of them have done it without the need of the hard sell. Marketing? So far, the designers haven't had to worry much about it. In the U.S., demand exceeds supply for many of the lines. Most companies don't even have New York showrooms, and while most do have New York press representatives, even they must be tracked down. Retailers must go to Tokyo, for the most part, to buy the lines, although several designers have begun showing at the semiannual ready-to-wear buying shows in Paris.

The Japanese fashion business is so new in the U.S. that there are few domestic experts. Sheila Bernstein, divisional vp-fashion merchandising with Associated Merchandising Corp. (AMC), is one of them. She and her staff follow the Japanese market for AMC, a national buying cooperative that represents major department stores. While the volume of

Source: Reprinted from the September 5, 1983, issue of *Advertising Age*. Copyright, Crain Communications, Inc., 1983.

Japanese apparel business done in this country is relatively small, the design influence has been felt.

"In Paris this year, there was much more black and gray," Ms. Bernstein says, adding that French designers showed apparel that was "clean and architectural looking," following the lead of the Japanese.

The Japanese designers pick their U.S. outlets carefully. Their apparel is in boutique areas of large, urban department stores and in specialty stores. Barney's in New York was among the first retailers to emphasize the designers, as was Charivari, a group of high-fashion stores on Manhattan's Upper West Side.

Also, the cost of the apparel limits its market. As Ms. Bernstein explains, duty and import costs force the price of a $100 item in Japan up to $150 to $200 in the U.S. Over-all prices range from $100 to $600.

The designers are becoming aware of this problem, and some have responded by lowering their prices slightly, or adding less expensive lines.

Among the designers considered part of the Japanese new wave are Miyake, Yamamoto, and Mitsuhiro Matsuda. But the one who has most captured the imagination of the fashion industry is Rei Kawakubo, the ascetic designer who runs Comme des Garcons (French for "like the boys"). In a country where few women hold executive positions, Ms. Kawakubo, 40, founded and built an influential company with estimated worldwide sales in 1982 of $27 million, according to *Women's Wear Daily*.

It was her apparel that recently drew press reaction ranging from wild accolades to "bag lady look" sneers. The clothing is severe, in neutral colors—usually black. She disdains traditional concepts, like sleeves and waistlines, and uses draping and knots to style the cloth-

ing. Fabrics are cotton and silk; wrinkles are part of the look.

The no-nonsense style of her apparel is carried over to the way she runs her company. She controls every aspect of the business, from design to distribution. She reportedly does no media advertising in Japan; at the moment she plans none in the U.S. Her only publicity is a black-and-white booklet of photos of her apparel issued several times a year.

In Japan, Ms. Kawakubo owns 20 shops and has franchised 30. Last December, she opened her first boutique outside Japan, in Paris. And now, she has made an agreement with Diane Benson, the woman behind New York's two Dianne B. shops, to open a New York store.

Diane Benson opened her trendsetting Madison Ave. boutique in 1977 and was, she says, among the first to carry the Issey Miyake line. "I took lots of Miyake markdowns" before the line caught on, Ms. Benson recalls. She discovered Comme des Garcons four years ago while on a buying trip in the Orient. "I was drawn to the clothes because of their durability and design," says Ms. Benson, who herself designs a line, Dianne B., for Cygne Designs. At that time, nobody at Comme des Garcons "spoke English; they weren't prepared to export."

Ms. Benson has bought the franchise for the first Comme des Garcons shop in the U.S. It will be the only Comme des Garcons shop outside Japan to carry all the company's lines—Comme des Garcons (women's wear), Homme (men's wear), Tricot (knitwear) and, exclusively in the U.S., Robe de Chambre, all-cotton lounging apparel. Says Ms. Benson with a grin, "I hope all the people who are buying condos in Soho won't be able to live without this Robe de Chambre."

As she explains, it's far from the normal franchiser-franchisee relationship; Rei Kawakubo insisted on calling the shots. "She talked me into things I never thought anyone would talk me into," Ms. Benson says.

The Soho store, scheduled to open in late summer, is of a radically different design. Ms. Benson calls it "a temple, of sorts." It's a cavernous rectangular space—bigger than a bowling alley. Ms. Kawakubo insisted that the skylight windows be covered over (this in New York, where space and light are at a premium). She decreed that clothes will be displayed only halfway along each of the two longer walls and only one item of each style will be hung. Salespeople will have assisting "runners," whose job will be to go to the hidden downstairs stockroom and retrieve the garments.

On the selling floor will be two rough-hewn black sculptural tables—one 16 ft. long, the other 32 ft. There will also be a concrete bench. Cut into the middle of the floor space is a large square; steps from its rim will descend into a second selling space, where a lean selection of men's apparel will be displayed, some on hangers, others on concrete shelving.

Ms. Kawakubo prohibited a traditional cash register. Instead, a special wrap desk/table was designed with a cash drawer and numerical keyboard, hidden from customers. Salespeople dressed in Comme des Garcons apparel will carry small telephones that can be plugged into hidden wall jacks; there will be no other phones.

Think Zen monastery, and you've got the picture.

Ms. Benson is no stranger to innovation; her Soho shop on West Broadway broke tradition with its pastel geometric interior and innovative use of selling space. But while she's uneasy about the rigid restrictions imposed by Ms. Kawakubo, she is putting her faith in the designer's judgment.

And Comme des Garcons is backing it with a guarantee: "They've agreed that if the store doesn't work, they'll redo it at their expense," she says. But she's optimistic about its success. "It's going to be so divine," Ms. Benson predicts.

No advertising *per se* is planned for the shop—the doors will just open—but there are plans to send a Christmas catalog to those on Ms. Benson's retail mailing list. The catalog—in a 12-postcard format—is scheduled to be advertised in *Artforum* and *Interview*.

Clothing prices will start at $100, with the average cost for an outfit (top and bottom) at $300. This is no problem in Soho, where expensive boutiques are the norm; price resistance is virtually nonexistent.

But Comme des Garcons and the other Japanese designer apparel is priced out of the reach of most American consumers. AMC's Ms. Bernstein believes this will change. "The Japanese have maximized their business in Japan," she says. "There's a limited market there, so where do they go?

"As with electronics and cars, apparently the major market for them will be the U.S.," she believes, predicting that more Japanese apparel companies will enter the American market. "I think you will see a giant increase within five years."

The Benetton Group

What Is Benetton?

The Benetton Group, a privately owned company based in Treviso, Italy, just outside Venice, is the world's largest knitwear manufacturer. Founded in 1964 as a family enterprise consisting of a sister and three brothers, Benetton and its subsidiaries design, manufacture and market a diversified range of knitwear and casual clothing for women, men and children, principally under the Benetton, Sisley and 012 trademarks.

Benetton sells its clothes in 53 countries on all five continents through over 3000 franchised retail outlets worldwide, including 1250 in Italy and over 250 in North America. Today, it is a complex industrial company worth approximately $320 million.

History

Benetton, called the "Italian miracle of the century," traces its roots to Giuliana Benetton, whose interest in knit-making flourished during her teenage years, when she began working in a sweater shop in Ponzano, Italy.

Her brilliant designs, full of bright pastel colors and soft textures, impressed her brother Luciano. Sensing the potential market for his sister's homemade sweaters, Luciano said, "You design the sweaters; I'll worry about selling them." With imaginative insight, Luciano began selling the sweaters to many local merchants, while attending the 1960 Summer Olympic Games in Rome.

Luciano's fascination with his sister's craft served as the catalyst for Benetton's phenomenal growth. Demand from merchants grew, and in 1964, all three of her brothers, spurred on by the enthusiasm for Giuliana's vibrant, stylish knitwear, joined in the sales and marketing of her designs to form Benetton.

In 1968, Giuliana, Luciano, Gilberto and Carlo opened their first store in Belluno, Italy—north of Treviso—thus launching their big business of manufacturing woolen garments. By 1978, there were 1000 stores in Italy. Benetton's extensive network of international franchised shops today extends throughout Europe, with recent expansion into the United States, Canada and Japan. Since January 1985, Benetton has opened additional stores in Budapest, Hungary; Belgrade, Yugoslavia; and Sophia, Bulgaria, as well as being invited to open stores in Moscow and Shanghai. Outside of Italy, France is Benetton's largest market, followed by Germany and the United States.

Over the last two decades, the Benetton Group has been transformed from a small family operation into a vast industrial company. Since 1972, the family has conducted business out of a beautifully restored 17th-century villa called "Villa Minelli." The villa governs 10 other factories, which manufacture Benetton's colorful and lively apparel 24 hours a day; seven factories operate in Italy, with one each in France, Scotland and Spain.

The Benetton Group has established one of the most technologically sophisticated computerized information systems utilized in the clothing and textile industry. In fact, by mid-1985, a new establishment will be opened in Castrette (Treviso), which will be totally automated, with just two people to oversee the operation.

Each of the four family members are equal

Source: Press release by Sally Fischer, Benetton.

partners in the company and have played a crucial role to ensure the success and steady progress of Benetton's operations: Luciano is the managing director and serves as the company spokesman, Giuliana is the chief designer, Gilberto is financial director and Carlo is the production manager.

The Benetton clan has a total of 15 children, ranging in ages from 1 to 25, to contribute to the continued success of this fashion empire.

Financial Profile

Benetton's dramatic growth started in 1978, when it tackled the export market. During the 10-year period from 1975 to December 31, 1984, revenues from exports have grown from approximately 2 percent in 1978 to approximately 55 percent in 1984.

Recently, the company has experienced tremendous growth in its U.S. market. Last year, Benetton rang up over $300 million in world sales. According to Francesco Della Barba, executive vice president for U.S. operations, 1984 sales were roughly 8 percent of total sales, compared with Italy's contribution of 45 percent of total sales for the same period.

Della Barba forecasts that sales in the United States for 1985 will be 11.4 percent of total worldwide sales. In addition, he states that "total sales should grow by 58 percent from 1984 to 1985 in our U.S. market." Della

Barba attributes Benetton's successful penetration of the U.S. apparel market to America's fascination with the "made in Italy" look. "Benetton offers good-looking, high-quality, colorful, attractive and universal clothes. We are probably the only manufacturer that can sell its products to the entire world!"

The Benetton Group owns 49 percent of Fiorucci, and recently the Benetton family bought controlling stock in Calzaturificio di Varese, a shoe company.

Product Line

Last year Benetton shipped over 39 million garments—a variety of 400 styles in over 300 colors. The rainbow of products include woolen, cotton and denim casual wear for both adults and children. In addition to its three trademarks, Benetton, Sisley, and 012, Benetton markets clothing under the Tomato, Merceria, My Market and Fantomax trademarks. Its shoes, from Calzaturificio di Varese, will be offered in the United States by the end of 1985.

The latest challenge for Benetton will be its entry into the mail-order catalog business, beginning with distribution of 500,000 fall/winter catalogs between July 15th and October 1st. Della Barba feels that this move represents "a great potential and an alternative to retailing, given that the United States is the only nation where the mail-order business is booming."

German Fashion: Making It a Business
by Wendy Green

Systems-oriented and profit-motivated, West German apparel manufacturers are making their presence increasingly felt in the U.S. sportswear market. Industry giants such as

Escada AG and Mondi are leading the parade, but a number of smaller West German designer firms are out to grab a piece of the U.S. action as well.

Source: *Women's Wear Daily*, December 30, 1985. Reprint permission granted.

"More and more people are discovering the German manufacturers," says Ellin Saltzman, senior vice president and corporate fashion director of Saks Fifth Avenue. "Their quality and detailing are simply excellent. They've done their research and are filling a void here. It seems the German fashion industry has come into its own."

Escada AG is perhaps the best known and most successful of the West German imports—with distribution in 25 countries from Europe to East Asia, Australia, South Africa and the Americas and an average yearly wholesale volume of more than $110 million.

"Profitability is the name of the game," says Steven Lubinski, vice chairman and treasurer of SRB Fashion International, Escada AG's American subsidiary. "We function as a business first. We run on information—information that we analyze to make good marketing decisions. Marketing has gotten us where we are and I wouldn't be surprised if SRB became a $75 million company in three to five years."

Marketing continues as the key to Escada AG's success, says Lubinski; no move is made without the appropriate research and planning. Everything from demographic, consumer and store surveys to the latest Parisian runway fashions are interpreted and applied to the company's worldwide marketing strategy.

"The American market is just one part of our global strategy," says Wolfgang Ley, chairman and chief executive officer of Escada AG. "We are more international than German, really, and we cater to the sophisticated and affluent customer worldwide. We are heading toward a standardization of fashion style so it doesn't matter where the company or customer originated. It's the clothes that count."

Like many West German lines, Escada AG is quick to emphasize its "European styling" while downplaying its Germanic roots. Although an impressive 75 percent of Escada's volume is exported, the company still finds itself fighting the stereotype of West German fashion as nothing more than dowdy, derivative basics.

"We are in no way related to the old German look of dull green coats," says Ley, who, with his wife Margaretha, founded Escada AG in Munich in 1977. He had been working in retailing and manufacturing; she was chief design director at Mondi—another big West German fashion firm. They met, married and decided to create a collection of designer sportswear that would appeal to women from Bavaria to Boston. They called it Escada after a horse they had bet and won on in Spain. The line sold in West Germany, expanded into Europe, then Canada, and by October 1981 Ley was market-testing in the US. SRB Fashion International was formed in December that year and opened for fall in March 1982.

In its first year, SRB brought in $2,300,000 in volume, "but we didn't expect that kind of growth and it took time to adjust," recalls Lubinski. "There was a lot of turmoil and inefficiency at first, buyers didn't know where to put us, we had to find qualified people fast, but we made it. We found loyal stores and a following and now we're in a period of stabilization. We're cutting back on weak accounts and building on our strong ones."

Today SRB does an average of more than $40 million wholesale, making it one of Escada AG's most profitable subsidiaries. SRB carries three labels, each aimed at a different market.

Escada is the biggest and the most successful of the three. Its elegantly tailored sportswear ranges from $49 for a cotton T to $579 for a leather jacket, wholesale, and is responsible for two-thirds of SRB's volume. Laurel offers career-oriented customers sportswear at $39 for a cotton tank to $279 for a leather jacket, while Crisca's trendy but not junior fashion is priced at $39 for a cotton T to $129 for a wool jacket. All are designed by Margaretha Ley's international design team in Munich and produced in Bavaria at the company's high-tech headquarters. Wolfgang Ley is a devout believer in computer technology. "Our (Japanese) knitting machines are some of the most advanced in the world," he boasts. Another favorite, a layout computer, has the ability to produce 34,000 colors and full-color printouts. Color is very important to Escada— it organizes all three lines around color stories.

Margaretha Ley designs 22 color groups of 22 to 27 pieces each for Escada, two seasons a year. Each group is self contained, offering sportswear as well as coordinating accessories manufactured for Escada. Everything from gloves, scarves and jewelry (made in West Germany) to shoes (manufactured in Italy) carry forward the group theme. The same holds true for Laurel and Crisca. Subsidiaries and agencies may pick up whichever groups they like; SRB brings back about a dozen for the American market each season.

"Buyers must buy a merchandising concept," says Gloria Gelfand, president of SRB. "They can't just buy our sweaters because that wouldn't represent the collection and stores correctly. We don't dictate to our stores, we emphasize what we know they'll do best with."

Although some retailers resist this highly structured system of preselected fashion, most praise it, noting that it seems only to increase sales.

"We do phenomenally well with Escada— better than with any other designer line, German or American," says Bill Dodson, president of Lilly Dodson in Richardson, Tex. Approximately $1,500,000 of the store's $5,500,000 yearly retail volume comes from Escada. "Escada is flamboyant without being outrageous, and it changes significantly every season, much more so than most American designers. It keeps the store fresh."

"Escada's packaging works well for us," agrees Sydney Bachman vice president and fashion director at Bergdorf Goodman. "they deliver it as a group, the customer sees it all together and it creates multiple sales because they buy complete outfits. The Escada customer always wants to look dressed up, even if she's just wearing pants, like Crystal on 'Dynasty'; so when she buys trousers she'll buy a shirt and jacket to go with it."

Bergdorf's opened a 1,230-square-foot Escada boutique this summer, and Saks Fifth Avenue has a 1,200-square-foot version on the second floor. In addition, Escada is carried by 250 accounts from Neiman-Marcus in Dallas to I. Magnin, San Francisco, and Bonwit Teller, New York.

Backing up each store are Escada's hefty retail catalogs, a $2 million advertising budget, store clinics and 120 trunk shows a season—all designed to drive home Ley's design concepts.

"This is the bible of our business," says Gelfand, pointing to the slick, 182-page four-color spring-summer catalog that Escada sends to retailers. The catalogs are used to train salespeople on how to show the collection, and to preview the line with customers. Similar but smaller catalogs are done for Laurel and Crisca. "Every salesperson in every store has one of these."

Plans include a petite division for fall 1986, a New York communications center to be linked via satellite with the main computer center in Munich, further expansion into Italy and France and an Escada boutique to open in Seoul, South Korea, in 1986.

"We plan to grow," says Ley. "Whether through takeovers or by our own design, we intend to enter new markets whenever we see a niche we might fill."

But Escada AG isn't the only fashion firm

with an international appetite. Munich-based Mondi of America and Bruestle are aiming at the same market.

"We're supplying the whole world," says Herwig Zahm, owner and chairman of Bruestle and Mondi of America. "We're trying to make internationally appealing clothes for the women in London, Paris or New York. We're very export-minded and are already in practically every Western country, from Australia to England, but we left the biggest for last. We're just building up our U.S. market now."

Seven years ago Mondi brought its tailored sportswear—wholesaling from $50 to $225—to America. Two years ago it introduced Bruestle, an $80 to $350 line of ladylike sportswear, followed a year later by Nic, its $25 to $75 junior line and this spring by Slendor and Mondi Men at $50 to $225.

Like Escada AG, Mondi backs up its sportswear collections with slick catalogs and sells its clothes in coordinated, predesigned packages that offer everything from jackets to socks and shoes. For spring, the 360-piece Mondi collection has 10 different groups available; the 250-piece Bruestle line offers eight. Mondi is carried by Neiman-Marcus in Dallas; I. Magnin in San Francisco; Lord & Taylor in New York and several hundred specialty stores. Approximately 200 specialty stores carry the Bruestle line. Together, the two bring in approximately $30 million in American sales annually, representing 15 percent of the company's international volume.

Also eagerly competing for attention in the U.S. are other established West German lines. The 50-year-old Basler, 20-year-old Britt and 20-year-old L'Estelle entered America last year while the 26-year-old Steilmann company and the 37-year-old Strehle firm with its G.D. and Strenesse collections arrived two years ago. And then there is Bleyle of America. They have been in the U.S. for 30 years and, even though the U.S. line is designed and manufactured in Georgia, the company's worldwide headquarters is in Stuttgart.

Wolfgang Ley remains unfazed by his compatriot competitors. "We have no German rivals," he claims. "Italian designer lines are our main competition. It will take other German firms years to reorganize and understand the U.S. consumer and retail infrastructure. This is not just a matter of exporting. If German lines are to sell here, they have to adapt their methods and markets to Americans—not the other way around. What is wonderful about America is that there is always room for a good product. Find a good product and you will find success. Liz Claiborne and Esprit, they are models of success. I admire success greatly."

Endnotes

1. "Chambre Syndicale Forms Non-couture Section," *Women's Wear Daily,* October 3, 1984.
2. "The Paris Couture," *New York Times Magazine,* September 16, 1984.
3. "An Arab Princess Is a Beautiful Bride," *Wall Street Journal,* November 5, 1985, p. 1.

4. "French Couture Sales Jump 35 Percent in 1984," *Women's Wear Daily*, February 7, 1985.
5. Couture Sales: Chambre Syndicale de la Couture. *Women's Wear Daily*, Feb. 3, 1986.
6. "Designers Grumble but Fashion Goes On," *Women's Wear Daily*, July 26, 1976.
7. "Voice of the Couture," *Vanity Fair*, December 1984, p. 132.
8. "New York Pret—French Fashion," *Women's Wear Daily*, September 11, 1985, p. 25; and "French Build in U.S. with Medium Prices," *Women's Wear Daily*, December 27, 1985; "France," *Women's Wear Daily*, September 16, 1986.
9. Dr. Liberati, Deputy Trade Commissioner, Italian Trade Council, New York, in a telephone interview, November 6, 1985.
10. "London," *Women's Wear Daily*, March 18, 1986, p. 15.
11. *Ibid.*
12. "Trade Fairs and Exhibitors in the Federal Republic of Germany," 1984 brochure.
13. "Japanese Fashions," *Women's Wear Daily*, September 10, 1985, p. 6.
14. *Ibid.*
15. *Ibid.*
16. T. H. White, "The Danger from Japan," *New York Times Magazine*, July 28, 1985, pp. 40–42.
17. "Hong Kong: "Battling to Keep the SA Dollars," *Women's Wear Daily*, November 13, 1984.
18. Estelle Hamburger, *Fashion Business: It's All Yours*. New York: 1976. Garfield Press, 1976.
19. *Focus: Economic Profile of the Apparel Industry*. New York: Dun & Bradstreet, 1985; and "China's Textile Exports Seen Rising," *Women's Wear Daily*, January 12, 1986.
20. Mary Ellen Bernard, executive vice-president and general manager of Frederick Atkins, Inc., at the Fashion Institute of Technology's Fashion Seminar in New York, October 1985.

Selected Bibliography

Charles-Roux, Edmonde. *Chanel*. New York: Alfred A. Knopf, 1975.

DeGraw, Imelda G. *25 Years/25 Couturiers*. Denver: Art, 1975.

deMarly, Diana. *The History of Haute Couture, 1850–1950*. London: B. T. Batsford Ltd., 1980.

Dior, Christian. *Christian Dior & I*. New York: E. P. Dutton, 1957.

Keenan, Brigid. *Dior in Vogue*. New York: Harmony Books, 1981.

Lambert, Eleanor. *World of Fashion: People, Places, Resources*. New York: Bowker, 1976.

Lynam, Ruth, ed. *Couture*. Garden City, N.Y.: Doubleday, 1972.

Madsen, Axel. *Living for Design.* New York: Delacorte, 1979.

Milbank, Carolyn R. *Couture: The Great Designers.* New York: Steward D. Tabori and Chang, 1985.

Poiret, Paul. *Kings of Fashion.* Philadelphia: J. B. Lippincott, 1931.

Quant, Mary. *Quant by Quant.* New York: Putnam, 1966.

Saint Laurent, Yves. *Yves Saint Laurent.* New York: Metropolitan Museum of Art, distributed by Crown Publishers, 1983.

Saunders, Edith. *The Age of Worth.* Bloomington, Ind.: University Press, 1955.

Schiaparelli, Elsa. *Shocking Life.* New York: E. P. Dutton, 1954.

Vecchio, Walter and Robert Riley. *The Fashion Makers, A Photographic Record.* New York: Crown Publishers, 1968.

Trade Associations

Board of Trade, Export Services Division, Hillgate House, 35 Old Bailey, London EC 4, England.

Camera Nazionale della Moda Italiana, 00187 Roma, Via Lombardia, 44, Italy.

Centro Di Firenze Per La Moda Italiana, Vitale Gramsci 9/A, Florence, Italy.

Chambre Syndicale de La Couture Parisienne, 100 Rue Du St. Honoré, 75008 Paris, France.

Clothing Export Council of Great Britain, 54 Grosvenor Street, London, WIXODB, England.

Fédération Française des Industries de Prêt-à-Porter Féminin, 69 Rue de Richelieu, Paris 75002, France.

Trade Publications

Femme-Lines, 225 East 36th Street, New York, N.Y. 10016.

Women's Wear Daily, 7 East 12th Street, New York, N.Y. 10003.

CHAPTER REVIEW AND LEARNING ACTIVITIES ....

Key Words and Concepts

Define, identify, or briefly explain the following:

Caution fee	Haute couture
Chambre Syndicale	IGEDO
Couturier	Imports
Dusseldorf	Low-wage production centers
Fashion center	Prêt-à-porter
Fédération Française du Prêt à Porter Feminin	Trade showing
Franchised boutique	

Review Questions on Chapter Highlights

1. Name the three categories of foreign fashion producers and explain how each is different.
2. What is a haute couture house, and do its operations differ from those of an American apparel company? Are there haute couture houses in the United States? Prove and explain your answer.
3. What is the Prêt-à-Porter division of the Chambre Syndicale de la Couture Parisienne and why did it come into existence?
4. What are the major sources of income for haute couture houses?
5. List the major European ready-to-wear fashion centers and give the reasons for the importance of each. What are the secondary European centers and for what are they known?
6. What is the fashion importance of Japan today? Give examples that support your answer.
7. What is Asia's Bermuda Triangle and what is its importance to the United States?
8. Name some additional low-wage apparel production centers in the Orient and explain the reasons for their emergence.
9. Discuss the following statement made by a major retailer: "Where there is a sewing machine we'll go."
10. Why are all foreign governments so eager to develop the apparel industry in their respective countries? Is the United States as active as foreign governments in its support of our domestic apparel industry? Explain your answer.
11. Select any one reading in this chapter and explain how it illustrates the text of this chapter.

Applications for Research and Discussion

1. Analyze your own wardrobe for apparel and accessories that were made in a foreign country. Make a list of the countries of origin and the type of merchandise from each. Were you aware of the country of origin at the time of purchase and did it influence your purchase decision?
2. Select a particular category of merchandise (men's or women's). Shop several retail stores and compare their foreign-made merchandise with domestically produced products that retail at about the same price. Consider workmanship, styling, fit, value, and other comparative factors. As a customer, which would you prefer to buy and why?
3. Research both free-standing shops and departments in large stores that bear the name of a foreign fashion producer (i.e., Benetton, Rive Gauche, etc.). Discuss their fashion importance in your community. Who is their target customer?

8

IMPORTS

Imports and exports have always been a major consideration of nations. Each country tries to sustain and expand its economy by exporting products it has in abundance or can produce efficiently and importing those it needs or

...chandise is concerned, international trade in the ...to the country's beginnings. As far back as the ...nventories of our sailing ships listed silks from ...s from England, damasks and velvets from Italy, ...e laces and fabrics from Paris. In the nineteenth ...he latest French fashions were imported by Ameri- ...d as models of the garments they would create for ...hen advanced printing techniques made possible ...smakers turned to such early European magazines ...*uarest* to see what was being worn in London and ...ey saw. Early American fashion retailers, such as ...and Marshall Field of Chicago, bought the models ..., such as Worth and Doucet, as well as European ...opy couture styles in their workrooms.

...roductive capacity and creative talent abound in ...U.S. textile firms, apparel producers, and retailers ...countries to purchase merchandise for resale, or for ...rve new fashion ideas.

...s the penetration of imports into the United States, ...cedures involved, and the applicable government ...deal with the importing operations of well-known ...etailers.

IMPORT PENETRATION BY FOREIGN PRODUCERS ....

There is no question that the penetration of textile, apparel, and accessories imports is a problem shared by every segment of the American fashion industry, as has been discussed in previous chapters. Since 1980, imports have increased faster than domestic consumption, resulting in a decline in the demand for domestically produced fashion goods.

Apparel/Textile Trade Deficit

A **trade deficit** is the amount by which the value of **imports** exceeds **exports**. In 1985, textile and apparel imports combined amounted to $21,300 billion, compared with exports of $3100 billion. The trade deficit of $18,200 billion was close to 13 percent of the total U.S. trade deficit for that year and an all-time high.[1]

Imports versus Domestic Production

The market share of imports in several merchandise categories, as noted in previous chapters, has equaled and even exceeded domestic production. For example, imports of women's and girls' woven blouses and shirts stood at 8,587,000 dozen, well above domestic production of 5,671,000 dozen in 1984; imports of wool knit shirts and blouses rose to 639,000 dozen compared with U.S. production of only 500,000 dozen. In the sweater category, government data showed domestic production of women's and girls' man-made fiber

GROWTH OF IMPORTS OF SELECTED WOMEN'S AND CHILDREN'S WEAR (IN THOUSANDS OF UNITS)

Category	Year 1980	Year 1985
Coats and jackets	42,879	71,007
Suits	1,715	6,916
Dresses	24,453	47,101
Blouses and shirts	379,169	542,276
Sweaters	149,955	242,368
Skirts	14,774	45,392
Slacks and shorts	168,036	265,970
Raincoats	6,696	11,460
Intimate apparel	216,452	353,420

Source: U.S. Bureau of the Census (imports for consumption); U.S. Industrial Outlook 1986.

sweaters to be only 5,200,000 dozen, while imports surged to almost 9 million dozen.[2]

It is estimated that in the not-too-distant future, if the present rate of growth is sustained, **import penetration** will account for 65.2 percent for men's, women's, and children's wear. That is, for every 1000 units produced in this country, an additional 652 will be imported.[3] As Sol Chaikin, then president of the ILWGU, said, "No industry in America has been harder hit by Asian competition than the American garment industry, which has lost 155,000 jobs in the last six years."[4]

REGULATION OF IMPORTS ....

The international trading policy of the United States has generally been based on the principle that high tariffs and excessive restrictions of foreign goods will lower our standard of living for the following reasons:

- Trade barriers mean high prices for consumers, since decreased competition will allow domestic firms to charge higher prices.
- Domestic producers who are incapable of meeting competition are not entitled to special consideration by the government.
- Nations affected by restrictive import measures taken by this country may retaliate against what they consider to be American protectionism, and thus damage the export prospects of other industries in this country.
- Trade restraints to protect one industry, such as textiles and apparel, may save some jobs but increase unemployment in others as foreign countries retaliate by buying less from the United States. Also, domestic firms that rely on imports would be less able to compete and would lose business.

In 1947, the United States and other major trading nations entered into the General Agreement on Tariffs and Trade (known as GATT). This is a multilateral agreement designed to liberalize and govern world trade. Within the framework of GATT, there are many different trading agreements and rules, some of which are entered into by two or more countries, and some of which are unilateral.

The Multi-Fiber and Textile Arrangement

Until the 1970s, the dollar volume of U.S. purchases from foreign producers was relatively insignificant and therefore created little or no real disruption of our domestic textile and apparel industries. As imports began to swell and penetration reached flood level, the U.S. government moved to control the growth rate of imports by keeping it equal to the growth rate of domestic production. The most important outcome of this was the multilateral Multi-

Fiber Textile Arrangement **(MFA).** This provides an umbrella under which nations may negotiate and implement bilateral trade agreements.

The MFA first became effective in 1974 and was renewed, with some revisions, in 1977, to cope with the problem of increased penetration into the apparel/textile industry. The MFA sets general rules for the kinds of actions countries can take to protect their industries from disruption by rising imports. Under its provisions, the United States (or any other nation) can control disruptive imports by consulting with the exporting nations individually and entering into bilateral agreements, which establish import quotas. Such agreements provide for a somewhat orderly development of trade and offer some relief to a country that is being overwhelmed by imports.

The MFA, however, is not without shortcomings, and it does not give American producers the measure of relief they need. In many categories of apparel, the permitted level of imports remains high enough to disrupt domestic production. A further weakness is that MFA assumes levels of domestic growth beyond what is actually occurring, and thus lets imports continue at a disproportionate level. Another shortcoming is that MFA limits the quantity or number of units brought into the United States rather than the cost value of the merchandise. Foreign producers are thus encouraged to shift into higher-priced items if they choose to do so, thereby cutting even more deeply into the dollar value of the domestic market.

At the time of this writing, the MFA is up for revision. Most of the low-wage apparel producing nations want it scrapped, whereas the United States and European countries favor a more stringent trade agreement that would include such measures as surcharges on exports from low-wage countries.

Quotas and Bilateral Trade Agreements

Quotas are quantitative restrictions placed on exporting countries on the number of units of specific items that may be shipped to a particular importing country over a specified period of time. With some regulated exceptions, which will be explained below, a foreign producer cannot ship goods into the United States without a quota.

The United States negotiates separate bilateral treaties with each of the textile/apparel exporting nations. These **bilateral treaties** establish country-by-country quotas, or annual maximums, on hundreds of categories in cotton, wool, man-made fiber textiles, and apparel. Each bilateral agreement establishes the quota level on a category-by-category basis, specifies the growth factors to be applied to each quota year, and provides for establishing new quotas in cases in which the bilateral agreement does not provide for a particular import category. The negotiating of bilateral agreements is the responsibility of the office of the U.S. Trade Representative. The Customs Service is responsible for keeping track of import levels and quota levels.

When more goods are presented for entry into the United States than the quota level allows, that merchandise is denied entry and is warehoused at the port of entry, at the expense of the importer.

Quotas, which vary for different merchandise categories and for different countries, are specified in numerical units first by fiber square yardage equivalents (SYE) and then translated into apparel categories. For example, Hong Kong has the largest quota allocation for natural fiber garments, whereas Taiwan and South Korea have the biggest quotas for man-made fibers. Usually, the exporting country administers its own quota and makes allocations to individual producers based on their past export performance. Allocations can be lost if they are not used within the designated quota year. Manufacturers, however, can and do sell unused quota to other companies and thus maintain their export rights for subsequent years.

In Hong Kong particularly, the system has given rise to quota brokers, who deal independently in unused or excess quotas. In some cases, a manufacturer who has large quota allotments can make more profit from selling part or all of his quota than from actually producing apparel.

Several areas in the world, however, have no quota restrictions at all—for example, the European Economic Community (EEC). Exemptions are based on the assumption that (1) these are high-wage industrialized countries whose products are not price-competitive with domestic goods, (2) our exports to these countries balance our imports from them, and (3) their import penetration is not large enough to cause domestic market disruption.

Also exempt from U.S. quotas are countries in the Caribbean Basin or in Central America—this is because the regions are not considered to constitute major apparel-producing centers. Many countries in Africa and Asia that are not yet in the industrialized or even in the developing stage are exempt as well. Our relations with these exempt areas are in marked contrast with the quota restrictions we place on more than 90 percent of the garments imported from Taiwan, Hong Kong, and South Korea, our three biggest sources of supply.

"GETTING AROUND" THE QUOTAS

From time to time, the White House has announced programs to tighten the administration of the textile agreements in order to control an excessive influx of imports, yet little has been accomplished toward stemming the tide. U.S. importers, whether retailers, wholesale importers, or manufacturers, have been getting around quotas with impunity. Production has been transferred to countries with unused or excess quotas, or to developing countries without quotas. In addition, countries with used-up quotas are illegally transshipping through countries with quota availability.

In a sense, quotas have created opportunities for many of the low-wage producing countries in Asia. As the demand for inexpensive imports grows,

QUOTAS FOR SALE

Source: Reprinted with permission of RWP: Hva Shak Company.

U.S. manufacturers have of necessity sought sources beyond the quota-limited facilities of Hong Kong, Taiwan, and South Korea. However, as the volume of garment production inevitably shifts from the Asian triangle to other emerging low-wage countries, new trade agreements are bound to follow. And with them will come the added headache of quotas.

In this day and age, obtaining the best quality and prices is not always the only concern of U.S. buyers. The problem of available quotas now complicates the procedure. For buyers who are interested in importing goods to America, availability centers on quotas—spelled with a capital "Q."

NEW COUNTRY-OF-ORIGIN RULES

To curtail quota evasion by diversion and transshipment through second countries on categories covered by treaties, new country-of-origin laws were established by the United States in January of 1985. The new rules set up criteria for determining which country was truly the country of origin for incoming merchandise—and thus which country's quota was involved.

Traditionally, it had been accepted as legitimate practice for two or more foreign countries to contribute to the making of some apparel categories. For example, in the case of a knitted sweater, yarn could be spun in one country, dyed in another, knit into panels for back, front, and sleeves in a third, and then finally assembled into a garment, labeled, and exported in a fourth. Hong Kong, for instance, has functioned as the assembler and shipper for much of its knitwear, using panels knitted in mainland China.

The new rules say that the first manufacturing steps determine a garment's origin. It must carry an import label bearing that country's name and be subject to that country's quota limitations. In the example of Hong Kong, cited above, the sweaters are now regarded as having originated in China and would be counted against China's quota, even though Hong Kong does the finishing and shipping. The problem for Hong Kong is that China's quota is insufficient.

These new U.S. rules have affected such countries as Hong Kong, Pakistan, South Korea, Taiwan, and Indonesia. They are now exploring and investing in other low-wage countries that are producing below their quota levels or are quota free. Among this latter category are the Caribbean countries, Sri Lanka, Mauritius, Thailand. As production shifts, however, quotas for such countries are inevitable, and may even result in some shift of production back to the United States.

Simultaneously with the new country of origin laws, a new textile and apparel law was passed which required that all clothing and household fabrics made in this country are now required to carry a label saying "Made in USA." The law also requires that all mail-order ads identify which items are

EXAMPLE OF "MADE IN THE USA" LABEL

Source: Reprinted with permission of Crafted with Pride in the USA Council, Inc.

manufactured in the United States and which in foreign countries. The intent of this legislation was to fill a void in existing labeling requirements and provide the federal government with ways to prevent fraudulently or unmarked foreign goods.

Taxes on Imports: Tariffs/Duties

In addition to the restraints imposed by import quotas, most fashion goods are subject to an import tax. Among the rare exceptions are leather and furs. This tax on imports, known as a **duty** or **tariff,** is established and regulated by the U.S. government, paid by the importer, and collected by the U.S. Customs Service. The amount varies for different categories of merchandise, but it is generally *ad valorem*, or a percentage of the first or invoice cost. Its primary purpose, of course, is to increase the eventual selling price of imported goods and thus protect domestic industries. For many fashion categories, however, from the low-wage countries, even with the addition of taxes and shipping costs, the final landed cost in the United States is often considerably less than for domestically produced apparel of equal quality.

The countries from which we import tend to impose tariffs that are highly restrictive. They use excise taxes and other trade barriers that make this country's goods economically unsuitable for sale within their borders. Some, like Brazil, for example, keep the products of other countries, including the United States, from entering its country.

Preferential Programs: Exemptions from Tariffs and/or Quotas

The U.S. government also has a number of programs that are designed to stimulate the trade and economy of developing countries around the world. Such countries receive preferential treatment and exemption from quotas.

GENERAL SYSTEM OF PREFERENCES (GSP)

The GSP, which became effective in 1976 and expired in 1985, allowed merchandise from beneficiary countries to come in without quota restrictions or tariffs. These are developing countries or dependent countries and territories throughout the world. The original list consisted of 112 countries in Central America, Africa, Asia, the Caribbean Basin, and the Far East. Since 1976, however, some of those on the original list became highly industrialized and were removed from the preferred group—Taiwan, South Korea, and Sri Lanka, for example. Current lists were maintained and published in *Importing*, a periodical of the Department of the Treasury, U.S. Customs Service.

TARIFF SCHEDULE 807

Section 807 of the U.S. Tariff Schedule provides for special duty treatment of garments that have been cut within this country, shipped abroad for further processing, and then reimported directly into the United States.

Under 807, a domestic manufacturer can design and cut garments in a U.S. plant and ship the cut materials to a low-wage country for sewing exactly as if he were using a domestic factory as contractor. Under this procedure, the only duty paid on the returning goods is a very low one—a tax only on the value added by the low-wage foreign country. In effect, if ten dollar's worth of cut materials go out of the United States, and the labor abroad costs one dollar, only that one dollar is taxed when the goods return.

THE CARIBBEAN BASIN INITIATIVE

The **Caribbean Basin Initiative** (CBI), which was passed by Congress in 1983, permits almost all manufactured or semimanufactured goods produced in Caribbean and Central American countries to come into the United States without quota restrictions. The legislation was intended to stimulate exports from that area into the United States, and thus spark a boom in manufacturing investments. In conjunction with the CBI, Caribbean countries recognized this potential for growth and adjusted their laws to provide incentives for industrialization. Among these incentives are duty-free importation of equipment, low factory rentals, and tax-free profits for a specified number of years.

Investors in Caribbean producing plants include some Asian companies whose quotas are limited in their own countries and who are using Caribbean plants either to break into the U.S. market or simply to increase their export capabilities in general.

Textile and Apparel Trade Enforcement Act of 1985 (HRI562)

Introduced into Congress in 1985, this Textile and Apparel Trade Enforcement Act was presented by its proponents as a way to "promote orderly nondisruptive future growth of world trade in fibers, textiles and apparel products."[5] Essentially, its purpose was to do the following:

- *Roll back imports* from the major exporting nations of South Korea, Taiwan, and Hong Kong from their 1984 levels by some 24 percent and assign them a 1 percent annual growth thereafter.
- *Limit 1985 imports* from China, Japan, Pakistan, Indonesia, India, the Philippines, Thailand, Brazil, and Singapore, to 1984 levels, with a 1 percent annual increase in their quotas for 1986 and 1987.
- Require an import license as a prerequisite for all imports, including those from Canada, the European Economic Community (EEC), and all other quota-free countries.
- *Vary quota restrictions* on imports from nations classified as "nonmajor exporters" of textiles and apparel, depending on whether their exported products equal 40 percent of U.S. domestic production of like merchandise during the preceding year. Whenever the 40 percent threshold is reached, a product would be classified as "import sensitive" and an import quota would be imposed.

**THIS ACT WAS VETOED BY
PRESIDENT REAGAN**

> # S680/HR1562:
>
> *An urgent, rational bill that
> will put an end to uncon-
> trolled imports of apparel &
> textiles, stop the erosion of
> our industry, save two mil-
> lion American jobs. And
> still give the nations of the
> world, poorer ones espe-
> cially, legitimate access to
> our market.*

- *Expansion of quotas on textiles,* so that silk, linen, and rami would be subject to the square yards equivalents (SYE) quotas imposed on cotton, wool, and synthetic fiber merchandise.

Although passed by both houses of Congress, this bill was vetoed by President Reagan in December, 1985, an action which the industry termed "appalling." After the veto, its Congressional supporters rescheduled an override vote on the bill for August 6, 1986 in an attempt to defeat his veto. This attempt failed by eight votes, reflecting the split between protectionists and free traders. The industry has vowed to intensify their lobbying efforts for further protectionist trade measures.

WHO IMPORTS AND WHY

There are many reasons for the rise of imports, but primarily they stem from the intense competition that characterizes the fashion industry. Basically, producers and retailers alike import textiles, apparel, and accessories for the same reasons:

- *Lower prices.* On the price front, the domestic industry has a twofold disadvantage. Labor costs are higher than in the low-wage countries discussed previously and the domestic producer does not enjoy tax exemptions, rebates, preferential financing schemes, and other profit cushions that foreign governments provide their exporting entrepreneurs.

- *Foreign expertise and capabilities.* Many foreign countries have productive capabilities and expertise that we do not possess. For example, European countries have generations of skills behind them in such hand operations as laces, embroideries, beading, hand-finished buttonholes, hand-knitted sweaters, and hand-loomed woolens, to name a few. Italy and Switzerland are outstanding examples. And the highly individual patterns of true fishermen's sweaters are, of course, from Ireland. Also in the category of goods that American producers either cannot produce at all or cannot do as well as foreign makers are such items as the cashmeres of Scotland and China, the soft-as-butter leathers of Spain, and the silks of Italy and China.
- *Exclusive rights.* Foreign purchases also give American companies an opportunity to avoid sameness—assortments that are too much like those of their competitors. American retailers are always in search of new and different merchandise to which they can get exclusive rights, particularly if they can secure these rights without making the massive purchases often required by large, volume-minded American apparel producers. The exclusive item, not available in competing stores, permits the retailer to generate storewide excitement and at the same time to obtain a higher markup percentage because the merchandise is free from competition. Similarly, it is almost impossible for apparel producers to obtain exclusivity of fabrics from American textile producers without committing themselves to the purchase of huge runs far in advance of their selling season. Foreign producers of apparel or textiles, who are generally not as large as American manufacturers, do not need or demand big commitments.

  Joan Vass, a leading American designer of high-priced fashions, explains it this way: "I'm as patriotic as the next guy, but my designs come first. . . . I employ only forty people here and the United States mills aren't interested in selling to me. I'm too small for them. Also, U.S. mills do high volume, and volume doesn't always allow for luxurious materials. America simply doesn't make as good a product as Italy or Japan."[6]
- *Fashion cachet of Europe.* Not to be underestimated as a reason for importing fashion goods is the glamour associated with European fashions and labels. From its inception, the U.S. fashion business has been influenced by foreign fashions and has found inspiration across the Atlantic. It is true that today a circle of American designers get adoring treatment from American retailers and their customers, yet what comes from the European fashion centers will probably always have a special cachet just because of its origin.

In short, whenever the domestic market is unable to meet a fashion need, whether it be price, exclusivity, or technical expertise, the use of imports has become a means of coping with the need. No matter what the reason, and no matter whether a producer or a retailer is doing the importing, it is obvious that foreign purchases are deemed profitable to U.S. importers.

Imports by Retailers

A retail firm's success ultimately rests on the strength, balance, and competitiveness of its merchandise assortment. A major responsibility of retail buyers and merchandise managers is therefore, to seek ideal assortments *wherever* they can find them. In many situations, imports are an essential ingredient of the retail product mix because they can provide distinctive, competitive, and profitable merchandise.

Although exact figures are not available, a published research study reports that imports by retailers account for 50 percent of America's apparel imports.[7] It is also estimated, however, that goods of foreign origin account for only 15 to 20 percent of store inventories.[8]

IMPORT BUYING METHODS

Not all foreign purchases by retailers are made in a single pattern. Procedures vary and may involve anything from sending representatives abroad to placing an order with a foreign source at a showroom in the United States. Among the most common means are the following:

- *Foreign trade shows in the United States.* Many foreign producers exhibit their collections in the United States. Such showings may be at international trade shows staged in this country, or in single-nation shows sponsored by a particular country to court foreign buyers. (Examples of such shows were discussed in the previous chapter.) Buyers who are unable or unwilling to make trips overseas do their buying at such shows.
- *Foreign producers' showrooms in the United States.* Many large overseas producers maintain their individual sales forces in showrooms in New York City, as well as in major regional apparel marts, for the convenience of retailers.
- *Store-owned foreign buying offices.* Many large retailers maintain offices, independently or in conjunction with their buying offices in the United States, in major cities of Europe and the Orient, such as Florence, Paris, London, Hong Kong, and Tokyo. These offices keep their principals updated on new producers, important new products, and fashion developments. In addition, they place orders as requested and handle the forms and other procedures that are involved, such as letters of credit, quality control checks, and follow-through on shipping arrangements and delivery dates. Retailers who maintain such offices include, for example, Sears, J. C. Penney, Macy's, The May Company, and Saks-Fifth Avenue. Also maintaining foreign offices for the benefit of the retailers they serve are such buying offices as Frederick Atkins and the Associated Merchandising Corporation.

AD BY FOREIGN COMMISSIONAIRE

- *Foreign commissionaires and agents.* Retailers, particularly those of smaller size who are not represented by their own foreign offices in a particular country, use **commissionaires** and agents. These functionaries assist store buyers when they make direct visits to the countries concerned. In return for a fee (i.e., a commission), they direct visiting buyers to suitable producers, handle the necessary export forms, and follow through on delivery and shipping arrangements.

- *Foreign trade showings.* Practically every European country and some Far Eastern fashion centers hold seasonal, semiannual group showings in March/April and in October. These shows are attended by thousands of visiting buyers from all over the world who come to buy or observe new developments in foreign fashions and products, or do both. Purchases that are made are followed up by either commissionaires or the foreign buying office serving the store concerned. These shows, which are both national and international in nature, were discussed in the preceding chapter.

SPECIFICATION BUYING FOR PRIVATE LABELS

The move toward import buying by retailers has been accelerated by the renewed retail trend toward featuring private-label merchandise. Merchants have become disenchanted with designer-name products and national brands because these widely distributed products have lost much of their exclusivity. Designer names and national brands turn up in off-price discount stores that have multiplied like fried chicken and hamburger outlets.

Such store-name or private brand goods, more often than not, are made overseas by producers who offer better comparative values in terms of styling, or price, or sometimes both. Nearly all private-label merchandise is made to the specifications of the importing retailer (or retail buying group). In **specification buying,** the buyer plans the styles and designs to be produced. This is done sometimes by describing the garment, and sometimes by supplying an actual sample for copying or adaptation. The merchant may even supply the fabric, not necessarily from the country in which the garment is to be made. Also specified by the purchaser are the garment's measurements, its trimmings, the quantity, and the negotiated wholesale price. In effect, the retailer fulfills the function of an apparel jobber, and the foreign producer the function of a contractor. In this way, U.S. retailers can enjoy both exclusive styles and the favorable prices that are possible when merchandise is made to specifications by lower-cost producers in the Far East.

Imports by Producers

Even if all retailers were to purchase exclusively from domestic sources, imports would still be a major factor in their merchandise assortments, because U.S. manufacturers also import. The retailer who purchases these imports does so, not necessarily because they are imports, but because they satisfy a need in the merchandise assortment and can be sold profitably at a price point attractive to the store's customers.

DIRECT IMPORTS BY PRODUCERS

Producers do direct importing of textiles and apparel for the same reasons that apply to retailers—price advantage, exclusivity of product, foreign expertise, and any other fashion or quality factors that may be absent from domestic markets. Fabric mills import yarns not readily available in this country. Fabric jobbers and apparel manufacturers import silks and certain luxurious fabrics, that are not produced here. Many sportswear apparel companies import sweaters or leather items to coordinate with their domestically produced skirts, slacks, and other separates. There are also some U.S. based companies that specialize in importing finished products, such as dresses and skirts, and market them domestically under their own names.

OFFSHORE PRODUCTION

Despite the continuing outcry over the amount of direct importing done by retail buyers, American producers have been steadily increasing their own import practices by having their merchandise produced abroad. For example, of the 25 million units that the firm of Liz Claiborne manufactured in 1984, some 84 percent were produced in 23 Far Eastern plants; 80 percent of the fabrics were of overseas origin.[9]

Another example is Kayser-Roth. In addition to manufacturing in 165 domestic factories, the firm contracts out 25 percent of its output to offshore factories. Many of the high-priced designer-name firms, such as Calvin Klein, have their merchandise produced by both domestic and foreign contractors—the latter primarily in the Far East. In fact, 70 percent of Calvin Klein's highest-priced merchandise is produced in Hong Kong. In contrast, 81 percent of his lower-priced Puritan division merchandise is produced domestically.[10]

OFFSHORE PRODUCTION IN INDIA AND SOUTH AMERICA

Pisces Fashions Ltd.
India

Looking for importers/wholesalers for woven sleep and loungewear production. We have 10 years experience with top corporations in U.S. market.
NY contact: 212 789-1234. Overseas: 25 W. Gandhi Plaza, Delhi, India. 543-5454. TELEX: 33-7711.

TEE SHIRTS IN SOUTH AMERICA

Large tee shirt manufacturer, high-volume production, offers high-quality services in manufacturing or silk-screening tee shirts on any textiles. Contact Tee-Shirts, 8998 Carnation St., Wolfburg, NY 11666.

SECTION 807: VALUE-ADDED DUTY

It will be recalled from earlier discussions in this chapter that Section 807 of the tariff schedule imposes only a very small value-added duty on merchandise cut in the United States but contracted out for further stages of production to some other country. According to a sourcing study by Kurt Salmon Associates, Section 807 production operations accounted for 12.6 percent of U.S. imports, and the number is expected to increase. This is because the low-wage foreign countries being used in this way are not affected by restrictive import laws and are given preferential quota and duty treatment by the United States. Among these countries are the Dominican Republic, Mexico, Haiti, and Costa Rica, where the average hourly wage is lower than in the Far East.

The recent entrance of textile firms into the apparel manufacturing field, as noted in Chapter 3, operates under the 807 tariff schedule.

The following reaction of the ILGWU to the increase in 807 operations is of interest: "The increased resort of off-shore production under 807, a euphemism for imports, has led some to view this form of importing as somehow healthier for the U.S. than other forms of importing. This, of course, is nonsense, except for the individual firm doing the importing."[11]

807 PRODUCTION IN COSTA RICA AND DOMINICAN REPUBLIC

807 PRODUCTION

Open capacity in D.R. for established women's sportswear manufacturer. Top quality, fast production, Florida cutting facilities. Contact Ms. Mandez, 315 666-4433.

807 PRODUCTION

Open capacity for men's suits in Costa Rica. American management available, quality sewing, fast turnaround. Contact Suzanne Wong, 202 123-2439.

PROTECTIONISM VERSUS FREE TRADE

The penetration of imports into the U.S. fashion business has given rise to a highly vocal battle between advocates of protectionism and of free trade. **Protectionism** means the reduction, limitation, or exclusion of foreign goods. **Free trade** means avoiding protectionist measures and letting goods flow freely among countries.

On the protectionist side are the American producers of apparel, accessories, and textiles, the two major industry unions (the ILGWU and the ACTWU), and the industry's trade associations. All are strenuously lobbying in Washington for more protection from imports. On the other side are the retailers and their trade associations, and organized consumer groups. These spokespersons adamantly believe that the public wants and should have imported products. One result is that, in 1985, there were some 300 bills pending in Congress pertaining to regulation of imports! Other industries, too, are in the fray—industries that do have entry into markets abroad and fear they will lose them if protectionism is invoked on behalf of fashion industries.

In addition to their lobbying efforts, both sides exhort the general public

PROTECTIONISM: "CRAFTED WITH PRIDE IN USA" COUNCIL

Source: Reprinted with permission of Crafted with Pride in the USA Council, Inc.

to add its voice. Statements are made in newspapers and on TV, petitions are circulated, consumer surveys are made, and demonstrations are held.

To finance these efforts, American retailers formed the Retail Industry Trade Action Coalition (RITAC) in 1985 to fight for freer international trade in textiles and apparel. Its membership consists of 20 leading retail firms and 8 retail trade associations. Similarly, the fiber producers, fabric mills, and apparel manufacturers have formed and are supporting the Crafted with Pride in USA Council and launched a public information campaign to heighten consumer awareness of the "Made in the USA." label and to educate retailers on the bottom-line advantages of domestically produced goods. These advantages include timeliness, reduced handling costs, geographic proximity, and flexibility.

How the problem will be resolved is uncertain at this point. The arguments both for and against imports are valid and rational. One thing, however, is certain: the problem will not be easily cured and will continue to involve many compromises to satisfy retailers, importers, foreign exporters, workers, labor unions, textile producers, apparel and accessory manufacturers, U.S. legislators—and the consumer.

GLOBAL SOURCING: AN INTERNATIONAL FASHION MIX ....

Despite the growing protectionist movement in the United States, most industry observers do not foresee a swing back to exclusively domestic sourcing. Quite the contrary. Retailers seem determined to find new import sources to avoid quotas and maintain a flow of goods into their stores. Similarly, domestic producers seem to be increasing the 807 and other offshore production activities.

Many industry professionals agree that the trend toward global sourcing will be heightened if the Congress passes laws to roll back quotas of current major suppliers. A spokesperson for Liz Claiborne, Inc., which sources internationally, points out that "anyone who's prudent will look to other countries." His own company has already formed relationships in Israel and Ireland, as other bases for sourcing.[12] And Norman Hinerfeld, chairman of the executive committee of Kayser-Roth, forecasted: "Where today you have about 35 actually exporting countries, in ten years you will probably have about 65."[13]

The fashion business has indeed become a global one, involving a merchandise mix that ranges from anything to everything and comes from anywhere to everywhere. Today, American retail buyers and producers range all over the world to visit fashion markets: to Europe for small quantities of high-priced goods; to the Orient for lower-cost orders in depth; to emerging

GLOBAL SOURCING: AN INTERNATIONAL FASHION MIX

**U.S. Imports of Cotton, Wool, and Man-Made Fiber Apparel
from Selected Countries, 1964–1984
(in millions of SYE)[a]**

	1964	1968	1974	1978	1980	1982	1983	1984
Hong Kong	168	321	369	695	628	690	761	815
Taiwan	36	148	422	608	670	748	867	936
Korea	11	144	294	458	494	576	643	684
People's Republic of China	0	0	8	63	166	357	430	444
Subtotal	215	613	1,093	1,824	1,958	2,371	2,701	2,879
% of total	38%	53%	56%	63%	68%	70%	69%	61%
Japan	197	313	164	170	82	76	96	138
% of total	35%	27%	8%	6%	3%	2%	3%	3%
Philippines	44	43	102	158	148	161	177	234
India	—	—	27	77	69	73	106	131
Indonesia	—	—	—	—	5	38	46	129
Singapore	—	23	90	85	71	82	89	128
Sri Lanka	—	—	1	10	43	59	66	108
Thailand	—	—	42	46	35	53	66	106
Dominican Republic	—	—	6	35	59	76	76	94
Mexico	—	13	91	91	92	56	60	86
Haiti	—	—	41	53	58	54	60	68
Macao	—	—	12	37	43	43	50	61
Subtotal	—	—	412	592	623	695	793	1,145
% of total	—	—	21%	20%	21%	20%	20%	24%
All other countries	—	—	268	315	221	240	297	560
% of total	—	—	15%	11%	8%	8%	8%	12%
Total all countries	561	1,153	1,937	2,901	2,884	3,382	3,894	4,722
	100%	100%	100%	100%	100%	100%	100%	100%

[a]Square yards equivalent; this is a means of measuring quantity by using the fabric content rather
than the number of units involved.
Authors' note: Silk, linen, and ramie unreported since they were quota-free.
Source: Office of Textiles and Apparel, Department of Commerce.

countries that have not yet been affected by quotas; and to domestic market
centers within the United States.

A chart accompanying this chapter illustrates, in terms of square yard
equivalents, how our global sources of supply have grown, and how the
relative importance of various areas have changed over the past several years.

U.S. PENETRATION OF FOREIGN MARKETS ·

American textile and apparel producers have been unable to match their exports to the rising tide of imports. This is not simply a matter of this country's cost of production versus the costs in other countries; it is also a matter of trade barriers, such as excise taxes, value-added taxes, and restrictive quotas, often imposed by the very countries that enjoy a large share of the U.S. market. With these barriers, plus shipping costs, plus the differential in cost of production, and the high world value of the American dollar, our domestically produced fashion merchandise has been priced out of many potential foreign markets.

Joint Ventures and Foreign Licensing Pacts

Some of our major textile and apparel producers have found ways to penetrate foreign markets in spite of the obstacles just mentioned. One method is to **license** foreign producers in return for a percentage of their wholesale sales. A second is to enter into a **joint venture,** or partnership arrangement with a foreign producer. A third method is to establish *wholly owned manufacturing plants* in foreign countries. Some U.S. companies use one, two, or all three of these methods, the choice depending on how the particular method works in relation to the international trade rules of the country concerned. A domestic company doing business in three or more foreign markets may use all three methods, each in a different area.

LICENSING AGREEMENTS

Licensing is a relatively uncomplicated way for a domestic manufacturer to cultivate foreign markets, and it is the least costly. Entering into a legal arrangement, the U.S. company gives the right to use its manufacturing process or its trademark name, or both, to a foreign producer. In return, it receives a fee or royalty percentage on wholesale sales.

The foreign producer gains production expertise and the use of a well-known name, or both. The licensing American firm gains entry into a foreign market at little risk or financial investment. Among the firms that have such licensing arrangements are Healthtex and Carter, in the children's wear field. Enormous amounts of women's and men's clothing and accessories are also produced and sold in Japan and European countries that bear the names of well-known French, Italian, and American designers or the brand names of their companies.

JOINT-OWNERSHIP VENTURES

A joint venture in the context of foreign trade consists of a partnership between a U.S. company and a foreign producer. In many countries, such an arrangement is a requirement for penetrating anti-import barriers. Under joint ownership ventures, the U.S. company provides designs, patterns, technical expertise, and the use of its name. The foreign partner then employs his own country's labor to produce and market the merchandise.

A notable example is the U.S.-based firm of Esprit, which has established Esprit Far East in Asia through a partnership with Michael Ying of Hong Kong. The Asian partner owns half the company and serves as its managing director. Esprit Far East is a major exporter of women's and children's casual apparel. Ninety-five percent of its merchandise is produced in Asia. Hong Kong manufactures the bulk of the output, and the balance is contracted out to factories in Taiwan, Singapore, and to a lesser extent in Malaysia, China, and Macao. The U.S. company, however, is involved in every operational step, from design to patterns, to fabric, to quota, to shipping arrangement. Most of the elements that constitute the garments are purchased in Asia—even zippers, labels, and buttons.

Another example of a joint venture is the arrangement between the French silk producer, J. Brochier Soieries, based in Lyons, France, and the China Silk Company, to manufacture silk fabrics for export. Still other such joint ventures exist between Blue Bell, Inc., the producer of Wrangler jeans, and companies in Italy and Spain.[14]

Direct Ownership of Production Facilities

The third method of penetrating a foreign market is by a 100 percent investment in a foreign-based assembly or production facility. Some foreign countries, for economic reasons, offer investment incentives to U.S. companies to establish wholly owned subsidiaries within their borders. As in the case of joint ventures, the foreign facility provides employment to the host country's own labor and often uses the local materials.

For example, Burlington Industries has such manufacturing facilities of its own in Ireland, France, England, Germany, Italy, and Mexico. Another example is Wrangler Jeans, which has facilities in Scotland and Malta and, until recently, also had manufacturing units in Belgium and the Ivory Coast.

Direct Exports

Along with foreign licensing, joint ventures, and foreign subsidiaries, some U.S. companies also do direct exporting to other areas where the tariff and other trade barriers are less restrictive. The volume involved is relatively small, because of the high cost of the domestic product and the trade barriers involved. Nevertheless, there are foreign consumers who are eager to buy products that are uniquely American and who covet the "Made in the U.S.A." label.

Our exports are so small in relation to our imports of textiles and apparel that our balance of trade (imports versus exports) had been consistently worsening since the late 1970s. Seeking to correct this situation, our government has from time to time launched efforts to increase exports. As one example among several, the Department of Commerce's Bureau of Export Development in 1979 formalized and put into effect a Textile and Apparel Export Expansion Program whose purpose was to increase the amount of direct exporting done by U.S. apparel companies.

The ineffectiveness of programs such as this is clearly evidenced by the fact that our apparel and textile trade deficit continued to rise. From a little more than $1.5 billion in 1970, the combined apparel/textile trade deficit reached $18.2 billion in 1985, as previously noted.

How effective future regulations, if any, will be in improving the apparel/textile balance of trade remains to be seen. One conclusion, however, is fairly certain: the real problem our domestic industry will continue to face is that of import penetration. No matter how much exports may increase, it is most unlikely that they will ever counterbalance the penetration of imports into the American fashion economy.

In the opinion of one financial expert, the decrease in exports has contributed more to the trade deficit than the imports themselves. Testifying before a House subcommittee against possible protectionist legislation, Stuart Tucker, of the Overseas Development Council, said: "Most of the international trade bills presented to Congress concerning the trade imbalance do not attack the root of the trade deficit."[15]

One indication of the nature of the problem is that, of the 40 countries that accounted for over 90 percent of U.S. imports in 1984, only nine bought more from the United States than they sold to it. And of the top 20 trading partners, the United States had a trade surplus with only four.[16]

The trade imbalance is not a problem that will be easily solved. It is one that the best minds in industry and government will have to wrestle with, probably for a long time to come.

Readings

Using foreign manufacturing facilities can be like entering a strange new world, whose intricacies must be mastered. The same is true with purchasing lines from European sources. These articles tell how the fashion business copes.

Sourcing in the Far East—Esprit's Way

Producing 95 percent of its goods in Asia, Esprit has found its best course is to work closely with relatively few factories and to involve itself in every phase of production and shipping.

Asian Bargains

K Mart deals with many countries in the Orient, and in so doing copes with other cultures, import limitations, and a variety of problems unique to the Asian experience.

Hong Kong . . . Better!

Hong Kong is upgrading the styling and quality of its merchandise and has become the number one source in Asia for many U.S. merchants.

Europe for Sale

European manufacturers, seeking to make it easy for U.S. buyers to deal with them, use representatives in America to handle all the problems of importing for the retailers to whom they sell.

Sourcing in the Far East—Esprit's way

by Paul Charles Ehrlich

"Running all over the world looking for cheap deals is not my idea of being an efficient buyer. You wind up a spectator, a refugee, a buyer on the run with very little clout in the market."

This bit of apparel wisdom comes from Michael Ying, managing director and a 50 percent owner of Esprit's Asian operation—Esprit Far East. While American buyers scour the globe in an often exhausting search for an ever-spreading range of sourcing countries, Esprit has maintained a philosophy of "less is more."

For this major exporter of sporty and casual women's apparel, manufacturing success tends not to be based strictly on price points, that is, whether a blouse can be made more cheaply in Indonesia or South Africa. Rather, emphasis is placed on maintaining direct control over a consolidated base of factories. Little is left to agents or third parties. Esprit gets involved in each step of production—from thread to fabric to quotas to shipping.

"You can go to a cheap country and pay nothing, but you wind up with nothing." Ying explained. "also, when you're spread out you open yourself up to more mistakes because you have less control over production."

Ying estimated overseas sales this fiscal year ending June 30 should be about $400 million, out of total worldwide sales of about $700 million. Total worldwide sales last year were about $450 million, he said.

In 1971, after labor problems in San Francisco, Esprit started its production overseas. Today, about 95 percent of Esprit's apparel is made in Asia, with the bulk of it produced in Hong Kong. Esprit is considered the largest single apparel exporter from the colony, with about 24 million items shipped over the last year to international markets. There is also some production in Taiwan and Singapore and, to a lesser extent, in Malaysia, China and Macao.

"We have found that these markets, and especially Hong Kong, provide the quality and efficiency that we require," Ying said. "Instead of looking for new areas, we are trying to improve production by working closer with a limited number of factories. Shortening the chain of command is one of the keys."

Esprit has had trailblazing experiences with factories in places with inexpensive labor. The company had buying offices in New Delhi and Sri Lanka in the mid-Seventies and early Eighties but shutdown operations because of problems with quality and delivery.

"We got great prices but little else," Ying said. "No fabric would arrive because of a flood. Or the fabric would come but we couldn't get the goods cut in time. What good are cheap prices to a customer who won't get the goods when he needs them?"

Operations in Hong Kong have also been trimmed and tightened. A few years ago, Esprit subcontracted its large volume to about 200 different factories. The number has since been halved, although larger orders than ever before are being placed.

"We are able to do more and get a better product," the managing director said. "Working with fewer factories also enables us to build a stronger relationship with the manufacturer."

Firm control and factory loyalty enables

Source: *Women's Wear Daily*, June 26, 1985. Reprint permission granted.

Esprit to operate on amazingly fast lead times of 30 to 35 days. By comparison, many retailers work on lead times of two to four months from order to arrival. Furthermore, Esprit produces about 800 different styles a season that are shipped in relatively small quantities throughout the season. Thus, timing is important, Ying says, because stores are working with limited stocks. The process also saves Esprit warehouse costs, he added.

Before placing an order, Esprit directly sources all the ingredients that comprise a garment: fabric, buttons, zippers, labels and so forth. Most of these items are purchased in Asia. About 85 percent of Esprit's garments use natural fibers such as cotton and wool. About 50 percent of the fabrics come from China and the rest from Japan. While supplies have been reliable in recent years, China is increasing fabric costs.

Esprit also arranges exporting quotas beforehand.

"Many companies get stuck because they leave it to factories to get the quotas," Ying explained. "But when it gets time to ship goods, quota prices may have gone up or there are none available."

Because of the company's long-term performance in Hong Kong, Esprit has acquired about one million dozen quotas for popular items such as blouses, shirts, sweaters and pants.

Another one million dozen are bought in the open market.

In Hong Kong, quotas are traded like commodity futures.

"When we finally have everything in our hands we can go to the factory and say, 'Start sewing tomorrow,' " Ying said.

Ying declined to discuss the potential impact of the Textile and Apparel Trade Enforcement Act now before the U.S. Congress, a bill that would cut back imports significantly. He deferred comment on that matter to Esprit San Francisco headquarters. (Esprit has been quite active in opposing the bill, taking on the task of organizing West Coast companies to fight it. Last month it held a meeting at its San Francisco headquarters to inform the California business community of the problems faced by apparel importers because of the bill.)

Esprit's consolidated approach toward manufacturing is also reflected in the way it markets apparel. In the Seventies, the company was called Esprit de Corp. and featured seven different brands of apparel, such as Sweet Baby Jane blouses and Plain Jane dresses. Each line had a different image and although sales were good—about $120 million in 1979—the overall results were unsatisfactory.

"The image wasn't clear," Ying explained. "It was hard to promote seven brands at the same time. Fashion was changing to a more complete look that provided coordinated products. So, we gave all the lines one identity."

In 1979, the company decided to merge the lines and promote one name: Esprit. A massive promotion campaign was launched to push the Esprit "look."

In addition to its wholesaling efforts, Esprit has opened its own retail outlets. One recently opened in Los Angeles. There are also stores in San Francisco, New Orleans and Melbourne and two in Hong Kong. A third store is scheduled to open here in September, and Singapore is slated for a 12,000-square-foot store before year end

Esprit's next target will likely be Taiwan, Ying said. He has rejected Japan for now because the enormous size of the market requires a large staff to oversee operations.

Ying said Esprit has been eyeing China's domestic market, but "conditions are not yet right." China requires production to be made in the country, of which a sizable portion must be exported. Ying said China's limited quota supply makes such an arrangement not viable.

Asian Bargains
K mart Apparel Buyers Hopscotch the Orient to Find Quality Goods
by Steve Weiner

Back home in New Jersey, Joseph Antonini wouldn't rate more than a glance and a smile of greeting while on a factory tour. So Mr. Antonini is clearly embarrassed by what is happening here [i.e., South Korea].

As he rides up to the Hanil Synthetic Fiber Industrial Co. plant, security guards straighten and bark a word that sounds like "choof." Workers spring to open Mr. Antonini's door, and dozens of applauding Hanil office workers crowd around, hailing the startled visitor. Mr. Antonini and his associate, Ronald L. Buch, are handed large floral displays.

"Can you beat that?" asks Mr. Antonini, the president of K mart Apparel Corp.

Gulping Potent Liquor

Lots of people are trying. A few days earlier, Mr. Antonini survived a 21-course banquet in his honor at a Chinese clothing factory. Then there was the *mao-tai* party, an affair of fortitude at which toasts were continually exchanged in gulped servings of the potent Chinese liquor. "I tasted that for days," Mr. Antonini says.

This is an Asian buying trip. It sounds like great fun, but it is serious business for the 30 or so buyers of K mart Apparel, the clothing arm of the U.S. discount chain. The buyers, often with their bosses in tow, scour a dozen Asian nations for 1985 fall merchandise worth hundreds of millions of dollars. They look for bargains, but they also use the trip to make contacts for new sources of supply and to learn what the competition is doing.

It is a demanding, ritualized process of negotiating to the third decimal point by day, cementing deals, and then renewing good will at night in an atmosphere of luxury, power and privilege.

All the 'The Pencil'

"It can go to your head," notes Mr. Antonini, a 20-year K mart veteran who remembers living in one-room apartments as a young store manager. Now he and his buyers fly first class, stay only in luxury hotels and drive around Hong Kong in Mercedes-Benz limousines. In Hong Kong a merchandise source treats Mr. Antonini to a $400 bottle of wine at dinner. And in Japan, a source serves him rich meals of Kobe beef at $200 a plate.

Indeed, those with "the pencil"—the buyers' term for the authority to order merchandise—are treated royally. "But once you lose the pencil, it's over," says the wife of one K mart executive. "You've got to understand it's for the pencil, not you."

Those pencils are busiest through late fall when hundreds of apparel retailers and importers descend on Asian capitals to compete for the best values and the vendors' production time. "It's like a convention of old buddies from Seventh Avenue," says a buyer, referring to the New York City street at the center of the garment industry.

The lure is quality, often superior to that of U.S. products at prices held down by low Asian pay scales. Japan, Hong Kong, Taiwan and South Korea—the Big Four of Asian countries from which the U.S. imports consumer goods—produce some of the world's best merchandise, from fabrics to electronic goods.

Adding Quality

Even developing nations, such as Bangladesh, Mauritius and Indonesia, find it relatively easy to produce apparel that appeals to the U.S. market. "You can add a dollar's worth of quality for 10 cents of cost," says Gil Waschman, senior vice president for non-apparel goods at Target Stores, a Dayton-Hudson Corp. unit.

But Asian buying is fraught with difficulties. Travel can be arduous. Communication can be sticky. "Our buyers learned that the Japanese say yes often," says Michael Rouleau, a former Target executive vice president. "But it's 'Yes, we can,' or 'Yes, we can't.' You have to learn which yes it is."

A tricky problem is dealing with the quotas. The U.S. limits apparel and textile imports through a combination of treaties and unilateral embargos. Each nation has its own system for allocating its quota. That confusing system bedevils buyers trying to secure sources of supply. Target bought wool sweaters from China for several years, but because of pricing and quota limits, China refused to make any more for 1984. Wal-Mart Store Inc.'s shirt importer had to scramble last fall when Indonesian production was unexpectedly embargoed by the U.S., for a time trapping 480,000 dress shirts. "You don't control your own destiny in these places," says a spokesman for the importer.

After months of planning, K mart begins a part of its Asian buying trip in Europe. As part of its goal to offer more up-scale merchandise, K mart sends Mr. Buch and several others to gather sweater designs from London, Paris and other European fashion capitals. They buy 80 examples of the latest in "leading edge" fashions, including sweaters with harsh geometric patterns, clashing colors or unusual features, such as ribbed shoulders or quilted yokes. K mart intends to sell acrylic and wool-blend versions of the sweaters in its stores in about a year. (The company says it isn't doing anything illegal because fashion designs aren't protected by the law and because K mart is "emulating" or improving, not copying, the designs.)

K mart knows that nine out of 10 of its customers will be attracted to the flashy look but will take the basic cardigan and pullover anyway. "You must have both," says Mr. Buch, vice president and general merchandise manager. "We spend more time working on 2,000-dozen fashion sweaters than we do on 20,000-dozen basics," he says.

The buyers' next stop is Korea. They want to compare the sweater-maker Hanil's ability to make complicated sweaters with that of a competing factory in Taiwan that has done superior work with difficult designs. K mart also needs to review Hanil's progress on many of the retailer's basic sweaters.

But there is a catch. The Korean government requires its manufacturers to negotiate prices higher than a national-average benchmark price for their goods each year. Hanil made about three million sweaters for K mart last year, but the Korean government said it must cut production by 120,000 sweaters because last year it negotiated prices that were too low.

K mart makes Hanil strut its stuff. In an office crammed with thousands of sweaters, Gary Kovie, a senior buyer, compares each original with Hanil's copies. The manufacturer hasn't done well on every complicated, high-fashion design. He examines an original Claude Montana ski sweater, with bold X's and O's marching across the chest. Hanil's sample is short several characters, and those that are there are the wrong size.

But the Korean company does well on the more-basic patterns. Mr. Kovie makes changes nonetheless. He snips a yarn from one sweater and asks that it be used in another. Styles are rebuilt; crew-neck sweaters become V-necks, sleeveless sweaters sprout sleeves. He holds up a ski sweater with a snowflake design on the chest and shoulders. Picking up yarns of blue, white, navy and gray, he decides which could substitute for the colors in the patterns. "The white might show through too much," offers a K mart staffer.

Sometimes Mr. Buch, the boss, intervenes. "Don't get too wild now," he tells Mr. Kovie, who is looking at a striped sweater. "Black and gray is more salable than black and red," he says. Mr. Kovie changes the color combination.

Reproducing a Crack

Like other companies, K mart takes an active role in the manufacturing process. Failure to be specific can produce startling results. One year, a gift-ware buyer was horrified when an Asian factory, faithful to a demitasse sample damaged during shipment from Europe, reproduced thousands with a tiny crack down the side. And Target was astonished when the maker of an inflatable rubber boat put it in a box with a Chinese sampan on the cover.

The laborious sweater-ordering process goes on for days, punctuated only by breaks for Cokes or coffee—the Americans won't drink the water because they fear they will get sick—or glances at a ball game on television.

Throughout the process, prices are negotiated. K mart can win low prices because its immense orders keep the knitting machines running longer and more efficiently. It also

takes delivery of merchandise earlier, helping factories through slack periods. The formula works with Hanil. In the first step of negotiations, Hanil accepts K mart's first price without the usual haggling, Mr. Antonini says. By the time the process ends in early January, Hanil has won half of K mart's imported-sweater production, including four of 12 contested fashion designs.

Evenings are often a welcome respite. Daewoo Corp., a large Korean industrial concern that makes shirts for K mart sponsors the first formal dinner, at the Seoul Hilton, where a three-foot carved ice tower supports the K mart corporate symbol. The buyers and executives are served from a French menu that includes frog-leg consomme, and fish and scallop with watercress sauce. Toasts and testimonials are mixed in with small talk. Mr. Buch raises his glass and toasts "the good times, when prices could have risen but didn't, and the bad times, when we both took risks to help each other." The buyers say the evening was comparatively tame. Last year, Kim Woo Chong, Daewoo's chairman, entertained K mart in his hotel penthouse with South Korea's finest opera singer.

Socializing Required

Business is rarely discussed at the dinners— similar ones are given in Taiwan, Hong Kong and Japan. Rather, buyers say they go not to make deals but because attendance is expected. "The socializing is part of the process," says Mr. Buch. "If we didn't go to dinner, it would be an insult."

Two K mart and Daewoo incidents illustrate how the Asian trade is built on business and personal relationships. K mart helped Daewoo get its start in the apparel business with a pattern of early and steady orders. This paid off for K mart in 1983, when Daewoo initially said it couldn't meet the retailer's shirt-production needs. But Mr. Buch was able to obtain the needed additional shirts by personally intervening with Daewoo's chairman in a half-hour meeting in which they relived old times.

Daewoo has reciprocated with small favors of its own. When Norman Milley, the president of K mart stores, complained that the company's shirts wouldn't fit his 15-inch neck and 44-inch waist, Daewoo made up a special batch of shirts with a 15-inch neck, medium yoke and extra-large body.

The Korean buying trip also gives the K mart buyers a chance to see what competitors are doing. On a courtesy tour of a Daewoo shirt plant, Mr. Buch admires a crisply packaged K mart Ketch brand shirt. He also examines a shirt made by Daewoo under the Oleg Cassini label that can sell in department stores for twice the price of the Ketch shirt. Mr. Buch tells the Daewoo executive that the shirts are of nearly equal quality, and the executives agree. "This is why I'll have an 8% market share in dress shirts in three years," he says.

("Our shirt is better made, has a better finish, than the K mart shirt," asserts George W. Camacho, vice president and sales manager of Burma Bibas Inc., the holder of the Oleg Cassini dress-shirt license. "They may be made in the same factory, but our construction is different.")

In Hong Kong, the K mart shirt buyers keep busy. K mart wants Smart Shirts Ltd., a unit of St. Louis-based Kellwood Co., to make some of its sport shirts. Smart Shirts asks whether K mart needs all of its previously committed production time, an indication that Smart Shirts wants to make expensive shirts for others. (R.H. Macy Co.; Saks Fifth Avenue, a unit of B.A.T. Industries PLC; and Lands' End are among its customers.) But K mart says it does need the production time, and Smart Shirts agrees to honor its commitment.

K mart quickly agrees to Smart Shirts's price of about $5 a long-sleeve shirt, even though it is higher than it would like. K mart gets the concession that the pattern on the pockets, flaps and seams will match the pattern on each shirt, a feature that normally costs 12½ cents a shirt more. Usually, protracted discussions on prices are the rule. Haggling over details as small as a dyed snap can be important. For instance, a retailer can save three cents a garment, or $36,000 on a typical order, by insisting that the snap be part of the deal, not an extra.

Retailers enjoy a handsome profit by buying shirts in Asia. T. F. Ying, the president of Smart Shirts, says the average polyester shirt takes about $1.50 of material. Fine cotton would cost between $4 and $6. Special features raise the cost: 20 cents a shirt extra for single-needle tailoring or 30 cents a shirt extra for 16 to 18 stitches an inch instead of 12. Thus, a chiefly cotton dress shirt selling for more than $20 in a U.S. department store can cost as little as $5 to buy from an Asian manufacturer.

On the Japanese leg of the trip, K mart executives visit several Osaka-area trading companies. Labor costs in Japan are about 25% higher than in Taiwan or Korea, some manufacturers say. K mart deals with trading companies that contract orders out to neighboring nations, often at lower prices than what K mart could negotiate by itself. But this year, prices are higher than usual at some suppliers, and the trip hasn't been fruitful quickly.

A courtesy call at Hamamatsu Chuo Orimono K. K., a trading house known more simply by Westerners as Rainbow, helps K mart's score. The sales manager, during an otherwise dull showing of basic corduroy merchandise, holds up a pair of pants that he says Rainbow obtained for Lane Bryant, a unit of Limited Inc. and a major U.S. chain specializing in quality clothes for large women.

"You make that to Lane Bryant specification?" asks Mr. Antonini. Rainbow does.

K mart has accidentally found a supply of pants that match Lane Bryant stock and that it could sell at discount prices. "Would you make the same thing for us?" Mr. Antonini asks. The sales manager agrees, and Mr. Antonini later sends a buyer to Rainbow to clinch the deal. "You never know what you'll find," he says.

Bargain-Basement Prices

Buyers find bargains for themselves, too. One brings home a fur coat from Seoul, which he says he got for a bargain-basement price. Another traveler gets pearls in Hong Kong and a $500 watch he says would cost twice that in the U.S. The buyers wear trophies from past overseas trips, like custom-made suits and gold Rolex watches.

By late December, almost all of K mart's commitments for fall 1985 are made. Imports make up two-thirds of its sweater line; 100% of the dress shirts are from Asia and Mauritius. (About 10% of all merchandise is imported.) All the buyers were able to find supplies, and prices ranged from 2% below last year's to 5% above. "It was a good trip," Mr. Antonini says.

But next fall's selling season remains uncertain. No one knows whether consumers will be in the buying mood. K mart's more affluent customers might be turned off by the washable-blend sweaters demanded by its low-income and moderate-income shoppers. And lower-income customers might not like the designer knock-offs. Success is selling 80% of any style at its normal price. "Anything less than that can chip at profitability," says Mr. Buch.

"There's been a lot written about the uncertainty of 1985," says Mr. Buch. "Buying isn't a science. It's a crapshoot. You can never be sure you're right."

Hong Kong . . . Better!
by Joan Bergmann

Quick, what do you think of when someone says "Hong Kong?"

If you are a retailer, the automatic answer used to be sweaters—or, perhaps, knitwear.

But all that is changing.

Talk to Elsa Cheng, who is the Hong Kong-based divisional manager for Associated Merchandising Corp.'s mass merchant member-client stores—including Mervyn's, Bradlees, Target, Richway and Jamesway—and her answer is that sweaters may still be Number One, but with an important difference. That difference is better—better styling, better finishing, better blends.

What is more, she is looking more to Hong Kong for her stores' requirements in other items, too—chiefly jackets and men's sport shirts.

Talk to Allied Stores' J. W. Herbst, vice president/Far East Administration, and he will point to Allied's longstanding involvement with Hong Kong, as evidenced by the Orient Expressed store-wide promotions staged by Jordan Marsh/Boston in 1981 and even earlier by The Bon, Seattle, in 1979.

But the biggest change Herbst observes in Hong Kong is the strong shift in the fashion direction of upper moderate and better. Hong

Source: *STORES Magazine*, December 1984. Reprinted with permission. National Retail Merchants Association. Copyright © 1986.

Kong, he adds, has become "very important" for all types of knits, particularly sportswear.

Talk to David Cohen, managing director, Asia, for May Department Stores International, and he will state that "Hong Kong will always be Number One," no matter where else May goes for sourcing for its private label business, and that sportswear is by far the biggest classification.

Talk to R. A. Goshorn, general manager, K mart Far East Ltd., and he acknowledges that, as K mart upgrades, it will be looking more and more to Hong Kong. Up to now, he observes, K mart has relied heavily on Hong Kong for both knit and woven blouses. But now K mart will be looking to Hong Kong resources, in addition, for color and styling direction.

At BATUS, whose divisions include Saks Fifth Avenue, Marshall Field, Gimbels and Kohl's, the market representative for dresses, Lynda DaCostra, says Hong Kong is becoming a major resource for better dresses—both knits and silks.

These executives for some of the nation's biggest department, discount, and specialty store companies, were interviewed by STORES during the Hong Kong Women's Sportswear Show, September 30–October 3, in Hong Kong.

The four-day event, which included a gala fashion show and an exhibition, drew more than 2,700 registrants—both retailers and manufacturers—from all over the world.

What they saw was more than sportswear. In the big fashion show, in the individual designer shows, and in the exhibit booths, the range of merchandise offerings included dresses, suits, and evening wear, as well as basic shirts, pajamas, pants and shorts.

And, although Bangladesh industry is only two or three years old as a major force, he points out, "They are doing everything." The reason is that government insists that knitting and sewing all be done there—sort of its own country-of-origin regulations.

Discussing how May works with Hong Kong, Cohen describes a process typical of most major American retail corporations. He says, "At May, we work with our New York design people, who provide us with the specifications and designs for our own label programs."

These, then, are taken to the factories May knows can best execute them.

May, Cohen adds, has not reached the point of having its own designers in Hong Kong. "We have one design person here, however, who we use to watch the specifications on colors."

In women's sportswear, May uses Hong Kong for both knits and wovens. Cohen expects wovens to continue to be hot as a category for Fall 1985, which is the season his office has been working on. The tricky part of wovens, he points out, is the long lead time in getting yarn-dyed fabric from Japan—"they're taking around five months." With wovens, he adds, there is a seven month minimum from the time of placing the order to shipping, whereas sweaters and other knits turn around much faster, with only a three or four month period between placing the order and shipping.

For Cohen, dresses are "not important" as a Hong Kong-sourced category. He calls dresses "treacherous" as an all-import program because of the need to be right in picking the winning fabrics nine months in advance.

"If you are talking about Italian fabrics, for example, it means you must make the trip to Italy, pick out the fabrics, then find the right manufacturer in Hong Kong—and then you still have to sell the idea to the stores!" he adds.

But dresses are what BATUS' DaCostra

works on during her semiannual Hong Kong trips. "Hong Kong is a major resource for better dresses, particularly knits and silks," she says.

How does she work with Hong Kong? "We come up with the ideas before we get there. We send over our development books based on information we are getting from our stores. Often we will send samples to Hong Kong before we come over." Her itinerary usually includes Japan, Korea, Taiwan and, finally, Hong Kong.

Her evaluation of Hong Kong as a source: "It is becoming a lot more sophisticated and, at the same time, it is causing more problems than ever before." The main problem? "Quota, of course."

How does DaCostra put together a corporate program for such a diverse group of stores? "We look to Saks for fashion direction. Saks does a lot of its own private label as well."

But, she adds, in the final analysis, the BATUS store group is really not that different, because all are fairly conservative.

BATUS' private label dress program, she adds, is "still in its infancy," and she expects it to grow, with Hong Kong playing an increasingly important role. "The quality here is very good, and they can do most of the things we need."

Hong Kong, Cheng says, is particularly good for her clients, which are upscale discount companies. "Hong Kong has upgraded a lot. The workmanship is excellent, and the detailing is superb. The service is good; shipments are prompt." What is also good, she adds, is that a lot of resources have become more flexible, and are willing to accept orders for smaller quantities.

"Our stores have upgraded their requirements and their standards. They used to come to Hong Kong looking mainly for price points. That is changing," she adds.

How does she work with her client-stores? "Even before they arrive, we are receiving Telexes about their requirements. We do the ground work here and make up samples for them to evaluate," she says.

Too, K mart is upgrading, Lam hurries to add, in both the quality of piece goods and in styling while, at the same time, trying to keep prices at reasonable levels. All of K mart's business in Hong Kong in apparel is private label, Lam points out. The Hong Kong office does not, however, do any programs for K mart's new Designer Depot division, which works independently.

In addition to Hong Kong, the K mart people are trying programs in Bangladesh and Mauritius, but Hong Kong will continue to be important, they agree, especially in areas like misses blouses and tops in both knits and wovens.

K mart Apparel buyers go to the Far East three or four times a year, including swings to Korea, Japan, Taiwan, Singapore, Pakistan, Indonesia and Malaysia. The Third World countries today are shopped primarily for basics, with little style merchandise purchased there.

How does K mart work with Hong Kong manufacturers? "Our buyers give their manufacturers a sample and ask them to make it up," Lam answers. But, he observes, some of the vendors are moving into positions themselves to be able to create the kind of merchandise they know K mart needs.

Of all the companies interviewed for this article, Allied Stores has perhaps made the most visible commitment to Hong Kong, as noted, through its Orient Expressed promotions, complete with special events, in-store designer appearances, demonstrations of arts and crafts and the like.

Allied's Herbst points out that starting in the late 1950s, Allied began sending buying teams to Japan and then on to Hong Kong, which has since superseded Japan in importance in the apparel areas. Today Hong Kong is Allied's most important source in all types of knits, particularly sportswear, in the budget, moderate, upper moderate and better areas.

Herbst cites the strong shift in favor of better merchandise, which, he says, gives Hong Kong an edge, and a greater degree of penetration in Allied stores.

Allied was among the first of American retail companies to put a spotlight on Hong Kong designers, even creating special shops for them, he observes, citing Eddie Lau as an important example, "We no longer consider him a 'young designer.' He is established."

A buying office such as Allied Stores International, which is owned by Allied and based in Hong Kong "assumes the important role as an extended arm of the main office, especially at a time when the company is making intensified efforts in developing private label programs," Herbst points out.

What distinguishes Hong Kong from the volume markets, Herbst adds, is "the creativity of its resources and its quality control standards." He is especially enthusiastic about its creativity in children's wear and in moderate-to-better knit dresses.

As for the future, Herbst says, "Hong Kong will maintain the role it has played all along. We have fared very well in our business relationships in Hong Kong, which have been cultivated over many years. The closeness between our vendors and ourselves is precious. Hong Kong will play an increasingly important role to Allied Stores."

Europe for Sale
by Stan Gellers

To wide-eyed European manufacturers shopping a hectic MAGIC or NAMSB show for the first time, it would seem that the streets of America are truly paved with gold. The temptations are manifold: All those dollars to be spent . . . all those potential customers . . . all those malls across a country bountiful in shoppers with insatiable fashion appetites.

For many European companies that have made the giant step to sell the land of plenty, the U.S. has been a bonanza. These firms entered this market with their own agents, or an American subsidiary and showroom. They had telex machines to tap out crucial reports on the state of an order, or they warehoused their inventories in this country, enabling them to speed orders to stores almost overnight.

But for overseas companies that lacked the above "musts," and for those that tried to go it alone, America has been as much of a bust as Europe has been to those many U.S. retailers who tried to buy abroad without agents at their elbows to guide them.

Failures like these, however, are apparently in the minority, because imports of apparel are absolutely booming. The U.S. Department of Commerce's Census Bureau supplies some startling figures.

For the month of December 1984 alone, exports from the European economic community increased by close to 60 percent over the

Source: *Daily News Record*, April 29, 1985. Reprinted with permission.

previous year. The big gainer was Italy during the first 10 months of last year, accounting for about 80 percent of total men's wear imported from Europe—followed by France, the United Kingdom and Spain, in that order.

Certainly, the high and mighty dollar had much to do with the growth in U.S. imports, which amounted to a staggering, if not chilling, multibillion-dollar figure last year. Despite efforts of both government and industry to stem the flow of imports, the increases continue to mount. The reason is simple: Europe is one big, fat bargain for American apparel retailers.

As a result, U.S.-based agents repping European lines are gleefully watching the rising tide of orders from merchants who want the built-in sales and prestige of a label from Western Europe. But selling the U.S. market hasn't been all fun and games.

"I first began bringing in Factice young men's and junior sportswear myself from France when I got the beat of American retailers' sense of timing," says Natalie Azani, who distributes the line in North America. "They simply didn't want to buy European merchandise six months in advance. Two to three months are about as far as they want to extend themselves. What did this mean for me? Becoming a stock house with practically immediate deliveries."

Azani explains that her company literally "owns the merchandise," and because of the cash flow generated by immediate availability, the operation can afford the luxury of shipping by air. She goes on to say that many other French companies have been knocking on her door, looking for reps in this country. "I'm not contemplating any additions myself, but we'd like the extra competition. There's safety in numbers, and the more European companies American retailers see, the more likely they are to spend."

Barbara Kramer of Fundamentals says her sales organization works with U.S. importers who, in turn, bring in the merchandise. "It's the only way to do it," she insists. "If an American store buys direct, that means it will have to get its own letter of credit, then hassle for deliveries, etc."

Part of the reason for the success of European companies in the U.S. is that they've carefully worked out the mechanics. Kramer continues, "Buying through an agent or rep, a merchant knows that everything is done for them. The buying procedure is exactly like it is when they're working with a domestic maker. The billing and warehousing is done here, and merchandise is shipped directly to the store. That means no telexes, no overseas phone calls . . ."

Completely open to the idea of repping for European companies "who are searching us out," Kramer notes that her agency just signed on Studio 55, an Italian progressive fashion sport shirt company. "This one came over the transom from the New York importer we've been working with," she says.

The way Studio 55 linked up with a sales organization—through a mutual contact—is typical of how overseas companies try to avoid difficult situations.

"Many of the problems faced by exporters parallel those U.S. stores have to cope with when they try to buy on their own. There's often a language barrier, costly phone calls to check on orders, difficulties in arranging for payment without a U.S. rep or a factor—plus additional paperwork."

Guiseppi Finizio of Itlatex, which acts as an agent and importer, reveals what it's like to be on the other side of the table in a showroom. "There's more competition among the importers, but more customers," he says. "A few years ago, there may have been several hundred lines to worry about. Now there are 1,000 or more. To tell the truth, Europe has to sell the U.S. because its own business is soft."

Describing the problems of selling American stores, Finizio immediately mentions slow payments: 110 days compared to 60 days in Italy. "The Americans can only compare with the French in being late. Then, the market segment is limited—18 cities, at best."

The agent also stresses that he can't sell basics to the U.S. "They can be made cheaper here or in the Orient. Classics are something else. Italy is always a year ahead of the U.S., and there's the danger of being rejected. To sell this country, you have to have patience and capital."

No matter what the mechanics of selling are, they require personal involvement in the U.S. In some cases, a member of a European company moves to the U.S. and opens a branch. In others, the company hires a U.S. agent or rep, plus the brokers, factors and importers, to step in and fill the breach.

"A European company must have a presence here to succeed," insists Ken Wade, who began GB Clothing on the West Coast two years ago and later signed on New York-based Fundamentals to rep the company in the East.

GB, which was awarded the coveted Queen's Award for Exports in England, first tested the export market on the Continent and in the Middle East. One of the main factors that drove the company to the U.S. was the increasing value of the American dollar against the pound. Wade claims that U.S. buyers could hardly pass up the contemporary fashions at "bargain" prices. The company's trousers, for example, retail at about $60. Sport coats are $140 to $160, and woven sport shirts are in the $50 to $55 range.

Agents point out that a European company's wholesale prices reflect a variety of overhead costs. Included are agent's fees (about 8 to 15 percent), built-in operating costs, contribution to showroom rent, trade show fees, extra sample lines and so on.

Even with these cost cushions, agents and reps in the U.S. think twice about signing on a new line. "And the calls come through every day," says Gregory Schmitz, who, with Lucille Morsut, reps three lines (GS from India, Milano Due from Turkey and Prima from Uruguay). He adds, "The bottom line is this: if you take on a line, will you make money? If not, the merchandise just takes up valuable space."

Discussing the risks that European companies face when trying to break into the U.S. market, Schmitz admits that more than one company has been burned. "It's the same old story. A U.S. agent asks for financial support—rent, a draw, etc.—and then doesn't deliver. About the only assurance a foreign company has is to rely on word-of-mouth recommendations from the retailers or wholesalers they already know."

Naturally, there are exceptions. Major retailers have turned into manufacturer/importers in their overseas trading. Medium-sized specialty stores have also saved cash buying directly from mills in Europe.

"We started buying on our own two years ago, getting our own letters of credit, and so on," reports Charles Alberts, general merchandise manager at the Barons chain based in Miami. "Our first experiment was an order for 150 dozen with a Spanish sport shirt company. They've been so successful that today we're up to 15,000 units. And with the dollar as strong as it is, we've been able to slash our prices from $65 to $47.50 and maintain the same margins."

Buying directly, of course, saves the extra cost of paying off an agent. Alberts' only warning is that a U.S. retailer has to order "meaningful quantities."

But the European trade groups with offices in this country caution that there's much greater insurance dealing with a U.S. rep. The agencies insist that on-site American representation is vital, expensive as it may be.

The French Fashion & Textile Center helps

manufacturers from France make American connections, according to Barbara Wise, the agency's marketing coordinator. "It can be word-of-mouth, meeting an agent at a trade show, or a direct recommendation from a U.S. retailer who buys from them."

Often, says Wise, a company hasn't enough money to set up shop on its own, man the showroom, and pump in all of the systems necessary to sell the U.S.

"Another important consideration is that the company that wants to sell the U.S. understand what the mentality is like. This is why we organize study groups to come over and visit MAGIC or NAMSB. This tells a manufacturer why and how they have to adapt their product to the needs of the American market."

The British and Spanish trade groups also take active roles in helping manufacturers from their respective countries make American stores regular customers. They do everything from screening potential exporters, their product mix and market prospects.

The British Trade Development Office helps companies from the U.K. by coming up with fairly exhaustive market studies for a very modest fee. A. Paul Ceurvorst, deputory director and consul in New York, says they cover such points as the size of market for the particular product, domestic production and imports of the product, methods of distribution, typical markups, discounts, U.S. regulations that affect the product, and what American retailers and consumers think of the product.

"Most important, we tell the management of these companies how their products should be modified for the U.S. market," he says. And when all signals are go, the British agency helps find the company representation in this country.

The British are clearly typical of all the Europeans looking eagerly toward America. Ceurvorst reports that during the first six months of 1984, there were more inquiries from companies seeking to crash the U.S. market than in the entire previous year. Many of those have already succeeded—and there are many more waiting in the wings.

Endnotes

1. *U.S. Industrial Outlook 1986.*
2. *U.S. Industrial Outlook 1985.*
3. "Conditions in the Women's Apparel Industry," Research Department, International Ladies Garment Workers Union, October 15, 1985.
4. T. H. White, "The Danger from Japan," *New York Times Magazine*, July 28, 1985.
5. Senator Strom Thurmond in "Textile Import Bill Survives First Senate Test," *Women's Wear Daily*, October 3, 1985.
6. "Jean Vass Wants the Best She Can Get," *Women's Wear Daily*, September 18, 1985.
7. 1983 Research Study published by Summerour and Associates, Inc.
8. "The Costs of Protectionism: Textile and Apparel Import Quotas," pamphlet issued by National Retail Merchants Association, New York.

9. "Block Those Quotas," *Stores Magazine*, National Retail Merchants Association, September 1985.
10. "Calvin's SEC Filing Details Dollars," *Women's Wear Daily*, August 7, 1985.
11. "Conditions in the Women's Garment Industry," September 1985, ILGWU, New York.
12. Arthur Ortenberg, vice-president of Liz Claiborne, Inc. in "Sportswear," *Women's Wear Daily*, June 17, 1985.
13. *Ibid*.
14. *Women's Wear Daily*, March 5, 1985.
15. "U.S. Export Decline Blamed for Deficit," *Women's Wear Daily*, July 26, 1985.
16. *Ibid*.

Selected Bibliography

Cateora, Philip. *International Marketing*, 5th ed. Homewood, Il: R. D. Irwin, 1983.
Importing into the United States. Washington, D.C.: Department of the Treasury, U.S. Custom Service, 1984.
Magee, Stephen P. *International Trade*. Reading, Mass.: Addison-Wesley, 1980.
Majoro, Simon. *International Marketing*. Boston: Allen & Unwin, 1982.
Woronoff, John. *World Trade War*. New York: Praeger, 1984.

Trade Associations

China External Trade Development Council, 41 Madison Avenue, New York, N.Y. 10016.
French Fashion and Textile Center, 200 Madison Avenue, New York, N.Y. 10016.
Hong Kong Trade Development Council, 548 Fifth Avenue, New York, N.Y. 10022.
Israel Trade Center, 350 Fifth Avenue, New York, N.Y. 10010.
Italian Trade Center, 499 Park Avenue, New York, N.Y. 10022.
Japanese Trade Center, 1221 Avenue of the Americas, New York, N.Y. 10019.
Korea Trade Promotion Center, 460 Park Avenue, New York, N.Y. 10022.
Taiwan Trade Information, 41 Madison Avenue, New York, N.Y. 10016.

Trade Publications

Apparel Import Digest, American Apparel Manufacturers Association, 1611 North Kent Street, Arlington, Va. 22209.
Focus, American Apparel Manufacturers Association, 1611 North Kent Street, Arlington, Va. 22209.

CHAPTER REVIEW AND LEARNING ACTIVITIES ....

Key Words and Concepts

Define, identify, or briefly explain the following:

Asian Bermuda Triangle	Joint venture
Bilateral treaty	Licensing agreement
Caribbean Basin Initiative	MFA
Developing country	Offshore production
Duties	Protectionism
Export	Quotas
Foreign commissionaires	Specification buying
Free trade	Tariffs
Global sourcing	Tariff Schedule 807
Imports	Trade deficit
Import penetration	

Review Questions on Chapter Highlights

1. Why has the traditional international trading policy of the United States been based on the principle that excessive import restrictions will lower our standard of living?
2. What are the regulations that pertain to imports and what is the importance of each?
3. What countries have quota exemptions and why?
4. What is the Caribbean Basin Initiative and why would an Asian country own production plants in this area?
5. What type of domestic companies import and why?
6. Describe the various methods used by retailers to buy foreign merchandise.
7. What is specification buying? How is it done, who does it, and why?
8. Name several major American apparel producers who produce "offshore" and explain why they use foreign contractors instead of domestic ones.
9. Are you a "protectionist" or a "free trader"? What are the reasons for your position?
10. In view of the productive capacity and creative talent in the U.S. fashion industry, why is our fashion trade deficit so big?
11. Do you agree with the statement that "U.S. apparel and textile exports will never counterbalance the penetration of imports?" Explain why.
12. Some of our textile and apparel producers have found ways to penetrate foreign markets other than exporting directly. List those ways and explain each one.

Applications for Research and Discussion

1. Research new import regulations either passed or pending other than those described in this chapter.
2. Research current activities of organized protectionist groups (i.e., similar to the "Crafted with Pride" council) and organized free trade groups (i.e., similar to RITAC) and describe their activities.
3. "The People's Republic of China is considered to be a 'sleeping giant' with the potential to become a major exporter to the United States." Research the current status of China's textile/apparel industry and their exports.

9

THE RETAILERS OF FASHION

Eventually all merchandise that is designed and produced must reach the ultimate consumers, and that is the role and responsibility of **retailers.** In the course of buying and selling goods that are acceptable to their customers, they also serve the industry as a series of listening posts on the consumer front. At the same time they act as a medium for disseminating information and stimulating demand for fashion products.

Historically, new and different retailing formats have come into being in response to changing social and economic conditions, and each has initiated certain operational methods that distinguished it from previously existing types. This chapter discusses different types of retailing, the circumstances and period of their origin, and the part that each plays in the business of fashion. The readings that follow the text illustrate the fashion operations of leading companies in their respective fields.

FASHION RETAILING IN THE PAST

In the early 1800s, there were only about 10 million people in the United States, and most were farmers or pioneers moving westward with the frontier. Except for the few cities established along the Atlantic coast, the country was rural. Transportation was by foot, on horseback, or by horse and wagon. Roads, such as they were, were little more than Indian trails through the wilderness. Retailers who functioned in this environment were small country stores and trading posts, or itinerant peddlers. The last-named group traveled from farm to farm, offering for sale such small conveniences as cutlery, tools, buttons, combs, hand mirrors, needles, and thread. They were welcome visitors to frontier people, because they brought with them bits of news and a touch of civilization.

The retailing of ready-to-wear was still in the future, awaiting the development of factory produced textile and apparel.

Early Retailing of Ready-to-Wear

It was not until late in the nineteenth century that significant amounts of ready-made clothing became available for sale in stores. Before that, the fashion operations of stores in the growing cities consisted only of selling fabrics, trimmings, and made-to-order clothing.

The early years of ready-to-wear retailing were difficult ones for merchants. Like the apparel producers, they brought little or no fashion experience to their efforts in behalf of "ready-made store clothing." Both retailers and producers had to learn about apparel fashion by trial and error. Although custom-made clothing remained important into the 1920s, it was steadily giving way before the growing and constantly improving ready-to-wear manufacturing industry. At the same time, retailers were learning to deal in ready-to-wear. By the 1920s men's, women's, and children's apparel departments were firmly established in all big-city department and specialty stores, and ready-to-wear was also available through mail-order catalogs to customers in outlying areas.

In the early days of ready-to-wear retailing, owners of the great fashion stores worked creatively with manufacturers to produce ready-to-wear designs that would meet the fashion needs of their customers. Many retailers helped manufacturers to get started by bringing them Paris models to copy and providing them with substantial orders. The retailer at that time was the main source of fashion information for consumers as well as manufacturers. There were few movies, few telephones, no television, and only a few publications to keep people up-to-date on what should be produced or worn. Long before the fashion show, the bridal counselor, and the college shop were commonplace; several prominent stores were publishing fashion brochures that they mailed to their customers. Lord & Taylor began such a publication in 1881, John Wanamaker in 1909, Marshall Field and Company in 1914. As fashion traveled its long, slow route from Paris to Podunk, customers looked to their oracles, their favorite stores, for advice on what to wear.

DIVERSITY OF FASHION RETAILING TODAY . . . .

Until the mid-1900s, fashion merchandise as we know it today was retailed primarily either by big-city department and specialty stores or by small apparel shops in communities of almost any size. There were other sources of apparel and accessories, such as mail-order sellers, chain stores, and discount operations, but they dealt in low-to-popular-priced merchandise in which fashion was not a major concern.

As consumers became more affluent, better educated, and more sophisticated, fashion rather than need became the force behind discretionary spending. In the 1960s, the projection of a "fashion image" became a major objective for retailers. The retailing of fashion proliferated at all price levels, and every conceivable type of retailer jumped into the business of fashion spelled with a capital "F."

Today the retail marketers of fashionable merchandise come in an almost infinite variety of shapes, sizes, locations, pricing strategies, merchandise assortments, and customer services—all competing for a share of the fashion pie.

DEPARTMENT STORES

A **department store** is defined by the Bureau of the Census as a retail establishment that employs 25 people or more and that carries a wide variety of merchandise lines, including (1) men's, women's, and children's apparel; (2) furniture and home furnishings; and (3) household linens and fabrics. In the trade, however, several other criteria are applied: related categories of merchandise are offered for sale in separate departments; each department is managed as a separate profit center; responsibilities for stocking the department are delegated to a buyer; customers are offered many services, such as credit, return privileges, deliveries, and telephone and mail order. There are usually also such specialized services as restaurants, beauty salons, and jewelry repair, among others.

Origin of Department Stores

Most of our large and best-known department stores were founded in the middle and late nineteenth century, when mass production was developing and cities were growing. Some of their founders began as peddlers before they opened a store. Some examples are Aaron Meier, whose small general store in Portland, Oregon, was opened in 1857 and later developed into Meier & Frank; Morris Rich, who peddled notions in Ohio and then moved on to Georgia to open Rich's of Atlanta in 1867; Adam Gimbel, whose descendants built the Gimbel organization on the foundation of the store he opened in Vincennes, Indiana, in 1842. Others had their beginnings as small dry goods stores such as Macy's, New York, that opened in 1858 for the sale of feathers, hosiery, and gloves and added new lines as increasing mass production made them possible.[1]

Department Stores Today

In the fashion business, the department store not only represents an impressive volume of sales, but also is a medium for exposing merchandise to the customer, often with considerable drama.

The typical department store chooses as its target group of customers people of middle to upper middle class, with fairly large discretionary incomes. The fashion appeal of such a store stems from the breadth of assortment it offers in middle to upper-middle prices and in national brand and designer names, often augmented by its own brand name. Browsing

ORGANIZATION CHART OF A TYPICAL LARGE DEPARTMENT STORE

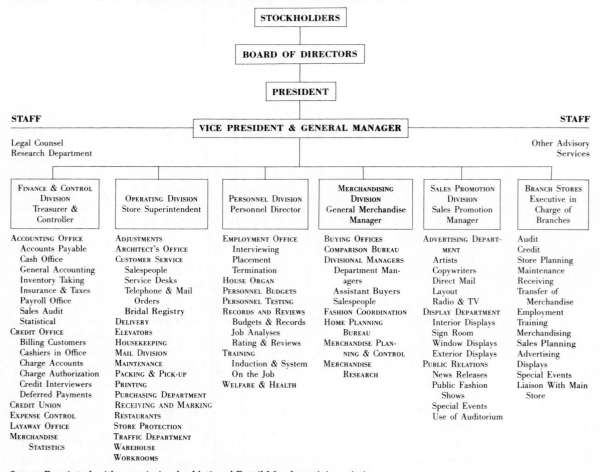

Source: Reprinted with permission by National Retail Merchants' Association.

among its broad stocks and guided by its advertising and displays, the customer can develop his or her own ideas of what to buy. When the choice has been made, the purchase can be consummated with confidence because of the store's refund policies. The offer of money back if the merchandise fails to please has been a cornerstone of department store policy for more than a century.

It is not uncommon for department stores to stage fashion shows, within the store, and also outside for clubs and charities. Their advertising and displays bring customer traffic and, since these stores cover so many fields of merchandise, they can generate more traffic than a specialized clothing store. The combination of customer traffic and appealing displays often prompts, say, a woman who has come seeking a lamp for her living room to purchase fashion items for herself, even though these were not on her shopping list. Department stores cater chiefly to women and typically do more than half of their total volume in apparel and accessories for women, men, and children.

BRANCHES: FROM SUBURBAN TO NATIONAL

In retailing, when a store well established in one location opens an additional facility in another but operates it from the original parent or flagship store, the new addition is called a **branch.** Just as the branches of a tree depend on the trunk for nourishment and growth, so do branch stores depend on the buyers, promotion executives, and other members of the parent store's management team for merchandise and direction.

Where customers go, stores go. When young city families moved out to new suburbs in vast numbers in the 1950s, retailers in the central cities moved out to serve them in branches—free standing at first, but later in the shopping centers that soon developed. By the early 1970s, branches had proliferated to the point that collectively they began contributing more than half the parent firm's total volume. By the late 1970s, suitable suburban areas had been exploited to the full by some stores, and these began to expand around the country, into other metropolitan areas. Thus, we find New York's Lord & Taylor with branches in Connecticut, New Jersey, Pennsylvania, Virginia, and Maryland. Dillard's of Little Rock, Arkansas, has branches in Texas, Missouri, New Mexico, Oklahoma, Florida, Kansas, and Ohio. Bloomingdale of New York has branches in Massachusetts, New Jersey, Pennsylvania, Texas, Florida, and the Washington, D.C. area. And, as a possible indication of things to come, J. W. Robinson's of Los Angeles is developing five branches in Japan.

STORE OWNERSHIP GROUPS

The founding fathers to today's great department stores operated family-owned and family-run single-unit stores. Today, by means of mergers and acquisitions, nearly every such store is part of a **store ownership group,** which is a corporation that owns a number of autonomously operated retail organizations. Each store division retains its local identity and independence,

STORE OWNERSHIP GROUPS

Companies	Sales in Billions of Dollars (Year Ending 1985)
Federated	$9,978.0
Dayton–Hudson	8,793.3
May Dept. Stores*	5,027.6
Associated Dry Goods*	4,363.0
Allied Stores	4,135.4
R. H. Macy	4,505.8
Carter Hawley Hale	3,977.9
Batus	2,175.0

Source: Annual Reports.
*May Dept. Stores and Associated Dry Goods Merged in 1986.

has its own branches, has its own buyers and merchandise mix, operates under its own name, and presents itself to customers much as if it were still an independently owned institution. Few customers realize that, for example, Lord & Taylor's of New York, Robinson's of Los Angeles, L. S. Ayres of Indianapolis, and Hahne & Company in New Jersey are among the stores owned by Associated Dry Goods Corporation. Similarly, Federated Department Stores owns Bloomingdale's of New York, Sanger Harris in Texas, Burdine's in Florida, and Lazarus in Ohio.

The oldest and largest of such groups is the Federated Department Stores, Inc., incorporated in 1929 by a merger of Filene's of Boston, Lazarus of Columbus, and Abraham & Straus of Brooklyn, soon joined by Bloomingdale's of New York. During the decade that followed, other corporate ownership groups were formed, such as Allied Stores, Associated Dry Goods, and the R. H. Macy organization. The trend continued, giving birth to such organizations as Dayton–Hudson and Carter–Hawley–Hale. In 1986 Associated Dry Goods was acquired by the May Department Store group. As the end listing in this chapter shows, few indeed of this country's largest department stores are now independently owned.

APPAREL SPECIALTY STORES: LARGE AND SMALL

In contrast to the department store's wide range of merchandise and broad appeal, a **specialty store** is a retail establishment that either deals in a single category of merchandise (as jewelry, shoes, furniture, apparel, etc.) or specializes in related categories—for example, clothing and accessories for men, women, or children, or sporting equipment and active sports apparel. The focus of their business, as to targeted customers and merchandise assortment, is well defined.

Such stores vary widely in size and range from small **Mom-and-Pop stores** to large departmentized firms. Among consumers, the larger versions are often mislabeled department stores, because they carry wide assortments in the merchandise categories in which they specialize, offer extensive customer services, and are also organized by departments. To qualify as department stores, however, they would have to carry furniture and home appliances beyond the token assortments of linens and giftwares that some of them offer.

Large or small, the specialty shops play an important role in the retailing of fashion today. The fashion impact of giants like Saks-Fifth Avenue and Neiman Marcus makes a great contribution, but so also does the small, independently owned shop that offers convenience, friendliness, and an assortment carefully tuned to the wants of its clientele.

Large Departmentalized Specialty Stores

Like the department stores, many of today's large and prestigious specialty shops began in the second half of the 1800s as small, independently owned enterprises, in small towns or in the then-developing cities. Some expanded into department stores; others simply broadened their assortments in specialized merchandise categories. Filene's of Boston, for example, was founded in 1873 in Lynn, Massachusetts, by William Filene, who later bought a men's store in that city, a dry goods store in Bath, Maine, and two stores in Boston—one specializing in gloves, and the other in laces. Similarly, I. Magnin of San Francisco had its beginnings in 1880, in the modest home of Isaac and Mary Ann Magnin, where wealthy San Francisco ladies came for Mrs. Magnin's exquisite, hand-made, embroidered, and lace-trimmed lingerie, christening dresses, and spectacular made-to-order bridal gowns.[2]

Like the department stores, almost every one of these great specialty stores is now part of a store ownership group. To cite examples, Saks-Fifth Avenue is owned by Batus (British American Tobacco, U.S.); Filene's and I. Magnin, by Federated Stores; Neiman Marcus and Bergdorf Goodman, by Carter Hawley Hale. And also like department stores, they operate branch stores, either in local suburbs or nationally, or both.

Unlike department stores, however, they are completely dedicated to fashions in the rise and peak stages, and their assortments are both broad and deep in the upper-middle to highest-price ranges. Therein lies their competitive strength. They are highly focused on their targeted customers; they develop salespeople who are fashion knowledgeable and helpful; and they provide personalized customer services.

Retail authorities, even in 1978, foresaw the future of the apparel specialty store business as bright for the next several decades.[3] So far, their forecast has been correct.

Small Apparel Specialty Shops

It would be hard to find a town so small, or a city so big, that it is without independently owned, small Mom-and-Pop apparel or accessories shops. These are the stores owned and managed by one or two people and employing fewer than three salespeople. Without having branches or being a part of a chain, each of the stores so defined generally has annual sales volume of half a million dollars or less. The attrition rate among them is high, but so also is the rate of replacement by new entrepreneurs. Their collective impact in the fashion business, however, is important. Bureau of the Census figures continue to show that a substantial part of fashion retailing is done in just such outlets.

From the consumers' point of view, small fashion retailers offer convenience of location and intimate knowledge of their customers' needs and tastes. Their owners know the way of dressing in the communities they serve, and more often than not, they will buy with individual customers in mind.

From the producer's point of view, according to manufacturers interviewed by the authors, the importance of these stores goes far beyond the amount of business they place. For one thing, they are loyal to the firms from which they buy. In the larger stores, the buyers may not be the same from one year to the next, and they do not have that same loyalty.

With some quite large manufacturing firms, such as Russ Togs, for example, small specialty shops may account for a major portion of their business. With others, such as Liz Claiborne or Esprit, the minimum quantities demanded on an order will rule out the small retailer entirely. For the industry as a whole, which is a stronghold of small manufacturing firms, the collective buying power of the small, specialized apparel retailers is invaluable.

Boutiques

The term **boutique** is French for a little shop, and for many years it referred only to those intimate shops within Paris couture houses where the customer could buy perfumes and accessories carrying the house label. In the United States the term boutique designates a small shop that carries highly individualized and specialized merchandise intended for a narrow, well-defined customer segment.

The proliferation of boutiques in the United States (and in London, where the trend began) was an outgrowth of the antiestablishment "do your own thing" attitudes of the 1960s. Some of today's boutiques, like their 1960s forerunners, cater to the avant garde young, others to more mature customers. Many feature merchandise at astronomical prices; others sell at more moderate levels. Some deal only in designer clothes; others deal in hand-crafted fashions; some deal in trendy accessories; and still others deal in antique clothing.

The early independently owned boutiques of the 1960s were often established by creative fashion enthusiasts to sell merchandise that expressed their individual point of view—even if they had to design or possibly produce the merchandise themselves. Generally the merchandise was too advanced, too limited in appeal, for large stores to handle; only boutiques could do the job.

Independently owned boutiques made such an important place for themselves in the mid-1960s that large stores sought ways to appeal to boutique customers. Many stores established and still maintain groups of small, highly specialized shops on their floors in which they feature merchandise assortments keyed to a particular "total look" in apparel and accessories.

The boutique approach gained further impetus as European couture designers ventured into ready-to-wear and established their own boutiques, either free standing, or within stores selected for the franchise, or both. Among the luminaries whose ready-to-wear is offered in boutiques, independent or within larger stores, are Cardin, Givenchy, Valentino, Yves St. Laurent for his Rive Gauche collections, and such Americans as Calvin Klein, Ralph Lauren, Anne Klein, Donna Karan, and Perry Ellis. In addition, many foreign ready-to-wear designers have entered the U.S. market by way of their own boutiques in fashionable areas—for example, the Soprani boutique on Rodeo Drive in Los Angeles and the Giorgio Armani on New York's Madison Avenue.

Today, the boutique concept is widely accepted and used by most large department and specialty stores, not only for current fashions, but also for bath accessories, gourmet food and cookwear, and whatever else captures customer interest.

CHAIN STORE RETAILERS

A **chain** is understood to be a retail organization that owns and operates a string of similar stores, all merchandised and controlled from a central headquarters office. Multistore chains developed during the late 1800s, as transportation and communication improved. Among the early chains were the A & P (Great Atlantic & Pacific Tea Company), Woolworth's, and J. C. Penney. Each started with a single store, gradually added others, and demonstrated the feasibility of the multistore concept and the economies of centralized buying.

In the trade, the characteristics that distinguish chain stores from department and departmentized specialty stores are as follows:

- There is no one big city flagship or main parent store, as in the case of a multiunit department store with branches.
- The store units are standardized and uniform in physical appearance and in the merchandise they carry.
- The buying is done by buyers in the chain's central office, and each buyer is responsible for a specific category of merchandise—as contrasted with buying for an entire department.
- Merchandise is distributed to the units of a chain from its central or regional warehouses.
- The buying function is separate from the selling function.
- Selling is the responsibility of centralized sales managers and the managers of the individual store units.

Such highly centralized, uniform store operation is quite different from what prevails among department and specialty stores that have branches, or autonomously operated retail stores that are part of the ownership groups discussed earlier.

Fashion Retailing by Chain Stores

Chains that sell apparel are either (1) general merchandise retailers, like Sears and Montgomery Ward, whose product categories are similar to those of department stores, or (2) **specialized apparel** and/or accessory **chains** that focus on one or more related categories of apparel, just as nonchain specialty stores do. They may be national, regional, or local in location.

As an indication of their importance, consider the following facts:

- The Big Four of retailing—the four largest general merchandise chains—are Sears, K mart, J. C. Penney, and Montgomery Ward. Their combined 1985 annual merchandise sales of $68 billion amounted to 59 percent more than the total $42.7 billion retail sales of the eight largest store ownership groups. Sears, in fact, is the largest retailer in the world, with retail sales of over $26 billion.

THE "BIG FOUR" MASS MERCHANTS

Company	1985 Sales	Number of Stores
Sears Roebuck	$26,552,300,000	799
K-Mart	22,420,000,000	2065
J. C. Penney	13,747,000,000	1479
Montgomery Ward	5,383,000,000	315

Source: Annual Reports.

- In addition to their nonstore divisions, which contribute 15 to 20 percent of their total volume, their full-line merchandise stores number 799 for Sears, 2065 for K mart, 1479 for Penney, and 315 for Ward's.
- The combined sales of the top six specialized apparel nondiscount chains are $5.6 billion. These chains, operating 6,260 stores among them, are Petrie, The Limited, The Gap, Casual Corners, Brooks Fashions, and Charming Shops. All are largely in shopping malls. Their individual sales and number of store units are illustrated in this chapter.

SPECIALIZED APPAREL CHAINS

In terms of the fashion business, the decade of the 1920s was the beginning of chain store retailing. Before then, there were a few retail chains of "waist stores," as blouse shops were then called. Their targeted market was the low-income customers seeking prices below those offered in department and specialty stores. In about 1919, as blouses went out of fashion, producers of waists began to make low-priced dresses that the waist chains added to their assortments. With department and specialty stores catering to middle- and upper-middle-income families, there was little competition for chains featuring low-priced apparel. This period saw the start of many low-priced apparel chains that catered to the new class of "working women" who had entered the work force during the manpower shortage of World War I.

A notable example of an early waist chain is the Lerner Shops, which got its start in those years and, by 1984, had 800 stores, with sales of $700 million, primarily in low-priced fashions.[4] Other types of chains that sprang up and developed in that post-World-War-I period included millinery chains, men's hat chains, and family clothing stores. Fashion leadership was not their forte. In 1985 this chain was acquired by the Limited.

Chains took a different direction in the 1970s. There are now new specialized apparel chains, quite different from any of their predecessors. Regional or national in scope, they operate stores of relatively small individual size, and feature highly selective lines of contemporary and often trendy fashions in middle price ranges. Their aim is toward mainstream American juniors, misses, and young men's sportswear customers.

Today's apparel chains derive their strength from their ability to focus on a particular segment of the consumer market and the fashion interests of that market. Unlike department stores, they are not burdened by the need to serve a broad section of the public; they concentrate strictly on the consumer audience they have marked out for themselves. As in all chain retailing, their operations are highly centralized; their store units are generally uniform in design and merchandise presentation; and they usually operate under the same name in all locations. Typical are the Gap, the Limited, and Casual Corners. Also in this field is Petrie, but unlike the others, it operates many of its 1370 stores under different names.

Such chains feature mainly their own private brands. Their buying power

SOME OF THE SPECIALIZED APPAREL CHAINS

Company	No. of Stores	1985 Sales in millions	Ownership
The Limited	2397	$2,387	Public
Petrie Stores	1370	1,161	Public
The Gap	647	648	Public
Casual Corner	515	624	U.S. Shoe
Brooks Fashion Stores	781	436	Dylex
Charming Shoppes	550	392	Public
Chess King	517	206	Melville Shoe
Merry-Go-Round	334	164	Public
The Children's Place	159	158	Federated

Source: Stores, August, 1986.

is so large that they can specify color, patterns, styles, fabrics, and whatever else they consider important. Today, they are not just stores that are selling fashion, but it is their *au courant* fashions that are selling their stores.

These specialized apparel chains have become an increasing source of competition to department and large specialty stores since their merchandise categories and price ranges are within the scope of these older forms of fashion retailing. Thus, in 1979, the president of the R. H. Macy group told a stockholders meeting that the growing competition from these chains was felt most directly in junior apparel, misses sportswear, and young men's sportswear—three categories, he said, that represented 30 percent of that store group's business.[5]

The inroads made on the fashion market by apparel specialty chains have impelled some of the giant store ownership groups to develop or acquire such chains of their own. Thus, for example, Allied Stores acquired the Plymouth chain; Federated Stores obtained the Children's Place; and Associated Dry Goods bought the Sycamore Apparel chain. At the upper end of the price scale, Neiman Marcus, owned by Carter Hawley Hale, is being converted into a national specialty apparel chain.

APPAREL RETAILING BY GENERAL MERCHANDISE CHAINS

The mass general merchandising chains have also become a factor in fashion distribution. The Penney chain had apparel and accessories from the start, but Montgomery Ward and Sears had functioned primarily as catalog houses until the 1920s. With transportation improving and the rural customer no longer completely dependent on the mails, they moved into store operations. Sears began in 1925, with a single store located in its Chicago mail-order facility. Ward's soon followed. Both companies started with stores that featured equipment and supplies primarily of interest to men. Only gradually did their stores move into apparel, and then it was for their typical customer, of modest means and modest clothing budget.

It was not until the 1960s that the big general merchandising chains came of age as major factors in the fashion business. In response to the increased affluence and greater fashion awareness of their targeted customers, they broadened their assortments and extended their price ranges upward. They also gave prime main floor locations to apparel and accessories.

Glamorous names were brought into their stocks through licensing agreements. Where once the customer saw only store-name labels in garments made to the retailer's specifications, now she was offered Halston III collections in Penney's, or Cheryl Tieg and Stephanie Powers in Sears, or the Designer Depot in K mart.

With their enormous buying power, these great chains can have merchandise produced to their specifications and styled exclusively for them. They may not have, or even attempt to have, the fashion authority and leadership shown by department and specialty stores and by the new breed of specialized apparel chains. But what they can do, and do very well, is move a great deal of merchandise and control a substantial percentage of the fashion market. It is generally estimated in the trade that apparel and accessories represent, at the very least, 25 percent of these chains' total volume. On that basis, the combined fashion goods business of the big four amounts to many billions of dollars, a decidedly important share of the fashion market.

MAIL-ORDER HOUSES: NONSTORE RETAILING

By Census definition and trade usage today, a **mail-order house** is a retail establishment that does the bulk of its selling to the consumer primarily through the medium of a catalog as a result of orders placed mainly by mail or phone. The concept of selling through a catalog rather than over the counter of a store was pioneered by Aaron Montgomery Ward in 1872, to be followed by Richard Sears, who issued the first Sears Roebuck & Company catalog in 1893, although he had been in business before that time.

Among the conditions that paved the way for this nineteenth-century innovation in retailing was the then predominantly rural nature of the country. Stocks of country stores were limited, and transportation to the developing fashionable city stores was difficult. More to the point, rural free delivery had just been introduced by the Post Office.

These early catalogs were the standbys of rural customers for generations. Although the fashions offered were not exciting, the prices and assort-

1897 SEARS, ROEBUCK CATALOG PAGE

TAILOR MADE WALKING or BICYCLE SUITS

SUITS FOR HIGH SUMMER WEAR.

24980 Made of Washable Linen Crash, Blazer style with newest sleeves and cuffs, very finest skirt. Price.....................$3.15

24981 Very Stylish, made of high grade plaid washable linen crash, big sailor collar fancy front. Our price, only...............$4.00

24982 This Beautiful Summer Suit, is made of fancy checked washable linen crash, sailor collar and fronts of white linen, newest sleeves and cuffs. Very rich. Price............................$4.25

24983 $5.00 Would not be too much for this Elegant Suit, made of fancy washable linen crash, big sailor collar, front and cuffs of blue linen, making a very pretty combination. Price only...$5.00

BICYCLE SUITS.

24989 Consists of five pieces, Jacket, Skirt, Bloomers, Leggins and Cap, made of Austrian covert cloth in brown or gray mixtures. Blazer Jacket very nobby. Price..........................$3.75

24990 This Nobby Suit (illustrated) is made of five pieces in double breasted Reefer style, full skirt in either tan or gray mixed Austrian covert cloth. Would be cheap at $7.50. Only...$4.00

24991 Very Similar to 24993, made of very stylish novelty cloth, in five pieces consisting of cap, jacket, skirt, leggins and bloomers. Only..$4.25

24992 Blazer Style made of Imported Tiger Cloth, consisting of five pieces. Material durable and will outwear any material. Others sell it for $8.00, we sell it for............................$4.75

24993 This Handsome Suit (illustrated) is made of brown or blue Repellant cloth, bound in leather all around and consists of five pieces, jacket, half lined with silk. Can't be beat.............$6.75

Source: The 1897 Sears, Roebuck Catalog.

ments surpassed those in rural stores and they were a delight to the country clientele they were intended to serve. In the eyes of these customers, the catalogs indeed earned the name that came to be applied to them: "the wish book." So well, indeed, did the mail-order houses meet the needs and broadening interests of rural customers that by 1895 the Sears catalog consisted of 507 pages, and the company's annual sales exceeded $750,000.[6]

As one early mail-order company, Jones Post & Co., told its customers: "Your home, or ranch, or farm, is never so far distant that you are shut out from the great throbbing world with its mammoth commercial establishments. No longer are you forced to be satisfied with the small stock and slim assortment (of country stores) from which to make your selection at exorbitant prices."[7]

Catalog Retailing Today

Whether one calls it direct marketing, catalog retailing, mail-order retailing or nonstore retailing, the fact remains that there is tremendous activity in an old form of retailing: selling by mail or telephone from catalogs.

Industry estimates are that American consumers are currently buying $37 billion of consumer products (exclusive of services) from mail-order catalogs. Of this, $25 billion is believed to be from specialty catalogs and the remaining $12 billion from general merchandise catalogs.[8] A recent survey also revealed that, of the eight billion catalogs mailed in 1985, proven catalog customers receive an average of 200 catalogs each year.[9] Sears alone publishes and distributes 54 different catalogs a year, amounting to a total of 300 million.[10]

Catalog sales have been increasing rapidly and show every sign of continuing to do so. This phenomenon is a result of several factors: the rise of two-earner families, in which neither spouse has much time for shopping in stores; affluent singles, whose active working and social lives leave little room for shopping; the time crunch for working mothers; crowded stores; and the often inexperienced and hard-to-find store salespeople. To reach these busy spenders, retailers have increasingly resorted to the mails. The result has been an explosion not only in the number of catalog operations located throughout the United States but also in the variety of goods that can be bought from them. Everybody and his brother is in the catalog business, ranging from the Metropolitan Museum of Art in New York, through TWA, American Express, the Collins Street Bakery (which sells fruitcake from Texas), and Nestle's, which has a 14-page catalog featuring high-priced European chocolates.

The largest in terms of dollar sales are the general merchandise catalogs of Sears and J. C. Penney. Beamed nowadays at mainstream America, they sell everything to furnish a home, clothe a family, and provide equipment for hobby activities. Sears has catalog sales of $2.83 billion dollars. Penney's are $1.74, or about 10 percent of their total volume. Since Montgomery Ward discontinued its catalog, Spiegel has stepped into third place, with sales of $1 billion in 1985.[11] The merchandise featured ranges through innumerable categories, including some that are new, indeed. An Ambience edition catalog of Spiegel's featured a red fox coat for $5695, a linen top for $225, and a $185 skirt by French designer Castelbajac.

Mail-Order Apparel Specialists

In recent years, there has been a proliferation of specialized apparel mail-order houses, each of which focuses its effort on a specific segment of the consumer market. Some, like the Horchow Collection, concentrate on very high-priced, sophisticated, luxury items of wearing apparel and accessories. Other similar successful operations of this type are Trifles and Js. A. Bank

EXAMPLES OF MAIL ORDER SPECIALISTS

Banana Republic Clothing. Authentic, classic, comfortable travel and safari clothing in natural fabrics for men and women. Bush jackets, safari bags, multi-pocketed vests, unique sweaters, bush hats, khaki trousers and shorts. Year's subscription: **$1.00.**

Horchow. Select gifts as unique as the individuals on your gift list from the Horchow Christmas catalogues. Fashions, linens, decoratives, accessories, jewelry, and collectibles. Mail or toll-free phone. For a full year of catalogues, send **$3.00.**

L. L. Bean. Send for our Christmas 1986 Catalog. Features a full range of products for men and women who enjoy the outdoors. L. L. Bean pays all regular postage and guarantees 100% satisfaction. **Gratis.**

Source: As advertised in consumer publications.

Clothiers. Another group of apparel catalog retailers specializes in classic and sporty looks for men and women. Perhaps the best-known of this type is L. L. Bean, Inc., of Freeport, Maine, whose sales are estimated at $344 million.[12] Others in this category include Banana Republic, Talbot's, Johnny Appleseed, Dunham's, Eddie Bauer, Land's End, and Carroll Reed. Trendier and more fashion-forward types of apparel are emphasized in the catalogs of the French Boot Shop, Honeybee, and Nancy's Choice. Relatively new and even more specialized is Victoria's Secret, which features high-priced, sexy-looking intimate apparel. There are also catalogs devoted to off-size apparel, such as Kings Size for men and Lane Bryant for women.

In fact, mail-order sellers, of both apparel and other consumer products, have multiplied to such a degree that there is even a publication called a *Catalog of Catalogs* for consumers (and readers of this book) who want information about the various mail-order houses and the merchandise they feature. There is also a company, called *The Buyers Marketplace Catalogs,* which markets catalogs of different mail-order companies by advertising in various consumer publications.

At this point, it may be well to reread the definition of mail-order retailers at the head of this section. Some catalog retailers, like L. L. Bean or Carroll Reed, may have one or more retail stores, but if the bulk of their business is done through catalog sales, they are considered mail-order retailers.

CATALOG OPERATIONS OF CONVENTIONAL RETAILERS

Today, catalog addict customers not only hear from specialized mail-order companies such as Spiegel, Penney, L. L. Bean, and American Express, but they also hear from Bloomingdale's, Macy's, Neiman Marcus, Saks-Fifth Avenue, and countless other department and specialty stores through the country. Every year, department and specialty stores generally issue 6 to 20 catalogs each, with circulation figures ranging from 100,000 to 1 million.[13]

Originally, the primary purpose of such store catalogs was to draw customers into the store. Nowadays, the same elements that led to the growth of mail-order houses have encouraged conventional retail stores to increase the frequency of their mail-order catalogs and improve the efficiency with which they handle mail and telephone responses. The reasons, of course, are the time crunch affecting working women and the growing competition from catalogs of the kinds just discussed. These days, mail and telephone-order business accounts for a more and more substantial portion of the conventional store's business. Precise figures are not readily available, but this may illustrate the point: Bloomingdale-by-Mail (the store's catalog division) is now referred to as the second largest "store" in that multiunit operation, with sales in 1985 of an estimated $60 million. Neiman Marcus and Saks-Fifth Avenue are each believed to do about $50 million a year from catalogs.[14]

DISCOUNTING RETAILERS ....

Shortly after World War II, discount retailing changed the face of the retail world by adopting techniques originated by food **supermarkets** in the 1930s. Those techniques entailed offering lower prices to depression-weary customers by using self-selection selling, low-rent locations, inexpensive functional decor, and cash and carry terms.

Discount retailers today are not easily defined—or, indeed, easily named. They are called off-price stores, underselling retailers, promotional stores, and volume merchandisers. As generally understood in the trade, however, the term **discounter** applies to an "underselling" retail establishment that uses self-service combined with such other expense-saving techniques as no free deliveries, no mail or telephone orders, low-rent locations, and limited return privileges. By eliminating customer services and reducing other operational expenses, they operate profitably on markups lower than those that prevail among other types of retailers.

The success of discounters in the 1950s stemmed from their selling of nationally advertised branded appliances at prices below the manufacturers' suggested retail prices. This was in the period just after World War II, when men returning from military service spearheaded a boom in family formation, suburban living—and babies. The two-earner household in that period was relatively rare, and incomes had to be stretched to accommodate the pent-up demand for everything young families needed, from refrigerators to ready-to-wear. As the suburban communities burgeoned, so did the discounters. They opened stores in both cities and suburbs, and broadened their merchandise assortments to include low-priced, unbranded apparel.

As these households and their children prospered, many of them retained their active interest in buying at favorable prices. They were in a position to enjoy the good life—but they enjoyed it more at a bargain. This was in marked contrast with the attitude of earlier generations, among whom comfortable incomes were equated with freedom from price consciousness. Underselling retailing in various forms became more and more firmly entrenched in the 1960s, 1970s, and 1980s, without regard to business cycles, employment statistics, or consumer income figures.

Proliferation of Off-Price Apparel Discounters

Underselling stores that offer quality and fashion apparel have been on the scene for many years, but only recently have they blossomed into a major force in retailing. One of the earliest among them, Loehman's, was founded in Brooklyn in 1920, and is now a national chain of 84 stores. Others that came into the field later followed the same course, starting as individual stores and developing into national chains.

GROWTH OF OFF-PRICE RETAIL SALES

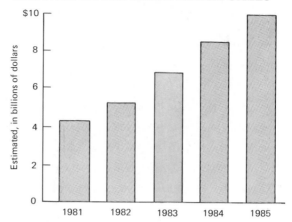

Source: Reprinted with permission by Management Horizons Inc./Alex Brown and Sons Inc.

Known in the trade today as **"off-price" retailers,** the fashion apparel discounters came into their own in the late 1970s, achieving an annual growth rate of 23.1 percent between 1979 and 1983—a much faster rate than was exhibited by more conventional appeal retailers. Industry authorities expect that off-price specialty retailing will continue to grow and gain an ever-larger share of the fashion business. What distinguishes these new fashion discounters from their predecessors is that the present-day stores specialize in high-quality, brand and designer-name clothing, at deeply discounted prices.

The target customers of these operations are the price-conscious middle-class. Among them are also consumers who formerly bought top-quality merchandise without really questioning price. When apparel prices skyrocketed, some of these consumers sought the discounters—not for cheaper grades of merchandise, but for the familiar "names" and qualities at lower prices. For example, they are willing to spend $100 on a dress, sweater, or handbag, but they want one that normally sells for $150 to $200 in department and specialty stores.

Currently, the largest and most successful of such discounters is Marshall's, which started with one store in Beverly, Massachusetts, and now operates more than 200 stores across the country. The company's financial reports indicate sales of well over $1 billion a year. Other big names in this category are listed in a chart in this chapter.

The impact of off-price apparel retailing on conventional retailers has been more than just competition. Today, one can walk into well-known

THE BIG NAMES IN BARGAIN CLOTHES

Company	Sales, 1985 (add 000,000)	Number of Outlets	Ownership
Marshall's	1,375	247	Melville
T.J. Maxx	840	191	Zayre Corp.
Loehmann's	360	82	Associated Dry Goods/May Co.
Burlington Coat Factory	352	76	Public
Hit or Miss	260	428	Zayre
Syms	215	15	Public
Ross Stores	376	107	Public
Filene's Basement	213	17	Federated

Source: Stores, July 1986

department and specialty stores at the height of the selling season and find numerous markdowns and off-price sales.

Another response to this form of competition has been that store ownership groups have developed or acquired such discounting operations of their own. For example, Federated Stores has launched a chain of off-price stores under the name of Filene's Basement, and Associated Dry Goods has acquired the Loehman chain.

In addition to the off-price specialized apparel retailers, there are general merchandise discounting chains, all of which sell large quantities of apparel and accessories at prices lower than those of conventional department and chain stores. K mart, for example, reports sales of $22 billion a year. Wal-Mart Stores, second largest of this type, reports annual sales of $8.4 billion.[15] Other giant discounters include Caldors (acquired by Associated Dry Goods), Ames Department Stores, Jamesway, and Family Dollars.

The distinction between conventional and discount reatiling is getting smaller, and it becomes increasingly harder to determine where conventional retailing ends and off-price operations begin.

The Lowered Costs of Discounting

Regardless of the kinds of merchandise being discounted, the economics of discount operations is basically the same. Operating expenses are kept low by holding customer services (salespeople, telephone ordering, delivery, etc.) to a minimum; locations are in less expensive areas; advertising is minimal; extraneous departments (jewelry repair, travel bureaus, etc.) are eliminated. These economies permit profitable operation at markups far below what conventional retailers require. Merchandise can therefore be priced at from 20 to 30 percent below what prevails in conventional stores.

Both conventional and discount stores often buy from the same whole-sale sources, but more often than not the off-price retailers actually pay less than other types for identical merchandise. They are not rigid about sizes, styles, and colors at any given time, nor with continuity of brand and designer merchandise. They simply make opportune buys when and where they are available.

The typical purchasing operation of large discounters was aptly described by Marshall's in an advertising supplement issued when its Dallas store was opened in 1980. Under a headline proclaiming "Brand Names for Less," the copy asked, "What's the Secret Behind Marshall's?" And the supplement answered:

> There's no secret—we pay less, so you pay less. . . . Department store buyers order their merchandise a season ahead. Our buyers wait until the season begins. That's when we can buy the same merchandise at lower wholesale prices. Manufacturers sell at lower wholesale prices during the season because they've overproduced, missed a delivery date or need to make room for the next season's line. We also keep our overhead costs down. When you're in a department store, notice the carpeting, expensive lighting and elaborate displays. Those extras can add to the cost of your purchase. Our stores are clean, neat and pleasant to shop without the extras. And, we're sure, smart shoppers would rather have value than decor.

Off-price stores also may specify ahead for goods to be made during what would otherwise be a dead, between-seasons time for producers. Sometimes, manufacturers schedule part of their regular production for discounters, but insist that the brand name not be advertised and that it should not be sold in the trading area of the maker's regular accounts. A final virtue of the discounter—they pay promptly, and do not ask for advertising allowances, the privilege of returning slow sellers, or similar concessions that major conventional stores may request.

Factory Outlets

A newly important form of off-price apparel retailing is booming across the country—**factory outlets** selling top brand and designer-name clothing. Such outlets have been around for many years, but until recently they were located in out-of-the-way factory towns and served as a dumping ground for old stuff and odds and ends of factory stock.

Today, such outlets have upgraded their physical appearance, services, and merchandise assortments. They have become a means by which manufacturers can turn a profit on excess inventory resulting from irregulars, incomplete assortments, returns from retailers, orders canceled because of delays in production, and slow-selling numbers. Some outlets even buy closeouts from other companies to balance their stocks; still others produce merchandise specifically for their outlet stores.

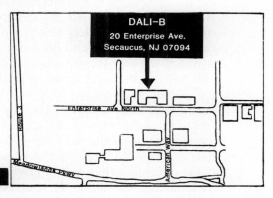

Originally located on the factory grounds, these outlets now tend to be clustered in outlying areas not in conflict with the shopping areas of their major retail accounts. In some communities, hundreds of factory outlet stores are set up in special areas, where the consumer finds everything from children's clothing to home furnishings. Most such factory outlet areas are in the East, where the greatest number of apparel producers are located. Among the largest such areas are those in Secaucus, New Jersey; Reading, Pennsylvania; Utica, New York; Murfreesboro, Tennessee; and Freeport, Maine.

Factory outlets generally do very little advertising, thus avoiding conflict with their retail accounts, but they do leave labels in the garments. Seasonal goods arrive about a month after the producer has shipped to his regular retail customers. For example, fall clothes will be delivered to the outlets in late August rather than July as with traditional retailers. Retail selling prices are usually lower even than those of the off-price retailers, since the merchandise reaches the consumer directly from the maker.

Among the factory outlets are some run by designer-owned companies: Ralph Lauren, in Freeport, Maine; Liz Claiborne and Anne Klein, in Reading, Pennsylvania; and Calvin Klein, in Secaucus, New Jersey. Manhattan Industries, in its outlets, has Perry Ellis, Henry Grethel, and John Henry merchandise. Many, if not all, well-known brand-name manufacturers are also in the factory outlet business—among them, Levi Strauss, Cluett Peabody, Healthtex, Arrow Shirts, and Country Miss. Generally, producers have several outlets in different areas; Country Miss, for instance, has 56 throughout the East.

DESIGNERS/MANUFACTURERS INTO FRANCHISED RETAILING ....

The proliferation of designer and manufacturer wholly owned and franchised boutiques is changing the landscape of fashion retailing in America. One indication of how franchised fashion retailing is growing is to be found in the operations in the field of Benetton, an Italian manufacturing company. From one franchised outlet in Italy, opened in 1968, Benetton's franchised shops have grown to 2664 stores in 53 countries around the world. Its first franchised store in the United States was opened in 1980; in 1985 there were 400 in operation, and by 1988 there are expected to be 1000 in this country.[16] A second and equally important indication that franchised fashion operations may well become the next area of growth in the fashion business was the following trade announcement by Esprit in December 1985: "It is our intention to open a franchising program with separate units of our Esprit Better Sportswear, Esprit Sport, Esprit Kids, and Esprit de Corp/Shoes."[17]

Franchised Retailing

Franchised operations are familiar to the public through such organizations as fast-food outlets like MacDonald's and Kentucky Fried Chicken, through automobile dealerships, restaurants such as the Howard Johnson's, and national networks of real estate offices like Century 21.

In a **franchise** arrangement, the **franchisor** (a parent company) provides a **franchisee** (owner-operator of a retail unit) with exclusive use of an established name in a specific trading area, plus assistance in organizing, training, merchandising, and management, in return for a stipulated consideration. The nature of the agreement varies widely from company to company. For example, the franchising company may provide an operating program complete in every detail, or the agreement may simply specify that the franchisor will provide merchandise for the franchisee. The uniform appearance of many franchised retail outlets often gives the impression to the public that they constitute a chain, but in actuality, each store is run by an individual entrepreneur who owns the business, meets his or her obligation to the franchisor, and retains the remaining profits.

Beginning in the late 1960s, franchising arrangements began to be visible in the apparel retailing field. Among the earliest and most successful are the maternity shop franchises such as Lady Madonna and Maternally Yours. Other examples are the Tennis Lady shops and the hundreds of Athlete's Foot franchised outlets.

American Designer-Name Franchised Boutiques

As described in the previous chapter, European ready-to-wear designers have been operating their own name boutiques—both wholly owned and franchised—for the last two decades, among them the Rive Gauche franchised boutiques of Yves St. Laurent and the Nouvelle Boutiques of Givenchy. In the 1980s American designers began to follow their lead with a vengeance, and today American designer-franchised boutiques are burgeoning in major cities throughout the United States. An outstanding example is Ralph Lauren who has pioneered a $100 million retail business with his countrywide 49 franchised Polo/Ralph Lauren shops to date, with more in the offing.[18] Among other American designers who are following in his footsteps are Donna Karan, Norma Kamali, and Elie Tahari, with undoubtedly many more to come.

Most European and American designers generally explain that they are operating retail stores "in order to show the consumers and their regular accounts the most creative way to merchandise their lines and reinforce an image."[19] What they are actually doing, however, is taking control of their own destiny and expanding their business by entering the field of fashion retailing.

It is interesting to note the mixed reaction of department and specialty store executives to the retail boutiques that are controlled by the same designers from whom they buy. Some say that their stores "offer a broader spectrum of price points and attract a wider customer base." Another says, however, that "although designer name clothes are important to our store, designer controlled boutiques do cut into our business."[20] In either case, the growth and future role of stores controlled by fashion manufacturers is one that bears watching.

DIFFERENT TYPES OF SHOPPING CENTERS TODAY ·

A major retail phenomenon growing out of the migration to suburbia that followed World War II was the development and proliferation of shopping centers. A **shopping center** is a preplanned, architecturally coordinated grouping of retail stores, plus a parking area that is generally larger than the area occupied by the stores themselves. Medical facilities, banks, restaurants, and sometimes theaters and skating rinks, may be part of the mix offered the shopper. These centers were (and still are) usually developed by real estate interests and occasionally by the real estate divisions of very large retailers. The centers have their own managements, promotional activities, and merchants' associations to weld their stores into a cohesive group.

Since the 1960s, when shopping centers first hit their stride, they have provided a prime area of expansion for department stores, chain stores, large and small specialty stores, and off-price retailers. By the mid-1980s, there were an estimated 25,000 centers. California, with almost 1700, has the largest number, followed by Texas, Florida, and New York, with some 600 to 700 each. The largest single center is the Del Amo Fashion Center in Torrance, California, with 2,650,000 square feet of selling space. Next in size are Lakewood Center Mall, Lakewood, California, and Roosevelt Field Mall, in Garden City, New York.[21]

Numbers alone do not tell the whole story of shopping centers, however. Over the years, they have changed from open-air centers, laid out horizontally with on-site parking into multilevel, enclosed, and climate-controlled **malls,** where shoppers can spend an entire day, shopping, resting, eating, even skating or seeing motion pictures. And they are no longer purely suburban phenomena; they are now in center city areas—often those associated with urban renewal enterprises. An outstanding example of an urban enterprise is Trump Tower, located on Fifth Avenue in New York. This is a 68-story building consisting of 49 floors of apartments, 13 floors of office space, and a 6-floor atrium around which are some of the most prestigious fashion stores in the world. Another example is the Water Tower in Chicago.

Another change—where at first shopping centers contained a heterogeneous mixture of small retail establishments and branches of big-city stores, today there are smaller, specialized centers that contain a homogeneous mix of tenants, all targeted toward the same segment of the consumer market. There are malls containing only factory outlets, such as the Mid-America mall near Chicago. And there are malls whose tenants are all high-priced specialty stores, such as the Galleria in Dallas, the Worth Street Plaza in Palm Beach, Florida, and a Design Center in New Jersey. There are even "themed" malls, such as a shopping center in Dallas that specializes in a Hispanic theme, and one in California whose tenants all specialize in early American crafts.

Today, the United States is saturated with malls and centers of many types, differing dramatically from their predecessors in location, tenant mix, and architectural and physical layout. Back in the 1960s, when shopping centers first appeared in numbers, it was feared that their proliferation would "overstore" communities and lead to ruin. Hasn't happened yet!

OTHER TYPES OF RETAIL FORMATS

One cannot ignore several other types of retailing, even though these do not deal in apparel to any noticeable extent. Among them are the early nonstore operations of producers who sell directly to consumers, the catalog warehouses that developed in the 1970s, the wholesale price clubs that emerged in the 1980s, and the newest type of all—electronic retailing, which has been predicted to be the wave of the future.

Direct Selling: Door-to-Door and Party Plans

Modern versions of the early peddlers are the **direct-selling retailers** who operate without stores. A *direct-selling* establishment is one that sells merchandise by contacting customers through either *door-to-door* approaches or some form of *in-home party plan*. Direct selling is not new in the fashion field; in the period before World War II, silk hosiery and custom-made foundation garments were successfully sold this way.

Door-to-door retailing encompasses many different types of products. Working on commission, a salesperson calls on a customer at home and attempts to make the sale. In the household goods field, such names as Electrolux and Fuller Brush are familiar; they use this method exclusively. In fashion-related fields, Avon is perhaps the best-known operation of this kind. Starting with door-to-door selling of cosmetics, it now includes jewelry as well as other accessories in its merchandise mix.

The *party plan* of selling depends on the company's representative getting a local woman to organize a party of her friends and neighbors, at which the salesperson presents the company's merchandise. The hostess receives a gift, usually provided by the salesperson. This method of selling in the home is most closely associated with Tupperware, but it has also been used effectively in the fashion field by firms such as Sarah Coventry for jewelry and Bee-Line, a seller of moderately priced staple apparel for the family.

In most instances, salespeople who represent direct-selling firms use a company-produced catalog to supplement the relatively limited assortment of samples from which they sell.

Flea Market Retailers

A **flea market** is a location, either indoors or out, in which a wide variety of independent sellers rent space on a temporary basis. Flea markets are growing all over the country, both in number and in size. Some are open every day, others only on the weekend. Any vendor may sell at these markets. All that is needed is merchandise, new or used, and the money to rent a booth or table.

The merchandise offered for sale may be new or old, antiques and near-antiques, clothing, accessories, furniture, kitchen utensils, hand-crafted and ready-made products, high-priced and penny-priced merchandise. The variety is infinite—and this is part of the attraction for shoppers hunting for possible treasure, bargains, or unique items.

Catalog Showroom Retailers

A **catalog showroom retailer** is an underselling company that sells from a catalog and also maintains a showroom where samples of the merchandise can be seen and ordered. There are no deliveries, but usually the purchases can be picked up immediately at the showroom or from an adjoining ware-house. Very large, prepackaged stocks of the catalog items are on hand.

The mainstay of the merchandise assortment is usually branded house-wares, appliances, TVs, stereo equipment, electronics, toys, and sporting goods at prices well below those prevailing in conventional stores. Items of apparel, cosmetics, children's sleepers, men's underwear, and jewelry are also carried, but usually not featured or listed in the catalogs. Prices reflect the low operating costs. In addition to their bare-bones operation, catalog show-rooms are usually in low-rent areas. Few salespeople are needed, because customers select their items from samples and catalogs, then make out purchase slips and pick up their packages from the warehouse.

Stores of this type began in the late 1960s and achieved a growth rate ranging from 30 to 40 percent annually. The largest of these is Best Products Co., whose annual financial reports indicate that there are 199 showrooms, with total sales of $2.2 billion. The second largest is Service Merchandise, with 154 units and sales of $1.4 billion.[22] Some of these companies now have mail-order divisions.

The impact of such stores on the fashion business has been neglible thus far; but so was the impact of other forms of underselling stores at first. Whether or not these minimum-service retailers will make a place for themselves in fashion remains to be seen.

Warehouse Clubs: Selling in Bulk

Retailers who specialize in bulk sales of nationally branded merchandise at deeply discounted prices are so new that they do not yet have a clearly recognized name. Called "wholesale clubs," **"warehouse clubs,"** or "buying clubs," they are springing up all over the country and selling merchandise in bulk to member customers at an unheard of 10 percent markup. Although they deal primarily in commodities, some are already selling basic apparel and footwear, sheets, towels, and other home textiles.

Membership in these retailing clubs is generally restricted to small businesses, called wholesale members, who pay an initial fee of $25 to join, and also to individuals who belong to certain associations and are known as group members. Group members do not pay a membership fee but pay an additional 5 percent above the club's 10 percent markup.

Wholesale members are the backbone of the warehouse clubs' clientele, accounting for approximately 60 percent of their business. These are small Mom-and-Pop retailers—food stores, drugstores, restaurants, hardware stores—who either cannot meet the minimum order requirements of conventional wholesalers or who want to do fill-in buying.

Little or no advertising, stark industrial decor, low-rent locations, cash-and-carry transactions, and very fast inventory turn keep their expense rate down to 8 percent of their total sales—far lower than for any other type of retailing. The largest of them all is San Diego's Price Co., whose sales reached $1.4 billion from 20 stores in their fiscal year ended August 1985.[23]

Inspired by the success of the Price Co., many large and well-established retailers such as K mart, Wal-Mart, and Zayre's are jumping into this newest retail format and opening their own warehouse clubs. A recent editorial in *Stores Magazine,* official magazine of the National Retail Merchants Association, asked: "What do warehouse clubs have to do with your business?" The answer was: "Would anyone venture to say that the $7 billion in new business generated by warehouse clubs are dollars that would not have been spent in your stores?"[24]

Electronic Retailing: Computerized Selling

A relatively new development in the world of retailing is *teleshopping,* or reaching out to the thousands of users of home computers to have them do their shopping through interactive computers. In fact, some authorities expect that by early in the twenty-first century almost all food and other basic household needs will be bought through in-home television computer systems and many other shopping choices will be made by viewing assortments, prices, and brands on a television screen.[25]

In its current state, which is clearly its infancy, **electronic retailing** is being used mostly for selling durable, brand-name products that have strong consumer identification.

An example of one of the most successful electronic operations is Compu-Card International, which describes itself as a hybrid of retailing and high technology.[26] Using their system, consumers order goods by telephone and home computer, tapping into a centralized video catalog. This features 60,000 brand-name products at prices that are discounted as much as 50 percent below manufacturers' suggested retail prices. Founded in 1973 by Walter Forbes, by 1985 it had become a publicly held company with some million members nationwide, each of whom pays a nominal membership fee of $25 a year.

Those who believe that electronic marketing is the wave of the future project that 2 million households will be shopping electronically by 1990.[27]

Of particular significance to the world of fashion is the stated opinion of the highly respected senior vice-president and marketing director of Saks-Fifth Avenue, one of our most prestigious specialty stores. He said, "The [fashion] industry will be revolutionized by electronic retailing. This will start with staple stocks and eventually move into some form of ready-to-wear. At this point, however, video is not a viable system for fashion merchandise, which requires more than the present video text appearing on screens. . . . If the TV picture is sufficiently improved and the consumer becomes fully adjusted to the medium—these will happen eventually—the possibilities for our kind of store are very promising."[28]

RESURGENCE OF PRIVATE LABELS: RETAILERS INTO MANUFACTURING ....

Today the fashion business is inundated with so many different labels and names that it is hard to know whether a specific name is that of a producer, a designer, or a store's private label. **Private-label** merchandise refers to goods that are produced exclusively for one retailer, and it carries only the name of the store that sells it or a brand name that is owned by the store.

In the late 1970s as designer and manufacturer's brand names proliferated, it seemed as if every type of retailer was featuring the same nationally advertised names—department and specialty stores, mail-order houses, chain store retailers, and hordes of off-price specialists who were underselling these well-known names. To regain their exclusivity and freedom from price competition, many large department and specialty stores increasingly devel-

SELECTED EXAMPLES OF PRIVATE LABELS

Store	Private Label
Dayton–Hudson	Boundary Waters
Macy's	Club House
Neiman Marcus	Red River
Saks-Fifth Avenue	Privé Collection
Broadway Store	Rio Bravo Western
Lord & Taylor	Private Editions
Belk Stores	Jonathan Stewart
Bloomingdales	Young East Sider

oped and promoted their own privately labeled fashion merchandise in men's, women's, and children's apparel and accessories. These private-brand products are not intended to completely eliminate the national brands or designer names that they have been featuring; they carry the outside names and their own side by side. The proportion of private to other labels varies from store to store, of course, but it is generally estimated that private labels, on an average, account for 20 to 25 percent of sales in those categories that are affected.

Today, because of private-label operations, many large retailers are involved in manufacturing. Some have established special divisions that work with manufacturers or contractors in this country and abroad in the production of private-brand merchandise by means of specification buying. It is generally estimated that about 70 percent is produced offshore in low-wage foreign countries. Many retailers have also established **product development** departments to create specific lines. Macy's, for example, has even run help-wanted advertisements for what they describe as "designer merchandisers."

In addition, many major domestic manufacturers with strong national brands of their own are producing private-label merchandise. Rather than lose business to foreign sources, they are supplying retailers with exclusive merchandise to be sold under the store's own labels. Examples include the Mansco division of Manhattan Industries and the Blue Bell American division of Blue Bell (producers of Wrangler jeans). Even a top fashion company like Tahari has entered the field and produces for accounts such as Saks-Fifth Avenue.

Still another development is a relatively new and accelerating trend toward licensing and using a designer or other well-known name as one of a store's private labels. Some examples are the Halston III line for J. C. Penney, the Album Collection by Kenzo for the Limited chain stores, the Jaclyn Smith line for K mart, and the Cheryl Tiegs and Stephanie Powers lines for Sears Roebuck, and there will undoubtedly be more to come.

MAJOR FACTORY OUTLET CENTERS

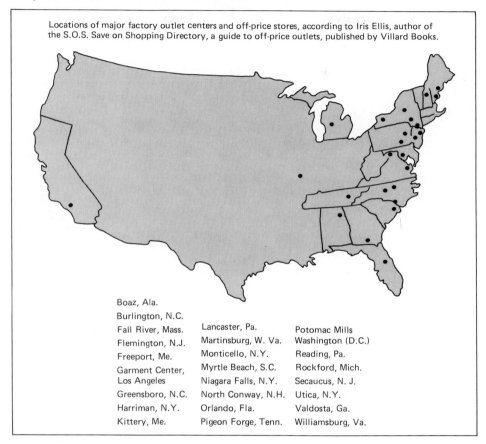

Locations of major factory outlet centers and off-price stores, according to Iris Ellis, author of the S.O.S. Save on Shopping Directory, a guide to off-price outlets, published by Villard Books.

Boaz, Ala.
Burlington, N.C.
Fall River, Mass.
Flemington, N.J.
Freeport, Me.
Garment Center, Los Angeles
Greensboro, N.C.
Harriman, N.Y.
Kittery, Me.

Lancaster, Pa.
Martinsburg, W. Va.
Monticello, N.Y.
Myrtle Beach, S.C.
Niagara Falls, N.Y.
North Conway, N.H.
Orlando, Fla.
Pigeon Forge, Tenn.

Potomac Mills
Washington (D.C.)
Reading, Pa.
Rockford, Mich.
Secaucus, N. J.
Utica, N.Y.
Valdosta, Ga.
Williamsburg, Va.

The private-label operations of retailers are progressing on many fronts and have without a doubt, added a new dimension to the business of fashion. Whether or not a revulsion by customers against the "name game" will set in remains to be seen. When it comes to fashion, nothing is forever.

CUSTOMERS CHANGE RETAILING . . . .

Each decade has seen changes not only in the fashions that people buy, but also in the ways in which significant numbers of people prefer buying it. To retailers, alert to the changing preferences of their customers, this has meant that no one way of doing business can serve all customers, or even all the

DOMESTIC MANUFACTURER SEEKS PRIVATE-LABEL WORK

Source: Reprinted with permission by Spitalnick and Company.

customers within the portion of the public served by particular types of stores.

Fashion is no longer the exclusive province of a few retailers or types of retailers. It is every retailer's business today, and there is enough fashionable merchandise and enough fashion demand to invite the attention of all merchants.

In their efforts to respond to the public's changing demands, many once widely separate kinds of retailing now overlap, competing with one another for various segments of the fashion market. For example, specialized apparel chains are going after department store customers, department stores are going after off-price business, and underselling retailers are going after everybody's business.

In retailing, as in fashion itself, the customer calls the tune. Just as fashions keep changing to reflect changes in consumer life-styles and values, so also does the retailing of fashion continue to change to adapt to customer preferences. If this means that new forms of retailing are called for, they will come forth. If it means that prevailing forms must change or segment their pattern of operation, those changes or segmentations will occur. Just as any fashion will die when it no longer appeals to a significant portion of the public, so will any form of retailing wither if it should fail to meet the needs and wants of any significant portion of its clientele.

THE TOP 50 DEPARTMENT STORES IN THE U.S.

Rank	Company (headquarters)	Ownership	Stores	Volume (000,000)
1.	Dillard's, Little Rock	(Ind)	101	$1,601.4
2.	Dayton Hudson, Minneapolis	(DH)	37	1,447.9
3.	Macy's New York	(RHM)	21	1,383*
4.	Bamberger's, New Jersey	(RHM)	23	1,297*
5.	Macy's California	(RHM)	25	1,199*
6.	The Broadway, Southern California	(CHH)	41	990
7.	Bloomingdale's, New York	(Fed)	15	955.2
8.	Lazarus, Columbus	(Fed)	31	856.2
9.	Marshall Field, Chicago	(Bat)	21	805
10.	May Co. California	(May)	35	784.2
11.	Abraham & Straus, Brooklyn	(Fed)	15	767.5
12.	Lord & Taylor, New York	(ADG)	44	760
13.	Burdine's, Miami	(Fed)	29	757.5
14.	Bullock's, California	(Fed)	27	712.3
15.	Emporium-Capwell, San Francisco	(CHH)	22	690
16.	Foley's, Houston	(Fed)	17	680.3
17.	Rich's, Atlanta	(Fed)	17	647.0
18.	Macy's Atlanta	(RHM)	26	625
19.	Hecht's, Washington, D.C.	(May)	23	567.8
20.	J. W. Robinson's, Los Angeles	(ADG)	22	560
21.	Jordan Marsh, Boston	(All)	18	550
22.	The Bon, Seattle	(All)	39	490
23.	Gimbels East, New York	(Bat)	20	480
24.	Woodward & Lothrop, Washington, D.C.	(Ind)	16	470.4
25.	Famous-Barr, St. Louis	(May)	17	460.5

Rank	Company (headquarters)	Ownership	Stores	Volume (000,000)
26.	Sanger Harris, Dallas	(Fed)	18	450.7
27.	John Wanamaker, Philadelphia	(CHH)	16	450
28.	Sterns, New Jersey	(All)	17	430
29.	L.S. Ayres, Indianapolis@	(ADG)	25	430
30.	Kaufmann's, Pittsburgh	(May)	18	423.9
31.	Carson Pirie Scott, Chicago	(Ind)	20	406
32.	Joske's, Texas	(All)	27	400
33.	Strawbridge & Clothier, Philadelphia	(Ind)	12	380
34.	P. A. Bergner, Milwaukee	(Ind)	31	356
35.	Filene's, Boston	(Fed)	16	353.5
36.	Maas Brothers, Tampa	(All)	21	340
37.	Thalhimer's, Richmond	(CHH)	25	335
38.	Hess's, Allentown, Pa.	(CAC)	39	330.7
39.	Gayfer's, Mobile, Ala.	(MS)	11	320
40.	McAlpin, Cincinnati	(MS)	9	300
41.	Higbee's, Cleveland	(IEPL)	11	280.8
42.	D. H. Holmes, New Orleans	(Ind)	17	272.8
43.	Jordan Marsh Florida	(All)	16	260
	Boscov's, Reading, Pa.	(Ind)	11	260
45.	B. Altman, New York	(Ind)	7	250
46.	May Company, Cleveland	(May)	10	238.6
47.	Frederick & Nelson, Seattle	(Bat)	15	230
	Weinstock's, Sacramento	(CHH)	12	230
49.	Elder-Beerman, Dayton	(Ind)	24	220.9
50.	G. Fox & Co., Hartford	(May)	8	219.1

Source: Reprinted with permission by *Stores Magazine,* July, 1986

Authors Note: In 1986 Bambergers name was changed to Macy's, New Jersey; also Gimbels went out of business.

Ownership Code: **ADG,** Associated Day Goods; **ALL,** Allied Stores; **BAT,** Batus Retail Group; **CAC,** Crown American Corp; **CHH,** Carter Hawley Hale, **DH,** Dayton Hudson; **FED,** Federated Stores; **IEPL,** IEPL Holding Co; **IND.,** Independent; **MAY,** May Department Stores; **MS,** Mercantile Stores; **RHM,** R.H. Macy Co. Inc.

Readings ....

The many different faces of fashion retailing are illustrated in these readings: department and specialty stores, mail-order retailers, apparel specialty chains, shopping malls, and off-price retailing, among others—plus the importance of all.

Limited Is a Clothing Retailer on the Move

Leslie H. Wexner, chairman and founder of the Limited, has built an empire by departing from "conventional wisdom" and doing things in his own innovative way.

Marshalls Offers Bargain Fun in the Racks

Marshalls, the largest off-price apparel chain in the country, appeals to its budget- and fashion-conscious customers by making bargain hunting fun.

The Metamorphosis of Spiegel

A "Plain Jane" mail-order company has transformed itself into catalog chic—an inside look at how they did it.

Neiman's Takes Aim at $1 Billion

Once the exclusive domain of the very rich, Neiman Marcus is now going after the "just rich" from coast to coast.

Sam Walton of Wal-Mart: Just Your Basic Homespun Billionaire

Building a $6 billion retail empire as a larger version of a small town dime store has not changed its special down home character.

Making It Unique

What's unique about Unique? The store is always looking for a new twist and then gets it on the rack before conventional retailers place their orders.

Limited Is a Clothing Retailer on the Move

by Jolie Solomon

When R. H. Macy & Co. announced its $3.58 billion leveraged buyout last week, the Wall Street rumor mill soon had other major retailers up for sale. High on the list of rumored acquirers is Leslie H. Wexner, chairman of Limited Inc.

Mr. Wexner, whose family controls 35.1% of Limited, won't comment, and he hasn't made any moves to satisfy the gossips. But the very appearance of his name indicates his stature and marks progress from just 18 months ago when Limited's unsuccessful bid to buy the much larger Carter Hawley Hale Stores Inc. shocked the market and triggered a wave of David and Goliath analogies.

Last week, however, the retailer capped its 2,400-plus store empire with the purchase of New York's tony Henri Bendel shop, which Limited plans to expand internationally. That added the top layer to Limited's nationwide collection of specialty women's apparel stores, which include large-size discount stores, Victoria's Secret lingerie shops and the trendsetting Limited chain for the 18-to-35-year-old set. Next week the company will open a showpiece, seven-level Manhattan store in a restored landmark building on upper Madison Avenue.

Limited's prospects appear, well, unlimited. How did the company, which started 22 years ago as a single suburban store near Columbus, Ohio, begin to set trends for others in the fiercely competitive and fickle fashion field? And, more importantly, can it keep it up?

Mr. Wexner, the 48-year-old billionaire founder, usually gets the credit for the company's success. But behind his oft-cited marketing prowess are a series of deliberate strategies that enabled Limited to squeeze out or buy up many competitors.

New York Office

To help keep a closer eye on the industry which Limited has said repeatedly it wants to lead, the company next year will move into a newly purchased townhouse on New York's Upper East Side that will serve as its corporate offices there. "We want to tap more into world resources," says Mr. Wexner, chatting recently in the study of his suburban Columbus mansion.

He and other top officers already spend 75% of their time in makeshift quarters at the Limited divisions based in New York. But the company needs "a presence" in the city, albeit secluded and "low-profile," Mr. Wexner adds. The company will retain its extensive office and distribution facilities at its headquarters here. But the home-away-from-home also is intended to give the financial community more access to Limited.

So far, that community almost seems to worship Limited. "I'm always asking myself where Limited could fall down," says Art

Source: *Wall Street Journal*, October 31, 1985. Reprinted with permission.

Charpentier of Goldman, Sachs & Co. "It's very difficult to find any place that they seem vulnerable. What it says is that (if they trip up) it's going to be a bolt out of the blue. There'll be people who said they anticipated it."

About the only criticism competitors and other retail observers can muster suggests that Limited's corporate culture, while a strength, is so intense that it produces some management turnover. Also, the company's market domination alienates vendors who, analysts add, can't do much about it.

"Look what happened to those who tried to sue Limited" last summer when it abruptly canceled orders for its newly acquired Lerner division, says one industry executive, requesting anonymity because she is wary of Mr. Wexner's "power." Vendors backed off, she says. "They need to eat, too."

Lawsuit over Inventory

The acquisition of Lerner, which turned out to have serious inventory problems, added a note of rancor to Limited's story this year. Limited is in the early stages of a lawsuit against Rapid-American Corp., which sold the unit. The suit claims that Rapid-American failed to disclose accounting information on the inventory.

But analysts say Limited is ahead of schedule in turning Lerner around. And, despite the concern's frustrated attempt to buy Carter Hawley Hale, it rarely stumbles. Including the 800-store Lerner division, the company for the current fiscal year expects to report $2.5 billion in sales, up 87% from sales of $1.34 billion last year, on which the company earned $92.5 million, or 77 cents a share. Analysts project full-year earnings of about $1.10 to $1.15 a share.

"The only thing that worries me is Les Wexner being hit by a beer truck," says Al Pennington, president of a consulting firm bearing his name.

But Limited's success can be traced to more than Mr. Wexner's fashion eye, manic devotion to work and management touch. It also reflects, for example, Limited's intense ownership ethic (along with management, 25% of Limited employees own more than half of the company's stock) and an international manufacturing organization that, consultants say, gives Limited a critical edge over competitors in supply, pricing and timing.

Add to that Limited's willingness to leverage itself repeatedly to grab more segments of the consolidating specialty retail market, suggests Phil Barach, chairman of U.S. Shoe Corp., a competitor, who says his company moves like a "turtle," compared with Limited.

At a retail seminar earlier this year, David Kollat, a Limited executive vice president, scoffed at projections of a no-growth decade ahead for women's apparel. "We'll grow at the expense of our competitors," listeners recall him saying.

Mr. Wexner bases the company's success on its departures from "conventional wisdom." He cites its refusal to rapidly rotate buyers the way department stores do, and even the flashy, American-style interior of its offices in Hong Kong, where, he says, most Americans opt to blend in with more subtle Oriental styles.

It is not that "Limited does anything different from the rest. They just do it better," says Chris Schwartz, vice president for corporate development at Dylex Ltd., a Toronto-based specialty retailer with 2,700 stores that recently bought such Limited competitors as the Foxmoor chain.

A case in point is Mast Industries, Limited's manufacturing and buying arm, whose purchase by Limited in 1978 was heavily criticized. Traditionally, says Martin Trust, who founded Mast and now heads it, many retailers have jumped into the retail supply cycle late, bought through third-party "hired guns"—often on a one-order basis—and depended on New York middleman suppliers along with the rest of the retail herd. "In the old days, it was OK to chase the market," says New York retail consultant Carol Farmer.

She says more retailers will begin to do as Mast does: Keep the retailer involved from the sewing machine on up. Mast helps Limited marketing people track and predict trends, locates countries and manufacturers, and will even set up in business a promising entrepreneur or buy machinery for a small, undercapitalized manufacturer. Full-time quota specialists try to stay ahead of the international protectionist game by buying up production "options." As a result, say industry sources, Mast has long-term relationships that speed delivery to its stores and preempt other retailers.

To illustrate Mast's power, competitors point to the "shaker" sweater, a V-necked, brightly colored, oversize garment that Limited predicted, after test marketing last year, would be a must-have item for millions of young women.

Ms. Farmer, who worked for Lerner before Limited bought it, says Limited seemed suddenly to have "jillions" of the sweaters in its stores, forcing Lerner's and others into frantic, costly catch-up efforts.

The 20% of Mast's output that goes to outsiders, including some Limited competitors, helps keep Mast up to date on the rest of the industry, says Mr. Trust. But the 25% of Limited divisions' apparel that Mast supplies is the bulk of its projected $400 million in sales this year. By contrast, Dylex's product sourcing division, which some say also is very progressive, will do only $200 million.

Mast's quick production turnarounds fit what Robert Morosky, vice chairman, describes as an important Limited strategy: flexibility. More interested in controlling budgets and employees, he says, many retailers won't allow quick reversals or unexpected budget increases. Limited gives buyers and other employees the authority to make quick decisions without layers of approvals. Accounting employees, for example, can offer suppliers prepayment in exchange for discounts, an independence other retailers wouldn't grant to mere "bookkeepers," he says.

Dylex's Mr. Schwartz says the company has managed to maintain an unusual "entrepreneurial zeal." But the culture isn't for everyone. One top retail executive turned down a job with Limited, citing the company's single-mindedness, time demands and requirement that employees not stray outside Limited's very closed society. "I'm too old to join a monastery," the executive told Limited.

Whether the culture and systems can be maintained as Limited grows is an open question. "If they acquired (a big department store company) and got really leveraged, it could backfire," at least temporarily, says Mr. Pennington, the consultant.

But Mr. Morosky, the Mast vice chairman, says he is unfazed by leverage levels like the 121% of debt relative to equity that Limited recorded when it acquired Lerner. That figure is now down to 70%. And Mr. Wexner vows to get into the department store business, either through acquisition or a joint venture.

He does concede that it is dangerous to see success as "a self-fulfilling prophecy." Goldman Sachs's Mr. Charpentier says he thinks Limited got that message back in the late 1970s when management problems hurt earnings. "They know that if they're going to drive at 150 mph, they not only have to have the best engine, but the best steering and brakes and suspension and rollbar—and fire extinguisher."

Marshalls Offers Bargain Fun in the Racks

by Lori Kesler

Marshalls stores don't have flashy personalities. In fact, they may remind you of somebody's dear old Aunt Alice.

You know the type. She's sort of plain and, well, she hasn't really dressed up since the last family wedding. Yet those close to Aunt Alice know she has surprisingly good taste.

She buys spiffy sports outfits for her nieces and classic preppy stuff for her nephew. She just doesn't spend much money on pretty things for herself.

Marshalls, the largest off-price apparel chain in the country, carefully nurtures the same kind of no-nonsense image.

Don't look here for stylish window displays. In fact, don't look for displays at all, because what you'll find, instead, are rows of brand name clothes, some with Pierre Cardin and Christian Dior labels, hanging from plain wire hangers on long skeletal pipe racks.

"We keep the stores simple and basic by design," says John Arruda, vp-advertising and sales promotion. "It keeps overhead down."

It also convinces bargain hungry shoppers this is their kind of place. Because Marshalls deals in off-season merchandise, overruns and irregulars, store inventory changes drastically from week to week.

While many shoppers might see this as a real inconvenience, others view it as a sort of challenge. Hard-core enthusiasts visit Marshalls every few days to see what's new. Some even know the truck delivery schedules and regularly arrive just in time to get first grab at new stock.

A typical Marshalls store has about 30,000 sq. ft. of men's and women's wear, children's apparel, lingerie and accessories, shoes, domestics, giftware and jewelry. It averages about $6.8 million in sales annually and sells its merchandise for 20% to 50% off. Irregulars, which make up about 15% of the stock, are sometimes reduced even more.

Marshalls' president, Frank H. Brenton, expects sales this year to top $1.1 billion, up from $830 million last year and $618 million in 1981. There are currently 152 stores across the U.S., and the company plans to have a total of 175 stores open by the year's end.

Woburn, Mass.-based Marshalls, now owned by Melville Corp. in Harrison, N.Y., was started in 1956 by two men—one in the war surplus business, Norman Barron, and the other, Alfred Marshall, a soft goods merchant. They opened a store in Beverly, Mass., but the company really didn't grow much beyond that region until Melville bought it in 1976.

"Melville had the foresight to see this was a good concept," Mr. Brenton says. "They put some money behind Marshalls and it really started to move."

By the time Mr. Brenton joined the company in 1978, its sales volume had reached $240 million annually. Sales continue to grow at about 30% a year, well above the over-all 18% rate for Melville, which also owns Thom

McAn, Foxmoor and Kay-Bee Toy & Hobby Shops.

Industry expert Alton Doody, president of the Doody Co. in Columbus, O., refers to off-price retailing as "the fundamental trend in apparel retailing in the 1980s," and he says Marshalls is well positioned to take advantage of its spreading popularity.

"Marshalls is sort of the K mart of this new business," he says. "It's well managed and well financed, and it'll be a major factor for many years."

The Marshalls chain has taken commanding lead of the mass market off-price category and has inspired such apparent imitators as Zayre Corp.'s T. J. Maxx and F. W. Woolworth's J. Brannam, both started in the late 1970s.

Marshalls' quarter century of experience gives it an edge over the newcomers. In a market where classic off-price bargains are becoming increasingly scarce, Marshalls gets the goods by knowing how to play the game.

"We treat our vendors very well," Mr. Brenton says. "We're aware that we need them more than they need us. If we want to buy X number of an item, but they want to sell more, we'll take what they want. We'll clean up the entire lot.

"And when we make a bad buy, we eat it. We don't ask for a markdown allowance. Also, we pay on time."

One insider agrees: "When a deal's a deal, they pay. That's not always true these days with department stores."

Then, too, says Mr. Brenton, if a vendor "has a problem somewhere, we won't push his goods in that area. It's a two-way street. They know we have integrity and we'll stand by them when they need us. As a result, maybe they'll cut heavier for us than they normally would."

Marshalls pioneered this way of doing business with manufacturers, says Mr. Doody.

"They offered them controlled distribution," he says, "and that's probably the single most important key to Marshalls' success.

"If a manufacturer has a strong account [regular retail outlet] in a certain city, Marshalls doesn't place its merchandise there. If it's sort of in between, the clothes appear unbranded. If there's nobody in town that means anything to the manufacturer, the clothes appear branded."

Marshalls' size and longevity give it some other advantages, too. Instead of using brokers, it employs its own buyers, said to be among the top in the field.

And it has five regional warehouses. "A lot of companies have one distribution center for the entire country and they sort everything through there. Our setup gives us a big advantage," Mr. Brenton says. "We can get goods in and out in 48 hours if we have to."

Some manufacturers resist selling to off-pricers. A few have their own factory outlets "and others are just stubborn," Mr. Brenton says. "They don't like to deal with off-pricers. But there aren't too many of them left."

Off-pricers tend to search out low-rent locations, and Marshalls usually moves its stores into existing buildings that meet its 30,000-sq.-ft. space requirement. The bulk of its stores are in strip centers, although it has a few free-standing buildings and some stores in shopping centers where it can afford the rent.

In its stores, Marshalls marks merchandise with tags listing regular retail price and "our price."

"They're pretty up front with the customer," says John Leffler at Management Horizons, a research company in Columbus, O. "Lots of tags will say 'irregular' or 'past season.'" Company officials say Marshalls often buys current goods right after a season opens, so an item marked "past season" may turn up on its racks shortly after it appears in the department stores.

Marshalls tries to educate the public about its way of doing business via advertising and consumer guides distributed in-store. The uninitiated customer may be disappointed at first if she can't walk in and immediately find a blouse in a particular color, size or style, Mr. Arruda says. "But when she discovers she can get substantial savings by shopping regularly at Marshalls, she may decide the benefits outweigh the inconvenience," he says.

Marshalls' advertising, about 80% institutional, has used the same theme—"brand names for less"—in print, radio and TV for years. The ad budget amounts to about 2% of the sales volume. The stores never run sales because "we're not promotional. We're selling a concept," Mr. Brenton says.

Marshalls' advertising aims for consistency. "We don't change every six months, and we don't keep looking for a new handle or promotional device. We don't manufacture hype or try to create three-day excitement," says Mr. Arruda.

"We have our way of doing business, and it's been pretty much the same over the years," he says. "Despite the temptation to keep changing, we try to keep it simple and consistent—and that's not easy."

Marshalls' officials say some imitators have copied their concept almost exactly—from store size and location to instore configuration. But Marshalls, with its national penetration, won't be easy to catch. And anyway, there's plenty of room for expansion, notes Mr. Doody, because he figures the off-price market will be able to hold well over 1,000 stores of this type in five years.

However, he predicts that as it evolves, Marshalls probably will stock more "planned assortment"—that is, merchandise purchased on a regular basis with no price advantage. Then a customer looking for bargains can also pick up other merchandise—underwear, for example—that isn't necessarily a closeout. "That's a predictable part of the life cycle," Mr. Doody says.

Perhaps so, but Mr. Brenton insists the only "true off-pricers" in the business are the companies that deal primarily in closeouts and overruns. And he seems to think some of the newcomers don't quite fit the bill. "Those that buy current goods and discount 20% to 25% don't qualify as true off-pricers."

And the Marshalls customer is different from theirs because "she sacrifices getting current merchandise for price," Mr. Brenton says. "When somebody's buying a $75 dress, it better be just right. For $39, she's not quite as fussy."

The Metamorphosis of Spiegel
by Winston Williams

Spiegel Inc. spawned a daily ritual at the fashionable Oak Brook Shopping Center when the catalogue house moved its offices to this western suburb of Chicago seven years ago.

Rubbing elbows with the crowds of picky buyers are curious Spiegel executives who meticulously search the racks at such tony establishments as I. Magnin, Marshall Field's, Lord

Source: *New York Times*, July 5, 1984. Excerpted with permission.

& Taylor, Saks, Bonwit Teller and Neiman Marcus, looking for ideas for the resurgent Spiegel catalogue.

Indeed, Spiegel has seen more than its surroundings change since it moved from a converted warehouse on Chicago's West Side to a shiny glass and metal high-rise that towers above the neighboring retail stores.

Henry A. Johnson, Spiegel's lean president and chief executive officer, dapper and elegant in a pink shirt and pink tie, called the move a crucial one. "We needed a new environment," the 65-year-old executive said, referring to the company's former digs. "You should have seen the place. We didn't even have air conditioning. We were trying to upgrade ourselves. But how could we attract quality people in an environment like that?"

And upgrade Spiegel did. Pursuing a daring strategy that some skeptics say is still loaded with risks, Spiegel, once the perennial Plain Jane in the catalogue industry, has dramatically transformed its image. The company that once sold a decidedly homely line of goods on "easy-credit" terms to low-income shoppers in distant regions has evolved in the last few years into a purveyor of quality goods to fashion-conscious career women.

By aggressively pursuing this "upscale" market, offering more select goods and revamping its catalogue, Spiegel has fulfilled Mr. Johnson's ambition of making it a "fine department store in print." In the process, it has propelled itself into the pace-setting position as trend-maker in the booming catalogue business.

The change in the catalogue is striking. The brightly-colored polyester leisure suits, the socks, the plain men's underwear and the cheap furniture that once crammed its catalogue pages are gone, replaced by luxuriant furs, sleek attaché cases, lacy lingerie and trendy goods bearing snob labels such as Liz Claiborne, Ralph Lauren and Bill Blass.

And the change is just as apparent in the company's balance sheet. In the past few years, sales have grown spectacularly, in the range of 25 to 30 percent a year, and earnings have surged.

Profits, after being stuck for several years between $2 million and $3 million on flat revenues of about $260 million, began to pick up in 1981. By 1983, the company says, its pre-tax profits had more than doubled from the year before, to $22.5 million, on revenues of $513 million, compared with pre-tax earnings of $10.1 million, on revenues of $394 million in 1982.

Its parent company—the giant, privately held West German retailer Otto-Versand G.m.b.H.—does not release profit figures on a quarterly basis, but it reports that sales this year were up 22 percent through May. The average value of each order has also soared—an important measure, since it can cost just as much to fill a cheap order as an expensive one.

And Spiegel's praises are being sung from widely diverse corners of the retail trade. Donald Peters, president of local 743 of the United Brotherhood of Teamsters, which represents Spiegel's work force, called the changes "very positive," adding: "Now I wonder why anybody ever bothered to look at those old catalogues."

Roberta Wexler, information director for the Direct Marketing Association, an industry trade group, agreed: "Spiegel certainly identified the working woman market and has run with it. The management there deserves all the glory they're getting."

But the highest form of flattery is coming from Spiegel's competitors. Sears, J. C. Penney and Montgomery Ward—which still surpass No. 4 Spiegel in overall catalogue sales—are now putting more emphasis on expensive merchandise and designer labels in their own catalogues. In addition, they are following Spiegel's lead in experimenting with a growing number of small specialty catalogues, zeroing in on such markets as children's clothes and gourmet cooking utensils.

These larger competitors, however, have managed to contain their enthusiasm for Spiegel's approach. The company's rapid growth, they say, has not been entirely problem-free. Surging volume has caught the company short-staffed on several occasions, leading to long order delays.

In other instances, Spiegel has misjudged the demand for certain items, ending up with too few of some and too many of others—causing surpluses that are dumped at distressed prices at the company's three national surplus outlets.

Such miscalculations are common in the retailing business, but Spiegel's skeptics say the company could be making a bigger and potentially much more grave error by betting the company's entire store on the trendy and fickle upscale market. That segment, they say, is becoming saturated as new entrants rush willy-nilly into the catalogue business—including such glossy, and relatively new, competitors as Honeybee, Conran's and F.B.S.

"When you go for a niche, you're assuming that the niche is always going to be there and that you're going to dominate it," said G. Joseph Reddington, vice president of marketing at Sears, Roebuck & Company. "In many ways, that's riskier than being a general merchandiser. We've got a broader base."

But for Mr. Johnson, an energetic man who gestures and draws diagrams as he talks, finding the appropriate niche was the only course to pursue when he left Avon Products Inc. in 1976 to turn around the flagging, century-old Spiegel, which was struggling to hang onto its No. 4 position in the catalogue industry.

"One of the first things I decided was that we couldn't be fourth on the totem pole and be a me-too'er at the same time," he said. "We

had to find a way of being unique in the market." He perceived that the explosion of two-income families meant, in addition to growing incomes, less time for women to shop.

But the Spiegel of seven years ago was ill-equipped to take advantage of this insight. Its customers were concentrated in small rural communities in the South and the Midwest. They relied heavily on Spiegel's "easy-credit" policy, which allowed monthly installment payments as low as $7. Its homespun catalogues simply marched out the merchandise, with no effort at stylish layout or glossy presentation.

Still, Spiegel might have continued to muddle through with its old formula had it not been for a radical shrinking of its customer base. Many loyal customers were forsaking Spiegel for the ubiquitous discount stores, such as K mart, that have sprouted in the last 15 years. And the children of its bread-and-butter customers were growing up, becoming better educated and moving on to more sophisticated shopping pastures.

"You could feel the market slipping away from you, drying up" said Edward J. Spiegel, vice president of marketing and a great-grandson of founder Joseph Spiegel. "It was a frustrating thing not to be able to move fast enough to stop it."

In the mid-1970s, interest rates rose so sharply that financing Spiegel's credit accounts, which turned over an average of once every 18 months, became costly. And profits, when there were some, were meager. The Beneficial Corporation, which had bought the company in 1965, became frustrated, too. It decided to hire Mr. Johnson to whip the company into good enough shape to sell it.

Mr. Johnson began his retailing career right out of high school, when he took a job as an office boy at Montgomery Ward's mail order operation in Chicago for $14 a week. After the war he returned to Ward's, where he became an assistant buyer before joining Alden's, the now-defunct cataloguer, as head furniture buyer.

He rose to vice president before joining Avon in 1974 as head of its Avon Fashions mail-order operation. Studying at night, he earned an undergraduate degree in business from Northwestern University and an M.B.A. from the University of Chicago.

His new way of doing things included closing more than 200 order stores throughout country, where customers could come in, view a few samples and place orders. Spiegel aimed at a new, more affluent, market, but the strategy at first did not succeed—the company's customers dropped by half a million, to a low of 2.7 million. (That number is now back up to 3.8 million.)

A period of stagnant revenues also followed the wave of changes, and employment continued to fall off—from 7,000 in 1976, when Mr. Johnson arrived, to a low of 3,500 in 1981. Since then, the pickup in business has pushed employment to 4,200 and the company said it is likely to rise.

While many employees were let go in the company's revamping, many new ones were brought on board, including buyers and advertising specialists hired from leading department stores and trained in the mail-order business.

Eugene Bilan, a specialist in writing copy for catalogues, said he was recently recruited "to create excitement in the catalogues every 20 pages or so"—for example, by tossing in enticing photos of $3,800 diamond necklaces. "This is a hot place to work right now," said Mr. Bilan, whose 20 years on the retailing circuit includes stints at Neiman-Marcus and Bloomingdale's.

The catalogue has started to feature the work of the country's most successful fashion photographers—artists such as James Moore

and Herb Ritts. The book is less cluttered, and the presentations are slicker, with greater use of bold and imaginative graphics. The number of specialty catalogues—including books featuring seasonal and children's clothes, Norma Kamali fashions and items for large women—has expanded to more than a dozen. The new Spiegel features toll-free telephone numbers for placing orders, and advertisements for the catalogue in Vogue and other high-fashion magazines.

Now 90 percent of its customers are in its new target group. Its average buyer is a 39-year-old working woman from a 2.8-member household with an annual family income of $38,000. Had the company continued its old ways, executives say, its average buyer today would be from a larger, less-educated blue-collar household with income of $18,000.

The company's new look, in fact, runs the risk of alienating a large chunk of traditional catalogue buyers, the customers who have formed the backbone of the mail-order business.

"In the last few years they've gone a little far out for me; I'm more conservative than that," said Myrtis Fryer, a widowed nurse in remote Petersburg, Alaska, who has shopped by catalogue for many years. She added, however, that the books excite her teen-age daughter.

To replace the Mrs. Fryers of the catalogue world, Spiegel is trying to attract more women such as Diane Sievers, a young paralegal who works for an insurance company in Northampton, Mass. She orders increasingly by mail because her busy schedule limits her shopping time.

"They seem to carry name-brand products cheaper than I can get in the stores around here," she said. (The company says its prices are generally comparable to most retailers'.)

Spiegel's current management, which was left intact by its new owner, is delighted over its partnership relationship with Otto-Versand, which purchased the company from Beneficial in 1982 for an undisclosed sum. Spiegel now has the financial muscle to finance its receivables of $350 million easily. And because its parent is privately held, the cataloguer is not pressured for quick results, Mr. Johnson said. He has said he hopes to make Spiegel a billion-dollar company, and internal projections are that the company will reach that sales level by 1988.

The German connection is a source of technology and capital for Spiegel as well. The company is now trying to improve productivity and reduce costs at its main distribution center in Chicago, where much of the processing is still done manually. A new $20 million highly automated order-filling system is being installed at its 12-story Chicago warehouse.

Now, with its turnaround firmly established, Spiegel is continuing to concentrate on marketing. It worries little about the shakeout that is predicted for the mail-order industry, believing its organization still has a vast market to tap.

"Our shoppers now are with us because of their lifestyle, not because they can't get credit anywhere else," said Mr. Spiegel, the marketing executive. "The trend toward more working women is going to continue. The better part of the risk is behind us."

Neiman's Takes Aim at $1 Billion
by Pat Kivests

After a decade of rapid-fire expansion, Neiman-Marcus is aiming to be the nation's dominant high fashion specialty retailer by minding the store once again.

Once the preeminent family-owned operation that carved its niche catering to Texas's oil-bred carriage trade, the 21-unit Dallas-based division of Carter Hawley Hale tripled its size in the last nine years, adding 14 stores in markets as diverse as Boston and Beverly Hills, Calif.

Ringing in a healthy $238 a square foot in 1984, sales climbed to $750 million with an operating profit conservatively estimated at over $82 million, or more than 10.9 percent of sales. By the end of 1985, with the addition of its 22nd unit in Palo Alto, Calif., sources say Neiman's will reach $840 million in sales and will give Saks Fifth Avenue a run for its money in the high stakes specialty store business.

By 1987, Neiman-Marcus could easily be a $1 billion operation.

"If you will excuse the play on words," says Richard Marcus, chairman, "Neiman-Marcus is emerging from an intensive period of expansion and entering an era of mining the store. During the expansion, we realize now, there were many things left undone, many opportunities missed. A weak-performing store or department, for example, tended to get put off from the herd mentally. Expansion," he says, "became a distraction."

Accordingly, the store is gearing down its rate of store expansion to gear up for what top management hails as a new era of enhancement and concentrated productivity.

Source: *Women's Wear Daily*, April 3, 1985. Reprinted with permission.

Directing its energies inward, management intends to intensify businesses at which Neiman's traditionally has excelled, such as high-end designer dresses, gifts, cosmetics and shoes; to develop businesses in areas where it has fallen short, such as designer sportswear, contemporary sportswear and fashion accessories, and to win over the upscale customer of tomorrow—a contemporary-minded individual in the broadest sense of the word contemporary, who has a large expendable income and who is as much attuned to MTV as to public television. That customer is also, by Neiman's own admission, one the retailer largely has failed to address.

David Dworkin, the former Batus executive who spent six years with Saks and five months with Marshall Field's before assuming the post of president in February 1984, is largely credited with recharting Neiman's course by strategizing merchandising divisions, adapting an aggressive stance in inventory ownership and implementing a formidable marketing and promotional campaign (boosting what was a meager advertising budget 10-fold, according to some sources inside the company) to back up new merchandising positions. Even *Imprint,* the glossy fashion magazine published quarterly by N-M has become an integral part of the store's marketing strategy by reflecting, in its advertising and editorial content, both the concepts and merchandise Neiman's is aggressively stressing.

In addition, Neiman's will launch an intensive two-week television campaign this summer in metropolitan Chicago, where the store operates three units. More image-oriented than product-oriented, the campaign will consist of 100 60-second, 30-second and 10-second spots. Similar campaigns are expected to follow in California and in Texas. The campaign also marks a significant change in the way Neiman's, which has traditionally relied heavily on local newspaper advertising to reach its customers, will attempt to reach its customers in the future.

"Our strategy is to remain dominant in the carriage trade—second to none—but there are businesses beyond that within the demographics of the Neiman's customer and we're in the position to capture them," says Dworkin.

N-M has no intention of allowing its high-end designer business—which several resources praised as the finest in the country—to slip for a moment. Neiman's high-end salon, which is still a service-driven department where a significant amount of merchandise is sold by conscientious sales associates even before it reaches the sales floor, has increased its depth and breadth of resources.

A stronger stock position has been taken with major designers such as Galanos. Fresh, fashionably outspoken resources, such as Tony Chase, which "speak to a new customer or address the traditional customer who is hungry for newness," have been added, according to Ann Keenes, senior vice president and general merchandise manager overseeing high-end designer dresses.

At the same time, to facilitate the development of businesses that had been allowed to languish, Dworkin divided and realigned the responsibilities of Neiman's three senior vice presidents and general merchandise managers last June and added a fourth executive to their ranks. The action, he says, allowed each to focus more logically on a given merchandising category and to select and aggressively tackle weaker segments for development.

Contemporary sportswear is an example. "When we reorganized last spring, we realized we were nowhere in the contemporary market," recalls Dworkin. " 'What does the upbeat Eighties woman who wears Calvin Klein during the week want to wear on the weekend?' we asked ourselves."

The answer led to a new department and

a new merchandising concept called Nuvo Etc.

The department has become a gathering place for creative energies and a focus for Neiman's in terms of how the customer of the Eighties and Nineties wants to buy her clothes and how a retailer should sell and merchandise them to meet her needs. It is expected to represent at least 8 percent of total sales in 1985, or approximately $67 million, according to sources. More important, however, management expects the area—which is a cohesive, tightly edited combination of what was once the junior and contemporary departments—will more than double its volume within a year and a half.

"We're planning it with a liberal open-to-buy without a ceiling," says Dworkin. "I don't want to put a cap on where it might go."

He adds that Nuvo is not an attempt to expand the customer base in a conventional way. "We're not expanding our base by seeking a moderate customer, a junior customer or a contemporary customer per se. We see Nuvo as reflecting a contemporary thrust in our society that cuts across age barriers."

Resources include In Wear, Esprit, Danny Noble, Leon Max, Norma Kamali, K-Factory and Betty Jackson. For fall 1985, Marilyn Kaplan, senior vice president and general merchandise manager overseeing the area, says Nuvo will take an aggressive stand in imports, augmenting its domestic assortment with fresh goods from Italy, London and Paris.

"The goal," she says, "is to add excitement, to avoid the pedestrian and to be forward without being so crazy that one has to be drunk or drugged to appreciate the clothes."

While Nuvo is a prime example of Neiman's bid to tread authoritatively into areas where it once just tiptoed, there are other categories strategically geared for growth that are no less significant.

Cosmetics, long a strong suit, generated 10 percent of sales last year, or $75 million, and is expected to record a 17 percent to 20 percent increase in 1985. In 2½ years, says one insider, Neiman's expects cosmetics to be a $100 million business.

Shoes, another high profile department for Neiman's, generated 8.2 percent of sales last year and will be intensified at the upper end, where key resources include Andrea Pfister, Walter Steiger, Maude Frizon and Charles Jourdan pump, retailing for $155, notes Ron Frasch, senior vice president and general merchandise manager for cosmetics, women's shoes and accessories. Frasch, who joined Neiman's from Saks last spring, adds that a layer of new resources—including Seducta and Kenneth Cole—will be added this year to relate to the Nuvo attitude carried over from rtw.

Fashion jewelry, an abysmally underdeveloped department in the past, will receive a substantial boost. In 1985, the category's gross dollar margin will exceed total sales for all of 1983, says Frasch. Neiman's expects to see a 30 percent increase by ushering in upscale contemporary resources such as Stephen Dweck, Ben Amun and Richard Serbin.

The biggest accessories news, however, is Neiman's introduction of a contemporary gold jewelry department that will offer the designs of Serbin, Ben Amun and a select few others in 14-karat gold. The move, Frasch believes, will give Neiman's an edge on the competition. Filling the void that exists between fashion and precious jewelry, the collection will open in 10 stores this spring and will be heralded by an eight-page gold book to be dropped this month. Retail price points will run from $100 to $2,000, with the majority of pieces in the $800 to $1,200 range.

On a broader front, Neiman's will undertake the renovation and reallocation of space in 10 of its units during the next three years. All changes will be made on the basis of merchandising strategies and never will be done solely for cosmetic reasons. At NorthPark, Neiman's largest-volume store with estimated sales in excess of $65 million last year, a 56,600-square-foot third floor was completed last October, boosting the unit's size 27 percent to 224,000 square feet. NorthPark is soon expected to be Neiman's first $100 million store.

Other strong units include the downtown Dallas flagship and Prestonwood stores, both estimated to be in the $60 million range; its Houston store at the Galleria, also in the $60

million range; Beverly Hills, which does in excess of $51 million; and San Francisco, estimated to bring in more than $46 million.

Weaker units, one source speculates, include the San Diego store at $19 million and the Newport Beach, Calif., unit at $21 million.

Despite industry rumblings about the White Plains, N.Y., store, both Dworkin and Marcus maintain that it is a profitable entity with a continuous upside potential.

Sam Walton of Wal-Mart: Just Your Basic Homespun Billionaire

Sam M. Walton is nothing if not intense. The energetic founder of Wal-Mart Stores Inc. seems unable to walk, drive—or even fly—past one of his stores or anyone else's without counting the number of cars in the parking lot. He was once so busy counting that he crashed his car into the back of a Wal-Mart truck. Walton's neighbors in the tiny Ozark town of Bentonville, Ark., couldn't resist ribbing him about this during a parade in his honor in 1983: One of the 10 floats was a wrecked car welded to the back of a Wal-Mart truck.

It was the kind of small-town joke Walton could appreciate. But if you think he is merely a well-liked local merchant, think again. At 67, Walton is one of the most successful—and innovative—retailers around. From a single five-and-dime in Newport, Ark., he now counts among his empire 817 Wal-Mart off-price department stores, most of them purposely located in small towns across the South and Southwest. With $6.4 billion in sales in fiscal 1985, Wal-Mart is second only to K mart Corp. (sales: $23 billion) among discounters—

and closing fast. "I foresee him becoming the No. 1 discounter in the country," says Herbert Fisher, chairman of Jamesway Corp., a Secaucus (N.J.) discount chain. "Sam is a living legend."

Preacher Man

There is little about Walton that reflects his amazing success. Though he is one of the wealthiest men in America—the Walton family's 39% stake in Wal-Mart shares is worth $2.5 billion—he lives a simple existence. He drives a beat-up 1978 Ford pickup and doesn't seem to mind that his bird dogs have chewed its interior or that the tires are bald. Visitors to Bentonville often mistake Wal-Mart's office building, with its lobby decorated in Early Bus Station, for a warehouse.

Walton's eccentricities, however, are also his strength. He seems to run Wal-Mart like a larger version of his original dime store. He doesn't bother with pricy industry consultants and marketing gurus. Instead, he relies on the

Source: Excerpted from the October 14, 1985 issue of *Business Week,* by special permission. © 1985 by McGraw-Hill, Inc.

seat-of-the-pants judgments of his employees and his own ability to keep a close eye on other regional retail chains.

He drives himself and his company with an almost evangelical fervor. At store openings, Walton leads Wal-Mart cheers that begin "Give me a W, give me an A." To many of his loyal employees, who participate in a generous profit-sharing plan, Walton has the air of a fiery Baptist preacher. Says Paul R. Carter, a Wal-Mart executive vice-president: "Mr. Walton has a calling."

The gospel according to Sam is paying off. As other retailers struggle, Wal-Mart regularly posts nearly 35% annual sales gains. Profits have soared an average of 37% a year since 1975. And Wal-Mart beats the industry in profitability. Its five-year return on equity is over 35%. No wonder Wall Street accords Wal-Mart a price-earnings multiple of 24, the highest of any company its size.

Walton isn't satisfied. Through his new, highly profitable string of Sam's Wholesale Clubs, he is moving aggressively into deep discounting. With 19 of the warehouse outlets in operation and four more on the drawing boards, Wal-Mart will pass San Diego's Price Club as the largest of the deep discounters.

Yet Wal-Mart is at a critical juncture. While the company is opening 115 new stores this year and establishing beachheads in the upper Midwest and the Rocky Mountain region, some analysts doubt that Wal-Mart will be able to keep expanding and maintain its fat margins. And many worry that the company will lose its unique character should Walton retire.

No Apologies

Walton brushes aside such concerns. "There is no limit to our growth unless we stumble or don't do our job," he says. And there is little indication that he is contemplating retirement—or even knows the meaning of the word. Says Ferold G. Arend, who retired as president in 1983: "Sam is just as active in the company as ever." The Wal-Mart air force is constantly ferrying top management to and from the stores. Walton, a pilot himself, sets the pace. Traveling at least three days a week, he visits all of his stores at least once each year. And he drops in on hundreds of his competitors for good measure.

Walton doesn't need to apologize for doing things his way. From the flag-waving store openings to Walton's recent "Buy American" campaign to a corporate environment that is at once folksy and fiercely competitive, Walton's company is a product of his all-American persona.

He got his retailing roots from his father, who scraped through the Depression in Columbia, Mo., by trading whatever he could get his hands on. Young Walton paid his way through the University of Missouri by operating a paper route. But the foundation of his retailing philosophy was the early J. C. Penney stores. As a management trainee for the Penney store in Des Moines in the 1930s, he adopted the company's tenet of never placing profits before people. Drafted in 1942, he spent the war stateside in the Military Police.

Small-Town Success

After the war, Walton opened his first store in Newport. Though successful, he was forced to move across the state and start over when his landlord refused to renew the lease in 1951. His Bentonville-based variety store chain flourished under the care of Walton and his younger brother James, known as Bud. Perhaps by accident, Walton hit upon the tactic that has sustained him ever since—selling name-brand merchandise at a discount in small-town America.

The first Wal-Mart opened in Rogers, Ark., in 1962. Progress was slow until the company went public in 1970. Today, 100 shares of the first issue—then worth $1,600—would be worth about $300,000 after splits. Investment banker Jackson T. Stephens, a Wal-Mart director, wasn't surprised at Wal-Mart's growth. "Sam has the ability to concentrate on his business to a greater extent than anyone else I have ever met," he says.

Walton was absolutely convinced in the late 1950s that discounting would transform retailing, but there was nothing else dogmatic about his approach. He prowled New England, the cradle of off-pricing. "He visited just about every discounter in the U.S.," says William F. Kenney, the retired president of the now-defunct Kings Department Stores. "He would introduce himself as a little country boy from Arkansas."

In fact, Walton was then the largest franchisee of Ben Franklin variety stores. In 1962 he journeyed to Chicago to try to persuade the Franklin people to join him in discounting. They declined. But one Franklin executive, Donald G. Soderquist, now an executive vice-president at Wal-Mart, bumped into Walton the next day in one of the first K marts to open in the Chicago suburbs. "Here he was, 25 mi. from our offices, and he was talking to a clerk. He was writing in a little notebook, and at one point he got down on his knees to look under the display cabinet. I said: 'Mr. Walton, what are doing?' He said: 'Just part of the education process, Don.' "

Walton's cadre suggested several innovations that would prove crucial to Wal-Mart's success. Arend prevailed on Walton to open warehouses as a more economical means of distribution than shipping directly to the stores. Walton relented eventually, and today the company's highly automated distribution centers are a key element of its strategy: Wal-Mart clusters 150 stores around a warehouse, with no store more than a few hours distant.

The hubs are a principal reason Wal-Mart can make money in towns as small as 5,000 people.

In 1975, Vice-Chairman Jack Shewmaker convinced Walton that computer terminals in every store would pay a handsome return. Today the company's state-of-the-art computer system does everything from tracking inventory to planning new stores. And Wal-Mart is installing a satellite-based private network to link the stores more closely and is experimenting with video conferences.

Spare a Dime?

Walton has a reputation as a penny pincher. During buying trips to New York in the company's early days, Arend recalls, Walton would exhort his executives to search out the one great buy that would pay for the trip. Enfield remembers that Walton would stride toward a pay phone immediately after landing during a trip through the Midwest. He then would ask Enfield for change. "I began carrying a roll of dimes," he says.

Such frugality extends throughout the company. Like many companies, Wal-Mart gathers its far-flung management once a year. Not many, however, charter buses to bring them in. To keep his people focused on the bottom line, Walton insists that all employees have access to complete financial results. Each month, Soderquist sends out monthly summaries ranking every department in every store. The overachievers are recognized and rewarded—and the laggards, while seldom fired, are sometimes demoted.

Quirkiness

The troops are encouraged to produce a steady flow of ideas. The Wal-Mart planning process begins when store managers ask every clerk what he or she can do to improve the operation of the store. Everyone learns the value of "LTC," company shorthand for a low threshold for change. If a policy doesn't seem to be working, Wal-Mart executives want to make sure their employees are not afraid to challenge and change it. Bentonville executives also keep in touch by spending one week each year in the stores performing an hourly job.

Walton is showing his usual quirkiness in designating an heir apparent. The choice: Shewmaker, 47, or President David D. Glass, 49. But the wily chairman is not tipping his hand as to which. To keep things confused, Walton had them switch jobs last year. Shewmaker, now chief financial officer, is reporting to Glass, the chief operating officer. Walton described it at the time as cross-pollination. But Arend isn't buying. "He is throwing them at each other," Arend says. "He did the same thing to me."

"Pretty Prudish"

Walton is unabashedly old-fashioned. Although the company liberalized its hiring of the elderly—around the time Walton turned 65—women have yet to enter the senior ranks at Wal-Mart. At its annual store manager's conference, Wal-Mart schedules programs for managers' wives. They are urged to speak their minds on life with a Wal-Mart store manager. "They do, too," says Shewmaker. The program, of course, presumes that Wal-Mart managers are male and that their wives do not have careers of their own.

Company policy forbids employees, even single ones, to date one another without authorization from the executive committee. Women are scarce even in the ranks of merchandise buyers. There were only six female buyers as recently as five years ago. There are 12 today, 17% of the total. Walton resisted urgings by Arend last year to name a woman to the board of directors. "Sam is really pretty prudish," says Enfield.

Wal-Mart stock took a pounding a few years ago when news leaked out that Walton had a mild form of leukemia. The condition was arrested with only a change in diet and is since in remission. Many at Wal-Mart quietly began to contemplate carrying on without Sam. The future, however, will probably include a Walton. His eldest son, Robson, 40, is expected to assume a top role. But if family history is a precedent, Sam Walton has several years left on the team. His father, Thomas, died last year at 93, occasioning a rare, brief bout of depression in Walton. He hung his father's cane on the wall in his office.

Walton emerged from his slump with his optimism intact. He found that pessimism didn't pay in 1983, when he was so convinced that his company was going to have a disappointing year that he promised Wal-Mart employees he would do the hula on Wall Street if they surpassed his meager expectations. Things turned out better than he expected—and Walton did his dance in a grass skirt. Chances are, he will not make that kind of mistake again. As Sam Walton likes to say, it's a big sky out there.

Making It Unique

The seed was planted when Harvey Russack first started selling recycled denim jeans on a downtown street corner in the late Sixties. Now, the 14-year-old Unique Clothing Warehouse has blossomed into an $8 million to $10 million specialty store that is plugged into a brand new group of customers.

What makes its success story a benchmark in retailing is that it acknowledges and caters to a generation nurtured on the visual rock boom. Rock video, with its succession of graphic images and rock stars whose personae are as closely identified with their clothes as with their music—often more so—has been the catalyst for this generation.

Whereas plenty of baby boomers are Madonna fans, most of them are too conservative to rush out and dress up like her. Not so the current crop of teenagers who can't wait to get decked out in the latest look. And so, for the first time since the Sixties, there is a recognizable generation gap in the way people dress.

Unique keeps on top of this, says head buyer Elyse Adams, by watching what the kids in the street wear and listening to what its customers say. "They know what they want before SA does. For instance, when a new video airs on MTV, you can feel the effects immediately. People come in asking for black lace corsets, like Madonna, or whatever they want. We have a paper and pencil by the time clock and encourage our employees to write down what they ask for," says Adams.

The 13-year-old who wants to look like Cyndi Lauper one month and Madonna the next requires a range of fashion merchandise, and she can find it at Unique. Moreover, she can afford to. Almost nothing at Unique costs more than $50, and the average price range is $9.99 to $29.99 for a pair of pants or $9.99 to $14.99 for a shirt. The very hottest fad, such as the Edie Sedgwick silver wig, is stocked well before it hits the mainstream market. The first day that Unique placed the Sedgwick wigs on the floor, they sold out of an initial 24-piece order. The store has been selling Hawaiian print shorts since December, regularly moving out about 100 pieces a week.

When you walk into Unique's main store at 726 Broadway, it does look reminiscent of a warehouse, chock full of such diverse items as pith helmets, prom dresses—the latest version made from plastic garbage bags—chewing gum and fruit bracelets, paper leis and brightly dyed athletic apparel. Rock music blares from an advanced 32-speaker sound system that rivals that of many nightclubs. The average age of the sales staff is 20, while the age range of the primary group of customers is 13 to 25.

Although at first glance the merchandise seems to be unrelated, it is actually sorted into colorful themes on the wide-open selling floor. The notable lack of departments or classifications favored by traditional stores allows red brassieres to be sold next to cotton trousers, and cocktail dresses to hang on the rack next to pajamas.

This uninhibited mix epitomizes the way a customer might assemble a look or select an item. The store supports no designer names or dictates, preferring to interpret its own version of hot fashion by mixing trendy items and

Source: *Women's Wear Daily,* June 10, 1985. Reprinted with permission.

looks. A Unique label is sewn into almost everything the store sells. Although Adams won't reveal her resources, which number over a thousand, she says many of them are far from SA or any other traditional market.

Russack, who has overseen dramatic merchandise changes in his store during the last decade and a half—from vintage clothing to reworked denim—took on a business partner, Richard Wolland, three years ago. Wolland's previous retail experience was as store manager for Korvettes. He and Russack delegate most of the creative authority to the small, young staff led by Adams.

The Unique operation includes three stores: the main store at 726 Broadway, which is the newest and the fastest paced; the original store at 718 Broadway, about five feet away, which is connected to the third unit, a men's store. Russack and Wolland plan to add 15,000 square feet to the 11,000-square-foot new store by 1986 and see the possibility of doubling volume.

The most immediate merchandising story is featured in the floor-to-ceiling front windows of the new store, which might reflect, for example, what Adams calls "the black and white Sixties story"—a loosely translated melange of miniskirts, geometric print dresses, stirrup pants, vinyl hotpants and midriff tops. A black sleeveless turtleneck dress with round cutouts at the waist at $39.99 and another sleeveless version with a white stripe down the front at $30.99 sold out, at 12 units each, in one day. "The whole Sixties Twiggy thing came in and flew out," Adams says.

The lifespan of any front window story is about one week, including weekends. What hasn't sold is rotated to the inner racks and, soon after, is marked down. "If something isn't moving, we put in on sale even if it is in season. We don't like to wait," says Adams. In the meantime, shipments are received and put out on the floor daily to fill the voracious appetites of two separate stores that repeat very little merchandise except best-selling items.

The Unique basics are a large collection of perennial bestsellers, such as T-shirts, sweats and jeans, garment-dyed in a wide variety of bright colors. Russak started dyeing and overdyeing garments more than 10 years ago and even briefly wholesaled the inexpensive sportswear to Macy's New York and other large department stores.

Now, Adams and staff are always looking for a new twist, such as dyeing huge quantities of men's boxer shorts when the men's underwear trend hit, or overdyeing batches of paisley print pajamas. The strength of this grouping is evident in the sales tally of athletic T-shirts in May—6,000 in four weeks.

Unique's reaction to trends is quicker than a traditional specialty store, partially because there is a minimum of bureaucracy. The store's policy is to see virtually "everyone who knocks on our door with merchandise," Adams says.

As much to support local artists as to make a profit, Russack has allocated an "artwear" department stocked with garments made by local artists and sold on a consignment basis.

With expansion, Russack and company are thinking about adding housewares, more accessories, toys and more shoes. But the emphasis of the store will remain on fashion.

In the end, says Russack, "We go by what we like. The Unique style is something that makes avant-garde accessible. I want Unique to be synonymous with change."

There is only one change, perhaps, that puzzles Russack. "I remember when we carried only natural fibers. Synthetics were taboo. Now," he says, "people can't get enough of doubleknit polyester."

Endnotes

1. Leon Harris, *The Merchant Princes*. New York: Harper & Row, 1979.
2. *Ibid.*
3. Malcolm McNair and Eleanor May, "The Next Revolution of the Retailing Wheel," *Harvard Business Review*, September–October 1978.
4. "The Super Specialists," *Stores Magazine,* August 1986.
5. *Ibid.*
6. *Merchants to the Millions.* Sears Roebuck & Co. Publication Service, Department 703, Chicago, Ill.
7. Claudia B. Kidwell and Margaret C. Christman, *Suiting Everyone: The Democratization of Clothing in America,* published for the National Museum of History and Technology by the Smithsonian Institution Press, Washington, D.C., 1974, p. 62.
8. "Mail Order: Continuing Its Maturation, Competitiveness," *Direct Marketing,* July 1986.
9. "Competition Heating Up in Mail Order Fashions," *Mass Marketing,* August 26, 1986.
10. Telephone Interview with Mr. Jim Podany, Sears Roebuck & Co., July 7, 1986.
11. "Mail Order," *Direct Marketing.*
12. "The Rustic Pitch Pays Off in Catalog Sales for L. L. Bean," *U.S. News and World Report,* September 1985.
13. "Competition Heating Up in Mail Order Fashion," *Daily News Record,* August 26, 1985.
14. Sam Feinberg, "From Where I Sit," *Women's Wear Daily,* June 20, 1985.
15. 1985 Annual Reports.
16. "Benetton: Manufacturing Group Takes New Slant on Retailing," *Daily News Record,* May 24, 1985.
17. "Franchising," *Women's Wear Daily,* December 11, 1985.
18. "Fashioning a New Breed of Boutiques," *Women's Wear Daily,* January 13, 1986.
19. *Ibid.*
20. *Ibid.*
21. *The American Way,* December 1984; and Sam Feinberg, "From Where I Sit," *Women's Wear Daily.* July 16, 1985.
22. Annual reports to stockholders.
23. "Shopping at the Club," *Fortune,* December 24, 1985.
24. Editorial, *Stores Magazine,* September 1985, p. 6.
25. McNair and May, "The Next Revolution of the Retailing Wheel," *Harvard Business Review.*
26. "The Man Who Computerized Bargain Hunting," *Fortune,* July 9, 1984.

27. "Direct Marketing Goes Electronic," *Sales and Marketing Magazine,* June 14, 1985.
28. Sam Feinberg, "From Where I Sit," *Women's Wear Daily,* September 7, 1984.

Selected Bibliography

Allen, Randy L. *Bottom Line Issues in Retailing.* New York: Chilton Book Co., 1985.

Barmash, Isadore. *For the Good of the Company.* New York: Grosset and Dunlop, 1976.

Brough, James. *The Woolworths.* New York: McGraw-Hill, 1982.

Case, Margaret. *And the Price Is Right.* Cleveland: World, 1958.

Fairchild's Financial Manual of Retail Stores. New York: Fairchild Publications, published annually.

Ferkauf, Eugene. *Going into Business, How to Do It, by the Man Who Did It.* New York: Penfield Press, 1977.

Gold, Annalee. *How to Sell Fashion,* 2nd ed. New York: Fairchild Publications, 1978.

Graham, John W. and Susan K. *Selling; Selling by Mail; Direct Response Marketing for Small Business.* New York: Scribner & Sons, 1985.

Guberman, Reuben. *Handbook of Retail Promotion Ideas.* Reading, Mass.: Addison-Wesley, 1981.

Harris, Leon. *Merchant Princes.* New York: Harper & Row, 1979.

Hartley, Robert F. *Retailing: Challenge and Opportunity,* 2nd ed. Boston: Houghton Mifflin, 1980.

Herndon, Booton. *Satisfaction Guaranteed.* New York: McGraw-Hill, 1972.

Horchow, Roger. *Elephants in Your Mailbox.* New York: Times Books, 1980.

Kowinski, William S. *The Malling of America.* New York: Wm. Morrow Publishers, 1985.

Kroc, Ray. *Grinding It Out, the Making of McDonald's.* Chicago: Henry Regnery Co., 1977.

Mahoney, Tom and Leonard Sloane. *The Great Merchants,* 2nd ed. New York: Harper & Row, 1974.

Marcus, Stanley. *His and Hers: The Fantasy World of the Neiman Marcus Catalog.* New York: Viking Press, 1982.

Marcus, Stanley. *Minding the Store.* Boston: Little, Brown, 1974.

Marcus, Stanley. *Quest for the Best.* New York: Viking Press, 1979.

McCree, Cree. *Flea Market America: A Bargain Hunter's Guide.* Santa Fe: Muir, 1983.

National Retail Merchants Association. *The Buyers Manual.* New York: NRMA, 1979.

Nystrom, Paul H. *Fashion Merchandising*. New York: Ronald Press, 1932.

Ostrow, Rona and Sweetman R. Smith, *The Dictionary of Retailing*. New York: Fairchild Publications, 1985.

Pegler, Martin. *The Language of Store Planning and Display*. New York: Fairchild Publications, 1982.

Peters, Tom and Nancy Austin. *A Passion for Excellence: The Leadership Difference*. New York: Random House, 1985.

Segal, Marvin. *From Rags to Riches: Success in Apparel Retailing*. New York: John Wiley & Sons, 1982.

Stevens, Mark. *Like No Other Store in the World: The Inside Story of Bloomingdale's*. New York: Thomas Y. Crowell, 1979.

Stone, Elaine and Jean A. Samples. *Fashion Merchandising*, 4th ed. New York: McGraw-Hill, 1985.

Stutz, Geraldine. *Designing to Sell: A Complete Guide to Retail Store Planning and Design*. New York: McGraw-Hill, 1985.

Weil, Gordon L. *Sears, Roebuck, U.S.A.* New York: Stein & Day, 1977.

Trade Associations

Direct Selling Association, 1730 M Street N.W., Washington, D.C. 20036.

International Council of Shopping Centers, Inc., 665 Fifth Avenue, New York, N.Y. 10022.

Men's Retailers Association, 2011 Eye Street, N.W., Washington, D.C. 20006.

Menswear Retailers of America, 390 National Press Building, Washington, D.C. 20045.

National Mass Retailing Institute, 570 Seventh Avenue, New York, N.Y. 10018.

National Retail Merchants Association, 100 West 31st Street, New York, N.Y. 10001.

Trade Publications

Chain Store Age, 425 Park Avenue, New York, N.Y. 10022.

Department Store Guide, Inc., 425 Park Avenue, New York, N.Y. 10022.

Discount Merchandiser, 641 Lexington Avenue, New York, N.Y. 10022.

Discount Store News, 425 Park Avenue, New York, N.Y. 10022.

Franchising Today, 3106 Diablo Avenue, Haywood, Calif. 94545.

Franchising World, 1025 Connecticut Avenue N.W., Washington, D.C. 20036.

Merchandising, 1515 Broadway, New York, N.Y. 10017.

Retail Week, 370 Lexington Avenue, New York, N.Y. 10022.

Stores Magazine, 100 West 31st Street, New York, N.Y. 10001.

Women's Wear Daily, 7 East 12th Street, New York, N.Y. 10003.

CHAPTER REVIEW AND LEARNING ACTIVITIES ....

Key Words and Concepts

Define, identify, or briefly explain the following:

Apparel specialty chain
Boutique
Branch store
Catalog retailing
Catalog showroom
Chain store retailer
Department store
Direct seller
Discounter
Electronic retailing
Factory outlet
Flea market
Franchisee
Franchising
Franchisor
General merchandise retailer

Mail-order house
Marketing mix
Mom-and-pop store
National brand
Off-price retailer
Party plan
Private label
Product developer
Retailer
Shopping center
Shopping mall
Specialty store
Store ownership group
Supermarket
Warehouse club

Review Questions on Chapter Highlights

1. In what types of retail establishment do you prefer to shop and why? What types do you avoid and why?
2. Describe the targeted customer of the typical department store.
3. What is a store ownership group? Name the leading ownership groups in order of their sales volume and cite examples of their members.
4. What are the competitive advantages of apparel specialty stores as compared to department stores?
5. Compare the operations of a department store and its branches with chain store operations. How are they similar and how do they differ?
6. Explain the competitive strengths of specialized apparel chains and illustrate them from the text and the reading entitled "Limited Is a Clothing Retailer on the Move" at the end of this chapter.
7. Why is mail-order retailing so important today? Name different types of retailers who are in the mail-order business. Which type do you and your family prefer to buy from and why?
8. How can off-price retailers like Marshalls undersell conventionally priced retailers? What are their sources of supply?

9. How are large department and specialty stores meeting the competition of the underselling retailers?
10. How have shopping centers changed in the past two decades and why?
11. What is your opinion about the future importance of apparel selling by electronic retailers, price club, catalog showrooms, and others. Why?
12. Name the different types of retailers, give the approximate date of their emergence, and explain the social and economic factors that led to their development.
13. List the different types of retailing and explain the distinctive characteristics of each. Cite an example of each type in your own community.
14. Name and identify the different types of retailers featured in this chapter's readings.

Applications for Research and Discussion

1. Research your community for examples of franchised operations. List their names and explain why you believe they are franchises. Explain what a franchised operation is and how the entrepreneur becomes a franchisee. Would this be an interesting career for you personally? Why or why not?
2. Do a survey of two or more shopping centers/malls that are accessible to your community. Name and categorize the different types of retailing establishments in one of them. What are the similarities and differences between the two centers?
3. Shop several large department stores, specialty stores, and chains to find privately labeled apparel and accessories and answer the following:
(a) What is meant by a private label and how does it differ from a national brand?
(b) What private label names are being used by these stores?
(c) Compare the price, styling, quality, and fit of these private labels to national brand and designer-name goods. Do you think the private label developments are hurting the sale of national brand and designer names and why or why not?

10

AUXILIARY FASHION ENTERPRISES

Of vital importance in the fashion industry are the services of a variety of independently operated auxiliary enterprises that act as advisers, sources of information, and propagators of fashion news. Some of these enterprises devote their full energies to observing and analyzing the fashion scene, and assist producers and retailers in clarifying their own thinking about it. Others aid by getting a coherent fashion message to the consuming public, thus giving impetus to trends that appear to be in the making. Among these fashion business auxiliaries are fashion information and advisory services, the news media, fashion video producers, advertising and publicity specialists, resident buying offices, and others.

This chapter discusses such enterprises, how they function, and the part they play in the fashion business. The readings that follow the text are concerned with the activities of companies that operate in this segment of the fashion business.

FASHION INFORMATION AND ADVISORY SERVICES

Although all fashion producers and retailers of any size have experts of their own within their firms, many use outside specialized sources of fashion information against which to check their own analyses and conclusions.

Fashion Information Services

Beginning in the late 1960s and growing in importance ever since then, a number of comprehensive **fashion information services** have developed. Their clients are worldwide and include fiber companies, textile producers, producers of men's, women's, and children's wear, retailers, buying offices, and accessories and cosmetics companies. So all-pervading is the influence of fashion, however, that their clients also include some producers of small appliances; cars, home furnishings, and other consumer products.

REPORTS FROM IM INTERNATIONAL

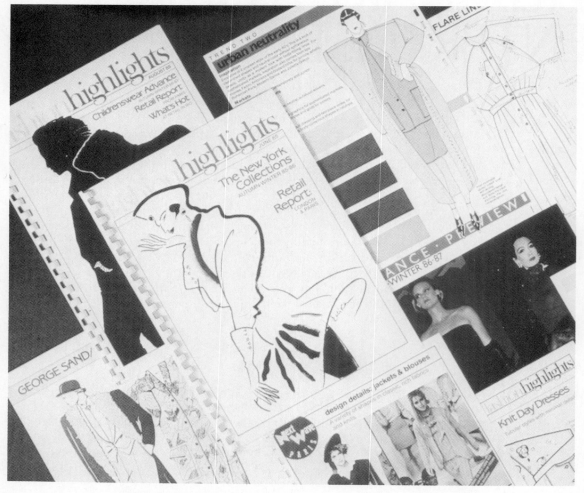

Source: Courtesy of IM International Publishing/Fashion Forecasters.

In a business environment where time and timing are ever more important, these services offer specific, timely, concise, and complete worldwide information, often tailored to each client's specific needs.

The number of firms offering these services is constantly increasing, but the following are among the most important:

- IM International, headquartered in London and New York. Their reports include a semiannual color report for fabrics and yarns, with predictions 18 months in advance of the season: a monthly action report, covering all important world markets and featuring forecasts on color, fabric, and silhouette; a monthly shopping sketch book, covering retail fashions in New York, London, Paris, Milan, and Los Angeles.

- Nigel French, headquartered in London. Their fabric reports cover the major fabric seasons, spring/summer and fall/winter, including the Interstoff and American fabric showings. They also issue separate color and knitwear brochures, report on New York and European designer collections, and present major season styling issues.
- The Fashion Service, known as TFS, the reports of which cover fashion information from all over the world. Their specific reports are covered in a reading in this chapter.
- Here and There, the reports of which cover U.S. ready-to-wear, couture collections, Japanese Pret collections, Italian and French knitwear shows, fabric fairs (Interstoff, Ideacomo, Premier Vision-Prato), and a special feature that translates high fashion looks for mass markets.
- Promostyl, which began as a children's wear service in 1967, now has offices or agents in 23 cities worldwide, and publishes 31 different handbooks annually. More information on this company will be found in a reading at the end of this chapter.

Other fashion information services include Pat Tunsky, Color Box, and Fashion Works, Inc. And the list grows from year to year!

Consultants

A **fashion consultant** is an independent individual or firm hired by fashion producers and/or retailers to assist them in some phase of their fashion operation. Probably the oldest still in existence is **Tobé Associates,** founded in 1927 by Mrs. Tobé to service retailers. The firm sends to its paying clients a multipage, illustrated weekly brochure that contains information on current and coming trends illustrated by specific style numbers with the names of the producers and the wholesale prices. As Tobé herself once described the function of her consulting firm,

We are the reporters and interpreters of the fashion world speaking to the fashion-makers and the fashion sellers. . . . Our job is to tell the makers what the sellers are doing and vice versa. Most of all, we interpret and evaluate for each what is happening to fashion itself. . . . We make it our business to stay abreast of those economic, social, and art trends which I maintain are the great formative currents of fashion. . . . From all these we try to pick the significant trends that will change our lives, and hence our fashions. . . . We keep an eye on what those in the fashion vanguard are wearing and doing and seeing. This not only means reporting on what smart people wear. . . . It also means keeping abreast of what plays, films, and TV presentations they are seeing, which are successful, where they travel, and what books they read. . . . All of this information flows into our offices, where it is digested, sorted out, evaluated, and then disseminated through a weekly report. . . . Our clients—department stores throughout America, specialty stores in Europe, a wool manufacturer in Finland, the Export Institute in Israel—they can all shop the Fifth Avenue stores, the Paris showings, the Seventh Avenue showings, without budging from their desks. They can keep track of resort life without going to Monaco or Florida or the Caribbean. They can read about the fads, as well as the foundations of fashion, without spending much time or effort in research.

So it is our business as a whole to interpret the current scene to the makers and sellers of fashion wares.[1]

Another example of a retail consultant is Merchandising Motivation, Inc. (MMI), which is operated on a similar but smaller scale. There are also many other consulting firms, usually headed by former fashion practitioners, whose services are available, for a fee, to retailers or producers, or both. These firms usually deal with specific areas of the fashion industry, such as accessories, fibers, fabrics, children's wear, and menswear.

RESIDENT BUYING OFFICES: MARKET REPRESENTATIVES

The **resident buying office** is almost entirely a twentieth-century phenomenon. It has gone through cycles that faithfully reflect the ups and downs in the fortunes of retailers and manufacturers. It performs a paid service for the retailer in helping him locate desirable goods in the market; it performs an equally important but unpaid service for manufacturers by bringing their merchandise to the attention of retailers when it meets their needs and standards.

Originally, almost every large store outside New York City was affiliated with an independent buying office, either serving that store alone or serving many noncompeting retailers. Buying office functions included reporting market information, acting as representative of its client stores, and performing related services for its retail clients. Today, as it did then, the buying office keeps stores informed of fashion, price, and supply developments, acting as eyes and ears for the client stores. Buying activities were and still are initiated by the store buyers; the office supplements but does not replace the store staff. The functions of the buying office have expanded over the years, reflecting changes in retail needs and in fashion markets, and they continue to change with the times.

Types of Resident Offices

Resident buying offices fall into two major categories: (1) those that are independently owned enterprises and are paid fees by the stores they serve; and (2) those that are store owned or corporate owned.

INDEPENDENTLY OWNED OR FEE OFFICES

Independently owned offices, also known as salaried or **fee offices,** are run as private enterprises. Member or subscribing stores pay a yearly fee, usually based on a percentage of annual sales volume. Most such offices concentrate on serving specialty stores that carry all or most types of apparel and accessories. Others specialize in such narrow categories as large, petite, or tall sizes, bridal wear, maternity wear, junior wear, off-price apparel, fabrics, accessories, men's and boys' wear, or home furnishings. A few concentrate on filling the needs of small department stores, representing them in all the markets of interest to these clients.

Among the independently owned offices currently in business are the following, shown with the date when each was established:

- Felix Lilienthal & Co., 1909
- Van Buren–Neiman Associates, 1910
- Anstandig, Blitstein and Zillinson, 1917
- Loweth-National Buying Service, 1927
- Jack Braunstein, 1932
- Carr Buying Office, 1933
- Jack D. Barzilay, 1935
- Youth Fashion Guild–Fashion Guild Corp., 1945
- IRS (Independent Retailers Syndicate), 1946
- Certified Buying Service, 1949
- Betty Cohn, 1950
- Steinberg-Kass, 1951
- Atlas Buying Corp., 1957

Those listed here are by no means identical in the markets they service. Atlas, for example, specializes in representing discount stores owned by department store chains. Youth Fashion Guild–Fashion Guild Corp. serves children's stores. Van Buren–Neiman Associates has as their clients primarily large, higher-priced apparel specialty stores. All of these offices have their headquarters in New York City. Many more offices, of course, are operating in the field. Still others have come and gone over the years, or have merged with others.

One independent office, Nurik & Goldberg, is unusual in that it is not paid by the stores it serves. Instead, manufacturers pay the office a commission based on the amount of orders placed. Stores using this service are generally small and distributed throughout the United States.

Mortality rates among independent buying offices tend to be high, even though, as our list shows, some have prospered over more than half a century. Reasons for failure include the following: (1) failure to provide stores with sufficient advice on markets and marketing strategy; (2) emphasis on catalog preparation and other revenue-producing services as an alternative to raising fees, and to the detriment of effective market coverage; (3) lessened need for merchants to visit the New York market because of the growth of regional markets.

STORE-OWNED OFFICES: COOPERATIVE OFFICES

Unlike the privately owned, profit-oriented fee offices, the resident offices that are store-owned are controlled and supported by the stores they serve. Their major objectives are to provide market expertise and whatever additional services the supporting stores require to assist them in operating profitably.

A **cooperative office** is one owned and maintained by a group of stores that it serves exclusively. This type of office is also known as an *associated office*. Membership in the store group is by invitation only, and all the participants in such groups are major retailers within their respective areas.

One of the major and best known of such offices is the Associated Merchandising Corporation (AMC), founded in 1918 by Filene's of Boston, F. & R. Lazarus of Columbus, Ohio, J. L. Hudson of Detroit, and Rike's of Dayton. Other stores, such as Abraham & Straus of Brooklyn, Bloomingdale's of New York, Shillito's of Cincinnati, Foley's of Houston, Sanger-Harris of Dallas, and Burdine's of Miami, soon joined. Membership grew, attracting foreign as well as U.S. stores. In October 1984, however, the Federated Department Stores ceased using the AMC's domestic service in favor of its own corporate office. Remaining AMC stores include Carson Pirie Scott, Higbee's, Hudson's Bay Company, Hutzler's, Strawbridge & Clothier, Woodward & Lothrop, Brandeis, Liberty House, Prange's, Godchaux/Maison Blanche, the Parisian, Boscov's, and Snyder's of Louisville, Kentucky. It is estimated that the total retail sales volume of AMC stores, excluding Federated, is $6 billion.[2]

The AMC considers itself "a retail marketing firm, specializing in worldwide marketing research." It does not use the term *buyer* to describe its

MEMBERS OF FREDERICK ATKINS INC., A COOPERATIVE BUYING OFFICE

frederick atkins inc.
member stores

ADAM, MELDRUM & ANDERSON CO., INC.	Buffalo, New York
B. ALTMAN & CO.	New York, New York
P. A. BERGNER & CO.	Milwaukee, Wisconsin
BUFFUMS	Long Beach, California
CARLISLE'S	Ashtabula, Ohio
T. A. CHAPMAN COMPANY	Milwaukee, Wisconsin
D & L STORES—WEATHERVANE	New Britain, Connecticut
DILLARD'S—LITTLE ROCK	Little Rock, Arkansas
DILLARD'S—FORT WORTH	Fort Worth, Texas
DILLARD'S—SAN ANTONIO	San Antonio, Texas
DILLARD'S—DIAMOND'S	Tempe, Arizona
DILLARD'S—ST. LOUIS	St. Louis, Missouri
THE ELDER-BEERMAN STORES CORP.	Dayton, Ohio
M. EPSTEIN, INC.	Morristown, New Jersey
GOTTSCHALK'S	Fresno, California
S. GRUMBACHER & SON	York, Pennsylvania
HARRIS	San Bernardino, California
HERBERGER'S	St. Cloud, Minnesota
HESS'S DEPARTMENT STORES, INC.	Allentown, Pennsylvania
D. H. HOLMES CO., LTD.	New Orleans, Louisiana
IVEY'S—CAROLINA	Charlotte, North Carolina
IVEY'S—FLORIDA	Orlando, Florida
HOWLAND/STEINBACH/HOCHSCHILD'S	White Plains, New York
LOVEMANS	Chattanooga, Tennessee
MARSHALL FIELD'S	Chicago, Illinois

June 1986

McCURDY & COMPANY, INC.	Rochester, New York
McRAE'S	Jackson, Mississippi
MILLER & PAINE	Lincoln, Nebraska
PALAIS ROYAL	Houston, Texas
W. S. PEEBLES & CO., INC.	South Hill, Virginia
PIZITZ	Birmingham, Alabama
PORTEOUS MITCHELL & BRAUN CO.	Portland, Maine
PROFFITT'S	Alcoa, Tennessee
ALBERT STEIGER, INC.	Springfield, Massachusetts
PAUL STEKETEE & SONS	Grand Rapids, Michigan
STONE & THOMAS	Wheeling, West Virginia
THIMBLES	New York, New York
YOUNKERS, INC.	Des Moines, Iowa
ZCMI	Salt Lake City, Utah

frederick atkins inc.
associate member stores

GONZALEZ PADIN CO., INC.	San Juan, Puerto Rico
ISETAN CO., LTD.	Tokyo, Japan
DAVID JONES, LTD.	Sydney, Australia
KARSTADT	Essen, Germany
TRIMINGHAM BROTHERS, LTD.	Hamilton, Bermuda

frederick atkins international
overseas offices commissionaires
telex ITT-421026 cable address atkinsinta

AUSTRIA, Vienna	J. Urban
BELGIUM, Brussels	F. Vervoort Buying Agency
BRAZIL, Rio de Janeiro	Armstrong Industries, Ltd.
DENMARK, Copenhagen	Kjellbergs Successors
ENGLAND, London	Ardil, Ltd.
FRANCE, Paris	E. Boas S.A.R.L.
GERMANY, Pforzheim	Henkel & Grosse
GREECE, Athens	Marketing, Inc.
HOLLAND, Amsterdam	G.A. Van de Pol
HONG KONG, Kowloon	William E. Connor (H.K.) Ltd.
INDIA, New Delhi	Ambiance India Private Ltd.
ISRAEL, Tel Aviv	Eran Enat Buying Office
ITALY, Florence	G.B. Giorgini, S.A.S.
JAPAN, Tokyo, Nagoya, Osaka	William E. Connor, Inc.
KOREA, Seoul	Regis Gard, Ltd.
PAKISTAN, Karachi	Possibilities Trading
PHILIPPINES, Manila	Southgate (H.K.) Ltd.
PEOPLE'S REPUBLIC OF CHINA	William E. Connor (H.K.) Ltd.
PORTUGAL, Lisbon, Oporto	Graham Limitada
SINGAPORE	William E. Connor (H.K.) Ltd.
SPAIN, Madrid	Cidon, S L
SRI LANKA, Colombo	Possibilities Trading
SWITZERLAND, Zurich	Rene E. Buser Buying Office
TAIWAN, Taipei	Eastwall Alliance (China Ltd.)
THAILAND, Bangkok	Export Development Corp.
URUGUAY, Montevideo	Carlos Hausner

Source: Reprinted with permission of Frederick Atkins Inc.

market representatives; they have such titles as product managers, merchandise analysts, and similar designations.

AMC member stores nowadays are offered a choice of four membership categories:

- Shareholder independents get domestic product development and overseas services.
- Federated Stores still receive product development and overseas services, but no domestic representation.
- Subscribers to Overseas Merchandising Services are nonshareholding mass-merchandising companies, such as Bradlee's, Gold Circle Stores, Mervyn's, Target Stores, and Jamesway.
- Overseas shareholder stores include such retailers as Harrod's, Galeries Lafayette, Matsuzakaya of Japan and Hong Kong, Nordiska of Sweden, and Truworth of South Africa, among others.

The other major cooperative buying office is Frederick Atkins, Inc., which describes itself as an "international research and merchandising organization, jointly owned by 45 independent department store groups in the

United States and nine major retailers outside of the United States who are associate members. The combined total annual sales volume of the member stores in the United States only is well over four billion dollars. The Atkins office is headquartered in New York City, where it occupies 110,000 square feet on four floors. The office is organized like a department store, with three main divisions: merchandising, operations, and finance. On the staff of more than 400 people are the counterparts of every major executive in a store."[3]

Some of the member stores at Atkins are Adam, Meldrum, and Anderson of Buffalo; B. Altman of New York, T. A. Chapman, Elder-Beerman, Gotts-chalk's, D. H. Holmes, Dillard's, Marshall Fields, McCurdy's, Charles A. Stevens, Younker's, Loveman's, Hess Brothers, Milwaukee Boston Store, and ZCMI. Overseas members include Isetan, Japan; David Jones, Australia; Trimingham, Bermuda. And many other domestic and foreign stores.

CORPORATE OFFICES

Another very important type of buying office is the **corporate office,** which is owned and financed by a store ownership group and serves only the stores of that group. Unlike the homogeneous mix of stores served by cooperative offices, some of the store ownership groups consist of both large and small stores. Examples are Federated Department Stores, May Department Stores, Allied Stores, Carter-Hawley-Hale, R. H. Macy & Co., Associated Dry Goods Corp., Mercantile Stores, T. Eaton, Belk Stores, and BATUS Retail. In the case of each of these corporate offices, the combined volume of the stores it represents makes it a very important factor in the marketplace.

The large cooperative and corporate buying offices may also maintain branch offices in other U.S. market centers, and in many foreign countries to assist their stores in import buying. For example, AMC has 23 foreign branch offices in cities such as Paris, Florence, Tel Aviv, Beirut, and Hong Kong, among others, as well as branch offices in Los Angeles and Washington, D.C. In addition, they use the services of commissionaires in foreign countries. Frederick Atkins has commissionaires in 27 European, Asian, and South American cities, to "help to develop and maintain foreign resource relationships, assist the office and store personnel on overseas trips, set up meetings, and follow through on orders after the buyers have left."[4]

Fashion Merchandising Services Provided

The degree, extent, and quality of services vary from one office to another, depending on its financial capabilities and the needs of its member stores. Essentially, however, they all serve the same function—to make available to their members complete and accurate merchandise information from all parts of the world. The president of Van Buren–Neiman, a major buying office, has

EXAMPLE OF A RESIDENT BUYING OFFICE BULLETIN

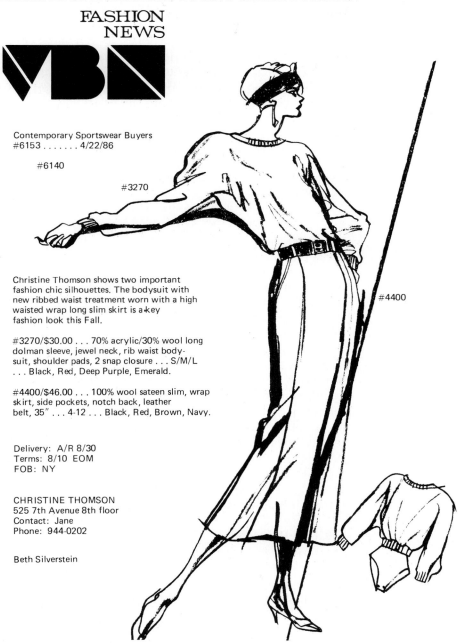

FASHION NEWS

VBN

Contemporary Sportswear Buyers
#6153 . . . . 4/22/86

#6140

#3270

Christine Thomson shows two important
fashion chic silhouettes. The bodysuit with
new ribbed waist treatment worn with a high
waisted wrap long slim skirt is a key
fashion look this Fall.

#3270/$30.00 . . . 70% acrylic/30% wool long
dolman sleeve, jewel neck, rib waist bodysuit, shoulder pads, 2 snap closure . . . S/M/L
. . . Black, Red, Deep Purple, Emerald.

#4400/$46.00 . . . 100% wool sateen slim, wrap
skirt, side pockets, notch back, leather
belt, 35" . . . 4-12 . . . Black, Red, Brown, Navy.

#4400

Delivery: A/R 8/30
Terms: 8/10 EOM
FOB: NY

CHRISTINE THOMSON
525 7th Avenue 8th floor
Contact: Jane
Phone: 944-0202

Beth Silverstein

Source: Van-Buren-Neiman Associates buying office. Reprinted with permission.

said: "The term buying office is an anachronism. Our office is a market researcher and consultant—an additional service tool, not a substitute for the stores we represent."[5]

MARKET INFORMATION.   Prior to each major selling season, market representatives cover the segments of the wholesale markets for which they are responsible and present written surveys to their member stores. These reports cover market conditions in general and analyze specific fashion classifications by trend, look, price lines, and resources. In addition, many offices hold semiannual fashion clinics or meetings in which they orally present this information and show samples. During the season, news bulletins go out continually, reporting new items, best sellers, price changes, fashion developments, supply conditions, important new resources, and/or other developments.

BUYING SERVICES.   When buyers of member stores are in the market themselves, the market representatives act as advisers and time savers by setting up appointments, recommending important suppliers, and sometimes accompanying them into the wholesale markets. When the store buyers return home, the office representative will, if requested, follow up on shipments of orders that store buyers have placed. During the season, if asked to do so by store buyers, they will place reorders and fill-in orders to ensure faster delivery. In addition, they may send out bulletins with suggested orders attached, to be confirmed by the store buyer. Sometimes store buyers may allocate a small portion of their available open-to-buy to their market representatives to be used at the latter's discretion for an important new fashion item. Some store buyers send copies of their orders to their resident offices to follow up on delivery. It must be emphasized again, however, that the role of a market representative is to service store buyers—not to substitute for or replace them. They do not have the "power to buy" except when given permission by the store to do so. All of the purchasing done by market representatives is ordered under the name of the member store and delivered to and paid for by that store. This procedure prevails in resident offices of all types—fee, associated, or corporate.

GROUP PURCHASING, PRIVATE LABEL, AND IMPORT PROGRAMS.   A **group purchase** is an order placed at the same time by a group of stores for the identical merchandise from the same supplier. Through domestic or foreign group purchases, all participants can benefit from the various advantages of large-quantity purchases: lower than regular prices, exclusive rights to the merchandise purchased, production of an item that is not otherwise available, a lower-priced "knock-off" of a fast-selling higher-priced style in which the buyers have confidence, the production of merchandise made to the exact specifications of the purchasing group, merchandise for a group mailing piece like a Christmas catalog, merchandise for a private label group program, or a combination of these advantages.

Many resident offices—both independent and store-owned—organize, coordinate, and implement such group buying activities for their members. However, such group purchasing programs must be supported by a sufficient number of stores to make them feasible. In addition, the merchandise selected for purchase must be agreed upon by, at the very least, a committee of the participating store buyers.

The private label program and philosophy of the AMC, for example, is explained by James L. Knabe, senior vice-president of merchandising, fashion, and research, thus: "[It is based on] a specialty store approach as well as department store needs, and we have brought in outside designers to develop private label programs in both soft and hard lines. Our idea is to create our own brands to supplement market offerings, not to replace them. Retailers have to be very careful to maintain the private label-to-brand balance, and yet to help identify the trends and market them in ways similar to the Limited and Esprit."[6]

In the same field, Frederick Atkins has a staff of 14 highly skilled, experienced buyers called **product developers,** whose single responsibility is to develop program merchandise, made to exact specifications, exclusively for member stores.[7] The sourcing for all these private-label goods is worldwide.

CENTRALIZED MERCHANDISING. Although declining in importance, some fee offices continue *centralized buying* of budget-priced ready-to-wear and accessories. This means that a market representative of the office makes the selection of styles for each store's stock within the framework of a budget allotment set by that participating store. The office orders the merchandise, and, guided by sales and stock reports from the store, reorders some styles and discontinues or replaces others. With the experience of many stores to draw on, the office has a national picture of fashion trends to guide its selections.

SALES PROMOTION. In addition to their buying activities, resident buying offices maintain departments that prepare catalogs and other direct mailing pieces for use by their member stores. Some offices also prepare advertising mats that suggest layouts and copy, supply stores with illustrated suggestions for visual merchandising, and provide a variety of other sales promotion aids. In addition, they prepare visual merchandise aids, develop marketing techniques, and keep member stores advised of emerging media and technology.

EXCHANGE OF INFORMATION. The exchange of merchandise information is a service provided by all types of offices. However, cooperative and corporate offices also consolidate merchandising, operating, and financial figures sent to them by their members and report these cumulative figures back to the stores in a form that enables those participating to compare their operations.

FASHION IN THE NEWS MEDIA ....

Fashion is news, and the news media cover it, both in editorial treatments and in paid advertising messages. This statement applies not only to newspapers and magazines but also to broadcast media. Thus, a vital means of communication between the industry and the consumer, and between related parts of the industry, is activated in the daily newspapers, news magazines women's and men's magazines, specialized fashion publications, those segments of the trade press that affect the fashion business, radio, and television. The impact is enormous.

Fashion Magazines

Fashion magazines, whose major activity is to report and interpret fashion news to the consumer, together with additional features for balanced reading fare, have been functioning in this country for more than a century. *Godey's Lady's Book,* which was started in 1830, carried pictures of the latest fashions, gave advice on fabrics, contained other helpful hints, and, of course, included advertising. Its distinguished editor, Sara Josepha Hale, gave early proof that a woman could have a successful career in the business world even in the days of hoopskirts and cinched waists. Its masculine counterpart, *Burton's Gentlemen's Magazine,* also had an editor whose name acquired luster: Edgar Allan Poe. His editorial career there was brief, however, from 1839 to 1840. The present-day roster of fashion magazines in the United States consists of highly specialized publications, each appealing to its own carefully delineated market. Examples include *Harper's Bazaar, Vogue,* and *L'Officiel,* American Edition, in the high-priced field; *Gentlemen's Quarterly, Playboy,* and *Esquire,* the masculine counterparts; *Details, Mademoiselle,* and *Glamour,* for college, career, and young married women, *Seventeen,* for teenaged girls.

ROLE OF FASHION MAGAZINES.   The role of fashion magazines is a many-sided one. As fashion reporters, their editors shop the wholesale markets both here and abroad, to select and feature styles they consider newsworthy for their individual audiences. As fashion influentials, these editors sometimes take an active part in the production of merchandise by working closely with manufacturers to create merchandise that they consider acceptable to their readers. They participate in distribution by contacting retailers and urging them to carry and promote the designs they feature and to emphasize the trends endorsed editorially. Finally, they provide their readers with information not only about the styles they recommend but also about who produces them and who sells them at retail.

An important tool of their activities, and of other consumer magazines that cover fashions to a lesser extent, is the **editorial credit.** This is how it operates: the editors select garments and accessories that, to their minds, exemplify fashion news. they photograph and show these styles in their pages, identifying the makers and naming one or more retail stores in which the consumer can buy them, and usually citing the approximate price. The magazine's sponsorship and the editorial mention encourage the makers to produce the garments in good supply, the retailers to stock them, and the customer to buy. Even in stores that do not have editorial credits for it, a fashion item featured in a strong magazine may be given special attention. If the magazine concerned has a good following among the store's customers, the editorial sponsorship becomes a selling point of the garment not only to consumers but also to the merchant. The style is then stocked, advertised, and displayed and the magazine's name is usually featured in ads and displays. Hangtags on the garment and magazine blow-ups in the displays remind the customer that this is the style she or he saw in the publication. The magazine, of course, provides the tags and the blow-ups.

DEPENDENCE ON ADVERTISING REVENUE

Like most publications, fashion magazines derive their principal revenue from the sale of advertising space. In 1985, a single black-and-white page in *Vogue, Seventeen, Mademoiselle,* or *Bazaar* ranged from $10,400 to $15,400, and a four-color page began at $16,200 and went up to $22,000.[8] In general magazines like *Reader's Digest* or women's magazines like *McCall's*, the rates were about $90,000 a page in black and white. Naturally, a high ratio of advertising to editorial pages means a prosperous magazine. Although conditions vary from issue to issue and from year to year, advertising generally accounts for nearly half the total number of pages in a consumer fashion magazine.

Dependency on dollars from advertisers instead of dollars from subscribers is not always conducive to unbiased fashion reporting; it can result in a conflict between editorial comment and advertising interests. Editorial mentions of merchandise bring to producers highly desirable publicity and prestige, since the editorial pages tend to have more authority in the reader's eyes than do pages devoted to paid advertising. Thus, firms that buy space in a magazine and contribute toward keeping it profitable are likely to protest if they are not given adequate editorial attention. Such a clash of interests often makes objective fashion reportage difficult, if not impossible.

The money the advertiser spends for his page is, in simplest terms, spent to influence customers to buy his product. If a publication can show tangible evidence that it can move merchandise into the retail store and then out into the consumer's hands, its chances of selling advertising space improve.

Magazines confirm that to attract advertisers, nothing is more important to fashion magazines than their relation to stores. This fact accounts for the increasingly large staffs of departments almost unknown to their readers—promotion and merchandising. The merchandising editors act as the liaison between the fashion editors, the advertising staff, and the retail stores. Their job is to ensure that editorialized and advertised merchandise will be placed

*Back-to-school is an
$8.7 billion celebration
when you're*

®*seventeen*

*M*ajoring in merchandise:
Going back to school is the most
important shopping time of the year for
America's young women. And last year
they spent more than 8.7 billion dollars
getting ready for it.

To reach these eager shoppers just
when they're entering the biggest shopping season of the year, there's really
only one magazine. The magazine they
believe in: Seventeen.

The August back-to-school issue of
Seventeen will be our biggest, brightest
ever. Packed with new ideas in clothes,
cosmetics, footwear, and accessories.
Backed by the biggest retail promotion
in which more than 600 tie-in stores
participate with fashion shows, window
displays, and twice the local tie-in advertising than they gave to all other fashion
magazines combined.

If you'd like to be a part of this vital,
eager market, call Bob Bunge at
212-407-9782.

Ready to wear:
Young American
women spent over
$4.7 billion last fall.
Plus $927 million
on accessories.

®*seventeen*

**BECAUSE
SHE BELIEVES
IN US,
SHE'LL BELIEVE
IN YOU.**

Color her loyal: A
Yankelovich study
proves that 41% of
women 20 to 34 still
use the same brand
of mascara they first
chose as teenagers.

Sleepwear and intimate apparel:
An advertiser's dream, they spent
$739 million last year.

Best foot forward: Last year
American teenagers spent $985
million on footwear.

© Triangle Communications, Inc. 1985

Source: Reprinted with permission of Triangle Communications Inc.

444

in retail stores where readers can buy it. They do this by telling the retailers what the magazine is featuring and why—and where to purchase it. Then they list for their readers' information the names of stores where the merchandise can be found. This service to the reader also helps to impress the advertisers with the magazine's selling power among retailers.

SERVICES TO THE INDUSTRY. The closer their relationship with both the producers and retailers, the easier it is for magazines to attract advertising. To cement these relationships, many free services are offered by fashion publications. Their staff members keep fabric and apparel producers informed on new trends and advise them on ways and means of selling merchandise. The fashion editors encourage them to manufacture items for which they anticipate a demand and, secure in the knowledge that the items will be featured by the editors, the producers will plunge ahead. The merchandising and promotion departments provide advertisers with "as advertised" blow-ups to distribute to their retail accounts. In addition, most magazines that are active in fashion prepare, well in advance of each season, fashion forecasts of their color predictions for the guidance of manufacturers and retailers alike. These forecasts show the colors, specific styles, and resources that will be featured in the magazine.

In developing a close relationship with retail stores, the fashion magazines make themselves a source of information for them. To make their editorialized and advertised merchandise desirable to retailers and, ultimately, to their customers, the merchandising departments prepare elaborate retail store kits that, along with the list of sources for featured garments, contain suggestions for advertising, fashion shows, and display. The kits also include selling aids such as hangtags, signs, and other promotional materials. If an important retailer requests the service, the magazine will send a representative to commentate a fashion show. Members of the magazine staff are also available in their offices at almost any time to show samples of merchandise to retailers who call, and thus encourage buyers to visit the producers of the featured apparel and accessories.

Most of the consumer magazines, including those primarily concerned with fashion, also maintain research departments. A function of these departments is to survey the readers of the magazine and compile information about their buying power, living patterns, and merchandise preferences. *Glamour*, for example, surveys young career women and college students periodically and compiles reports for retailers and manufacturers about what these women buy, how much they spend, and similar information. The fashion magazines, then, not only interpret the fashion for their readers but also interpret their readers for their industry. In the process, they serve as a clearinghouse for information in the fashion field.

Compared with consumer magazines of general interest, such as *Reader's Digest*, with a circulation of more than 18 million in 1985, or women's magazines like *McCall's* with a circulation of about 6.2 million, the fashion magazines have small circulations. *Vogue* and *Harper's Bazaar* have circulations of 1,109,000 and 732,147, respectively; *Mademoiselle* has 1,163,000. *Seventeen*, the largest, has a circulation of 1,695,000.[9] Their influence in the fashion business, individually and collectively, is great and far out of proportion to their actual circulation. Fashion editors ignore styles and designers in whom they have little faith but give a great amount of free publicity to those that they favor. Ordinarily, however, what they do is try to pick the most dramatic, the most exciting fashions—not always the most wearable, but the ones that will attract attention.

Newspapers and General Magazines

As mentioned earlier, almost all newspapers devote space to fashion. Coverage varies, of course, both in amount and depth. A paper with the facilities of the *New York Times* may have its experts report on the Paris openings and express opinions that are read by consumers and trade professionals alike. A small-town paper, on the other hand, may assign its society editor to fill out the women's page with items about fashion, clipped from what the wire services send, what comes in by way of press releases, or what the local retailers supply. Each paper's policy and the interests of its readers determine how much space the publication devotes to fashion news.

Among magazines not in the fashion-magazine category, there is also coverage of fashion, and it varies with the nature of the publication. Fashion editors of such media, looking at the fashion scene through the eyes of their average reader, will select for illustration and comment only the items of interest to the young mother, working women, the ageless city sophisticate, the sportsman, the young male executive, or whoever the particular audience may be.

Some of the general magazines show merchandise and give editorial credit; others, like the *New Yorker*, show no merchandise but discuss what the shops are showing. The activities of their fashion editors, as in the case of newspapers, vary according to the importance that each publication and its readers attach to fashion information.

Trade Publications

There is a special field of journalism known as **trade** or business publishing. Some business newspapers and magazines in the fashion field concern themselves with a particular classification of merchandise, from raw material to the sale of the finished product. These publications are not addressed to the ultimate consumer but to the fashion professionals concerned with the manufacturing and distribution of that merchandise. Typical examples are *Textile Age,* and *Bobbin Magazine.* Other business publications devote themselves to only one aspect of production or retailing and have a horizontal readership. Examples of these publications are *Stores* magazine, which goes to department store management, and *Chain Store Age*, for chain store management. Fairchild's *Women's Wear Daily*, which is published five times a week, covers the fashion waterfront in the women's fashion business—raw materials, manufacturing, retailing, and how the trend setters among the consuming public dress. Founded in 1890 by E. W. Fairchild, it has headquarters in New York City and maintains offices in cities throughout the United States and Europe—even in Asia. *Women's Wear Daily* reports collections, trade conventions, fashion events, new technical developments at all stages of production, personnel changes at the executive level, the formation of new fashion businesses—and the wardrobes and activities of prominent individuals. It is often called the industry's "bible" and no women's fashion enterprise is without its copy of *Women's Wear Daily*. The Fairchild counterpart for the textile and men's wear industry is the *Daily News Record*.

Business publications are not aimed at the general public and are inclined to discourage subscriptions from people not active in the fields they serve. They seldom appear on newsstands, except for the Fairchild dailies in the garment district. Their circulations are quite small compared with those of consumer magazines, and their advertising rates are correspondingly small, under $6585 a page. *Women's Wear Daily*, with a circulation of 62,920 in 1985, is a giant in the field. The *Daily News Record* has a circulation of 23,113, with a black-and-white rate of $5760 a page.[10]

The capacity of trade papers for disseminating fashion information is out of all proportion to their size. Their readership, it should be kept in mind, is concentrated among people dealing in the merchandise they cover. They talk shop to such people. And, in terms of the amount of merchandise involved, when a manufacturer or merchant responds to information on fashion, that response moves a lot of merchandise.

Trade paper editors are usually in their markets every day of the business year, and they cover every nook and cranny of their fields. They analyze

THE FASHION INDUSTRY'S "BIBLE"

Source: Masthead/reprinted with permission of *Women's Wear Daily*.

fashion trends for their readers and show sketches or photos of actual merchandise, identified as to source and style number, to assist buyers and store owners in keeping abreast of the flow of new products. In addition, trade publications discuss business conditions and contain articles on how to manufacture, promote, or sell the trade's products. They analyze and report on foreign markets, cover conventions and other meetings of interest to the trade, report on legislative developments of interest, and write up merchandising and promotion operations of retail stores.

Solid market research is also part of a trade publication's work. These magazines and papers make estimates of the size of their markets, survey subscribers on buying responsibilities and attitudes toward current problems, publish directories of manufacturers, help retailers and manufacturers find sources of supply, and report on seminars and conventions appropriate to their fields.

Within their particular fields, trade paper editors and reporters are extremely well informed. Reading their articles is like listening to a group of experts indulging in shop talk.

Television: Broadcast and Closed Circuit

The impact of television advertising is enormous, but the medium is expensive to use and, until fairly recently, one saw and heard little more of fashion advertising on the home screen than the institutional messages of fiber companies or the local promotions of retailers. In the late 1970s, retailers such as J. C. Penney, Kinney Shoes, Macy's, Carson Pirie Scott, to name but a few, began to use network TV advertising to tell their fashion stories. Today, however, both retailers and producers are harnessing the power of network TV. New brands of jeans, notably Jordache and Calvin Klein, got off to explosive starts through saturation use of this medium.

As the 1980s progressed, a new element was added: video presentations, used both on the TV channels and in the stores themselves to revolutionize customer perception of fashion. A major AMC executive has called the use of closed-circuit in-store video presentations "the single most influential selling tool of the 1980's."[11]

Sears, an early user of this medium, has had on-the-floor videos since 1977. Each Sears store, depending on its size, has one to four portable 19-inch VCR units that have been used to sell everything from fashion to tractors. Sears produces its tapes in Chicago and sends them out on a monthly schedule coordinated with advertising and display materials.[12] Other stores that are active in this field include Neusteter, Denver, whose in-store productions are called Video Log; and Marshall Field, which buys rock productions from a firm called Video Pool (who themselves buy the production from music and fashion video companies).

Since MTV and its superstars like Madonna, Cindy Lauper, and Michael

AN FTV VIDEO PRODUCER

One West 37th St., New York, N.Y. 10018 (212) 869-4666 Telex 225707

Source: Reprinted with permission by *Video Fashion Monthly.*

Jackson have demonstrated how quickly they can create demand for new fashions, stores have been paying close attention to the impact those small screens can have on their customers. Videotapes of models going down the runway are now old hat compared with the new fashion tapes, in which entertainment is the key word, and the emphasis is on imagination and excitement, not merely the particular outfits. Norma Kamali, Willi Smith, Henry Grethel, Hartmarx, and Daniel Hechster are just a few of the firms now producing videos featuring their clothes. Exotic backgrounds are part of the effort—Kenya, Mexico, the Swiss Alps, for instance—for these fashion television videos (FTV).

The future for this new form of promotion seems as unlimited as the customers' appetite for something new and different. A reading at the end of this chapter describes the 40 videotapes produced each year by *Videofashion Monthly*, one of the pioneers in this new industry. Another company in this area is Vidcat—the Video Catalog Company—which produces point-of-sale entertainment, training, and educational videos.

ADVERTISING AND PUBLICITY AGENCIES ....

There are two ways in which producers and retailers use space in print media or time in broadcast media to get their message across to the trade or to the public. One way is paid **advertising.** The other is **publicity**—time or space given without charge by the medium because it considers the message newsworthy.

Advertising Agencies

An **advertising agency** is a service agency whose original function was simply to prepare and place ads in magazines or newspapers for its clients. Today its job encompasses much more: research of the client's consumer markets, advice on promotional needs, planning of promotional campaigns, preparation of print and broadcast advertising, preparation of selling manuals, creation of selling aids, labels, signs, and packaging—anything that helps to increase the sale of the client's product and makes the advertising itself more effective.

An advertising agency may consist of one talented, hard-working executive with a few small clients, or it may be an organization with a staff of hundreds and clients with hundreds of millions of dollars to spend each year. Approximately 65 percent of agencies' revenue is derived primarily from commissions. These are paid, not by the client, but by the media from whom the agencies purchase advertising space or time. Custom has fixed the rate at 15 percent. The balance of their income is received directly from clients, generally in the form of fees for special services such as market research, and as part of the cost for producing a product for the client—for example, photography, typography, art, and layout.

When an advertising agency bids for a client's account, it studies the firm's operation thoughtfully and draws up a presentation that outlines the campaign the agency suggests and the varied services that the agency performs. When awarded the account, the agency may delve into package design, market research, the creation of selling aids and sales training material—plus its original function of preparing and placing advertising in publications, in broadcast media, and, in some cases, in transit and outdoor media.

In the fashion industries, it is usually only the largest producers of nationally distributed merchandise who make use of advertising agencies. These include some makers of finished apparel plus the giant fiber and fabric sources. Retailers, whose audience is local or regional, usually maintain their own complete advertising departments that handle their day-to-day newspaper advertisements. This does not by any means imply that retailers are small advertisers. One of the country's four largest spenders for advertising is a retailer, Sears, Roebuck & Company. It is second only to Procter & Gamble, and is followed by Beatrice Foods and General Motors.[13]

FASHION EXPERTISE.   Some agencies, often among the smallest in the field, specialize in fashion accounts. In such agencies, and in those of the larger ones that serve fashion accounts, it is important to have personnel who are expert in the language and background of the fashion business: account executives who work with clients and coordinate what is done, art directors who visualize the fashion advertising, copywriters who are familiar with fashion appeals, and stylists or fashion coordinators who are responsible for the fashion slant of the ads.

The work of the fashion expert in an agency is not necessarily limited to fashion accounts. If a man's or woman's figure appears in an ad for automobiles, cigarettes, or soap, it is most likely that a fashion adviser has checked the model's outfit to make sure it is in tune with the current fashion picture as well as with the occasion and level of society that is being represented.

Agency people also realize that fashion is a quick way to identify with whatever group of customers the advertiser seeks to reach: young, dashing, mature, conservative, or whatever. This is especially noticeable in television advertising, where the advertiser has only a few seconds in which to establish rapport with the particular viewers he wishes to influence. Compare the clothing of the characters in an investment firm's commercials, for example, with those of the characters in commercials for soft drinks. The one seeks to project a conservative image, the other a carefree, young, and with-it attitude.

Thus, the advertising agency, whether or not it has a fashion account on its roster of clients, becomes involved, directly or indirectly, in the business of fashion.

Publicity and Public Relations Firms

Publicity, unlike advertising, cannot be controlled in relation to where, when, and how a particular message will appear—if, indeed, it appears at all. The publicity practitioner's control over the fate of the story he or she wishes to place with a medium rests primarily in the ability to convince the particular editor that the material is truly news of interest to that medium's audience.

Publicity's purpose, like that of advertising, is to enhance the client's sales appeal to potential customers. The space or time supplied by the media, in this case, is free, but the public relations firm's services are not. Working on a fee basis, with provision for expenses, the publicity agency develops news stories around the client's product or activities and makes these stories available to editors and broadcasters.

The key word in effective publicity is "news." The publicity expert's first job is to find or "create" news value in a product, activity, or personality to be publicized. Next, he or she considers the media that might conceivably find this news of interest to their readers and writes the story (called a press release) in a form appropriate to the media that constitute the target. If they are likely to use illustrations, a suitable photograph may be included.

Typically, publicity activities include getting editorial mentions in consumer and trade publications, "plugs" on television and radio, school and college tie-ins, running fashion shows or other events, often with admission charges that go to a charity organization, feature articles in newspapers and magazines, and anything else that makes the products or the client's name better known and more readily accepted by the consumer—or by an industry, if that industry is the client's customer.

The publicity firm does more than merely use its contacts to place material for its client. It also prepares press releases, distributes photographs, writes radio and TV scripts, sometimes works out an elaborate fashion show, and hires and coaches professional actors to sing, dance, and model for the audience. If a medium, whether print or broadcast, is working on a special feature touching the client's field, the public relations people swing into action to provide the writer of the feature with facts, photos, and other help. Many fashion editors in smaller towns depend on press releases and photographs for the content of their fashion pages.

A broader term than publicity is public relations. A public relations firm does not limit its efforts to getting the client or the product mentioned in the media through press releases and similar efforts. It may supply expert advice on how to improve the client's public image and may develop some potent but less obvious ways of getting publicity for the client: suggesting him or her as a speaker at conventions of appropriate groups, having the client give scholarships and establish awards and foundations, for instance.

There are many independent publicists and public relations agencies who specialize in fashion publicity. As in the case of advertising agencies, their clients are generally fiber, fabric, or apparel producers instead of retailers, since retailers usually maintain their own internal publicity staffs. Insofar as the fashion business is concerned, the public relations and publicity fraternity performs the very useful function of feeding information about the industry to the news media and thus stimulates business by keeping fashion in the limelight.

THE FASHION GROUP

The Fashion Group is a professional association of women who represent every phase of fashion manufacturing, retailing, merchandising, advertising, publishing, and education. Organized in 1930 its purpose was, and is, to serve as a national and international clearinghouse for the exchange of information about what is going on in the business of fashion.

Headquartered in New York, it has 34 regional chapters in major cities throughout the United States and foreign countries with a membership that exceeds 5000. Qualifications for membership consist of a minimum of five years' executive experience in the industry, meritorious performance, and recommendation by two current members.

OTHER FASHION ENTERPRISES

There are enterprises of many other types that play important behind-the-scenes roles in the business of fashion. Their activities, however, are too varied and too highly specialized to be described in detail. For example, display consultants design and construct fashion display materials for manufacturers, retailers, and fashion magazines. Consultants in the fields of sales promotion or marketing are also retained on a fee basis by manufacturers and retailers. Market research agencies do consumer surveys for retail stores, publications, and manufacturers, or retail surveys for producers. Among the research agencies who do work for the fashion field are Audits and Surveys, which has made some interesting studies of the buying patterns of retail store customers, and Yankelovich, Skelly and White, who are noted for their demographic and psychographic research.

There are many **trade associations,** each one serving businesses and business executives with interests in common. Each organization is set up as a medium for such purposes as, for example, disseminating trade and technical information, doing research into markets or methods of operation, analyzing relevant legislation, doing public relations work for the industry or trade, lobbying on political matters. In addition to those that have been mentioned in preceding chapters, other examples are the National Retail Merchants Association (to which most department and apparel specialty stores belong); the American Apparel Manufacturers Association; the American Textile Manufacturers Institute; and too many more to be enumerated here. There are also associations of publicity and advertising specialists, of menswear buyers, and fashion designers, among others.

In short, there is a whole arsenal of auxiliary services that contribute to making the fashion business what it is today and that will undoubtedly contribute to its growth in the future.

Readings ....

The readings in this section take us inside some of the enterprises that work behind the scenes to serve the fashion business. They spot fashion trends early, and help manufacturers and retailers respond to these trends at the right time for their target customer.

Who Decides Next Year's Fashions?
Ever wonder where clothes designers, manufacturers, and retailers get their ideas for tomorrow's colors, fabrics, shapes, and styles? This reading takes you behind the scenes with the decision makers.

T.F.S.—The Fashion Service
A relatively new, important fashion information service, with a reputation for being fast to spot new trends, describes its services to its subscribers.

Videofashion Monthly
The world's largest producer and distributor of fashion and life-style video programs details their service, which provides subscribers a front seat to the top designer collections every season, every month.

Organization of Frederick Atkins, Inc.
This major cooperative buying office, headquartered in New York City, organizes its office to match the stores it services. Here is a blueprint of their internal structure and how it functions.

Mademoiselle: Editors and Departments and What They Do
Everything you have always wanted to know about a fashion magazine—who does what and how—is outlined for you in this reading.

Who Decides Next Year's Fashions?
by David Colker

Leigh Simpson has seen the future, and it's black. "Looking forward two years, we're coming up on a time when people will be questioning the 'Me Generation' attitude that we've seen so far in the eighties," she says energetically. "That means things are going to be more expressive of the individual, more spiritual, serious, non-ornamented. You're going to see lots of black."

Simpson is not, like your run-of-the-mill prognosticator, concerned with the fertility of Princess Di, the marital status of Elizabeth Taylor or an impending visit by aliens from another planet. Furthermore, she cannot tell you how you'll fare in love, commerce or at the racetrack. And you won't find her wearing a turban unless the wraparound hats become all the rage.

Simpson is in the business of forecasting fashion.

"What we do at my company is look at everything going on—movies, MTV, politics, attitudes, the economy, whatever—and try to see how they will affect fashion a couple of years from now," she explains. "It's a creative process. It doesn't have anything to do with being psychic, but it's not exactly a science, either."

It does, however, have a lot to do with business. As amorphous as this "creative" process sounds, it's an increasingly vital one for thousands of designers, manufacturers, buyers and retailers all over the world. People have a heightened awareness of design these days, and the latest trends are so quickly disseminated via the mass media that there is a volatile turnover in fashion preferences.

Businesses in which color dye, fabric and shape choices must be made up to eighteen months in advance, however, are not equipped to make quick changes in their product lines. That's where forecasting services—such as Simpson's New York–based IM International, the Paris-based Promostyl, London-based Nigel French and a handful of smaller companies—come into the picture.

Fashion forecasting for the United States used to be easy. A couple of decades ago you could tell what was going to hit big here in two years by simply taking note of what was currently popular in the fashion capitals of Europe. "In the sixties when I was on a long trip to Europe," Simpson says, "everyone I knew in the industry, from designers to manufacturers, wanted me to send them sketches from the boutiques. They wanted me to tell them which fabrics were selling, which colors."

When she got home, Simpson recognized the need for a service that would provide that information, and in 1969 she opened IM International. But over the years, fashion forecasting became much more complicated. "The time gap has certainly narrowed," she says. "Gone are the days when you could look at what was happening over there and just add two years. As New York designers became more and more important, fashion became much more international. Now they're usually still a bit ahead in Europe, but we're almost working on the same time frame."

Europe still lays claim to the largest forecasting company—Promostyl, which began as a children's wear service in 1967 and now has offices or exclusive agents in twenty-three cit-

Source: *Republic Airlines Magazine,* October 1985. Reprinted courtesy *Republic Magazine* carried aboard Republic Airlines © 1985. East/west Network, Inc. publisher.

ies worldwide. Its forecasting covers a broad base of topics—each year the company makes available thirty-one different "trend books" covering everything from basic men's, women's and children's wear to fabric and color guides, accessories, ski clothing and beachwear. The information found in these books does not come cheap; it ranges from an annual subscription price for the fabric service (which includes spring and fall trend books, plus a bimonthly newsletter) of $2,550 down to the men's shirt forecasting (including two trend books and *Early Fabric Direction* and *Color, Fabric and Silhouette Reconfirmation* newsletters) for $1,050.

The subscriber to any Promostyl service also gets the right to consult with the staff at any of the companies' worldwide offices. In New York, that staff is quite young—none of the sales representatives is over thirty. "Fashion comes from the young," says sales rep Allisson Savicz with a note of pride. "They are the most innovative, and they have a lot of influence. The older generation might laugh at us, but you watch and see if touches of the Madonna look don't show up in coming years in the more mature women's line."

There is no formal forecasting done out of the New York office. "That's all coordinated at the company headquarters in Paris," says Lesa Salvani, the director of Promostyl USA. "But we do have input." That input doesn't generally come from anyone the public might identify as a trendsetter. "Most of the people the public knows are having their clothes put together by someone else," declares sales rep Joseph Ieraci. "They might dress well, but in an outfit by Armani or someone like that. The real individualists, the people making a real fashion statement, are putting together things for themselves."

Indeed, the attitude around Promostyl seems to be that once someone is known to the masses, that person is no longer able to be considered individualistic enough to be a trendsetter. "Madonna is old news," declares Savicz about the pop singer who wears lingerie as outer garments. "That was the kind of look we were seeing five years ago in New York. When you're talking about trends, she isn't important."

"We make it a point to cover the streets," explains sales rep Carolyn Lettieri. A fast-talking, energetic finishing school graduate who wrote articles for *Seventeen* magazine before joining Promostyl, Lettieri doesn't mean the kind of streets her finishing school background would suggest. "When I first came to New York, I thought Manhattan was where it was all happening. But when I was riding the subways, I started noticing that the kids from the Bronx and Brooklyn were the ones who were really pulling it together. The heavy belts, the ripped T-shirts, the funky way they tied their shoelaces—it all looked great. And it wasn't long before that look started to come into the general market."

Salvani says that some U.S. cities outside New York are important in a limited way for spotting trends. "San Francisco is turning out an interesting crop of designers and Los Angeles is becoming more important, but when I walk down Melrose [currently considered the hippest street in L.A.], it looks like London two years ago."

Still, Salvani does consider L.A. to be important in one area. "Let's face it, Jane Fonda had a great influence on fashion in recent years," she allows. "The whole aerobics thing that spawned a kind of 'life-style fashion' came out of the West Coast. But it took the Europeans to discover it, take it back to Europe, rework it into fashion and sell it back to us."

You won't, for the most part, find radically forward-looking togs on Promostyl staff members, who mostly dress for the office in a conservatively stylish manner befitting young men and women meeting clients from the Midwest. The one exception is Ieraci, a former bank teller from Pittsburgh, who wears triangular metal clips fastened onto the tips of his shirt collar and a string tie. "It's 'Cowboy,' " Ieraci explains, "a small trend that's coming up." He says that this look is not to be confused with the Western wear craze that hit the country a few years ago. " 'Western' is like *Dallas.* " 'Cowboy' is like Roy Rogers and Howdy Doody," he explains.

The slender, bespectacled Ieraci enjoys adding these touches to his outfits, and he wears them well—because he avoids using more than just a touch of Cowboy, the look is interesting and jaunty rather than ostentatious. But by the time the rest of us are not-as-artfully adding Cowboy to our get-ups, he'll have moved onto something new. "In the fall when everyone starts wearing this stuff," Ieraci notes matter-of-factly, "I'll have it out of my system."

Over at IM International, when it comes to forecasting, they have simple and they have complicated. The service's two thousand subscribers in forty countries have the choice of receiving either a comprehensive report that provides about 125 pages per month on predictions, the latest in color and fabric information and news from the hot fashion capitals; or a much smaller monthly magazine that is far less technical. The price, of course, is adjusted accordingly. An annual subscription to the more comprehensive of the publications, *The Action Report,* costs $3,500 per year, while the smaller one, called *Fashion Highlights,* runs $300.

Within a year, IM International plans to be the first forecaster to break into the consumer market. "Everyone who comes through the office, whether they were in the fashion business or not, loves to leaf through the smaller publication," Simpson says. "And all the time they are asking us if they could take a copy home. So we have decided to get into the business of putting out a home version of the magazine." The subscription and newsstand prices of the publication have not yet been fixed—they will surely be far less than the $300 a year charged for its current industry version—but don't expect the magazine to come cheap. "We'll be aiming at the dual-income home market," she says.

Although IM International's service is mostly concerned with women's wear, with a lesser focus on men's and children's fashion, some of its clients are not in the clothing business at all. Major cosmetic firms, for example, use the prediction books to help them choose upcoming colors. Auto manufacturers have also signed up. "Surveys show that the American woman plays a big role in choosing the family car," Simpson says. "So it's important that the exterior and interior color be appealing."

Even toy companies are on the roster. "The ten-year-old kids are pretty hip these days," she says. "They want their Barbies to look hip, too."

IM International projects, at most, about two years into the future. "Right now, we're working on Spring/Summer '87," Simpson says. "When we work that far ahead, we do colors first, because that's the first part of the industry to gear up. Next comes fabrics."

How, exactly, do they do it? "Well, there is a lot of brainstorming in which we sit around and take a look at everything that's going on, everything that will have an effect on that time frame. 'We immerse ourselves in thinking ahead.

"Sometimes we have an easier time talking about what is going to happen in two years than what is happening right this second. We live in that time frame."

Simpson comes down to earth, however, to talk about current trends and how they evolved. She traces the rise of a softer, more feminine look back, to some degree, to Nancy

Reagan. "When she came on the scene, so did the high-fashion couturiere, and this was important because the couturiere had not been important for many years. This brought on a more elegant, refined look in clothing."

Other factors contributed to the trend. "In the years when equality between the sexes was being stressed, women were wearing suits and ties like men," says Promostyl's Savicz. "Now we've gotten to the point where women don't feel they have to compete so strongly. They have the confidence to walk around, socially and professionally, in a floral outfit. They aren't afraid to be more feminine."

Along these lines, Promostyl is predicting that the fashion themes for next summer will include "Rough Romantics," using cotton "treated in a rustic/romantic way with casual mixtures of patterns and textures"; "Paris Picnic," featuring kitchen gingham and picnic checks "inspired by country afternoons in the forties"; "Royal Hippie," with gleaming paisley prints and tapestry flowers in audacious mixtures inspired by the sassy splendor of the seventeenth century; and "Hybrid Chic," a savage and sophisticated mix of noble shapes and sorcerer's prints.

Like most trends in fashion, the softer, more muted look will eventually affect the industry across the board. Simpson points out that punk, which was featured in IM International predictions as far back as 1974, is still an influence, as is MTV, the sixties revival and the "Body Beautiful" look. "Now that women and men are spending up to two hours a day in the gym, they want to show off their work," Simpson says. "That means a degree of bareness will continue to be used, as well as body knits and other revealing fashion."

Sometimes trends arise suddenly from hit movies or TV shows. *Flashdance,* of course, had a big impact, and currently men are starting to borrow touches from the flashy style of Don

Johnson and Philip Michael Thomas on "Miami Vice."

"I just got done with a trend for women for Autumn/Winter '86–87," Simpson notes, "that has a bit of militarism mixed with a feminine look. Something like a lace skirt worn with combat boots or maybe a sexy top worn under a combat jacket. I wouldn't say that *Rambo* was the specific influence for this, but I wouldn't say it wasn't, either."

For Spring '86, Promostyl is predicting a heavy Indian influence. "I'm sure movies like *Gandhi* and *A Passage to India* had something to do with that," Ieraci says. The firm also is forecasting more somber, medieval touches showing up in fashion.

All this is leading to the darker, more spiritual trend that both IM International and Promostyl see in our fashion future. "People will be asking more and more if the world is going in the right direction," Simpson predicts. "I don't want to get too psychological here, but a lot of people will be looking for inner response, rather than looking outward toward politics or clothing to solve their problems."

Simpson and the folks at Promostyl admit that no matter how far out their predictions might get, they are, to a degree, self-fulfilling. If the many clients of these services create clothing in line with the forecasts, the predictions will naturally come true. Indeed, Promostyl has a staff of house designers in Europe and the United States to create clothes for private labels, and, naturally, these designers have a tendency to put out the look Promostyl forecasters are promoting.

But the forecasters maintain that fashion is still volatile enough to keep them on their toes. And besides, Savicz declares, even though large sums of money are involved, it's important to keep what they are doing in perspective. "One day we got a panic call from a woman who owns a clothing shop," she says. "I just heard that lavender is dead!" she screamed. 'My whole children's line is in lavender! What am I going to do?'

"You know, if you take fashion that seriously, you're really in trouble. We have to keep reminding ourselves that fashion is fantasy and fun, and that's all it is."

T.F.S.—The Fashion Service

Info-Flash Womenswear

Monthly reporting of important fashion information from the fashion capitals of the world, that keeps abreast of current and ongoing trends in the industry. Tracking, reporting and editing those trends into fashion action points.

- Unique T.F.S. folio format!
- Sketches, photos, slides, audio cassettes, samples, swatches.
- Colour 'chips', posters!
- Monthly!
- Slide presentations of the big current events!
- Fast! On the spot!

REPORTING ON:

Retail: A sketched report of the hot fashion merchandise almost every month from a selection of fashion cities (London, Paris, Milan, Rome, Florence, Tokyo, New York). A focus on the hot looks and the hot items for the season. Twice yearly, at the beginning of the major retail seasons, a bonanza retail report.

Street Scenes: Black and white photographs or colour slides of what the avant garde and trendy fashion set are wearing now.

Samples: A selection of merchandise that reflects the current hot looks and items at retail now and that go forward. On figure illustrations show the item as part of the important total look, ad flat pattern drawings give all the measurements and details. Actual garments can be viewed in the New York Fashion Office. Minimally five times a year. Special 'Samples Flashes' for instant hot items.

Wholesale: Written text, sketched or photographed and fabric or colour swatched (when appropriate) reports covering the major fabric, ready-to-wear and accessory fairs around the world. (Includes Premier Vision, Interstoff, Pitti Filati, Porte de Versailles PRET, Igedo, SEHM, Parisian Haute Couture, European Designer Collections, New York Designer Collections.*) Reported on as the events happen!

Memo: A special feature included several times a year, consisting of a written and illustrated and/or swatched editorial on important fashion ideas that should have extra emphasis and development.

• **Special Issues . . .** Part of the yearly schedule, but issues that deal primarily with single subjects as highlighted below:

Designer R-T-W Collections: Twice yearly coverage of the designer shows in Milan,

London and Paris. 100 colour slides, with drawings of those slides for easy reference; text report on the fashion news in silhouette, looks, items, fabrics and colours (separate colour swatched section). Audio cassette gives recorded commentary for slides. Complete and released one week after collections!

St. Tropez Resort Report: An annual issue that deals with the big fashion news from this trendy summer hot spot. Includes colours slides (with drawings) and black & white photographs of the major looks and items as worn by the fashion set on the street; major coverage of what's retailing in the boutiques; a selection of samples. Audio cassette gives recorded commentary for slides. Released July 1!

• **Slide Presentations . . .** Twice yearly presentations of European design ready-to-wear collections. Twice yearly presentations of New York designer shows. Twice yearly presentations of Parisian Haute Couture collections. Annual presentation of the hot looks on the streets and in the boutiques in Saint Tropez. (Available in the New York Office, or by special arrangement with the London Office.)

Forecast Womenswear

Quarterly forecasting of important advance fashion colours, fabrics, trends & items. Informs of future trends in the industry on a seasonal basis. Projecting, creating, merchandising and visualizing that information into fashion action points.

• Unique T.F.S. folio format!
• Sketches, swatches, colour yarns, posters, audio cassettes!
• Seasonal consultations!
• Advanced! Accurate!

FORECASTING:

Colours: Four seasonal Folios containing advanced colour projections for Spring, Summer, Autumn and Winter. Each folio includes colour cards swatched with yarns, plus an extra set of yarns. Three to six cards per season. Five to ten colours per card. Merchandised into fashion colour stories and enhanced with colour mood photography.

Fabrics: Four seasonal Folios containing advanced fabric projections for Spring, Summer, Autumn and Winter. Each folio includes mini posters with sketches, text and swatches. Ten to fifteen mini posters per season. Three to four swatches per poster. Merchandised into fashion fabric stories on fibre, base cloth, print and pattern direction.

Trends/Looks: Four trends per season for Spring, Summer, Autumn and Winter. First previewed in mini poster format, contained in a folio. Highlighting the key information about advanced fashion looks. Fully developed in individual booklet format containing comprehensive information on colour, fabric and styling. Accompanied by an audio cassette trend seminar and illustrated poster as overview.

Items/Design: Original T.F.S. designs throughout the Forecast. On-the-figure illustrations and off-figure croquis sketches visualize all the trends and looks. Each trend booklet contains a "Design File" section, organized by merchandising classification: Tops, Bottoms, Jackets/Coats, Dresses, Knits, Body-Lounge-Swimwear, Accessories & Footwear.

Seasonal Consultations: Personal meetings with a T.F.S. director to focus advanced seasonal information on colour, fabric and trends for clients' individual needs.

What & When . . . Two-part information kits, each season:

Part One: includes colour folio, fabric folio and trend preview folio.
Part Two: includes trend and design booklets, audio cassette, poster.
Spring Part One: January 15
Spring Part Two: February 5
Summer Part One: May 15
Summer Part Two: May 30
Autumn Part One: June 25
Autumn Part Two: July 20
Winter Part One: October 5
Winter Part Two: October 30

Info-Flash Menswear

Monthly reporting of important fashion information from the fashion capitals of the world, that keeps abreast of current and on going trends in the industry. Tracking, reporting and editing those trends into fashion action points.

- Unique T.F.S. folio format!
- Sketches, photos, slides, audio cassettes, samples, swatches, colour 'chips,' posters!
- Slide presentations of the big current events!
- Fast! On the spot!

REPORTING ON:

Retail: A sketched report of the hot fashion merchandise almost every month from a selection of fashion cities (London, Paris, Milan, Florence, New York). A focus on the hot looks and the hot items for the season. Twice yearly, at the beginning of the major retail seasons, a bonanza retail report.

Street Scenes: Black and white photographs or colour slides of what the avant garde and trendy fashion set are wearing now.

Samples: A selection of merchandise that reflects the current hot looks and items at retail now and that go forward. On figure illustrations show the item as part of the important total look, and flat pattern drawings give all the measurements and details. Actual garments can be viewed in the New York Fashion Office. Minimally five times a year. Special 'Samples Flashes' for instant hot items.

Wholesale: Written text, sketched or photographed and fabric or colour swatched (when appropriate) reports covering the major fabric and ready-to-wear fairs around the world. (Includes Premier Vision, Interstoff, Pitti Filati, SEHM, European Designer Collections*). Reported on as the events happen!

- **Memo:** A special feature included several times a year, consisting of a written and illustrated and/or swatched editorial on important fashion ideas that should have extra emphasis and development.

- **Special Issues . . .** Part of the yearly schedule, but issues that deal primarily with single subjects as highlighted below:

Designer R-T-W Collections: Twice yearly coverage of the designer shows in Milan and Paris. 80 colour slides, with drawings of those slides for easy reference; text report on the fashion news in silhouette, looks, items, fabrics and colours (with colour swatches).

St. Tropez Resort Report: An annual issue that deals with the big fashion news from this trendy summer hot spot. Includes colours slides (with drawings) and black & white photographs of the major looks and items as worn by the fashion set on the street; major coverage of what's retailing in the boutiques; a selection of samples. Audio cassette gives recorded commentary for slides. *Released July 1!*

• **Slide Presentations:** Twice yearly presentations of Italian and French designer ready-to-wear shows. Annual presentation of the hot looks on the streets and in the boutiques in Saint Tropez. (Available in the New York Office, or by special arrangement with the London Office.)

T.F.S. Show-Time

Timely slide showings covering the major events in the fashion calendar. Tracking, reporting and editing current and ongoing trends into fashion action points.
Nine important shows annually!
Multi-screen!
Timely!
Succinct & scintillating!

PROGRAMME:
European Designer Collections (Womens): Twice yearly presentation of the latest, most important and fashion forward information from the designer ready-to-wear shows in Paris, London and Milan. Trended and edited for fashion action! Featuring 280 colour slides.
European Designer Collections (Mens): Twice yearly presentation of the latest, most important and fashion forward information from the Italian and French designer ready-to-wear shows. Trended and edited for fashion action! Featuring 160 colour slides.
New York Designer Collections (Womens): Twice yearly presentation of the latest and most important information from the New York ready-to-wear showings. Trended and edited for fashion action! Featuring 280 colour slides.

Parisian Haute Couture Collections: Twice yearly presentation of the most important looks from the most prestigious names in fashion. Trended and edited for fashion action! Featuring 280 colour slides.
Saint Tropez Resort (Womens & Mens): Annual presentation of the hot looks on the streets and in the boutiques of this trendy fashion hot spot! Trended and edited for fashion action! Featuring 160–280 colour slides.

AVAILABLE TO PURCHASE AS SELF-CONTAINED PRODUCTS . . . OR VIEWING AVAILABLE ON AN ANNUAL SUBSCRIPTION BASIS.

As Self-Contained Products: Each show package includes 160 to 280 colour slides (numbered and ready for traying), audio cassette with voice over commentary, typewritten script of same commentary.

Special Fabric Package

Specially selected segments of T.F.S. forecast and info-flash publications regarding advanced and current fabric information.

• Unique T.F.S. folio format.
• Seasonal fabric forecast.
• Premiere vision and Interstoff newsflashes and swatched reports.
• Slide presentations of the big current events!
• Seasonal consultations!
Fast! On the spot! Advanced!
Accurate!

FORECASTING:
Fabrics: Four seasonal Folios, taken from the T.F.S. Forecasts, containing advanced fabric projections for Spring, Summer, Autumn and Winter. Each folio includes mini

posters with sketches, text and swatches. Ten to fifteen mini posters per season. Three to four swatches per poster. Merchandised into fashion fabric stories on fiber, base cloth, print and pattern direction.

REPORTING ON:

Major Fabric Fairs: twice yearly issues, taken from T.F.S. Info-Flash, covering Premier Vision and Interstoff. Written text, colour photo collages and fabric swatches that report on those seasonal fabric exhibitions.

Consultations & Presentations: Four seasonal consultations with T.F.S. directors on advance trend information, an overview of the seasons. Nine slide presentations annually (includes—Designer Shows, St. Tropez, Couture, Menswear).

Videofashion Monthly

Right now there's a communications revolution going on all around you. It's called VIDEO.

In your neighborhood, your living room, your office or store—from the phenomenon of MTV and fashion music videos to video sales displays, merchandising meetings and more—video is changing the way our world communicates.

And what happens when this high tech boom meets the ever-dynamic, always moving world of high fashion?

The answer: *Videofashion Monthly*—the first fashion magazine on videocassette. *Videofashion Monthly* gives you the opportunity to discover, utilize and profit from the thriving video medium and your video equipment right now by capturing the action, vitality, the trend-setting power and glamorous beauty of this fast-paced world we call fashion.

Think of *Videofashion Monthly* as a *Vogue* or *Harper's Bazaar*—on video! Each month, in an exciting and different 30-minute video program, *Videofashion Monthly* details the news, the directions, the behind-the-scenes insights and expert analyses of what's happening in fashion around the world. Month-to-month, you'll see regular departments, special features, short takes and unique fashion events.

But, unlike any other publication you've ever seen before, *Videofashion Monthly* moves, talks, vibrates with activity. Print commentary glides across the screen of your monitor as you view top-fashion mannequins walking, swirling, modeling the latest looks. Just think—you'll finally get to see the back of the dress!

Videofashion Monthly puts fashion into action. It'll boost your business, add new excitement to your organization, provide a unique and valuable merchandising tool. It's made for anyone in the fashion stream or related areas. Imagine: The latest technology bringing the heartbeat and hub of our industry "live" to you, your associates, your customers, across a monitor or screen!

Videofashion Monthly has the world of fashion covered. There are twelve timely issues a year . . . six international reports on videocassettes for each of the Spring/Summer and Fall/Winter seasons. You get the reports from today's fash-

Source: *Videofashion Monthly,* promotional brochure. Reprinted with permission.

ion capitals: New York, Milan, Paris, Japan and London. And, every season there's a special report, too—featuring the stars, covering the world, tracking all that's happening in a great, in-depth summary program.

Videofashion Monthly is your front row seat to the top designer collections and fashion extravaganzas every season, every month. "Turn on" an issue. Here's just some of what you'll find:

- *Fashion News* . . . Hemlines rising? Waistlines dropping? Right before your eyes, watch the top runway looks formulate into the season's best-selling, stylemaking trends as our expert commentators and sharp-eyed editors present what's hot from such names as: *Giorgio Armani, Oscar de la Renta, Karl Lagerfeld, Kenzo, Krizia, Anne Klein* and many, many more. From haute-couturiers of style like *Yves Saint Laurent* to rising stars like *Stephen Sprouse*, they're all in *Videofashion Monthly*.

- *Designer Profiles* . . . Right from the experts' mouths: Watch and listen to the purveyors of fashion in exclusive interviews that disclose their individual design philosophies, industry predictions and good design business sense. In past seasons, we've visited the homes, studios and boutiques of such fashion celebrities as: *Halston, Louis Vuitton, Gianni Versace, Zandra Rhodes* and others. Wait till you see who's coming next!

- *Video*Cover*Girl of the Month* . . . Who's that face? That body? That model who highlights those clothes like no one else? On each *Videofashion Monthly* program, you'll meet top cover girls from the hottest modeling agencies—*Diane deWitt of Ford, Ines de la Fressange of Legends, Pat Cleveland of Zoli, Jerry Hall of Ford*, to name a few—as they reveal their personal experiences from the other side of the cameras in the glamorous, demanding, profitable and strenuous fashion business.

- *Beauty* . . . It's said that a hairstyle and makeup are a woman's most essential fashion accessory. To show why and how it's done, you'll hear from the hair and makeup experts from around the world, watch them work, get their professional secrets. A sampling of the smart and famous who have shown up on *Videofashion Monthly* already: *Alexandre de Paris, Linda Mason, Way Bandy, Lydia Snyder, Diego de la Palma Makeup Studio of Italy, Robert Wren,* and many more.

- *How To's* . . . Because the best fashion transcends the towering world of couture into the homes and lives of everyday people, every *Videofashion Monthly* is information-packed with great ideas for personal style. Each videocassette issue pinpoints the silhouette, the accessory, the MUST-BUY necessity that'll pull the right look together that season. They're the kind of tips and cues your customers, colleagues and sales force will be using to make *your* season a total success.

- *And* . . . There's music . . . narration . . . on-screen print keynoting major fashion points. Slow motion, freeze frames and close-ups allow you to see the clothes, study the details, examine their drape and movement, practically feel the fabrics and textures. This and even more turns every *Videofashion Monthly* videocassette into a full color, multi-dimensional, high-impact show.

Videofashion Monthly informs, motivates and entertains you and everyone you do business with and for. Watch it in your office. Share it with others. Show it again and again—at your sales meeting, on your selling floor, in your reception area. Use it to gather vital data and generate sales. *Videofashion Monthly* video programs delight and enhance. They easily adapt to the merchandising methods you may already be using.

And, that's not all. If you choose to become a continuing *Videofashion Monthly* subscriber—and after you get your first videocassette we're sure you will—you'll be able to receive large discounts on other kinds of fashion programming from VIDEOFASHION, INC. We have been making fashion programs since 1976 and are now the largest fashion video company in the world. Today, no one has a more complete historical and current video library of designer shows, fashion and beauty information than does VIDEOFASHION, INC. We've even moved into menswear programming. You'll find our programs distributed and viewed in 22 countries of the world.

Four Reasons Why We Can Be Your Complete Fashion Resource on Videocassette:

1. *Videofashion Monthly* gives you 12 information-packed, exciting and entertaining magazine-format programs every year to keep customers, students, colleagues up to date on international fashion, shopping and beauty trends.
2. *Videofashion News* is a separate series of 6 half-hour programs produced each fashion season highlighting the most important and trend-setting examples of clothing from almost 90 designers shows. It is the first news service on videocassette geared directly to members of the fashion industry and related businesses. Twice a year—for Spring/Summer and again for Fall/Winter—we bring you right to where fashion history is being made: on the runways of the most important designer shows around the world. You see the new season BEFORE it's in the consumer magazines, BEFORE merchandise is in the stores, BEFORE many of the business decisions that shape *your* season have been made.

   With *Videofashion News,* the latest fashions come alive! Unlike a still photograph, you see actual moving footage of the runway shows as they were presented. You view the styles from every angle . . . see how the fabrics flow on the body . . . you're so close to the action, you can practically feel the textures of the clothes through the viewing screen! The new shapes and silhouettes take form before your very eyes as you watch how colors, lengths and proportions work together to create the most current fashion stories.
3. *Videofashion Men* is a videomagazine covering the very latest in International Menswear. Produced on a quarterly basis, the four half-hour programs each year contains regular "Departments" like Fashion News, Designer Profiles, Video*Cover* Portraits, Special Features, Must Buys, etc. Now, at last there's a fashion magazine about men on video. *Videofashion Men* picks up where *GQ* and *M* leave off.
4. *Videofashion Specials* are now being offered for the first time. We have 12 newly edited programs for immediate delivery: *Introduction to World Fashion, Video*Cover*Girls, The Art of Dressing, The Making of a Model, American Designers, Milan Designers, Paris Designers, Turning Japanese, The London Influence, Shopping the World, The Beauty Makers,* and *The Future of Fashion.* Each special is approximately 30-minutes in length and presents a dynamic and different view of fashion for anyone who wants to be informed about the fashion business today.

Organization of Frederick Atkins, Inc.

Frederick Atkins, Inc. is an international research and merchandising organization, jointly owned by forty-five independent department store groups in the United States. There are nine major retailers outside of the United States who are associate members. The combined total annual sales volume of the member stores in the United States only is well over four billion dollars. The Atkins office is headquartered in New York City at 1515 Broadway, where it occupies 110,000 square feet on four floors.

The office is organized like a department store, with three main divisions: Merchandising, Operations and Finance. On the staff of more than 400 people are the counterparts of every major executive in a store.

Frederick Atkins, Inc. has the following major divisions: Merchandising; Sales Promotion; Research; Accounting/Imports/Data Processing; Operating; Personnel/Communications; California Division; Frederick Wholesale Corporation.

Merchandising includes: Ready-To-Wear; Accessories; Shoes, Intimate Apparel; Children's; Men's & Boys'; Imports; Home Fashions/Home & Leisure; Budget Store; Fashion.

A brief description of these major divisions is given in the following pages.

STATEMENT OF PURPOSE

Frederick Atkins, Inc. is an international merchandising and marketing organization. It is a cooperative association, owned by a group of general merchandise retailers and operated by a professional staff that has expertise in retail management and in the merchandise categories sold in the stores.

The primary purpose of Frederick Atkins, Inc. is to assist its members in improving their sales, market share, profitability and image within each store's trading area. To these ends, Frederick Atkins provides its members with information and services related to (a) merchandise markets, (b) management and operation of a retail business, (c) advertising and merchandise presentation and (d) consumer attitudes and purchasing patterns.

A. Merchandise & Marketing

Frederick Atkins makes available to its members a broad spectrum of new marketing and merchandising concepts and directions that stores should be aware of in advance of competition.

Merchandise, sales promotion and fashion information is gathered from all foreign and domestic markets and transmitted on a daily basis via written and oral communications. Other reports and studies are prepared on both a regular and on an as-needed basis; these reports and studies concern markets, merchandise, presentation, sales promotion and merchandising techniques.

In addition to its information services, Frederick Atkins provides its members with a number of specialized merchandising services, such as import merchandise opportunities, provided through its 25 foreign commissionaires. Through its subsidiary organization, Frederick Wholesale Corporation, Frederick Atkins makes merchandise available from both domestic and foreign markets, and at a price

Source: Frederick Atkins. Reprinted with permission.

consistent with the quality standards of Atkins member stores.

B. Management and Operations

Frederick Atkins seeks to provide its members with the means to operate their businesses profitably and efficiently within the context of current economic and social conditions. It provides professional advice and information on a wide variety of subjects, including finance and economics, management information systems, marketing, personnel management and executive placement.

C. Cooperation In addition to its responsibility to provide information and services designed to enable the stores to maintain leadership in fashion and in the creative, innovative art of retailing, Frederick Atkins also functions as a forum for the exchange of ideas, techniques and information among the stores.

MERCHANDISING

The merchandising divisions are set up exactly the same as the stores, with General Merchandise Managers, Divisional Merchandise Managers and Buyers who are called Market Representatives.

The Market Representatives provide the stores with complete merchandising and research reports on all markets and activities covered by full-line department stores. They also provide the stores with prototype department reports which include resource structures, merchandise classifications mix, fashion trends and operating information, customer profiles and promotional and display ideas. This report is provided as a tool to help new buyers learn the business, and as an aid for established buyers to compare an existing business with that which is typical of an Atkins store.

The merchandising divisions also provide the stores with T.I.P.'s (Trend Intensification Program). T.I.P.'s are designed to help the stores zero in on major trends which are important in several classifications, or fashion silhouettes and materials that offer large volume or profit potential.

The merchandising divisions also prepare department intensification studies and comprehensive reports on emerging classifications and underdeveloped resources. In addition, Atkins undertakes major in-depth studies of key classifications, such as sportswear, as well as all aspects of retail operations.

FASHION

The Fashion Office at Frederick Atkins, Inc. operates as an arm of Merchandising, working directly with Divisional Merchandise Managers and Market Representatives in all areas of Soft Goods. The primary functions of the department are thorough market coverage, trend evaluation and timely communication of trend to member stores. Trends are interpreted from a merchandising standpoint and sent directly to those merchandisers responsible for implementation at retail as well as to store personnel in the creative services such as Directors of Sales Promotion, Advertising and Display.

Trends are ascertained by working with designers and manufacturers several months before each season both in the New York and California markets and by Spring and Fall attendance at the Pret-A-Porter collections in Milan, Florence, Paris, and London. Fabric and color news, projected through two major reports a year, is based on information gathered from American manufacturers of yarns and textiles and by attendance at Interstoff, the international fabric show at Frankfurt, Germany.

Two Fashion Directions Meetings are held each year: one in March for Fall Trend Projections and the other in September for Spring. These meetings, attended by 700 member store Presidents, General Merchandise Managers, Divisionals, and Buyers are regarded by both the stores and the office as the official "kick-off" for the next season. In-depth Fashion Trend Evaluations Books are then sent to the stores well in advance of actual buying periods and cover both Ready-to-Wear and Accessories.

Frequent communiques as to specific items and trend categories are mailed on a continuing basis in the form of Forward Fashion News bulletins, Action Items, and New Resource reports.

SALES PROMOTION

The Senior Vice President, Sales Promotion works closely with the member stores in all areas of advertising, publicity, public relations, special events, visual merchandising, and marketing techniques, plus emerging media and technology.

Through meetings, special reports and the regular exchange of ideas and information, member stores are kept informed of trends in sales promotion throughout the country and of new programs being developed by the Atkins Office, various communications media, manufacturers, and other industry groups.

The Direct Mail department offers an optional service to member stores that enables them to work together to produce top quality catalogs and statement enclosures. Through this program, stores with relatively small mailing lists compete successfully with the largest stores in their trading areas.

The Sales Promotion division is also responsible for the development, design and control of all Atkins Private Brand labels and packaging.

FREDERICK WHOLESALE CORPORATION (FWC)

The Frederick Wholesale Corporation is a wholly owned subsidiary of Frederick Atkins, Inc., established for the purpose of purchasing merchandise and supplies in bulk quantities for resale to retail stores throughout the United States. In this manner, Frederick Wholesale Corporation is able to offer to its customers savings not normally available on an individual basis.

All FWC merchandise, whether it carries an Atkins private label or a famous national brand, has the endorsement of store buyers whose advisory committees are totally involved in the selection and development of the programs.

To support group buying functions, FWC has a Quality Control Division which helps the advisory committees and the Atkins import buyers and market representatives evaluate merchandise to ensure that the member stores' high quality standards are maintained. All programs are tested prior to formal adoption, and again before delivery to the stores. The Quality Control Division has developed a very sophisticated program which requires our resources to adhere to our exacting specifications. All Atkins program coordinators have participated in a vigorous training program to ensure expertise in specification buying.

An office and showroom are maintained by Frederick Wholesale at 1515 Broadway, New York, New York 10036.

Mademoiselle: Editors and Departments and What They Do
The Editorial Staff

The EDITOR-IN-CHIEF heads the magazine. She has the final editorial word and determines the final result of the magazine. She reads every piece of copy, sees every proof, approves every photograph, sketch and layout, presides at most office conferences, and is liaison between management and the other editors. Her job is to create, together with the staff, a profitable product for MADEMOISELLE's publishers, The Condé Nast Publications Inc. The profit comes from attracting—and holding—readers and advertisers. With the staff, she must create editorial themes, feature ideas and beauty, health and fashion portfolios for forthcoming issues. She must also spot upcoming trends far enough in advance to make production deadlines. (MADEMOISELLE works roughly three months ahead of actual publication.) The Editor-in-Chief has other varied duties. They include fashion plans with manufacturers, discussing business problems, talking with experts in every field, meeting with staff and free-lance writers, and attending fashion shows. She is the chief representative for the magazine—speaking before fashion organizations, making guest appearances on radio and television programs, and serving on various boards and committees.

The MANAGING EDITOR focuses and coordinates the efforts of all the magazine's departments. She works closely with the Editor-in-Chief in planning and organizing the magazine from cover models and cover copy to theming issues to mapping out each issue's format. She keeps track of budget, or the number of pages allotted each issue, supervises deadlines, and keeps art, layouts, copy and proof moving. She edits all copy (including beauty and fashion) and often writes for the magazine. In the absence of the Editor-in-Chief, she becomes head of the staff.

Features are supervised and handled by the FEATURES EDITOR. These include articles that are of general interest, preferably those that are controversial and devoted to women's current concerns of work, relationships and sense of self. A staff of feature writers contributes ideas and articles; some articles are commissioned from free-lance writers. Chapters from forthcoming nonfiction books, articles from agents and occasionally unsolicited manuscripts are also used. The Feature Editor is responsible for the monthly columns and contributors.

The ART DIRECTOR is responsible for the physical appearance of the magazine. She works closely with the Editor-in-Chief, Managing Editor and departmental editors in planning editorial features. The Art Department is responsible for the "face" of MADEMOISELLE, and constantly strives for exciting typographical approaches to layouts. The Art Director selects photographers and/or free-lance artists for each feature, approves the selection of models for fashion layouts, chooses the illustrations or photographs to be used with each feature, and arranges these with blocks of copy to form the layouts. This department prepares a maquette (a small dia-

Source: *Mademoiselle Magazine*. Reprint permission granted.

gram organizing the space allotted each month to each department). From the resulting paste-ups and through several series of photostats a loose-bound version of the issue (the dummy) is prepared. In addition, the Art Director sees the portfolios of dozens of aspiring illustrators and photographers.

The FASHION EDITOR'S basic function is to interpret fashion news in terms of MADE-MOISELLE's readership interest and salability. The department is made up of several Associate Fashion Editors and each one is responsible for a specific area of the fashion market (shoes, lingerie, sportswear, coats, dresses, suits, accessories and men's wear). This department helps select clothes and models, presides over photographic sittings, works with the Art Department and the fashion copy writers, and makes presentations to the fashion trade and retail executives.

The BEAUTY AND HEALTH EDITOR and the BEAUTY MARKETING EDITOR and their assistants are responsible for the editorial beauty pages, as well as many health, diet and fitness pages. They help select models, supervise photography sittings, work closely with the Art Department on photographs and layouts, approve beauty copy and conduct beauty makeovers. The Beauty Editors report and create new looks which complement the new fashions. The Beauty Marketing Editor is specifically responsible for keeping MADEMOISELLE in touch with the ever-expanding beauty industry. She keeps abreast of the endless developments in the field of beauty and researches new products.

The CAREER EDITOR and her assistant keep track of women and their careers as they write in-depth profiles of young women in specific job fields, research and write articles about job trends, salary scales, management training courses and techniques for finding a job or leaving one.

The MEDICAL EDITOR and her assistant supervise the "Health Guide" that's in each issue and keep tabs on medical trends. The articles include the latest information on contraception, nutrition, infertility, diet, how to prevent a cold or survive one, how to talk back to your doctor, as well as tips on exercise and sports, beating the heat or cold, how often to have a checkup, etc.

The COPY EDITOR and her associates are in charge of writing some of the health and all of the fashion, beauty and home furnishings copy that appears on the editorial pages of the magazine. The department receives all of the essential information (description, prices, fabric credits, stores) from various departments and layouts from the Art Department to help them write the text copy and blurbs.

The HOME & FOOD EDITOR is responsible for MADEMOISELLE's pages which cover the at-home life: entertaining, table settings, gift ideas, food, decorating, and furniture. The Environments Editor interprets merchandise and decorating trends to the readers, covers the home furnishings market and represents MADEMOISELLE at trade functions.

The FABRIC EDITOR and her assistants are responsible for reporting and developing trends in the fabric market. They work closely with fabric mills and designers, offering suggestions for fabrics or reporting on their discoveries. The Fabric Editor may design material herself, which is then manufactured by a mill and sent to a ready-to-wear house to become a garment that is rightfully called MADEMOISELLE's own. This department usually works a year in advance, making predictions about fabric trends for upcoming seasons. They prepare a fabric bulletin board for use by the garment industry, designers and stores throughout the country who come to MADEMOISELLE rather than cover the market themselves.

The ENTERTAINMENTS EDITOR covers the arts: theatre, film, dance, music, literature and visuals. She researches and writes material for the Entertainments section and some other features in the magazine.

The TRAVEL EDITOR and her assistant report on the most interesting vacation possibilities here and abroad in a monthly column. They present in-depth pieces on places to visit, ways to travel, things to buy, the "in" spots of a particular season, or little-known locales of surprising interest. They also advise readers requesting information on any aspect of travel. This department often ties in with the Fashion Department to illustrate, for example, "Where to Ski and What to Wear." They are also invaluable in feeding information on the young women's travel habits and plans to all members of the travel industry.

The FICTION EDITOR spends hours upon hours reading all material submitted to this department—unsolicited manuscripts as well as those sent by agents, college literary magazines, galleys of forthcoming books and European fiction. MADEMOISELLE has the reputation for discovering new writers and for publishing stories that are later selected for inclusion in anthologies. MADEMOISELLE is always on the lookout for new talent and sponsors the annual College Fiction Competition. Fiction entries number close to a thousand.

The SHOPPING EDITOR is responsible for MADEMOISELLE's monthly "Mailway Catalogue" section, selecting merchandise from the best and most original products available through specialty stores, boutiques and mail-order houses.

The PRODUCTION EDITOR and her department are responsible for the physical execution of every page of MADEMOISELLE. They edit all copy for errors in spelling, punctuation, construction and grammar, serving as a liaison between the editorial staff and the printers in Chicago. They take the copy from original edited text to the final proofs by ordering type, assuring adherence to alloted space and coordinating the type and illustration. The Production Editor must also see that all proofs are approved by the proper editors and that all deadlines are met.

The EDITORIAL PRODUCTION COORDINATOR is responsible for the magazine's release on time. Coordinating corporate production schedules for the art, copy and production departments, she makes sure that the schedules are adhered to. She coordinates the art and editorial units through all states of production, acting as a liaison between departments as well as a link between the corporate production department and the magazine staff.

The READER MAIL CORRESPONDENT deals exclusively with the readers—the magazine's continual source of feedback opinion. She answers any queries readers might have about MADEMOISELLE—from fashion advice to circulation figures. In addition, she selects reader mail for publication in the column, "From You to Us."

THE BUSINESS STAFF

The PUBLISHER of the magazine works very closely with the Editor-in-Chief but specifically represents the financial, business end of MADEMOISELLE. He is the final "decision maker" for the magazine's relations with the business community. His primary goal is to increase advertising revenue, thus keeping the profit margin healthy.

The ADVERTISING DIRECTOR and his staff of (ADVERTISING REPRESENTATIVES) have the responsibility of selling advertising space in MADEMOISELLE. Sales representatives solicit business from companies whose products can best and most logically be merchandised to the 18-to-34-year-old age group, MADEMOISELLE's readership. Each sales representative covers a specific market—fashion, beauty, travel, schools, etc. The sales representative is a good-will ambassador, the legman between client and magazine.

THE PROMOTION STAFF

The PROMOTION DIRECTOR and her assistants, together with the PROMOTION ART DIRECTOR and the PROMOTION COPY CHIEF, maintain a department that is much like a small advertising agency with MADEMOISELLE as its sole account. It consists of copy writers, publicists, artists and liaison people, and a marketing staff, who work with stores, manufacturers and advertisers. The general purpose is to promote the magazine at every possible level. Promotion pieces, trade ads and presentations are directed to advertisers and potential advertisers. This department also prepares all the sales tools for the advertising department. Merchandising aids specialists carry on a campaign to supply manufacturers and retailers with tie-in material—counter cards, blowups, reprints for mailing, hang tags, etc. The Promotion Director supervises all special projects such as fashion shows, exhibits and promotional films.

The PUBLICITY/CAREER MARKETING MANAGER'S job is two-fold. As Career Marketing Manager she works with a panel of college students and career women who do product research for MADEMOISELLE's advertisers, keeping them up-to-date on their likes and dislikes. As Career Manager she reports to advertisers on MADEMOISELLE readers' shopping habits, product preferences and services they may require. She also heads MADEMOISELLE's "Career Network," a panel of successful working women in 25 major cities across the country. In her Publicity

Manager capacity, she and her assistant publicize each issue of the magazine at every possible communications level. She prepares news releases for the media—newspapers, syndicates, trade publications, radio and television. She initiates special publicity projects, as well as publicizes the magazine's regular features. She is the official hostess for the magazine—and does everything from giving tours to planning parties.

THE MERCHANDISING DEPARTMENT

The MERCHANDISING DIRECTOR and her associates work with retail stores across the country that use MADEMOISELLE promotions throughout the year. MADEMOISELLE maintains a showroom where top store executives come to preview merchandise that will be featured in future issues of the magazine. (MADEMOISELLE was the first magazine to offer on-page merchandising for fashions, i.e., to list retail stores, colors, sizes, fabrics, prices, etc. If the stores decide to carry the merchandise shown in the fashion editorial pages, they may be credited in the magazine.) For each garment, five retail stores across the country and one New York store are listed. MADEMOISELLE also helps retail stores promote the magazine's editorial choices via fashion shows, window displays and other promotional aids. The MERCHANDISE CREDIT COORDINATOR keeps in constant touch with stores across the country checking and rechecking to make certain the clothes shown editorially are readily available to readers. This department also keeps in contact with manufacturers to make sure clothes are actually made and delivered.

The WESTERN EDITOR works with stores and shop markets for editorial merchandise so that the New York City branch is aware of fashion markets and retail patterns across the country. The Western Editor keeps up good public relations with both manufacturers and retailers in addition to keeping the New York staff alerted to market and fashion news in their territory. MADEMOISELLE's fashion directions are passed on to markets and stores by this editor.

Endnotes

1. Address before Harvard Graduate School of Business Administration, Cambridge, Mass., April 25, 1957. Reprinted with permission of the late Tobé Coller Davis in the 1965 edition of this book.
2. Samuel Feinberg, "From Where I Sit," *Women's Wear Daily*, December 2, 1985.
3. *Organization of Frederick Atkins, Inc. Handbook.* New York: Frederick Atkins.
4. *Ibid.*
5. Samuel Feinberg, "From Where I Sit," *Women's Wear Daily*, December 22, 1985.
6. Feinberg, "From Where I Sit," December 2, 1985.
7. *Organization of Frederick Atkins, Inc. Handbook.*
8. Standard Rate and Data Service (a reference service for advertisers) provides information on rates and circulation and brings figures up to date periodically. These amounts are from the August 1986 issue.
9. *IMS/Ayer Directory of Publications*, 1985 annual edition.
10. *Ibid.*
11. "Dressing Up with FTV," *Newsweek*, January 7, 1985.
12. Lewis A. Spalding, "Taped for Success," *Stores*, May 1985.
13. *Fortune Magazine*, April 1986.

Selected Bibliography

Beaton, Cecil. *The Best of Beaton.* New York: Macmillan, 1968.

Brady, James. *Superchic.* Boston: Little, Brown, 1974.

Cahan, Linda, and Joseph Robinson. *A Practical Guide to Visual Merchandising.* New York: John Wiley and Sons, 1984.

Ehrenkranz, Lois B., and Gilbert R. Kahn. *Public Relations/Publicity: A Key Link to Communication.* New York: Fairchild Publications, 1983.

Howell, Georgina. *In Vogue; Sixty Years of International Celebrities and Fashion from British Vogue.* New York: Schocken, 1976.

Kelly, Katie. *The Wonderful World of Women's Wear Daily.* New York: Saturday Review Press, 1972.

Pegler, Martin M. *Visual Merchandising and Display.* New York: Fairchild Publications, 1983.

Snow, Carmel. *The World of Carmel Snow.* New York: McGraw-Hill, 1962.

Winters, Arthur and Stanley Goodman. *Fashion Advertising and Sales Promotion,* 6th ed. New York: Fairchild Publications, 1984.

Trade Associations

American Advertising Federation, 1225 Connecticut Avenue N.W., Washington, D.C. 20036.

American Association of Advertising Agencies, 666 Third Avenue, New York, N.Y. 10017.

The Fashion Group, Inc., 9 Rockefeller Plaza, New York, N.Y. 10020.

Magazine Publishers Association, Inc., 575 Lexington Avenue, New York, N.Y. 10010.

Public Relations Institute, 350 West 57th Street, New York, N.Y. 10019.

Public Relations Society of America, 845 Third Avenue, New York, N.Y. 10022.

Trade Publications

Advertising Age, 740 North Rush Street, Chicago, Ill. 60611.

Fashion Calendar, 185 East 85th Street, New York, N.Y. 10028.

Public Relations Journal, 845 Third Avenue, New York, N.Y. 10022.

Standard Rate and Data Service, Inc., 5201 Old Orchard Road, Skokie, Ill. 60076.

Visual Merchandising, 407 Gilbert Avenue, Cincinnati, Ohio 45202.

CHAPTER REVIEW AND LEARNING ACTIVITIES ....

Key Words and Concepts

Define, identify, or briefly explain the following:

Advertising	Group purchase
Advertising agency	Market representative
Corporate buying office	Merchandising editor
Cooperative buying office	Product developer
Daily News Record	Publicity
Editorial credit	Resident buying office
Fashion consultant	Tobé Associates
The Fashion Group	Trade association
Fashion information service	Trade publication
Fashion magazine	*Women's Wear Daily*
Fee office	

Review Questions on Chapter Highlights

1. List the different types of information provided by a fashion information service. What types of firms subscribe to them? Why and how are they used?
2. Why would a Japanese company and an American company subscribe to and utilize the *same* fashion information service?
3. Name and briefly explain the different types of buying offices. What function do they all serve?
4. Could the services of a New York buying office help you, as an out-of-town store buyer, do a better job, and if so, how? Could the services of a New York buying office help you, as a New York store buyer, and why or why not?
5. Using the reading "Organization of Frederick Atkins, Inc." (see the chapter readings preceding), describe the specific types of merchandising and fashion information that they send to their stores.
6. Explain the relationship and services of a fashion magazine to each of the following: (a) apparel producers, (b) retailers, (c) consumers.
7. What types of information are found in trade publications such as *Women's Wear Daily* and *Daily News Record*? How does a trade publication differ from a fashion magazine?
8. Why and how are retailers using closed circuit television?
9. Citing an example of each, explain the similarities and differences between advertising and publicity. Do you think that one is more effective in selling fashion merchandise than the other? Why?
10. What is a trade association? Give the names of trade associations that have been mentioned in previous chapters in this book and describe their activities.

Applications for Research and Discussion

1. Research current costs of a page of black-and-white advertising and a page of four-color advertising in both fashion and general-interest monthly magazines. How do you think the costs are justified in relation to potential return on investment?
2. Survey large stores in your immediate vicinity to investigate present use of closed circuit in store video presentations. In what types of stores and/or departments are they found most frequently? What is your opinion about their efficacy as a selling tool? Why?
3. Assume you hold an executive position in the fashion field. Identify your job and research the trade publications that you would find most helpful in successfully accomplishing your job. Describe the type of information that they provide and bring in three examples of articles that you consider particularly valuable. Explain your choices.

THE INFLUENTIAL DESIGNERS

These are the people who have had the greatest design impact on the fashion industry during this century. Some of them are superb craftsmen and women whose knowledge of fabric, cut, and production have enabled millions to be clothed with taste and style. Others have raised fashion design to the level of art. In all cases, they have either created lasting trends, established standards of excellence, or been a major influence on future generations.

ADOLFO   Began as milliner, added separates, custom blouses, long skirts in late '60s . . . devoted following of status dressers.

GILBERT ADRIAN   MGM's top designer, 1923–1939, for stars such as Crawford, Hepburn, Garbo . . . wide shoulders, tailored suits.

AZZEDINE ALAIA   Sexy clothes that cling to every curve from this contemporary Paris ready-to-wear designer.

WALTER ALBINI   Early Italian rtw designer.

HARDY AMIES   British couturier for men and women, noted for his tailored suits, coats, cocktail and evening dresses.

GIORGIO ARMANI   Major Italian rtw force for men and women . . . beautifully tailored clothes . . . now at peak of his powers.

LAURA ASHLEY   Romantic Victorian looks in fabrics and fashion . . . built a London-based empire in clothes and home furnishings.

CRISTOBAL BALENCIAGA   One of century's greatest . . . innovations include semifit jacket, cocoon coat, balloon skirt, bathrobe coat, pillbox hat . . . disciples include Givenchy, Courreges, Ungaro.

PIERRE BALMAIN   Opened own Paris house in 1945 . . . classic daytime looks, extravagant evening gowns.

Source: WWD: 75 Years in Fashion 1910–1985. Reprint permission granted.

PATRICK DE BARENTZEN   "Daring" member of Italian couture in the '60s . . . whimsical . . . enormous Infanta skirts.

JEAN BARTHET   Influential milliner of the '50s and '60s . . . customers ranged from Princess Grace to Sophia Loren.

BILL BLASS   Mr. Fashion Right . . . taste, durability and a consistent high level of talent since the late '50s.

MARC BOHAN   Joined House of Dior in the early '60s and has been there ever since.

DONALD BROOKE   Most successful period was the '60s . . . also did much work for Broadway stage.

STEPHEN BURROWS   Body-conscious clothes in vibrant colors . . . noted for his draped matte jerseys.

ROBERTO CAPUCCI   Started in Rome at age 21 . . . very hot in the '50s . . . known for drapery, imaginative cutting.

JOHN CAVANAUGH   One of Britain's best in the '50s . . . headed Curzon St. . . . known for nipped-waist, full-skirt New Look.

PIERRE CARDIN   King of the licensing game . . . top innovator of the '50s and '60s, became first Paris couturier to sell his own rtw . . . now involved in everything from rock to restaurants.

HATTIE CARNEGIE   Influential in the '30s and '40s . . . began as milliner, then designed custom and rtw . . . influenced Norell, Trigere, McCardell.

BONNIE CASHIN   An American sportswear original—casual country and travel clothes in wool jersey, knits, tweeds, canvas, leather.

ANTONIO DEL CASTILLO   The Infanta silhouette . . . designed for Lanvin from 1950–1963, then opened his own house in Paris.

COCO CHANEL   Chanel No. 5 . . . the house on the rue Cambon . . . the Chanel suit: braid-trim, collarless jacket, patch pockets . . . feminism before it was fashionable . . . the one and only.

ALDO CIPULLO   Jeweler for Cartier's in the '70s . . . elegance, but with a light approach.

LIZ CLAIBORNE   Contemporary sportswear . . . executive dressing . . . great commercial success.

OSSIE CLARK   Enfant terrible of British fashion in the '60s . . . HotPants, maxi coats . . . started '40s revival in 1968.

SYBIL CONNOLLY   Ireland's most prestigious designer.

ANDRES COURREGES   The Basque tailor . . . hot in the '60s, with suits and roomy coats . . . Tough Chic . . . the great white way.

ANGELA CUMMINGS   Designed jewelry for Tiffany's, now on her own . . . inventive and tasteful.

LILLY DACHE   From the '30s to '50s, U.S.'s top milliner . . . draped turbans, brimmed hats, snoods . . . fantasies for films.

DONALD DAVIES   English shirtmaker who is based in Dublin and went to shirtdresses in the '60s . . . he used featherweight Irish tweed in a variety of colors.

JEAN DRESSES Designed from 1925–1965 . . . his Jean Dresses Diffusion, a lower-price line for America, the start of mass production by a French couturier.

CHRISTIAN DIOR Launched the New Look in 1947, becoming fashion's most famous name until his death 10 years later.

PERRY ELLIS Appeared in the '70s as one of the avant-garde young sportswear designers . . . gave classics a high-fashion twist.

ALBERTO FABIANI One of Italy's top couturiers of the '50s . . . "surgeon of coats and suits" . . . conservative tailoring . . . wed Simonetta Visconti.

JACQUES FATH Enfant terrible, showman, ran own Paris house from 1937–1954 . . .sexy clothes, hourglass shapes, plunging necklines.

GIANFRANCO FERRE Architectural approach has turned him into one of Italy's leading rtw designers.

SALVATORE FERRAGAMO Italian shoemaker who became international success . . . pioneer of wedge heel, platform sole, Lucite acrylics heel.

ANNE FOGARTY Spearheaded the revolution in junior sizes in the early '50s.

FONTANA SISTERS One of Italy's leading couture houses in the '50s, started by mother, Amabile, in 1907, continued by daughters Zoe, Micol and Giovanna.

MARIANO FORTUNY Mushroom-pleated silk tea gowns . . . his clothes now are collector's items.

FEDERICO FORQUET Big in the '60s in Rome, noted for coats and suits in blocks of bold color . . . went into interior design in 1972.

JAMES GALANOS Born in Philadelphia, studied in New York, worked in Paris, opened own business in Los Angeles . . . one of America's most elegant fashion creators.

IRENE GALITZINE Palazzo pajamas of the '60s an important concept . . . now in cosmetics, furs, linens.

JEAN-PAUL GAULTIER One of Paris's trendiest and more controversial rtw designers for men and women.

RUDI GERNREICH Avant-garde sportswear . . . maillots . . . topless swimsuit, 1964 . . . see-through blouses . . . the No-Bra.

HUBERT DE GIVENCHY A major couturier since he opened own House in Paris in '52 . . . influenced by Balenciaga . . . most famous client: Audrey Hepburn.

ALIX GRES Originally a sculptress . . . couturiere since 1934 . . . known for statuesque and molded gowns "sculpted" on live model.

ALDO GUCCI Head of Florence-based family business . . . Manufacturer and retailer of leathers, luggage and apparel . . . GG.

HALSTON Began as milliner at Bergdorf's, did Jacqueline Kennedy's pillbox hat, 1961 . . . opened couture business in '68, rtw in '72 . . . simple classics . . . now designs collection for J. C. Penney.

NORMAN HARTNELL London's biggest couture house in the '30s . . . coronation gowns for Queen Elizabeth.

EDITH HEAD   Probably Hollywood's best-known designer.

JACQUES HEIM   Successful Paris couturier from 1923 until the early '60s . . . designer of Atome, the first bikini.

BARBARA HULANICKI   Mod look, the early '60s . . . a founder of Biba . . . the Total Look: coordinated color in clothes, cosmetics, hose.

IRENE   Top designer for movie stars for many decades, also had own rtw business in the '60s.

CHARLES JAMES   The Eccentric One . . . ran own custom business in the '40s and '50s . . . innovative shapes . . . the Dali of design.

MR. JOHN   One of America's best-known milliners, especially in the '40s and '50s—the heyday of hats.

BETSEY JOHNSON   Big in the '60s . . . low prices, off-beat fashions . . . designed for Paraphernalia, co-founded Betsey Bunky Nini.

STEPHEN JONES   London's extraordinary milliner who designs hats for such notables as Lady Di.

NORMA KAMALI   Her contemporary sweatshirt clothes made high fashion affordable by a young audience.

JACQUES KAPLAN   Headed Georges Kaplan, new York furrier . . . innovator and promoter . . . a pioneer of "fun" furs.

DONNA KARAN   Anne Klein's assistant, then her successor . . . now on her own . . . high-fashion, elegant sportswear.

REI KAWAKUBO   Comme des Garcons . . . one of the first of the New Wave from Japan in the '80s.

KENZO   Left Japan for Paris in 1965 . . . light, whimsical rtw.

EMMANUELLE KHANH   One of the first major rtw designers in Paris in the '60s . . . kicky, young clothes.

CHARLES KLEIBACKER   Journalism, show business, then fashion . . . opened own business in New York in 1960 . . . known for bias cuts.

ANNE KLEIN   A major American sportswear designer . . . associated with Junior Sophisticates, 1951–1964 . . . classic sportswear.

CALVIN KLEIN   Pure American looks in sportswear and rtw . . . clean lines, sophistication and a wide range of prices.

KARL LAGERFELD   Outspoken, controversial, avant-garde . . . designed for Chloe, now for Fendi and Chanel as well as his own firm.

JEANNE LANVIN   One of earliest Paris couturiers . . . peak years between two World Wars . . . her perfumes: My Sin and Arpege.

RALPH LAUREN   Noted for his Americana-influenced designs . . . the western look for men and women.

LUCIEN LELONG   Great name in Paris couture from the '20s to '40s . . . didn't design, himself, but inspired workers such as Dior, Balmain, Givenchy and Schlumberger.

JEAN LOUIS   Not only a successful Hollywood designer, but also headed his own couture firm.

MAINBOCHER One of America's first custom designers . . . dressed Duchess of Windsor . . . specialized in quiet quality.

GERMANA MARUCELLI Avant-garde Milanese couturier of the '50s and '60s.

VERA MAXWELL Pioneer of American sportswear.

CLAIRE MCCARDELL Perhaps the most profound influence on American sportswear design . . . hot in the '40s and '50s.

MARY MCFADDEN Socialite who first started designing exotic jewelry . . . her pleated evening dresses became the rage in the late '70s.

MISSONI One of the early Italian rtw families . . . known for knits in original colors and designs.

ISSEY MIYAKE Avant-garde Japanese designer, predated Japan's New Wave.

CAPT. EDWARD MOLYNEUX From the '20s to '40s, his purity of line drew the rich and famous to his Paris salon. Brief revival in the '60s.

CLAUDE MONTANA Contemporary French rtw . . . big shoulders . . . leathers . . . architectural shapes.

HANAE MORI Comes from Japan, shows in France . . . tasteful clothes in beautiful colors . . . innovative beading.

DIGBY MORTON Early British couturier . . . opened house in 1933 . . . specialized in tailored suits, cableknit sweaters, Donegal tweeds.

THIERRY MUGLER Tongue-in-chic fashion from one of Paris's New Wave designers.

JEAN MUIR Started in the '60s in London . . . elegant, intricately detailed young clothes.

NORMAN NORELL Brought American fashion to the level of Paris couture.

FRANK OLIVE Sophisticated and slick hats have been his forte since the '60s.

ANDRE OLIVER Associated with Pierre Cardin since 1955 . . . created clothes for men and women.

PAQUIN One of the first Paris couturiers . . . house opened in 1891 and lasted until 1956.

MOLLIE PARNIS One of the most successful women designers and manufacturers on SA.

JEAN PATOU A businessman and showman as well as a designer of elegant, ladylike couture clothes in the '20s and '30s.

MME. PAULETTE Leading American milliner in the '50s and '60s . . . associated with Saks Fifth Avenue.

SYLVIA PEDLAR Put high fashion into loungewear . . . founded Irish Lingerie and designed there 40 years.

ELSA PERETTI Revolutionary jewelry designer . . . diamonds by the yard . . . made small diamonds fashionable . . . innovator in silver.

ROBERT PIQUET Ran his Paris couture house from 1933 to 1951 . . . influenced Givenchy and Dior, both of whom were employed by him.

PAUL POIRET One of first French couturiers to free women from constraints of underpinnings . . . leader of early 20th century.

THEA PORTER Anti-establishment London designer of the '60s and '70s . . . fantasy long clothes . . . Orientalia.

ANNA POTOK A key influence in fur design . . . founder of Maximilian.

EMILIO PUCCI His prints on thin silk jerseys revolutionized Italian fashion in the '50s and '60s.

LILLY PULITZER Her printed-cotton shift, the "Lilly," swept the nation in the '60s and '70s . . . floral prints . . . Palm Beach.

MARY QUANT A miniskirt pioneer synonymous with the "swinging London" look of the '60s . . . Carnaby St.

MADELEINE DE RAUCHE Renowned sportswoman who created sports clothes for herself and friends . . . made functional clothes in the '30s.

OSCAR DE LA RENTA Came to U.S. to work for Elizabeth Arden in the early '60s . . . one of SA's "luxury" designers.

ZANDRA RHODES A London original . . . outrageous evening looks . . . fantasy colorings for hair and makeup.

JACQUELINE DE RIBES A socialite-turned-designer . . . her love of couture quality is reflected in her rtw.

NINA RICCI Opened her house in Paris in 1932 . . . dressed mature, elegant women . . . pioneered showing lower-priced clothes in a boutique . . . her fragrance: L'Air du Temps.

MARCEL ROCHAS Elegant French Couture of the '30s and '40s . . . packaged a perfume called Femme in black lace.

SONIA RYKIEL The genius of sweater dressing.

YVES SAINT LAURENT One of the century's greatest influences on fashion and taste.

COUNT FERNANDO SARMI Beautiful evening clothes . . . chief designer at Elizabeth Arden, 1951–1959, then head of his own business.

JEAN-LOUIS SCHERRER His soft, refined dresses popular in the '60s . . . opened own Paris house in 1962.

ELSA SCHIAPARELLI The Great Schiap . . . one of the true avant-garde designers in Paris from the '30s to '50s.

JEAN SCHLUMBERGER Legendary jeweler whose exuberant fantasies have pleased women such as Bunny Mellon and Babe Paley since the late '40s.

MILA SCHOEN Important Italian designer of the '60s and '70s.

KEN SCOTT Expatriate from Indiana who settled in Milan . . . fabric and dress designer since 1956 . . . Art Nouveau influenced.

SIMONETTA One of the first of the Italian couture designers . . . married Albert Fabiani.

ADELE SIMPSON One of SA's durables . . . in her own business since 1949 . . . known for conservative good taste.

STEPHEN SPROUSE Contemporary, controversial designs, strongly influenced by the '60s.

GUSTAVE TASSELL Started own business in Los Angeles, 1959 . . . refined, no-nonsense clothes.

PAULINE TRIGERE A pioneer American couturiere . . . started own business in 1942, still going strong.

EMANUEL UNGARO Once known as "the young terrorist" of fashion, now does some of the most seductive clothes in Paris.

VALENTINA Russian-born, opened own couture business in America in 1928 . . . dramatic clothes . . . dressed Garbo, whom she resembled.

VALENTINO The Chic . . . one of the most important European couturiers since the mid-'60s . . . taste, elegance, timelessness.

PHILIPPE VENET Givenchy's master tailor, 1953–1962, then opened own business . . . noted for lean suits, rounder shoulders.

GIANNI VERSACE Italian rtw . . . an innovator for men and women in leathers and other fabrics.

SALLY VICTOR From mid-'30s to mid-'60s, one of America's most prominent milliners.

MADELEINE VIONNET The inventor of the bias cut and a major influence on fashion since early in the century.

DAVID WEBB Known for his enamel-and-jeweled bracelets in the '60s.

JOHN WEITZ Women's sportswear with men's-wear look . . . big in the '50s and '60s . . . now only in men's wear . . . once "designed" a cigar.

VIVIENNE WESTWOOD Contemporary, controversial English designer . . . runs World's End, off-beat London boutique.

B. H. WRAGGE Owner-designer of Sydney Wragge, pioneered concept of sportswear separates . . . important in the '40s and '50s.

CHARLES FREDERICK WORTH Dressmaker for Empress Eugenie and "founder" of French couture when he opened his own house in 1858.

YOHJI YAMAMOTO Oversize, dramatic Japanese clothes.

BEN ZUCKERMAN The master tailor . . . major influence on American coats and suits.

B

SOURCES OF CURRENT STATISTICAL INFORMATION

FROM THE U.S. GOVERNMENT

- *Statistical Abstract of the United States*. Annual. Provides historical as well as fairly current data on a wide variety of subjects. Uses both government and private sources. From the U.S. Department of Commerce, Washington, D.C. 20233. In most libraries.
- *Survey of Current Business*. Monthly. Provides little historical data but much fairly current data from a variety of sources. U.S. Department of Commerce.
- *U.S. Industrial Outlook*. Annual. Provides quite current figures and interpretive comment on many industries, but may not cover every industry each year. U.S. Department of Commerce.
- *Population Profile*. Annual. Summarizes data on population by age, sex, area, income level, and so on. U.S. Department of Commerce.
- *Monthly Labor Review*. Contains data on the work force, consumer price index, wholesale prices, and so on. U.S. Department of Labor, Washington, D.C. 20212.

The listed publications are a good starting point for research. For greater detail about specific subject areas, consult the following sources:

- *Industry production:* Write the Bureau of the Census, U.S. Department of Commerce, Washington, D.C. 20233, for whatever is currently available on the particular product, industry, or retail or wholesale operation with which you are concerned.

484

- *The consumer:* Contact the Bureau of the Census for its most recent population reports on whatever phase interests you most (income, education, ethnic origin, metropolitan area versus nonmetropolitan, etc.). For information on how much the public spends on various categories of goods and services, ask the Office of Business Economics, U.S. Department of Commerce, for its latest annual report on personal consumption expenditures. Also check the Bureau of Labor Statistics, U.S. Department of Labor, Washington, D.C. 20212, for possible studies of urban family budgets and expenditures.
- *Foreign trade:* Monthly reports, with annual figures in the December issue each year, from the Department of Commerce, Bureau of the Census. FT110, on imports and FT410 on exports are good starting points.

PRIVATE RESEARCH ORGANIZATIONS

Supported by their subscribers, private research organizations often develop useful research publications, some of which may be compendiums of statistics gathered from many sources.

- *Dun & Bradstreet Companies, Inc., 299 Park Avenue, New York, N.Y. 10017.* This is a credit reporting agency, primarily concerned with business enterprises. It makes special studies of various industries and publishes *Focus*, the economic profile sponsored by the Apparel Manufacturers Association of America.
- *Conference Board, 845 Third Avenue, New York, N.Y.* Funded by business firms, makes studies of economic conditions, consumer attitudes, and so on. Presents statistics from government sources in graphic form.
- *Standard & Poor, 25 Broadway, New York, N.Y.* A service subscribed to by financial and investment concerns to provide information on individual companies whose stocks are listed on the various exchanges. Has detailed information on producers and retailers; makes annual studies of textile and apparel industries, "Textiles, Apparel and Home Furnishings."

  Each chapter of the text includes a list of associations functioning in the field covered. For additional organizations, check with your library for its latest available directory of trade associations.

PERIODICALS

Publications that sell advertising usually have research departments, which are sources of information on the publication's readers and on the market it serves. Each chapter of the text includes an appropriate list. For additional sources, check with your library for its latest directory, such as *Ulrich's International Periodicals Directory, Standard Rate and Data Service,* or *IMS/Ayer Directory of Publications.*

C

CAREER OPPORTUNITIES IN FASHION

Fashion is everywhere, and so are career opportunities for those who combine a knowledge of the fashion business with their own talent, ambition, and ability. Consider that a fashion career may open up anywhere along the road from raw materials to the final consumer purchase; stores, mail-order houses, other forms of retailing, manufacturing companies, advertising agencies, newspapers, magazines, commercial photography studios, and public relations firms are among the student's targets in the quest for a foothold in fashion.

Personal attributes suggest the direction a beginner should take. An outgoing personality helps in sales work at all levels, in showroom work, in public relations, and especially in jobs such as that of fashion coordinator, in which one often needs persuasive skills to sell one's ideas to other executives in the organization. The gift of a great figure or a photogenic face can make modeling a possibility, and through that work, a chance to learn from inside many other phases of the fashion business. The visually creative people do well in design, display, advertising, photography, and sketching for designers and fashion information services. Analytical minds adapt well to the multiple problems of managing retail fashion assortments or planning factory production, and thrive on market research.

The rewards of fashion careers are as varied as the jobs themselves. Some pay fabulously; others provide only a modest living. Some positions demand worldwide travel, to buy or observe, or to do both. Others permit one to live at home and commute to an office, retail store, or manufacturing establishment. But all of them, and hundreds more, offer the student of fashion a

486

chance to work, learn, and grow in the endlessly exciting, unceasingly stimulating business of fashion.

The following is a guide to entry-level jobs in the fashion industry. It was prepared by Phyllis Madan and Marilyn Henrion of the Placement Department of the Fashion Institute of Technology, New York, which is affiliated with the State University of New York.

ENTRY-LEVEL JOBS FOR FASHION DESIGN GRADUATES ....

- Assistant designer
- Cutting assistant
- Sketching assistant
- Sketcher (assistant to designer)
- Sketcher/stylist
- Junior designer

The personal qualities needed for all of the following jobs in the design room are similar. Applicants must be well organized, flexible, fast workers, and have the ability to work under pressure in often cramped working conditions. Fashionable grooming and neat appearance are essential. Most jobs require creativity and a good eye for trends in silhouette, color, and fabric.

Assistant Designer

Responsibilities. Responsible for executing designers' ideas by creating a first pattern from slopers or draping. Instructs and supervises the work of samplehands. Often is required to keep records, order fabrics and trim, do follow-up and clerical work. Although job is primarily technical in nature, one may be asked to shop stores for trends, sketch, possibly consult with designer about fabric choices and designs.

Skills/Preparation Required. Fashion design degree, good knowledge of garment construction (sewing), strong technical skills (making first patterns, draping, and sketching). Beginners must have a portfolio.

Cutting Assistant

Responsibilities. Beginning assistant position in companies where there are several assistant designers. Cuts samples, alters patterns, generally assists in design room. Once ability is proven, may have opportunity to assist patternmaker or do draping.

Skills/Preparation Required. Fashion Design degree preferred, good pattern-making skills, draping skills helpful, knowledge of garment construction.

Sketching Assistant

Responsiblities. Sketches principally for designers' records—precise technical sketches of constructed garment swatched with fabric and trim. May sketch free-hand or with croquis. May sketch and prepare artwork for presentations. Writes specification sheets on how garments are constructed. Usually orders fabric, handles a variety of clerical and follow-up duties. May do market research.

Skills/Preparation Required. Fashion design degree necessary. Ability to do precise technical sketches rapidly. Portfolio required.

Sketcher (Assistant to Designer)

Responsibilities. Sketches free-hand illustration-quality sketches of designers' ideas, may be asked to contribute own design ideas, may deal with buyers, and do promotional work. Hours are often long and irregular. Must be available to run errands, and generally assist the designer.

Skills/Preparation Required. Fashion design degree a must. Ability to do free-hand illustration-quality sketches at a fast pace. Outstanding portfolio required.

Personal Qualities Required. Extremely high taste level as evidenced by personal appearance and portfolio. Awareness of new fashion trends both in the United States and in Europe. Must be articulate, poised, and able to deal with high-level executives.

Sketcher/Stylist

Responsibilities. Works directly with principals of firm. Shops stores for current trends, sketches ideas, works with patternmaker in developing these ideas, may or may not do technical work of draping and patternmaking. Participates in fabric selection, coordination of the line, and may be involved in working with buyers in merchandising the line.

Skills/Preparation Required. Fashion design degree, excellent portfolio, good eye for trends in silhouettes, color, and fabric.

Personal Qualities Required. See Sketcher/Assistant above.

Junior Designer

Responsibilities. Sketches original designs, executes own first pattern, frequently sews sample. Does market research in fabrics and trends. Must be able to provide company with new design ideas and make accurate predictions on what will be salable in coming season. Must be able to design garments within company's price range. Job is fast paced and a high-risk position since continuation of employment may be based on success of line.

Skills/Preparation Required. Fashion design degree required. Strong creative ability as well as excellent technical skills (draping, patternmaking, sewing). Good eye for trends (silhouette, color, fabric). Portfolio must show evidence of strong creative ability in designing coordinated line of apparel.

Personal Qualities Required. See Sketcher/Assistant above.

ENTRY-LEVEL JOBS FOR TEXTILE DESIGN GRADUATES

- Textile artist
- Colorist
- Assistant to stylist
- Embroidery designer
- Handweaver
- Silk screen artist

Jobs for textile design graduates may be found in textile mills, textile converting houses, textile design studios and vertical manufacturers (garment manufacturers who produce their own fabric).

Personal Qualities Required. The personal qualities required for all the jobs listed below are similar. On jobs other than those of a strictly technical nature, a high degree of creativity is a must as well as an excellent color sense and eye for fashion trends. Other requirements include neatness, ability to follow through on a job from start to finish, ability to follow instructions, and work at a fast pace. Interpersonal skills are required in those jobs involving public contact.

Textile Artist

Does original textile designs, may also do color combinations and repeats.

Colorist

Does various color combinations of existing designs.

Assistant to Stylist

Sets up appointments for stylist, acts as liaison with mills, works with clients and salespeople in stylist's absence, keeps clerical records.

Embroidery Designer

Does detailed technical drawings on graph paper of designs for lace and embroidery. Limited use of color.

Handweaver

Executes designer's ideas on hand loom.

Silk Screen Artist

Executes designer's ideas through silk screen process. They make screens as well as do the printing. After a time may be given opportunity to create own designs.

ENTRY-LEVEL JOBS FOR ADVERTISING DESIGN GRADUATES

- Paste-up and mechanical artist
- Layout artist
- Assistant art director

Jobs for advertising design graduates can be in either advertising or graphic design.

Advertising artists may work on trade or consumer accounts in advertising agencies, in-house advertising departments, or printing firms. They may work in print (magazine or newspaper) or television advertising.

Graphic designers develop "collateral material," which may consist of brochures, annual reports, packaging, logos and trademarks, corporate image projects, and so on. They also may work in publishing, doing editorial layout for books and magazines.

Board persons do the finished art to prepare the work for the printer. They may work in either advertising or graphic design.

Paste-up/Mechanical Artist

Responsibilities. Prepares art for printer by pasting together elements of layout (type, ilustration, photography), does color separations using T-square and ruling pen. May work for advertising agency, graphic design studio, service studio, printer, publication, or in-house corporate art department.

Skills/Preparation Required. Advertising design degree or illustration degree. Must have taken course in paste-ups and mechanicals and have portfolio demonstrating precision and accuracy in executing mechanicals and color separations.

Personal Qualities Required. Ability to work quickly under pressure and meet deadlines, neatness, accuracy, precision, thoroughness, ability to follow instructions, good at details.

Layout Artist

Responsibilities. Designs layout for ads, usually under the supervision of the art director. Specifies type face, does "comp" rendering to indicate what finished ad will look like when printed. May do own mechanicals.

Skills/Preparation Required. Advertising design degree, portfolio demonstrating advertising layouts, thorough knowledge of type faces, skill at "comp" rendering and mechanicals.

Personal Qualities Required. Ability to work quickly under pressure and meet deadlines, ability to take direction and criticism.

Assistant Art Director

Responsibilities. Works directly with art director. May perform any or all of the following duties depending on the size and structure of the agency or firm: assist in developing concepts for advertising campaigns, rough and finished "comp" renderings, specifying type, mechanicals, paste-ups, layout, graphic design.

Skills/Preparation Required. Advertising design degree, strong portfolio indicating thorough development of creative concepts through fast, crisp, "comp" renderings.

Personal Qualities Required. Poise, self-confidence, persuasiveness, thoroughness, ability to take criticism and direction, ability to communicate ideas.

Alternate Entry Jobs for Advertising Design Graduates

Because of the highly competitive nature of most of the above jobs, graduates sometimes begin their careers by accepting nonart positions in the field, such as guy/gal friday, advertising assistant, or advertising production/traffic assistant.

ENTRY-LEVEL JOBS FOR FASHION ILLUSTRATION GRADUATES

- Free-lance illustrator
- Staff illustrator
- Sketcher

Free-Lance Illustrator

Responsibilities. Jobs in illustration tend to be free lance rather than full-time. Free-lance illustrators may do work for advertising agencies, retail stores, manufacturers, textile and fiber houses, pattern companies, display houses, and publications.

Skills/Preparation Required. Illustration degree required. Must have excellent portfolio indicating distinctive illustration style and creativity. Should be well organized and have ability to run own free-lance business (negotiating contracts, setting rates, billing, keeping own records).

Personal Qualities Required. Ability to work rapidly under pressure of deadlines, good follow-through, creativity, aggressiveness, self-motivation.

Sketcher

Responsibilities. Apparel manufacturers may hire sketchers on a free-lance or full-time basis to sketch garments for their records. These sketches are not used for reproduction and are not considered illustration. They must show clear details of garment construction. In full-time positions other duties such as clerical work may be included in the job.

Skills/Preparation Required. Illustration or fashion design degree, knowledge of garment construction, ability to do detailed sketches with tight hand.

Personal Qualities Required. Flexibility, ability to work rapidly under pressure, good communication skills.

ENTRY-LEVEL JOBS FOR FASHION BUYING AND MERCHANDISING GRADUATES

Retail Stores

- Executive trainee
- Assistant store manager
- Department manager

Buying Offices

- Distributor/planner trainee
- Buyer's clerical

Manufacturers/Textile Firms

- Showroom trainee
- Sales trainee (See description in Textile Technology section.)
- Assistant piece goods buyer (See description in Textile Technology section.)
- Merchandising assistant
- Production assistant
- Shopper/stylist trainee

Miscellaneous Areas

- Assistant to fashion coordinator
- Assistant to photo stylist

Executive Trainee (Retail Stores)

Responsibilities. The type of training program varies with each store. Upon completion of the program, trainees are placed in various progressive assignments in merchandising and/or management. Often a new assignment may necessitate a transfer to a branch store. In recruiting executive trainees, a store's goal is to hire and train potential buyers and managers. All jobs in retailing require long hours, which include nights and weekends.

Skills/Preparation Required. Fashion buying and merchandising degree is necessary. Some stores may require a four-year degree. Applicants must have excellent grades, especially in retail math. Prior retail store experience is desirable.

Personal Qualities Required. Maturity, high energy level, flexibility, decisiveness, initiative and leadership ability, stress tolerance, risk-taking ability, and self-confidence. Must be goal-oriented, a self-starter, and have excellent grooming and fashion sense.

Assistant Store Manager (Retail Stores)

Responsibilities. Assists stores, boutiques, and chain stores to hire candidates who have an interest in store management. Functions include supervising and scheduling salespeople, seeing that merchandise is displayed properly, opening and closing the store, inventory and stock control, and so on. Candidates must be willing to function in a sales capacity as well. In most cases training is informal and occurs on the job. Advancement is usually to store manager and possibly area supervisor in the case of a chain store operation. As in any store job, hours include nights and weekends. These positions are management jobs and do not lead to buying in most cases.

Skills/Preparation Required. Fashion buying and merchandising degree, ability to work with figures and deal firmly with suppliers. Previous work experience either in a retail store or of a clerical nature desirable. In some cases light typing is required.

Personal Qualities Required. Good memory, good handwriting, outgoing personality, fashionable appearance, physical stamina, good communication and interpersonal skills.

Buyer's Clerical (Buying Offices)

Responsibilities. Keeps all clerical records for buyer, such as unit control, answers phones, follows up on shipments. Training is on-the-job and advancement can ultimately lead to buyer or market representative. This position is usually the entry job in the larger buying offices, absorbing many of the clerical duties, which are usually handled by the assistant buyer in a smaller office. Job is found both in chain and resident buying offices. In large central buying offices it is frequently the only entry position, with assistant buyer as the first promotional step.

Skills/Preparation Required. Same as for Executive Trainee (retail stores).

Personal Qualities Required. Sames as for Executive Trainee (retail stores).

Distributor/Planner Trainee (Chain Offices)

Responsibilities. Responsible for determining allocation of merchandise to various store units. Works with computer printouts and unit control records. Has frequent contact with buyers, merchandise managers and store personnel. This is an office job found in large chain buying offices. Advancement can lead to a position as head distributor/planner, controller, or buyer.

Skills/Preparation Required. Fashion buying and merchandising degree, prior work experience, excellent math, analytical and organizational skills.

Personal Qualities Required. The ability to communicate well both in person and on the phone, good memory, decisiveness, thoroughness.

Showroom Trainee (Apparel/Textile Firms)

Responsibilities. This entry position involves diversified duties depending on the size and nature of the company. Job can include any or all of the following duties: reception, answering phones, dealing with buyers on the phone and in person, writing up orders, follow-up work, filing, keeping records, learning to show and sell the line to clients, occasional modeling of garments. Job can lead to showroom sales, merchandising, production, or piece goods buying.

Skills/Preparation Required. Degree preferred but not always necessary. Previous sales experience beneficial, course in salesmanship helpful, typing skills sometimes required.

Personal Qualities Required. Excellent appearance and grooming, strong fashion sense, outgoing personality, must be poised, articulate, quick-thinking, socially at ease, and self-confident.

Merchandising Assistant (Apparel/Textile Firms)

Responsibilities. Works with the merchandiser developing the line for the coming season. Assists in determining the merchandise to be included in line and the price points of merchandise based on trends, cost factors, and production considerations. Has contact with clients, the design, production and piece goods staff, and the sales force. Recordkeeping responsibilities are usually included. Job can lead to merchandiser, stylist, piece goods buyer, or salesperson.

Skills/Preparation Required. Fashion buying and merchandising or fashion design degree. Analytical and organizational skills.

Personal Qualities Required. Good fashion sense including style, color, and fabric knowledge, self-confidence, thoroughness, high stress tolerance, the ability to communicate well, good appearance, good at details.

Production Assistant (Apparel/Textile Firms)

Responsibilities. Assists production manager in keeping records that relate to production of merchandise such as sales records, cutting records, inventory control, shipping records. Keeps clients informed on progress of orders. Expedites work flow and deliveries. Job involves heavy phone contact, details, and figure work.

Skills/Preparation Required. Apparel production management or fashion buying and merchandising degree preferred. Mathematical and organizational skills.

Personal Qualities Required. Accuracy, assertiveness, thoroughness, high stress tolerance, neat handwriting, ability to communicate well over the telephone.

Shopper/Stylist Trainee (Apparel/Textile Firms)

Responsibilities. Major responsibility is to do market research, bringing back information on current trends in style, fabric, color, and to give direction for future line. May also be involved in production, merchandising, piece goods buying and even showroom sales. These jobs are ordinarily found in small companies that do not have a design staff, but may also exist as a supplement to the design staff in a larger organization. Can lead to position as stylist or merchandiser.

Skills/Preparation Required. Fashion buying and merchandising or fashion design degree. Sketching ability usually necessary.

Personal Qualities Required. Strong sense of fashion trends in style, color, fabric, good knowledge of textiles, resourcefulness, flexibility, imagination, assertiveness. Must be very observant and have excellent communication skills.

Assistant to Fashion Coordinator

Responsibilities. Assists fashion coordinator in a retail store, trade organization, buying office, textile firm, pattern company or manufacturer. Responsibilities usually include heavy typing and clerical duties, follow-up and detail work, scheduling appointments, running errands. May also involve market coverage, booking models, assisting in writing of fashion forecasts and fashion show preparations.

Skills/Preparation Required. Fashion buying and merchandising, advertising and communications, or fashion design degree. Organizational skill. Good typing, steno helpful. Previous work experience in some area of the fashion industry.

Personal Qualities Required. Excellent appearance, grooming and fashion sense, polished speaking voice, poise, thoroughness, flexibility, and the ability to communicate well.

Photo Stylist Trainee or Assistant Photo Stylist

Responsibilities. Job exists in photography studios and advertising agencies. While many of the jobs are free-lance assignments, there are some staff photo stylists. Duties include booking models, accessorizing clothing, obtaining props, pinning up hems, ironing garments, running errands, picking up and returning merchandise. Long hours required during heavy work periods.

Skills/Preparation Required. Fashion buying and merchandising, photography, or fashion design degree, fashion coordination course helpful.

Personal Qualities Required. Enthusiasm, stamina, flexibility, resourcefulness, high stress tolerance, strong sense of style and color.

ENTRY-LEVEL JOBS FOR TEXTILE TECHNOLOGY GRADUATES

- Assistant converter/converting clerk
- Assistant piece goods buyer
- Sales trainee
- Fabric technician
- Knit grapher
- Quality control trainee
- Assistant stylist

Assistant Converter/Converting Clerk

Responsibilities. Assists the converter in overseeing the various processes involved in the transition of greige goods to finished fabric (i.e., dyeing, printing, finishing processes). Keeps production and inventory records. Acts as liaison between mills and clients, expedites shipments and work flow, does follow-up work, has heavy phone contact, may do some costing.

Skills/Preparation Required. Textile technology, fashion buying and merchandising, or apparel production management degree, excellent math skills.

Personal Qualities Required. Good at details and figures, well organized, good communication skills, ability to work under pressure, assertiveness.

Assistant Piece Goods Buyer

Responsibilities. Keeps records of piece goods purchases and inventory, maintains swatch file and sample cuts, follows up on orders and shipments. Also may involve making piece goods substitutions and purchasing trims and notions under direction of the supervisor.

Skills/Preparation Required. Textile technology, fashion buying and merchandising, or apparel production management degree.

Personal Qualities Required. Well organized, good at details and follow-up, figure aptitude, assertiveness, neat handwriting.

Sales Trainee (Outside Sales)

Responsibilities. May work for textile firm, fiber or yarn producer, or apparel manufacturer. Trains for outside sales to retail stores, buying offices, manufacturers and textile firms. After training period, is assigned a territory (territory may be New York City or other area requiring relocation). Must carry sample case.

Skills/Preparation Required. Fashion Institute of Technology degree preferred, some sales background (retail or wholesale) very desirable.

Personal Qualities Required. Must be assertive, well-groomed, poised, mature, articulate, self-confident, highly competitive, self-starting, energetic, and have good interpersonal skills.

Fabric Technician

Responsibilities. Performs various lab tests on fabrics, yarns, fibers, and garments to determine durability, color fastness, shrinkage, and so on.

Skills/Preparation Required. Textile technology degree required.

Personal Qualities Required. Good at details, well organized, able to follow instructions and work alone. Some writing ability required for reports of findings.

Knit Grapher

Responsibilities. Graphs instructions for knit fabric designs.

Skills/Preparation Required. Textile technology degree or other degree with sufficient courses in knit technology, knowledge of knit machine capabilities.

Personal Qualities Required. Analytical ability, must be able to translate designer's ideas into precise instructions for factory production.

Quality Control Trainee

Responsibilities. Checks fiber, yarn, fabric, apparel to see that production specifications are met. Identifies problems and works with production staff to correct them. May write reports based on findings.

Skills/Preparation Required. Textile technology, apparel production management, or patternmaking technology degree.

Personal Qualities Required. Must have analytical skills, be good at details and follow-up.

Assistant Stylist

Responsibilities. Works with nonprint, knit, or woven fabric stylist or yarn stylist. Duties include fabric analysis, color research. May involve graphing for knits. Responsibilities might also include maintaining yarn and fabric swatch books, preparation of presentation boards.

Skills/Preparation Required. Textile technology degree required, excellent technical knowledge of fabric structure.

Personal Qualities Required. Must have good color sense, be well organized, good at details.

ENTRY-LEVEL JOBS FOR ADVERTISING AND COMMUNICATIONS GRADUATES

- Junior copywriter
- Public relations assistant/publicity assistant/special events assistant
- Editorial assistant/editorial trainee
- Media buyer trainee/media sales trainee

Junior Copywriter

Responsibilities. This job is found in advertising agencies and in-house corporate advertising departments. It is an entry-level position in copywriting. Employees are expected to write copy immediately, starting with small assignments. In addition, there may be some clerical duties.

Skills/Preparation Required. Advertising and communications degree, excellent grades, good typing skills, excellent portfolio of copy including completed advertising campaigns.

Personal Qualities Required. Creativity, maturity, ability to translate ideas into words fluently, ability to work quickly and under pressure of deadlines.

Public Relations Assistant/Publicity Assistant/ Special Events Assistant

Responsibilities. This job is found in public relations agencies and in-house publicity and special events departments. Entry jobs always include answering phones, scheduling appointments, typing, clerical duties; very often includes such tasks as making coffee, running errands, and so on. Job may also include writing press releases, working on trade shows, and assisting in planning presentations, campaigns, and special events.

Skills/Preparation Required. Advertising and communications degree, good typing, strong creative writing skills evidenced in portfolio of publicity campaigns.

Personal Qualities Required. Maturity, poise, creativity, flexibility, excellent grooming and fashion sense, strong interpersonal skills, good speaking voice, responsiveness to clients' needs, ability to think quickly and work under constant pressure of deadlines, high degree of initiative. Must be articulate.

Editorial Assistant/Editorial Trainee

Responsibilities. These jobs are found in trade and consumer publications. Entry jobs always involve clerical and/or secretarial duties. Some jobs may include working with photographers and models, writing editorial copy, researching the market for trends and news items.

Skills/Preparation Required. Advertising and communications degree, portfolio approved by departmental adviser. Good typing.

Personal Qualities Required. Maturity, poise, flexibility, thoroughness, excellent grooming and fashion sense, ability to work under constant pressure of deadlines, ability to spot trends and identify resources. Must be articulate.

Media Buyer Trainee/Media Sales Trainee

Responsibilities. These jobs are found in advertising agencies, marketing firms, publications, television and radio stations. Entry jobs are always clerical or secretarial in nature, working as an assistant to the media buying or sales staff. Duties may include answering phones, making appointments, client contact, typing contracts, and so on. May be trained to either sell or buy print space or broadcast time.

Skills/Preparation Required. Advertising and communications degree, good typing.

Personal Qualities Required. Self-confidence, self-motivation, outgoing personality, strong interpersonal skills, good telephone personality, business sense, high stress tolerance, mathematical and organization ability, detail oriented.

Alternative Entry Jobs for Advertising and Communications Graduates

Because of the highly competitive nature of this field, some graduates accept entry-level jobs such as advertising production assistants, secretaries, or guy/gal fridays in the advertising and communications field. Progress to the jobs described above depends on the candidates' qualifications and performance.

FASHION BUSINESS LANGUAGE GUIDE

ACCESSORIES All articles ranging from hosiery to shoes, bags, gloves, belts, scarves, jewelry, and hats, for example, worn to complete or enhance an outfit of apparel.

ACCESSORIZING The process of adding accessory items to apparel for display, for models in fashion shows, or for customers' clothes on request.

ACWTU Amalgamated Clothing Workers and Textile Union.

ADAPTATION A design that reflects the outstanding features of another design but is not an exact copy.

ADVERTISING A nonpersonal method of influencing sales through a paid message by an identified sponsor. Advertising appears in media such as newspapers, magazines, television, and radio.

ADVERTISING CREDIT The mention of a store name (one or several), in a producer's advertisement, as a retail source for the advertised merchandise.

APPAREL An all-embracing term that applies to men's, women's, and children's clothing.

APPAREL JOBBER A firm that generally handles all the processes but the sewing, and sometimes the cutting, and that contracts out these production processes to independently owned contractors.

APPAREL MANUFACTURER (i.e., inside shop) A firm that buys fabrics and does the designing, patternmaking, grading, cutting, sewing, and assembling of garments in factories that they own.

AVANT GARDE In any art, the most daring of the experimentalists; innovation of original and unconventional designs, ideas, or techniques during a particular period.

BOARDING (HOSIERY) Heat-setting process used to give hosiery a permanent shape.

BOUTIQUE From the French word meaning "little shop." A free-standing shop or an area within a retail store, devoted to specialized merchandise for special-interest customer.

BRANCH In retailing, an extension of a parent or flagship store, operated under the same name and ownership.

BRAND A trade name or symbol that distinguishes a product as that of a particular manufacturer or distributor.

BRIDGE JEWELRY Jewelry that in price and materials is between costume and fine jewelry.

BUYER An (retail) executive who is responsible for the selection and purchase of merchandise.

CATALOG SHOWROOM RETAILER An underselling establishment that prints and distributes a catalog and maintains a showroom where samples of the merchandise can be seen and ordered.

CAUTION French term for admission or entrance fee charged to trade customers by haute couture houses.

CHAIN STORES A retail organization that owns and operates a string of similar stores that are merchandised and controlled from a central headquarters office.

CHAMBRE SYNDICALE DE LA COUTURE PARISIENNE The French trade association that represents the haute couture houses of Paris.

CLASSIC A particular style that continues as an accepted fashion over an extended period of time.

COLLECTION A manufacturer's or designer's group of styles and/or design creations for a specific season. The season's total number of styles of designs, accumulated for presentation to buyers, constitutes a collection.

COMMISSIONARE An independent retailer's service organization that is foreign based and is used to represent importers abroad.

CONFINED A line or label that is sold to one retailer in a trading area on an exclusive basis.

CONGLOMERATE A company consisting of a number of subsidiary divisions in a variety of unrelated industries.

CONSUMER The ultimate user of goods or services.

CONSUMER OBSOLESCENCE The rejection of something that retains utility value in favor of something new.

CONTRACTOR (APPAREL) A manufacturing concern that does the sewing and often the cutting for other apparel producers (so-called because this work is done under a contractual arrangement).

CONTRACT TANNERS Business firms that contract hides and skins to the specification of leather converters.

CONVERTER (LEATHERS) A company that buys hides and skins, farms them out for processing to contract tanneries, and sells the finished product.

CONVERTER (TEXTILE) A firm that buys or handles the greige goods (i.e., unfinished fabrics) from mills and contracts them out to finishing plants to have them finished (i.e., dyed, printed, etc.).

COOPERATIVE ADVERTISING Advertising, the cost of which is shared by a firm and its customer for the benefit of both.

CORPORATION An artificial legal entity.

COST PRICE The price at which goods are billed to a store, exclusive of any cash discounts that may apply to the purchase.

COSTUME JEWELRY Jewelry made of nonprecious materials.

COUTURIER French word for (male) designer, usually one who has his own couture house. Couturière (female).

CRAZE A fad or fashion characterized by much crowd excitement or emotion.

CUSTOM MADE Apparel made to the order of individual customers; cut and fitted to individual measurements as opposed to apparel that is mass-produced in standardized sizes.

CUTTING-UP TRADES The segment of the fashion industries that produces apparel (i.e., apparel producers).

DEMOGRAPHICS The study of vital and social statistics of a population.

DEPARTMENT STORE A retail establishment that employs at least 25 people and that carries a wide variety of merchandise lines, including home furnishings, apparel for the family, and household linens and dry goods.

DESIGN An arrangement of parts, form, color, and line, for example, to create a version of a style.

DIRECT MARKETING A term that embraces direct mail, mail order, and direct response.

DIRECT SELLER A retailer that sells merchandise by contacting customers either through door-to-door approaches or through some form of in-home party plan.

DISCOUNTER (off-price) An "underselling" retail establishment that utilizes self-service combined with many other expense-saving techniques.

DISPLAY A visual presentation of merchandise or ideas.

DOMESTIC MARKET When referring to origin of goods, domestic means manufactured in one's own country as opposed to foreign made.

DOMESTICS Merchandise essentially for the home including sheets, pillows, towels, blankets, table linens, and other textile products.

EDITORIAL CREDIT The mention, in a magazine or newspaper, of a store name as a retail source for merchandise that is being editorially featured by the publication.

ELECTRONIC RETAILING Selling by means of an electronic device such as television or interactive computers.

ENTREPRENEUR A person who organizes, launches, and directs a business undertaking and assumes the financial risks and uncertainties of the undertaking.

EXCLUSIVITY   Allowing a business company sole use within a given trading area of a product.

EXPORTING   Selling goods and sometimes services to other countries.

FAD   A minor or short-lived fashion.

FACTOR   Financial institution that buys accounts receivable from sellers, assumes the risks and responsibilities of collection, and charges a fee for this service.

FACTORY   A manufacturing plant.

FACTORY OUTLET   A manufacturer-owned retail outlet whose major purpose is to dispose of manufacturer's excess inventory.

FASHION (OR FASHIONS)   The prevailing style(s) at any particular time. When a style is followed or accepted by many people, it is a fashion.

FASHION   A continuing process of change in the styles of dress that are accepted and followed by a large segment of the public at any particular time.

FASHION BULLETIN   Written report on significant fashions prepared by fashion specialists.

FASHION CLINIC   Meeting of a group of persons interested in fashion (under the direction of a fashion specialist) for the purpose of presenting and/or discussing significant fashion trends; clinics are usually held at the beginning of new fashion seasons.

FASHION CONSULTANT   A person who gives professional fashion advice or services.

FASHION COORDINATOR (OR DIRECTOR)   A person charged with the responsibility for keeping abreast of fashion trends and developments, and acting as a source of fashion information to others in his or her organization. Other responsibilities vary from place to place, as do job titles.

FASHION CYCLE   A term that refers to the rise, popularization, and decline of a fashion. It is usually represented visually by a wavelike curve.

FASHION FORECAST   A prediction as to which fashions and/or styles will be popular during a future period.

(THE) FASHION GROUP   A national association of women engaged in the fashion business.

FASHION IMAGE   The impression the consumer has of a retailer's position on fashion leadership, quality, selection, and prices.

(THE) FASHION PRESS   Reporters of fashion news for magazines, newspapers, broadcast media, and so on.

FASHION RETAILING   The business of buying fashion-oriented merchandise from a variety of resources and assembling it in convenient locations for resale to ultimate consumers.

FASHION SHOW OR SHOWING   Formal presentation of a group of styles, often in connection with showing the season's new merchandise.

FASHION TREND   The direction in which fashion is moving.

FLEA MARKET   A location in which a wide variety of independent sellers periodically rent space.

FRANCHISE   A contractual agreement between a wholesaler, manufacturer, or service organization (the franchisor) and an independent retailer who buys the right to use the franchisor's product or service for a stipulated fee. In return, the parent company provides assistance, guidelines, and established business patterns.

GARMENT CENTER (SA)   The area to the East and West of Seventh Avenue in New York City, in which many of the women's ready-to-wear industry showrooms are located.

GEMSTONES   A mineral found in nature that is used in jewelry because of its beauty, clarity, rarity, and other attributes.

GENERAL MERCHANDISE STORES   Retail stores that carry a wide range of merchandise lines including apparel, hardware, furniture, home furnishings, and many other products.

GREIGE GOODS   Unfinished fabrics.

HAUTE COUTURE   (literal French translation: "the finest dressmaking") As used in the fashion business, this refers to a firm whose designer creates a collection of original designs that are then duplicated for individual customers on a made-to-order basis.

HIDES   Animal skins that weigh over 25 pounds when shipped to a tannery.

HIGH FASHION   A fashion that is in the stage of limited acceptance.

I.L.G.W.U.   International Ladies' Garment Workers' Union.

INCOME   The returns that come in periodically from business, property, labor, or other sources, i.e., revenue.

INITIAL MARK-UP   (Mark on) The difference between the cost price of merchandise and its original retail price.

IMPORT   Merchandise brought in from a foreign country for resale or other purposes.

JOBBER   See Apparel Jobber.

JEWELRY   Articles of personal adornment made of either precious or nonprecious materials.

KIPS   Animal skins weighing from 15 to 25 pounds when shipped to a tannery.

KNOCK-OFF   The copying of another manufacturer's fashion design.

LANDED COST   The cost of an imported product, which includes the cost of the merchandise, transportation, and duty.

LAST   A form in the shape of a boot over which shoes are built.

LEAD TIME   Time necessary to produce merchandise from receipt of order to delivery time.

LEVERAGED BUYOUT (LBO)   The purchase of a public company's stock made by a group of investors who borrow money from an investment firm using the company's assets as collateral.

LICENSEE   The person or organization to whom a license is granted.

LICENSING   An arrangement whereby firms are given permission to produce and market merchandise that bears the name of a licensor, who receives a percentage of wholesale sales in return for the use of his or her name.

LICENSOR   The person or organization who grants a license.

LINE   A collection of styles and designs shown by a producer in a given season.

LINE-FOR-LINE COPY   Exact copy of a style originated by a foreign couturier.

MAIL ORDER   A firm that does the bulk of its sales through a catalog.

MALL   See Shopping Centers.

MARK-DOWN   Reduction from an original retail price.

MARKET   (1) A group of potential customers. (2) The place or area in which buyers and sellers congregate.

MARKETING   The total business interaction that involves the planning, pricing, promotion, and distribution of consumer-wanted goods and services for profit.

MARKET REPRESENTATIVE   A market specialist in a resident buying office who covers a narrow segment of the wholesale market and makes information about it available to client stores.

MARKET SEGMENTATION   Defining a target market.

MARKET WEEKS   Scheduled periods during which producers introduce their new lines for an upcoming season.

MART   A building or building complex housing both permanent and transient showrooms of producers.

MASS PRODUCTION   Production of goods in quantity—many at a time rather than one at a time.

MERCHANDISING   The activities involved in buying and selling: finding customers, providing them with what they want, when they want it, at prices they can afford, and are willing to pay.

MERGER   Acquisition of one company by another.

MODE   Synonym for a fashion.

MOM-AND-POP STORE   A small store generally operated by husband and wife with limited capital and few or no hired assistants.

NATIONAL BRAND   Brand owned by a manufacturer, which is a trade name or symbol, that is nationally advertised.

NEEDLE TRADES   Synonym for apparel industry.

N.R.M.A. (NATIONAL RETAIL MERCHANTS ASSOCIATION)   A trade association of the leading department, specialty, and chain stores in the United States.

OFF-PRICE RETAILING   The selling of brand and designer-named merchandise at lower than normal retail prices.

OFFSHORE PRODUCTION   Production of goods by a domestic manufacturer in a foreign country.

OPENINGS   Fashion showings of new collections by apparel producers at the beginning of a season.

OPEN-TO-BUY   The amount of money that a buyer may spend on merchandise to be delivered in a given month.

OUTSIDE SHOP   See Contractor.

PELT   Skin of a fur-bearing animal.

POLICY   A clearly defined course of action or method of doing business deemed necessary, expedient, or advantageous.

PRESS KIT   A collection of facts, figures, photographs, and other promotional materials assembled into a compact package and distributed to the press.

PRESS RELEASE   A written statement of news that has occurred or is about to occur, specifying the source of the information and the date after which its use is permissible.

PRÊt-À-PORTER   (French term meaning, literally, "ready-to-carry") French ready-to-wear apparel, as distinguished from couture clothes, which are custom made.

PRIMARY MARKET   Producers of fibers, textiles, leather, and furs.

PRIVATE LABEL   Merchandise that is produced exclusively for one retail firm and identified by one or more "names" or brands that are owned by the retailer.

PRODUCT DEVELOPER   A person employed by retailers to create private label merchandise for their exclusive use.

PROFIT   Total revenue and sales less all costs and expenses.

PSYCHOGRAPHICS   The study of people's attitudes and values.

PUBLIC CORPORATION   A business that sells shares of its stock on the public market to the public.

PUBLICITY   A nonpaid message—verbal or written—in public-information medium about a company's merchandise, activities, or services.

PUBLICLY OWNED   A corporation whose shares are available for sale by one of the major stock exchanges to any person who chooses to purchase these shares.

READY-TO-WEAR   Apparel that is mass produced in standardized sizes as opposed to apparel made to a customer's special order (custom made).

REORDER NUMBER   A style number that continues to be ordered by buyers.

RESIDENT BUYING OFFICE   A service organization located in a major market center that reports market information, acts as market representative, and renders other related services to a group of stores who have their own buyers.

RESOURCE   A vendor or source of supply.

RETAILING   The business of buying goods from a variety of resources for resale to ultimate consumers.

ROYALTY   A compensation paid to the owner of a right (name, brand, etc.) for the use of that right.

SALES PROMOTION Any activity that is used to influence the sale of merchandise, services, or ideas.

SAMPLE The model or trial garment (may be original in design, a copy, or an adaptation) to be shown to the trade.

SEASON In retailing a selling period.

SECONDARY MARKET Producers of finished consumer fashion products (dresses, coats, suits, accessories, and the like).

SELL THROUGH A measurement of the amount of merchandise sold of a particular merchandise category or style.

SEVENTH AVENUE An expression used as a synonym for New York City's women's apparel industry (actually, a street on which the showrooms of many garment manufacturers are located).

SHOPPING CENTERS A group of retail stores and related facilities planned, developed, and managed as a unit.

SHOWING See Fashion Show or Showing.

SILHOUETTE The overall outline or contour of a costume. Also frequently referred to as "shape" or "form."

SKU Stock-keeping unit.

SMART Having a fashionable appearance.

SOCIOECONOMICS Pertaining to a combination or interaction of social and economic factors.

SPECIALTY STORE A retail establishment that deals either in one category of merchandise or in related categories of merchandise.

STORE OWNERSHIP GROUP A retailing organization consisting of a group of stores that are centrally owned and controlled in terms of broad policy making but are operated autonomously.

STYLE (NOUN) A type of product with specific characteristics that distinguish it from another type of the same product.

STYLE (VERB) To give fashion features to an article or group of articles (as to style a line of coats and suits, for example).

STYLE NUMBER An identification number given to an individual design by a manufacturer. The retailer uses the number when ordering the item and for stock identification.

STYLIST One who advises concerning styles in clothes, furnishings, and the like.

STYLE PIRACY A term used to describe the use of a design without the consent of the originator.

TRADE ASSOCIATION A nonprofit voluntary association of businesses having common interests.

TRADE PUBLICATIONS Newspapers or magazines published specifically for professionals in a special field.

TRADE SHOW Periodic merchandise exhibits staged in various trading areas by groups of producers.

TRIANGLE FIRE A fire that occurred in the Triangle Shirtwaist factory in 1911 and took 146 lives. The tragedy was the turning point in the "sweatshop" era because it awoke the public conscience to the labor conditions in the garment industry.

TRUNK SHOW A producer's or designer's complete collection of samples brought into the store for a limited time to take orders from customers.

VENDEUSE French term meaning saleswoman.

VENDOR One who sells; resource from which a retailer buys goods.

VIDEO SHOPPING In home shopping using cable television or interactive home computers.

VOLUME Amount of dollar sales done in a given period by a retail store or other mercantile establishment.

WAREHOUSE CLUB A retail establishment that specializes in bulk sales of nationally branded merchandise at discount prices.

WOMEN'S WEAR DAILY Trade publication of the women's fashion industries. (The textile and menswear counterpart is the *Daily News Record*.)

INDEX*

---

*Bold face page indicates definition term or brief description about designer

511